Churchill's History
of the English-Speaking Peoples

Winston S. Churchill

CHURCHILL'S
History of the
English-Speaking
Peoples

ARRANGED FOR ONE VOLUME BY

Henry Steele Commager

Illustrated

DODD, MEAD & COMPANY

NEW YORK

Acknowledgment is made to *The Island Race* by Winston S.
Churchill for the use of several illustrations in this volume.

Printed in the United States of America
by Vail-Ballou Press, Inc., Binghamton, N. Y.

Preface

ENGLAND STARTED late in the race for empire and dominion. No one, looking at a map of Europe in the year 1500—which is about when the race for territory and colonies in Africa and Asia and the New World began—would have thought that it would be this little fog-bound island off the northern coast of Europe that would win out over all her rivals and extend her power, plant her institutions, impress her character on every continent and the islands of every sea. How remarkable it is that men and women on the prairies of western United States and Canada, in the Australian hinterland, on the streets of Toronto or of Bombay or of Johannesburg, speak the English language, and that English is rapidly coming to be the common language of the civilized world. Judges in San Francisco and Melbourne and Trinidad and Malta apply the English common law, and a hundred nations, new and old alike, chose to live under the English parliamentary system of government. These are triumphs that dwarf the military conquests of an Alexander, an Augustus, a Mohammed or a Napoleon.

The expansion of England—not of English rule alone, for that is already a thing of the past but of English law and institutions and culture —is, all in all, the most remarkable achievement of any one nation in recorded history.

Winston Churchill knew this, by instinct, by study, by experience—and all three were important in his political and his literary career. He was born to an Anglo-American, not just an English, heritage; as he said in his famous address to the United States Congress in December 1941 when he pointed out that his father was English, his mother American: "had it been the other way around I might have got here on my own." In the end, he did, for Congress made him an honorary citizen of the United States. . . . All his life he had studied the history not only of Britain, but of the Empire and the Commonwealth, and of the United States too: how moving are those words with which he greeted the news of Pearl Harbor:

Silly people might discount the force of the United States. Some said they were soft, others that they would never be united. They would fool around at a distance. They would never come to grips. . . . But I had studied the American Civil War, fought out to the last desperate inch. American blood flowed in my veins. . . . I went to bed, and slept the sleep of the saved and the thankful.

v

His own career, too—military, journalistic, political—had taken him to every part of the English-speaking world. He had fought in South Africa and the Sudan; he had played a decisive role in one war and the leading role in another. Twice—as First Lord of the Admiralty in World War I, and as Prime Minister in World War II—he had seen "the New World, with all its power and might, step forth to the rescue and liberation of the Old," and he was prepared to see the two nations, Britain and the United States, get "more and more mixed up together."

Like almost everything Winston Churchill wrote—the youthful *A Roving Commission;* that stirring account of fighting along the Nile, *The River War; The World Crisis,* which recorded the sweep and scope of the first World War; the six-volume biography of his ancestor, *Marlborough;* the vast six-volume panorama of the *Second World War*—*A History of the English-Speaking Peoples* was a very personal book. This history was a project long close to Churchill's heart and long in his mind, as well. He began work on it in the thirties, when he was out of office; he returned to it again after he had helped guide the English-speaking peoples to victory in the Second World War; it represented therefore almost two decades of thought and of writing.

It is a grave responsibility to cut and trim and arrange a classic, which has, after all, its own proportions and its own symmetry. But if the four-volume *A History of the English-Speaking Peoples* is to be made available in a single volume, there is no alternative. Needless to say I have scrupulously respected the original text: everything here is as Churchill wrote it. But I have reduced the book to approximately half its original length. Where I have dispensed with whole chapters, I have renumbered the remaining chapters consecutively; where, more commonly, I have omitted shorter passages, I have not used the customary ellipsis, for to have done so would be to have made almost every page unsightly. This book is not, after all, meant for scholars, who will go to the original, but for the large reading public which Churchill himself most wanted to reach and for young people, in school and out. In the selection of the material I have kept in mind the importance of continuity and have tried to retain enough material to present a continuous narrative. While Churchill was incapable of writing a dull paragraph, I have attempted to keep those chapters and passages which seem to have the greatest literary vigor and beauty. And as this book is designed primarily for American readers, I have given proportionately larger space to the story of the expansion of England, to the Empire, the Commonwealth, and the United States, than Churchill gave in the four volumes of the History.

HENRY STEELE COMMAGER

Amherst, Massachusetts

Contents

CONTENTS

CONTENTS

CONTENTS

BOOK XII   The Victorian Age

Illustrations

Maps and Genealogical Tables

Churchill's History
of the English-Speaking Peoples

Hadrian's Wall As It Appears Today

One of the largest and most significant remains of the Roman occupation of Britain is Hadrian's Wall which was built between AD 122 and 127 as a military barrier, seventy-three miles long, between the Tyne and the Solway. "It consisted of a stone rampart, eight to ten feet thick, sustained by seventeen forts, garrisoned each by an auxiliary cohort, about eighty castles and double that number of signal towers. In front of the wall was a thirty-foot ditch and behind it another." Although several times broken and pierced by Scottish raids and tribal attacks, the wall was continually strengthened and rebuilt. For almost two hundred years after the death of Hadrian in AD 138, there was near peace along the Roman Wall.

The Martyrdom of Thomas Becket, Archbishop of Canterbury, in Canterbury Cathedral, December 29, 1170. From an English Psalter, *circa* 1200.

BOOK ONE

The Island Race

CHAPTER ONE

Britannia

IN THE summer of the Roman year 699, now described as the year 55
before the birth of Christ, the Proconsul of Gaul, Gaius Julius Cæsar, turned
his gaze upon Britain. In the midst of his wars in Germany and in Gaul
he became conscious of this heavy Island which stirred his ambitions and
already obstructed his designs. To Cæsar the Island presented itself as an
integral part of his task of subjugating the Northern barbarians to the rule
and system of Rome. The land not covered by forest or marsh was verdant
and fertile. The climate, though far from genial, was equable and healthy.
The natives, though uncouth, had a certain value as slaves for rougher work
on the land, in mines, and even about the house. The Romans, however,
hated and feared the sea. By a supreme effort of survival they had two
hundred years before surpassed Carthage upon its own element in the
Mediterranean, but the idea of Roman legions landing in the remote, unknown, fabulous Island of the vast ocean of the North would create a novel
thrill and topic in all ranks of Roman society.

Thus, in this summer fifty-five years before the birth of Christ, Cæsar
withdrew his army from Germany, broke down his massive and ingenious
timber bridge across the Rhine above Coblenz, and throughout July
marched westward by long strides towards the Gallic shore somewhere
about the modern Calais and Boulogne.

In the early days Britain was part of the Continent. A wide plain joined
England and Holland, in which the Thames and the Rhine met together
and poured their waters northward. In some slight movement of the earth's
surface this plain sank a few hundred feet, and admitted the ocean to the
North Sea and the Baltic. Another tremor, important for our story, sundered
the cliffs of Dover from those of Cape Gris Nez, and the scour of the ocean
and its tides made the Straits of Dover and the English Channel. When did
this tremendous severance occur? Until lately geologists would have assigned it to periods far beyond Neolithic man. But the study of striped
clays, the deposits of Norwegian glaciers, shows layer by layer and year by
year what the weather was like, and modern science has found other
methods of counting the centuries. From these and other indications time
and climate scales have been framed which cover with tolerable accuracy

1

many thousand years of prehistoric time. These scales enable times to be fixed when through milder conditions the oak succeeded the pine in British forests, and the fossilised vegetation elaborates the tale. Trawlers bring up in their nets fragments of trees from the bottom of the North Sea, and these when fitted into the climatic scale show that oaks were growing on what is now sixty fathoms deep of stormy water less than nine thousand years ago. Britain was still little more than a promontory of Europe, or divided from it by a narrow tide race which has gradually enlarged into the Straits of Dover, when the Pyramids were abuilding and when learned Egyptians were laboriously exploring the ancient ruins of Sakkara.

The last of the successive waves of Celtic inroad and supersession which marked the Iron Age came in the early part of the first century B.C. "The Belgic tribes arrived in Kent and spread over Essex, Hertfordshire, and part of Oxfordshire, while other groups of the same stock . . . later . . . spread over Hampshire, Wiltshire, and Dorset and part of Sussex." [1] There is no doubt that the Belgae were by far the most enlightened invaders who had hitherto penetrated the recesses of the Island. They were a people of chariots and horsemen. They introduced for the first time a coinage of silver and copper. They established themselves as a tribal aristocracy in Britain, subjugating the older stock. This active, alert, conquering, and ruling race established themselves wherever they went with ease and celerity, and might have looked forward to a long dominion. But the tramp of the legions had followed hard behind them, and they must soon defend the prize they had won against still better men and higher systems of government and war.

Meanwhile in Rome, at the centre and summit, only vague ideas prevailed about the western islands. "The earliest geographers believed that the Ocean Stream encircled the whole earth, and knew of no islands in it." [2] Herodotus about 445 B.C. had heard of the tin of mysterious islands in the far West, which he called the Cassiterides, but he cautiously treated them as being in the realms of fable. However, in the middle of the fourth century B.C. Pytheas of Marseilles—surely one of the greatest explorers in history—made two voyages in which he actually circumnavigated the British Isles. He proclaimed the existence of the "Pretanic Islands Albion and Ierne," as Aristotle had called them. Pytheas was treated as a story-teller, and his discoveries were admired only after the world he lived in had long passed away. But even in the third century B.C. the Romans had a definite conception of three large islands, Albion, Ierne, and Thule (Iceland). Here all was strange and monstrous. These were the ultimate fringes of the world. Still, there was the tin trade, in which important interests were concerned, and Polybius, writing in 140 B.C., shows that this aspect at least had been fully

[1] Darby, *Historical Geography of England*, p. 42.
[2] *Antiquity*, vol. i, p. 189.

2

discussed by commercial writers.

Late in August 55 B.C. Cæsar sailed with eighty transports and two legions at midnight, and with the morning light saw the white cliffs of Dover crowned with armed men. He judged the place "quite unsuitable for landing." He therefore anchored till the turn of the tide, sailed seven miles farther, and descended upon Albion on the low, shelving beach between Deal and Walmer. But the Britons, observing these movements, kept pace along the coast and were found ready to meet him. There followed a scene upon which the eye of history has rested. The Islanders, with their chariots and horsemen, advanced into the surf to meet the invader. Cæsar's transports and warships grounded in deeper water. The legionaries, uncertain of the depth, hesitated in face of the shower of javelins and stones, but the eagle-bearer of the Tenth Legion plunged into the waves with the sacred emblem, and Cæsar brought his warships with their catapults and arrow-fire upon the British flank. The Romans, thus encouraged and sustained, leaped from their ships, and, forming as best they could, waded towards the enemy. There was a short, ferocious fight amid the waves, but the Romans reached the shore, and, once arrayed, forced the Britons to flight.

Cæsar's landing however was only the first of his troubles. His cavalry, in eighteen transports, which had started three days later, arrived in sight of the camp, but, caught by a sudden gale, drifted far down the Channel, and were thankful to regain the Continent. The high tide of the full moon which Cæsar had not understood wrought grievous damage to his fleet at anchor. "A number of ships," he says, "were shattered, and the rest, having lost their cables, anchors, and the remainder of their tackle, were unusable, which naturally threw the whole army into great consternation. For they had no other vessels in which they could return, nor any materials for repairing the fleet; and, since it had been generally understood that they were to return to Gaul for the winter, they had not provided themselves with a stock of grain for wintering in Britain."

The Britons had sued for peace after the battle on the beach, but now that they saw the plight of their assailants their hopes revived and they broke off the negotiations. In great numbers they attacked the Roman foragers. But the legion concerned had not neglected precautions, and discipline and armour once again told their tale. It shows how much food there was in the Island that two legions could live for a fortnight off the cornfields close to their camp.

The British again submitted. Their conqueror imposed only nominal terms. Breaking up many of his ships to repair the rest, he was glad to return with some hostages and captives to the mainland. He never even pretended that his expedition had been a success. To supersede the record of it he came again the next year, this time with five legions and some cavalry conveyed in eight hundred ships. Cæsar had marched twelve miles into the interior when he was recalled by the news that a great storm had shattered or damaged a large portion of his fleet. He was forced to spend ten days in hauling all his ships on to the shore. This done he renewed his invasion. But the British had found a leader in the chief Cassivellaunus, who was a master of war under the prevailing conditions. Using mobile forces and avoiding a pitched battle with the Roman legions, he escorted them on their inroad and cut off their foraging parties. None the less Cæsar captured his first stronghold; the tribes began to make terms for themselves; a well-conceived plan for destroying Cæsar's base on the Kentish shore was defeated. At this juncture Cassivellaunus, by a prudence of policy equal to that of his tactics, negotiated a surrender of hostages and a promise of tribute and submission, in return for which Cæsar was content to quit the Island.

In a dead calm, "he set sail late in the evening and brought all the fleet safely to land at dawn." This time he proclaimed a conquest. Cæsar had his triumph, and British captives trod their dreary path at his tail through the streets of Rome; but for nearly a hundred years no invading army landed upon the Island coasts.

Little is known of Cassivellaunus, and we can only hope that later defenders of the Island will be equally successful and that their measures will be as well suited to the needs of the time. The impression remains of a prudent and skilful chief, whose qualities and achievements, but for the fact that they were displayed in an outlandish theatre, might well have ranked with those of Fabius Maximus Cunctator.

CHAPTER TWO

Subjugation

DURING THE hundred years which followed Julius Cæsar's invasion the British Islanders remained unmolested. The Belgic cities developed a life of their own, and the warrior tribes enjoyed amid their internecine feuds the comforting illusion that no one was likely to attack them again.

In the year A.D. 41 the murder of the Emperor Caligula, and a chapter of accidents, brought his uncle, the clownish scholar Claudius, to the throne of the world. In this triumphant period there were always available for a new emperor a number of desirable projects, well thought out beforehand and in harmony with the generally understood Roman system, any one of which might catch the fancy of the latest wielder of supreme power.

The advantages of conquering the recalcitrant island Britannia were paraded before the new monarch, and his interest was excited. He was attracted by the idea of gaining a military reputation. He gave orders that this dramatic and possibly lucrative enterprise should proceed.

The internal situation favoured the invaders. Cunobelinus (Shakespeare's Cymbeline) had established an overlordship over the south-east of the Island, but in his old age dissensions had begun to impair his authority. Plautius and the legions arrived. The people of Kent fell back on the tactics of Cassivellaunus, and Plautius accordingly had much trouble in searching them out. Advancing along Cæsar's old line of march, he came on a river he had not heard of, the Medway. The Britons faced them on the second day, and were only broken by a flank attack, Vespasian—some day to be Emperor himself—having discovered a ford higher up. This victory marred the stage-management of the campaign. Plautius had won his battle too soon, and in the wrong place. Something had to be done to show that the Emperor's presence was necessary to victory. So Claudius, who had been waiting on events in France, crossed the seas, bringing substantial reinforcements, including a number of elephants. A battle was procured, and the Romans won. Claudius returned to Rome to receive from the Senate the title of "Britannicus" and permission to celebrate a triumph.

But the British war continued.

The conquest was not achieved without one frightful convulsion of revolt. The King of the East Anglian Iceni had died. His kingdom was plundered by centurions, his widow Boadicea (relished by the learned as Boudicca) was flogged, and his daughters outraged.

Boadicea's tribe, at once the most powerful and hitherto the most submissive, was moved to frenzy against the Roman invaders. They flew to arms. Boadicea found herself at the head of a numerous army, and nearly all the Britons within reach rallied to her standard. There followed an uprush of hatred from the abyss, which is a measure of the cruelty of the conquest. It was a scream of rage against invincible oppression and the superior culture which seemed to lend it power. "Boadicea," said Ranke, "is rugged, earnest and terrible." Her monument on the Thames Embankment opposite Big Ben reminds us of the harsh cry of liberty or death which has echoed down the ages.

The Britons were encouraged by omens. The statue of Victory fell face foremost, as if flying from the enemy. The sea turned red. Strange cries were heard in the council chamber and the theatre. The Roman officials, business men, bankers, usurers, and the Britons who had participated in their authority and profits, found themselves with a handful of old soldiers

5

in the midst of "a multitude of barbarians." Suetonius, the new governor, was a month distant. The Ninth Legion was a hundred and twenty miles away. There was neither mercy nor hope. The victorious Britons advanced. "Suetonius," says Tacitus, "undaunted, made his way through a hostile country to Londinium, a town which, though not dignified by the title of colony, was a busy emporium for traders." This is the first mention of London in literature. Though fragments of Gallic or Italian pottery which may or may not antedate the Roman conquest have been found there, it is certain that the place attained no prominence until the Claudian invaders brought a mass of army contractors and officials to the most convenient bridgehead on the Thames.

The citizens of London implored Suetonius to protect them, but when he heard that Boadicea had turned and was marching south he took the hard but right decision to leave them to their fate.

The slaughter which fell upon London was universal. No one was spared, neither man, woman, nor child. The wrath of the revolt concentrated itself upon all of those of British blood who had lent themselves to the wiles and seductions of the invader. This is probably the most horrible episode which our Island has known. We see the crude and corrupt beginnings of a higher civilisation blotted out by the ferocious uprising of the native tribes. Still, it is the primary right of men to die and kill for the land they live in, and to punish with exceptional severity all members of their own race who have warmed their hands at the invaders' hearth.

"And now Suetonius, making up a force of about ten thousand fully armed men, . . . resolved . . . for battle." The day was bloody and decisive. The barbarian army, eighty thousand strong, attended, like the Germans and the Gauls, by their women and children in an unwieldy wagon-train, drew out their array, resolved to conquer or perish. Here was no thought of subsequent accommodation. On both sides it was all for all. At heavy adverse odds Roman discipline and tactical skill triumphed. No quarter was given, even to women. Boadicea poisoned herself.

Suetonius now thought only of vengeance, and indeed there was much to repay. Reinforcements were sent by Nero from Germany, and all hostile or suspect tribes were harried with fire and sword. Yet even so their spirit was unbroken, and the extermination of the entire ancient British race might have followed but for the remonstrances of a new Procurator, supported by the Treasury officials at Rome, who saw themselves about to be possessed of a desert instead of a province. The Procurator, Julius Classicianus, whose tombstone is now in the British Museum, pleaded vehemently for the pacification of the warrior bands, who still fought on without seeking truce or mercy, starving and perishing in the forests and the fens. In the end it was resolved to make the best of the Britons. The Emperor

Nero sent a new Governor, who made a peace with the desperate tribesmen which enabled their blood to be perpetuated in the Island race.

In A.D. 78 Agricola, a Governor of talent and energy, was sent to Britannia. With military ability he united a statesmanlike humanity. In all he conducted six campaigns of expansion in Britannia. There was no safety or permanent peace for the British province unless he could subdue the powerful tribes and large bands of desperate warriors who had been driven northwards by his advance.

The decisive battle was fought at Mons Graupius, a place which remains unidentified, though some suggest the Pass of Killiecrankie. Tacitus describes in unconvincing detail the course of this famous struggle. The whole of Caledonia, all that was left of Britannia, a vast host of broken, hunted men, resolved on death or freedom, confronted in their superiority of four or five to one the skilfully handled Roman legions and auxiliaries, among whom no doubt many British renegades were serving. It is certain that Tacitus greatly exaggerated the dimensions of the native army in these wilds, where they could have no prepared magazines. The number, though still considerable, must have been severely limited. Apparently, as in so many ancient battles, the beaten side were the victims of misunderstanding and the fate of the day was decided against them before the bulk of the forces realised that a serious engagement had begun. Reserves descended from the hills too late to achieve victory, but in good time to be massacred in the rout. The last organised resistance of Britain to the Roman power ended at Mons Graupius. Here, according to the Roman account, "ten thousand of the enemy were slain, and on our side there were about three hundred and sixty men." Clive's victory at Plassey, which secured for the British Empire a long spell of authority in India, was gained against greater odds, with smaller forces and with smaller losses.

The way to the entire subjugation of the Island was now open but Caledonia was to Rome only a sensation and the remnants of the British fighting men were left to moulder in the Northern mists.

*   *   *

In the wild North and West freedom found refuge among the mountains, but elsewhere the conquest and pacification were at length complete and Britannia became one of the forty-five provinces of the Roman Empire. In all of them the principle was followed of adapting the form of government to local conditions. No prejudice of race, language, or religion obstructed the universal character of the Roman system. The only divisions were those of class, and these ran unchallenged throughout the ordered world. There were Roman citizens, there was an enormous mass of non-Roman citizens, and there were slaves, but movement to full citizenship was possible to fortunate members of the servile class. On this basis therefore the life of Britain now developed.

7

CHAPTER THREE

The Roman Province

FOR NEARLY three hundred years Britain, reconciled to the Roman system, enjoyed in many respects the happiest, most comfortable, and most enlightened times its inhabitants have ever had. In culture and learning the land was a pale reflection of the Roman scene, not so lively as the Gallic. But there was law; there was order; there was peace; there was warmth; there was food, and a long-established custom of life. The population was free from barbarism without being sunk in sloth or luxury. Some culture spread even to the villages. Roman habits percolated; the use of Roman utensils and even of Roman speech steadily grew. The British thought themselves as good Romans as any. Indeed, it may be said that of all the provinces few assimilated the Roman system with more aptitude than the Islanders. The British legionaries and auxiliaries were rated equal or second only to the Illyrians as the finest troops in the Empire. There was a sense of pride in sharing in so noble and widespread a system. To be a citizen of Rome was to be a citizen of the world, raised upon a pedestal of unquestioned superiority above barbarians or slaves. Movement across the great Empire was as rapid as when Queen Victoria came to the throne, and no obstruction of frontiers, laws, currency, or nationalism hindered it.

A poll in the fourth century would have declared for an indefinite continuance of the Roman regime. In our own fevered, changing, and precarious age, where all is in flux and nothing is accepted, we must survey with respect a period when, with only three hundred thousand soldiers, peace in the entire known world was maintained from generation to generation, and when the first pristine impulse of Christianity lifted men's souls to the contemplation of new and larger harmonies beyond the ordered world around them.

There are no signs that any large increase of population accompanied the Roman system. In more than two centuries of peace and order the inhabitants remained at about the same number as in the days of Cassivellaunus. The new society, with all its grace of structure, with its spice of elegance and luxury—baths, banquets, togas, schools, literature, and oratory —stood on no more sumptuous foundation than the agriculture of prehistoric times. The rude plenty in which the ancient Britons had dwelt was capable of supporting only to a moderate extent the imposing façade of Roman life.

We owe London to Rome. The military engineers of Claudius, the bureaucracy which directed the supply of the armies, the merchants who

8

followed in their wake, brought it into a life not yet stilled.

If a native of Chester in Roman Britain could wake up today [1] he would find laws which were the direct fulfilment of many of those he had known. He would find in every village temples and priests of the new creed which in his day was winning victories everywhere. Indeed the facilities for Christian worship would appear to him to be far in excess of the number of devotees. Not without pride would he notice that his children were compelled to learn Latin if they wished to enter the most famous universities. He might encounter some serious difficulties in the pronunciation. He would find in the public libraries many of the masterpieces of ancient literature, printed on uncommonly cheap paper and in great numbers. He would find a settled government, and a sense of belonging to a world-wide empire. He could drink and bathe in the waters of Bath, or if this were too far he would find vapour baths and toilet conveniences in every city. He would find all his own problems of currency, land tenure, public morals, and decorum presented in a somewhat different aspect, but still in lively dispute. He would have the same sense of belonging to a society which was threatened, and to an imperial rule which had passed its prime. He would have the same gathering fears of some sudden onslaught by barbarian forces armed with equal weapons to those of the local legions or auxiliaries. He would still fear the people across the North Sea, and still be taught that his frontiers were upon the Rhine. The most marked changes that would confront him would be the speed of communications and the volume of printed and broadcast matter. He might find both distressing. But against these he could set chloroform, antiseptics, and a more scientific knowledge of hygiene. He would have longer history books to read, containing worse tales than those of Tacitus and Dio. Facilities would be afforded to him for seeing "regions Cæsar never knew," from which he would probably return in sorrow and wonder. He would find himself hampered in every aspect of foreign travel, except that of speed. If he wished to journey to Rome, Constantinople, or Jerusalem, otherwise than by sea, a dozen frontiers would scrutinise his entry. He would be called upon to develop a large number of tribal and racial enmities to which he had formerly been a stranger. But the more he studied the accounts of what had happened since the third century the more satisfied he would be not to have been awakened at an earlier time.

* * *

Nevertheless the Roman Empire was an old system. Its sinews and arteries had borne the strain of all that the ancient world had endured. The Roman world, like an aged man, wished to dwell in peace and tranquility and to enjoy in philosophic detachment the good gifts which life has to bestow upon the more fortunate classes. But new ideas disturbed

[1] Written in 1939.

9

the internal conservatism, and outside the carefully guarded frontiers vast masses of hungry, savage men surged and schemed. The essence of the Roman peace was toleration of all religions and the acceptance of a universal system of government. Every generation after the middle of the second century saw an increasing weakening of the system and a gathering movement towards a uniform religion. Christianity asked again all the questions which the Roman world deemed answered for ever, and some that it had not thought of. The alternations between fanatic profligacy and avenging puritanism which marked the succession of the emperors, the contrast between the morals at the centre of power and those practised by wide communities in many subject lands, presented problems of ever-growing unrest. At the moment when mankind seemed to have solved a very large proportion of its secular difficulties and when a supreme Government offered unlimited freedom to spiritual experiment inexorable forces both within and without drove on the forward march. No rest; no stay. "For here have we no continuing city, but we seek one to come." Strange standards of destiny were unfurled, destructive of peace and order, but thrilling the hearts of men. Before the Roman system lay troubles immeasurable—squalor, slaughter, chaos itself, and the long night which was to fall upon the world.

We see these forces swelling like a flood against all the threatened dykes of the Roman world, not only brimming at the lip of the dam, but percolating insidiously, now by a breach, now by a mere ooze, while all the time men became conscious of the frailty of the structure itself. If the superior virtue of the legion failed all fell. Certainly from the middle of the second century all these disruptive forces were plainly manifest. However, in Roman Britain men thought for many generations that they had answered the riddle of the Sphinx. They misconceived the meaning of her smile.

CHAPTER FOUR

The Lost Island

WE CANNOT doubt that the second and to some extent the third century of the Christian era, in contrast with all that had gone before and most that was to follow, were a Golden Age for Britain. But by the early part of the fourth century shadows had fallen upon this imperfect yet none the less tolerable society. By steady, persistent steps the sense of security departed from Roman Britain. Its citizens felt by daily experience that the world-wide system of which they formed a partner province was in decline. They entered a period of alarm.

From the end of the third century, when Roman civilisation in Britain and the challenge to the supreme structure were equally at their height, inroads of barbarian peoples began, both from Europe and from the forlorn Island to the westward. The Scots, whom nowadays we call the Irish, and the Picts from Scotland began to press on Hadrian's Wall, to turn both flanks of it by sea raids on a growing scale. At the same time the Saxons rowed in long-boats across the North Sea and lay heavy all along the east coast from Newcastle to Dover. From this time forth the British countryside dwelt under the same kind of menace of cruel, bloody, and sudden inroad from the sea as do modern nations from the air.

Over this fertile, peaceful, ordered world lay the apprehension of constant peril. But like other systems in decay, the Roman Empire continued to function for several generations after its vitality was sapped. For nearly a hundred years our Island was one of the scenes of conflict between a dying civilisation and lusty, famishing barbarism. The Roman Britons were lively and audacious members of the Empire. They took a particularist view, yet wished to have a hand in the game themselves. As time passed the Roman garrison in Britain steadily became more British, and towards the end of the third century it assumed a strong national character. While glorying in the name of citizens and Romans, and having no desire for independence, both province and army adopted a highly critical attitude towards the Imperial Government. Emperors who disregarded British opinion, or sacrificed British interests, above all those who could be accused of neglecting the defences of the province, were the objects of active resentment. A series of mutinies and revolts aggravated the growing dangers of the times.

These were not merely mutinies of discontented soldiers. They were bold bids for control of the Roman Empire by legions only a few thousand strong, but expressing the mood, sentiments, and ambitions of the society in which they lived. They left the local scene for the supreme theatre, like players who wish to quit the provinces for the capital. Unhappily they took away with them at each stage important elements of the exiguous military forces needed to man the dykes.

*   *   *

Continuous efforts were made by the Roman-British community to repel inroads but although the process of wearing down was spread over many years, and misery deepened by inches, we must recognise in the year 367 circumstances of supreme and murderous horror. In that fatal year the Picts, the Scots, and the Saxons seemed to work in combination. All fell together upon Britannia. A wide-open breach was made in the defences, and murderous hordes poured in upon the fine world of country houses and homesteads. Everywhere they were blotted out. The ruins tell the tale. The splendid Mildenhall silver dinner service, now in the British Museum, is thought to have been buried at this time by its owners, when their villa was surprised by raiders. Evidently they did not live to dig it up again. The villa life of Britain only feebly recovered from the disaster. The towns were already declining. Now people took refuge in them. At least they had walls.

The pages of history reveal the repeated efforts made by the Imperial Roman Governments to protect Britannia. Again and again, in spite of revolts and ingratitude, officers and troops were sent to restore order or drive back the barbarians. But in these fatal years the civilised parts of the Island were stripped of their defenders, both in order to aid the Empire and to strike against it.

By the beginning of the fifth century all the legions had gone on one errand or another, and to frantic appeals for aid the helpless Emperor Honorius could only send his valedictory message in 410, that "the cantons should take steps to defend themselves."

A generation passed and a Gaulish chronicler records this sombre note in A.D. 441 or 442: "The Britons in these days by all kinds of calamities and disasters are falling into the power of the Saxons." What had happened? Something more than the forays of the fourth century: the mass migration from North Germany had begun. Thereafter the darkness closes in.

*   *   *

A broad question is keenly disputed. Did the invaders exterminate the native population, or did they superimpose themselves upon them and become to some extent blended with them? Here it is necessary to distinguish between the age of fierce forays in search of plunder and the age of settlement. Even where self-interest did not preserve the native villagers as labourers on Saxon farms we may cherish the hope that somewhere a maiden's cry for pity, the appeal of beauty in distress, the lustful needs of an invading force, would create some bond between victor and vanquished. Thus the blood would be preserved, thus the rigours of subjugation would fade as generations passed away. The complete obliteration of an entire race over large areas is repulsive to the human mind. There should at least have been, in default of pity, a hearing for practical advantage or the natural temptations of sex. Thus serious writers contend that the Anglo-Saxon conquest was for the bulk of the British community mainly a change of masters. The rich were slaughtered; the brave and proud fell back in large numbers upon the Western mountains. Other numerous bands escaped betimes to Brittany, whence their remote posterity were one day to return.

1 2

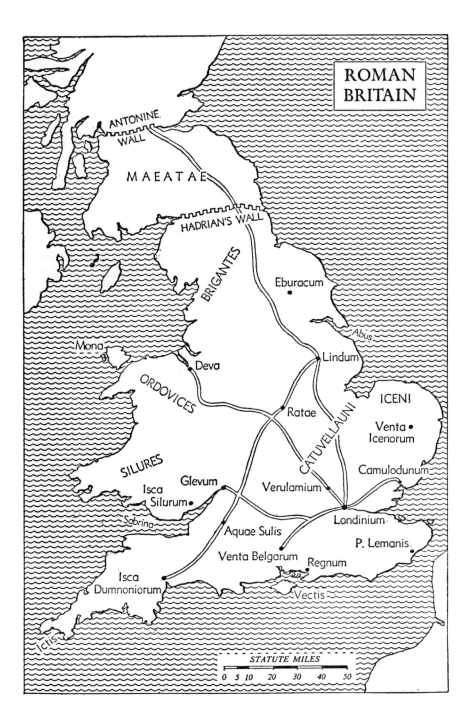

ROMAN BRITAIN

ANTONINE
WALL

MAEATAE

HADRIAN'S WALL

BRIGANTES

Eburacum

Abus

Mona

Deva

Lindum

ORDOVICES

ICENI

Ratae

Venta •
Icenorum

CATUVELLAUNI

SILURES

Glevum

Camulodunum

Isca
Silurum •

Verulamium

Sabrina

Londinium

Aquae Sulis

P. Lemanis.

Venta Belgarum

Regnum

Isca
Dumnoniorum

Vectis

Ictis

STATUTE MILES

0 5 10   20   30   40   50

The Saxon was moreover a valley-settler. His notion of an economic holding was a meadow for hay near the stream, the lower slopes under the plough, the upper slopes kept for pasture. But in many places a long time must have passed before these lower grounds could be cleared and drained, and while this work was in progress what did he live on but the produce of the upland British farms? It is more natural to suppose that he would keep his natives working as serfs on the land with which they were familiar until the valley was ready for sowing. Then the old British farms would go down to grass, and the whole population would cluster in the village by the stream or the spring. But the language of the valley-settlers, living in compact groups, would be dominant over that of the hill-cultivators, scattered in small and isolated holdings. The study of modern English place-names has shown that hill, wood, and stream names are often Celtic in origin, even in regions where the village names are Anglo-Saxon. In this way, without assuming any wholesale extermination, the disappearance of the British language can be explained even in areas where we know a British population to have survived. They had to learn the language of their masters: there was no need for their masters to learn theirs. Thus it came about that both Latin and British yielded to the speech of the newcomers so completely that hardly a trace of either is to be found in our earliest records.

There was no colour bar. In physical type the two races resembled each other and the probabilities are that in many districts a substantial British element was incorporated in the Saxon stock. The invaders themselves were not without their yearnings for settled security. The warriors returning from a six months' foray liked to sprawl in lazy repose. In the fifth century, as the pressure from the East grew harder and as the annual raiding parties returned from Britain with plunder and tales of wealth there was created in the ruling minds a sense of the difficulty of getting to the Island, and consequently of the security which would attend its occupation by a hardy and valiant race. Here, perhaps, in this wave-lapped Island men might settle down and enjoy the good things of life without the haunting fear of subjugation by a stronger hand, and without the immense daily sacrifices inseparable from military and tribal discipline on the mainland. To these savage swords Britain seemed a refuge. In the wake of the raiders there grew steadily the plan and system of settlement. Thus, with despair behind and hope before, the migration to Britain and its occupation grew from year to year.

CHAPTER FIVE

England

A RED sunset; a long night; a pale, misty dawn! But as the light grows it becomes apparent to remote posterity that everything was changed. Night had fallen on Britannia. Dawn rose on England, humble, poor, barbarous, degraded, and divided, but alive. Britannia had been an active part of a world state; England was once again a barbarian island. It had been Christian, it was now heathen. Its inhabitants had rejoiced in well-planned cities, with temples, markets, academies. They had nourished craftsmen and merchants, professors of literature and rhetoric. For four hundred years there had been order and law, respect for property, and a widening culture. All had vanished. The buildings, such as they were, were of wood, not stone. The people had lost entirely the art of writing. Some miserable runic scribblings were the only means by which they could convey their thoughts or wishes to one another at a distance. Barbarism reigned in its rags, without even the stern military principles which had animated and preserved the Germanic tribes. The confusion and conflict of petty ruffians sometimes called kings racked the land. There was nothing worthy of the name of nationhood, or even of tribalism; yet this is a transition which the learned men of the nineteenth century banded themselves together to proclaim as an onward step in the march of mankind. We wake from an awful and, it might well have seemed, endless nightmare to a scene of utter prostration. Nor did the seeds of recovery spring from the savage hordes who had wrecked the Roman culture. They would certainly have continued to welter indefinitely in squalor, but for the fact that a new force was stirring beyond the seas which, moving slowly, fitfully, painfully, among the ruins of civilisation, reached at length by various paths the unhappy Island, to which, according to Procopius, the souls of the dead upon the mainland were ferried over by some uncouth Charon.

When the evil days overtook the land and the long struggle with the Saxons was fought out, the British Church fell back with other survivors upon the western parts of the Island. British Christianity languished and might well have become moribund but for the appearance of a remarkable and charming personality.

St. Patrick was a Roman Briton of good family, dwelling probably in the Severn valley. His father was a Christian deacon, a Roman citizen, and a member of the municipal council. One day in the early fifth century there descended on the district a band of Irish raiders, burning and slaying. The young Patrick was carried off and sold into slavery in Ireland. For six years he tended swine, and loneliness led him to seek comfort in religion.

After many wanderings we find him in one of the small islands off Marseilles. Later he consorted with Bishop Germanus of Auxerre. He conceived an earnest desire to return good for evil and spread the tidings he had learned among his former captors in Ireland. After fourteen years Patrick sailed back in 432 to the wild regions which he had quitted. His success was speedy and undying. "He organised the Christianity already in existence; he converted kingdoms which were still pagan, he brought Ireland into connection with the Church of Western Europe, and made it formally part of universal Christendom." On a somewhat lower plane, although also held in perpetual memory, was the banishing of snakes and reptiles of all kinds from the Irish soil, for which from age to age his fame has been celebrated. It was therefore in Ireland and not in Wales or England that the light of Christianity now burned and gleamed through the darkness.

And it was from Ireland that the Gospel was carried to the North of Britain and for the first time cast its redeeming spell upon the Pictish invaders. Columba, born half a century after St. Patrick's death, but an offspring of his Church, and imbued with his grace and fire, proved a new champion of the faith. From the monastery which he established in the island of Iona his disciples went forth to the British kingdom of Strathclyde, to the Pictish tribes of the North, and to the Anglian kingdom of Northumbria. He is the founder of the Scottish Christian Church. Thus the message which St. Patrick had carried to Ireland came back across the stormy waters and spread through wide regions.

*   *   *

These were the days when it was the first care of the Bishop of Rome that all Christ's sheep should be gathered into one fold. Here in the North, where so much zeal and fervour were evident, the faith seemed to be awkwardly and above all separately planted.

For various reasons, including the spreading of the Gospel, it was decided in the closing decade of the sixth century that a guide and teacher should be sent to England to diffuse and stimulate the faith, to convert the heathen, and also to bring about an effective working union between British Christians and the main body of the Church. For this high task Pope Gregory, afterwards called "the Great," and the ecclesiastical statesmen gathered in Rome selected a trusty and cultured monk named Augustine. St. Augustine, as he is known to history, landed in Kent, and his arrival infused a mood of action. He converted King Ethelbert, who had for reasons of policy long meditated this step. Upon the ruins of the ancient British church of St. Martin he refounded the Christian life of Canterbury, which was destined to become the centre and summit of religious England.

From the title loosely accorded him of "Apostle of the English," Augustine enjoyed for many centuries the credit of having re-converted the once-

1 6

famous Roman province of Britannia to the Christian faith; and this halo has shone about him until comparatively recent times.

*   *   *

Almost a generation passed before Redwald, King of the East Angles, had established by a series of victories a wide dominion over the lands of Central England. With Redwald's aid the crown of Northumbria was gained by an exiled prince, Edwin, who by his abilities won his way, step by step, to the foremost position in England. He not only established his personal primacy, but the confederation founded by him foreshadowed the kingdom of all England.

We have a picture, agreeable and instructive, of Edwin: "There was then a perfect peace in Britain wheresoever the dominion of King Edwin extended, and, as it is still proverbially said, a woman with her new-born babe might walk throughout the Island from sea to sea without receiving any harm. That King took such care for the good of his nation that in several places where he had seen clear springs near the highways he caused stakes to be fixed with proper drinking vessels hanging on them for the refreshment of travellers, nor durst any man touch them for any other purpose than that for which they were designed, either for the great fear they had of the King or for the affection which they bore him."

Such in his heyday was the prince, and the ample kingdom of Northumbria, shaped like England itself in miniature, became Christian. But this blessed event brought with it swift and dire consequences. The drama unfolded with staggering changes of fortune. In 633 Penda, the heathen, made an unnatural alliance with Cadwallon, the Christian British King of North Wales, with the object of overthrowing the suzerainty of Edwin and breaking the Northumbrian power. Here for the first time noticed in history, British and English fought side by side. Politics for once proved stronger than religion or race. In a savage battle near Doncaster Edwin was defeated and slain, and his head—not the last—was exhibited on the ramparts of captured York. This sudden destruction of the greatest king who had hitherto ruled in the Island brought in recoil an equally speedy vengeance. Here at last was the chance, so long expected, of British vengeance upon their Saxon foes. Here was the faithful paying off of very old but very heavy debts. We might almost be seeing again the spirit of Boadicea.

The failure of Ethelbert's attempt to make a Christian reunion of England and Britain left the direction of the immediate future with the Northumbrian Court. It was to York and not to Canterbury that Rome looked, and upon English, not British, armies that the hopes of organised Christendom were placed.

Anglo-Saxon England was definitely rallied to the Christian faith. There was now no kingdom in which heathen practices prevailed. Indeed, apart from individuals, whose private adherence to Woden was overlooked,

1 7

the whole Island was Christian. But this marvellous event, which might have brought in its train so many blessings, was marred by the new causes of division which now opened between the English and British peoples. These differences persisted across the centuries, much debated by the parties concerned. The celebrated and largely successful attempt to solve them took place at the Synod of Whitby in 664. The importance of this event cannot be overrated. Instead of a religion controlled by the narrow views of abbots pursuing their strict rule of life in their various towns or remote resorts there was opened to every member of the English Church the broad vista of a world-state and universal communion. In Britain for the first time there was achieved a unity of faith, morals, and Church government covering five-sixths of the Island. The decisive step had been taken in the spiritual sphere. The Island was now entirely Christian, and by far the greater and more powerful part was directly associated with the Papacy.

Rome had little reason to be satisfied with the mission of Augustine. Fresh emissaries were chosen in 668 to carry the light into the Northern mists, one of them, a native of Asia Minor, Theodore of Tarsus. These missionaries were of a stronger type than their precursors, and their character and integrity shone before all. When they arrived at Canterbury there were but three bishops from all England to greet them. When their work was finished the Anglican Church raised its mitred front in a majesty which has not yet been dimmed. This remarkable Asiatic was the earliest of the statesmen of England, and guided her steps with fruitful wisdom.

* * *

Bede, a monk of high ability, working unknown in the recesses of the Church, now comes forward as the most effective and almost the only audible voice from the British islands in these dim times. The name of "the Venerable Bede" still carries with it a proud renown. He alone attempts to paint for us, and, so far as he can, explain the spectacle of Anglo-Saxon England, divided by tribal, territorial, dynastic, and personal feuds and striving for mastery by force and fraud. For almost exactly a hundred years, from 731 to 829, there was a period of ceaseless warfare, conducted with cruelty and rapine under a single creed.

The leadership of Saxon England passed for nearly eighty years to two Mercian kings. Ethelbald and Offa reigned each for forty years. The moral sense had grown so strong in matters of sex that Churchmen could now brand a king as licentious. Boniface from Germany censured Ethelbald for the "twofold sin" which he committed in nunneries by using the advantages of his royal position to gain himself favours otherwise beyond his reach.

* * *

After the shapeless confusion of darker centuries, obscure to history and meaningless to almost all who lived through them, we now see a purpose steadily forming. England, with an independent character and personality, might scarcely yet be a part of a world civilisation as in Roman times, but there was a new England, closer than ever before to national unity, and with a native genius of her own. Henceforward an immortal spirit stood for all to see.

CHAPTER SIX

The Vikings

AFTER THE fall of Imperial Rome the victorious barbarians were in their turn captivated and enthralled by the Gospel of Christ. Though no more successful in laying aside their sinful promptings than religious men and women are today, they had a common theme and inspiration. There was a bond which linked all the races of Europe. There was an international organisation which, standing erect in every country, was by far the most powerful, and indeed the only coherent surviving structure, and at the head of which the Bishop of Rome revived in a spiritual, or at least in an ecclesiastical form, the vanished authority of the Cæsars. The Christian Church became the sole sanctuary of learning and knowledge. It sheltered in its aisles and cloisters all the salvage of ancient days. It offered to men in their strife and error "the last solace of human woe, the last restraint of earthly power." Thus, while the light of pagan civilisation was by no means wholly extinguished, a new effulgence held, dazzled, and dominated the barbaric hordes, not only in our Island but throughout Europe. They were tamed and uplifted by the Christian revelation. Everywhere, from the Euphrates to the Boyne, old gods were forsworn, and a priest of Christ could travel far and wide, finding in every town an understanding brotherhood and a universal if sometimes austere hospitality.

Amid the turbulence and ignorance of the age of Roman decay all the intellectual elements at first found refuge in the Church, and afterwards exercised mastery from it. Here was the school of politicians. The virtual monopoly of learning and the art of writing made the Churchmen indispensable to the proud and violent chieftains of the day. The clerics became the civil servants, and often the statesmen, of every court. They fell naturally, inevitably, into the place of the Roman magistrates whose garb they wore, and wear today. Triumphant barbarism yielded itself insensibly to a structure, reliance upon which was proved on numberless occasions to give success in the unending struggle for power. After the convulsions and disorders of the Dark Ages, when at last daylight fell again on the British Island, she awoke to a world also profoundly changed, but devoid neither of form nor majesty. There was even a gentler breeze in the air.

The fervour of the converted heathen brought in its train mischiefs which opened new calamities. The Church was bound by its spirit to inculcate mildness and mercy. It was led by zeal and by its interests to fortify in every way the structure of its own power. The humility and faith of the descendants of the invaders soon exposed them, in their human frailty, to an organised exploitation which during the sixth and seventh centuries led in many countries to an engrossment by the Church of treasure and lands out of all proportion to its capacity to control events. We see, then, a Christendom pious but forward; spiritually united, but a prey to worldly feuds; in a state of grace, but by no means free from ambition.

Upon this revived, convalescent, loosely-knit society there now fell two blasting external assaults. The first, the Arabs, came from the East. For Britain was reserved the second invading wave. It came from the North. In Scandinavia the Vikings fitted out their long-boats for sea. This double assault by Arab infidels and Nordic pirates distracted the weakened life of Europe for ten generations. It was not until the eleventh century that the steel-clad feudalism of medieval Christendom, itself consisting largely of the converted descendants of the Vikings, assigned limits to the Arab conquests, and established at the side of the Christian Church ample and effective military power.

*   *   *

Measure for measure, what the Saxon pirates had given to the Britons was meted out to the English after the lapse of four hundred years. In the eighth century a vehement manifestation of conquering energy appeared in Scandinavia. Norway, Sweden, and Denmark threw up bands of formidable fighting men who, in addition to all their other martial qualities, were the hardy rovers of the sea. The causes which led to this racial ebullition were the spontaneous growth of their strength and population, the thirst for adventure, and the complications of dynastic quarrels. There was no question of the Danes or Norsemen being driven westward by new pressures from the steppes of Asia. They moved of their own accord. Their prowess was amazing. One current of marauding vigour stuck southwards from Sweden, and not only reached Constantinople, but left behind it potent germs which across the centuries influenced European Russia. Another contingent sailed in their long-boats from Norway to the Mediterranean, harried all the shores of the inland sea, and were with difficulty repulsed by the Arab kingdoms of Spain and the north coast of Africa. The third far-ranging impulse carried the Scandinavian buccaneers to the

British Isles, to Normandy, to Iceland, and presently across the Atlantic Ocean to the American continent.

* * *

The soul of the Vikings lay in the long-ship, the vessel which, in many different sizes, bore the Vikings to the plunder of the civilised world. Its picture rises before us vivid and bright: the finely carved, dragon-shaped prow; the high, curving stern; the long row of shields, black and yellow alternately, ranged along the sides; the gleam of steel; the scent of murder. Yet this superb instrument of sea-power would have been useless without the men who handled it. All were volunteers. Parties were formed under leaders of marked ability. In the sagas we read of crews of "champions, or merry men": a ship's company picked no doubt from many applicants, "as good at the helm or oar as they were with the sword." There were strict regulations, or early "Articles of War," governing these crews once they had joined. Men were taken between the ages of sixteen and sixty, but none without a trial of his strength and activity. No feud or old quarrel must be taken up while afloat or on service. No woman was allowed on board. News was to be reported to the captain alone. All taken in war was to be brought to the pile or stake, and there sold and divided according to rule. This war booty was personal; that is to say, it was not part of the property which passed by Scandinavian law to a man's kindred. He was entitled to have it buried with him.

When we reflect upon the brutal vices of these salt-water bandits, pirates as shameful as any whom the sea has borne, or recoil from their villainous destruction and cruel deeds, we must also remember the discipline, the fortitude, the comradeship and martial virtues which made them at this period beyond all challenge the most formidable and daring race in the world.

* * *

One summer's day, probably in 789, while "the innocent English people, spread through their plains, were enjoying themselves in tranquility and yoking their oxen to the plow," news was carried to the King's officer, the Reeve of Dorchester, that three ships had arrived on the coast. The Reeve "leapt on his horse and rode with a few men to the harbour (probably Portland), thinking that they were merchants and not enemies. Giving his commands as one who had authority, he ordered them to be sent to the King's town; but they slew him on the spot and all who were with him." This was a foretaste of the murderous struggle which, with many changes of fortune, was to harry and devastate England for two hundred and fifty years. It was the beginning of the Viking age.

It was not till 835 that the storm broke in fury, and fleets, sometimes of three or four hundred vessels, rowed up the rivers of England, France, and Russia in predatory enterprises on the greatest scale. For thirty years

Southern England was constantly attacked. Paris was more than once besieged. Constantinople was assaulted. The harbour towns in Ireland were captured and held. Dublin was founded by the Vikings under Olaf. In many cases now the raiders settled upon the conquered territory. The Swedish element penetrated into the heart of Russia, ruling the river towns and holding the trade to ransom. The Norwegian Vikings, coming from a still more severe climate, found the Scottish islands good for settlement. They colonised the Shetlands, the Faroes, and Ireland. They reached Greenland and Stoneland (Labrador). They sailed up the St. Lawrence. They discovered America; but they set little store by the achievement.

For a long time no permanent foothold was gained in Britain or France. It was not until 865, when resistance on the Continent had temporarily stiffened, that the great Danish invasion of Northumbria and Eastern England began.

Saxon England was at this time ripe for the sickle. The invaders broke in upon the whole eastern seaboard, once guarded by the "Count of the Saxon Shore," with its Imperial fortresses in ruins, buried already under the soil of centuries. No Roman galleys plied their oars upon the patrol courses. There was no Imperial Government to send a great commander or a legion to the rescue. But on all sides were abbeys and monasteries, churches, and even cathedrals, possessed in that starveling age of treasures of gold and silver, of jewels, and also large stores of food, wine, and such luxuries as were known. The pious English had accepted far too literally the idea of the absolution of sins as the consequence of monetary payment to the Church. Their sins were many, their repentances frequent, and the Church had thrived. Here were easy prizes for sharp swords to win.

*　　*　　*

The Danish raiders stayed longer every year. In the summer the fleets came over to plunder and destroy, but each year the tendency was to dally in a more genial and more verdant land. At last the warrior's absence on the raids became long enough and the conditions of his conquest sure enough for him to bring over his wife and family. Thus again behind piracy and rapine there grew the process of settlement. But these settlements of the Danes differed from those of the Saxons. Behind their frontier lines the soldiers of one decade were to become the colonists and landowners of the next. The Danish settlement in England was essentially military. They cut their way with their swords, and then planted themselves deeply in the soil. The warrior type of farmer asserted from the first a status different from the ordinary agriculturist. Without any coherent national organisation to repel from the land on which they had settled the ever-unknowable descents from the seas, the Saxons, now for four centuries entitled to be deemed the owners of the soil, very nearly succumbed completely to the Danish inroads. That they did not was due—as almost every critical turn of historic fortune has been due—to the sudden apparition in an era of confusion and decay of one of the great figures of history.

CHAPTER SEVEN

Alfred the Great

THE STORY of Alfred is made known to us in some detail in the pages of Asser, a monk of St. David's. In spite of ill-health, he was renowned as a hunter, and his father had taken him to Rome as a boy, so that he had a lively comprehension of the great world. Alfred began as a second-in-command to his elder brother, the King. There were no jealousies between them, but a marked difference of temperament. Ethelred inclined to the religious view that faith and prayer were the prime agencies by which the heathen would be overcome. Alfred, though also devout, laid the emphasis upon policy and arms.

The Danes had occupied London, not then the English capital, and their army, moving forward, met the forces of the Saxons on the Berkshire downs, and here, in January, 871, was fought the Battle of Ashdown.

The fight was long and hard, but at last the Danes gave way, and, hotly pursued, fled till nightfall; they fled through the night and the next day, and the whole breadth of Ashdown—meaning the Berkshire hills—was strewn with their corpses, among which were found the body of one of the Viking kings and five of his jarls.

The results of this victory did not break the power of the Danish army; in a fortnight they were again in the field. But the Battle of Ashdown justly takes its place among historic encounters because of the greatness of the issue. If the West Saxons had been beaten all England would have sunk into heathen anarchy. Since they were victorious the hope still burned for a civilised Christian existence in this Island. This was the first time the invaders had been beaten in the field. Alfred had made the Saxons feel confidence in themselves again. They could hold their own in open fight. The story of this conflict at Ashdown was for generations a treasured memory of the Saxon writers. It was Alfred's first battle.

King Ethelred soon fell sick and died. At twenty-four Alfred became King, and entered upon a desperate inheritance. To and fro the fighting swayed, with varying fortunes. In the summer, about a month after he had assumed the crown, Alfred sustained a definite defeat in the heart of his own country. On the morrow of this misfortune he thought it best to

23

come to terms while he still had an army. By an inglorious treaty and stubborn campaign Alfred secured five years in which to consolidate his power.

The reasons which led the Danes to make a truce with Alfred are hard to analyse at this date. Both sides liked war, and this had been ding-dong: there was little to show but scars and corpses on either side. But now in the last quarter of the century a subtle, profound change came over "the Great Heathen Army." Alfred and the men of Wessex had proved too stubborn a foe for easy subjugation. Some of the Danes wished to settle on the lands they already held; the rest were for continuing the war at a suitable moment till the whole country was conquered. Perhaps these two bodies acted in concert, the former providing a sure and solid base, the latter becoming an expeditionary force. Thus, after mauling the kingdom of Strathclyde and carrying off the stock and implements of agriculture nearly half of the sea-pirates settled themselves in Northumbria and East Anglia. Henceforward they began "to till the ground for a livelihood." Here was a great change. We must remember their discipline and organisation. The ships' companies, acting together, had hitherto fought ashore as soldiers. All their organisation of settlements was military. The sailors had turned soldiers, and the soldiers had turned yeomen. They preserved that spirit of independence, regulated only by comradeship and discipline for vital purposes, which was the life of the long-ship.

The whole of the East of England thus received a class of cultivator who, except for purposes of common defence, owed allegiance to none; who had won his land with the sword, and was loyal only to the army organisation which enabled him to keep it. From Yorkshire to Norfolk this sturdy, upstanding stock took root. As time passed they forgot the sea; they forgot the army; they thought only of the land—their own land. They liked the life. Although they were sufficiently skilful agriculturists, there was nothing they could teach the older inhabitants; they brought no new implements or methods, but they were resolved to learn.

The Danish differs in many ways from the Saxon settlement four hundred years earlier. There was no idea of exterminating the older population. The two languages were not very different; the way of life, the methods of cultivation, very much the same. The colonists—for such they had now become—brought their families from Scandinavia, but also it is certain that they established human and natural relations with the expropriated English. The blood-stream of these vigorous individualists, proud and successful men of the sword, mingled henceforward in the Island race. A vivifying, potent, lasting, and resurgent quality was added to the breed. As modern steel is hardened by the alloy of special metals in comparatively small quantities, this strong strain of individualism, based upon land-ownership, was afterwards to play a persistent part, not only in the blood but in the politics of England. The tribulations of another three hundred years did not destroy their original firmness of character nor their deep attachment to the conquered soil. All through English history this strain continues to play a gleaming part.

It remained only for conversion to Christianity to mingle these races inextricably in the soul and body of a nation. These considerations may aptly fill the five years' breathing-space which Alfred had gained by courageous fighting and politic Danegeld. In this interval Halfdene, the Viking king, departed from the scene. The tortured, plundered Church requited his atrocities by declaring that God punished him in the long run by madness and a smell which made his presence unendurable to his fellows.

*   *   *

Alfred's dear-bought truce was over. Guthrum, the new warleader of the mobile and martial part of the heathen army, proceeded to attack Alfred's kingdom by raid and storm from every quarter. The prudent King sought peace and offered an indemnity. The Danes took the gold, and "swore upon the Holy Ring" they would depart and keep a faithful peace. With a treachery to which all adjectives are unequal they suddenly darted away and seized Exeter. But let all heathen beware of breaking oaths! A frightful tempest smote the sea army. A hundred and twenty ships were sunk, and upwards of five thousand of these perjured marauders perished as they deserved. Thus their whole careful plan fell to pieces, and Alfred found his enemies in the summer of 877 in the mood for a new peace. They swore it with oaths of still more compliant solemnity, and they kept it for about five months.

Then in January 878 occurred the most surprising reversal of Alfred's fortunes. It was Twelfth Night, and the Saxons, who in these days of torment refreshed and fortified themselves by celebrating the feasts of the Church, were off their guard, engaged in pious exercises, or perhaps even drunk. Down swept the ravaging foe. The whole army, sole guarantee of England south of the Thames, was dashed into confusion. Many were killed. The most part stole away to their houses. Only a handful of officers and personal attendants hid themselves with Alfred in the marshes and forests. This was the darkest hour of Alfred's fortunes.

This is also the moment when those gleaming toys of history were fashioned for the children of every age. We see the warrior-king disguised as a minstrel harping in the Danish camps. We see him acting as a kitchen-boy to a Saxon housewife. "Alack, man, why have you not turned over the bread when you see that it is burning, especially as you so much like eating it hot." The misguided woman little thought that she was talking to King Alfred, who had fought so vigorously against the heathens and won so many victories over them. Low were the fortunes of the once ruthless English. Pent in their mountains, the lineal descendants of the Ancient Britons, slatternly, forlorn, but unconquered, may well have grinned.

Towards the end of Lent, Alfred, striving to take the field again, continued a brigand warfare against the enemy while sending his messengers to summon the "fyrd," or local militia, for the end of May. There was a general response; the King was loved and admired. The news that he was alive and active caused widespread joy. All the fighting men came back. After all, the country was in peril of subjugation, the King was a hero, and they could always go home again.

Battle must be sought before they lost interest. Alfred advanced to Ethandun and on the bare downs was fought the largest and culminating battle of Alfred's wars. All was staked. All hung in the scales of fate. On both sides the warriors dismounted; the horses were sent to the rear. The shield-walls were formed, the masses clashed against each other, and for hours they fought with sword and axe. But the heathen had lost the favour of God through their violated oaths; eventually from this or other causes they fled from the cruel and clanging field, and at the last, full of despair, begged for peace. They offered to give without return as many hostages as Alfred should care to pick and to depart forthwith.

But Alfred had had longer ends in view. It is strange that he should have wished to convert these savage foes. Baptism as a penalty of defeat might lose its spiritual quality. The workings of the spirit are mysterious, but we must still wonder how the hearts of these hard-bitten swordsmen and pirates could be changed in a single day. Alfred meant to make a lasting peace with Guthrum. He had him and his army in his power. He could have starved them into surrender and slaughtered them to a man. He wished instead to divide the land with them, and that the two races, in spite of fearful injuries given and received, should dwell together in amity. He received Guthrum with thirty prominent buccaneers in his camp. He stood godfather to Guthrum; he raised him from the font; he entertained him for twelve days; he presented him and his warriors with costly gifts; he called him his son.

This sublime power to rise above the whole force of circumstances, to remain unbiased by the extremes of victory or defeat, to persevere in the teeth of disaster, to greet returning fortune with a cool eye, to have faith in men after repeated betrayals, raises Alfred far above the turmoil of barbaric wars to his pinnacle of deathless glory.

The first result of this new unity was the recovery of London in 886. London had long been the emporium of Christian England. Ancient Rome had seen in this bridgehead of the Thames, at the convergence of all the roads and sea routes, the greatest commercial and military centre in the Island. Now the City was set on the road to becoming the national capital.

King Alfred's main effort was to restore the defences and the modesty of his reforms shows us the enormous difficulties which he had to overcome, and proves that even in that time of mortal peril it was almost impossible to keep the English under arms. He saw too the vision of English sea-power. To be safe in an island it was necessary to command the sea. He made great departures in ship design, and hoped to beat the Viking numbers by fewer ships of much larger size.

*　　*　　*

King Alfred's Book of Laws, or Dooms, attempted to blend the Mosaic code with Christian principles and old Germanic customs. He inverted the Golden Rule. Instead of "Do unto others as you would that they should do unto you," he adopted the less ambitious principle, "What ye will that other men should *not* do to you, that do ye not to other men." The Laws of Alfred, continually amplified by his successors, grew into that body of customary law which the Norman kings undertook to respect, and out of which, with much manipulation by feudal lawyers, the Common Law was founded.

The King encouraged by all his means religion and learning. Above all he sought the spread of education. Lastly in this survey comes Alfred's study of history. He it was who set on foot the compiling of the *Saxon Chronicle*. From King Alfred's time the entries are exact, often abundant, and sometimes written with historic grasp and eloquence.

We discern across the centuries a commanding and versatile intelligence, wielding with equal force the sword of war and of justice; using in defence arms and policy; cherishing religion, learning, and art in the midst of adversity and danger; welding together a nation, and seeking always across the feuds and hatreds of the age a peace which would smile upon the land.

This King, it was said, was a wonder for wise men. "From his cradle he was filled with the love of wisdom above all things," wrote Asser. The Christian culture of his Court sharply contrasted with the feckless barbarism of Viking life. The older race was to tame the warriors and teach them the arts of peace, and show them the value of a settled common existence. We are watching the birth of a nation.

The result of Alfred's work was the future mingling of Saxon and Dane in a common Christian England. In the grim time of Norman overlordship the figure of the great Alfred was a beacon-light, the bright symbol of Saxon achievement, the hero of the race. The ruler who had taught them courage and self-reliance in the eternal Danish wars, who had sustained them with his national and religious faith, who had given them laws and good governance and chronicled their heroic deeds, was celebrated in legend and song as Alfred the Great.

*　　*　　*

One final war awaited Alfred. Guthrum died in 891, and the pact which he had sworn with Alfred, and loosely kept, ended. Suddenly in the autumn of 892 a hostile armada of two hundred and fifty ships appeared carrying "the Great Heathen Army" that had ravaged France, to the invasion of England. The King, in ill-health, is not often seen in this phase at the head of armies; we have glimpses of him, but the great episodes of the war were centered, as they should be, upon the young leaders. There had been a re-gathering of wealth and food; there was a settled administration, and the allegiance of all was given to King Alfred. Unlike Charlemagne, he had a valiant son. At twenty-two Edward could lead his father's armies to the field.

In this cruel war the Vikings used three armies, but in the end they were fairly beaten in full and long fight by the Christians.

Alfred had well defended the Island home. He had by policy and arms preserved the Christian civilisation in England. He had built up the strength of that mighty South which has ever since sustained much of the weight of Britain, and later of her Empire. He had liberated London, and happily he left behind him descendants who, for several generations, as we shall see, carried his work forward with valour and success.

*   *   *

Alfred died in 899, but the struggle with the Vikings had yet to pass through strangely contrasted phases. Alfred's blood gave the English a series of great rulers, and while his inspiration held, victory did not quit the Christian ranks. In his son Edward, who was immediately acclaimed King, the armies had already found a redoubtable leader. A quarrel arose between Edward and his cousin, Ethelwald, who fled to the Danelaw and aroused the Vikings to a renewed inroad upon his native land. The eventual English victory was a milestone in the long conflict. Alfred's son was now undisputed King of all England south of the Humber, and the British princes of North and South Wales hastened to offer their per-petual allegiance. It seemed as if a broad and lasting unity was about to be reached. Edward the Elder reigned five years more in triumphant peace, and when he died in 925 his authority and his gifts passed to a third re-markable sovereign, capable in every way of carrying on the work of his father and grandfather.

CHAPTER EIGHT

The Saxon Dusk

ATHELSTAN, THE third of the great West Saxon kings, sought at first, in accordance with the traditions of his house, peaceful relations with the unconquered parts of the Danelaw; but upon disputes arising he marched into Yorkshire in 926, and there established himself. The whole of North Britain—Celtic, Danish, and Norwegian, pagan and Christian—together presented a hostile front under Constantine, King of the Scots, and Olaf of Dublin, with Viking reinforcements from Norway. The fight that followed is recorded for us in an Icelandic saga. According to the saga-man, Athelstan challenged his foes to meet him in a pitched battle, and to this they blithely agreed. The armies, very large for those impoverished times, took up their stations as if for Olympic Games, and much parleying accompanied the process. Tempers rose high as these masses of manhood flaunted their shields and blades at one another and flung their gibes across a narrow space; and there was presently a fierce clash. In this the English were worsted. But on the following day at Brunanburh the real trial of strength was staged. The rival hosts paraded in all the pomp of war, and then in hearty goodwill fell on with spear, axe, and sword. All day long the battle raged.

The victory of the English was overwhelming. Constantine, "the perjured" as the victors claimed, fled back to the North, and Olaf retired with his remnants to Dublin. Thus did King Alfred's grandson, the valiant Athelstan, become one of the first sovereigns of Western Europe. He styled himself on coin and charter *Rex totius Britanniae*.

*   *   *

Historians select the year 954 as the end of the first great episode in the Viking history of England. A hundred and twenty years had passed since the impact of the Vikings had smitten the Island. For forty years English Christian society had struggled for life. For eighty years five warrior kings— Alfred, Edward, Athelstan, Edmund, and Edred—defeated the invaders. The English rule was now restored, though in a form changed by the passage of time, over the whole country. Yet underneath it there had grown up, deeply rooted in the soil, a Danish settlement covering the great eastern plain, in which Danish blood and Danish customs survived under the authority of the English king.

In the brilliant and peaceful reign of Edgar (957–975) all this long building had reached its culmination. The reconquest of England was accompanied step by step by a conscious administrative reconstruction which has governed the development of English institutions from that day to this. Finally, with this military and political revival marched a great rebirth of monastic life and learning and the beginning of our native English literature. Another and happy, if incidental, result was to promote the production of splendid illuminated manuscripts which were much in demand in contemporary Europe. Many of these, designed for the religious instruction of the laity, mark, we are told, the first achievement of English as a literary language—the earliest vernacular to reach this eminence in the whole of Europe. From whatever point of view we regard it, the tenth century is a decisive step forward in the destinies of England. Despite the catastrophic decline of the monarchy which followed the death of Edgar, this organisation and English culture were so firmly rooted as to survive two foreign conquests in less than a century.

It must have seemed to contemporaries that with the magnificent coronation at Bath of Edward, son of Edgar, in 973, on which all coronation orders since have been based, the seal was set on the unity of the realm. Everywhere the courts are sitting regularly, in shire and borough and hundred; there is one coinage, and one system of weights and measures. The arts of building and decoration are reviving; learning begins to flourish again in the Church; there is a literary language, a King's English, which all educated men write. Civilisation had been restored to the Island. But now the political fabric which nurtured it was about to be overthrown. Hitherto strong men armed had kept the house. Now a child, a weakling, a vacillator, a faithless, feckless creature, succeeded to the warrior throne. Twenty-five years of peace lapped the land, and the English, so magnificent in stress and danger, so invincible under valiant leadership, relaxed under its softening influences. We have reached the days of Ethelred the Unready (978–1016). But this expression, which conveys a truth, means literally Ethelred the Ill-counselled, or Ethelred the "Redeless."

In 980 serious raids began again. The English were worsted, and then followed the most shameful period of Danegeld. Ethelred suspected a plot against his life. Panic-stricken, he planned the slaughter of all Danes in the south of England, whether in his pay or living peaceably on the land. This atrocious design was executed in 1002 on St. Brice's Day. Among the victims was Gunnhild, the wife of Pallig, one of the chief Vikings, and sister of Sweyn, King of Denmark. Sweyn swore implacable revenge, and for two years executed it upon the wretched Islanders. The fury of the avenger was not slaked by blood. It was baffled, but only for a space, by famine. At last Ethelred, for thirty-six thousand pounds of silver, the equivalent of three or four years' national income, bought another short-lived truce. It is vain to recount the long catalogue of miseries. In earlier ages such horrors remain unknown because unrecorded. Just enough flickering light plays upon this infernal scene to give us the sense of its utter desolation and hopeless wretchedness and cruelty.

But soon the young Danish prince, Canute, set forth to claim the English crown. At this moment the flame of Alfred's line rose again in Ethelred's son, Edmund—Edmund Ironside, as he soon was called. At twenty he was famous. Although declared a rebel by his father, and acting in complete disobedience to him, he gathered forces, and in a brilliant campaign struck a succession of heavy blows. He gained battles, he relieved London, he contended with every form of treachery; the hearts of all men went out to him. New forces sprang from the ruined land. Ethelred died, and Edmund, last hope of the English, was acclaimed King. In spite of all odds and a heavy defeat he was strong enough to make a partition of the realm,

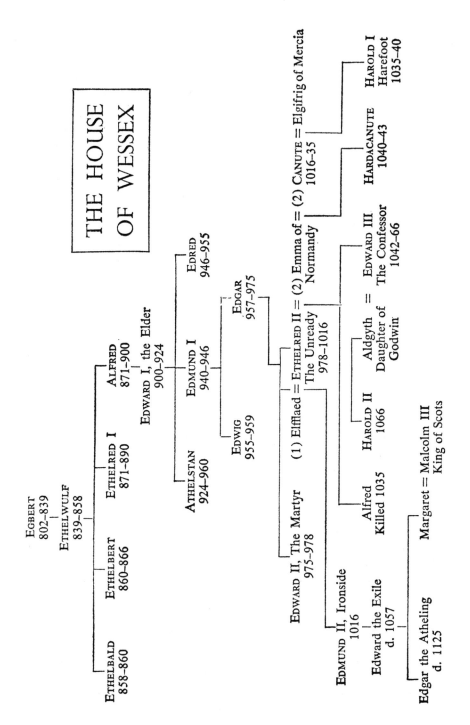

THE HOUSE
OF WESSEX

EGBERT
802–839

ETHELWULF
839–858

ETHELBALD   ETHELBERT   ETHELRED I   ALFRED
858–860   860–866   871–890   871–900

                              EDWARD I, the Elder
                                   900–924

ATHELSTAN   EDMUND I   EDRED
924–960   940–946   946–955

EDWIG   EDGAR
955–959   957–975

EDWARD II, The Martyr   (1) Elfflaed = ETHELRED II = (2) Emma of = (2) CANUTE = Elgifrig of Mercia
975–978   The Unready   Normandy   1016–35
                                   978–1016

EDMUND II, Ironside
1016

Alfred   Aldgyth   =   EDWARD III   HARDACANUTE   HAROLD I
Killed 1035   Daughter of   The Confessor   1040–43   Harefoot
                    Godwin   1042–66   1035–40

Edward the Exile   HAROLD II
d. 1057   1066

Margaret = Malcolm III
           King of Scots

Edgar the Atheling
d. 1125

31

and then set himself to rally his forces for the renewal of the struggle; but in 1016, at twenty-two years of age, Edmund Ironside died, and the whole realm abandoned itself to despair.

At Southampton, even while Edmund lived, the lay and spiritual chiefs of England agreed to abandon the descendants of Ethelred for ever and recognise Canute as King. All resistance, moral and military, collapsed before the Dane. There were three principles upon which sovereignty could be erected: conquest, which none could dispute; hereditary right, which was greatly respected; and election, which was a kind of compromise between the two. It was upon this last basis that Canute began his reign. Everyone knows the lesson he administered to his flatterers when he sat on the seashore and forbade the tide to come in. He made a point of submitting himself to the laws whereby he ruled. He even in his military capacity subjected himself to the regulations of his own household troops. At the earliest moment he disbanded his great Danish army and trusted himself broadly to the loyalty of the humbled English. He married Emma of Normandy, the widow of Ethelred, and so forestalled any action by the Duke of Normandy on behalf of her descendants by Ethelred.

Canute became the ruling sovereign of the North, and was reckoned as having five or six kingdoms under him. He was already King of Denmark when he conquered England, and he made good his claim to be King of Norway. Scotland offered him its homage. The Viking power, although already undermined, still stretched across the world, ranging from Norway to North America, and through the Baltic to the East. But of all his realms Canute chose England for his home and capital. He liked, we are told, the Anglo-Saxon way of life. He wished to be considered the "successor of Edgar," whose seventeen years of peace still shone by contrast with succeeding times. He ruled according to the laws, and he made it known that these were to be administered in austere detachment from his executive authority.

His remarkable achievements, under the blessing of God and the smiles of fortune, were in large measure due to his own personal qualities. Here again we see the power of a great man to bring order out of ceaseless broils and command harmony and unity to be his servants, and how the lack of such men has to be paid for by the inestimable suffering of the many.

* * *

Meanwhile across the waters of the English Channel a new military power was growing up. The Viking settlement founded in Normandy in the early years of the tenth century had become the most vigorous military state in France. In less than a hundred years the sea rovers had transformed themselves into a feudal society. It was from this virile and well-organised land that the future rulers of England were to come. Between the years

Runnymede, the "Charter" island in the Thames near London. Here, or in the adjacent meadow, on June 15, 1215, King John was forced to agree to the signing of the famous Magna Carta.

A Part of the "Articles of the Barons."

"The original articles on which Magna Carta is based exist today in the British Museum. They were sealed in a quiet, short scene which has become one of the most famous in our history. Afterwards the King returned to Windsor. Four days later, probably, the Charter itself was engrossed. In future ages it was to be used as the foundation of principles and systems of government of which neither King John nor his nobles dreamed."

1028 and 1035 the Viking instincts of Duke Robert of Normandy turned him seriously to plans of invasion. His death and his failure to leave a legitimate heir suspended the project, but only for a while.

In 1035 Canute died, and his empire with him. He left three sons, ignorant and boorish Vikings, and many thoughts were turned to the representatives of the old West Saxon line, Alfred and Edward, then living in exile in Normandy. The elder, Alfred, "the innocent Prince" as the chronicler calls him, hastened to England in 1036. A Wessex earl, Godwin, was the leader of the Danish party in England. He possessed great abilities and exercised the highest political influence. The venturesome Alfred was arrested and his personal attendants slaughtered. The unfortunate prince himself was blinded, and in this condition soon ended his days in the monastery at Ely. The guilt of this crime was generally ascribed to Godwin. The succession being thus simplified, Canute's sons divided the paternal inheritance. Sweyn reigned in Norway for a spell, but his two brothers who ruled England were short-lived, and within six years the throne of England was again vacant.

Godwin continued to be the leading figure in the land, and was now master of its affairs. There was still living in exile in Normandy Edward, the remaining son of Ethelred and Emma, younger brother of the ill-starred Alfred. The illustrious line of Alfred the Great was the oldest in Europe. A sense of sanctity and awe still attached to any who could claim descent from the Great King. Godwin saw that he could consolidate his power and combine both English and Danish support by making Edward King. Edward made no difficulty; he was welcomed home and crowned; and for the next twenty-four years, with one brief interval, England was mainly governed by Godwin and his sons.

According to tradition King Edward, called the Confessor, was a kindly, weak, chubby albino. His main interest in life was religious, and as he grew older his outlook was increasingly that of a monk. His saintliness brought him as the years passed by a reward in the veneration of his people, who forgave him his weakness for the sake of his virtues.

Meanwhile the Godwin family maintained their dictatorship under the Crown. Nepotism in those days was not merely the favouring of a man's own family; it was almost the only way in which a ruler could procure trustworthy lieutenants. The family tie, though frequently failing, gave at least the assurance of a certain identity of interest. Statistics had not been collected, but there was a general impression in these primitive times that a man could trust his brother, or his wife's brother, or his son, better than a stranger. We must not therefore hasten to condemn Earl Godwin because he parcelled out the English realm among his relations.

A crisis came in the year 1051, when the Norman party at Court suc-

33

ceeded in driving Godwin into exile. During Godwin's absence William of Normandy is said to have paid an official visit to the Confessor in England in quest of the succession to the Crown. Very likely King Edward promised that William should be his heir. But in the following year Godwin returned, backed by a force raised in Flanders, and with the active help of his son Harold. Together father and son obliged King Edward to take them back into power. Many of the principal Norman agents in the country were expelled, and the authority of the Godwin family was felt again throughout the land. The territories that they directly controlled stretched south of a line from the Wash to the Bristol Channel.

Seven months after his restoration Godwin died, in 1053. Since Canute first raised him to eminence he had been thirty-five years in public life. Harold, his eldest surviving son, succeeded to his father's great estates. He now filled his part to the full, and for the next thirteen adventurous years was the virtual ruler of England. In spite of the antagonism of rival Anglo-Danish earls, and the opposition of the Norman elements still attached to the Confessor's Court, the Godwins, father and son, maintained their rule under what we should now call a constitutional monarchy. A brother of Harold's became Earl of Mercia, and a third son of Godwin, Tostig, who courted the Normans, and was high in the favour of King Edward, received the Earldom of Northumbria, dispossessing the earls of those regions. But there was now no unity within the house of Godwin. Harold and Tostig soon became bitter foes. All Harold's competence, vigour, and shrewdness were needed to preserve the unity of the realm. Even so, as we shall see, the rift between the brothers left the land a prey to foreign ambitions.

*   *   *

The condition of England at the close of the reign of Edward the Confessor was one of widespread political weakness. Illuminated manuscripts, sculpture, metalwork and architecture of much artistic merit were still produced, religious life flourished, and a basis of sound law and administration remained, but the virtues and vigour of Alfred's posterity were exhausted and the Saxon monarchy itself was in decline. A strain of feeble princes, most of whom were short-lived, had died without children. Even the descendants of the prolific Ethelred the Unready died out with strange rapidity, and at this moment only a sickly boy and his sister and the aged sovereign represented the warrior dynasty which had beaten the Vikings and reconquered the Danelaw. The great earls were becoming independent in the provinces.

The Island had come to count for little on the Continent, and had lost the thread of its own progress. The defences, both of the coast and of the towns, were neglected. To the coming conquerors the whole system, social, moral, political, and military, seemed effete.

The figure of Edward the Confessor comes down to us faint, misty, frail.

The medieval legend, carefully fostered by the Church, whose devoted servant he was, surpassed the man. The lights of Saxon England were going out, and in the gathering darkness a gentle, grey-beard prophet foretold the end. When on his death-bed Edward spoke of a time of evil that was coming upon the land his inspired mutterings struck terror into the hearers. Only Archbishop Stigand, who had been Godwin's stalwart, remained unmoved, and whispered in Harold's ear that age and sickness had robbed the monarch of his wits. Thus on January 5, 1066, ended the line of the Saxon kings. The national sentiment of the English, soon to be conquered, combined in the bitter period that lay before them with the gratitude of the Church to circle the royal memory with a halo. As the years rolled by his spirit became the object of popular worship. His shrine at Westminster was a centre of pilgrimage. Canonised in 1161, he lived for centuries in the memories of the Saxon folk. The Normans also had an interest in his fame. For them he was the King by whose wisdom the crown had been left, or so they claimed, to their Duke. Hence both sides blessed his memory, and until England appropriated St. George during the Hundred Years' War, St. Edward the Confessor was the kingdom's patron saint. St. George proved undoubtedly more suitable to the Islander's needs, moods, and character.

BOOK TWO

The Making of the Nation

CHAPTER NINE

The Norman Invasion

ENGLAND, DISTRACTED by faction and rivalry at home, had for a long time lain under rapacious glare from overseas. The Scandinavians sought to revive the empire of Canute. The Normans claimed that their Duke held his cousin Edward's promise of the throne. William of Normandy had a virile origin and a hard career. The prize was large enough for the separate ambitions of both hungry Powers. Their simultaneous action in the opening stages was an advantage to be shared in common.

* * *

One morning Duke Robert of Normandy, the fourth descendant of Rollo, was riding towards his capital town, Falaise, when he saw Arlette, daughter of a tanner, washing linen in a stream. His love was instantly fired. He carried her to his castle, and, although already married to a lady of quality, lived with her for the rest of his days. To this romantic but irregular union there was born in 1027 a son, William, afterwards famous.

Duke Robert died when William was only seven, and in those harsh times a minor's hold upon his inheritance was precarious. The great nobles who were his guardians came one by one to violent ends, and rival ambitions stirred throughout Normandy. Were they to be ruled by a bastard? Was the grandson of a tanner to be the liege lord of the many warrior families? The taint of bastardy clung, and sank deep into William's nature. It embittered and hardened him. In 1047, when he was twenty, a formidable conspiracy was organised against him, and at the outset of the revolt he narrowly missed destruction. But at the Battle of Val-ès-Dunes, fought entirely on both sides by cavalry, the rebels were routed, and thenceforward, William's position as Duke of Normandy was secure.

In no part of the feudal world was fighting quality carried to a higher pitch than among the Normans. William was a master of war, and thereby gave his small duchy some of the prestige which England had enjoyed thirty years before under the firm and clear-sighted government of Canute. He and his knights now looked out upon the world with fearless and adventurous eyes. Good reasons for gazing across the Channel were added to the natural ambitions of warlike men. William watched every move on the part of the supporters of the Anglo-Danish party, headed by Godwin and his son Harold.

Fate played startlingly into the hands of the Norman Duke. On some visits of inspection, probably in 1064, Harold was driven by the winds on to the French coast, and was conducted to the Norman Court. A friendship sprang up between William and Harold. Politics apart, they liked each other well. He was honoured and knighted by William. But the Duke looked forward to his own future succession to the English crown. Here, indeed, was the prize to be won. Harold had one small streak of royal blood on his mother's side; but William, through his father, had a more pointed or at least less cloudy claim to the Island throne. This claim he resolved to assert. He invited Harold to make a pact with him whereby he himself should become King of England, and Harold Earl of the whole splendid province of Wessex, being assured thereof and linked to the King by marriage with William's daughter.

All this story is told with irresistible charm in the tapestry chronicle of the reign designed by English artists under the guidance of his half-brother, Odo, Bishop of Bayeux. It is, of course, the Norman version, and was for generations proclaimed by their historians as a full justification—and already even in those days aggressors needed justifications—of William's invasion of England. The Saxons contended that this was mere Norman propaganda, and there is the usual conflict of evidence. Nevertheless, it cannot be said that the bargain between the two men was unreasonable, and Harold probably at the time saw good prospects in it for himself. Later, Harold, liberated, was conducting the government of England with genuine acceptance and increasing success. When, at length, in January, 1066, Edward the Confessor died, absolved, we trust, from such worldly sins as he had been tempted to commit, Harold, at the beginning of the fateful year 1066, was blithely crowned King with all solemnity in Westminster Abbey.

This event opened again the gates of war. Every aspiring thane who heard the news of Harold's elevation was conscious of an affront, and also of the wide ranges open to ability and the sword.

*　　*　　*

Two rival projects of invasion were speedily prepared. The first was from Scandinavia. The successors of Canute in Norway determined to revive their traditions of English sovereignty. An expedition was already being organised when Tostig, Harold's exiled and revengeful half-brother, ousted from his Earldom of Northumbria, arrived with full accounts of the crisis in the Island and of the weak state of the defences. King Harold Hardrada set forth to conquer the English crown. He sailed at first to the Orkneys, gathering recruits from the Scottish isles and from the Isle of

Man. With Tostig he wended towards the north-east coast of England with a large fleet and army in the late summer of 1066.

Harold of England was thus faced with a double invasion from the north-east and from the south. In September, 1066, he heard that a Norwegian fleet, with Hardrada and Tostig on board, had sailed up the Humber, beaten the local levies under Earls Edwin and Morcar, and encamped near York at Stamford Bridge. He now showed the fighting qualities he possessed. The news reached him in London, where he was waiting to see which invasion would strike him first, and where. At the head of his Danish household troops he hastened northwards up the Roman road to York, calling out the local levies as he went. His rapidity of movement took the Northern invaders completely by surprise. Within five days of the defeat of Edwin and Morcar Harold reached York, and the same day marched to confront the Norwegian army ten miles from the city.

The battle began. The Englishmen charged, but at first the Norsemen, though without their armour, kept their battle array. After a while, deceived by what proved to be a feint, the common ruse of those days, they opened up their shield rampart and advanced from all sides. This was the moment for which Harold had waited. The greatest crash of weapons arose. Hardrada was hit by an arrow in the throat, and Tostig, assuming the command, took his stand by the banner "Land-ravager." In this pause Harold offered his brother peace, and also quarter to all Norsemen who were still alive; but "the Norsemen called out all of them together that they would rather fall, one across the other, than accept of quarter from the Englishmen." [1] Harold's valiant house-carls, themselves of Viking blood, charged home, and with a war shout the battle began again. At this moment a force left on board ship arrived to succour the invaders. They, unlike their comrades, were clad in proof, but, breathless and exhausted from their hurried march, they cast aside their ring-mail, threw in their lot with their hard-pressed friends, and nearly all were killed. The victorious Harold buried Hardrada in the seven feet of English earth he had scornfully promised him, but he spared his son Olaf and let him go in peace with his surviving adherents. Tostig paid for his restless malice with his life. Though the Battle of Stamford Bridge has been overshadowed by Hastings it has a claim to be regarded as one of the decisive contests of English history. Never again was a Scandinavian army able seriously to threaten the power of an English king or the unity of the realm.

At the moment of victory news reached the King from the South that "William the Bastard" had landed at Pevensey.

*   *   *

William the Conqueror's invasion of England was planned like a business enterprise. The resources of Normandy were obviously unequal to the task;

[1] From the *Heimskringla Saga,* by Snorre Sturlason.

but the Duke's name was famous throughout the feudal world, and the idea of seizing and dividing England commended itself to the martial nobility of many lands. The barons of Normandy at the Council of Lillebonne refused to countenance the enterprise officially. It was the Duke's venture, and not that of Normandy. But the bulk of them hastened to subscribe their quota of knights and ships. Brittany sent a large contingent. It must be remembered that some of the best stocks from Roman Britain had found refuge there, establishing a strong blood strain which had preserved a continuity with the Classic Age and with the British race. All France was deeply interested. Mercenaries came from Flanders, and even from beyond the Alps; Normans from South Italy and Spain; nobles and knights answered the advertisement. The shares in this enterprise were represented by knights or ships, and it was plainly engaged that the lands of the slaughtered English would be divided in proportion to the contributions, subject of course to a bonus for good work in the field. During the summer of 1066 this great gathering of audacious buccaneers, land-hungry, war-hungry, assembled in a merry company. Around St. Valery, at the mouth of the Somme, ships had been built in all the French ports from the spring onwards; and by the beginning of August nearly seven hundred vessels and about seven thousand men, of whom the majority were persons of rank and quality, were ready to follow the renowned Duke and share the lands and wealth of England.

But the winds were contrary. For six whole weeks there was no day when the south wind blew. The heterogeneous army, bound by no tie of feudal allegiance, patriotism, or moral theme, began to bicker and grumble. Only William's repute as a managing director and the rich pillage to be expected held them together. At length the whole fleet put to sea, with all their stores, weapons, coats of mail, and great numbers of horses. Special arrangements were made to keep the fleet together, the rendezvous being at the mouth of the Somme, and the Duke by night having a lamp of special brilliancy upon his masthead. The next morning all steered towards the English coast. The Duke, who had a faster vessel, soon found himself alone in mid-Channel. He hove to and breakfasted with his staff "as if he had been in his own hall." Wine was not lacking, and after the meal he expressed himself in enthusiastic terms upon his great undertaking and the prizes and profit it would bring to all engaged therein.

On September 28 the fleet came safely to anchor in Pevensey Bay. There was no opposition to the landing. The local "fyrd" had been called out this year four times already to watch the coast, and having, in true English style, come to the conclusion that the danger was past because it had not yet arrived had gone back to their homes. William landed, as the tale goes, and fell flat on his face as he stepped out of the boat. "See," he said, turning the omen into a favourable channel, "I have taken England with both my hands."

Meanwhile Harold and his house-carls, sadly depleted by the slaughter of Stamford Bridge, jingled down Watling Street on their ponies, marching night and day. On the morning of October 14, at the first streak of dawn, William set out from his camp at Pevensey, resolved to put all to the test; and Harold, eight miles away, awaited him in resolute array.

As the battle began Ivo Taillefer, the minstrel knight who had claimed the right to make the first attack, advanced up the hill on horseback, throwing his lance and sword into the air and catching them before the astonished English. He then charged deep into the English ranks, and was slain. The cavalry charges of William's mail-clad knights, cumbersome in manœuvre, beat in vain upon the dense, ordered masses of the English. Neither the arrow hail nor the assaults of the horsemen could prevail against them. William's left wing of cavalry was thrown into disorder, and retreated rapidly down the hill. On this the troops on Harold's right, who were mainly the local "fyrd," broke their ranks in eager pursuit. William, in the centre, turned his disciplined squadrons upon them and cut them to pieces. The Normans then re-formed their ranks and began a second series of charges upon the English masses, subjecting them in the intervals to severe archery. It has often been remarked that this part of the action resembles the afternoon at Waterloo, when Ney's cavalry exhausted themselves upon the British squares, torn by artillery in the intervals. In both cases the tortured infantry stood unbroken. Never, it was said, had the Norman knights met foot-soldiers of this stubbornness. They were utterly unable to break through the shield-walls, and they suffered serious losses from deft blows of the axe-men, or from javelins, or clubs hurled from the ranks behind. But the arrow showers took a cruel toll. So closely were the English wedged that the wounded could not be removed, and the dead scarcely found room in which to sink upon the ground.

The autumn afternoon was far spent before any result had been achieved, and it was then that William adopted the time-honoured ruse of a feigned retreat. He had seen how readily Harold's right had quitted their positions in pursuit after the first repulse of the Normans. He now organised a sham retreat in apparent disorder, while keeping a powerful force in his own hands. The house-carls around Harold preserved their discipline and kept their ranks, but the sense of relief to the less trained forces after these hours of combat was such that seeing their enemy in flight proved irresistible. They surged forward on the impulse of victory, and when half-way down the hill were savagely slaughtered by William's horsemen. There remained, as the dusk grew, only the valiant bodyguard who fought round the King and his standard. His brothers, Gyrth and Leofwine, had already been killed. William now directed his archers to shoot high into the air, so that the arrows would fall behind the shield-wall, and one of these pierced

Harold in the right eye, inflicting a mortal wound. He fell at the foot of the royal standard, unconquerable except by death, which does not count in honour. The hard-fought battle was now decided. The last formed body of troops was broken, though by no means overwhelmed. They withdrew into the woods behind, and William, who had fought in the foremost ranks and had three horses killed under him, could claim the victory. Nevertheless the pursuit was heavily checked. There is a sudden deep ditch on the reverse slope of the hill of Hastings, into which large numbers of Norman horsemen fell, and in which they were butchered by the infuriated English lurking in the wood.

The dead King Harold's naked body, wrapped only in a robe of purple, was hidden among the rocks of the bay. His mother in vain offered the weight of the body in gold for permission to bury him in holy ground. The Norman Duke's answer was that Harold would be more fittingly laid upon the Saxon shore which he had given his life to defend. The body was later transferred to Waltham Abbey, which he had founded. Although here the English once again accepted conquest and bowed in a new destiny, yet ever must the name of Harold be honoured in the Island for which he and his famous house-carls fought indomitably to the end.

* * *

The Normans introduced into England their system of land tenure based upon military service. A military caste was imposed from above. A revolution not only in warfare, but also in the upper reaches of society, had taken place. The Normans, a small minority, had destroyed the Saxon governing class and had thrust an alien domination upon England. They were administrators and lawyers rather than legislators. The whole system of Saxon local government, also of immense usefulness for the future— the counties, the sheriffs, and the courts—survived, and through this the King maintained his widespread contacts with the country. Thus in the future government of England both Norman and Saxon institutions were unconsciously but profoundly blended.

In the Norman settlement lay the germ of a constitutional opposition, with the effect if not the design of controlling the Government, not breaking it up. The seat of this potential opposition was found in the counties, among the smaller nobility and their untitled descendants, Justices of the Peace and knights of the shire. They were naturally for the Crown and a quiet life. Hence after centuries they rallied to the Tudor sovereigns; and in another age to the Parliament against the Crown itself. Whatever else changed they were always *there*. And the reason why they were there is that William found the old West Saxon organisation, which they alone could administer, exceedingly convenient. He did not mean to be treated as he had treated the King of France. He had seen, and profited by seeing, the mischief of a country divided into great provinces. The little provinces of England, with the King's officers at the head of each, gave him exactly the balance of power he needed for all purposes of law and finance, but were at the same time incapable of rebelling as units. The old English nobility disappeared after the Battle of Hastings. But all over Domesday Book the opinion of what we should later call the gentry of the shire is quoted as decisive.

The Conquest was the supreme achievement of the Norman race. It linked the history of England anew to Europe, and prevented for ever a drift into the narrower orbit of a Scandinavian empire. Henceforward English history marched with that of races and lands south of the Channel.

CHAPTER TEN

Growth Amid Turmoil

WILLIAM DIED at Rouen in 1087, leaving England to his son William, known as Rufus the Red. Rufus brought the Welsh marches and the Northern counties under his control. When he was killed in a hunting accident in the New Forest, he was succeeded by his younger brother Henry, who put down rebellion at home, defeated his brother Robert of Normandy, and once more united the two kingdoms of England and Normandy, with the capital now in London.

The Anglo-Norman State was now powerful. Henry was lord of England, Normandy, and Maine. But what may be judged malignant fortune now intervened. The King had a son, his heir apparent, successor indisputable. On this young man of seventeen many hopes and assurances were founded. In the winter of 1120 he was coming back from a visit to France in the royal yacht called the *White Ship*. Off the coast of Normandy the vessel struck a rock and all but one were drowned. None dared tell the King. When at last he heard the tidings "he never smiled again." This was more than the agony of parental grief for an only son. It portended the breakdown of a system and prospect upon the consolidation of which the whole life's work of Henry stood. The spectre of a disputed succession glared again upon England. The forces of anarchy grew, and every noble in his castle balanced his chances upon who would succeed to the Crown.

There were two claimants, each of whom had a fair share of right. King Henry in the grey close of his life set himself to fill the void with his daughter Maud as female king. Against her stood the claim of Stephen, son of the Conqueror's daughter Adela.

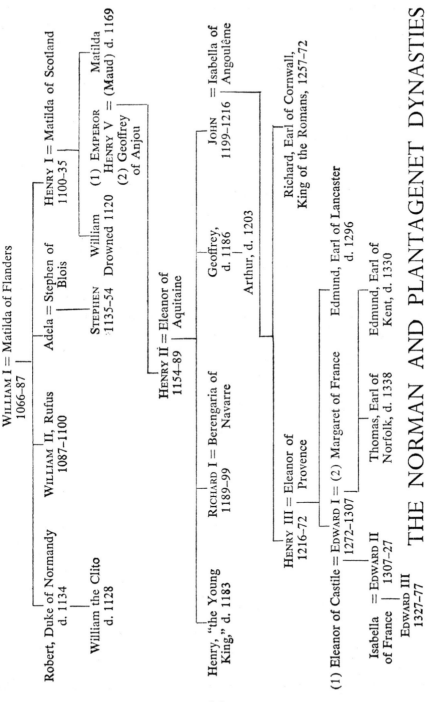

THE NORMAN AND PLANTAGENET DYNASTIES

43

After giving the Island thirty years of peace and order and largely reconciling the Saxon population to Norman rule, Henry I expired on December 1, 1135, in the confident hope that his daughter Maud would carry on his work. But she was with her husband in Anjou and Stephen was the first on the spot. Stephen quickly made terms with the Church, and, thus sustained, was crowned and anointed King. A succession established on such disputable grounds could only be maintained unchallenged by skilful sovereignty. The more we reflect upon the shortcomings of modern government the readier we shall be to make allowances for the difficulties of these times.

The Island dissolved into confused civil war. During the years that followed there was neither law nor peace in large parts of the country. It seemed that a divided succession had wrecked the work of the Norman kings. Over large parts of England fighting was sporadic and local in character. It was the central southern counties that bore the brunt of civil war. But these commotions bit deep into the consciousness of the people. It was realised how vital an institution a strong monarchy was for the security of life and property. No better reasons for monarchy could have been found than were forced upon all minds by the events of Stephen's reign. Men looked back with yearning to the efficient government of Henry I. But a greater than he was at hand.

*   *   *

In 1147 the leadership of Maud's party devolved upon her son. Henry Plantagenet was born to empire. To contemporaries he was best known as Henry Fitz-Empress; but he carried into English history the emblem of his house, the broom, the *Planta Genesta,* which later generations were to make the name of this great dynasty, the Plantagenets. He embodied all their ability, all their energy, and not a little of that passionate, ruthless ferocity which, it was whispered, came to the house of Anjou from no mortal source, but from a union with Satan himself.

When scarcely fifteen, in 1147, Henry had actively championed his claim to the English throne on English soil. His small band of followers was then defeated by Stephen's forces, and he took refuge in Normandy. For a few years of comparative peace King Stephen was left in uneasy possession. In the meantime Henry was invested by his parents in 1150 as Duke of Normandy. The next year his father's death made him also Count of Anjou, Touraine, and Maine. In his high feudal capacity Henry repaired to Paris to render homage to his lord the King of France, of which country he already possessed, by the accepted law of the age, a large part.

Louis VII was a French Edward the Confessor; he practised with faithful simplicity the law of Christ. All his days were spent in devotion, and his nights in vigil or penance. When he left his own chapel he would delay the whole Court by waiting till the humblest person present had preceded him.

These pious and exemplary habits did not endear him to his queen. Eleanor of Aquitaine was in her own right a reigning princess, with the warmth of the South in her veins. She had already complained that she had "married a monk and not a king" when this square-shouldered, ruddy youth, with his "countenance of fire," sprightly talk, and overflowing energy, suddenly presented himself before her husband as his most splendid vassal. Eleanor did not waste words in coming to a decision. The Papacy bowed to strong will and Eleanor obtained a divorce from Louis VII in 1152 on the nominal grounds of consanguinity. But what staggered the French Court and opened the eyes of its prayerful King was the sudden marriage of Eleanor to Henry two months later. Thus half of France passed out of royal control into the hands of Henry. Rarely have passion and policy flowed so buoyantly together. The marriage was one of the most brilliant political strokes of the age. Henry afterwards admitted his designs, and accepted the admiration of Europe for their audacity. He was nineteen and she was probably thirty; and, uniting their immense domains, they made a common cause against all comers.

War in all quarters lay before the royal pair. Everywhere men shook their heads over this concentration of power, this spectacle of so many races and states, sundered from each other by long feuds or divergent interests, now suddenly flung together by the hot blood of a love intrigue. From all sides the potentates confronted the upstart. The King of France, who certainly had every conceivable cause of complaint; King Stephen of England, who disputed Henry's title to the Norman duchy, though without force to intervene across the Channel; the Count of Champagne; the Count of Perche; and Henry's own brother, Geoffrey—all spontaneously, and with good reason, fell upon him. A month after the marriage his foes converged, but the youthful Duke Henry beat them back, ruptured and broken. He turned forthwith to England. It was a valiant figure that landed in January, 1153, and from all over England, distracted by civil wars, hearts and eyes turned towards him. Merlin had prophesied a deliverer; had he not in his veins blood that ran back to William the Conqueror, and beyond him, through his grandmother Matilda, wife of Henry I, to Cedric and the long-vanished Anglo-Saxon line? A wild surge of hope greeted him from the tormented Islanders, and when he knelt after his landing in the first church he found "to pray for a space in the manner of soldiers," the priest pronounced the wish of the nation in the words, "Behold there cometh the Lord, the Ruler, and the kingdom is in his hand."

There followed battles: Malmesbury, where the sleet, especially directed by Almighty God, beat upon the faces of his foes; Wallingford, where King Stephen by divine interposition fell three times from his horse before going into action. Glamour, terror, success, attended this youthful, puissant warrior, who had not only his sword, but his title deeds. The baronage saw their interest favoured by a stalemate; they wanted neither a victorious Stephen nor a triumphant Henry. The weaker the King the stronger the nobles. A treaty was concluded at Winchester in 1153 whereby Stephen made Henry his adopted son and his appointed heir. "In the business of the kingdom," promised Stephen, "I will work by the counsel of the Duke; but in the whole realm of England, as well in the Duke's part as my own, I will exercise royal justice." On this Henry did homage and made all the formal submissions, and when a year later Stephen died he was acclaimed and crowned King of England with more general hope and rejoicing than had ever uplifted any monarch in England since the days of Alfred the Great.

CHAPTER ELEVEN

Henry Plantagenet

THE ACCESSION of Henry II began one of the most pregnant and decisive reigns in English history. The new sovereign ruled an empire, and, as his subjects boasted, his warrant ran "from the Arctic Ocean to the Pyrenees." England to him was but one—the most solid though perhaps the least attractive—of his provinces. But he gave to England that effectual element of external control which, as in the days of William of Orange, was indispensable to the growth of national unity. He was accepted by English and Norman as the ruler of both races and the whole country. The memories of Hastings were confounded in his person, and after the hideous anarchy of civil war and robber barons all due attention was paid to his commands. Thus, though a Frenchman, with foreign speech and foreign modes, he shaped our country in a fashion of which the outline remains to the present day.

After a hundred years of being the encampment of an invading army, England became finally and for all time a coherent kingdom, based upon Christianity. Henry Plantagenet first brought England, Scotland, and Ireland into a certain common relationship. He relaid the foundations of a central power, based upon the exchequer and the judiciary. The King gathered up and cherished the Anglo-Saxon tradition of self-government under royal command in shire and borough. It is to him we owe the enduring fact that the English-speaking race all over the world is governed by the English Common Law rather than by the Roman.

A vivid picture is painted of this gifted and, for a while, enviable man:

square, thick-set, bull-necked, with powerful arms and coarse, rough hands; his legs bandy from endless riding; a large, round head and closely cropped red hair; a freckled face; a voice harsh and cracked. Intense love of the chase; other loves, which the Church deplored and Queen Eleanor resented; frugality in food and dress; days entirely concerned with public business; travel unceasing; moods various. It was said that he was always gentle and calm in times of urgent peril, but became bad-tempered and capricious when the pressure relaxed. Everything was stirred and moulded by him in England, as also in his other much greater estates, which he patrolled with tireless attention.

But this twelfth-century monarch, with his lusts and sports, his hates and his schemes, was no materialist; he was the Lord's Anointed, he commanded, with the Archbishop of Canterbury—"those two strong steers that drew the plough of England"—the whole allegiance of his subjects. The offices of religion, the fear of eternal damnation, the hope of even greater realms beyond the grave, accompanied him from hour to hour. At times he was smitten with remorse and engulfed in repentance. He drew all possible delights and satisfactions from this world and the next. He is portrayed to us in convulsions both of spiritual exaltation and abasement. This was no secluded monarch: the kings of those days were as accessible to all classes as a modern President of the United States. People broke in upon him at all hours with business, with tidings, with gossip, with visions, with complaints. Talk rang high in the King's presence and to His Majesty's face among the nobles and courtiers, and the jester, invaluable monitor, castigated all impartially with unstinted licence.

Few mortals have led so full a life as Henry II or have drunk so deeply of the cups of triumph and sorrow. In later life he fell out with Eleanor. When she was over fifty and he but forty-two he is said to have fallen in love with "Fair Rosamond," a damosel of high degree and transcendent beauty, and generations have enjoyed the romantic tragedy of Queen Eleanor penetrating the protecting maze at Woodstock by the clue of a silken thread and offering her hapless supplanter the hard choice between the dagger and the poisoned cup. Tiresome investigators have undermined this excellent tale, but it certainly should find its place in any history worthy of the name.

*   *   *

Such was the man who succeeded to the troubled and divided inheritance of Stephen. Already before his accession to the English throne Henry had fought the first of his many wars to defend his Continental inheritance. Ever since the emergence of the strong Norman power in North-West France, a hundred years before, the French monarchy had struggled ceaselessly against the encroachments of great dukedoms and countships upon the central Government. The Battle of Hastings had made the greatest French subject, the Duke of Normandy, also King of England; but Henry II's accession to the Island throne in 1154 threatened France with far graver dangers. Hitherto there had always been political relief in playing off overmighty subjects one against another. But when in one hour Henry II was King of England, Duke of Normandy, Lord of Aquitaine, Brittany, Poitou, Anjou, Maine, and Guienne, ruler from the Somme to the Pyrenees of more than half France, all balance of power among the feudal lords was destroyed.

Louis VII found instead of a dozen principalities, divided and jealous, one single imperial Power, whose resources far surpassed his own. He was scarcely the man to face such a combination. Yet weak as he appeared in his struggle with the enterprising and active Henry, the tide of events flowed with the compact French monarchy, and even Louis left it more firmly established than he found it.

How, we may ask, did all this affect the daily life of England, her history, and her common folk? For many generations their bravest and best were to fight and die by the marshes of the Loire or under the sun-baked hills of Southern France in pursuit of the dream of English dominion over French soil. For this two centuries later Englishmen triumphed at Crécy, Poitiers, and Agincourt, or starved in the terrible Limoges march of the Black Prince. For this they turned fertile France into a desert where even the most needed beasts died of thirst and hunger. Throughout the medieval history of England, war with France is the interminable and often the dominant theme. It groped and scraped into every reach of English life, moulding and fretting the shape of English society and institutions.

No episode opens to us a wider window upon politics of the twelfth century in England than the quarrel of Henry II with his great subject and former friend, Thomas Becket, Archbishop of Canterbury. We have to realise the gravity of this conflict. The military State in feudal Christendom bowed to the Church in things spiritual; it never accepted the idea of the transference of secular power to priestly authority.

Now a great personality stood at the summit of the religious hierarchy, Thomas Becket, who had been the King's friend, a faithful comrade and colleague in the common endeavour. It was by the King's direct influence and personal effort that Becket was elected Archbishop. From that moment all his gifts and impulses ran in another channel. Something like the transformation which later carried Henry V from a rollicking prince to the august hero-king overnight was now witnessed in Becket. He sought by extreme austerities to gather around himself the fame and honour of a saint. Becket pursued the same methods and ambitions in the ecclesiastical as previously he had done in the political sphere; and in both he excelled. He now championed the Church against the Crown in every aspect of their functions.

The struggle between Henry II and Becket is confused by the technical details over which it was fought. There was however good reason why the quarrel should have been engaged upon incidents of administration rather than upon the main principles which were at stake. Stephen in his straits had made sweeping concessions to the Church, whose political influence then reached its zenith. These concessions, Henry felt, compromised his royal rights. He sought to retrace thirty years and to annul the effects of Stephen's surrender. But Becket resisted.

Thus he ruptured that unity which had hitherto been deemed vital in the English realm, and in fact declared war with ghostly weapons upon the King. Stiff in defiance, Becket took refuge on the Continent in exile.

In Becket's absence, Henry resolved to secure the peaceful accession of his son, the young Henry, by having him crowned in his own lifetime. The ceremony was performed by the Archbishop of York, assisted by a number of other clerics. This action was bitterly resented by Becket as an infringement of a cherished right of his see. His welcome home after the years of exile was astonishing. He made a triumphal progress through London and then hotfoot he proceeded to excommunicate the clergy who had taken part in the crowning of young Henry. These unfortunate priests and prelates travelled in a bunch to the King, who was in Normandy. They told a tale not only of ecclesiastical challenge, but of actual revolt and usurpation. They said that the Archbishop was ready "to tear the crown from the young King's head."

Henry Plantagenet, first of all his line, with all the fire of his nature, received these tidings when surrounded by his knights and nobles. He was transported with passion. "What a pack of fools and cowards," he cried, "I have nourished in my house, that not one of them will avenge me of this turbulent priest!" Another version says "of this upstart clerk."

Four Knights had heard the King's bitter words spoken in the full circle. They travelled fast to the coast. They crossed the Channel. They called for horses and rode to Canterbury. There on December 29, 1170, they found the Archbishop in the cathedral. The scene and the tragedy are famous. He confronted them with Cross and mitre, fearless and resolute in warlike action, a master of histrionic arts. After haggard parleys they fell upon him, cut him down with their swords, and left him bleeding like Julius Cæsar, with a score of wounds to cry for vengeance.

This tragedy was fatal to the King. The murder of one of the foremost of God's servants, like the breaking of a feudal oath, struck at the heart of the age. All England was filled with terror. They acclaimed the dead Archbishop as a martyr; and immediately it appeared that his relics healed incurable diseases, and robes that he had worn by mere touch relieved minor ailments. Here indeed was a crime, vast and inexpiable. But it is proof of the quality of the age that these fierce contentions, shaking the souls of men, should have been so rigorously and yet so evenly fought out. In modern conflicts and revolutions in some great states bishops and archbishops have been sent by droves to concentration camps, or pistolled in the nape of the neck in the well-warmed, brilliantly lighted corridor of a prison. What claim have we to vaunt a superior civilisation to Henry II's times? We are sunk in a barbarism all the deeper because it is tolerated by moral lethargy and covered with a veneer of scientific conveniences.

*   *   *

Eighteen years of life lay before the King after Becket's death. In a sense, they were years of glory. All Europe marvelled at the extent of Henry's domains, to which he added the lordship of Ireland. Through the marriages of his daughters he was linked with the Norman King of Sicily, the King of Castile, and Henry the Lion of Saxony, who was a most powerful prince in Germany. Diplomatic agents spread his influence in the Lombard cities of northern Italy. Both Emperor and Pope invited him in the name of Christ and all Europe to lead a new Crusade and to be King of Jerusalem. Indeed, after the Holy Roman Emperor, Frederick Barbarossa, Henry stood next in Christendom. It was suspected by his contemporaries that his aim was to win for himself a kingdom in Italy and even to wear the imperial crown.

Yet Henry knew well that his splendour was personal in origin, tenuous and transient in quality; and he had also deep clouding family sorrows. During these years he was confronted with no less than four rebellions by his sons. For the three eldest he had provided glittering titles; Henry held Normandy, Maine and Anjou; Richard was given Aquitaine, and to Geoffrey went Brittany. These boys were typical sprigs of the Angevin stock. They wanted power as well as titles, and they bore their father no respect. Urged on by their mother, Queen Eleanor, who now lived in Poitiers apart from her husband, between 1173 and 1186 they rose in revolt in various combinations. On each occasion they could count on the active support of the watchful King of France. Henry treated his ungrateful children with generosity, but he had no illusions. The royal chamber at Westminster at this time was adorned with paintings done at the King's command. One represented four eaglets preying upon the parent bird, the fourth one poised at the parent's neck, ready to pick out the eyes. "The four eaglets," the King is reported to have said, "are my four sons who cease not to persecute me even unto death. The youngest of them, whom I now embrace with so much affection will sometime in the end insult me more grievously and more dangerously than any of the others."

So it was to be. John, whom he had striven to provide with an inheritance equal to that of his brothers, joined the final plot against him. In 1188 Richard, his eldest surviving son, after the death of young Henry, was making war upon him in conjunction with King Philip of France. Already desperately ill, Henry was defeated at Le Mans and recoiled to Normandy. When he saw in the list of conspirators against him the name of his son John, upon whom his affection had strangely rested, he abandoned the struggle with life. "Let things go as they will," he gasped. "Shame, shame on a conquered King." So saying, this hard, violent, brilliant and lonely man expired at Chinon on July 6, 1189. The pious were taught to regard this melancholy end as the further chastisement of God upon the murderer of Thomas Becket. Such is the bitter taste of worldly power. Such are the correctives of glory.

CHAPTER TWELVE

Coeur de Lion

WHEN, IN the midst of these surgings, Henry II died in sorrow and disaster, he made no attempt to prescribe the succession, and it passed naturally to Richard. The new King affected little grief at the death of a father against whom he was in arms. He knelt beside his bier no longer than would have been necessary to recite the Lord's Prayer, and turned at once to the duties of his realm. In spite of many harsh qualities, men saw in him a magnanimity which has added lustre to his military renown.

*   *   *

Richard I, with all his characteristic virtues and faults cast in a heroic mould, is one of the most fascinating medieval figures. He has been described as the creature and embodiment of the age of chivalry. In those days the lion was much admired in heraldry. When Richard's contemporaries called him "Coeur de Lion" they paid a lasting compliment to the king of beasts. Little did the English people owe him for his services, and heavily did they pay for his adventures. He was in England only twice for a few short months in his ten years' reign; yet his memory has always stirred English hearts, and seems to present throughout the centuries the pattern of the fighting man. In all deeds of prowess as well as in large schemes of war Richard shone. He was tall and delicately shaped; strong in nerve and sinew, and most dextrous in arms. He rejoiced in personal combat, and regarded his opponents without malice as necessary agents in his fame. He loved war, not so much for the sake of glory or political ends, but as other men love science or poetry, for the excitement of the struggle and the glow of victory.

Although a man of blood and violence, Richard was too impetuous to

5 1

be either treacherous or habitually cruel. He was as ready to forgive as he was hasty to offend; he was open-handed and munificent to profusion; in war circumspect in design and skilful in execution; in politics a child, lacking in subtlety and experience. His political alliances were formed upon his likes and dislikes; his political schemes had neither unity nor clearness of purpose. The advantages gained for him by military genius were flung away through diplomatic ineptitude. His life was one magnificent parade, which, when ended, left only an empty plain.

The King's heart was set upon the new Crusade. This task seemed made for him. It appealed to every need of his nature. To rescue the Holy Land from the pollution of the infidel, to charge as a king at the head of knightly squadrons in a cause at once glorious to man and especially acceptable to God, was a completely satisfying inspiration.

The glamours of chivalry illumine the tale of the Third Crusade. All the chief princes of Europe were now in line around the doomed stronghold of Saladin, rivalling each other in prowess and jealousy. The sanctity of their cause was no bar to their quarrels and intrigues. King Richard dominated the scene. Fighting always in the most dangerous places, striking down the strongest foes, he negotiated all the time with Saladin. An agreement was in fact almost reached. To save his garrison Saladin offered to surrender his Christian captives, to pay a large indemnity, and to give up the cross, captured by him in Jerusalem, on which Christ—though this after twelve hundred years was not certain—had suffered. But the negotiations failed, and Richard in his fury massacred in cold blood the two thousand Turkish hostages who had been delivered as guarantees. Within five weeks of his arrival he brought the two years' siege to a successful conclusion.

In the next year, 1192, the King felt it imperative to return home. The chief danger lay in the overmighty position of Prince John. The indulgence of Richard had allowed his brother to form a state within a state. Early in 1193 the King set out. Wrecked in the Adriatic, he sought to make his way through Germany in disguise, but his enemy the Duke of Austria was soon upon his track. He was arrested, and held prisoner in a castle. For many months his prison was a secret of the Imperial Court, but, as a pretty legend tells us, Blondel, Richard's faithful minstrel, went from castle to castle striking the chords which Richard loved best, and at last was rewarded by an answer from Richard's own harp.

* * *

Early in 1193, at a moment already full of peril, the grave news reached England that the King was prisoner "somewhere in Germany." There was general and well-founded consternation among the loyal bulk of his subjects. John declared that Richard was dead, appeared in arms, and claimed the crown. That England was held for Richard in his long absence against all these powerful and subtle forces is a proof of the loyalties of the feudal age. A deep sense of his heroic character and sacred mission commanded the allegiance of a large number of resolute, independent people whose names are unknown to history. John's forces melted. In April the strain was relieved by the arrival of authoritative news that Richard was alive. Prince John put the best face he could upon it and stole away to France.

*   *   *

The Holy Roman Emperor demanded the prodigious ransom of 150,000 marks, twice the annual revenue of the English Crown. One hundred thousand was to be ready in London before the King was liberated. Richard approved and the English Council agreed. Meanwhile Philip and John were active on the other side. They offered the Emperor 80,000 marks to keep the English King under lock and key till Michaelmas 1194, or 150,000 marks to deliver him into their hands. But the Emperor felt that his black-mailing honour was engaged to Richard, with whom he had, perhaps precipitately, settled the figure. Once Philip knew that the Emperor would not go back upon his bargain he sent John his notorious message: "Have a care—the Devil is unloosed."

The charge staggered the kingdom. Yet nothing was more sacred than the feudal obligation to ransom the liege lord, above all when he enjoyed the sanctity of a Crusader. At the end of 1193 the stipulated first instalment was paid, and Richard Coeur de Lion was released from bondage. He picked his way, we may be assured, with care across Europe, arriving again in London among citizens impoverished but still rejoiced to see him and proud of his fame.

The mere arrival of the mighty warrior in France was enough to restore the frontiers and to throw King Philip and his forces upon an almost abject defensive. John sought pardon from the brother and liege lord he had so foully wronged. He did not sue in vain. With the full knowledge that if John had had his way he would still be a captive in a German castle, dethroned, or best of all dead—with all the long story of perfidy and un-natural malice in his mind, Coeur de Lion pardoned John, embraced him in fraternal love, and restored him to some of his estates, except certain fortresses which the barest prudence obliged him to reserve. This gesture was admired for its grandeur, though not perhaps for its wisdom, by the whole society, lay and spiritual, of Christendom.

*   *   *

The five remaining years of Richard's reign were spent in defending his French domains and raising money for that purpose from England. In 1199, when the difficulties of raising revenue for the endless war were at their height, good news was brought to King Richard. It was said there had been dug up near the castle of Chaluz, on the lands of one of his vassals, a treasure of wonderful quality; a group of golden images of an emperor, his wife, sons, and daughters, seated round a table, also of gold, had been unearthed. The King claimed this treasure as lord paramount. The lord of Chaluz resisted the demand, and the King laid siege to his small, weak castle. On the third day, as he rode daringly near the wall, confident in his hard-tried luck, a bolt from a crossbow struck him in the left shoulder by the neck. The wound, already deep, was aggravated by the necessary cutting out of the arrow-head. Gangrene set in, and Coeur de Lion knew that he must pay a soldier's debt. He prepared for death with fortitude and calm, and in accordance with the principles he had followed. He arranged his affairs; he divided his personal belongings among his friends or bequeathed them to charity. He sent for his mother, the redoubtable Eleanor, who was at hand. He declared John to be his heir, and made all present swear fealty to him. He ordered the archer who had shot the fatal bolt, and who was now a prisoner, to be brought before him. He pardoned him, and made him a gift of money. For seven years he had not confessed, but now he received the offices of the Church with sincere and exemplary piety, and died in the forty-second year of his age on April 6, 1199, worthy, by the consent of all men, to sit with King Arthur and Roland and other heroes of martial romance at some Eternal Round Table, which we trust the Creator of the Universe in His comprehension will not have forgotten to provide.

The archer was flayed alive.

CHAPTER THIRTEEN

Magna Carta

THE CHARACTER of the prince who now ascended the throne was already known. Richard had embodied the virtues which men admire in the lion, but there is no animal in nature that combines the contradictory qualities of John. He united the ruthlessness of a hardened warrior with the craft and subtlety of a Machiavellian. His cruelties were conceived and executed with a cold, inhuman intelligence. Monkish chroniclers have emphasised his violence, greed, malice, treachery, and lust. But other records show that he was often judicious, always extremely capable, and on occasions even generous. He possessed an original and inquiring mind, and to the end of his life treasured his library of books. In him the restless energy of the Plantagenet race was raised to a furious pitch of instability. However, when the long tally is added it will be seen that the British nation and the English-speaking world owe far more to the vices of John than to the labours of virtuous sovereigns; for it was through the union of many forces against him that the most famous milestone of our rights and freedom was in fact set up.

Although Richard had declared John to be King there were two views upon the succession. Geoffrey, his elder brother, had left behind him a son, Arthur, Prince of Brittany. It was already possible to hold that this grandson of Henry II of an elder branch had a prior right against John, and that is now the law of primogeniture. Those who had supported Richard against his father, and John against Richard, found it logical to support Arthur against John. From the first John feared Arthur and found himself compelled to fight at even greater odds than his predecessors for his possessions on the Continent.

Arthur, hearing that his grandmother Eleanor was at the castle of Mirebeau in Poitou with a scanty escort, surrounded the castle, stormed the outworks, and was about to gain custody of this important and hostile old queen. John surprised Arthur and the besiegers, and, as he declared, "by the favour of God" got the lot; Arthur and all who stood with him.

Arthur, caught in open fight besieging his own grandmother, was a prisoner of war. The horrid crime of murder has often been committed for reasons of state upon lesser temptations than now assailed this exceptionally violent king. No one knows what happened to Arthur. An impenetrable veil descends upon the tragedy of Rouen. The officer commanding the fortress gave out that upon the King's order he had delivered his prisoner at Easter 1203 to the hands of agents sent by John to castrate him, and that Arthur had died of the shock. However it may be, Arthur was never seen again.

Although high nobles and common people in large numbers were in those times frequently put to death without trial and for reasons of hate or policy, the murder by a king of an equal confirmed the bad impression which all the world had formed of John. Moreover, the odious crime did not prevent but rather hastened the loss of Normandy.

Three months later the capital was taken, and Normandy finally became French.

No English tears need have been shed over this loss. The Angevin Empire at its peak had no real unity. Time and geography lay on the side of the French. The separation proved as much in the interest of England as of France. It rid the Island of a dangerous, costly distraction and entanglement, turned its thought and energies to its own affairs, and above all left a ruling class of alien origin with no interest henceforth that was not English or at least insular. These consolations did not however dawn on John's contemporaries, who saw only disastrous and humiliating defeat, and blamed a King already distrusted by the people and at variance with the nobility.

*   *   *

English society was steadily developing. All classes were needed by the new centralised Government; but John preferred to emphasise the more ruthless aspects of royal power. By systematic abuse of his feudal prerogatives John drove the baronage to violent resistance.

The Papal throne at this time was occupied by Innocent III, one of the greatest of the medieval Popes, renowned for his statecraft and diplomacy, and intent on raising to its height the temporal power of the Church. By a ruse he caused Stephen Langton, an English cardinal of highest character, to be selected Archbishop of Canterbury. In his wrath, and without measuring the strength of his opponents, the King proceeded to levy a bloodless war upon the Church. When John began to persecute the clergy and seize Church lands the Pope retaliated by laying all England under an interdict. For more than six years the bells were silent, the doors of the churches were closed against the devout; the dead must be buried in unconsecrated ground and without the last communion. Many of John's subjects were assured of damnation for themselves or their loved ones on this account alone.

The Pope, in 1209, took the supreme step of excommunication. The King's insecurity at home forced him to bow and Innocent rejoiced in victory upon his own terms. John, however, was not at the end of his devices, and by a stroke of cunning choice enough to be called political genius he turned defeat into something very like triumph. He offered to make England a fief of the Papacy, and to do homage to the Pope as his feudal lord. Innocent leapt at this addition to his worldly dignities. He forgave the penitent King; he took him and the realm of England under his special protection. He accepted the sovereignty of England from the hands of John, and returned it to him as his vassal with his blessing.

This turned the tables upon John's secular enemies. The barons found meagre comfort in the transformation. Their grievances remained unredressed, their anger appeased. King John, who had lain at Dover, quaking but calculating, may have laughed while he pulled all these strings and threw his enemies into confusion.

The disaffected barons drew together under the leadership of Stephen Langton. They formed plans to restrain the rule of a despotic and defeated King, and openly threatened revolt unless their terms were accepted. In place of the King's arbitrary despotism they proposed, not the withering anarchy of feudal separatism, but a system of checks and balances which would accord the monarchy its necessary strength, but would prevent its perversion by a tyrant or a fool. The leaders of the barons in 1215 groped in the dim light towards a fundamental principle. Government must henceforward mean something more than the arbitrary rule of any man, and custom and the law must stand even above the King. It was this idea, perhaps only half understood, that gave unity and force to the barons' opposition and made the Charter which they now demanded imperishable.

On a Monday morning in June, between Staines and Windsor, the barons and Churchmen began to collect on the great meadow at Runnymede. An uneasy hush fell on them from time to time. Many had failed to keep their tryst; and the bold few who had come knew that the King would never forgive this humiliation. He would hunt them down when he could, and the laymen at least were staking their lives in the cause they served. They had arranged a little throne for the King and a tent. This handful of resolute men had drawn up, it seems, a short document on parchment. Their retainers and the groups and squadrons of horsemen in sullen steel kept at some distance and well in the background. For was not armed rebellion against the Crown the supreme feudal crime? Then events followed rapidly. A small cavalcade appeared from the direction of Windsor. Gradually men made out the faces of the King, the Papal Legate, the Archbishop of Canterbury, and several bishops. They dismounted without ceremony. Someone, probably the Archbishop, stated briefly the terms that were suggested. The King declared at once that he agreed.

He said the details should be arranged immediately in his chancery. The original "Articles of the Barons" on which Magna Carta is based exist today in the British Museum. They were sealed in a quiet, short scene, which has become one of the most famous in our history, on June 15, 1215. Afterwards the King returned to Windsor. Four days later, probably, the Charter itself was probably engrossed. In future ages it was to be used as the foundation of principles and systems of government of which neither King John nor his nobles dreamed.

*   *   *

If we set aside the rhetorical praise which has been so freely lavished upon the Charter, and study the document itself, we may find it rather surprising reading. It is entirely lacking in any spacious statement of the principles of democratic government or the rights of man. It implies on the King's part a promise of good government for the future, but the terms of the promise are restricted to the observance of the customary privileges and interests of the baronial class.

The thirteenth century was to be a great age of Parliamentary development and experiment, yet there is no mention in Magna Carta of Parliament or representation of any but the baronial class. The great watchwords of the future here find no place. The actual Charter is a redress of feudal grievances extorted from an unwilling king by a discontented ruling class insisting on its privileges.

Magna Carta must not, however, be dismissed lightly. Even in its own day men of all ranks above the status of villeins had an interest in securing that the tenure of land should be secure from arbitrary encroachment. Therefore in securing themselves the barons of Runnymede were in fact establishing the rights of the whole landed class, great and small—the simple knight with two hundred acres, the farmer or small yeoman with sixty. And there is evidence that their action was so understood throughout the country. In 1218 an official endeavoured to upset by writ a judgment given in the county court of Lincolnshire. The victim was a great land-owner, but the whole county rallied to his cause and to the "liberty sworn and granted," stating in their protest that they acted "with him, and for him, and for ourselves, and the community of the whole realm."

If the thirteenth-century magnates understood little and cared less for popular liberties or Parliamentary democracy, they had all the same laid hold of a principle which was to be of prime importance for the future development of English society and English institutions. Throughout the document it is implied that here is a law which is above the King and which even he must not break. This reaffirmation of a supreme law and its ex-pression in a general charter is the great work of Magna Carta; and this alone justifies the respect in which men have held it. The reign of Henry II, according to the most respected authorities, initiates the rule of law. But the work as yet was incomplete: the Crown was still above the law; the legal system which Henry had created could become, as John showed, an instrument of oppression.

Now for the first time the King himself is bound by the law. The root principle was destined to survive across the generations and rise paramount long after the feudal background of 1215 had faded in the past. The Charter became in the process of time an enduring witness that the power of the Crown was not absolute.

And when in subsequent ages the State, swollen with its own authority, has attempted to ride roughshod over the rights or liberties of the subject, it is to this doctrine that appeal has again and again been made, and never, as yet, without success.

CHAPTER FOURTEEN

King Edward I and King Edward II

DURING THE long reign of Henry III (1216–1272), England was torn by dissension and civil war. His son Edward I, who ruled for thirty-five years, ushered in an era of peace and of orderly administration. Few princes had received so thorough an education in the art of rulership as Edward I when at the age of thirty-three his father's death brought him to the crown.

Of elegant build and lofty stature, a head and shoulders above the height of the ordinary man, with hair always abundant, which, changing from yellow in childhood to black in manhood and snow-white in age, marked the measured progress of his life, his proud brow and regular features were marred only by the drooping left eyelid which had been characteristic of his father. If he stammered he was also eloquent. There is much talk of his limbs. His sinewy, muscular arms were those of a swordsman; his long legs gave him a grip of the saddle, and the nickname of "Longshanks." The King delighted in war and tournaments, and especially in hawking and hunting. When he chased the stag he did not leave his quarry to the hounds, nor even to the hunting spear; he galloped at breakneck speed to cut the unhappy beast to the ground.

All this was typical of his reign. He presents us with qualities which are a mixture of the administrative capacity of Henry II and the personal prowess and magnanimity of Coeur de Lion. No English king more fully lived up to the maxim he chose for himself: "To each his own." He was animated by a passionate regard for justice and law, as he interpreted them, and for the rights of all groups within the community. Injuries and hostility roused, even to his last breath, a passionate torrent of resistance. But submission, or a generous act, on many occasions earned a swift response and laid the foundation of future friendship.

Here was a time of setting in order. The reign is memorable, not for the erection of great new landmarks, but because the beneficial tendencies of the three preceding reigns were extracted from error and confusion and organised and consolidated in a permanent structure. The framework and policies of the nation which we have seen shaping themselves with many fluctuations, now set and hardened into a form which, surviving the tragedies of the Black Death, the Hundred Years' War with France, and the Wars of the Roses, endured for the remainder of the Middle Age, and some of them for longer. In this period we see a knightly and bourgeois stage of society increasingly replacing pure feudalism. The organs of government, land tenure, the military and financial systems, the relations of Church and State, all reach definitions which last nearly till the Tudors.

*   *   *

The first eighteen years of the reign witnessed an outburst of legislative activity for which there was to be no parallel for centuries. Edward saw himself able to conciliate powerful elements and escape from awkward debts, by the simple and well-trodden path of anti-Semitism. The propaganda of ritual murder and other dark tales, the commonplaces of our enlightened age, were at once invoked with general acclaim. The Jews, held up to universal hatred, were pillaged, maltreated, and finally expelled the realm. Exception was made for certain physicians without whose skill persons of consequence might have lacked due attention. Once again the sorrowful, wandering race, stripped to the skin, must seek asylum and begin afresh. To Spain or North Africa the melancholy caravan, now so familiar, must move on. Not until four centuries had elapsed was Oliver Cromwell by furtive contracts with a moneyed Israelite to open again the coasts of England to the enterprise of the Jewish race. It was left to a Calvinist dictator to remove the ban which a Catholic king had imposed. The bankers of Florence and Siena, who had taken the place of the Jews, were in their turn under Edward I's grandson to taste the equities of Christendom.

* * *

Edward I was remarkable among medieval kings for the seriousness with which he regarded the work of administration and good government. Though the most orthodox of Churchmen, Edward did not escape conflict with the Church. Anxious though he was to pay his dues to God, he had a far livelier sense than his father of what was due to Cæsar.

* * *

At the beginning of the reign relations between England and France were governed by the Treaty of Paris. For more than thirty years peace reigned between the two countries, though often with an undercurrent of hostility. But the presence of the English in the South of France had been a standing challenge to the pride of the French and a bar to their national integrity. Finally the Parlement of Paris declared the Duchy of Gascony forfeit. Edward now realised that he must either fight or lose his French possessions.

By 1294 the great King had changed much from his early buoyant manhood. Alone, perplexed and ageing, he had to face an endless succession of difficulties. In June 1294 he explained the grounds of the quarrel with the French to what is already called "a Parliament" of magnates in London. His decision to go to war was accepted with approval, as has often been the case in more regularly constituted assemblies.

The war degenerated into a series of truces which lasted until 1303. Such conditions involved expense little less than actual fighting. These were years of severe strain, both at home and abroad, and especially with Scotland. Although the King did not hesitate to recall recurrent Parliaments to Westminster and explained the whole situation to them, he did not obtain the support which he needed. Parliament was reluctant to grant the new taxes demanded of it.

Edward to a greater extent than any of his predecessors had shown himself prepared to govern in the national interest and with some regard for constitutional form. It was thus ironical, and to the King exasperating, that he found the principles he had emphasised applied against himself. So the Crown was once again committed solemnly and publicly to the principles of Magna Carta, and the concession was made all the more valuable because remedies of actual recent abuses of the royal prerogative powers had been added to the original charters. Here was a real constitutional advance.

*　　*　　*

In their fatal preoccupation with their possessions in France the English kings had neglected the work of extending their rule within the Island of Great Britain. The Welsh wars of Edward reveal to us the process by which the military system of England was transformed from the age-long Saxon and feudal basis of occasional service to that of paid regular troops. At the same time a counter-revolution in the balance of warfare was afoot. The mailed cavalry which from the fifth century had eclipsed the ordered ranks of the legion were wearing out their long day. A new type of infantry raised from the common people began to prove its dominating quality. This infantry operated, not by club or sword or spear, or even by hand-flung missiles, but by an archery which, after a long development, concealed from Europe, was very soon to make an astonishing entrance upon the military scene and gain a dramatic ascendancy upon the battlefields of the Continent. Here was a prize taken by the conquerors from their victims. In South Wales the practice of drawing the long-bow had already attained an astonishing efficiency, of which one of the Marcher lords has left a record. One of his knights had been hit by an arrow which pierced not only the skirts of his mailed shirt, but his mailed breeches, his thigh, and the wood of his saddle, and finally struck deep into his horse's flank. This was a new fact in the history of war, which is also a part of the history of civilisation, deserving to be mentioned with the triumph of bronze over flint, or iron over bronze. For the first time infantry possessed a weapon which could penetrate the armour of the clanking age, and which in range and rate of fire was superior to any method ever used before, or ever used again until the coming of the modern rifle. The War Office has among its records a treatise written during the peace after Waterloo by a general officer of long experience in the Napoleonic wars recommending that muskets should be discarded in favour of the long-bow on account of its superior accuracy, rapid discharge, and effective range. Thus the Welsh war, from two separate points of departure, destroyed the physical basis of feudalism.

*　　*　　*

The great quarrel of Edward's reign was with Scotland. In the year 1286 Alexander III of Scotland, riding his horse over a cliff in the darkness, left as his heir Margaret his granddaughter, known as the Maid of Norway. Now the bright project arose that the Maid of Norway should at the same moment succeed to the Scottish throne and marry Edward, the King's son. Thus would be achieved a union of royal families by which the antagonism of England and Scotland might be laid to rest. Practically all the ruling forces in England and Scotland were agreed upon it. It was a dream, and it

61

passed as a dream. The Maid of Norway embarked in 1290 upon stormy seas only to die before reaching land, and Scotland was bequeathed the problem of a disputed succession, in the decision of which the English interest must be a heavy factor. Two men stood clearly forth, John Balliol and Robert Bruce. Bruce asserted his aged father's closeness in relationship to the common royal ancestor; Balliol, a more distant descendant, the rights of primogeniture. But partisanship was evenly balanced.

The English King discharged his function as arbitrator with extreme propriety. He pronounced in 1292 in favour of John Balliol, who inevitably became not merely his choice, but his puppet. So thought King Edward I, and plumed himself upon a just and at the same time highly profitable decision.

In their distress the Scottish baronage accepted King Edward's award, but they also furnished the new King John with an authoritative council of twelve great lords to overawe him and look after the rights of Scotland. Thus King Edward saw with disgust that all his fair-seeming success left him still confronted with the integrity of Scottish nationhood, with an independent and not a subject Government, and with a hostile rather than a submissive nation.

At this very moment the same argument of overlordship was pressed upon him by the formidable French king, Philip IV. The rest of Edward's reign was spent in a twofold struggle North and South, for the sake of which he had to tax his subjects beyond all endurance. Nothing else mattered; and the embryonic Parliamentary system profited vastly by the repeated concessions he made in the hope of carrying opinion with him. Thus we see the wise law-giver, the thrifty scrutineer of English finances, the administrative reformer, forced to drive his people beyond their strength, and in this process to rouse oppositions which darkened his life and clouded his fame.

To resist Edward the Scots allied themselves with the French. Since Edward was at war with France he regarded this as an act of hostility. Edward struck with ruthless severity. He advanced on Berwick. The city, then the great emporium of Northern trade, was unprepared, after a hundred years of peace, to resist attack. The English army, with hardly any loss, trampled down its improvised defences, and Berwick was delivered to a sack and slaughter which shocked even those barbaric times.

This act of terror quelled the resistance of the ruling classes in Scotland and Edward might flatter himself that all was over. It was only beginning. It has often been said that Joan of Arc first raised the standard of nationalism in the Western world. But over a century before she appeared an outlaw knight, William Wallace, arising from the recesses of South-West Scotland which had been his refuge, embodied, commanded, and led to victory the Scottish nation. Wallace had behind him the spirit of a race as stern and as resolute as any bred among men. He added military gifts of a high order. Out of an unorganised mass of valiant fighting men he forged, in spite of cruel poverty and primitive administration, a stubborn, indomitable army, ready to fight at any odds and mock defeat. The structure of this army is curious. Every four men had a fifth man as leader; every nine men a tenth; every nineteen men a twentieth, and so on to every thousand; and it was agreed that the penalty for disobedience to the leader of any unit was death. Thus from the ground does freedom raise itself unconquerable.

Warenne, Earl of Surrey, Edward's commander in the North, advanced at the head of strong forces upon Stirling. At Stirling Bridge, near the Abbey of Cambuskenneth, in September, 1297, he found himself in the presence of Wallace's army. Wallace watched with measuring eye the accumulation of the English troops across the bridge, and at the right moment hurled his full force upon them, seized the bridgehead, and slaughtered the vanguard of five thousand men. Warenne evacuated the greater part of Scotland. His fortress garrisons were reduced one after the other. The English could barely hold the line of the Tweed.

It was beyond the compass of King Edward's resources to wage war with France and face the hideous struggle with Scotland at the same time. He sought at all costs to concentrate on the peril nearest home. He entered upon a long series of negotiations with the French King which were covered by truces repeatedly renewed, and reached a final Treaty of Paris in 1303. Though the formal peace was delayed for some years, it was in fact sealed in 1294 by the arrangement of a marriage between Edward and Philip's sister, the young Princess Margaret, and also by the betrothal of Edward's son and heir, Edward of Carnarvon, to Philip's daughter Isabella. This dual alliance of blood brought the French war to an effective close in 1297, although through Papal complications neither the peace nor the King's marriage was finally and formally confirmed until 1299. By these diplomatic arrangements Edward from the end of 1297 onwards was able to concentrate his strength against the Scots.

Wallace was now the ruler of Scotland, and the war was without truce or mercy. Edward hastened to the scene of disaster, and with the whole feudal levy of England advanced against the Scots. The Battle of Falkirk in 1298, which he conducted in person, bears a sharp contrast to Stirling Bridge. Wallace, now at the head of stronger powers, accepted battle in a withdrawn defensive position. He had few cavalry and few archers; but his confidence lay in the solid schiltrons (or circles) of spearmen, who were invincible except by actual physical destruction. The armoured cavalry of the English vanguard were hurled back with severe losses from the spear-points. But Edward, bringing up his Welsh archers in the intervals between horsemen of the second line, concentrated a hail of arrows upon particular points in the Scottish schiltrons, so that there were more dead and wounded than living men in these places. Into the gaps and over the carcasses the knighthood of England forced their way. Once the Scottish order was broken the spearmen were quickly massacred. The slaughter ended only in the depths of the woods, and Wallace and the Scottish army were once again fugitives, hunted as rebels, starving, suffering the worst of human privations, but still in arms.

The Scots were unconquerable foes. It was not until 1305 that Wallace was captured, tried with full ceremonial in Westminster Hall, and hanged, drawn, and quartered at Tyburn. But the Scottish war was one in which, as a chronicler said, "every winter undid every summer's work." Wallace was to pass the torch to Robert Bruce.

* * *

In the closing years of Edward's life he appears as a lonely and wrathful old man. Few dared to oppose the old King, but he had little love or respect.

A new champion of the grand Northern race now appeared in arms. King Edward was old, but his will-power was unbroken. When the news came that Bruce had been crowned at Scone his fury was terrible to behold. He launched a campaign in the summer of 1306 in which Bruce was defeated and driven to take refuge off the coast of Antrim. Here, according to the tale, Bruce was heartened by the persistent efforts of the most celebrated spider known to history.

Edward was now too ill to march or ride. He conjured his son to carry his bones in the van of the army which should finally bring Scotland to obedience, and to send his heart to Palestine with a band of a hundred knights to help recover the Sacred City. Neither wish was fulfilled by his futile and unworthy heir.

* * *

Edward I was the last great figure in the formative period of English law. By his statutes, necessary bounds were fixed to the freedom of the Common Law which, without conflicting with its basic principles or breaking with the past, imparted to it its final form. In the constitutional sphere the work of Edward I was not less durable. By the end it was fairly settled in the customs and traditions of England that "sovereignty," to use a term which Edward would hardly have understood, would henceforward reside not in the Crown only, nor in the Crown and Council of the Barons, but in the Crown in Parliament.

The foundations of a strong national monarchy had been laid. Their continuous development and success depended upon the King's immediate successor. Idle weaklings, dreamers, and adventurous boys disrupted the nascent unity of the Island. Long years of civil war, and despotism in reaction from anarchy, marred and delayed the development of its institutions. But when the traveller gazes upon the plain marble tomb at West-

Joan of Arc by Jules Bastien-Lepage

Main Street of Domrémy-la-Pucelle, France. Joan of Arc was born in this village and was baptised in the old church on the left.

minster on which is inscribed, "Here lies Edward I, the Hammer of the Scots. Keep troth," he stands before the resting-place of a master-builder of British life, character, and fame.

Edward II's reign may fairly be regarded as a melancholy appendix to his father's and the prelude to his son's. A strong, capable King had with difficulty upborne the load. He was succeeded by a perverted weakling, of whom some amiable traits are recorded. But this was a reign which by its weakness contributed in the long run to English strength. The ruler was gone, the rod was broken, and the forces of English nationhood, already alive and conscious under the old King, resumed their march at a quicker and more vehement step.

Edward, however, was still in control of Government, although he was under their restraint. Troubles in France and war in Scotland confronted him. He resolved upon the conquest of the Northern kingdom. A general levy of the whole power of England was set on foot to beat the Scots. A great army crossed the Tweed in the summer of 1314. The new champion of Scotland, Robert the Bruce, now faced the vengeance of England.

On the morning of June 24 the English advanced, and a dense wave of steel-clad horsemen descended the slope, splashed and scrambled through the Bannock Burn, and charged uphill upon the schiltrons. The struggle was prolonged and covered the whole front. At length the appearance on the hills to the English right of the camp-followers of Bruce's army, waving flags and raising loud cries, was sufficient to induce a general retreat, which the King himself, with his numerous personal guards, was not slow to head. The retreat speedily became a rout. The Scots hurled themselves forward down the slope, inflicting immense carnage. No more grievous slaughter of English chivalry ever took place in a single day. The Scots claimed to have slain or captured thirty thousand men, more than the whole English army, but their feat in virtually destroying an army of cavalry and archers mainly by the agency of spearmen must nevertheless be deemed a prodigy of war.

*   *   *

In the long story of a nation we often see that capable rulers by their very virtues sow the seeds of future evil and weak or degenerate princes open the pathway of progress.

CHAPTER FIFTEEN

The Long-Bow

IT SEEMED that the strong blood of Edward I had but slumbered in his degenerate son, for in Edward III England once more found leadership equal to her steadily growing strength. Beneath the squalid surface of Edward II's reign there had none the less proceeded in England a marked growth of national strength and prosperity. The feuds and vengeances of the nobility, the foppish vices of a weak King, had been confined to a very limited circle. The English people stood at this time possessed of a commanding weapon, the qualities of which were utterly unsuspected abroad. The long-bow, handled by the well-trained archer class, brought into the field a yeoman type of soldier with whom there was nothing on the Continent to compare. An English army now rested itself equally upon the armoured knighthood and the archers.

The power of the long-bow and the skill of the bowmen had developed to a point where even the finest mail was no certain protection. At two hundred and fifty yards the arrow hail produced effects never reached again by infantry missiles at such a range until the American civil war. The skilled archer was a professional soldier, earning and deserving high pay. He went to war often on a pony, but always with a considerable transport for his comfort and his arrows. He carried with him a heavy iron-pointed stake, which, planted in the ground, afforded a deadly obstacle to charging horses. Behind this shelter a company of archers in open order could deliver a discharge of arrows so rapid, continuous, and penetrating as to annihilate the cavalry attack. Moreover, in all skirmishing and patrolling the trained archer brought his man down at ranges which had never before been considered dangerous in the whole history of war. Of all this the Continent, and particularly France, our nearest neighbour, was ignorant. In France the armoured knight and his men-at-arms had long exploited their ascendancy in war. The foot-soldiers who accompanied their armies were regarded as the lowest type of auxiliary. A military caste had imposed itself upon society in virtue of physical and technical assertions which the coming of the long-bow must disprove. The protracted wars of the two Edwards in the mountains of Wales and Scotland had taught the English many hard lessons, and although European warriors had from time to time shared in them they had neither discerned nor imparted the slumbering secret of the new army. It was with a sense of unmeasured superiority that the English looked out upon Europe towards the middle of the fourteenth century.

*   *   *

The guiding spirit of the new King was to revive the policy, assert the claims, and restore the glories of his grandfather. The quarrel with Scotland was resumed. Edward III routed the Scots at Halidon Hill. Here was a battle very different in character from Bannockburn. The power of the archers was allowed to play its part, the schiltrons were broken, but there was a price to pay. The descendants and followers of Robert Bruce took refuge in France. The contacts between Scotland and France, and the constant aid given by the French Court to the Scottish enemies of England, roused a deep antagonism. Thus the war in Scotland pointed the path to Flanders.

The wars of John and Henry III on the mainland disclose a perpetual struggle between the King and his nobles and subjects to obtain men and money. European adventure was regarded as a matter mainly of interest to a prince concerned with his foreign possessions or claims. Now we see the picture of the Estates of the Realm becoming themselves ardently desirous of foreign conquests. Edward III did not have to wring support from his Parliament for an expedition to France. On the contrary, nobles, merchants, and citizens vied with one another in pressing the Crown to act.

In 1336 Edward decreed an embargo on all exports of English wool, thus producing a furious crisis in the Netherlands. All streams of profit and ambition flowed into a common channel at a moment when the floodwaters of conscious military strength ran high, and in 1337, when Edward repudiated his grudging homage to Philip VI, the Hundred Years' War began. It was never to be concluded.

* * *

Edward slowly assembled the expeditionary army of England. This was not a feudal levy, but a paid force of picked men. Its backbone consisted of indentured warriors, recruited where and how their captains pleased. In consequence, far less than the legal quota of unreliable militia needed to be drawn from every shire. Both knights and archers embodied the flower of the nation, and the men who gathered in the Cinque Ports formed one of the most formidable and efficient invading armies history had yet seen. These preparations were well known in France, and the whole strength of the monarchy was bent to resist them.

Philip VI looked first to the sea. For many years there had been a warfare of privateers, and bitter hatred ruled between the maritime populations on both sides of the Channel. All the resources of the French marine were strained to produce a fleet; even hired Genoese galleys appeared in the French harbours. In Normandy plans were mooted for a counterinvasion which should repeat the exploits of William the Conqueror. But Edward had not neglected his sea-power. His interest in the Navy won him from Parliament early in his reign the title of "King of the Sea." He

6 7

was able to marshal a fleet equal in vessels and superior in men. A great sea battle was necessary before the transport of the English army to France and its maintenance there was feasible. In the summer of 1340 the hostile navies met off Sluys, and a struggle of nine hours ensued. "This battle," says Froissart, "was right furious and horrible, for battles by sea are more dangerous and fiercer than battles by land, for at sea there is no retreat or fleeing; there is no remedy but to fight and abide the fortune." The French admirals had been ordered, under pain of death, to prevent the invasion, and both sides fought well; but the French fleet was decisively beaten and the command of the Channel passed into the hands of the invading Power. The seas being now open, the army crossed to France. At Cadzand the landing was opposed. Large bodies of Genoese cross-bowmen and men-at-arms awaited the disembarkation. But the English archers, shooting from the ships at long range, cleared the shores and covered the invading troops.

Joined with the revolted Flemings, Edward's numbers were greatly augmented, and this combined force, which may have exceeded twenty thousand, undertook the first Anglo-Flemish siege of Tournai. The city was stubbornly defended, and as the grip of famine tightened upon the garrison the horrible spectacle was presented of the "useless mouths" being driven forth into No Man's Land to perish by inches without pity or relief. But the capture of this fortress was beyond Edward's resources in money and supplies. The power of the archers did not extend to stone walls; the first campaign of what was a great European war yielded no results, and a prolonged truce supervened.

This truce was imposed upon the combatants through lack of money, and carried with it no reconciliation. On the contrary, both sides pursued their quarrel in secondary ways. The French wreaked their vengeance on the burghers of the Netherlands, whom they crushed utterly. The English retaliated as best they could. There was a disputed succession in Brittany, which they fomented with substantial aids. The chronic warfare on the frontiers of Gascony continued. Both sides looked forward to a new trial of strength. Well-trained men, eager to fight, there were in plenty, but to maintain them in the field required funds, which to us seem pitifully small, but without which all was stopped. How could these resources be obtained? The Jews had been exploited, pillaged, and expelled in 1290. The Florentine bankers, who had found the money for the first invasion, had been ruined by royal default. The main effort, not only of the Court but of Parliament, was to secure the modest sums of ready money without which knights could not ride nor archers draw their bows. But here a fertile source was at hand. The wealthier and best-organised commercial interest in England was the wool trade, eager to profit from war. A monopoly of wool merchants was created, bound to export only through a particular town to be prescribed by the King from time to time in accordance with his needs and judgment. This system, which was called the Staple, gave the King a convenient and flexible control. By taxing the wool exports which passed through his hands at the Staple port he was assured of an important revenue independent of Parliament. Moreover, the wool merchants who held the monopoly formed a corporation interested in the war, dependent on the King, and capable of lending him money in return for considerate treatment. This development was not welcomed by Parliament, where the smaller wool merchants were increasingly represented. They complained of the favour shown to the monopolists of the Staple, and they also pointed to the menace to Parliamentary power involved in the King's independent resources.

By the spring of 1346 Parliament had at length brought itself to the point of facing the taxation necessary to finance a new invasion. The army was reconstituted, more efficiently than before, its old elements were refreshed with carefully chosen levies. In one wave twenty-four hundred cavalry, twelve thousand archers, and other infantry sailed, and landed unopposed at St. Vaast in Normandy on July 12, 1346. Their object this time was no less than the capture of Paris by a sudden dash. The secret was well kept; even the English army itself believed it was going to Gascony. The French could not for some time collect forces sufficient to arrest the inroad. Caen fell, and Edward advanced, burning and laying waste the country, to the very walls of Paris. But by this time the whole power of the French monarchy had gathered against him. A huge force which comprised all the chivalry of France and was probably three times as big as Edward's army assembled in the neighbourhood of St. Denis. Against such opposition, added to the walls of a fortified city, Edward's resources could not attempt to prevail. King Philip grimly invited him to choose upon which bank of the Seine he would fight a pitched battle.

The thrust had failed and retreat imposed itself upon the army. The challenger was forced to quit the lists at a pace which covered sixty miles in four days. The French army moved on a parallel line to the southward and denied the Seine valley to the retreating English. They must now make for the Somme, and hope to cross between Amiens and the sea. Our generation has become familiar with this stretch of the river, which flows through broad morasses, in those days quite undrained and passable only by lengthy causeways and bridges. All these were broken or held by the levies of Picardy. Four separate attempts to find a passage failed. The vanguard of the French main army was already at Amiens. Edward and the English host, which had tried so audacious, even foolhardy, a spring, now seemed penned in a triangle between the Somme, the seashore, and the French mass. No means had been found to bring the fleet and its transports to any suitable harbour. To cross the Somme near the mouth was a desperate enterprise. The ford was very lengthy, and the tides, violent and treacherous, offered only a few precarious hours in any day.

Moreover, the passage was defended by strong forces popularly estimated to have been upwards of twelve thousand men. "The King of England," says Froissart, "did not sleep much that night, but, rising at midnight, ordered his trumpet to sound. Very soon everything was ready; and, the baggage being loaded, they set out about daybreak, and rode on until they came to the ford at sunrise: but the tide was at that time so full they could not cross." By the afternoon, at the ebb, the enemy's strength was manifest. But since to pause was to perish the King ordered his marshals to plunge into the water and fight their way across. The French resistance was spirited. The knighthood of Picardy rode out and encountered the English on the treacherous sands in the rising waters. "They appeared to be as fond of tilting in the water as upon dry land." By hard fighting, under conditions most deadly to men encased in mail, the passage was forced. At the landing the Genoese cross-bowmen inflicted losses and delayed the deployment until the long-bow asserted its mastery. Thus did King Edward's army escape.

Philip, at the head of a host between thirty and forty thousand strong, was hard upon the track. He had every hope of bringing the insolent Islanders to bay with their backs to the river, or catching them in transit. When he learned that they were already over he called a council of war. His generals advised that, since the tide was now in, there was no choice but to ascend to Abbeville and cross by the bridge which the French held there. To Abbeville they accordingly moved, and lay there for the night.

Edward and his army were intensely convinced of the narrowness of their deliverance. That night they rejoiced; the countryside was full of food; the King gathered his chiefs to supper and afterwards to prayer. But it was certain that they could not gain the coast without a battle. No other resolve was open than to fight at enormous odds. The King and the Prince of Wales, afterwards famous as the Black Prince, received all the offices of religion, and Edward prayed that the impending battle should at least leave him unstripped of honour. With the daylight he marshalled about eleven thousand men in three divisions. Mounted upon a small palfrey, with a white wand in his hand, with his splendid surcoat of crimson and gold above his armour, he rode along the ranks, "encouraging and entreating the army that they would guard his honour and defend his right." "He spoke this so sweetly and with such a cheerful countenance that all who had been dispirited were directly comforted by seeing and hearing him. . . . They ate and drank at their ease . . . and seated themselves on the ground, placing their helmets and bows before them, that they might be the fresher when their enemies should arrive." Their position on the open rolling downs enjoyed few advantages, but the forest of Crécy on their flanks afforded protection and the means of a final stand.

King Philip at sunrise on this same Saturday, August 26, 1346, heard
Mass in the monastery of Abbeville, and his whole army, gigantic for those
times, rolled forward in their long pursuit. Four knights were sent forth to
reconnoitre. About midday the King, having arrived with large masses on
the farther bank of the Somme, received their reports. The English were
in battle array and meant to fight. He gave the sage counsel to halt for the
day, bring up the rear, form the battleline, and attack on the morrow.
These orders were carried by famous chiefs to all parts of the army. But
the thought of leaving, even for a day, this hated foe, who had for so
many marches fled before overwhelming forces, and was now compelled
to come to grips, was unendurable to the French army. What surety had
they that the morrow might not see their enemies decamped and the field
bare? It became impossible to control the forward movement. All the roads
and tracks from Abbeville to Crécy were black and glittering with the
marching columns. King Philip's orders were obeyed by some, rejected by
most. While many great bodies halted obediently, still larger masses poured
forward, forcing their way through the stationary or withdrawing troops,
and at about five in the afternoon came face to face with the English army
lying in full view on the broad slopes of Crécy. Here they stopped.

King Philip, arriving on the scene, was carried away by the ardour of
the throng around him. The sun was already low; nevertheless all were
determined to engage. There was a corps of six thousand Genoese cross-
bowmen in the van of the army. These were ordered to make their way
through the masss of horsemen, and with their missiles break up the hostile array in preparation for the cavalry attacks. The Genoese had marched
eighteen miles in full battle order with their heavy weapons and store of
bolts. Fatigued, they made it plain that they were in no condition to do
much that day. But the Count d'Alençon, who had covered the distance on
horseback, did not accept this remonstrance kindly. "This is what one gets,"
he exclaimed, "by employing such scoundrels, who fall off when there is
anything for them to do." Forward the Genoese! At this moment, while
the cross-bowmen were threading their way to the front under many scorn-
ful glances, dark clouds swept across the sun and a short, drenching storm
beat upon the hosts. A large flight of crows flew cawing through the air
above the French in gloomy presage. The storm, after wetting the bow-
strings of the Genoese, passed as quickly as it had come, and the setting
sun shone brightly in their eyes and on the backs of the English. This, like
the crows, was adverse, but it was more material. The Genoese, drawing
out their array, gave a loud shout, advanced a few steps, shouted again,
and a third time advanced, "hooted," and discharged their bolts. Unbroken
silence had wrapped the English lines, but at this the archers, six or seven
thousand strong, ranged on both flanks in "portcullis" formation, who had

7 1

hitherto stood motionless, advanced one step, drew bows to the ear, and came into action. They "shot their arrows with such force and quickness," says Froissart, "that it seemed as if it snowed."

The effect upon the Genoese was annihilating; at a range which their own weapons could not attain they were in a few minutes killed by thousands. The ground was covered with feathered corpses. Reeling before this blast of missile destruction, the like of which had not been known in war, the survivors recoiled in rout upon the eager ranks of the French chivalry and men-at-arms, which stood just out of arrow-shot. "Kill me those scoundrels," cried King Philip in fury, "for they stop up our road without any reason." Whereupon the front line of the French cavalry rode among the retreating Genoese, cutting them down with their swords. In doing so they came within the deadly distance. The arrow snowstorm beat upon them, piercing their mail and smiting horse and man. Valiant squadrons from behind rode forward into the welter, and upon all fell the arrow hail, making the horses caper, and strewing the field with richly dressed warriors. A hideous disorder reigned. And now Welsh and Cornish light infantry, slipping through the chequered ranks of the archers, came forward with their long knives and, "falling upon earls, barons, knights, and squires, slew many, at which the King of England was afterwards exasperated." Many a fine ransom was cast away in those improvident moments.

In this slaughter fell King Philip's ally, the blind King of Bohemia, who bade his knights fasten their bridles to his in order that he might strike a blow with his own hand. Thus entwined, he charged forward in the press. Man and horse they fell, and the next day their bodies were found still linked. His son, Prince Charles of Luxembourg, who as Emperor-elect of the Holy Roman Empire signed his name as King of the Romans, was more prudent, and, seeing how matters lay, departed with his following by an unnoticed route. The main attack of the French now developed. The Count d'Alençon and the Count of Flanders led heavy cavalry charges upon the English line. Evading the archers as far as possible, they sought the men-at-arms, and French, German, and Savoyard squadrons actually reached the Prince of Wales's division. The enemy's numbers were so great that those who fought about the Prince sent to the windmill, whence King Edward directed the battle, for reinforcements. But the King would not part with his reserves, saying, "Let the boy win his spurs"—which in fact he did.

Another incident was much regarded. One of Sir John of Hainault's knights, mounted upon a black horse, the gift that day of King Philip, escaping the arrows, actually rode right through the English lines. Such was their discipline that not a man stirred to harm him, and, riding round the rear, he returned eventually to the French Army. Continuous cavalry charges were launched upon the English front, until utter darkness fell upon the field. And all through the night fresh troops of brave men, resolved not to quit the field without striking their blow, struggled forward, groping their way. All these were slain, for "No quarter" was the mood of the English, though by no means the wish of their King.

When night had fallen Philip found himself with no more than sixty knights in hand. He was slightly wounded by one arrow, and his horse had been shot under him by another. Sir John Hainault, mounting him again, seized his bridle and forced him from the field upon the well-known principle which, according to Froissart, he exactly expounded, of living to fight another day. The King had but five barons with him on reaching Amiens the next morning.

"When on this Saturday night the English heard no more hooting or shouting, nor any more crying out to particular lords, or their banners, they looked upon the field as their own and their enemies as beaten. They made great fires, and lighted torches because of the obscurity of the night. King Edward, who all that day had not put on his helmet, then came down from his post, and, with his whole battalion, advanced to the Prince of Wales, whom he embraced in his arms and kissed, and said, 'Sweet son, God give you good perseverance. You are my son, for most loyally have you acquitted yourself this day. You are worthy to be a sovereign.' The Prince bowed down very low, and humbled himself, giving all honour to the King his father."

On the Sunday morning fog enshrouded the battlefield, and the King sent a strong force of five hundred lancers and two thousand archers to learn what lay upon his front. These met the columns of the French rear, still marching up from Rouen to Beauvais in ignorance of the defeat, and fell upon them. After this engagement the bodies of 1,542 knights and esquires were counted on the field. Later this force met with the troops of the Archbishop of Rouen and the Grand Prior of France, who were similarly unaware of the event, and were routed with much slaughter. They also found very large numbers of stragglers and wandering knights, and "put to the sword all they met." "It has been assured to me for fact," says Froissart, "that of foot-soldiers, sent from the cities, towns, and municipalities, there were slain, this Sunday morning, four times as many as in the battle of the Saturday." This astounding victory of Crécy ranks with Blenheim, Waterloo, and the final advance in the last summer of the Great War as one of the four supreme achievements.[1]

*　　*　　*

Edward III marched through Montreuil and Blangy to Boulogne, passed through the forest of Hardelot, and opened the siege of Calais. Calais presented itself to English eyes as the hive of that swarm of privateers who were the endless curse of the Channel. Here on the nearest point of the

[1] Written in 1939.

73

Continent England had long felt a festering sore. Calais was what Dunkirk was to become three centuries later. The siege lasted for nearly a year. Every new art of war was practised by land; the bombards flung cannon-balls against the ramparts with terrifying noise. By sea elaborate barriers of piles stopped the French light craft, which sought to evade the sea blockade by creeping along the coast. All reliefs by sea and land failed. But the effort of maintaining the siege strained the resources of the King to an extent we can hardly conceive. When the winter came his soldiers demanded to go home, and the fleet was on the verge of mutiny. In England everyone complained, and Parliament was morose in demeanour and reluctant in supply. The King and his army lived in their hutments, and he never re-crossed the Channel to his kingdom. Machiavelli has profoundly observed that every fortress should be victualled for a year, and this precaution has covered almost every case in history.

Moreover, the siege had hardly begun when King David of Scotland, in fulfilment of the alliance with France, led his army across the Border. But the danger was foreseen, and at Neville's Cross, just west of the city of Durham, the English won a hard-fought battle. The Scottish King himself was captured, and imprisoned in the Tower. He remained there, as we have seen, for ten years until released under the Treaty of Berwick for an enormous ransom. This decisive victory removed the Scottish danger for a generation, but more than once, before and after Flodden, the French alliance was to bring disaster to this small and audacious nation.

Calais held out for eleven months, and yet this did not suffice. Famine at length left no choice to the besieged. They sued for terms. The King was so embittered that when at his demand six of the noblest citizens presented themselves in their shirts, barefoot, emaciated, he was for cutting off their heads. The warnings of his advisers that his fame would suffer in history by so cruel a deed left him obdurate. But Queen Philippa, great with child, who had followed him to the war, fell down before him in an edifying, and perhaps prearranged, tableau of Mercy pleading with Justice. So the burghers of Calais who had devoted themselves to save their people were spared, and even kindly treated. Calais, then, was the fruit, and the sole territorial fruit so far, of the exertions, prodigious in quality, of the whole power of England in the war with France. But Crécy had a longer tale to tell.

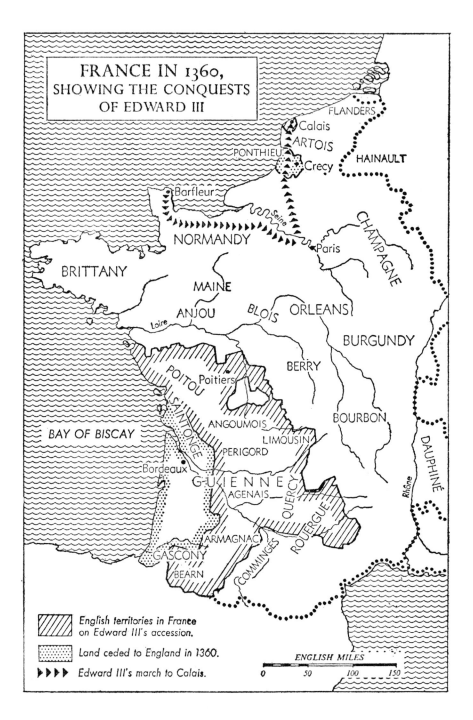

FRANCE IN 1360,
SHOWING THE CONQUESTS
OF EDWARD III

FLANDERS

Calais
ARTOIS
PONTHIEU
Crecy
HAINAULT

Barfleur
Seine
NORMANDY
Paris
CHAMPAGNE

BRITTANY

MAINE

ANJOU
Loire
BLOIS
ORLEANS

BERRY
BURGUNDY

POITOU
Poitiers

SAINTONGE
ANGOUMOIS
BOURBON
LIMOUSIN

BAY OF BISCAY
PERIGORD

Bordeaux
G·U·I·E·N·N·E
AGENAIS
QUERCY
DAUPHINÉ
Rhône

ROUERGUE

ARMAGNAC
COMMINGES
GASCONY
BEARN

English territories in France
on Edward III's accession.

Land ceded to England in 1360.

▶ ▶ ▶ ▶ Edward III's march to Calais.

ENGLISH MILES
0   50   100 _ _ _ 150

75

CHAPTER SIXTEEN

The Black Death

WHILE FEATS of arms and strong endeavours held the English mind, a far more deadly foe was marching across the continents to their doom. Christendom has no catastrophe equal to the Black Death. Vague tales are told of awful events in China and of multitudes of corpses spreading their curse afar. The plague entered Europe through the Crimea, and in the course of twenty years destroyed at least one-third of its entire population. The privations of the people, resulting from ceaseless baronial and dynastic wars, presented an easy conquest to disease. The records in England tell more by their silence than by the shocking figures which confront us wherever records were kept. We read of lawsuits where all parties died before the cases could be heard; of monasteries where half the inmates perished; of dioceses where the surviving clergy could scarcely perform the last offices for their flocks and for their brethren. A whole generation is slashed through by a hideous severance.

The character of the pestilence was appalling. The disease itself, with its frightful symptoms, the swift onset, the blotches, the hardening of the glands under the armpit or in the groin, these swellings which no poultice could resolve, these tumours which, when lanced, gave no relief, the horde of virulent carbuncles which followed the dread harbingers of death, the delirium, the insanity which attended its triumph, the blank spaces which opened on all sides in human society, stunned and for a time destroyed the life and faith of the world. This affliction, added to all the severities of the Middle Ages, was more than the human spirit could endure. The Church, smitten like the rest in body, was wounded grievously in spiritual power. If a God of mercy ruled the world, what sort of rule was this? It seemed to be the death rattle of the race.

But at length the plague abated its force. The tumours yielded to fomentations. Recoveries became more frequent; the resistant faculties of life revived. The will to live triumphed. The scourge passed, and a European population, too small for its clothes, heirs to much that had been prepared by more numerous hands, assuaging its griefs in their universality, turned with unconquerable hope to the day and to the morrow.

Philosophers might suggest that there was no need for the use of the destructive mechanism of plague to procure the changes deemed necessary among men. A more scientific reagent was at hand. Gunpowder which, according to some authorities, Edward had fired at Crécy and against Calais, was soon decisively to establish itself as a practical factor in war and in human affairs based on war.

*   *   *

The calamity which fell upon mankind reduced their numbers and darkened their existence without abating their quarrels. The war between England and France continued in a broken fashion, and the Black Prince, the most renowned warrior in Europe, became a freebooter. In 1355 an ambitious strategy was adopted. The Black Prince would advance northward from the English territories of Gascony and Aquitaine towards the Loire. His younger brother, John of Gaunt, Duke of Lancaster, struck in from Brittany. The two forces were to join for a main decision, but all this miscarried, and at Poitiers the Prince was brought to bay. Even on the morning of his victory his vanguard was already marching southwards in retreat.

The great merit of the Black Prince is that he did not rest upon the lessons of the past or prepare himself to repeat the triumphs of a former battle. He therefore did the opposite to what military convention, based upon the then known facts, would have pronounced right.

The French nobility left their horses in the rear. The Black Prince had all his knights mounted. A deadly toll was taken by the archers upon the whole front. The French chivalry, encumbered by their mail, plodded ponderously forward amid vineyards and scrub. Many fell before the arrows, but the arrows would not have been enough at the crisis. It was the English spear and axe men who charged in the old style upon ranks disordered by their fatigue of movement and the accidents of the ground. At the same time, in admirable concert, a strong detachment of mounted knights, riding round the French left flank, struck in upon the harassed and already disordered attack. The result was a slaughter as large and a victory as complete as Crécy, but with even larger gains. The whole French army was driven into ruin. The Black Prince, whose record is dinked by many cruel acts of war, showed himself a paladin of the age when, in spite of the weariness and stresses of the desperate battle, he treated the captured monarch with all the ceremony of his rank, seated him in his own chair in the camp, and served him in person with such fare as was procurable. Thus by genius, valour, and chivalry he presents himself in a posture which history has not failed to salute.

At Crécy France had been beaten on horseback; at Poitiers she was beaten on foot. These two terrible experiments against the English bit deep into French thought. But, as has been wisely observed, the trees do not grow up to the sky. For a long spell the French avoided battles. The triumph and the exhaustion of England were simultaneously complete. It was proved that the French army could not beat the English, and at the same time that England could not conquer France. The main effort of Edward III, though crowned with all the military laurels, had failed.

* * *

The renewal in 1369 of serious fighting in Aquitaine found England exhausted and disillusioned. The clergy claimed exemption from taxation, though not always successfully, and they could often flaunt their wealth in the teeth of poverty and economic dislocation. Churchmen were ousting the nobility from public office and anti-clerical feeling grew in Parliament. The King was old and failing, and a resurgence of baronial power was due. John of Gaunt set himself to redress the balance in favour of the Lords by a carefully planned political campaign against the Church. Ready to his hand lay an unexpected weapon, a distinguished Oxford scholar named Wyclif. Wyclif was indignant at the corruption of the Church, and saw in its proud hierarchy and absolute claims a distortion of the true principles of Christianity. He declared that dominion over men's souls had never been delegated to mortals. Though Pope and King was each in his sphere supreme, the final appeal was to Heaven, not to Rome.

Wyclif's doctrine opened deep rifts. It involved reducing the powers of the Church temporal in order to purify the Church spiritual. John of Gaunt was interested in the first, Wyclif in the second. The Church was opposed to both. Wyclif resolved to appeal to the people. Finally, with his students he took the tremendous step of having the Bible translated into English. The spirit of early Christianity now revived the English countryside with a keen, refreshing breeze after the weariness of sultry days. But the new vision opened to rich and poor alike profoundly disturbed the decaying society to which it was vouchsafed. The powers of Church and State were soon to realise their danger.

* * *

Edward III's long reign had reached its dusk. The glories of Crécy and Poitiers had faded. The warlike King, whose ruling passions were power and fame, who had been willing to barter many prerogatives for which his ancestors had striven in order to obtain money for foreign adventure, was now in old age a debtor to time and fortune. Harsh were the suits they laid against him. He saw the wide conquests which his sword and his son had made in France melt like snow at Easter. A few coastal towns alone attested the splendour of victories long to be cherished in the memories of the Island race. Queen Philippa, his loving wife, had died of plague in 1369. Even before her death the old King had fallen under the consoling thrall of Alice Perrers, a lady of indifferent extraction, but of remarkable wit and capacity, untrammelled by scruple or by prudence. The spectacle of the famous King in his sixties, infatuated by an illicit love, jarred upon the haggard yet touchy temper of the times. Here was something less romantic than the courtly love that had been symbolised in 1348 by the founding of the Order of the Garter. Nobles and people alike would not extend to the mistress of the King's old age the benefits of the commanding motto of the Order, *Honi soit qui mal y pense*.

The King, at length worn down by war, business, and pleasure, subsided into senility. He had reached the allotted span. He celebrated the Jubilee of his reign. The last decade was disparaging to his repute. Apart from Alice, he concentrated his remaining hopes upon the Black Prince; but this great soldier, renowned throughout Europe, was also brought low by the fatigues of war, and was sinking fast in health. In 1376 the Black Prince expired, leaving a son not ten years old as heir apparent to the throne. King Edward III's large share of life narrowed sharply at its end. Mortally stricken, he retired to Sheen Lodge, where Alice, after the modern fashion, encouraged him to dwell on tournaments, the chase, and wide plans when he should recover. But hostile chroniclers have it that when the stupor preceding death engulfed the King she took the rings from his fingers and other movable property in the house and departed for some time to extreme privacy. We have not heard her tale, but her reappearance in somewhat buoyant situations in the new reign seems to show that she had one to tell. All accounts, alas! confirm that King Edward died deserted by all, and that only the charity of a local priest procured him the protection and warrant of the Church in his final expedition.

The Black Prince's son was recognised as King by general assent on the very day his grandfather died, no question of election being raised, and the crown of England passed to a minor.

BOOK THREE

The End of the Feudal Age

CHAPTER SEVENTEEN

King Richard II and the Social Revolt

JOHN OF GAUNT, Duke of Lancaster, younger brother of the Black Prince, uncle of the young King Richard II, was head of the Council of Regency and ruled the land. Both the impact and the shadow of the Black Death dominated the scene. A new fluidity swept English society. The pang of almost mortal injury still throbbed, but with it crept a feeling that there was for the moment more room in the land. A multitude of vacant places had been filled, and many men in all classes had the sense of unexpected promotion and enlargement about them. A community had been profoundly deranged, reduced in collective strength, but often individually lifted.

In the economic and social sphere there arose a vast tumult. The Black Death had struck a world already in movement. Ever since the Crown had introduced the custom of employing wage-earning soldiers instead of the feudal levy the landed tie had been dissolving. Why should not the noble or knight follow the example of his liege lord? Covenants in which a small landowner undertook to serve a powerful neighbour, "except against the King," became common. The restriction would not always be observed. The old bonds of mutual loyalty were disappearing, and in their place grew private armies, the hired defenders of property, the sure precursors of anarchy.

In medieval England the lords of the manors had often based their prosperity on a serf peasantry, whose status and duties were enjoined by long custom and enforced by manorial courts. Around each manor a closely bound and self-sufficient community revolved. Although there had been more movement of labour and interchange of goods in the thirteenth and early fourteenth centuries than was formerly supposed, development had been relatively slow and the break-up of the village community gradual. The time had now come when the compartments of society and toil could no longer preserve their structure. The convulsion of the Black Death violently accelerated this deep and rending process. Nearly one-third of the population being suddenly dead, a large part of the land passed out of cultivation. The survivors turned their ploughs to the richest soils and quartered their flocks and herds on the fairest pastures. Many landowners abandoned ploughs and enclosed, often by encroachment, the best grazing. At this time, when wealth-getting seemed easier and both prices and profits ran high, the available labour was reduced by nearly a half. Small-holdings were deserted, and many manors were denuded of the peasantry who had served them from time immemorial. Ploughmen and labourers found themselves in high demand, and were competed for on all sides. They in their turn sought to better themselves, or at least to keep their living equal with the rising prices. The poet Langland gives an unsympathetic but interesting picture in *Piers Plowman:*

> Labourers that have no land, to live on but their hands,
> Deigned not to dine a day, on night-old wortes.
> May no penny ale him pay, nor a piece of bacon,
> But it be fresh flesh or fish, fried or baked,
> And that chaud and plus-chaud, for chilling of their maw,
> But he be highly-hired, else will he chide.

But their masters saw matters differently. They repulsed fiercely demands for increased wages; they revived ancient claims to forced or tied labour. The pedigrees of villagers were scrutinised with a care hitherto only bestowed upon persons of quality. The villeins who were declared serfs were at least free from new claims. Assertions of long-lapsed authority, however good in law, were violently resisted by the country folk. They formed unions of labourers to guard their interests. There were escapes of villeins from the estates, like those of the slaves from the Southern states of America in the 1850's.

Many vehement agitators, among whom John Ball is the best known, gave forth a stream of subversive doctrine. The country was full of broken soldiers, disbanded from the war, and all knew about the long-bow and its power to kill nobles, however exalted and well armed. The preaching of revolutionary ideas was widespread, and a popular ballad expressed the response of the masses:

> When Adam delved, and Eve span,
> Who was then a gentleman?

This was a novel question for the fourteenth century, and awkward at any time. The rigid, time-enforced framework of medieval England trembled to its foundations.

These conditions were by no means confined to the Island. Across the Channel a radical and democratic movement, with talk much akin to that of our own time, was afoot. All this rolled forward in England to the terrifying rebellion of 1381. It was a social upheaval, spontaneous and widespread, arising in various parts of the country from the same causes, and united by the same sentiments. That all this movement was the direct consequence of the Black Death is proved by the fact that the revolt was most fierce in those very districts of Kent and the East Midlands where the death-rate had been highest and the derangement of custom the most violent. It was a cry of pain and anger from a generation shaken out of submissiveness by changes in their lot, which gave rise alike to new hope and new injustice.

* * *

Throughout the summer of 1381 there was a general ferment. In May violence broke out in Essex. It was started by an attempt to make a second and more stringent collection of the poll-tax which had been levied in the previous year. The turbulent elements in London took fire, and a band under one Thomas Faringdon marched off to join the rebels. In Kent, after an attack on Lesnes Abbey, the peasants marched through Rochester and Maidstone, burning manorial and taxation records on their way. At Maidstone they released the agitator John Ball from the episcopal prison, and were joined by a military adventurer with gifts and experience of leadership, Wat Tyler.

The royal Council was bewildered and inactive. Early in June the main body of rebels from Essex and Kent moved on London. Here they found support. John Horn, fishmonger, invited them to enter; the alderman in charge of London Bridge did nothing to defend it, and Aldgate was opened treacherously to a band of Essex rioters. For three days the city was in confusion. Foreigners were murdered; the Savoy palace of John of Gaunt was burnt; Lambeth and Southwark were sacked. This was the time for paying off old scores. But the loyal citizen body rallied round the mayor, and at Smithfield the King faced the rebel leaders. Among the insurgents there seems to have been a general loyalty to the sovereign. Their demands were reasonable but disconcerting. They asked for the repeal of oppressive statutes, for the abolition of villeinage, and for the division of Church property. In particular they asserted that no man ought to be a serf or do labour services to a *seigneur,* but pay fourpence an acre a year for his land and not have to serve any man against his will, but only by agreement. While the parley was going on Tyler was first wounded by Mayor Walworth and then smitten to death by one of the King's squires. As the rebel leader rolled off his horse, dead in the sight of the great assembly, the young King met the crisis by riding forward alone with the cry, "I will be your leader. You shall have from me all you seek. Only follow me to the fields outside." But the death of Tyler proved a signal for the wave of reaction. The leaderless bands wandered home and spread a vulgar lawlessness through their counties. They were pursued by reconstructed authority. Vengeance was wreaked.

The rising had spread throughout the South-West. There were riots in

Bridgewater, Winchester, and Salisbury. In Hertfordshire the peasants rose against the powerful and hated Abbey of St. Albans, and marched on London under Jack Straw. There was a general revolt in Cambridgeshire, accompanied by burning of rolls and attacks on episcopal manors. The Abbey of Ramsey, in Huntingdonshire, was attacked, though the burghers of Huntingdon shut their gates against the rioters. In Norfolk and Suffolk, where the peasants were richer and more independent, the irritation against legal villeinage was stronger. The Abbey of Bury St. Edmunds was a prominent object of hatred, and the Flemish woollen-craftsmen were murdered in Lynn. Waves of revolt rippled on as far north as Yorkshire and Cheshire, and to the west in Wiltshire and Somerset.

After Tyler's death the resistance of the ruling classes was organised. Letters were sent out from Chancery to the royal officials commanding the restoration of order, and justices under Chief Justice Tresilian gave swift judgment upon insurgents. The King, who accompanied Tresilian on the punitive circuit, pressed for the observance of legal forms in the punishment of rebels. Nevertheless the reaction was, according to modern examples, very restrained. Not more than a hundred and fifty executions are recorded in the rolls. There was nothing like the savagery we have seen in many parts of Europe in our own times. Law re-established ruled by law. Even in this furious class reaction no men were hanged except after trial by jury. In January 1382 a general amnesty, suggested by Parliament, was proclaimed. But the victory of property was won, and there followed the unanimous annulment of all concessions and a bold attempt to re-create intact the manorial system of the early part of the century. Yet for generations the upper classes lived in fear of a popular rising and the labourers continued to combine. Servile labour ceased to be the basis of the system. The legal aspect of serfdom became of little importance, and the development of commutation went on, speaking broadly, at an accelerated pace after 1349. Such were the more enduring legacies of the Black Death.

In the charged, sullen atmosphere of the England of the 1380's Wyclif's doctrines gathered wide momentum. But, faced by social revolution, English society was in no mood for Church reform. All subversive doctrines fell under censure, and although Wyclif was not directly responsible or accused of seditious preaching the result was disastrous to his cause. The landed classes gave silent assent to the ultimate suppression of the preacher by the Church.

Wyclif appealed to the conscience of his age. Baffled, though not silenced, in England, his inspiration stirred a distant and little-known land, and thence disturbed Europe. Students from Prague had come to Oxford, and carried his doctrines, and indeed the manuscripts of his writings, to Bohemia. From this sprang the movement by which the fame of John Huss eclipsed that of his English master and evoked the enduring national consciousness of the Czech people.

By his frontal attack on the Church's absolute authority over men in this world, by his implication of the supremacy of the individual conscience, and by his challenge to ecclesiastical dogma Wyclif had called down upon himself the thunderbolts of repression. But his protest had led to the first of the Oxford Movements. The cause, lost in his day, impelled the tide of the Reformation. Lollardy, as the Wyclif Movement came to be called, was driven beneath the surface. The Church, strengthening its temporal position by alliance with the State, brazenly repelled the first assault; but its spiritual authority bore henceforward the scars and enfeeblement resulting from the conflict.

Cruel days lay ahead. The political tradition was to be burned out in the misery of Sir John Oldcastle's rebellion under Henry V. But a vital element of resistance to the formation of a militant and triumphant Church survived in the English people. A principle had been implanted in English hearts which shaped the destiny of the race.

*   *   *

The King was now growing up. His keen instincts and precocious abilities were sharpened by all that he had seen and done. In the crisis of the Peasants' Revolt the brunt of many things had fallen upon him, and by his personal action he had saved the situation on a memorable occasion. It was the King's Court and the royal judges who had restored order when the feudal class had lost their nerve. Yet the King consented to a prolonged tutelage. John of Gaunt quitted the realm to pursue interests abroad. He left behind him his son, Henry, a vigorous and capable youth, to take charge of his English estates and interests.

It was not till he was twenty that Richard II determined to be complete master of his Council, and in particular to escape from the control of his uncles. The accumulation of Household and Government offices by the clique around the King and his effeminate favourite affronted the feudal party, and to some extent the national spirit. A purge of the Civil Service, supposed to be the source alike of the King's errors and of his strength, was instituted; and we may note that Geoffrey Chaucer, his equerry, but famous for other reasons, lost his two posts in the Customs.

The Lords Appellant, divided as they were, shrank from deposing and killing the King; but they drew the line at nothing else. They forced him to yield at every point. The victory of the old nobility was complete. Only the person of the King was respected, and that by the narrowest of margins. Richard, forced not only to submit but to assent to the slaughter of his friends, buried himself as low as he could in retirement.

We must suppose that this treatment produced a marked impression upon his mind. It falls to the lot of few mortals to endure such ordeals. He brooded upon his wrongs, and also upon his past mistakes. He saw in the triumphant

8 4

lords men who would be tyrants not only over the King but over the people. He laid his plans for revenge and for his own rights with far more craft than before. For a year there was a sinister lull.

* * *

On May 3, 1389, Richard took action which none of them had foreseen. Taking his seat at the Council, he asked blandly to be told how old he was. On being answered that he was three-and-twenty he declared that he had certainly come of age, and that he would no longer submit to restrictions upon his rights which none of his subjects would endure. He would manage the realm himself; he would choose his own advisers; he would be King, indeed. This stroke had no doubt been prepared with the uncanny and abnormal cleverness which marked many of Richard's schemes. It was immediately successful.

Richard used his victory with prudence and mercy. In October, 1389, John of Gaunt returned from Spain, and his son, Henry, now a leading personage, was reconciled to the King. The terrible combination of 1388 had dissolved. The machinery of royal government, triumphant over faction, resumed its sway, and for the next eight years Richard governed England in the guise of a constitutional and popular King.

This was an age in which the masses were totally excluded from power, and when the ruling classes, including the new middle class, even in their most deadly quarrels, always united to keep them down. Richard had solemnly promised the abolition of serfdom. He had proposed it to Parliament. He had been overruled. He had a long memory for injuries. Perhaps also it extended to his obligations.

The patience and skill with which Richard accomplished his revenge are most striking. So hard had the Estates pressed the royal power, now goading it on and now complaining of results, that we have the unique spectacle of a Plantagenet king lying down and refusing to pull the wagon farther over such stony roads. But this did not spring from lack of mental courage or from narrowness of outlook. It was a necessary feature in the King's far-reaching designs. He wished beyond doubt to gain absolute power over the nobility and Parliament. Whether he also purposed to use this dictatorship in the interests of the humble masses of his subjects is one of the mysteries, but also the legend, long linked with his name. His temperament, the ups and downs of his spirits, his sudden outbursts, the almost superhuman refinements of his calculations, have all been abundantly paraded as the causes of his ruin. But the common people thought he was their friend. He would, they imagined, had he the power, deliver them from the hard oppression of their masters, and long did they cherish his memory.

* * *

While the lords were at variance the King sought to strengthen himself. In 1388 it was with amazement that they saw him advancing upon them in cold hatred rarely surpassed among men. Arundel and some others of his associates were declared traitors and accorded only the courtesy of decapitation. Warwick was exiled to the Isle of Man. Gloucester, arrested and taken to Calais, was there murdered by Richard's agents. A stigma rested henceforward on the King similar to that which had marked John after the murder of Arthur. But for the moment he was supreme as no King of all England had been before, and still his wrath was unassuaged.

Parliament was called only to legalise these events. It was found to be so packed and so minded that there was nothing they would not do for the King. Never has there been such a Parliament. With ardour pushed to suicidal lengths, it suspended almost every constitutional right and privilege gained in the preceding century. It raised the monarchy upon a foundation more absolute than even William the Conqueror, war-leader of his freebooting lieutenants, had claimed. All that had been won by the nation through the crimes of John and the degeneracy of Edward II, all that had been conceded or established by the two great Edwards, was relinquished.

The relations between Gaunt's son, Henry, the King's cousin and contemporary, passed through drama into tragedy. Henry believed himself to have saved the King from being deposed and murdered by Gloucester, Arundel, and Warwick in the crisis of 1388. Very likely this was true. Since then he had dwelt in familiarity and friendship with Richard. These two young men had lived their lives in fair comradeship.

A quarrel arose between Henry and Thomas Mowbray, now Duke of Norfolk. Trial by battle appeared the correct solution, but the King, exasperating the spectators of all classes who had gathered in high expectation to see the sport, cast down his wardour, forbade the combat, and exiled Mowbray for life and Henry for a decade. Both lords obeyed the royal commands. Mowbray soon died; but Henry, astounded by what he deemed ingratitude and injustice, lived and schemed in France.

*   *   *

The year which followed was an unveiled despotism, and Richard, so patient till his vengeance was accomplished, showed restlessness and perplexity, profusion and inconsequence, in his function. During 1398 there were many in the nation who awoke to the fact that a servile Parliament had in a few weeks suspended many of the fundamental rights and liberties of the realm. Hitherto for some time they had had no quarrel with the King. They now saw him revealed as a despot.

In February of 1399 died old John of Gaunt, "time-honoured Lancaster." Henry, in exile, succeeded to vast domains, not only in Lancashire and the north but scattered all over England. Richard, pressed for money, could not refrain from a technical legal seizure of the Lancaster estates in spite of his promises; he declared his cousin disinherited. And forthwith, by a fatal misjudgment of what was stirring in the land, the King set forth upon a punitive expedition, in Ireland.

The moment had come; the coast was clear, and the man did not tarry. In July Henry of Lancaster, as he had now become, landed in Yorkshire. From York Henry marched across England, amid general acclamation.

It took some time for the news of Henry's apparition and all that followed so swiftly from it to reach King Richard in the depths of Ireland. He hastened back, though baffled by stormy seas. What he saw convinced him that all was over. The whole structure of his power, so patiently and subtly built up, had vanished as if by enchantment. At Flint Castle he submitted to Henry, into whose hands the whole administration had now passed. He rode through London as a captive in his train. He was lodged in the Tower. His abdication was extorted; his death had become inevitable. The last of all English kings whose hereditary right was indisputable disappeared for ever beneath the portcullis of Pontefract Castle. Henry, by and with the consent of the Estates of the Realm and the Lords Spiritual and Temporal, ascended the throne as Henry IV, and thereby opened a chapter of history destined to be fatal to the medieval baronage. Although Henry's lineage afforded good grounds for his election to the Crown, and his own qualities, and still more those of his son, confirmed this decision, a higher right in blood was to descend through the house of Mortimer to the house of York, and from this after a long interval the Wars of the Roses broke out upon England.

*   *   *

The character of Richard II and his place in the regard of history remain an enigma. That he possessed qualities of a high order, both for design and action, is evident. That he was almost from childhood confronted with measureless difficulties and wrongful oppressions against which he repeatedly made head is also plain. The injuries and cruelties which he suffered at the hands of his uncle Gloucester and the high nobility may perhaps be the key to understanding him. The unhappy people, already to be numbered by the million, looked to Richard with hopes destined to be frustrated for centuries. All through the reign of Henry IV the conception they had formed of Richard was idealised. He was deemed, whether rightly or wrongly, a martyr to the causes of the weak and poor. Statutes were passed declaring it high treason even to spread the rumour that he was still alive.

We have no right in this modern age to rob him of this shaft of sunlight which rests upon his harassed, hunted life. There is, however, no dispute that in his nature fantastic error and true instinct succeeded each other with baffling rapidity. He was capable of more than human cunning and patience, and also of foolishness which a simpleton would have shunned.

8 7

He fought four deadly duels with feudal aristocratic society. In 1386 he was overcome; in 1389 he was victorious; in 1397-1398 he was supreme; in 1399 he was destroyed.

*   *   *

All power and authority fell to King Henry IV, and all who had run risks to place him on the throne combined to secure his right, and their own lives. But the opposite theme endured with strange persistency. The Court of France deemed Henry a usurper. Yet many agreeable qualities stand to his credit. All historians concur that he was manly, capable, and naturally merciful. In the hour of his accession he was still the bold knight, surprisingly moderate in success, averse from bloodshed, affianced to growing constitutional ideas, and always dreaming of ending his life as a Crusader. But the sullen, turbulent march of events frustrated his tolerant inclinations and eventually soured his generous nature.

*   *   *

Richard's death was announced in February, 1400. Whether he was starved, or, as the Government suggested, went on hunger strike, or whether more direct methods were used, is unknowable. The walls of Pontefract have kept their secret. But far and wide throughout England spread the tale that he had escaped, and that in concealment he awaited his hour to bring the common people of the time to the enjoyment of their own.

All this welled up against Henry of Bolingbroke. He faced continual murder plots. Trouble with the Welsh deepened into a national insurrection. His most serious conflict was with the Percys. These lords of the Northern Marches, the old Earl of Northumberland and his fiery son Hotspur, had for nearly three years carried on the defence of England against the Scots. They had played a great part in placing Henry on the throne. But Edmund Mortimer, Hotspur's brother-in-law, had joined Glendower in rebellion, and the family were now under suspicion. They held a great independent power, and an antagonism was perhaps inevitable. Hotspur raised the standard of revolt. But at Shrewsbury on July 21, 1403, Henry overcame and slew him in a small, fierce battle. The old Earl, who was marching to his aid, was forced to submit, and pardon was freely extended to him.

At the same time the King's health failed. He was said to be smitten with leprosy, and this was attributed to the wrath of God. He was physically a broken man. Henceforward his reign was a struggle against death as well as life. By submissions Henry became the least of kings. But he had transferred an intolerable task to others. They were increasingly unworthy of the trust.

The life and reign of King Henry IV exhibit to us another instance of the vanities of ambition and the harsh guerdon which rewards its success. He had had wrongs to avenge and a cause to champion. He had hardly dared at first to aim at the crown, but he had played the final stake to gain it. He had found it less pleasing when possessed. Not only physically but morally he sank under its weight. His years of triumph were his years of care and sorrow. But none can say he had not reason and justice behind his actions, or that he was not accepted by the country at large. Upon his death a new personality, built upon a grand historic scale, long hungry for power, ascended without dispute the throne not only of England, but very soon of almost all Western Christendom.

CHAPTER EIGHTEEN

The Empire of Henry V

A GLEAM of splendour falls across the dark, troubled story of medieval England. In 1843 Henry V was King at twenty-six. The romantic stories of his riotous youth and sudden conversion to gravity and virtue when charged with the supreme responsibility must not be pressed too far. If he had yielded to the vehement ebullitions of his nature this was no more than a pastime, for always since boyhood he had been held in the grasp of grave business.

In the surging realm, with its ailing King, bitter factions, and deep social and moral unrest, all men had for some time looked to him; and succeeding generations have seldom doubted that according to the standards of his day he was all that a king should be. His face, we are told, was oval, with a long, straight nose, ruddy complexion, dark, smooth hair, and bright eyes, mild as a dove's when unprovoked, but lion-like in wrath; his frame was slender, yet well-knit, strong and active. His disposition was orthodox, chivalrous, and just. He came to the throne at a moment when England was wearied of feuds and brawls and yearned for unity and fame. He led the nation away from internal discord to foreign conquest; and he had the dream, and perhaps the prospect, of leading all Western Europe into the high championship of a Crusade. Council and Parliament alike showed themselves suddenly bent on war with France. As was even then usual in England, they wrapped this up in phrases of opposite import. Bishop Beaufort opened the session of 1414 with the exhortation "While we have time, let us do good to all men." This was understood to mean the speedy invasion of France.

During the whole of 1414 Henry V was absorbed in warlike preparations by land and sea. He reorganised the Fleet. Instead of mainly taking over and arming private ships, as was the custom, he, like Alfred, built many vessels for the Royal Navy. He had at least six "great ships," with about fifteen hundred smaller consorts. The expeditionary army was picked and trained with special care. In spite of the more general resort to fighting on foot, which had been compelled by the long-bow, six thousand archers, of whom half were mounted infantry, were the bulk and staple of the army, together with two thousand five hundred noble, knightly, or otherwise substantial warriors in armour, each with his two or three attendants and aides.

The English army of about ten thousand fighting men sailed to France on August 11, 1415, in a fleet of small ships, and landed without opposition at the mouth of the Seine. Harfleur was besieged and taken by the middle of September. The King was foremost in prowess:

> Once more unto the breach, dear friends, once more;
> Or close the wall up with our English dead.

In this mood he now invited the Dauphin to end the war by single combat. The challenge was declined. The attrition of the siege, and disease, which levied its unceasing toll on these medieval camps, had already wrought havoc in the English expedition. The main power of France was now in the field. The Council of War, on October 5, advised returning home by sea.

But Henry V, leaving a garrison in Harfleur, and sending home several thousand sick and wounded, resolved, with about a thousand knights and men-at-arms and four thousand archers, to traverse the French coast in a hundred-mile march to his fortress at Calais, where his ships were to await him. All the circumstances of this decision show that his design was to tempt the enemy to battle. This was not denied him. Marching by Fécamp and Dieppe, he had intended to cross the Somme at the tidal ford, Blanchetaque, which his great-grandfather had passed before Crécy. Falsely informed that the passage would be opposed, he moved by Abbeville; but here the bridge was broken down. He had to ascend the Somme to above Amiens by Boves and Corbie, and could only cross at the ford of Béthencourt. All these names are well known to our generation. On October 20 he camped near Péronne. He was now deeply plunged into France. It was the turn of the Dauphin to offer the grim courtesies of chivalric war. The French heralds came to the English camp and inquired, for mutual convenience, by which route His Majesty would desire to proceed. "Our path lies straight to Calais," was Henry's answer. This was not telling them much, for he had no other choice. The French army, which was already interposing itself, by a right-handed movement across his front, fell back before his advance-guard behind the Canche River. Henry, moving by Albert, Frévent, and Blangy, learned that they were before him in apparently overwhelming numbers. He must now cut his way through, perish, or surrender. When one of his officers, Sir Walter Hungerford, deplored the fact "that they had not but one ten thousand of those men in England that do no work today," the King rebuked him and revived his spirits in a speech to which Shakespeare has given an immortal form:

> If we are marked to die, we are enough
> To do our country loss; and if to live,
> The fewer men, the greater share of honour.

"Wot you not," he actually said, "that the Lord with these few can overthrow the pride of the French?" [1] He and the "few" lay for the night at the village of Maisoncelles, maintaining utter silence and the strictest discipline. The French headquarters were at Agincourt, and it is said that they kept high revel and diced for the captives they should take.

The English victory of Crécy was gained against great odds upon the defensive. Poitiers was a counter-stroke. Agincourt ranks as the most heroic of all the land battles England has ever fought. It was a vehement assault. The French, whose numbers have been estimated at about twenty thousand, were drawn up in three lines of battle, of which a proportion remained mounted. With justifiable confidence they awaited the attack of less than a third their number, who, far from home and many marches from the sea, must win or die. Mounted upon a small grey horse, with a richly jewelled crown upon his helmet, and wearing his royal surcoat of leopards and lilies, the King drew up his array. The archers were disposed in six wedge-shaped formations, each supported by a body of men-at-arms. At the last moment Henry sought to avoid so desperate a battle. Heralds passed to and fro. He offered to yield Harfleur and all his prisoners in return for an open road to Calais. The French prince replied that he must renounce the crown of France. On this he resolved to dare the last extremity. The whole English army, even the King himself, dismounted and sent their horses to the rear; and shortly after eleven o'clock on St. Crispin's Day, October 25, 1415, he gave the order, "In the name of Almighty God and of Saint George, Avaunt Banner in the best time of the year, and Saint George this day be thine help." The archers kissed the soil in reconciliation to God, and, crying loudly, "Hurrah! Hurrah! Saint George and Merrie England!" advanced to within three hundred yards of the heavy masses in their front. They planted their stakes and loosed their arrows.

The French were once again unduly crowded upon the field. They stood in three dense lines, and neither their cross-bowmen nor their battery of cannon could fire effectively. Under the arrow storm they in their turn moved forward down the slope, plodding heavily through a ploughed field already trampled into a quagmire. Still at thirty deep they felt sure of

[1] *Gesta Henrici V*, English Historical Society, ed. B. Williams.

breaking the line. But once again the long-bow destroyed all before it. Horse and foot alike went down; a long heap of armoured dead and wounded lay upon the ground, over which the reinforcements struggled bravely, but in vain. In this grand moment the archers slung their bows, and, sword in hand, fell upon the reeling squadrons and disordered masses. Then the Duke of Alençon rolled forward with the whole second line, and a stubborn hand-to-hand struggle ensued, in which the French prince struck down with his own sword Humphrey of Gloucester. The King rushed to his brother's rescue, and was smitten to the ground by a tremendous stroke; but in spite of the odds Alençon was killed, and the French second line was beaten hand to hand by the English chivalry and yeomen. It recoiled like the first, leaving large numbers of unwounded and still larger numbers of wounded prisoners in the assailants' hands.

Now occurred a terrible episode. The French third line, still intact, covered the entire front, and the English were no longer in regular array. At this moment the French camp-followers and peasantry, who had wandered round the English rear, broke pillaging into the camp and stole the King's crown, wardrobe, and Great Seal. The King, believing himself attacked from behind, while a superior force still remained unbroken on his front, issued the dread order to slaughter the prisoners. Then perished the flower of the French nobility, many of whom had yielded themselves to easy hopes of ransom. Only the most illustrious were spared. The desperate character of this act, and of the moment, supplies what defence can be found for its ferocity. It was not in fact a necessary recourse. The alarm in the rear was soon relieved; but not before the massacre was almost finished. The French third line quitted the field without attempting to renew the battle in any serious manner.

Henry, who had declared at daybreak, "For me this day shall never England ransom pay," had decisively broken in open battle at odds of more than three to one the armed chivalry of France. In two or at most three hours he had trodden underfoot at once the corpses of the slain and the will-power of the French monarchy.

After asking the name of the neighbouring castle and ordering that the battle should be called Agincourt after it, Henry made his way to Calais, short of food, but unmolested by the still superior forces which the French had set on foot. Within five months of leaving England he returned to London, having, before all Europe, shattered the French power by a feat of arms which, however it may be tested, must be held unsurpassed. He rode in triumph through the streets of London with spoils and captives displayed to the delighted people. He himself wore a plain dress, and he refused to allow his "bruised helmet and bended sword" to be shown to the admiring crowd, "lest they should forget that the glory was due to God alone." The victory of Agincourt made him the supreme figure in Europe.

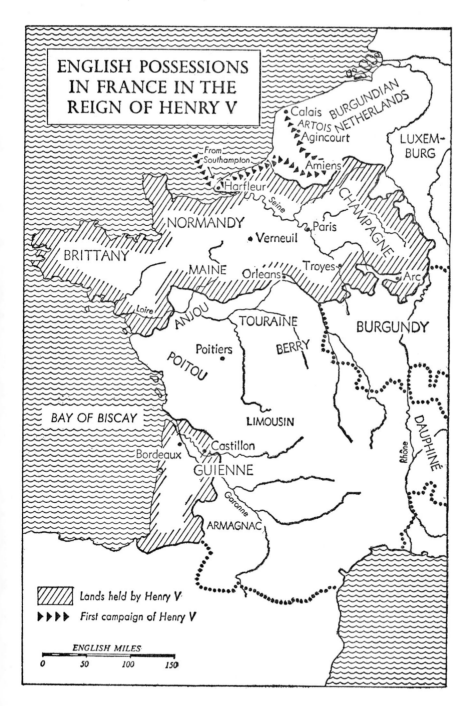

ENGLISH POSSESSIONS
IN FRANCE IN THE
REIGN OF HENRY V

Calais
BURGUNDIAN
ARTOIS NETHERLANDS
Agincourt
LUXEM-
BURG
From
Southampton
Amiens
CHAMPAGNE
Harfleur
Seine
NORMANDY
Paris
Verneuil
BRITTANY
MAINE
Orleans
Troyes
Arc
Loire
ANJOU
TOURAINE
BURGUNDY
BERRY
Poitiers
POITOU
LIMOUSIN
BAY OF BISCAY
DAUPHINÉ
Castillon
Rhône
Bordeaux
GUIENNE
Garonne
ARMAGNAC

///// Lands held by Henry V

▶▶▶▶ First campaign of Henry V

ENGLISH MILES
0   50   100   150

9 3

This was the boldest bid the Island ever made in Europe. Henry stood, and with him his country, at the summit of the world. He was himself endowed with the highest attributes of manhood. Ruthless he could also be on occasion, but the Chroniclers prefer to speak of his generosity and of how he made it a rule of his life to treat all men with consideration. He was more deeply loved by his subjects of all classes than any King has been in England. Under him the English armies gained an ascendancy which for centuries was never seen again.

*   *   *

But glory was, as always, dearly bought. The imposing Empire of Henry V was hollow and false. Where Henry II had failed his successor could not win. When Henry V revived the English claims to France he opened the greatest tragedy in our medieval history. Agincourt was a glittering victory, but the wasteful and useless campaigns that followed more than outweighed its military and moral value, and the miserable, destroying century that ensued casts its black shadow upon Henry's heroic triumph.

And there is also a sad underside to the brilliant life of England in these years. If Henry V united the nation against France he set it also upon the Lollards. We can see that the Lollards were regarded not only as heretics, but as what we should now call Christian Communists. They threatened nothing less than a revolution in faith and property. As early as 1410 we have a strange, horrible scene, in which Henry, then Prince of Wales, was present at the execution of John Badby, a tailor of Worcestershire. He offered him a free pardon if he would recant. Badby refused and the faggots were lighted, but his piteous groans gave the Prince hope that he might still be converted. He ordered the fire to be extinguished, and again tempted the tortured victim with life, liberty, and a pension if he would but retract. But the tailor, with unconquerable constancy, called upon them to do their worst, and was burned to ashes, while the spectators marvelled alike at the Prince's merciful nature and the tailor's firm religious principles. Such fearful obsessions weighed upon the age, and Henry, while King of the world, was but one of its slaves. This degradation lies about him and his times, and our contacts with his personal nobleness and prowess, though imperishable, are marred.

Fortune, which had bestowed upon the King all that could be dreamed of, could not afford to risk her handiwork in a long life. In the full tide of power and success he died at the end of August, 1422, of a malady contracted in the field. He died with his work unfinished. He had once more committed his country to the murderous dynastic war with France. He had been the instrument of the religious and social persecution of the Lollards. Perhaps if he had lived the normal span his power might have become the servant of his virtues and produced the harmonies and tolerances which mankind so often seeks in vain. But Death drew his scythe across these

94

prospects. The gleaming King, cut off untimely, went to his tomb amid the lamentations of his people, and the crown passed to his son, an infant nine months old.

CHAPTER NINETEEN

Joan of Arc

A BABY was King of England, and two months later, on the death of Charles VI, was proclaimed without dispute the King of France. Bedford and Gloucester, his uncles, became Protectors, and with a Council comprising the heads of the most powerful families attempted to sustain the work of Henry V. A peculiar sanctity enshrined the hero's son, and the glory of Agincourt played radiantly around the cradle of Henry VI. Nurses, teachers, and presently noble guardians, carefully chosen for the boy's education and welfare, were authorised to use "reasonable chastisement" when required. But this was little needed, for the child had a mild, virtuous, honest, and merciful nature. His piety knew no bounds, and was, with hunting and a taste for literature, the stay and comfort of his long, ignominious, and terrifying pilgrimage. Through his father he inherited the physical weakness of the house of Lancaster, and through his mother the mental infirmities of Charles VI. He was feeble alike in body and mind, unwise and unstable in his judgments, profuse beyond his means to his friends, uncalculating against his enemies, so tender-hearted that it was even said he would let common thieves and murderers live, yet forcd to bear the load of innumerable political executions. Flung about like a shuttlecock between the rival factions; presiding as a helpless puppet over the progressive decay of English society and power; hovering bewildered on the skirts of great battles; three times taken prisoner on the field; now paraded with all kingly pomp before Parliaments, armies, and crowds; now led in mockery through the streets; now a captive; now a homeless fugitive, hiding, hunted, hungry; afflicted from time to time by phases of total or partial idiocy, he endured in the fullest measure for nearly fifty years the extreme miseries of human existence, until the hand of murder dispatched him to a world which he was sure would be better, and could hardly have been worse than that he had known. Yet with all his shame of failure and incompetence, and the disasters these helped to bring upon his country, the English people recognised his goodness of heart and rightly ascribed to him the quality of holiness. They never lost their love for him; and in many parts of the country wherever the house of Lancaster was stubbornly defended he was venerated both as saint and martyr.

* * *

At the time of the great King's death the ascendancy of the English arms in France was established. Nothing could stand against the English archers.

The English attempt to conquer all vast France with a few thousand archers led by warrior nobles reached its climax in the triumph of Verneuil. There seemed to the French to be no discoverable way to contend against these rugged, lusty, violent Islanders, with their archery, their flexible tactics, and their audacity, born of victories great and small under varying conditions and at almost any odds. Yet the Dauphin, soon to be King Charles VII, stood for France, and everywhere, even in the subjugated provinces, a dull, deep sense of nationality, stirring not only in gentlefolk, but in all who could rise above the submerged classes, centred upon him.

* * *

There now appeared upon the ravaged scene an Angel of Deliverance, the noblest patriot of France, the most splendid of her heroes, the most beloved of her saints, the most inspiring of all her memories, the peasant Maid, the ever-shining, ever-glorious Joan of Arc. In the poor, remote hamlet of Domremy, on the fringe of the Vosges Forest, she served at the inn. She rode the horses of travellers, bareback, to water. She wandered on Sundays into the woods, where there were shrines, and a legend that some day from these oaks would arise one to save France. In the fields where she tended her sheep the saints of God, who grieved for France, rose before her in visions. St. Michael himself appointed her, by right divine, to command the armies of liberation. Joan shrank at first from the awful duty, but when he returned attended by St. Margaret and St. Catherine, patronesses of the village church, she obeyed their command. There welled in the heart of the Maid a pity for the realm of France, sublime, perhaps miraculous, certainly invincible.

Like Mahomet, she found the most stubborn obstacle in her own family. But the saints no doubt felt bound to set her fair upon her course. She made a perilous journey across France. She was conducted to the King's presence in the immense stone pile of Chinon. There, among the nobles and courtiers in the great hall, under the flaring torches, she at once picked out the King, who had purposely mingled with the crowd. "Most noble Lord Dauphin," she said, "I am Joan the Maid, sent on the part of God to aid you and the kingdom, and by His order I announce that you will be crowned in the city of Rheims." She fascinated the royal circle. When they set her astride on horseback in martial guise it was seen that she could ride. As she couched her lance the spectators were swept with delight.

Policy now, if not earlier, came to play a part. The supernatural character of the Maid's mission was spread abroad. To make sure that she was sent

King Henry VIII by Hans Holbein il Giovane

"We must credit Henry's reign with laying the basis of sea-power, with a revival of Parliamentary institutions, with giving the English Bible to the people, and above all with strengthening a popular monarchy under which succeeding generations worked together for the greatness of England while France and Germany were racked with internal strife."

Catherine of Aragon (1485–1536),
a portrait by Michael Sittow, *circa* 1502

Anne Boleyn (1507–36),
a drawing by Holbein

THE WIVES OF HENRY VIII

Jane Seymour (d. 1537),
a drawing by Holbein

Anne of Cleves (1515–57),
a painting by Holbein

Catherine Howard (d. 1542),
from a miniature by Holbein

Catherine Parr (1512–48),
an engraving after the Holbein paintir

by Heaven and not from elsewhere, she was examined by a committee of theologians, by the Parlement of Poitiers, and by the whole Royal Council. She was declared a virgin of good intent, inspired by God. Indeed, her answers were of such a quality that the theory has been put forward that she had for some time been carefully nurtured and trained for her mission. This at least would be a reasonable explanation of the known facts.

Orleans in 1429 lay under the extremities of siege. The Maid now claimed to lead a convoy to the rescue. In armour plain and without ornament, she rode at the head of the troops. She restored their spirits; she broke the spell of English dominance. She captivated not only the rough soldiery but their hard-bitten leaders. Her plan was simple. She would march straight into Orleans between the strongest forts. But the experienced captain, Dunois, brought her by other ways into the besieged town almost alone. She was received with rapture and the convoy marched for a whole day between the redoubts of the English while they gaped at it dumbfounded.

The report of a supernatural visitant send by God to save France, which inspired the French, clouded the minds and froze the energies of the English. The sense of awe, and even of fear, robbed them of their assurance. Dunois returned to Paris, leaving the Maid in Orleans. Upon her invocation the spirit of victory changed sides, and the French began an offensive which never rested till the English invaders were driven out of France.

She now told Charles he must march on Rheims to be crowned upon the throne of his ancestors. The idea seemed fantastic: Rheims lay deep in enemy country. But under her spell he obeyed, and everywhere the towns opened their gates before them and the people crowded to his aid. With all the pomp of victory and faith, with the most sacred ceremonies of ancient days, Charles was crowned at Rheims. By his side stood the Maid, resplendent, with her banner proclaiming the Will of God. If this was not a miracle it ought to be.

Joan now became conscious that her mission was exhausted; her "voices" were silent; she asked to be allowed to go home to her sheep and the horses of the inn. All adjured her to remain.

But the attitude both of the Court and the Church was changing towards Joan. Up to this point she had championed the Orleanist cause. After her "twenty victories" the full character of her mission appeared. It became clear that she served God rather than the Church, and France rather than the Orleans party.

Indeed, the whole conception of France seems to have sprung and radiated from her. Thus the powerful particularist interests which had hitherto supported her were estranged. Meanwhile she planned to regain Paris for France. When in May, 1430, the town of Compiègne revolted against the decision of the King that it should yield to the English, Joan with only six hundred men attempted its succour. She had no doubt that the enterprise was desperate. It took the form of a cavalry sortie across the long causeway over the river. The enemy, at first surprised, rallied, and a panic among the French ensued. Joan, undaunted, was bridled from the field by her friends. She still fought with the rearguard across the causeway. The two sides were intermingled. The fortress itself was imperilled. Its cannon could not fire upon the confused *mêlée*. Flavy, the governor whose duty it was to save the town, felt obliged to pull up the drawbridge in her face and leave her to the unfriendly Burgundians.

She was sold to the rejoicing English for a moderate sum. To Bedford, the Commander-in-Chief, and his army she was a witch, a sorceress, a harlot, a foul imp of black magic, at all costs to be destroyed. But it was not easy to frame a charge; she was a prisoner of war, and many conventions among the warring aristocrats protected her. The spiritual arm was therefore invoked. The Bishop of Beauvais, the learned doctors of Paris, pursued her for heresy. She underwent prolonged inquisition. The gravamen was that by refusing to disown her "voices" she was defying the judgment and authority of the Church. For a whole year her fate hung in the balance, while careless, ungrateful Charles lifted not a finger to save her. There is no record of any ransom being offered. Joan had recanted under endless pressure, and had been accorded all the mercy of perpetual imprisonment on bread and water. But in her cell the inexorable saints appeared to her again. Entrapping priests set her armour and man's clothes before her; with renewed exaltation she put them on. From that moment she was declared a relapsed heretic and condemned to the fire. Amid an immense concourse she was dragged to the stake in the market-place of Rouen. High upon the pyramid of faggots the flames rose towards her, and the smoke of doom wreathed and curled. She raised a cross made of firewood, and her last word was "Jesus!" History has recorded the comment of an English soldier who witnessed the scene. "We are lost," he said. "We have burnt a saint." All this proved true.

Joan was a being so uplifted from the ordinary run of mankind that she finds no equal in a thousand years. The records of her trial present us with facts alive today through all the mists of time. Out of her own mouth can she be judged in each generation. She embodied the natural goodness and valour of the human race in unexampled perfection. Unconquerable courage, infinite compassion, the virtue of the simple, the wisdom of the just, shone forth in her. She glorifies as she freed the soil from which she sprang. All soldiers should read her story and ponder on the words and deeds of the true warrior, who in one single year, though untaught in technical arts, reveals in every situation the key of victory.

Joan of Arc perished on May 29, 1431, and thereafter the tides of war flowed remorselessly against the English. The boy Henry was crowned in Paris in December amid chilly throngs. The whole spirit of the country was against the English claim. Burgundy became definitely hostile in 1435. Bedford died, and was succeeded by lesser captains. The opposing Captain-in-Chief, Dunois, instead of leading French chivalry to frontal attacks upon the English archer array, acted by manœuvre and surprise. The French gained a series of battles. Here they caught the English men-at-arms on one side of the river while their archers were on the other; there by a cannonade they forced a disjointed English attack. The French artillery now became the finest in the world. Seven hundred engineers, under the brothers Bureau, used a heavy battering-ram of twenty two inches calibre, firing gigantic stone balls against the numberless castles which the English still held. Places which in the days of Henry V could be reduced only by famine now fell in a few days to smashing bombardment. All Northern France, except Calais, was reconquered. Even Guienne, dowry of Eleanor of Aquitaine, for three hundred years a loyal, contented fief of the English Crown, was overrun. By the end of 1453, through force or negotiation, the English had been driven off the Continent. Of all their conquests they held henceforward only the bridgehead of Calais, to garrison which cost nearly a third of the revenue granted by Parliament to the Crown.

CHAPTER TWENTY

The Wars of the Roses

AS HENRY VI grew up his virtues and simpleness became equally apparent. As time passed he showed a feebleness of mind and spirit and a gentleness of nature which were little suited to the fierce rivalries of a martial age. Opinion and also interests were divided upon him. Flattering accounts of his remarkable intelligence were matched by other equally biased tales that he was an idiot almost incapable of distinguishing between right and wrong. Modern historians confirm the less complimentary view.

The loss of France, as it sank in year by year, provoked a deep, sullen rage throughout the land. A strong sense of wounded national pride spread among the people. Where were the glories of Crécy and Poitiers? Where were the fruits of famous Agincourt? All were squandered, or indeed betrayed, by those who had profited from the overthrow and murder of good King Richard. Exactly how the forces worked is unknown; but slowly, ceaselessly, there grew in the land, not only among the nobility and gentry, strong parties which presently assumed both shape and organisation.

At twenty-three it was high time that King Henry should marry. The

Earl of Suffolk was sent to France to arrange a further truce, and it was implied in his mission that he should treat for a marriage between the King of England and Margaret of Anjou, niece of the King of France. This remarkable woman added to rare beauty and charm a masterly intellect and a dauntless spirit. Like Joan the Maid, though without her inspiration or her cause, she knew how to make men fight. Even from the seclusion of her family her qualities became well known. Was she not then the mate for this feeble-minded King? Would she not give him the force that he lacked? And would not those who placed her at his side secure a large and sure future for themselves?

Suffolk was enthralled by Margaret. He made the match; and in his eagerness, by a secret article, agreed without formal authority that Maine should be the reward of France. The marriage was solemnised in 1445 with such splendour as the age could afford. Suffolk was made a marquis, and several of his relations were ennobled. The King was radiantly happy, the Queen faithfully grateful. But the secret slumbered uneasily.

It soon appeared that immense forces of retribution were on foot. When in 1448 the secret article became public anger was expressed on all sides. England had paid a province, it was said, for a princess without a dowry; traitors had cast away much in the field, and given up the rest by intrigue. At the root of the fearful civil war soon to rend the Island there lay this national grief and wrath at the ruin of empire. All other discontents fused themselves with this. The house of Lancaster had usurped the throne, had ruined the finances, and had sold the conquests. From these charges all men held the King absolved alike by his good heart and silly head. But henceforward the house of York increasingly becomes a rival party within the State.

As the process of expelling the English from France continued fortresses fell, towns and districts were lost, and their garrisons for the most part came home. The speed of this disaster contributed powerfully to shock English opinion and to shake the very foundations of the Lancastrian dynasty. The King was a helpless creature, respected, even beloved, but no prop for any man. Parliament was little more than a clearing-house for the rivalries of nobles. England, enormously advanced as it was in comprehension, character, and civilisation, was relapsing from peace and security into barbaric confusion.

* * *

It was upon this community that the agonies of the Wars of the Roses were now to fall. The need of all men and their active desire was for a strong and capable Government. Some thought this could be obtained only by aiding the lawful, established regime. Others had been for a long time secretly contending that a usurpation had been imposed upon them which had now become incompetent. The claims and hopes of the opposition to

100

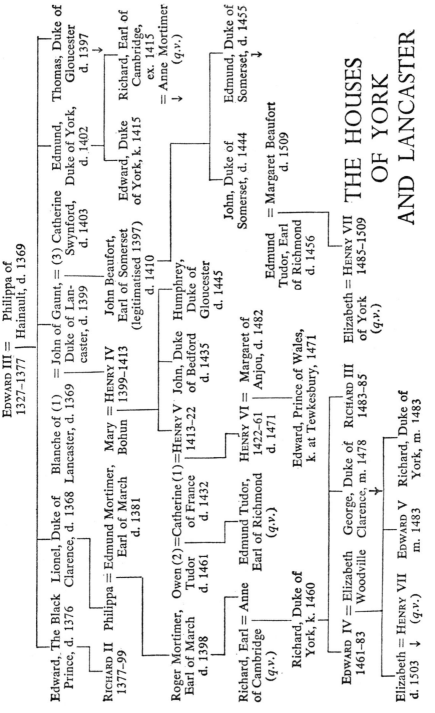

THE HOUSES
OF YORK
AND LANCASTER

EDWARD III = Philippa of
1327–1377 | Hainault, d. 1369

Edward, The Black Prince, d. 1376

Lionel, Duke of Clarence, d. 1368

Blanche of (1) Lancaster, d. 1369 = John of Gaunt, Duke of Lancaster, d. 1399 = (3) Catherine Swynford, d. 1403

Edmund, Duke of York, d. 1402

Thomas, Duke of Gloucester d. 1397

RICHARD II 1377–99

Philippa = Edmund Mortimer, Earl of March d. 1381

Mary = HENRY IV Bohun 1399–1413

John Beaufort, Earl of Somerset (legitimatised 1397) d. 1410

Richard, Earl of Cambridge, ex. 1415 = Anne Mortimer (q.v.)

Edward, Duke of York, k. 1415

Roger Mortimer, Earl of March d. 1398

Owen (2) = Catherine (1) = HENRY V Tudor of France 1413–22 d. 1461 d. 1432

John, Duke of Bedford d. 1435

Humphrey, Duke of Gloucester d. 1445

John, Duke of Somerset, d. 1444

Edmund, Duke of Somerset, d. 1455

Richard, Earl = Anne of Cambridge (q.v.)

Edmund Tudor, Earl of Richmond (q.v.)

HENRY VI = Margaret of 1422–61 Anjou, d. 1482 d. 1471

Edmund = Margaret Beaufort Tudor, Earl d. 1509 of Richmond d. 1456

Richard, Duke of York, k. 1460

Edward, Prince of Wales, k. at Tewkesbury, 1471

George, Duke of Clarence, m. 1478

RICHARD III 1483–85

Elizabeth = HENRY VII of York 1485–1509 (q.v.)

EDWARD IV = Elizabeth 1461–83 Woodville

EDWARD V m. 1483

Richard, Duke of York, m. 1483

Elizabeth = HENRY VII d. 1503 (q.v.)

101

the house of Lancaster were embodied in Richard, Duke of York, first Prince of the Blood. Around him and beneath him there gathered an immense party of discontent, which drove him hesitantly to demand a place in the Government, and eventually, through Queen Margaret's increasing hostility, the throne itself.

In these conditions the character of Richard of York deserves close study. He was a virtuous, law-respecting, slow-moving, and highly competent prince. Every office entrusted to him by the Lancastrian regime had been ably and faithfully discharged. Thus we see on the one side a weak King with a defective title in the hands of personages discredited by national disaster, and on the other an upright and wise administrator supported by a nation-wide party and with some superior title to the crown. Anyone who studies the argument which now tore the realm will see how easily honest men could convince themselves of either cause.

All England was divided between these two conceptions. Although the Yorkists predominated in the rich South, and the Lancastrians were supreme in the warlike North, there were many interlacements and overlaps. While the townsfolk and the mass of the people, upon the whole, abstained from active warfare in this struggle of the upper classes, their own opinion was also profoundly divided. Thus Europe witnessed the amazing spectacle of nearly thirty years of ferocious war, conducted with hardly the sack of a single town, and with the mass of the common people little affected and the functions of local government very largely maintained.

*   *   *

York felt himself the weaker. He was constitutionally averse from violence. Every effort was made to prevent bloodshed. Parleys were unending. But York stood for a cause; he was supported by the Commons; half the nation was behind him. Then in quick succession a series of grave events occurred. The disasters culminated in France. In this situation the King went mad. Suddenly his memory failed. He recognised no one, not even the Queen. He could eat and drink, but his speech was childish or incoherent. He could not walk. For another fifteen months he remained entirely without comprehension. The pious Henry had been withdrawn from the worry of existence to an island of merciful oblivion. His body gaped and drivelled over the bristling realm. When these terrible facts became known Queen Margaret aspired to be Protector. But the adverse forces were too strong for the Lancastrian party to make the challenge. Moreover, she had another preoccupation. On October 13 she gave birth to a son.

Hitherto neither side had been inclined to go to extremes. If Lancaster ruled during the life of Henry, York would succeed at his death, and both sides could accommodate themselves to this natural and lawful process. Now it seemed there would be a Lancastrian ascendancy for ever. Surprises continued. When it was generally believed that Henry's line was extinct he had produced an heir. When he seemed to have sunk into permanent imbecility he suddenly recovered. At Christmas, 1454, he regained all his faculties. He inquired whether he had been asleep and what had happened meanwhile. Margaret showed him his son, and told him she had named him Edward.

*   *   *

The Red Rose of Lancaster bloomed again. York ceased legally to be Protector from the moment that the King's mental recovery was known; he made no effort to retain the power. Nevertheless York's lords agreed upon a resort to arms and moved towards London, with St. Albans as their point of concentration. The King's army got there first. It was a collision rather than a battle; but it was none the less decisive. Not more than three hundred men perished in this clash at St. Albans, but these included an extraordinary proportion of the nobles on the King's side. The Yorkish triumph was complete. They had now got the King in their hands. Margaret and her child had taken sanctuary. The victors declared their devotion to the royal person and rejoiced that he was rid of evil counsellors. Upon this Parliament was immediately summoned in the King's name.

*   *   *

St. Albans was the first shedding of blood in strife. The Yorkists gained possession of the King. But soon we see the inherent power of Lancaster. In a few months they were as strong as ever. Continual trials of strength were made. There were risings in the country and grim assemblies of Parliament. The spectacle was displayed to the Londoners of the King being escorted to Westminster by a procession in which the Duke of York and Queen Margaret walked side by side, followed by the Yorkist and Lancastrian lords, the most opposed in pairs. Solemn pledges of amity were exchanged; the Sacrament was taken in common by all the leaders; all sought peace where there was no peace. A so-called compromise was attempted. Henry was to be King for life; York was to conduct the government and succeed him at his death. All who sought a quiet life for the nation hailed this arrangement. But the settlement defied the fact that Queen Margaret, with her son, the Prince of Wales, was at liberty at Harlech Castle, in Wales. The King in bondage had disinherited his own son. The Queen fought on.

At Wakefield on December 30, 1460, the first considerable battle was fought. The Lancastrians, with superior forces, caught the Yorkists by surprise, when many were foraging, and a frightful rout and massacre ensued. The Duke of York was killed; his son, eighteen years old, was flying, but the new Lord Clifford, remembering St. Albans, slaughtered him with joy, exclaiming, "By God's blood, thy father slew mine; and so will I do thee, and all thy kin." Henceforward this was the rule of the war. The heads of the three Yorkist nobles were exposed over the gates and walls of York. The great Duke's head, with a paper crown, grinned upon the landscape, summoning the avengers.

Hitherto the struggle had been between mature, comfortable magnates, deeply involved in State affairs and trying hard to preserve some limits. Now a new generation took charge. There was a new Lord Clifford, a new Duke of Somerset, above all a new Duke of York, all in the twenties, sword in hand, with fathers to avenge and England as the prize. The Yorkists under their young Duke now marched but Queen Margaret forestalled him, and on February 17, at the second Battle of St. Albans, she inflicted a bloody defeat. King Henry had been carted to the scene. There, beneath a large tree, he watched what happened with legitimate and presently unconcealed satisfaction. Among the many captains of consequence whom Margaret put to death in cold blood the next morning two cases need special consideration. King Henry said he had asked two knights to bide with him and they had done so for his own safety. Queen Margaret produced her son Edward, now seven years old, to whose disinheritance the King had perforce consented, and asked this child, already precociously fierce, to pronounce. "Fair son, with what death shall these two knights die whom you see there?" "Their heads should be cut off" was the ready answer. As Sir Thomas Kyriel was being led away to his doom he exclaimed, "May the wrath of God fall on those who have taught a child to speak such words." Thus was pity banished from all hearts, and death or vengeance was the cry.

*   *   *

Margaret now had her husband safe back in her hands, and with him the full authority of the Crown. The road to London was open, but she did not choose to advance upon it. This was the turning-point in the struggle. Nine days after the second Battle of St. Albans Edward of York entered London. The pretence of acting in the King's name could serve no longer. As he saw it, his father had been ruined and killed through respect for the majesty of Henry VI. He and his friends would palter no longer with such conceptions. Forthwith he claimed the crown; and such was the feeling of London and the strength of his army, now upon the spot, that he was able to make good show of public authority for his act. He declared himself King, and on March 4, 1461, was proclaimed at Westminster with such formalities as were possible. Henceforward Edward IV declared that the other side were guilty of treason, and that he would enforce upon them every penalty. These assertions must now be made good, and King Edward IV marched north to settle once and for all with King Henry VI.

On March 29 one of the most ruthless battles on English soil was fought. For six hours the two sides grappled furiously, with varying success. All hung in the balance until late in the afternoon, when the arrival of the Duke of Norfolk's corps upon the exposed flank of the Lancastrians drove the whole mass into retreat, which soon became a rout. The pursuit was carried on far into the night. Margaret and her son escaped to York, where King Henry had been observing the rites of Palm Sunday. Gathering him up, the imperious Queen set out with her child and a cluster of spears for the Northern border. The flower of the Lancastrian nobility and knighthood fell upon the field. For all prisoners there was but death. When Edward reached the town of York his first task was to remove the heads of his father and others of Margaret's victims and to replace them with those of his noblest captives. Three months later, on June 28, he was crowned King of Westminster, and the Yorkist triumph seemed complete. Not only the throne but one-third of the estates in England changed hands. It was measure for measure.

* * *

After this the Lancastrian cause was sustained by the unconquerable will of Queen Margaret. Never has her tenacity and rarely have her vicissitudes been surpassed in any woman. Margaret, as Queen of England and Princess of France, was an outstanding personage in the West of Europe. Her qualities of courage and combativeness, her commanding, persuasive personality, her fury against those who had driven her and her husband from the throne, produced from this one woman's will-power a long series of desperate, forlorn struggles after the main event had been decided.

The behaviour of Edward at this moment constitutes a solid defence for his character. This voluptuous young King, sure of his position, now showed a clemency unheard of in the Wars of the Roses. Many of the Lancastrian nobles were pardoned and Sir Ralph Percy, on swearing allegiance, was not merely allowed to go free, but restored to his estates.

Edward's magnanimity and forgiveness were ill repaid. When Margaret returned with fresh succours from France and Scotland in 1463 Percy opened the gates. Again the banner of Lancaster was raised. Edward's experiment of mercy in this quarrel was now at an end, and the former rigours were renewed in their extreme degree. Lancastrian nobles and knights by dozens and half-dozens were put to death. There was nothing for it but to still these unquiet spirits. Poor King Henry was at length tracked down in Lancashire and conveyed to London. This time there was no ceremonial entry. With his feet tied by leather thongs to the stirrups, and with a straw hat on his head, the futile but saintly figure around whom such storms had beaten was led three times round the pillory, and finally hustled to the Tower, whose gates closed on him, yet not—this time—for ever.

CHAPTER TWENTY-ONE

The Adventures of Edward IV

KING EDWARD IV had made good his right to the Crown upon the field. He was a soldier and a man of action; in the teeth of danger his quality was at its highest. In war nothing daunted or wearied him. Long marches, hazardous decisions, the marshalling of armies, the conduct of battles, seemed his natural sphere. The worse things got the better he became. But the opposite was also true. He was at this time a fighting man and little more, and when the fighting stopped he had no serious zest for sovereignty. The land was fair; the blood of youth coursed in his veins; all his blood debts were paid; with ease and goodwill he sheathed his sharp sword. It had won him his crown; now to enjoy life.

The successes of these difficult years had been gained for King Edward by the Neville family. In the first part of his reign England was therefore ruled by the two brothers, Warwick and Northumberland. The King did not quarrel with this. In all his reign he never fought but when he was forced; then he was magnificent. Let Warwick and Northumberland and other anxious lords carry the burden of State, and let the King be merry. For a while this suited all parties. The victors divided the spoil; the King had his amusements, and his lords their power and policy.

Thus some years slipped by, while the King, although gripping from time to time the reins of authority, led in the main his life of pleasure. One day the King a-hunting was carried far by the chase. He rested for the night at a castle. In this castle a lady of quality, niece of the owner, had found shelter. Elizabeth Woodville, or Wydvil, was the widow of a Lancastrian knight, "in Margaret's battle at St. Albans slain." There was high as well as ordinary blood in Elizabeth's veins; but she was an austere woman, upright, fearless, chaste, and fruitful. She and her two sons were all under the ban of the attainder which disinherited the adherents of Lancaster. The chance of obtaining royal mercy could not be missed. The widow bowed in humble petition before the youthful conqueror, and, like the tanner's daughter of Falaise, made at first glance the sovereign her slave.

The Lady Elizabeth observed the strictest self-restraint, which only enhanced the passion of the King. He gave her all his love, and when he found her obdurate he besought her to share his crown. He spurned the counsels of prudence and worldly wisdom. Why conquer in battles, why be a king, if not to gain one's heart's desire? But he was well aware of the dangers of his choice. His marriage in 1464 with Elizabeth Woodville was a secret guarded in deadly earnest. The statesmen at the head of the Government, while they smiled at what seemed an amorous frolic, never dreamed it was a solemn union, which must shake the land to its depths.

*   *   *

Warwick's plans for the King's future had been different. Isabella of the house of Spain, or preferably a French princess, were brides who might greatly forward the interests of England. A royal marriage in those days might be a bond of peace between neighbouring states or the means of successful war. Warwick used grave arguments and pressed the King to decide. Edward seemed strangely hesitant, and dwelt upon his objections until the Minister, who was also his master, became impatient. Then at last the truth was revealed: he had for five months been married to Elizabeth Woodville. Here then was the occasion which sundered him from the valiant King-maker. Warwick had deep roots in England, and his popularity was unbounded. But no one knew better than he that there slept in Edward a tremendous warrior, skilful, ruthless, and capable when roused of attempting and of doing all.

The clash came over foreign policy. In this sad generation England, lately the master, had become the sport of neighbouring states. With the instinct which afterwards ruled our Island for so many centuries, Edward sought to base English policy upon the second strongest state in Western Europe. He could no doubt argue that to be the ally of France was to be in the power of France, but to be joined with Burgundy was to have the means of correcting if not of controlling French action. Amid his revelries and other hunting he nursed a conqueror's spirit. Never should England become a vassal state; instead of being divided by her neighbours, she would herself, by dividing them, maintain a balance. At this time these politics were new; but the stresses they wrought in the small but vehement world of English government can be readily understood nowadays.

The offended chiefs took deep counsel together. Edward continued to enjoy his life with his Queen and, now and again, with others. Warwick had gained the King's brother, Clarence, to his side by whispering that but for this upstart brood of the Woodvilles he might succeed Edward as King. When all was ready Warwick struck. A rising took place in the North. As soon as the King had been enticed northwards by the rebellion, Warwick and Clarence defeated him with a merciless slaughter.

Edward, trying to rally his scattered forces, found himself in the power of his great nobles. His brother, Richard of Gloucester, known to legend as "Crookback" because of his alleged deformity, seemed his only friend. He was conveyed to Warwick's castle and there kept in honourable but real restraint. At this moment Warwick the King-maker had actually the two rival Kings, Henry VI and Edward IV, both his prisoners. This was a remarkable achievement for any subject.

But the relations between Warwick and the King did not admit of simple solutions. The King found it convenient in his turn to dissemble. He professed himself convinced that Warwick and Clarence were right. He undertook to amend his ways, and after he had signed free pardons to all who had been in arms against him he was liberated.

In March, 1470, under the pretence of suppressing a rebellion in Lincolnshire, the King called his forces to arms. At Losecoat Field he defeated the insurgents, and in the series of executions which had now become customary after every engagement he obtained a confession which accused both Warwick and Clarence of treason. He marched against them, and they fled, astounded that their own methods should be retorted upon themselves. The King-maker found himself by one sharp twist of fortune deprived of almost every resource he had counted upon as sure. He in his turn presented himself at the French Court as a suppliant.

But this was the best luck Louis XI had ever known. Now here in France were the leaders of both the parties that had disputed England for so long. Margaret was dwelling in her father's Anjou. Warwick, friend of France, vanquished in his own country, had arrived at Honfleur. With gusto the stern, cynical, hard-pressed Louis set himself to the task of reconciling and combining these opposite forces.

King Edward was by now alarmed and vigilant, but he could scarcely foresee how many of his supporters would betray him. Fitzhugh, his cousin, started a new insurrection in Yorkshire. Warwick and Clarence landed at Dartmouth in September, 1470. Kent and other southern counties rose in his behalf. Warwick marched to London. He brought the miserable Henry VI from his prison in the Tower, placed a crown on his head, paraded him through the capital, and seated him upon the throne.

The major part of Edward's kingdom seemed to have turned against him; he deemed it his sole hope to fly beyond the seas. He had but one refuge— the Court of Burgundy; and with a handful of followers he cast himself upon his brother-in-law.

*   *   *

Meanwhile the King-maker ruled England, and it seemed that he might long continue to do so. He had King Henry VI a puppet in his hand. The unhappy man, a breathing ruin sitting like a sack upon the throne, with a crown on his head and a sceptre in his hand, received the fickle caresses of Fortune with the same mild endurance which he had shown to her malignities.

Both sides now concentrated all their strength, and again large armies were seen in England. Throughout the land no one could see clearly what was happening, and the Battle of Barnet, which resolved their doubts, was itself fought in a fog. There the cry of treason ran through Warwick's hosts. Outnumbered, his ranks broken, he sought to reach his horse. He would have been wise in spite of taunts to have followed his usual custom of mounting again on the battle-day after walking along the lines; for had he escaped this zigzag story might have ended at the opposite point. But the King-maker, just as he was about to reach the necessary horse, was overtaken by the Yorkists and battered to death. He had been the foremost champion of the Yorkist cause. He had served King Edward well. He had received ill-usage from the youth he had placed and sustained upon the throne. By his depraved abandonment of all the causes for which he had sent so many men to their doom he had deserved death; and for his virtues, which were distinguished, it was fitting that it should come to him in honourable guise.

* * *

On the very day of Barnet Margaret at last landed in England. On learning that Warwick was slain and his army beaten and dispersed the hitherto indomitable Queen had her hour of despair. The King-maker aberration had been excised. The struggle was once again between Lancaster and York. Edward strove to cut Margaret off from Wales. Both armies marched incessantly. May 3 brought them to battle at Tewkesbury.

The Lancastrians were scattered or destroyed. The Prince of Wales, fighting valiantly, was slain on the field, according to one chronicler, crying in vain for succour to his brother-in-law, the treacherous Clarence. Margaret was kept for a show, and also because women, especially when they happened to be queens, were not slaughtered in this fierce age.

Richard of Gloucester hastened to London. He had a task to do at the Tower. As long as the Prince of Wales lived King Henry's life had been safe, but with the death of the last hope of Lancaster his fate was sealed. On the night of May 21 the Duke of Gloucester visited the Tower with full authority from the King, where he probably supervised the murder of Henry VI, the melancholy spectator who had been the centre of fifty years of cruel contention.

* * *

The rest of the reign of Edward IV may be told briefly. The King was now supreme. His foes and his patrons alike were dead. He was now a matured and disillusioned statesman. He had every means of remaining complete master of the realm while leading a jolly life. He made his administration live thriftily, and on his death he was the first King since Henry II to leave not debts but a fortune.

The King's brother, Clarence, was already in the Tower. How he died is much disputed. Some say the King gave him his choice of deaths. Certainly Edward did not intend to have a grisly public spectacle. According to Shakespeare the Duke was drowned in a butt of Malmsey wine. This was certainly the popular legend believed by the sixteenth century. Why should it not be true? At any rate no one has attempted to prove any different tale.

"False, fleeting, perjured Clarence" passed out of the world astonished that his brother should have so long a memory and take things so seriously.

Queen Elizabeth over the course of years had produced not only five daughters, but two fine boys, who were growing up. In 1483 one was twelve and the other nine. The succession to the Crown seemed plain and secure. The King himself was only forty. In another ten years the Yorkist triumph would have become permanent. But here Fate intervened, and with solemn hand reminded the pleasure-loving Edward that his account was closed. His main thought was set on securing the crown to his son, the unfledged Edward V; but in April, 1483, death came so suddenly upon him that he had no time to take the necessary precautions. Although always devoted to Queen Elizabeth, he had lived promiscuously all his life. She was in the Midlands, when, after only ten days' illness, this strong King was cut down in his prime. The historians assure us that this was the penalty of debauchery. It may well have been appendicitis, an explanation as yet unknown. He died unprepared except by the Church, and his faithful brother Richard saw himself suddenly confronted with an entirely new view of his future.

CHAPTER TWENTY-TWO

Richard III

THE KING died so suddenly that all were caught by surprise. A tense crisis instantly arose. His eldest son, Edward, dwelt on the Welsh border under the care of his uncle, the second Lord Rivers. A Protectorate was inevitable. There could be no doubt about the Protector. Richard of Gloucester, the King's faithful brother, renowned in war, grave and competent in administration, in possession of all the chief military offices, stood forth without compare, and had been nominated by the late King himself. Around him gathered most of the old nobility. They viewed with general distaste the idea of a King whose grandfather, though a knight, had been a mere steward to one of their own order. They deplored a minority and thereafter the rule of an unproved, inexperienced boy-King. They were, however, bound by their oaths and by the succession in the Yorkist line that their own swords had established.

For three weeks both parties eyed one another and parleyed. It was agreed in April that the King should be crowned at the earliest moment, but that he should come to London attended by not more than two thousand horsemen. Richard then rode with his power to Stony Stratford, arrested the commanders of the two thousand horse, forced his way to the young King, and told him he had discovered a design to seize the Government and oppress the old nobility. On this declaration Edward V took the only positive action recorded of his reign. He wept. Well he might.

The next morning Duke Richard presented himself again to Edward. He embraced him as an uncle; he bowed to him as a subject. He announced himself as Protector. He dismissed the two thousand horsemen to their homes; their services would not be needed. To London then! To the coronation! Thus this melancholy procession set out.

The Queen, who was already in London, had no illusions. She took sanctuary at once with her other children at Westminster, making a hole through the wall between the church and the palace to transport such personal belongings as she could gather.

The report that the King was in duress caused a commotion in the capital. "He was to be sent, no man wist whither, to be done with God wot what." [1] But Lord Hastings reassured the Council that all was well and that any disturbance would only delay the coronation, upon which the peace of the realm depended. The Archbishop of York, who was also Chancellor, tried to reassure the Queen. "Be of good cheer, madam," he said, "for if they crown any other than your son whom they now have with them, we shall on the morrow crown his brother whom you have with you here." He even gave her the Great Seal as a kind of guarantee. He was not in any plot, but only an old fool playing for safety first and peace at any price. Presently, frightened at what he had done, he managed to get the Great Seal back.

The King arrived in London only on May 4, and the coronation, which had been fixed for that date, was necessarily postponed. He was lodged at the Bishop of London's palace, where he received the fealty of all the lords, spiritual and temporal. But the Protector and his friends felt that it was hardly becoming that he should be the guest of an ecclesiastic, and when the Queen's friends suggested that he might reside at the Hospital of the Knights of St. John in Clerkenwell Richard argued that it would be more fitting to the royal dignity to dwell in one of his own castles and on his own ground. The Tower was a residence not only commodious but at the same time safe from any popular disorder. To this decision the lords of the Council gave united assent, it not being either easy or safe for the minority to disagree. With much ceremony and protestations of devotion the child of twelve was conducted to the Tower, and its gates closed behind him.

London was in a ferment, and the magnates gathered there gazed upon each other in doubt and fear. The next step in the tragedy concerned Lord Hastings. He had played a leading part in the closing years of Edward IV. After the King's death he had been strong against the Woodvilles; but he

[1] More.

111

was the first to detach himself from Richard's proceedings. It did not suit him, nor some of the other magnates, that all power should rapidly be accumulating in Richard's hands. He began to be friendly with the Queen's party, still in the sanctuary of Westminster Abbey. Of what happened next all we really know is that Hastings was abruptly arrested in council at the Tower on June 13 and beheaded without trial on the same day. Sir Thomas More late in the next reign wrote his celebrated history. In it Richard is evil incarnate, and Henry Tudor, the deliverer of the kingdom, all sweetness and light. The opposite view would have been treason. Not only is every possible crime attributed by More to Richard, and some impossible ones, but he is presented as a physical monster, crookbacked and withered of arm. No one in his lifetime seems to have remarked these deformities, but they are now very familiar to us through Shakespeare's play.

More's tale has priority. We have the famous scene at the Council in the Tower. It was Friday, June 13. Richard arrived in the Council chamber about nine, apparently in good humour. "My lord," he said to Bishop Morton, "you have very good strawberries in your garden at Holborn. I pray you let us have a mess of them." The Council began its business. Richard asked to be excused for a while; when he returned between ten and eleven his whole manner was changed. He frowned and glared upon the Council, and at the same time clusters of armed men gathered at the door. "What punishment do they deserve," demanded the Protector, "who conspire against the life of one so nearly related to the King as myself, and entrusted with the government of the realm?" There was general consternation. Hastings said at length that they deserved the punishment of traitors. "That sorceress my brother's wife," cried Richard, "and others with her —see how they have wasted my body with sorcery and witchcraft." So saying, he is supposed to have bared his arm and showed it to the Council, shrunk and withered as legend says it was. In furious terms he next referred to Jane Shore, with whom Hastings had formed an intimacy on the late King's death. Hastings, taken aback, replied, "Certainly if they have done so heinously they are worth a heinous punishment." "What?" cried Crookback. "Dost thou serve me with 'ifs' and 'ands'? I tell thee they have done it, and that I will make good upon thy body, traitor!" He struck the Council table with his fist, and at this signal the armed men ran in, crying "Treason!" and Hastings, Bishop Morton, and the Archbishop of York with some others were seized. Richard bade Hastings prepare for instant death. "I will not dine until I have his head." There was barely time to find a priest. Upon a log of wood which lay by chance in the Tower yard Hastings was decapitated. Terror reigned.

Meanwhile, the Queen and her remaining son still sheltered in sanctuary. Richard felt that it would be more natural that the two brothers should be together under his care, and he moved the Council to request the Queen to give him up. Having no choice, the Queen submitted, and the little prince of nine was handed over in Westminster Hall to the Protector, who embraced him affectionately and conducted him to the Tower, which neither he nor his brother was ever to leave again.

On June 25, 1483, Parliament met, and petitioned Richard to assume the crown. The coronation was fixed for July 6, and pageants and procession diverted the uneasy public. The King now had a title acknowledged and confirmed by Parliament, and upon the theory of the bastardy of Edward's children he was also the lineal successor in blood. Thus the whole design seemed to have been accomplished. Yet from this very moment there began that marked distrust and hostility of all classes towards King Richard III which all his arts and competence could not allay. Richard held the authority of government. He told his own story with what facilities were available, and he was spontaneously and almost universally disbelieved. Meanwhile he laboured to make the best impression, righting wrongs, settling disputes, granting favours, and courting popularity. Yet he could not escape the sense that behind the displays of gratitude and loyalty which naturally surrounded him there lay an unspoken challenge to his Kingship. Feeling already ran high against him, and on all men's lips was the demand that the princes should be liberated.

So we come to the principal crime ever afterwards associated with Richard's name. His interest is plain. His character was ruthless. It is certain that the helpless children in the Tower were not seen again after the month of July, 1483. According to Thomas More's story, Richard resolved in July to extirpate the menace to his peace and sovereignty presented by the princes. When they were asleep two assassins pressed the pillows hard down upon their faces till they were suffocated, and their bodies were immured in some secret corner of the Tower.

In the reign of Charles II, when in 1674 the staircase leading to the chapel in the White Tower was altered, the skeletons of two young lads, whose apparent ages fitted the two princes, were found buried under a mass of rubble. They were examined by the royal surgeon, and the antiquaries reported that they were undoubtedly the remains of Edward V and the Duke of York. Charles accepted this view, and the skeletons were reburied in Henry VII's Chapel at Westminster with a Latin inscription laying all blame upon their perfidious uncle "the usurper of the realm."

The popular demand for the release of the princes was followed by a report of their death. When, how, and by whose hand the deed had been done was not known. But as the news spread like wildfire a kind of fury seized upon many people. Although accustomed to the brutalities of the long civil wars, the English people of those days still retained the faculty of horror; and once it was excited they did not soon forget. A modern dictator with the resources of science at his disposal can easily lead the public on from day to day, destroying all persistency of thought and aim, so that memory is blurred by the multiplicity of daily news and judgment baffled by its perversion. But in the fifteenth century the murder of the two young princes by the very man who had undertaken to protect them was regarded as an atrocious crime, never to be forgotten or forgiven. In September Richard in his progress reached York, and here he created his son Prince of Wales, thus in the eyes of his enemies giving confirmation to the darkest rumours.

He proceeded in the new year to inaugurate a series of enlightened reforms in every sphere of Government. But all counted for nothing. The hatred which Richard's crime had roused against him throughout the land remained sullen and quenchless, and no benefits bestowed, no sagacious measures adopted, no administrative successes achieved, could avail the guilty monarch. Even Richard's own soul rebelled against him. He was haunted by fears and dreams. He saw retribution awaiting him round every corner. "I have heard by creditable report," says Sir Thomas More, "of such as were secret with his chamberers, that after this abominable deed done he never had quiet in his mind, he never thought himself sure. Where he went abroad, his eyes whirled about, his body privily fenced, his hand ever on his dagger, his countenance and manner like one always ready to strike again. He took ill rest at nights, lay long waking and musing; sore wearied with care and watch, he rather slumbered than slept. Troubled with fearful dreams, suddenly sometimes started he up, leapt out of his bed and ran about the chamber. So was his restless heart continually tossed and tumbled with the tedious impression and stormy remembrance of his most abominable deed."

*   *   *

A terrible blow now fell upon the King. In April, 1484, his only son, the Prince of Wales, died and his wife, Anne, the daughter of the King-maker, whose health was broken, could bear no more children. Henry Tudor, Earl of Richmond, now became obviously the rival claimant and successor to the throne. Richmond could trace his descent through his mother from Edward III, and on his father's side had a shadowy claim to descent from the legendary ancient kings of Britain, including King Arthur.

All hopes in England were now turned towards Richmond, and it was apparent that the marriage which had been projected between him and Edward IV's eldest daughter Elizabeth offered a prospect of ending for ever the cruel dynastic strife of which the land was unutterably weary. As the months passed many prominent Englishmen, both Yorkist and Lancastrian, withdrew themselves from Richard's baleful presence, and made their way to Richmond, who from this time forth stood at the head of a combination which might well unite all England.

All through the summer Richmond's expedition was preparing at the mouth of the Seine, and the exodus from England of substantial people to join him was unceasing. The suspense was wearing to Richard. He felt he was surrounded by hatred and distrust, and that none served him but from fear, or hope of favour. His dogged, indomitable nature had determined him to make for his crown the greatest of all his fights.

Richmond embarked at Harfleur with his Englishmen, Yorkist as well as Lancastrian, and landed at Milford Haven on the 7th of August. Kneeling, he recited the psalm *Judica me, Deus, et decerne causam meam.* He kissed the ground, signed himself with the Cross, and gave the order to advance in the name of God and St. George. Such were his assurances of support that he proclaimed Richard forthwith usurper and rebel against himself.

*　　*　　*

For all his post-horses it was five days before the King heard of the landing. He gathered his army and marched to meet his foe. At this moment the attitude of the Stanleys became of decisive importance. They had been entrusted by the King with the duty of intercepting the rebels should they land in the West. Sir William Stanley, with some thousands of men, made no attempt to do so. Richard thereupon summoned Lord Stanley, the head of the house, to his Court, and when that potentate declared himself "ill of the sweating sickness" he seized Lord Strange, his eldest son, to hold him answerable with his life for his father's loyalty. This did not prevent Sir William Stanley with the Cheshire levies from making friendly contact with Richmond. But Lord Stanley, hoping to save his son, maintained till the last moment an uncertain demeanour.

The city of York on this occasion stood by the Yorkist cause. The Duke of Norfolk and Percy, Earl of Northumberland, were Richard's principal adherents. "The Catte and the Ratte" had no hope of life but in their master's victory. On August 17, thus attended, the King set forth towards Leicester at the head of his army. Their ordered ranks, four abreast, with the cavalry on both flanks and the King mounted on his great white charger in the centre, made a formidable impression upon beholders. And when on Sunday, August 21, 1485, this whole array came out of Leicester to meet Richmond near the village of Market Bosworth it was certain that a decisive battle impended on the morrow.

Appearances favoured the King. He had ten thousand disciplined men under the royal authority against Richmond's hastily gathered five thousand rebels. But at some distance from the flanks of the main army, on opposite hill-tops, stood the respective forces, mainly from Lancashire and Cheshire, of Sir William Stanley and Lord Stanley, the whole situation resembling, as has been said, four players in a game of cards. Richard, according to the Tudor historians, although confessing to a night of frightful dreams and demon-hauntings, harangued his captains in magnificent style. "Dismiss all

1 1 5

fear. . . . Every one give but one sure stroke and the day is ours. What prevaileth a handful of men to a whole realm? As for me, I assure you this day I will triumph by glorious victory or suffer death for immortal fame." He then gave the signal for battle, and sent a message to Lord Stanley that if he did not fall on forthwith he would instantly decapitate his son. Stanley, forced to this bitter choice, answered proudly that he had other sons. The King gave orders for Strange's execution. But the officers so charged thought it prudent to hold the stroke in suspense till matters were clearer. "My lord, the enemy is past the marsh. After the battle let young Stanley die."

But even now Richmond was not sure what part Lord Stanley and his forces would play. When, after archery and cannonade, the lines were locked in battle all doubts were removed. The Earl of Northumberland, commanding Richard's left, stood idle at a distance. Lord Stanley's force joined Richmond. The King saw that all was lost, and, shouting "Treason! Treason!" hurled himself into the thickest of the fray in the desperate purpose of striking down Richmond with his own hand. He actually slew Sir William Brandon, Richmond's standard-bearer, and laid low Sir John Cheney, a warrior renowned for his bodily strength. He is said even to have reached Richmond and crossed swords with him. But at this moment Sir William Stanley's three thousand, "in coats as red as blood," fell upon the struggling Yorkists. The tides of conflict swept the principals asunder. Richmond was preserved, and the King, refusing to fly, was borne down and slaughtered as he deserved.

> One foot I will never flee, while the breath is my breast within.
> As he said, so did it he—if he lost his life he died a king.

Richard's crown, which he wore to the last, was picked out of a bush and placed upon the victor's head; and Henry Tudor became King of England. Richard's corpse, naked, and torn by wounds, was bound across a horse, with his head and long hair hanging down, bloody and hideous, and in this condition borne into Leicester for all men to see.

*   *   *

Bosworth Field may be taken as closing a long chapter in English history. Though risings and conspiracies continued throughout the next reign the strife of the Red and the White Rose had in the main come to an end. Neither won. A solution was reached in which the survivors of both causes could be reconciled. The marriage of Richmond with the adaptable Princess Elizabeth produced the Tudor line, in which both Yorkists and Lancastrians had a share. The revengeful ghosts of two mangled generations were laid for ever. Richard's death also ended the Plantagenet line. For over three hundred years this strong race of warrior and statesmen kings, whose gifts and vices were upon the highest scale, whose sense of authority and Empire had been persistently maintained, now vanished from the fortunes of the

Island. The Plantagenets and the proud, exclusive nobility which their system evolved had torn themselves to pieces. The heads of most of the noble houses had been cut off, and their branches extirpated to the second and third generation. An oligarchy whose passions, loyalties, and crimes had for long written English history was subdued. Sprigs of female or bastard lines made disputable contacts with a departed age. As Coeur de Lion said of his house, "From the Devil we sprang and to the Devil we shall go."

At Bosworth the Wars of the Roses reached their final milestone. In the next century the subjects of the Tudors liked to consider that the Middle Ages too had come to a close in 1485, and that a new age had dawned with the accession of Henry Tudor. Modern historians prefer to point out that there are no sharp dividing lines in this period of our history, and that Henry VII carried on and consolidated much of the work of the Yorkist Kings. Certainly the prolongation of strife, waste, and insecurity in the fifteenth century had aroused in all classes an overpowering desire for strong, ordered government. The Parliamentary conception which had prevailed under the house of Lancaster had gained many frontiers of constitutional rights. These were now to pass into long abeyance. Not until the seventeenth century were the old maxims, "Grievances before supply," "Responsibility of Ministers in accordance with the public will," "The Crown the servant and not the master of the State," brought again into the light, and, as it happened, the glare of a new day. The stir of the Renaissance, the storm of the Reformation, hurled their new problems on the bewildered but also reinspired mortals of the new age upon which England entered under the guidance of the wise, sad, careful monarch who inaugurated the Tudor dictatorship as King Henry VII.

BOOK FOUR

Renaissance and Reformation

CHAPTER TWENTY-THREE

The Round World

WE HAVE now reached the dawn of what is called the sixteenth century, which means all the years in the hundred years that begin with fifteen. The name is inevitable in English, but confusing. It covers a period in which extraordinary changes affected the whole of Europe. Some had been on the move for a long time, but sprang into full operative force at this moment. For two hundred years or more the Renaissance had been stirring the thought and spirit of Italy, and now came forth in the vivid revival of the traditions of ancient Greece and Rome, in so far as these did not affect the foundations of the Christian faith. Literature, philosophy, and art flowered under classical inspiration, and the minds of men to whom study was open were refreshed and enlarged. These were the humanists, who attempted a reconciliation of classical and Christian teachings, among the foremost of whom was Erasmus of Rotterdam. To him is due a considerable part of the credit for bringing Renaissance thought to England. Printing enabled knowledge and argument to flow through the many religious societies which made up the structure of medieval Europe, and from about 1450 onwards printing presses formed the core of a vast ever-growing domain. There were already sixty universities in the Western world, from Lisbon to Prague, and in the early part of the new century these voluntarily opened up broader paths of study and intercourse which rendered their life more fertile and informal. In the Middle Ages education had largely been confined to train-ing the clergy; now it was steadily extended, and its purpose became to turn out not only priests but lay scholars and well-informed gentlemen. The man of many parts and accomplishments became the Renaissance ideal.

This quickening of the human spirit was accompanied by a questioning of long-held theories. For the first time in the course of the fifteenth cen-tury men began to refer to the preceding millennium as the Middle Ages. Though much that was medieval survived in their minds, men felt they were living on the brink of a new and modern age. It was an age marked not only by splendid achievements in art and architecture, but also by the beginnings of a revolution in science associated with the name of Coperni-cus. That the earth moved round the sun, as he conclusively proved and Galileo later asserted on a celebrated occasion, was a novel idea that was to have profound effects upon the human outlook. Hitherto the earth had been thought of as the centre of a universe all designed to serve the needs of man. Now vast new perspectives were opening.

The urge to inquire, to debate, and seek new explanations spread from the field of classical learning into that of religious studies. Greek and even Hebrew texts, as well as Latin, were scrutinised afresh. Inevitably this led to the questioning of accepted religious beliefs. The Renaissance bred the Reformation. In 1517, at the age of thirty-four, Martin Luther, a German priest, denounced the sale of Indulgences, nailed his theses on this and other matters on the door of Wittenberg Castle church, and embarked on his venturesome intellectual foray with the Pope. What began as a protest against Church practices soon became a challenge to Church doctrine. In this struggle Luther displayed qualities of determination and conviction at the peril of the stake which won him his name and fame. He started or gave an impulse to a movement which within a decade swamped the Continent, and proudly bears the general title of the Reformation. It took different forms in different countries, particularly in Switzerland under Zwingli and Calvin. The latter's influence spread from Geneva across France to the Netherlands and Britain, where it was most strongly felt in Scotland.

*　　*　　*

While the forces of Renaissance and Reformation were gathering strength in Europe the world beyond was ceaselessly yielding its secrets to European explorers, traders, and missionaries. From the days of the ancient Greeks some men had known in theory that the world was round. Now in the sixteenth century navigations were to prove it so.

Italian geographers and navigators had for some time been trying to find a new sea-route to the Orient, but although they had much experience of shipbuilding and navigation from the busy traffic of the Eastern Mediterranean they lacked the capital resources for the hazard of oceanic exploration. Portugal was the first to discover a new path. Helped by English Crusaders, she had achieved her independence in the twelfth century, gradually expelled the Moors from her mainland, and now reached out to the African coastline. Prince Henry the Navigator, grandson of John of Gaunt, had initiated a number of enterprises. Exploring began from Lisbon. All through the later fifteenth century Portuguese mariners had been pushing down the west coast of Africa, seeking for gold and slaves, slowly extending the bounds of the known world, till, in 1487, Bartholomeu Diaz rounded the great promontory that marked the end of the African continent. He called it "the Cape of Storms," but the King of Portugal with true insight renamed it "the Cape of Good Hope." The hope was justified; in 1498 Vasco da Gama dropped anchor in the harbour of Calicut; the sea-route was open to the wealth of India and the Farther East.

*　　*　　*

119

An event of greater moment for the future of the world was meanwhile taking shape in the mind of a Genoese named Christopher Columbus. Brooding over the dreamlike maps of his fellow-countrymen, he conceived a plan for sailing due west into the Atlantic beyond the known islands in search of yet another route to the East. He married the daughter of a Portuguese sailor who had served with the Navigator, and from his father-in-law's papers he learnt of the great oceanic ventures. In 1486 he sent his brother Bartholomew to seek English backing for the enterprise. Bartholomew was captured by pirates off the French coast, and when he finally arrived in England and won the notice of Henry Tudor, the new King, it was too late. Christopher, however, had gathered the support of the joint Spanish sovereigns, Ferdinand of Aragon and Isabella of Castile, and under their patronage in 1492 he set sail into the unknown from Palos, in Andalusia. After a voyage of three months he made landfall in one of the islands of the Bahamas. Unwittingly he had discovered, not a new route to the East, but a new continent in the West, soon to be called America.

It was nearly a hundred years before England began to exert her potential sea-power. Her achievements during this period were by comparison meagre. The merchants of Bristol tried to seek a north-west passage beyond the Atlantic to the Far East, but they had little success or encouragement. Their colleagues in London and Eastern England were more concerned with the solid profits from trade with the Netherlands. Henry Tudor, however, appreciated private enterprise, provided it did not involve him in disputes with Spain. He financed an expedition by John Cabot, who in 1497 struck land near Cape Breton Island. But there was little prospect of trade, and an immense forbidding continent seemed to block further advance. On a second voyage Cabot sailed down the coast of America in the direction of Florida, but this was too near the region of Spanish efforts. Upon Cabot's death the cautious Henry abandoned his Atlantic enterprise.

*   *   *

The arrival of the Spaniards in the New World and their discovery of precious metals had led them into wordy conflict with the Portuguese. As one of the motives of both countries was the spreading of the Christian faith into undiscovered heathen lands, they appealed to the Pope, in whose hands the gift of new countries was at this time conceived to lie. By a series of Bulls in the 1490's the Borgia Pope Alexander VI drew a line across the world dividing the Spanish and Portuguese spheres. This remarkable dispensation stimulated the conclusion of a treaty between Spain and Portugal. A north-south line 370 leagues west of the Azores was agreed upon, and the Portuguese felt entitled to occupy Brazil.

Although the Portuguese were first in the field of oceanic adventure their country was too small to sustain such efforts. It is said that half the population of Portugal died in trying to hold their overseas possessions. Spain soon overtook them. In the year of Columbus's first voyage, Granada, the only Moorish city which survived on Spanish soil, had fallen to the last great Crusading army of the Middle Ages. Henceforward the Spaniards were free to turn their energies to the New World. In less than a generation a Portuguese captain, in Spanish pay, Magellan, set out on the voyage to South America and across the Pacific that was to take his ship round the globe. Magellan was killed in the Philippines, but his chief officer brought his ship home round the Cape of Good Hope. The scattered civilisations of the world were being drawn together, and the new discoveries were to give the little kingdom in the northern sea a fresh importance. Here was to be the successor of both Portugal and Spain, though the time for entering into the inheritance was not yet. But now the spices of the East were travelling by sea to the European market at Antwerp. The whole course of trade was shifted and revolutionised. The overland route languished; the primacy of the Italian cities was eclipsed by North-West Europe; and the future lay not in the Mediterranean, but on the shores of the Atlantic, where the new Powers, England, France, and Holland, had ports and harbours which gave easy access to the oceans.

*　　*　　*

The wealth of the New World soon affected the old order in Europe. In the first half of the sixteenth century Cortes overcame the Aztec empire of Mexico and Pizarro conquered the Incas of Peru. The vast mineral treasures of these lands now began to pour across the Atlantic. By channels which multiplied gold and silver flowed into Europe. So did new commodities, tobacco, potatoes, and American sugar. The old continent to which these new riches came was itself undergoing a transformation. After a long halt its population was again growing and production on the farms and in the workshops was expanding. There was a widespread demand for more money to pay for new expeditions, new buildings, new enterprises, and new methods of government. The manipulation of finance was little understood either by rulers or by the mass of the people, and the first recourse of impoverished princes was to debase their currency. Prices therefore rose sharply, and when Luther posted his theses at Wittenberg the value of money was already rapidly falling.

As ever in times of rapid inflation, there were much hardship and many difficulties in adjustment. But a strong sensation of new growth and well-being abounded, and ultimately every class benefited by the general amelioration. For a world which, a century before, had lost perhaps a third of its population by the Black Death there was a wonderful stimulus of mind and body. Men were groping their way into a larger age, with a freer interchange of more goods and services and with far greater numbers taking an effective part. The New World had opened its spacious doors, not only geographically by adding North and South America as places for

1 2 1

Europe to live in, but by enlarging its whole way of life and outlook and the uses it could make of all it had.

CHAPTER TWENTY-FOUR

The Tudor Dynasty

FOR A generation and more the English monarchy had been tossed on the rough waters of a disputed succession. On August 22, 1485, Henry Tudor, Earl of Richmond, had won a decisive victory near the small Midland town of Market Bosworth, and his rival, the usurper Richard III, was slain in the battle. In the person of Henry VII a new dynasty now mounted the throne, and during the twenty-four years of careful stewardship that lay before him a new era in English history began.

Henry's first task was to induce magnates, Church, and gentry to accept the decision of Bosworth and to establish himself upon the throne. He was careful to be crowned before facing the representatives of the nation, thus resting his title first upon conquest, and only secondly on the approbation of Parliament. At any rate, Parliament was committed to the experiment of his rule. Then he married, as had long been planned, the heiress of the rival house, Elizabeth of York.

Legislation was passed stating that all who gave their allegiance to the King for the time being—that is, to the King upon the throne—should be secure in their lives and property. This idea of an actual King as distinct from a rightful King was characteristic of the new ruler. Sure of himself, he did not shrink from establishing his power upon a practical basis. He put down disorder in the countryside and co-operated with Parliament. Henry's careful attention to this body sprang from a real community of interests, the need for settled government. If this was despotism, it was despotism by consent. It was impossible to govern England from London in the fifteenth century. The machinery of administration was too primitive.

Henry had many reasons to feel his throne shake a little beneath him. The Wars of the Roses had weakened English authority in Wales but it was in Ireland that their effects were most manifest. But a powerful ally was at hand. Artillery, which had helped to expel the English from France, now aided their incursion into Ireland. The cannons spoke to Irish castles in a language readily understood. But the cannons came from England.

The Irish could use but could not make them. Now in the advance of culture precedence was regulated by gunpowder.

* * *

Henry's dealings with Scotland are characteristic of his shrewd judgment. He took the first steps to unite England and Scotland by marrying his daughter Margaret to James IV in 1502, and there was peace in the North until after his death.

With France too his policy was eminently successful. He realised that more could be gained by the threat of war than by war itself. Henry gained both ways. Like Edward IV, he pocketed not only a considerable subsidy from France, which was punctually paid, but also the taxes collected in England for war.

Henry VII as a statesman was imbued with the new, ruthless political ideas of Renaissance Europe. He strove to establish a strong monarchy in England, moulded out of native institutions. Like his contemporary, Lorenzo de' Medici in Florence, Henry worked almost always by adaptation, modifying old forms ever so slightly, rather than by crude innovation. And always at the centre was the King himself, the embodiment of direct personal government, often authorising or auditing expenditure, even the most trifling, with great sprawling initials which may still be seen at the Record Office in London. Henry VII was probably the best business man to sit upon the English throne.

He was also a remarkably shrewd picker of men. Daily, in all his leisure, he made notes on political affairs, on matters which required attention, "especially touching persons," whom to employ, to reward, to imprison, to outlaw, exile, or execute. Like the other princes of his age, his main interest, apart from an absorbing passion for administration, was foreign policy. Diplomacy, he considered, was no bad substitute for the violence of his predecessors, and early, accurate, and regular information was essential to its conduct. A spy system was organised and foreign intelligence. Though personally frugal, he maintained a calculated pageantry; he wore magnificent clothes, superb jewels, rich and glittering collars, and moved in public under a canopy of state, waited upon by noblemen, with a Court where about seven hundred persons dined daily in the Tower at his expense, entertained by jesters, minstrels, huntsmen, and his famous leopards.

His achievement was massive and durable. He built his power amid the ruins and ashes of his predecessors. He thriftily and carefully gathered what seemed in those days a vast reserve of liquid wealth. He trained a body of efficient servants. He magnified the Crown without losing the co-operation of the Commons. He identified prosperity with monarchy. Among the princes of Renaissance Europe he is not surpassed in achievement and fame. From the picture in the National Portrait Gallery his quick, hard grey eyes look out from an arched setting. Delicate, well-kept hands rest lightly upon the bottom of the frame. His lips are set tight, with a faint smile breaking the corners. There is an air of disillusionment, of fatigue, of unceasing vigilance, and above all of sadness and responsibility. Such was the architect of the Tudor monarchy, which was to lead England out of medieval disorder into greater strength and broader times.

CHAPTER TWENTY-FIVE

King Henry VIII

THE AGE in which the young King Henry VIII grew up was, when seen from the perspective of later centuries, one in which an old order was dying. But it scarcely seemed so to those who lived in it. The change most visible to the eyes of a ruler was the creation of the modern European state system. In his world of growing power the King of England had to move and act with far fewer resources than his neighbours. His subjects numbered not many more than three millions. He had smaller revenues, no standing army, no state apparatus answerable only to the royal will. And yet by the mere proximity of France and the Imperial Netherlands England was forced to play a part in European politics. Her King was involved in wars and negotiations, shifts in alliances and changes in the balance of power, of which he had had little experience and could only in a secondary degree affect.

*   *   *

Henry in his maturity was a tall, red-headed man who preserved the vigour and energy of ancestors accustomed for centuries to the warfare of the Welsh marches. His massive frame towered above the throng, and those about him felt in it a sense of concealed desperation, of latent force and passion. A French ambassador confessed, after residing for months at Court, that he could never approach the King without fear of personal violence. Although Henry appeared to strangers open, jovial, and trustworthy, with a bluff good humour which appealed at once to the crowd, even those who knew him most intimately seldom penetrated the inward secrecy and reserve which allowed him to confide freely in no one. To those who saw him often he seemed almost like two men: one the merry monarch of the hunt and banquet and procession, the friend of children, the patron of every kind of sport; the other the cold, acute observer of the audience chamber or the Council, watching vigilantly, weighing arguments, refusing except under the stress of great events to speak his own mind. On his long hunting expeditions, when the courier arrived with papers, he swiftly left his companions of the chase and summoned the "counsellors attendant" for what he was wont to call "London business."

Bursts of restless energy and ferocity were combined with extraordinary patience and diligence. Deeply religious, Henry regularly listened to sermons and wrote more than one theological treatise of a high standard. He was accustomed to hear five Masses on Church days, and three on other days.

An indefatigable worker, he digested a mass of dispatches, memoranda, and plans each day without the help of his secretary. He wrote verses and composed music. Profoundly secretive in public business, he chose as his advisers men for the most part of the meanest origin: Thomas Wolsey, the son of a poor and rascally butcher of Ipswich, whose name appears on the borough records for selling meat unfit for human consumption; Thomas Cromwell, a small attorney; Thomas Cranmer, an obscure lecturer in divinity. Like his father he distrusted the hereditary nobility, preferring the discreet counsel of men without a wide circle of friends.

This enormous man was the nightmare of his advisers. Once a scheme was fixed in his mind he could seldom be turned from it; resistance only made him more stubborn; and, once embarked, he always tended to go too far unless restrained. The only secret of managing him, both Wolsey and Cromwell disclosed after they had fallen, was to see that dangerous ideas were not permitted to reach him. But arrangements of this sort could not be complete. His habit was to talk to all classes—barbers, huntsmen, his "yeoman cook to the King's mouth"—and particularly anyone, however humble, connected with the sea, to ferret out opinions, and ride off on hunting expeditions which sometimes lasted for weeks. Each summer he went on progress through the country, keeping close to the mass of his subjects, whom he understood so well.

Almost his first act, six weeks after the death of his father in 1509, was to marry his brother Arthur's widow, Princess Catherine of Aragon. He was aged eighteen and she was five years and five months older. Catherine was at Henry's side during the first twenty-two years of his reign, while England was becoming a force in European affairs, perilous for foreign rulers to ignore. Until she reached the age of thirty-eight she remained, apart from three or four short lapses, the mistress of his affections, restrained his follies, and in her narrow way helped to guide public affairs between the intervals of her numerous confinements. Henry settled down to married life very quickly, in spite of a series of misfortunes which would have daunted a less robust character. The Queen's first baby was born dead, just after Henry's nineteenth birthday; another died soon after birth a year later. In all there were to be five such disappointments.

CHAPTER TWENTY-SIX

Cardinal Wolsey

HENRY LOOKED to the defences of the realm, and took measures to strengthen his navy. Then he sought and obtained a favorable peace treaty with France, thereby securing exactly double the amount of annual tribute that had been paid to his father. The crowning event of the peace was the marriage between Henry's young sister, Mary, and Louis XII himself. She was seventeen, he was fifty-two. The marriage ultimately bore tragic fruit; a grandchild was the Lady Jane Grey, who was for ten days to be Queen of England.

Among those who had crossed with the bridal retinue to France was a young girl named Mary Boleyn. She was one of three nieces of the Duke of Norfolk, all of whom successively engaged the dangerous and deadly love of Henry VIII. Mary and her sister Anne had been educated in France at an expensive academy attached to the French Court. On her return to England Mary became the King's mistress. Anne continued her studies in France.

Wolsey was richly rewarded for foreign successes, particularly in France, and for fourteen years in the King's name was the effective ruler of the realm. He owed his position not only to his great capacity for business, but to his considerable personal charm. He had "an angel's wit," one of his contemporaries wrote, for beguiling and flattering those whom he wished to persuade. In the King's company he was brilliant, convivial, and "a gay seeker out of new pastimes." All this commended him to his young master. Other would-be counsellors of Henry's saw a different side of the Cardinal's character. At the height of his influence Wolsey enjoyed an income equivalent to about £500,000 a year in early twentieth-century money. He kept one thousand servants, and his palaces surpassed the King's in splendour. These counts against him gradually added up in the course of years. But for the time being—and it was for a long time, as Chief Ministers go—he successfully held in his grasp an accumulation of power that has otherwise probably never been equalled in England.

The King's popularity rose with the achievements of his reign. Successes abroad enabled Wolsey to develop Henry VII's principles of centralised government. Thus it was that this system of arbitrary government, however despotic in theory, however contrary to the principles believed to lie behind Magna Carta, in fact rested tacitly on the real will of the people. The Tudors were, indeed, the architects of an English system of local government which lasted almost unchanged until Victorian times.

*　　*　　*

1 2 6

Within a few years of his accession Henry embarked upon a programme of naval expansion, while Wolsey concerned himself with diplomatic manœuvre. Henry had already constructed the largest warship of the age, the *Great Harry*, of fifteen hundred tons. The fleet was built up under the personal care of the sovereign, who was not content until England commanded the Narrow Seas. Wolsey's arrangements for the foreign service were hardly less remarkable. The dispatches of this period, at the height of the Renaissance, are as closely knit and coloured as any in history; each event, the size of armies, rebellions in Italian cities, movements within the College of Cardinals, taxes in France, is carefully weighed and recorded. For some years, at least, Wolsey was a powerful factor and balancing weight in Europe.

The zenith of this brilliant period was reached at the Field of the Cloth of Gold in June, 1520, when Henry crossed the Channel to meet his rival, Francis I of France, for the first time. Henry's main perplexity was, we are told, about his appearance; he could not decide how he would look best, in his beard as usual or clean-shaven. At first he yielded to Catherine's persuasion and shaved. But directly he had done so he regretted the step and grew the beard again. It reached its full luxuriance in time to create a great impression in France.

At the Field of the Cloth of Gold, near Guîsnes, the jousting and feasting, the colour and glitter, the tents and trappings, dazzled all Europe. It was the last display of medieval chivalry. Many noblemen, it was said, carried on their shoulders their mills, their forests, and their meadows. But Henry and Francis failed to become personal friends. At Guîsnes he attempted to outdo Francis both by the splendour of his equipment and the cunning of his diplomacy. Relying on his great physical strength, he suddenly challenged Francis to a wrestling match. Francis seized him in a lightning grip and put him on the ground. Henry went white with passion, but was held back. Although the ceremonies continued Henry could not forgive such a personal humiliation. Within a month he had concluded an alliance with the Emperor; only six weeks later the Imperial armies won an overwhelming victory over the French at Pavia, in Northern Italy. But although Francis himself was taken prisoner and crushing terms of peace were imposed on France, England did not share in the spoils of victory. Henry could no longer turn the scales in Europe. The blame was clearly Wolsey's, and the King decided that perhaps the Cardinal had been given too free a hand. He insisted on visiting the great new college which Wolsey was building at Oxford, Cardinal College, destined to become Christ Church, the largest and most richly endowed in the university. When he arrived he was astonished at the vast sums which were being lavished upon the masonry. "It is strange," he remarked to the Cardinal, "that you have found so much money to spend upon your college and yet could not find enough to finish my war." He decided Wolsey would have to be sacrificed to preserve the popularity of the monarch.

Wolsey crossed the Channel to conduct prolonged negotiations for a treaty of alliance with France. While he was away Henry became openly infatuated with Anne Boleyn. Since she had returned from school in France Anne had grown into a vivacious, witty woman of twenty-four, very slender and frail, with beautiful black eyes and thick black hair so long that she could sit on it, which she wore flowing loose over her shoulders. She had a fiery temper, was outspoken and domineering, and although not generally liked soon gained a small following.

We first hear of Anne Boleyn in a dispatch dated August 16, 1527, four months after Henry had begun proceedings for the annulment of his marriage. Did he plan the divorce and then find Anne? Or had he arranged to marry Anne from the beginning? We shall never know, for Henry was very secretive in his private matters. "Three may keep counsel," he observed a year or two later, "if two be away; and if I thought my cap knew my counsel I would cast it into the fire and burn it."

Henry had been carefully guarded by Wolsey and Catherine. The appearance at Court of a lady with whom he spent hours at a time created an extraordinary stir. Together Anne and Henry arranged to send a special royal ambassador to Pope Clement VII, independently of the resident ambassador chosen by Wolsey, to seek not only annulment of the King's marriage, but also a dispensation to marry again at once. The Pope was now practically a prisoner of Charles V, who was determined that Henry should not divorce his aunt. The refusal followed.

At the same time the King had the writs sent out for a Parliament, the first for six years, to strengthen his hand in the great changes he was planning. Norfolk and Gardiner, not Wolsey, completed the arrangements. Wolsey retired in disgrace to his diocese of York. On one occasion he came to Grafton to see the King. But when he entered he found that Anne was there, Norfolk insulted him to his face, and he was dismissed without an audience.

On October 9, 1529, Wolsey's disgrace was carried a step farther. Anne determined to ruin him. She had set her heart on York Place, the London residence of the Archbishops of York, which was, she decided, of a convenient size for her and Henry; large enough for their friends and entertainments, yet too small to permit Queen Catherine to live there, also. Anne and her mother took the King to inspect the Cardinal's goods in York Place, and Henry was incensed by the wealth which he found. The judges and learned counsel were summoned and the King asked how he could legally obtain possession of York Place, which had been regarded as belonging to the Archbishops of York in perpetuity. The judges advised that Wolsey should make a declaration handing over York Place to the King and his successors. A judge of the King's Bench was accordingly

Queen Elizabeth I (1533–1603) by an unknown artist

The Execution of Mary, Queen of Scots.

A drawing showing three stages of the event. At the upper left Mary is led into the hall. In the center her attendants remove her outer robe. At the upper right may be seen the headsman's ax.

sent to Wolsey. A member of his household, George Cavendish, has left an account of the Cardinal's last days. According to him Wolsey said, "I know that the King of his own nature is of a royal stomach. How say you, Master Shelley? May I do it with justice and conscience, to give that thing away from me and my successors which is none of mine?" The judge explained how the legal profession viewed the case. Then said the Cardinal, "I will in no wise disobey, but most gladly fulfil and accomplish his princely will and pleasure in all things, and in especial in this matter, inasmuch as ye, the fathers of the law, say that I may lawfully do it. Howbeit I pray you show his Majesty from me, that I most humbly desire his Highness to call to his most gracious remembrance that *there is both Heaven and Hell.*"

Henry cared nothing for the fulminations of a Cardinal. Threats merely made him take more sweeping measures. As Wolsey journeyed back to London, where the cell in the Tower was being placed in readiness, he fell ill, and when he neared Leicester Abbey for the night he told the monks who came out to greet him, "I am come to leave my bones among you." Soon afterwards he died; and they found next to his body a shirt of hair, beneath his other shirt, which was of very fine linen holland cloth. This shirt of hair was unknown to all his servants except his chaplain.

With the death of the Cardinal political interests hitherto submerged made their bid for power. The ambition of the country gentry to take part in public affairs in London, the longing of an educated, wealthy Renaissance England to cast off the tutelage of priests, the naked greed and thirst for power of rival factions, began to shake and agitate the nation. Henry was now thirty-eight years old.

CHAPTER TWENTY-SEVEN

The Break with Rome

THE APPEAL to the Pope for a divorce having failed, Dr. Cranmer, a young lecturer in divinity at Cambridge and a friend of the Boleyns, made a helpful new suggestion, that the question whether the King had ever been legally married should be withdrawn from the lawyers and submitted to the universities of Europe. Cranmer's idea proved a great success, and the young lecturer was rewarded with an appointment as Ambassador to the Emperor. The King determined to mark his displeasure with the Pope by some striking measure against the power of the Church of England.

Early rumblings of a Reformation had been silenced by the then immovable power of Wolsey. Now the Commons eagerly resumed their interrupted task. From the outset the Reformation House of Commons acquired a corporate spirit, and during its long life, longer than any previous Parliament, eagerly pursued any measure which promised revenge. Hostility to the Episcopate smouldered and marked the Commons for more than a hundred years.

Parliament was now to hear and disseminate the royal view on the divorce. Lord Chancellor More came down to the House and said, "There are some who say that the King is pursuing a divorce out of love for some lady, and not out of any scruple of conscience; but this is not true," and he read out the opinions of twelve foreign universities and showed a hundred "books" drawn up by doctors of strange regions, all agreeing that the King's marriage was unlawful.

Throughout these proceedings Queen Catherine remained at Court. The King, although he rode and talked openly with Anne, left Catherine in charge of his personal wardrobe, including supervision of the laundry and the making of his linen. When he required clothes he continued to apply to Catherine, not Anne. Anne was furiously jealous, but for months the King refused to abandon his old routine. Finally, about the middle of July, Anne took the King on a long hunting expedition, longer than any they had ever made together. Catherine waited, day after day, until a month had gone by. At last the messenger came. Henceforward she and her daughter Mary were banished from Court.

*   *   *

The winter of 1531–1532 was marked by the tensest crisis of Henry's reign. A form of excommunication, or even interdict, had been drafted in Rome, ordering the King to cast off his concubine Anne within fifteen days. The shadow of Papal wrath hung over England. But, as in the dark days in the early part of the reign, the King pursued his inflexible course to the end. Opposition merely confirmed him in his plans. The Annates Bill (the first year's income which the bishops paid to Rome on consecration) was drafted as a fighting measure, in case the worst occurred. It armed the King for a greater struggle with the Papacy than had preceded Magna Carta.

This was the most difficult Bill which Henry ever had to steer through Parliament. At last he thought of an entirely new expedient—the first public division of the House. "He thought of a plan that those among the Members who wished for the King's welfare and the prosperity of the kingdom (as they call it) should stand on one side of the House and those who opposed the measure on the other. For fear of the King's indignation a number of them went over," and the Bill was passed.

Sir Thomas More resigned the Lord Chancellorship as a protest against royal supremacy in spiritual affairs. He had tried to serve his sovereign faithfully in everything; now he saw that Henry's courses must inevitably conflict with his own conscientious beliefs. Thus the English Reformation was a slow process. An opportunist King measured his steps as he went, until England was wholly independent of administration from Rome. Wolsey had done much to prepare the way. He had supported the Papacy during some of its most critical years, and in return had been allowed to exercise wide and sweeping powers which were usually reserved to the Pope himself or to one of his visiting legates. England therefore was more accustomed than any other province of Christendom to Papal jurisdiction being vested in one of its own priests, and this made it easier to transfer it to the Crown.

Confident that he could carry through even the most startling appointment to Canterbury, the King recalled Cranmer from his embassy. Cranmer had been married twice. Since the marriage of priests was still illegal in England, Cranmer's wife went ahead in disguise. A week later he was offered the Archbishopric of Canterbury. He accepted. Henceforward, until Henry died, Cranmer's wife was always hidden, and if she accompanied him was obliged, according to popular repute, to travel with the luggage in a vast chest specially constructed to conceal her.

A month later Henry secretly married Anne Boleyn. The breach between England and Rome was complete.

About ten days later the royal commissioners waited on Queen Catherine. Every sort of reason was advanced why she should renounce her title voluntarily. She refused to resign. But the Commissioners had still another announcement to make. Catherine was in any case Queen no longer, for the King was already married to Anne Boleyn. Thus Henry's secret marriage became known. Catherine's marriage with Henry had existed in fact but not in law; it was void from the beginning; and five days afterwards the marriage with Anne was declared valid. Queen Anne Boleyn was crowned on June 1 in Westminster Abbey.

The following month it became clear that the new Queen was expecting a child. As the confinement approached a magnificent and valuable bed, which had lain in the Treasury since it had formed part of a French nobleman's ransom, was brought forth, and in it on September 7, 1533, the future Queen Elizabeth was born.

Although bonfires were lighted there was no rejoicing in Henry's heart. "Do you wish to see your little daughter?" the old nurse asked, according to one account. "My daughter, my daughter!" replied the King in a passion. "You old devil, you witch, don't dare to speak to me!" He galloped at once away from Greenwich, away from Anne, and in three days had reached the residence of a worthy old courtier, Sir John Seymour, who had a pretty daughter, a former Maid of Honour to Queen Catherine. Jane

Seymour was about twenty-five, and although she was attractive no one considered her a great beauty. But she was gay and generally liked, and Henry fell in love with her.

Sir Thomas More was confined in the Tower for many months. At his trial he offered a brilliant defence, but the King's former trust in him had now turned into vengeful dislike. Under royal pressure the judges pronounced him guilty of treason. More was executed in July. For his fate the King must bear the chief responsibility; it is a black stain on his record. Shortly afterwards Henry was excommunicated and in theory deprived of his throne by the Pope. More stood forth as the defender of all that was finest in the medieval outlook. He represents to history its universality, its belief in spiritual values, and its instinctive sense of other-worldliness. Henry VIII with cruel axe decapitated not only a wise and gifted counsellor, but a system which, though it had failed to live up to its ideals in practice, had for long furnished mankind with its brightest dreams.

*   *   *

Jane Seymour was installed at Greenwich. Through her serving-man, who had been taken into the pay of the Imperial Ambassador, we have a story of the royal courtship. One day the King sent a page down from London with a purse full of gold and a letter in his own handwriting. Jane kissed the letter, but returned it to the page unopened. Then, falling on her knees, she said, "I pray you beseech the King to understand by my prudence that I am a gentlewoman of good and honourable family, without reproach, and have no greater treasure in the world than my honour, which I would not harm for a thousand deaths. If the King should wish to make me a present of money, I beg him to do so when God shall send me a husband to marry." The King was greatly pleased. She had, he said, displayed high virtue, and to prove that his intentions were wholly worthy of her he promised not to speak to her in future except in the presence of her relations.

In January, 1536, Queen Catherine died. If the King was minded to marry again he could now repudiate Queen Anne without raising awkward questions about his earlier union. It was already rumoured by the Seymour party that in her intense desire for an heir Queen Anne had been unfaithful to the King soon after the birth of Elizabeth, with several lovers. If proved, this offence was capital. The Queen had accordingly been watched, and one Sunday two young courtiers, Henry Norris and Sir Francis Weston, were seen to enter the Queen's room, and were, it was said, overheard making love to her. The following Sunday a certain Smeaton, a gentleman of the King's chamber, who played with great skill on the lute, was arrested as the Queen's lover.

Anne was placed under arrest, and kept under guard until the tide turned to take her up-river to the Tower. So quickly had the news spread that large crowds collected along the river-bank, and were in time to watch her barge rowing rapidly up-stream.

The special commissioners of treason appointed the previous week, including Anne Boleyn's father, and the entire bench of judges except one, formed the court for the trial of Anne's lovers. A special jury consisting of twelve knights had been summoned, and found the prisoners guilty. They were sentenced to be hanged, drawn, and quartered, but execution was deferred until after the trial of the Queen. This opened the following Monday in the Great Hall of the Tower. She was charged with being unfaithful to the King; promising to marry Norris after the King was dead; giving Norris poisoned lockets for the purpose of poisoning Catherine and Mary; and other offences, including incest with her brother. The Queen denied the charges vigorously, and replied to each one in detail. The peers retired, and soon returned with a verdict of guilty. The Queen was to be burnt or beheaded, at the King's pleasure.

Anne received the sentence with calm and courage. She declared that if the King would allow it she would like to be beheaded like the French nobility, with a sword, and not, like the English nobility, with an axe. Her wish was granted; but no executioner could be found in the King's dominions to carry out the sentence with a sword, and it was found necessary to postpone the execution while an expert was borrowed from St. Omer. During Thursday night she slept little. Distant hammering could be heard from the courtyard of the Tower, as a low scaffold, about five feet high, was erected for the execution. In the morning the public were admitted to the courtyard.

On May 19, 1536, the headsman was already waiting, leaning on his heavy two-handed sword, when the Constable of the Tower appeared, followed by Anne in a beautiful night robe of heavy grey damask trimmed with fur, showing a crimson kirtle beneath. She had chosen this garment in order to leave her neck bare. A large sum had been given to her to distribute in alms among the crowd. "I am not here," she said to them simply, "to preach to you, but to die. Pray for the King, for he is a good man and has treated me as well as could be." Then she took off her pearl-covered headdress, revealing that her hair had been carefully bound up to avoid impeding the executioner.

"Pray for me," she said, and knelt down while one of the ladies-in-waiting bandaged her eyes. Before there was time to say a Paternoster she bowed her head, murmuring in a low voice, "God have pity on my soul." "God have mercy on my soul," she repeated, as the executioner stepped forward and slowly took his aim. Then the great blade hissed through the air, and with a single stroke his work was done.

As soon as the execution was known Henry appeared in yellow, with a feather in his cap, and ten days later was privately married to Jane Seymour. Jane proved to be the submissive wife for whom Henry had always longed and Henry spent a happy eighteen months with her. She was the only Queen whom Henry regretted and mourned, and when she died, still aged only twenty-eight, immediately after the birth of her first child, the future Edward VI, Henry had her buried with royal honours in St. George's Chapel at Windsor. He himself lies near her.

CHAPTER TWENTY-EIGHT

The End of the Monasteries

THOUGH ALL had been bliss at Court while Jane was Queen, rural England was heavy with discontents. Henry was increasingly short of revenue and Church properties offered a tempting prize. The idea of suppression of monasteries was not altogether new: Wolsey had suppressed several small houses to finance his college at Oxford, and the King had since suppressed over twenty more for his own benefit. Parliament made little difficulty about winding up the smaller houses, when satisfied that their inmates were either to be transferred to large houses or pensioned off.

The King had now a new chief adviser. Thomas Cromwell, in turn mercenary soldier in Italy, cloth agent, and moneylender, had served his apprenticeship in statecraft under Wolsey, but he had also learned the lessons of his master's downfall. Ruthless, cynical, Machiavellian, Cromwell was a man of the New Age. Perhaps his greatest accomplishment was his inception of the Government service of modern England. Cromwell is the uncommemorated architect of our great departments of State. As First Minister, he handled the dissolution of the monasteries with conspicuous, cold-blooded efficiency. The main result was in effect, if not in intention, to commit the landed and mercantile classes to the Reformation settlement and the Tudor dynasty.

The Reformation is sometimes blamed for all the evils attributed to the modern economic system. Yet these evils, if such they were, had existed long before Henry VIII began to doubt the validity of his marriage to Catherine of Aragon. Thomas More, who did not live to see events run their course, had already in *Utopia* outlined to his contemporaries the sharp features of the new economy.

Complete printed Bibles, translated into English by Tyndal and Coverdale, had appeared for the first time late in the autumn of 1535, and were now running through several editions. The Government enjoined the clergy to encourage Bible-reading. Cromwell ordered the Paternoster and Com-mandments to be taught in the mother tongue instead of in Latin. Next year *The Institution of a Christian Man,* prepared by Cranmer for popular edification, displayed a distinct leaning to the New Opinion. Here indeed was a change and a revelation. Henry directed that every parish in the country should purchase a Bible of the largest volume in English, to be set up in each church, where the parishioners might most commodiously re-sort to the same and read it. Six copies were set up in St. Paul's, in the City of London, and multitudes thronged the cathedral all day to read them, especially, we are told, when they could get any person that had an audible voice to read aloud. This Bible has remained the basis of all later editions, including the Authorised Version prepared in the reign of James I.

*   *   *

Up to this point Thomas Cromwell had consistently walked with suc-cess. But he now began to encounter the conservatism of the older nobility. They opposed the doctrinal changes of Cranmer and his following. France and the Emperor might invade England and execute the sentence of deposi-tion which the Pope had pronounced. The King himself was anxious to avoid a total religious cleavage with the European Powers. These large is-sues were to be resolved like so much of the action of this memorable reign, as a result of the conjugal affairs of the King.

An alliance with the princes of Northern Germany against the two Catholic monarchs of France and Spain now seemed imperative, and ne-gotiations for a marriage between Henry and Anne, the eldest Princess of Cleves, were hurried on. Anne's charms, Cromwell reported, were on everybody's lips. "Everyone," he announced, "praises her beauty both of face and body. One says she excels the Duchess of Milan as the golden sun does the silver moon." Anne spoke only German, spent her time chiefly in needlework, and could not sing or play any instrument. She was thirty years old, very tall and thin, with an assured and resolute countenance, slightly pockmarked, but was said to possess wit and animation, and did not over-indulge in beer.

On New Year's Day of 1540 Henry hurried to visit her. But on seeing her he was astonished and abashed. Embraces, presents, compliments, all carefully arranged, were forgotten. He mumbled a few words and returned to his barge. Privately he dubbed her "the Flanders Mare."

But the threat from abroad compelled the King to fulfil his contract. Since he now knew as much about the Canon Law on marriage as anyone in Europe, he turned himself into the perfect legal example of a man whose marriage might be annulled. The marriage was never consummated.

Norfolk and Gardiner, the chief schemers for power, now saw their chance to break Cromwell, as Wolsey had been broken, with the help of a new lady. Yet another of Norfolk's nieces, Catherine Howard, was pre-

1 3 5

sented to Henry at Gardiner's house, and captured his affections at first sight. In June, 1540, the King was persuaded to get rid of Cromwell and Anne together. Anne agreed to have her marriage annulled, and Convocation pronounced it invalid. She lived on in England, pensioned and in retirement, for another seventeen years. A few days after Cromwell, condemned for heresy and treason, was executed on July 28, Henry was privately married to his fifth wife, Catherine Howard.

Catherine, about twenty-two, with auburn hair and hazel eyes, was the prettiest of Henry's wives. His Majesty's spirits revived, his health returned, and he went down to Windsor to reduce weight. But wild, tempestuous Catherine was not long content with a husband nearly thirty years older than herself. Her reckless love for her cousin, Thomas Culpeper, was discovered, and she was executed in the Tower in February, 1542, on the same spot as Anne Boleyn. The night before the execution she asked for the block so that she could practise laying her head upon it, and as she mounted the scaffold said, "I die a Queen, but would rather die the wife of Culpeper. God have mercy on my soul. Good people, I beg you to pray for me."

Henry's sixth wife, Catherine Parr, was a serious little widow from the Lake District, thirty-one years of age, learned, and interested in theological questions, who had had two husbands before the King. She married Henry at Hampton Court on July 12, 1543, and until his death three years later made him an admirable wife, nursing his ulcerated leg, which grew steadily worse and in the end killed him. She contrived to reconcile Henry with the future Queen Elizabeth; both Mary and Elizabeth grew fond of her, and she had the fortune to outlive her husband.

*   *   *

The brilliant young Renaissance prince had grown old and wrathful. The pain from his leg made Henry ill-tempered; he suffered fools and those who crossed him with equal lack of patience. Suspicion dominated his mind and ruthlessness marked his action. At the time of his marriage with Catherine Parr Henry was engaged in preparing the last of his wars. The roots of the conflict lay in Scotland. In the autumn of 1542 an expedition under Norfolk had to turn back at Kelso, principally through the failure of the commissariat, which, besides its other shortcomings, left the English army without its beer, and the Scots proceeded to carry the war into the enemy's country. Their decision proved disastrous. Badly led and imperfectly organised, they lost more than half their army of ten thousand men in Solway Moss and were utterly routed. The news killed James V, who died leaving the kingdom to an infant of one week, Mary, the famous Queen of Scots. At once the child became the focus of the struggle for Scotland.

Once again England and the Empire made common cause against the French, and in May, 1543, a secret treaty was ratified between Charles V and Henry. Throughout the year, and well into the spring of 1544, the preparations continued. While Scotland was left to Edward Seymour, brother of Queen Jane, and now Earl of Hertford, the King himself was to cross the Channel and lead an army against Francis in co-operation with an Imperial force from the north-east.

The plan was excellent, but the execution failed. Henry and Charles distrusted each other; each suspected the other of seeking a separate peace. Wary of being drawn too deep into the Emperor's plans, Henry sat down to besiege Boulogne. The town fell on September 14, and Henry was able to congratulate himself on at least one tangible result from his campaign. Five days later the Emperor made his peace with Francis, and refused to listen to Henry's complaints and exhortations. Meanwhile the English in Scotland, after burning Edinburgh and laying waste much country, ceased to make headway, and in February, 1545, were defeated at Ancrum Moor.

Henry's position was extremely grave. Without a single ally, the nation faced the possibility of invasion from both France and Scotland. The crisis called for unexampled sacrifices from the English people; never had they been called upon to pay so many loans, subsidies, and benevolences. To set an example Henry melted down his own plate and mortgaged his estates. Henry completely failed in Scotland. He would make no generous settlement with his neighbours, yet he lacked the force to coerce them. For the next fifty years they were to tease and trouble the minds of his successors.

On Thursday the 27th of January, 1547, the King was dying. The physicians dared not tell him so, for prophesying the King's death was treason by Act of Parliament. Shortly before midnight the King awoke. He sent for Archbishop Cranmer. When he came Henry was too weak to speak; he could only stretch out his hand. In a few minutes the Supreme Head had ceased to breathe.

*   *   *

Henry's rule saw many advances in the growth and the character of the English state, but it is a hideous blot upon his record that the reign should be widely remembered for its executions. Two Queens, two of the King's chief Ministers, a saintly bishop, numerous abbots, monks, and many ordinary folk who dared to resist the royal will were put to death. Almost every member of the nobility in whom royal blood ran perished on the scaffold at Henry's command. Roman Catholic and Calvinist alike were burnt for heresy and religious treason. These persecutions, inflicted in solemn manner by officers of the law, perhaps in the presence of the Council or even the King himself, form a brutal sequel to the bright promise of the Renaissance. The sufferings of devout men and women among the faggots, the use of torture, and the savage penalties imposed for even paltry crimes, stand in repellent contrast to the enlightened principles of humanism. Yet his subjects did not turn from Henry in loathing. He succeeded in maintaining order amid the turmoil of Europe without army or police, and he imposed on England a discipline which was not attained elsewhere. A century of religious wars went by without Englishmen taking up arms to fight their fellow-countrymen for their faith. We must credit Henry's reign with laying the basis of sea-power, with a revival of Parliamentary institutions, with giving the English Bible to the people, and above all with strengthening a popular monarchy under which succeeding generations worked together for the greatness of England while France and Germany were racked with internal strife.

CHAPTER TWENTY-NINE

The Protestant Struggle

THE ENGLISH Reformation under Henry VIII had received its guiding impulse from the King's passions and his desire for power. He still deemed himself a good Catholic. However, none of his Catholic wives had borne him a son. Catherine of Aragon had given birth to the future Queen Mary, Anne Boleyn to the future Queen Elizabeth; but it was Jane, daughter of the Protestant house of Seymour, who had produced the future Edward VI. Fears of a disputed succession lay deeply engraved in Henry VIII and in his whole people. Henry wanted his own way on his throne and in his choice of consort, but he saw no need to change the faith or even the ritual to which his subjects had been born. With the new reign a deeper and more powerful tide began to flow. The guardian and chief counsellor of the child-king was his uncle, Edward Seymour, now Duke of Somerset. He and Cranmer proceeded to transform the political reformation of Henry VIII into a religious revolution. The Book of Common Prayer, in shining English prose, was drawn up by Cranmer and accepted by Parliament in 1549. Then followed the Forty-two Articles of Religion, and a second Prayer Book, until, on paper at least, England became a Protestant State.

Somerset was merely one of the regents appointed under Henry's will, and his position as Protector, at once dazzling and dangerous, had little foundation in law or precedent. Rivals crowded jealously upon him. The pale child Edward VI, who was constitutionally consumptive, might not live long. The next Protestant heir was Princess Elizabeth.

Far more serious were the distresses and discontents in the country-side. The life and economy of medieval England were fast dissolving. Landlords saw that vast fortunes could be made from wool, and the village communal strips barred their profits. Warfare had been going on for decades between landowner and peasantry. Slowly and surely the rights and privileges of the village communities were infringed and removed. Common land was seized, enclosed, and turned to pasture for flocks. Dissolution of the monasteries removed the most powerful and conservative element in the old system, and for a time gave fresh impetus to a process already under way. The multiplication of enclosures caused distress throughout the realm. In some counties as much as one-third of the arable land was turned over to grass, and the people looked in anger upon the new nobility, fat with sacrilegious spoil, but greedy still.

Two rebellions broke out. The Catholic peasantry in the South-West rose against the Prayer Book, and the yokels of the Eastern Counties against the enclosing landlords. John Dudley, Earl of Warwick, now seized his opportunity. He was a self-seeking, vigorous man, and the champion of wealth and property. Now he was given command of the troops to suppress the rising. The precise fire-drill of Warwick's best troops shattered the peasant array. Three thousand five hundred were killed. There were no wounded. Warwick had by accident made his mark as a strong man.

Somerset's enemies claimed the credit for restoring order. They blamed the rising in the East on his enclosure commissions and his sympathy for the peasants, and the rebellion in the West on his religious reforms. His foreign policy had driven the Scots into alliance with France, and he had lost Henry's one conquest, Boulogne. Warwick became the leader of the Opposition. "The Lords in London," as Warwick's party were called, met to take measures against the Protector. No one moved to support him. They quietly took over the government. After a spell in the Tower, Somerset, splendidly garbed as for a state banquet, was executed on Tower Hill. This handsome, well-meaning man had failed completely to heal the dislocation of Henry's reign and fell a victim to the fierce interests he had offended. Nevertheless the people of England remembered him for years as "the Good Duke." The nominal King of England, Edward VI, was a cold, priggish invalid of fifteen. In his diary he noted his uncle's death without a comment.

* * *

The Government of Warwick, now become Duke of Northumberland, was held together by class resistance to social unrest. His three years of power displayed to the full the rapacity of the ruling classes. Thomas More's definition of government as "a conspiracy of rich men procuring their own commodities under the name and title of a commonwealth" fitted England very accurately during these years.

One gleam of enterprise distinguishes this period. It saw the opening of relations between England and a growing new Power in Eastern Europe, hitherto known as Muscovy, but soon to be called Russia. A small group of Englishmen conceived the idea of seeking a north-eastern passage to Asia through Arctic waters. Upon the northern coasts of Asia there might be people who would buy cloth and other English products. As early as 1527 a small book had appeared prophesying such a discovery. One phrase rings out: "There is no land uninhabitable nor sea unnavigable." In 1553 an expedition was financed by the Muscovy Company of Merchant Adventurers with the backing of the Government. Sebastian Cabot, a wise old seaman who some fifty years earlier had accompanied his father on his voyage to Newfoundland, was brought in as Governor of the company. In May three ships set sail under Hugh Willoughby and Richard Chancellor. Willoughby perished with his crew off Lapland, but Chancellor wintered in Archangel, and in the spring pushed overland to the Court of Ivan the Terrible at Moscow. The monopoly of the German Hansa towns, which had long blocked English merchants throughout Northern Europe, was now outflanked and trade began with Russia.

Under the Succession Act of 1543 the next heir to the throne was Princess Mary, the Catholic daughter of Catherine of Aragon. Northumberland might well tremble for the future. Nothing remained but to effect a military *coup* when the young King died. A desperate scheme was evolved. Ou July 6, 1553, Edward VI expired, and Lady Jane Grey, named in Henry VIII's will as next in line after his own children, was proclaimed Queen in London. The only response to this announcement was gathering resistance: Northumberland was too much hated throughout the land. The common people flocked to Mary's support. In August Mary entered London with Elizabeth at her side. Lady Jane and her husband were consigned to the Tower. In vain Northumberland grovelled. But nothing could save him from an ignominious death.

*   *   *

Mary Tudor who now became Queen was probably the most unhappy and unsuccessful of England's sovereigns. As with Catherine, her mother, religion dominated her being, and Catherine's divorce and the break with Rome brought tragic and catastrophic change. She had clung to her confessors and her chapel throughout the reign of Edward VI, and was naturally feared by the ruling group of Protestant politicians in London.

Secure upon the throne, Mary proceeded to realise the wish of her life —the restoration of the Roman communion. The most urgent question was whom Mary should marry. Mary's eyes were fixed overseas, she worked fast, and was soon promised to the Emperor's son, the future Philip II of Spain. When news of the Spanish betrothal reached the people, ugly stories of the Inquisition and the coming of Spanish troops passed from mouth to mouth. The Commons came in deputation to beg the Queen not to violate the feelings of the nation, but Mary had all the obstinacy of the

1 4 0

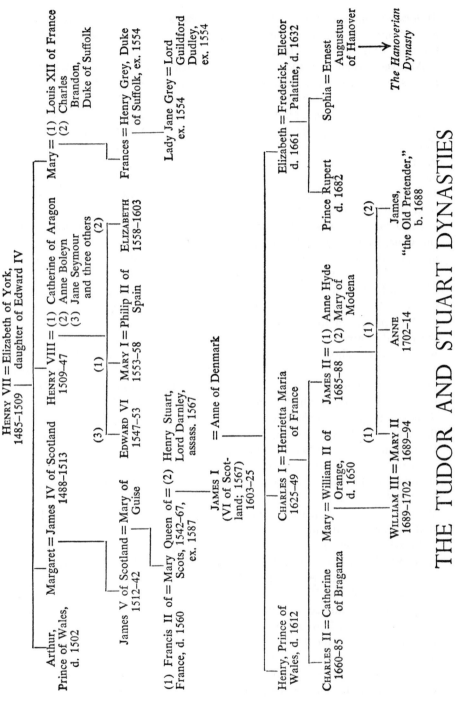

HENRY VII = Elizabeth of York,
1485–1509 | daughter of Edward IV

Arthur,
Prince of Wales,
d. 1502

Margaret = James IV of Scotland
1488–1513

James V of Scotland = Mary of
1512–42   Guise

(1) Francis II of = Mary Queen of = (2) Henry Stuart,
France, d. 1560   Scots, 1542–67,   Lord Darnley,
                   ex. 1587   assass. 1567

JAMES I
(VI of Scot-
land; 1567)
1603–25

= Anne of Denmark

HENRY VIII = (1) Catherine of Aragon
1509–47   (2) Anne Boleyn
           (3) Jane Seymour
               and three others

(3)

EDWARD VI
1547–53

(1)

MARY I = Philip II of
1553–58   Spain

(2)

ELIZABETH
1558–1603

Mary = (1) Louis XII of France
       (2) Charles
           Brandon,
           Duke of Suffolk

Frances = Henry Grey, Duke
          of Suffolk, ex. 1554

Lady Jane Grey = Lord
ex. 1554   Guildford
                 Dudley,
                 ex. 1554

Elizabeth = Frederick, Elector
d. 1661   Palatine, d. 1632

Prince Rupert
d. 1682

Sophia = Ernest
         Augustus
         of Hanover

→ The Hanoverian
  Dynasty

CHARLES I = Henrietta Maria
1625–49   of France

Henry, Prince of
Wales, d. 1612

Mary = William II of
       Orange,
       d. 1650

CHARLES II = Catherine
1660–85   of Braganza

JAMES II = (1) Anne Hyde
1685–88   (2) Mary of
               Modena

(1)

WILLIAM III = MARY II
1689–1702   1689–94

(1)

ANNE
1702–14

(2)

James,
"the Old Pretender,"
b. 1688

THE TUDOR AND STUART DYNASTIES

141

Tudors and none of their political sense. She was now on the threshold of her dreams—a Catholic England united in intimate alliance with the Catholic Empire of the Hapsburgs.

All eyes turned to Princess Elizabeth in watchful retirement at Hatfield. Events began to move fast. In the West, a rising was precipitated and soon after the Spanish match was proclaimed, rebellion broke out yet again in Southern England. The Capital was in alarm. Mary, bitter and disappointed with her people, and knowing she had failed to win their hearts, showed she was not afraid. In a stirring speech at Guildhall she summoned the Londoners to her defence. Straggled fighting took place in the streets, and the Queen's men cut up the intruders. This sealed the fate of Lady Jane Grey and her husband. In February, 1554, the two walked calmly to their death on Tower Hill.

Elizabeth's life was now in great danger. But, fearlessly and passionately, she denied all disloyal dealings. Perhaps Mary believed her. At any rate, after some months she was released and sent to Woodstock, where, in quiet and pious seclusion, she awaited the turn of fortune. In July, 1554, Mary and Philip were married in accordance with the rites of the Catholic Church.

Mary had been for ever odious in the minds of a Protestant nation as the Bloody Queen who martyred her noblest subjects. Generations of Englishmen in childhood learnt the sombre tale of their sacrifice from Foxe's *Book of Martyrs,* with its gruesome illustrations. These stories have become part of the common memory of the people—the famous scenes at Oxford in 1555, the faggots which consumed the Protestant bishops, Latimer and Ridley, the pitiful recantation and final heroic end in March, 1556, of the frail, aged Archbishop, Cranmer. Their martyrdom rallied to the Protestant faith many who till now had shown indifference.

These martyrs saw in vision that their deaths were not in vain, and, standing at the stake, pronounced immortal words. "Be of good comfort, Master Ridley," Latimer cried at the crackling of the flames. "Play the man. We shall this day light such a candle, by God's grace, in England as I trust shall never be put out."

In vain the Queen strove to join English interests to those of the Spanish state. She had married to make England safe for Catholicism, and she had sacrificed what little personal happiness she could hope for to this dream. As the wife of the King of Spain, against the interests of her kingdom, and against the advice of prudent counsellors, among them Cardinal Pole, she allowed herself to be dragged into war with France, and Calais, the last possession of the English upon the Continent, fell without resistance. This national disgrace, this loss of the symbol of the power and glory of medieval England, bit deep into the hearts of the people and into the conscience of the Queen. Hope of a child to secure the Catholic succession was unfulfilled. Her unhappiness was hardly redeemed by one vision of accomplishment. Yet, unchronicled and without praise, her reign witnessed one modest achievement, which has rarely received the attention of historians. Mary's Ministers, during her brief reign, embarked upon a major task of retrenchment and reform; by the time of her death they had done much to purge the government of the corrupt extravagance of Northumberland's régime.

Philip retired to the Netherlands and then to Spain, aloof and disappointed at the barrenness of the whole political scheme. Surrounded by disloyalty and discontent, Mary's health gave way. In November, 1558, she died, and a few hours later, in Lambeth Palace, her coadjutor, Cardinal Pole, followed her. The tragic interlude of her reign was over. It had sealed the conversion of the English people to the Reformed faith.

*　　*　　*

In its beginning the Protestant Reformation in Europe had been a local revolt against the abuses of an organisation. But this motive was removed when after some years the Catholic Church set its house in order. What remained was the insurgence of the Northern races against the entire apparatus of the Roman Church in so far as this seemed to conflict with the forward movement of the human mind. The Christian revelation could now be borne forward into ages that no longer required the moulds into which the barbaric conquerors of the ancient world had, necessarily and beneficently, been constrained after the collapse of the Roman Empire. Until the reign of Henry VIII there lay beneath the quarrels of the nobility, the conflicts between King and Church, between the ruling classes and the people, a certain broad unity of acceptance. The evils and sorrows of the medieval ages had lasted so long that they seemed to be the inseparable conditions of existence in a world of woe. No one had novel remedies or even consolations to propose. With the Reformation there came a new influence, cutting to the very roots of English life, stirring the souls of all classes to action or resistance, and raising standards for which great and small alike were prepared to suffer or inflict the worst extremities. The old framework, which, in spite of its many jars, had held together for centuries, was now torn by a division in which all other antagonisms of class and interest were henceforward to be ranged and ruled. Hitherto, amid their quarrels and tribulations, there had been one people and one system. Henceforward, for many generations to come, not only England but all the countries of Europe were to range themselves for or against the Protestant Reformation.

The violence of this convulsion can hardly be measured by us today, and it followed in England a less destructive course than in Germany or France. This was because the issue came to a head at a comparatively early stage, and under the strong government of the Tudors. Neverthe-

1 4 3

less the doctrinal revolution enforced by Cranmer under Edward VI, and the Counter-Revolution under Mary, exposed our agitated Islanders in one single decade to a frightful oscillation. Here were the citizens, the peasants, the whole mass of living beings who composed the nation, ordered in the name of King Edward VI to march along one path to salvation, and under Queen Mary to march back again in the opposite direction; and all who would not move on the first order or turn about on the second must prove their convictions, if necessary, at the gibbet or the stake. Thus was New England imposed on Old England; thus did Old England in terrible counter-stroke resume a fleeting sway; and from all this agony there was to emerge under Queen Elizabeth a compromise between Old and New which, though it did not abate their warfare, so far confined its fury that it could not prove mortal to the unity and continuity of national society.

CHAPTER THIRTY

Good Queen Bess

ELIZABETH WAS twenty-five years old when, untried in the affairs of State, she succeeded her half-sister Mary on November 17, 1558. It was England's good fortune that the new Queen was endowed by inheritance and upbringing with a combination of very remarkable qualities. There could be no doubt who her father was. A commanding carriage, auburn hair, eloquence of speech, and natural dignity proclaimed her King Henry's daughter. Other similarities were soon observed: high courage in moments of crisis, a fiery and imperious resolution when defied, and an almost inexhaustible fund of physical energy. She enjoyed many of the same pastimes and accomplishments as the King had done—a passion for the chase, skill in archery and hawking, and in dancing and music. She could speak six languages, and was well read in Latin and Greek. As with her father and grandfather, a restless vitality led her hither and thither from mansion to mansion, so that often none could tell where in a week's time she might be sleeping.

A difficult childhood and a perilous adolescence had been Elizabeth's portion. At one stage in her father's lifetime she had been declared illegitimate and banished from Court. During Mary's reign, when her life might have been forfeited by a false step, she had proved the value of caution and dissemblance. When to keep silence, how to bide her time and husband her resources, were the lessons she learnt from her youth. Many historians have accused her of vacillation and parsimony. Certainly these elements in her character were justly the despair of her advisers. The royal treasury, however, was never rich enough to finance all the adventurous projects urged upon her. Nor was it always unwise amid the turbulent currents of the age to put off making irrevocable decisions. The times demanded a politic, calculating, devious spirit at the head of the state, and this Elizabeth possessed. She had, too, a high gift for picking able men to do the country's work. It came naturally to her to take the credit for their successes, while blaming them for all that went wrong.

In quickness of mind the Queen was surpassed by few of her contemporaries, and many envoys to her Court had good reason to acknowledge her liveliness of repartee. In temperament she was subject to fits of melancholy, which alternated with flamboyant merriment and convulsive rage. Always subtle of intellect, she was often brazen and even coarse in manners and expression. When angered she could box her Treasurer's ears and throw her slipper in her Secretary's face. She was outwardly very free in her more tender relations with the opposite sex, so that, in the words of an illustrious counsellor, "one day she was greater than man, and the next less than woman." Nevertheless she had a capacity for inspiring devotion that is perhaps unparalleled among British sovereigns. There may be something grotesque to modern eyes in the flattery paid her by the Court, but with her people she never went wrong. By instinct she knew how to earn popular acclaim. In a sense her relationship with her subjects was one long flirtation. She gave to her country the love that she never entirely reposed in any one man, and her people responded with a loyalty that almost amounted to worship. It is not for nothing that she has come down to history as Good Queen Bess.

Elizabeth had been brought up a Protestant. She was a paragon of the New Learning. Around her had gathered some of the ablest Protestant minds: most important of all, William Cecil. Of sixteenth-century English statesmen Cecil was undoubtedly the greatest. He possessed a consuming thirst for information about the affairs of the realm, and was to display immense industry in the business of office. Cautious good judgment marked all his actions. It was a tremendous burden which the young Queen imposed upon her First Minister, then aged thirty-eight. Their close and daily collaboration was to last, in spite of shocks and jars, until Cecil's death, forty years later.

Religious peace at home and safety from Scotland were the foremost needs of the realm. So closely were Church and State involved that disobedience to the one was a challenge to the other. The idea that a man should pick and choose for himself what doctrines he should adhere to was almost as alien to the mind of the age as the idea that he should select what laws he should obey and what magistrates he should respect. The most that could be allowed was that he should outwardly conform and think what he liked in silence. But in the great turmoil of Europe silence was impossible. Men talked: secretly to one another, openly in their writings, which were now printed in a thousand copies, kindling excitement and curiosity wherever they were carried. Even if it were granted that Affairs of State could only be lawfully debated by those called thereto, common men could still search the Scriptures, and try the doctrines of the Church, its government, its rites and ceremonies, by the words of the Evangelist and Apostles.

It is at this point that the party known as the Puritans, who were to play so great a role in the next hundred years, first enter English history. Democratic in theory and organisation, intolerant in practice of all who differed from their views, the Puritans challenged the Queen's authority in Church and State, and although she sought for freedom of conscience and could maintain with sincerity that she "made no windows into men's souls," she dared not let them organise cells in the body religious or the body politic. A discordant and vigorous minority could rupture the delicate harmony that she was patiently weaving. Protestantism must be saved from its friends.

The Reformation in Europe took on a new aspect when it came to England. The gentry in Parliament fell into two great divisions, those who thought things had gone far enough, and those who wanted to go a step farther. It was the future distinction of Cavalier and Puritan, Churchman and Dissenter, Tory and Whig. But for a long time it was subdued by common horror of a disputed succession and a civil war, and by the rule that only the Crown could initiate policy and public legislation.

                    *   *   *

The immediate threat lay north of the Border. French troops supported the French Queen Mother in Scotland. A powerful Puritan party among the Scottish nobility, abetted by the persecuted preachers, were in arms against them, while John Knox raised his harsh voice against foreign rule and from exile in Geneva poured forth his denunciations of "the monstrous regiment of women." He meant of course that rule by women seemed to him unnatural. Elizabeth watched these doings with interest and anxiety. If the French party got control of Scotland their next move would be against her throne. Knox was permitted to return to his native land by way of England, and his preachings had a powerful effect. A small English army intervened on the Scottish Protestant side, and at this moment the Queen Mother Mary of Guise died. Elizabeth's efforts had been modest, but they prevailed. The Protestant cause in Scotland was assured for ever.

The delicate question of the Queen's marriage began to throw its shadow across the political scene, but Elizabeth could wait her time. In vain the Houses of Parliament begged their Virgin Queen to marry and produce an heir. Elizabeth was angry. She would admit no discussion. Her policy was to spend her life in saving her people from such a commitment, and using her potential value as a match to divide a European Combination against her.

*   *   *

In the last half of the sixteenth century women for a time controlled three countries—France, England, and Scotland. But of the three only the grip of Elizabeth held firm. Mary Stuart, Queen of Scots, was a very different personality from Elizabeth, though in some ways her position was similar. She was a descendant of Henry VII; she held a throne; she lived in an age when it was a novelty for a woman to be the head of a state. Her presence in Scotland disturbed the delicate balance which Elizabeth had achieved. She knew that Mary was incapable of separating her emotions from her politics. Mary had married her cousin, Henry Stuart, Lord Darnley, a weak, conceited youth who had both Tudor and Stuart blood in his veins. The result was disaster. The old feudal factions, now sharpened by religious conflict, seized Scotland in their grip. Mary's power melted slowly and steadily away. Her husband became a tool of her opponents. In desperation she connived at his murder, and in 1567 married his murderer, a warlike Border lord, Bothwell, whose unruly sword might yet save her throne and her happiness. But defeat and imprisonment followed, and in 1568 she escaped into England and threw herself upon the mercy of the waiting Elizabeth.

Mary in England proved even more dangerous than Mary in Scotland. She became the focus of plots and conspiracies against Elizabeth's life. The survival of Protestant England was menaced by her existence. There was always a danger so long as Mary lived that public discontent or private ambition would use her and her claims to destroy Elizabeth. In 1569 the threat became a reality. That year the Earls of Northumberland and Westmoreland led a rising in the North. The rebels planned to hold the North of England and wait to be attacked. They were far from sure of each other. In the South the Catholic lords made no move. There seems to have been no common plan of action, and the rebel forces scattered into small parties in the northern hills. Ignominiously they dribbled across the Border to safety, and the first act of the widespread Catholic conspiracy against Elizabeth was over. After twelve years of very patient rule she was unchallenged Queen of all England.

But Rome was prompt to retaliate. In February, 1570, Pope Pius V issued a Bull of excommunication against Elizabeth. From this moment Spain, as head of Catholic Europe, was supplied with a spiritual weapon should the need for attack arise. A terrible event followed later in Paris. By a sudden massacre of the Huguenots on the eve of the feast of St. Bartholomew, August 23, 1572, the Guises, pro-Spanish and ultra-Catholic,

147

recaptured the political power. Elizabeth was now driven to giving secret subsidies and support to the French Huguenots and the Dutch. Protestantism would only survive in Europe if England gave it encouragement and aid. In the long run there could be no compromise with the Catholics. By the Massacre of St. Bartholomew, the Queen was compelled to move into a cold war in the Netherlands, and an undeclared war at sea, until she was confronted with the massive onslaught of an Armada.

Most of the Puritans had at first been willing to conform to Elizabeth's Church settlement in the hope of transforming it from within, but they now strove to drive the Government into an aggressive Protestant foreign policy, and at the same time secure their own freedom of religious organisation. Their position in the country was strong. They had allies at Court and Council, like Walsingham, with whom the Queen's favourite, Leicester, was now closely associated. In the towns and counties of South-Eastern England they were vociferous. In defiance of the Church Settlement they began to form their own religious communities, with their own ministers and forms of worship. Their aim and object was nothing less than the establishment of a theocratic despotism. Like the Catholics they held that Church and State were separate and independent. Unlike them, they believed the seat of Church authority lay in the council of elders, the Presbytery, freely chosen by the flock, but, once chosen, ruling with unlimited scope and supplanting the secular power over a large area of human life.

To such men the Elizabethan Settlement, the Anglican Church, with its historic liturgy and ceremonial, its comprehensive articles and its episcopal government, were abhorrent because unscriptural, as Calvin interpreted Scripture. It had indeed some of the weaknesses of a compromise. Moreover, outside London, the universities, and a few great towns, the average parson in the early years of Elizabeth's reign was not an impressive figure. Sometimes he had kept his benefice by conforming under Edward VI, changing his creed under Mary, and finally accepting what a rural bench once described as "the religion set forth by Her Majesty" as the only way of earning a living. With barely enough Latin to read the old service books, and scarcely literate enough to deliver a decent sermon, he was no match for the controversialists and disputants charged with enthusiasm and new ideas, eloquent preachers, scurrilous pamphleteers, who were stealing his flock from him, and implanting in them novel and alarming notions about the rights of congregations to organise themselves, to worship in their own way, and to settle their own Church order. And why not, some day, their own political order? If not in England, perhaps in another land? A crack was opening in the surface of English society, a crack which would widen into a gulf. The Lutheran Church fitted well enough with monarchy, even with absolutism, but Calvinism, as it spread out over Europe, was a dissolving agency, a violent interruption of historic continuity, and with the return and resurgence of the exiles who had fled from Mary Tudor an explosive element was lodged in the English Church and State which ultimately was to shatter both. Elizabeth knew that the Puritans were perhaps her most loyal subjects, but she feared that their violent impulse might not only provoke the European conflict she dreaded, but imperil the very unity of the realm. Neither she nor her government dared yield a fraction of their authority. This was no time for religious war or upheaval at home.

*   *   *

The Catholic onslaught gathered force. About the year 1579 missionaries of a new and formidable type began to slip into the country. These were the Jesuits, dedicated to re-establishing the Catholic faith throughout Christendom. They were fanatics, indifferent to personal danger, and carefully chosen for their work. By their enemies they were accused of using assassination to achieve their aims and a number of plots against Elizabeth's life were uncovered.

The conspiracies naturally focused upon the person of Mary Queen of Scots, long captive. She was the heir to the English throne in the event of Elizabeth's removal from the world. Elizabeth herself was reluctant to recognise the danger to her life, yet the plots sharpened the question of who should succeed to the English throne. The death of Mary would make her son James the heir to the crown of England, and James was in safe Calvinist hands in Scotland. To avoid having another Catholic Queen it was only necessary to dispose of Mary before the Jesuits, or their allies, disposed of Elizabeth. The Council now concentrated their efforts on persuading the Queen that Mary must die. Plying her with evidence of Mary's complicity in the numerous conspiracies, they pressed hard on Elizabeth's conscience; but she shrank from the calculated shedding of royal blood.

A voluntary association of Protestant gentry was formed in 1585 for the defence of Elizabeth's life. In the following year evidence of a conspiracy, engineered by one Anthony Babington, an English Catholic, was laid before the Council by Walsingham. One of his agents had mingled with the conspirators for over a year. Mary's connivance was undeniable. Elizabeth was at last persuaded that her death was a political necessity. After a formal trial Mary was pronounced guilty of treason. Parliament petitioned for her execution, and Elizabeth at last signed the death warrant. Within twenty-four hours she regretted it and tried, too late, to stop the execution. She had a natural horror of being responsible for the judicial murder of a fellow sovereign, although she knew it was essential for the safety of her country. She was anxious that the supreme and final decision should not rest upon her.

The scene of Mary's death has caught the imagination of history. In the early morning of February 8, 1587, she was summoned to the great hall

149

of Fotheringay Castle. Accompanied by six of her attendants, Mary appeared at the appointed hour soberly clad in black satin. In the quietness of the hall she walked with stately movements to the cloth-covered scaffold erected by the fireplace. The solemn formalities were smoothly completed. But the zealous Dean of Peterborough attempted to force upon the Queen a last-minute conversion. With splendid dignity she brushed aside his loud exhortation. "Mr. Dean," she said, "I am a Catholic, and must die a Catholic."

Mary had arrayed herself superbly for the final scene. As she disrobed for the headsman's act, her garments of black satin, removed by the weeping handmaids, revealed a bodice and petticoat of crimson velvet. One of her ladies handed her a pair of crimson sleeves, which she put on. Thus the unhappy Queen halted, for one last moment, standing blood-red from head to foot against the black background of the scaffold. There was a deathly hush throughout the hall. She knelt, and at the second stroke the final blow was delivered. The awed assembly had fulfilled its task. In death the majestic illusion was shattered. The head of an ageing woman with false hair was held up by the executioner. A lapdog crept out from beneath the clothes of the bleeding trunk.

As the news reached London bonfires were lit in the streets. Elizabeth sat alone in her room, weeping more for the fate of a Queen than a woman. The responsibility for this deed she shifted with an effort on to the shoulders of her masculine advisers.

CHAPTER THIRTY-ONE

The Spanish Armada

WAR WAS now certain. The chances were heavily weighted in favour of Spain. From the mines of Mexico and Peru there came a stream of silver and gold which so fortified the material power of the Spanish Empire that King Philip could equip his forces beyond all known scales. The position was well understood in the ruling circles of England. So long as Spain controlled the wealth of the New World she could launch and equip a multitude of Armadas; the treasure must therefore be arrested at its source or captured from the ships which conveyed it across the oceans. In the hope of strengthening her own finances and harassing the enemy's preparations against the Netherlands and ultimately against herself, Elizabeth had accordingly sanctioned a number of unofficial expeditions against the Spanish coasts and colonies in South America. Gradually these expeditions had assumed an official character, and the Royal Navy surviving from the days of Henry VIII was rebuilt and reorganised by John Hawkins, son of a Plymouth merchant, who had formerly traded with the Portuguese possessions in Brazil. In 1573 he was appointed Controller of the Navy. He had, moreover, educated an apt pupil, a young adventurer from Devon, Francis Drake.

This "Master Thief of the unknown world," as his Spanish contemporaries called Drake, became the terror of their ports and crews. With the ships that Hawkins had built the English seamen knew they could fight and sink anything the Spaniards might send against them.

Meanwhile Elizabeth's seamen had been gaining experience in unexplored waters. A Devon gentleman, Humphrey Gilbert, was the first to interest the Queen in finding a route to China, or Cathay as it was called, by the North-West. His ideas inspired the voyages of Martin Frobisher, to whom the Queen granted a licence to explore. The Court and the City financed the expedition, and two small ships of twenty-five tons sailed in search of gold. Having charted the bleak coasts round Hudson Straits Frobisher came back. High hopes were entertained that the samples of black ore he brought with him might contain gold. There was disappointment when the ore was assayed and proved worthless. No quick riches were to be gained from adventures in the North-West.

Gilbert, however, was undaunted. He was the first Englishman who realised that the value of these voyages did not lie only in finding precious metals. There were too many people in England. Perhaps they could settle in the new lands. The idea of planting colonies in America now began to take hold of men's imaginations. A few bold spirits were already dreaming of New Englands that would arise across the ocean. At first they had strictly practical aims in mind. In the hope of transporting the needy unemployed to the New World, and of finding new markets among the natives for English cloth, Gilbert himself obtained a charter from Elizabeth in 1578, "to inhabit and possess at his choice all armed and heathen lands not in the actual possession of any Christian peoples." With eleven ships manned by many gentlemen adventurers, including his own stepbrother, Walter Raleigh, of whom more hereafter, he made several hopeful voyages, but none met with success.

In 1583 Gilbert took possession of Newfoundland in the Queen's name, but no permanent settlement was made. Resolved to try again in the following year, he set out for home. The little convoy encountered terrible seas, "breaking short and high pyramid-wise." Gilbert's ship, the *Squirrel,* suddenly disappeared. Walter Raleigh tried to continue Gilbert's work. In 1585 a small colony was established on Roanoke Island, off the American continent, and christened Virginia in honour of the Queen. But by now the threat from Spain was looming large, and to meet it all endeavour was concentrated at home. Colonial efforts were postponed for another twenty years by the Spanish War. In national resources the struggle that broke out was desperately unequal, but the Queen's seamen had received an unrivalled training which was to prove England's salvation.

*　　*　　*

The Spaniards had long contemplated an enterprise against England. Preparations were delayed by Drake's famous raid on Cadiz in 1587. In this "singeing of the King of Spain's beard" a large quantity of stores and ships was destroyed. Nevertheless, in May, 1588, the Armada was ready. A hundred and thirty ships were assembled, carrying twenty-five hundred guns and more than thirty thousand men, two-thirds of them soldiers. Their aim was to sail up the Channel, embark the expeditionary corps of sixteen thousand veterans from the Netherlands under Alexander of Parma, and land it on the south coast of England.

The command was entrusted to the Duke of Medina-Sidonia, who had many misgivings about the enterprise. His fleet was admirably equipped for carrying large numbers of men; it was strong in heavy short-range cannon, but weak in long-distance culverins—this was why the English kept out of range until the last battle. The seamen were few in proportion to the soldiers. These were recruited from the dregs of the Spanish population and commanded by army officers of noble families who had no experience of naval warfare. Many of the vessels were in bad repair; the provisions supplied under a corrupt system of private contract were insufficient and rotten; the drinking water leaked from butts of unseasoned wood. Their commander had no experience of war at sea, and had begged the King to excuse him from so novel an adventure.

The English plan was to gather a fleet in one of the south-western ports, intercept the enemy at the western entrance to the Channel, and concentrate troops in the south-east to meet Parma's army from the Flemish shore. It was uncertain where the attack would fall, but the prevailing westerly winds made it likely that the Armada would sail up the Channel, join Parma, and force a landing on the Essex coast.

The nation was united in the face of the Spanish preparations. Leading Catholics were interned in the Isle of Ely, but as a body their loyalty to the Crown was unshaken. An army was assembled at Tilbury which reached twenty thousand men, under the command of Lord Leicester. This, with the muster in the adjacent counties, constituted a force which should not be underrated. While the Armada was still off the coasts of England Queen Elizabeth reviewed the army at Tilbury and addressed them in these stirring words:

My loving people, who have been persuaded by some that are careful for our safety to take heed how we commit ourselves to armed multitudes, for fear of

1 5 2

treachery. But I assure you I do not desire to live to distrust my faithful and loving people. Let tyrants fear. I have always so behaved myself that, under God, I have placed my chiefest strength and safeguard in the loyal hearts and goodwill of my subjects; and therefore I am come amongst you, as you see, resolved, in the midst and heat of the battle, to live or die amongst you all, to lay down for my God, and for my kingdom, and for my people, my honour and my blood, even in the dust. I know I have the body of a weak and feeble woman, but I have the heart and stomach of a king, and of a king of England, too, and think foul scorn that Parma or Spain or any prince of Europe should dare to invade the borders of my realm; to which, rather than any dishonour shall grow by me, I myself will take up arms, I myself will be your general, judge and rewarder of every one of your virtues in the field. I know already for your forwardness you have deserved rewards and crowns; and we do assure you, in the word of a prince, they shall be duly paid you.

*   *   *

Hawkins's work for the Navy was now to be tested. He had begun over the years to revise the design of English ships from his experience of buccaneering raids in colonial waters. With ships built to weather any seas, Hawkins opposed hand-to-hand fighting and advocated battering the enemy from a distance with the new guns. The English sea-captains were eager to try these novel tactics against the huge overmasted enemy galleons. In spite of Hawkins's efforts only thirty-four of the Queen's ships, carrying six thousand men, could put to sea in 1588. A southerly gale stopped their attacking the Spanish coast, and they were driven into Plymouth with their supplies exhausted and scurvy raging through the ships.

In the event, they had plenty of time to consider their strategy. The Armada left the Tagus on May 20, 1588, but was smitten by storms. Two of their one-thousand-ton ships were dismasted. They put in to refit at Corunna, and did not set sail again until July 12. News of their approach off the Lizard was brought into Plymouth harbour on the evening of July 19. The English fleet had to put out of the Sound the same night. By difficult, patient, precarious tacking the English fleet got to windward, and for nine days hung upon the Armada as it ran before the westerly wind up the Channel, pounding away with their long-range guns at the lumbering galleons. They had gained the weather gauge. The Spaniards attempted a counter-attack with Neapolitan galleys, rowed by hundreds of slaves, but Drake, followed by Howard, swept in upon the main body, and, as Howard reported, "the Spaniards were forced to give way and flock together like sheep." The Channel passage was a torment to the Spaniards. The guns of the English ships raked the decks of the galleons, killing the crews and demoralising the soldiers. The English suffered hardly any loss.

The Spanish admiral then made a fatal mistake. He anchored in Calais Roads and the whole sea-power of England now combined. A council of war held in the English flagship during the evening of July 28 resolved to

1 5 3

attack. The decisive engagement opened. After darkness had fallen eight ships from the eastern squadron which had been filled with explosives and prepared as fire-ships were sent against the crowded Spanish fleet at anchor in the roads. Suddenly a series of explosions shook the air and flaming hulls drifted toward the anchored Armada. The Spanish captains cut their cables and made for the open sea. Collisions without number followed.

Medina now sent messengers to Parma announcing his arrival, and by dawn on July 29 he was off the sandbanks of Gravelines, expecting to find Parma's troops ready shipped in their transports. But there was no sail to be seen. The tides in Dunkirk harbour were at the neap. It was only possible to sail out with a favourable wind upon a spring tide. Neither condition was present. The army and the transports were not at their rendezvous. The Spaniards turned to face their pursuers. A desperate fight raged for eight hours, a confused conflict of ships engaging at close quarters. The official report sent to the English Government was brief: "Howard in fight spoiled a great number of the Spaniards, sank three and drove four or five on the banks." The English had completely exhausted their ammunition, and but for this hardly a Spanish ship would have got away. Yet Howard himself scarcely realised the magnitude of his victory. "Their force is wonderful great and strong," he wrote on the evening after the battle, "yet we pluck their feathers by little and little."

The tormented Armada now sailed northwards out of the fight. Their one aim was to make for home. The horrors of the long voyage round the north of Scotland began. Not once did they turn upon the small, silent ships which followed them in their course. Neither side had enough ammunition. Their ships had been shattered by the English cannonades and now were struck by the autumn gales. Sixty-five ships, about half of the fleet that had put to sea, reached Spanish ports during the month of October.

The English had not lost a single ship, and scarcely a hundred men. But their captains were disappointed. Half the enemy's fleet had got away. But to the English people as a whole the defeat of the Armada came as a miracle. For thirty years the shadow of Spanish power had darkened the political scene. A wave of religious emotion filled men's minds. One of the medals struck to commemorate the victory bears the inscription *"Afflavit Deus et dissipantur"*—"God blew and they were scattered."

Elizabeth and her seamen knew how true this was. The Armada had indeed been bruised in battle, but it was demoralised and set on the run by the weather. Yet the event was decisive. The new tactics of Hawkins had brought success. The nation was transported with relief and pride. Shakespeare was writing *King John* a few years later. His words struck into the hearts of his audiences:

> Come the three corners of the world in arms,
> And we shall shock them. Nought shall make us rue
> If England to itself do rest but true.

CHAPTER THIRTY-TWO

Gloriana

WITH 1588 the crisis of the reign was past. England had emerged from the Armada year as a first-class Power. She had resisted the weight of the mightiest empire that had been seen since Roman times. Her people awoke to a consciousness of their greatness, and the last years of Elizabeth's reign saw a welling up of national energy and enthusiasm focusing upon the person of the Queen. In the year following the Armada the first three books were published of Spenser's *Faerie Queene,* in which Elizabeth is hymned as Gloriana. Poets and courtiers alike paid their homage to the sovereign who symbolised the great achievement. Elizabeth had schooled a generation of Englishmen.

The success of the seamen pointed the way to wide opportunities of winning wealth and fame in daring expeditions. Before the reign came to a close another significant enterprise took its beginning. For years past Englishmen had been probing their way through to the East, round the Cape of Good Hope and overland across the expanses of the Middle East. Their ventures led to the founding of the East India Company. At the start it was a small and struggling affair, with a capital of only £72,000. Dazzling dividends were to be won from this investment. The British Empire in India, which was to be painfully built up in the course of the next three centuries, owes its origins to the charter granted by Queen Elizabeth to a group of London merchants and financiers in the year 1600.

The young men who now rose to prominence in the Court of the ageing Queen plagued their mistress to allow them to try their hand in many enterprises. The coming years resound with attacks upon the forces and allies of Spain throughout the world—expeditions to Cadiz, to the Azores, into the Caribbean Sea, to the Low Countries, and, in support of the Huguenots, to the northern coasts of France. The story is one of confused running fights, conducted with slender resources and culminating in a few great moments. The policy of the English Government was to distract the enemy in every quarter of the world. The Island was at last secure.

As the conflict with Spain drew inconclusively on, and both sides struck at each other in ever-growing, offensive exhaustion, the heroic age of sea fights passed away. One epic moment has survived in the annals of the English race—the last fight of the *Revenge* at Flores, in the Azores. "In the year 1591," says Bacon, "was that memorable fight of an English ship called the *Revenge,* under the command of Sir Richard Grenville, memorable (I say) even beyond credit and to the height of some heroical fable: and though it were a defeat, yet it exceeded a victory; being like the act of Samson, that killed more men at his death, than he had done in the time of all his life. This ship, for the space of fifteen hours, sate like a stag amongst hounds at bay, and was sieged and fought with, in turn, by fifteen great ships of Spain, part of a navy of fifty-five ships in all; the rest like abettors looking on afar off. And amongst the fifteen ships that fought, the great *San Philippo* was one; a ship of fifteen hundred tons, prince of the twelve *Sea Apostles,* which was right glad when she was shifted off from the *Revenge.* This brave ship the *Revenge,* being manned only with two hundred soldiers and marines, whereof eighty lay sick, yet nevertheless after a fight maintained (as was said) of fifteen hours, and two ships of the enemy sunk by her side, besides many more torn and battered and great slaughter of men, never came to be entered, but was taken by composition; the enemies themselves having in admiration the virtue of the commander and the whole tragedy of that ship."

It is well to remember the ordinary seamen who sailed in ships sometimes as small as twenty tons into the wastes of the North and South Atlantic, ill-fed and badly paid, on risky adventures backed by inadequate capital. These men faced death in many forms—death by disease, death by drowning, death from Spanish pikes and guns, death by starvation and cold on uninhabited coasts, death in the Spanish prisons. The Admiral of the English fleet, Lord Howard of Effingham, spoke their epitaph: "God send us to sea in such a company together again, when need is."

Victory over Spain was the most shining achievement of Elizabeth's reign, but by no means the only one. The repulse of the Armada had subdued religious dissension at home. Events which had swung England towards Puritanism while the Catholic danger was impending swung her back to the Anglican settlement when the peril vanished in the smoke of the burning Armada at Gravelines. But the fire was still dangerously smouldering when Elizabeth died.

*   *   *

Throughout Elizabeth's reign the weight and authority of Parliament had been steadily growing. Now the issue turned on monopolies. For some time the Crown had eked out its slender income by various devices, including the granting of patents of monopolies to courtiers and others in return for payment. Some of these grants could be justified as protecting and encouraging inventions, but frequently they amounted merely to unjustified privileges, involving high prices that placed a burden upon every citizen. In 1601 grievances flared up into a full-dress debate in the House of Commons. An angry Member read out a list extending from a patent for iron manufacture to a patent for drying pilchards. "Is not bread there?" shouted another back-bencher. The uproar in the House brought a stinging rebuke from Mr. Secretary Cecil. "What an indignity then is it," he exclaimed, "that when any is discussing this point he should be cried and coughed down. This is more fit for a grammar-school than a Parliament." But the

Queen preferred subtler methods. If the Commons pushed their proposals to a division the whole basis of her constitutional authority would be under fire. She acted swiftly now. Some monopolies were abolished forthwith. All, she promised, would be investigated. So she forestalled the direct challenge, and in a golden speech to a large gathering of her Commons summoned to her chamber she told them, "Though God hath raised me high, yet this I account the glory of my crown, that I have reigned with your loves." It was to be her last appearance in their midst.

The immense vitality displayed by the Queen throughout the troublous years of her rule in England ebbed slowly and relentlessly away. She lay for days upon a heap of cushions in her room. For hours the soundless agony was prolonged. The corridors without echoed with the hurrying of agitated feet. At last Robert Cecil dared to speak. "Your Majesty, to content the people you must go to bed." "Little man," came the answer, "is 'must' a word to use to princes?" The old Archbishop of Canterbury, Whitgift, her "little black husband," as she had once called him, knelt praying at her side. In the early hours of the morning of March 24, 1603, Queen Elizabeth died.

*　　*　　*

Thus ended the Tudor dynasty. For over a hundred years, with a handful of bodyguards, they had maintained their sovereignty, kept the peace, baffled the diplomacy and onslaughts of Europe, and guided the country through changes which might well have wrecked it. Parliament was becoming a solid affair based on a working harmony between Sovereign, Lords and Commons, and the traditions of English monarchical government had been restored and gloriously enhanced. But these achievements carried no guarantee of their perpetuation. The monarchy could only govern if it was popular. The Crown was now to pass to an alien Scottish line, hostile in political instincts to the class which administered England. The good understanding with Parliament which the Tudors had nourished came to a fretful close. The new kings soon clashed with the forces of a growing nation, and out of this conflict came the Civil War, the Republican interlude, the Restoration, and the Revolution settlement.

1 5 7

BOOK FIVE
The Civil War

CHAPTER THIRTY-THREE

The United Crowns

KING JAMES OF SCOTLAND was the only son of Mary Queen of Scots. He had been subjected from his youth to a rigid Calvinist upbringing which was not much to his taste. With little money and strict tutors he had long coveted the throne of England, but till the last moment the prize had seemed elusive. The struggle for power and favour between Essex and Robert Cecil might always have provoked Elizabeth, whom he knew only by intermittent correspondence, into some swift decision which would lose him the crown. But now all appeared settled. Cecil was his ally and skilful manager in the tense days after the Queen died. James was proclaimed King James I of England without opposition, and in April, 1603, began a leisurely journey from Holyrood to London.

He was a stranger and an alien, and his qualifications for governing England were yet to be tested. He detested the political ideas of his Calvinist mentors. He had fixed ideas about kingship and the divine right of monarchs to rule. He was a scholar with pretensions to being a philosopher, and in the course of his life published numerous tracts and treatises, ranging from denunciations of witchcraft and tobacco to abstract political theory. He came to England with a closed mind, and a weakness for lecturing. But England was changing. The habit of obedience to a dynasty had died with the last of the Tudors. The country gentlemen on whom the Tudors relied to maintain a balance against the old nobility, and on whom they had devolved the whole business of local government, were beginning to feel their strength. England was secure, free to attend to her own concerns, and a powerful class was now eager to take a hand in their management. On the other hand, James's title to the crown was not impeccable, and the doctrine of Divine Right, originally devised to justify the existence of national sovereignties against a universal Church or Empire, was called in to fortify his position. But how to reconcile a king claiming to rule by Divine Right and a Parliament with no other basis than ancient custom?

His first Parliament at once raised the question of Parliamentary privilege and Royal Prerogative. In dutiful but firm language the Commons drew up an Apology reminding the King that their liberties included free elections, free speech, and freedom from arrest during Parliamentary sessions. "The prerogative of princes," they protested, "may easily and daily grow, while the privileges of the subject are for the most part at an everlasting stand. . . . The voice of the people . . . in the things of their knowledge is said to be as the voice of God." James, like his son after him, treated these expressions of national grievance contemptuously, brushing them aside as personal insults to himself and mere breaches of good manners.

Hitherto James had been straitened; now he thought he was rich. The "beggarly Scotsmen" who had come South with him also enriched themselves. The expenses of the Court increased at an alarming rate. To his surprise James very soon found himself pressed for money. This meant frequent Parliaments.

The Catholics were anxious and hopeful. After all, the King's mother had been their champion. Their position was delicate. If the Pope would allow them to give their secular allegiance to the King, James might let them practise their own religion. But the Pope would not yield. He forbade allegiance to a heretical sovereign. Upon this there could be no compromise. Disappointment and despair led a small group of Catholic gentry to an infernal design for blowing up James and his whole Parliament by gunpowder while they were in session at Westminster. The chief plotter was Robert Catesby, assisted by Guy Fawkes, a veteran of the Spanish wars against the Dutch. The story reached Cecil, and the cellars of Parliament were searched. Fawkes was taken on the spot, and there was a storm of excitement in the City. James went down to open Parliament, and made an emotional speech upon what an honourable end it would have been to die with his faithful Commons. Kings, he said, were exposed to perils beyond those of ordinary mortals; only his own cleverness had saved them all from destruction. The House displayed an incomprehensible indifference, and, turning to the business of the day, discussed the petition of a Member who had asked to be relieved of his Parliamentary duties owing to an attack of gout. The anniversary, which even now is celebrated by bonfires and fireworks, was marred and enlivened until modern times by anti-Popery demonstrations.

* * *

At this time a splendid and lasting monument was created to the genius of the English-speaking peoples. Dr. John Reynolds of Oxford had asked, seemingly on the spur of the moment, if a new version of the Bible could be produced. The idea appealed to James. Here, thought James, was the chance to rid the Scriptures of propaganda and produce a uniform version which could be entrusted to all. Within a few months committees or "companies" were set up, comprising in all about fifty scholars and divines. About three years passed in preliminary research, and the main work did not get under way till 1607, but it was then accomplished with remarkable swiftness. The committees, though separated by considerable distances,

159

finished their task in 1609 and in 1611 the Authorised Version of the Bible was produced by the King's Printer.

It won an immediate and lasting triumph. Copies could be bought for as little as five shillings, and even with the inflated prices of today can still be purchased for this sum. It superseded all other versions. No new revision was deemed necessary for nearly three hundred years. In the crowded emigrant ships which sailed to the New World of America there was little room for baggage. If the adventurers took books with them they took the Bible, Shakespeare, and later *The Pilgrim's Progress,* and the Bible they mostly took with the Authorised Version of King James I. About ninety million complete copies are thought to have been published in the English language alone. It has been translated into more than seven hundred and sixty tongues. The Authorised Version is still the most popular in England and the United States. This may be deemed James's greatest achievement, for the impulse was largely his. The Scottish pedant built better than he knew. The scholars who produced this masterpiece are mostly unknown and unremembered. But they forged an enduring link, literary and religious, between the English-speaking peoples of the world.

*   *   *

James's foreign policy perhaps met the needs of the age for peace, but often clashed with its temper. To pose as Protestant champion in the great religious war now begun on the Continent might gain a fleeting popularity with his subjects, but would also deliver him into the hands of the House of Commons. Besides, the fortunes of war were notoriously uncertain. James seems genuinely to have believed in his mission as the Peacemaker of Europe, and also to have had a deep-rooted nervous dislike of fighting, founded in the tumultuous experiences of his youth in Scotland. He ignored the demand for intervention.

*   *   *

In the midst of these turmoils Sir Walter Raleigh was executed on Tower Hill to please the Spanish Government. Raleigh had been imprisoned at the beginning of the reign for conspiring to supplant James by his cousin, Arabella Stuart. This charge was probably unjust, and the trial was certainly so. Raleigh's dream of finding gold on the Orinoco River, which had cheered his long confinement, ended in disaster in 1617. This last expedition of his, for which he was specially released from the Tower, had merely affronted the Spanish governors of South America. The old capital sentence was now revived against him. His death on October 29, 1618, was intended to mark the new policy of appeasement and prepare the way for good relations with Spain. This deed of shame sets a barrier for ever between King James and the English people. There are others.

James and his Parliaments grew more and more out of sympathy as the years went by, but James found a brilliant supporter in the person of

King Charles I, from the Triple Portrait by Van Dyck

"At one o'clock in the afternoon Charles was informed that his hour had come. He walked through a window of the Banqueting House onto the scaffold.

"He resigned himself to death and assisted the executioner in arranging his hair under a small white satin cap. He laid himself upon the block and upon his own signal his head was struck off at a single stroke.

"An incalculable multitude had streamed to the spot, swayed by intense though inarticulate emotions. When they saw the severed head 'there was such a groan by the thousands then present,' wrote a contemporary diarist, 'as I never heard before and desire I may never hear again'."

Francis Bacon who maintained that the absolute and enlightened rule of the King with the help of his judges was justified by its efficiency. But his theories were unreal and widely unpopular.

At this point the Common Lawyers, headed by Chief Justice Coke, stepped to the forefront of English history. Coke, one of the most learned of English judges, gave a blunt answer to these controversies. He declared that conflicts between Prerogative and statute should be resolved not by the Crown but by the judges. It was a tremendous assertion, for if the judges were to decide which laws were valid and which were not they would become the ultimate lawgivers in the State. They would form a Supreme Court, assessing the legality of both royal and Parliamentary enactments.

Coke's high claims were not without foundation. They rested on the ancient tradition that law declared in the courts was superior to law published by the central authority. Coke himself was reluctant to admit that law could be made, or even changed. It existed already, merely awaiting revelation and exposition. If Acts of Parliament conflicted with it they were invalid. Thus at the beginning of his career Coke was not fighting on the same side as Parliament. In England his main assertions on behalf of fundamental law were overruled. It was to be otherwise in the United States.

James had no sympathy with these agitations. He did not care for compromise; but, shrewder than his son, he saw when compromise would suit him best. It was only the need of money that forced him to deal with Parliament at all. "The House of Commons," he once told the Spanish Ambassador, "is a body without a head. The Members give their opinions in a disorderly manner. At their meetings nothing is heard but cries, shouts, and confusion. I am surprised that my ancestors should ever have permitted such an institution to come into existence. I am a stranger, and found it here when I arrived, so that I am obliged to put up with what I cannot get rid of."

* * *

James was much addicted to favourites, and his attention to handsome young men resulted in a noticeable loss of respect for the monarchy. One of his favourites, Robert Carr, created Earl of Somerset by the King's caprice, was implicated in a murder by poison, of which his wife was undoubtedly guilty. Carr was succeeded in the King's regard by a good-looking, quick-witted, extravagant youth, George Villiers, soon ennobled as Duke of Buckingham. This young man quickly became all-powerful at Court, and in the affections of James. He formed a deep and honourable friendship with Charles, Prince of Wales. He accepted unhesitatingly the royal policy of a Spanish marriage, and in 1623 staged a romantic journey to Madrid for the Prince and himself to view the bride. Their unorthodox behaviour failed to impress the formal and ceremonious Court of Spain.

No sooner was the Spanish match broken off than Buckingham turned to France for a bride for Charles. When he and the Prince of Wales had passed through Paris on their way to Madrid, Charles had been struck by the charm of Marie de Medicis' daughter, Henrietta Maria, sister of Louis XII and then in her fourteenth year. Buckingham found the negotiations agreeable to the French Court, and especially to Queen Marie. A marriage with a Protestant princess would have united Crown and Parliament. But this was never the intention of the governing circle. A daughter of France seemed to them the only alternative to the Infanta. How could England face Spain alone? If we could not lean on Spain, it seemed that we must have France. The old King wanted to see his son married. He said he lived only for him. He ratified the marriage treaty in December, 1624. Three months later the first King of Great Britain was dead.

CHAPTER THIRTY-FOUR

The *Mayflower*

THE STRUGGLE with Spain had long absorbed the energies of Englishmen, and in the last years of Queen Elizabeth few fresh enterprises had been carried out upon the oceans. For a while little was heard of the New World. Hawkins and Drake in their early voyages had opened up broad prospects for England in the Caribbean. Frobisher and others had penetrated deeply into the Arctic recesses of Canada in search of a north-west passage to Asia. But the lure of exploration and trade had given way to the demands of war. The novel idea of founding colonies also received a setback. Gilbert, Raleigh, and Grenville had been its pioneers. Their bold plans had come to nothing, but they left behind them an inspiring tradition. Now after a lapse of time their endeavours were taken up by new figures, less glittering, more practical and luckier. Piecemeal and from many motives the English-speaking communities in North America were founded. The change came in 1604, when James I made his treaty of peace with Spain. Discussion that had been stimulated by Richard Hakluyt's *Discourse on Western Planting* was revived. Serious argument by a group of writers of which he was the head gained a new hearing and a new pertinence. For there were troubles in England. People reduced to beggary and vagabondage were many, and new outlets were wanted for the nation's energies and resources.

*   *   *

The steady rise in prices had caused much hardship to wage earners. Though the general standard of living improved during the sixteenth century, a wide range of prices rose sixfold, and wages only twofold. Industry was oppressed by excessive Government regulation. The medieval system of craftsmen's guilds, which was still enforced, made the entry of young apprentices harsh and difficult. The squirearchy, strong in its political alliance with the Crown, owned most of the land and ran all the local government. The march of enclosures, which they pursued, drove many English peasants off the land. The whole scheme of life seemed to have contracted and the framework of social organisation had hardened. There were many without advantage, hope, or livelihood under the new conditions. Colonies, it was thought, might help to solve these distressing problems.

The Government was not uninterested. Trade with lively colonies promised an increase in the customs revenue on which the Crown heavily depended. Merchants and the richer landed gentry saw new opportunities across the Atlantic for profitable investment, and an escape from cramping restrictions on industry and the general decline of European trade during the religious wars. Capital was available for overseas experiments. Raleigh's attempts had demonstrated the ill success of individual effort, but a new method of financing large-scale trading enterprises was evolving in the shape of the joint stock company. In 1606 a group of speculators acquired a royal charter creating the Virginia company. It is interesting to see how early speculation in its broadest sense begins to play its part in the American field.

A plan was carefully drawn up in consultation with experts such as Hakluyt, but they had little practical experience and underestimated the difficulties of the profoundly novel departure they were making. After all, it is not given to many to start a nation. It was a few hundred people who now took the first step. A settlement was made at Jamestown, in the Chesapeake Bay, on the Virginian coast, in May, 1607. By the following spring half the population was dead from malaria, cold, and famine. After a long and heroic struggle the survivors became self-supporting, but profits to the promoters at home were very small. Captain John Smith, a military adventurer from the Turkish wars, became the dictator of the tiny colony, and enforced harsh discipline. The marriage of his lieutenant John Rolfe with Pocahontas, the daughter of an Indian chief, caused a sensation in the English capital. But the London company had little control and the administration of the colony was rough-and-ready. The objects of the directors were mixed and ill defined. Some thought that colonisation would reduce

1 6 3

poverty and crime in England. Others looked for profit to the fisheries of the North American coast, or hoped for raw materials to reduce their dependence on the exports from the Spanish colonies. All were wrong, and Virginia's fortune sprang from a novel and unexpected cause. By chance a crop of tobacco was planted, and the soil proved benevolent. Tobacco had been introduced into Europe by the Spaniards and the habit of smoking was spreading fast. Demand for tobacco was great and growing, and the profits on the Virginia crop were high. Small-holders were bought out, big estates were formed, and the colony began to stand on its own feet. As it grew and prospered its society came to resemble the Mother Country, with rich planters in the place of squires. They were not long in developing independence of mind and a sturdy capacity for self-government. Distance from the authorities in London greatly aided them in this.

* * *

Beneath the drab exterior of Jacobean England, with favouritism at Court and humiliation in Europe, other and more vital forces were at work. The Elizabethan bishops had driven the nobler and tougher Puritan spirits out of the Established Church. But though they destroyed the organisation of the party small illegal gatherings of religious extremists continued to meet. There was no systematic persecution, but petty restrictions and spyings obstructed their peaceful worship. A congregation at Scrooby, in Nottinghamshire, led by one of their pastors, John Robinson, and by William Brewster, the Puritan bailiff of the manor of the Archbishop of York, resolved to seek freedom of worship abroad. In 1607 they left England and settled at Leyden, hoping to find asylum among the tolerant and industrious Dutch. For ten years these Puritan parishioners struggled for a decent existence. They were small farmers and agricultural workers, out of place in a maritime industrial community, barred by their nationality from the guilds of craftsmen, without capital and without training. The only work they could get was rough manual labour. They were persistent and persevering, but a bleak future faced them in Holland. They were too proud of their birthright to be absorbed by the Dutch. The authorities had been sympathetic, but in practice unhelpful. The Puritans began to look elsewhere.

Emigration to the New World presented itself as an escape from a sinful generation. There they might gain a livelihood unhampered by Dutch guilds, and practise their creed unharassed by English clerics. As one of their number records, "The place they had thoughts on was some of those vast and unpeopled countries of America, which are fruitful and fit for habitation; being devoid of all civil inhabitants; where there are only savage and brutish men, which range up and down little otherwise than the wild beasts of the same."

Throughout the winter of 1616–1617, when Holland was threatened with a renewal of war with Spain, there were many discussions among the anxious community.

Their first plan was to settle in Guiana, but then they realised it was impossible to venture out upon their own. Help must come from England. They accordingly sent agents to London to negotiate with the only body interested in emigration, the Virginia company. One of the members of its council was an influential Parliamentarian, Sir Edwin Sandys. Supported by the London merchant backers of the company, he furthered the project. Here were ideal settlers, sober, hard-working, and skilled in agriculture. They insisted upon freedom of worship, and it would be necessary to placate the Anglican bishops. Sandys and the emissaries from Holland went to see the King. James was sceptical. He asked how the little band proposed to support itself in the company's territory in America. "By fishing," they replied. This appealed to James. "So God have my soul," he exclaimed in one of his more agreeable remarks, " 'tis an honest trade! It was the Apostles' own calling."

The Leyden community was granted a licence to settle in America, and arrangements for their departure were hastened on. Thirty-five members of the Leyden congregation left Holland and joined sixty-six West County adventurers at Plymouth, and in September, 1620, they set sail in the *Mayflower,* a vessel of 180 tons.

After two and a half months of voyaging across the winter ocean they reached the shores of Cape Cod, and thus, by an accident, landed outside the jurisdiction of the Virginia company. This invalidated their patent from London. Before they landed there was trouble among the group about who was to enforce discipline. Those who had joined the ship at Plymouth were no picked band of saints, and had no intention of submitting to the Leyden set. There was no possibility of appealing to England. Yet, if they were not all to starve, some agreement must be reached.

Forty-one of the more responsible members thereupon drew up a solemn compact which is one of the remarkable documents in history, a spontaneous covenant for political organisation. "In the name of God, Amen. We whose names are under-written, the loyal subjects of our dread sovereign Lord, King James, by the grace of God, of Great Britain, France, and Ireland king, defender of the faith, etc. Having undertaken, for the glory of God, and advancement of the Christian faith, and honour of our king and country, a voyage to plant the first colony in the Northern parts of Virginia, do by these presents solemnly and mutually in the presence of God, and one of another, covenant and combine ourselves together into a civil body politic, for our better ordering and preservation and furtherance of the ends aforesaid; and by virtue hereof to enact, constitute, and frame such just and equal laws, ordinances, acts, constitutions, and offices, from time to time, as shall be thought most meet and convenient for the general good of the colony, unto which we promise all due submission and obedience."

In December on the American coast in Cape Cod Bay these men founded the town of Plymouth. The same bitter struggle with nature that had taken place in Virginia now began. There was no staple crop. But by toil and faith they survived. The financial supporters in London reaped no profits. In 1627 they sold out and the Plymouth colony was left to its own resources. Such was the founding of New England.

*   *   *

For ten years afterwards there was no more planned emigration to America; but the tiny colony of Plymouth pointed a path to freedom. In 1629 Charles I dissolved Parliament and the period of so-called Personal Rule began. As friction grew between Crown and subjects, so opposition to the Anglican Church strengthened in the countryside. Absolutism was commanding the Continent, and England seemed to be going the same way. Many people of independent mind began to consider leaving home to find freedom and justice in the wilds.

Just as the congregation from Scrooby had emigrated in a body to Holland, so another Puritan group in Dorset, inspired by the Reverend John White, now resolved to move to the New World. After an unhappy start this venture won support in London and the Eastern Counties among backers interested in trade and fishing as well as in emigration. Influential Opposition peers lent their aid. After the precedent of Virginia a chartered company was formed, eventually named "The Company of the Massachusetts Bay in New England." News spread rapidly and there was no lack of colonists. An advance party founded the settlement of Salem, to the north of Plymouth. In 1630 the Governor of the company, John Winthrop, followed with a thousand settlers. He was the leading personality in the enterprise. The uneasiness of the time is reflected in his letters, which reveal the reasons why his family went. "I am verily persuaded," he wrote about England, "God will bring some heavy affliction upon this land, and that speedily; but be of good comfort. . . . If the Lord seeth it will be good for us, He will provide a shelter and a hiding place for us and others. . . . Evil times are coming when the Church must fly into the wilderness." The wilderness that Winthrop chose lay on the Charles River, and to this swampish site the capital of the colony was transferred. Here from modest beginnings arose the city of Boston, which was to become in the next century the heart of resistance to British rule, and long remain the intellectual capital of America.

The Massachusetts Bay company was by its constitution a joint stock corporation, organised entirely for trading purposes, and the Salem settlement was for the first year controlled from London. But by accident or intent there was no mention in the charter where the company was to hold

166

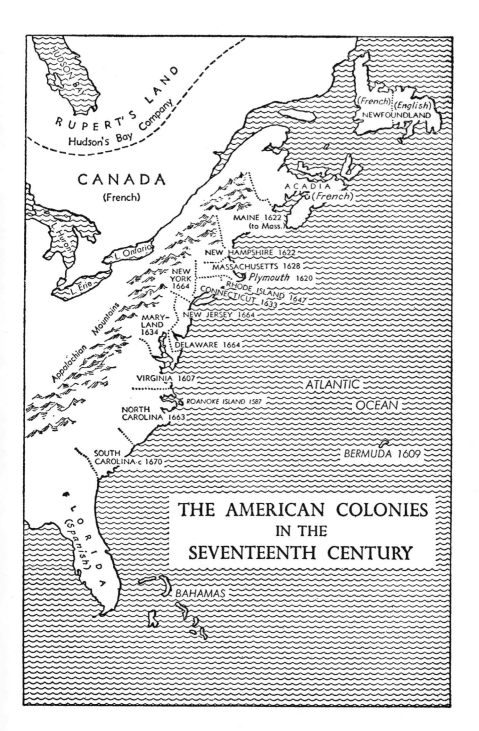

HUDSON BAY

RUPERT'S LAND
Hudson's Bay Company

CANADA
(French)

L. Ontario

L. Erie

Huron

Appalachian Mountains

(French) (English)
NEWFOUNDLAND

ACADIA
(French)

MAINE 1622
(to Mass.)

NEW HAMPSHIRE 1622

MASSACHUSETTS 1628

NEW YORK 1664

Plymouth 1620

RHODE ISLAND 1647

CONNECTICUT 1633

NEW JERSEY 1664

MARYLAND 1634

DELAWARE 1664

VIRGINIA 1607

ROANOKE ISLAND 1587

NORTH CAROLINA 1663

SOUTH CAROLINA c 1670

ATLANTIC

OCEAN

BERMUDA 1609

FLORIDA
(Spanish)

THE AMERICAN COLONIES
IN THE
SEVENTEENTH CENTURY

BAHAMAS

its meetings. Some of the Puritan stockholders realised that there was no obstacle to transferring the company, directors and all, to New England. A general court of the company was held, and this momentous decision taken. From the joint stock company was born the self-governing colony of Massachusetts. The Puritan landed gentry who led the enterprise introduced a representative system, such as they had known in the days before King Charles's Personal Rule. John Winthrop guided the colony through this early phase, and it soon expanded. Between 1629 and 1640 the colonists rose in numbers from three hundred to fourteen thousand. The resources of the company offered favourable prospects to small emigrants. In England life for farm labourers was often hard. Here in the New World there was land for every newcomer and freedom from all restrictions upon the movement of labour and such other medieval regulations as oppressed and embittered the peasantry at home.

The leaders and ministers who ruled in Massachusetts, however, had views of their own about freedom. It must be the rule of the godly. They understood toleration as little as the Anglicans, and disputes broke out about religion. By no means all were rigid Calvinists, and recalcitrant bodies split off from the parent colony when such quarrels became strident. Outside of the settlement were boundless beckoning lands. In 1635 and 1636 some colonists moved to the valley of the Connecticut River, and founded the town of Hartford near its banks. They were joined by many emigrants direct from England. This formed the nucleus of the settlement of the River Towns, later to become the colony of Connecticut. There, three thousand miles from home, enlightened rules of government were drawn up. A "Fundamental Order" or constitution was proclaimed, similar to the Mayflower compact about fifteen years before. A popular Government, shared in by all the freemen of the colony, was set up, and maintained itself in a modest way until its position was formally regularised after the Restoration of the Stuart monarchy.

The founders of Connecticut had gone out from Massachusetts to find new and larger lands in which to settle. Religious strife drove others beyond the bounds of the parent colony. A scholar from Cambridge, Roger Williams, had been forced to leave the university by Archbishop Laud. He followed the now known way to the New World, and settled in Massachusetts. The godly there seemed to him almost as oppressive as the Anglican Church in England. Williams soon clashed with the authorities, and became the leader of those idealists and humbler folk who sought escape from persecution in their new home overseas. The magistrates considered him a promoter of disorder, and resolved to send him back to England. Warned in time, he fled beyond their reach, and, followed at intervals by others, founded the town of Providence, to the south of Massachusetts. Other exiles from Massachusetts, some of them forcibly banished, joined his settlement in 1636, which became the colony of Rhode Island. Roger Williams was the first political thinker of America, and his ideas influenced not only his fellow colonists, but the revolutionary party in England. In many ways he foreshadowed the political conceptions of John Milton. He was the first to put into practice the complete separation of Church from lay government, and Rhode Island was the only centre in the world at that time where there was complete religious toleration. This noble cause was sustained by the distilling and sale of spirits, on which the colony thrived.

By 1640 five main English settlements had thus been established in North America: Virginia, technically under the direct rule of the Crown, and administered, somewhat ineffectually, by a standing committee of the Privy Council since the company's charter was abrogated in 1624; the original Pilgrim settlement at Plymouth, which, for want of capital, had not expanded; the flourishing Massachusetts Bay colony, and its two off-shoots, Connecticut and Rhode Island.

* * *

Two other ventures, both essentially commercial, established the English-speaking peoples in the New World. Since Elizabethan days they had often tried to get a foothold in the Spanish West Indies. In 1623, on his way back from a fruitless expedition to Guiana, a Suffolk gentleman named Thomas Warner explored one of the less inhabited West Indian islands. He deposited a few colonists on St. Christopher, and hurried home to get a royal patent for a more extensive enterprise. This achieved, he returned to the Caribbean, and, though much harassed by Spanish raids, he established the English in this disputed sea. By the 1640's Barbados, St. Christopher, Nevis, Montserrat, and Antigua were in English hands and several thousand colonists had arrived. Sugar assured their prosperity, and the Spanish grip on the West Indies was shaken. There was much competition and warfare in the succeeding years, but for a long time these island settlements were commercially much more valuable to England than the colonies in North America.

Another settlement of this period was sponsored by the monarchy. In theory all land settled by Englishmen belonged to the King. He had the right to grant such portions as he chose either to recognised companies or to individuals. Just as Elizabeth and James had granted industrial and commercial monopolies to courtiers, so now Charles I attempted to regulate colonial settlement. In 1632 George Calvert, Lord Baltimore, a Roman Catholic courtier who had long been interested in colonisation, applied for a patent for settling in the neighbourhood of Virginia. It was granted after his death to his son. The terms of the patent resembled the conditions under which land was already held in Virginia. It conferred complete proprietary rights over the new area, and tried to transport the manorial system to the New World. The government of the colony was vested in the Baltimore family, who had supreme power of appointment and regulation. Courtiers and merchants subscribed to the venture, and the new colony was named Maryland in honour of Charles's Queen, Henrietta Maria. Although the proprietor was a Roman Catholic there was a tolerant flavour about its government from the beginning, because Baltimore had only obtained his patent by proclaiming the religion of the Established Church as the official creed of the new settlement. The aristocratic nature of the régime was much modified in practice, and the powers of the local administration set up by Baltimore increased at the expense of his paper rights.

In these first decades of the great emigration over eighty thousand English-speaking people crossed the Atlantic. Never since the days of the Germanic invasions of Britain had such a national movement been seen. Saxon and Viking had colonised England. Now, one thousand years later, their descendants were taking possession of America. Many different streams of migrants were to make their confluence in the New World and contribute to the manifold character of the future United States. But the British stream flowed first and remained foremost. From the beginning its leaders were out of sympathy with the Government at home. The creation of towns and settlements from the wilderness, warfare with the Indians, and the remoteness and novelty of the scene widened the breach with the Old World. During the critical years of settlement and consolidation in New England the Mother Country was paralysed by civil war. When the English State again achieved stability it was confronted with self-supporting, self-reliant communities which had evolved traditions and ideas of their own.

CHAPTER THIRTY-FIVE

Charles I and Buckingham

OF THE many descriptions of Charles I at the beginning of his reign none is more attractive than the cameo which we owe to Ranke. He was, he says, "in the bloom of life: he had just completed his twenty-fifth year. He looked well on horseback: he was expert in knightly exercises. He was one of those young men of whom it is said that they have no fault. His strict propriety of demeanour bordered on maiden bashfulness: a serious and temperate soul spoke from his calm eyes." He had, however, suffered from infantile paralysis and spoke with a stammer.

A great political and religious crisis was overhanging England. Already in King James's time Parliament had begun to take the lead, not only in levying taxes but increasingly in the conduct of affairs, and especially in foreign policy. The furious winds of religious strife carried men's thoughts afar. The English people felt that their survival and their salvation were bound up for ever with the victory of the Reformed Faith, and they watched with straining, vigilant eyes every episode which marked its advance or misfortune. An intense desire for England to lead and champion the Protestant cause wherever it was assailed drove forward the Parliamentary movement with a force far greater than would ever have sprung merely from the issues which were now opening at home.

The secular issues were nevertheless themselves of enormous weight. Men looked back to earlier times. Great lawyers like Coke directed their gaze to the rights which they thought Parliament had possessed under the Lancastrian kings. They spoke of Magna Carta, and even of still more ancient rights in the mists of Anglo-Saxon monarchy. The past seemed to them to provide almost a written Constitution, from which the Crown was now threatening to depart. But the Crown also looked back, and found many precedents of a contrary character. Both King and Parliament had a body of doctrine upon which they dwelt with sincere conviction. This brought pathos and grandeur to the coming struggle.

A society more complex than that of Tudor England was coming into existence. Trade, both foreign and internal, was expanding. Coal mining and other industries were rapidly developing. Larger vested interests were in being. In the van stood London, ever-glorious champion of freedom and progress; London, with its thousands of lusty, free-spoken prentices and its wealthy City guilds and companies. Outside London many of the landed gentry, who supplied numerous Members to Parliament, were acquiring close connections with new industry and trade. In these years the Commons were not so much seeking to legislate as trying to wring from the Crown admissions of ancient custom which would prevent before it was too late all this recent growth from falling under an autocratic grip.

The men at the head of this strenuous and, to our time, invaluable movement were notable figures. Coke had taught the later Parliaments of James I the arguments upon which they could rest and the methods by which they might prevail. His knowledge of the Common Law was unique. Two country gentlemen stand with him: one from the West, Sir John Eliot, a Cornishman; the other, Thomas Wentworth, a Yorkshire squire. Behind them at this time, lacking nothing in grit, were leaders of the Puritan gentry, Denzil Holles, Arthur Hazelrigg, John Pym—Pym was eventually to go far and to carry the cause still farther. He was a Somerset man, a lawyer, strongly anti-High Church, and with an interest in colonial ventures. Here was a man who understood every move in the political game, and would play it out remorselessly.

*   *   *

The Parliaments of James, and now those of Charles, were for war and intervention in Europe. They sought to use the money power to induce the King and his Ministers to tread these dangerous paths for they knew that the stresses of war would force the Crown to come to them. King Charles and Buckingham were high-spirited men in the ardour of youth. The King was affronted by the manner in which he had been slighted in Madrid. He was for war with Spain.

The war went badly. Buckingham led an expedition but it accomplished nothing. On his return Parliament resolved to unseat the glittering, profuse, incompetent Minister. Buckingham was impeached, and to save his friend the King hastily dissolved Parliament.

A new complication was now added to the scene. The powerful French Minister, Cardinal Richelieu, was determined to curb the independence of the Huguenots. English sympathies naturally lay with these French Protestants. In 1627 a considerable force was despatched under Buckingham to help the Rochelais. It landed off the coast in the Île de Ré, failed to storm the citadel, and withdrew in disorder. Thus Buckingham's military efforts were once more marked by waste and failure.

The King was torn between the grinding need of finding money for the war and the danger that Parliament would again impeach his friend. In his vexation, he resorted to dubious methods of raising money. He demanded a forced loan; and when many important persons refused to pay he threw them into prison. At Coke's prompting the Commons now went on to frame the Petition of Right. Its object was to curtail the King's Prerogative.

We reach here, amid much confusion, the main foundation of English freedom. The right of the Executive Government to imprison a man, high or low, for reasons of State was denied; and that denial, made good in painful struggles, constitutes the charter of every self-respecting man at any time in any land. Trial by jury of equals, only for offences known to the law, if maintained, makes the difference between bond and free. But the King felt this would hamper him, and no doubt a plausible case can be advanced that in times of emergency dangerous persons must be confined. The terms "protective arrest" and "shot while trying to escape" had not yet occurred to the mind of authority. We owe them to the genius of a later age.

*   *   *

Both sides pressed farther along their paths. The King, having got his money, dwelt unduly upon the assurances he had received from the judges that his Prerogative was intact. The Commons came forward with further complaints against the growth of Popery and Arminianism (the form of High Church doctrine most directly opposed to Calvinism), about the mismanagement of the war, and about injury to trade and commerce from naval weakness in the Narrow Seas. They renewed their attack on Buckingham, asking the King whether it was consistent with his safety, or the safety of the realm, that the author of so many calamities should continue to hold office or remain near his sacred person. But now the King and Buckingham hoped that a second and successful expedition would relieve the Huguenots in La Rochelle. Charles dismissed the Houses. Before he had need of them again he and his cherished Minister would present them with a military or diplomatic result in which all could rejoice. Far better to rescue Protestants abroad than to persecute Catholics at home. A King who had delivered La Rochelle could surely claim the right to exercise indulgence even to Papists in his own land. This was not a discreditable position to take up; but Fate moved differently.

Buckingham himself was deeply conscious of the hatreds of which he was the object, and it is clear that in putting himself at the head of a new expedition to La Rochelle he hoped to win again for himself some national backing, which would at least divide his pursuers. But at the moment when his resolves were at their highest, as he was about to embark at Portsmouth, commander-in-chief of a formidable armament, with new engines for breaking the boom which Richelieu had built across the beleaguered harbour, he was stabbed to death by a fanatical naval lieutenant.

The death of Buckingham was a devastating blow to the young King. At the same time it immensely relieved his public difficulties, for much of the anger of the Parliament died with the favourite; and it brought for the first time a unity into his married life. Hitherto he had been morally and mentally dominated by "Steenie," the beloved friend of his boyhood and youth, to whom he confided his inmost thoughts. For three years he had lived in cold estrangement from the Queen. It was even said that the marriage had never been consummated. The death of Buckingham was the birth of his love for his wife. Little but storm lay before them, but henceforth they faced it together.

* * *

It had become plain to all that King and Commons could not work together on any terms. Parliament was dissolved and the period of King Charles's Personal Rule began.

CHAPTER THIRTY-SIX

The Personal Rule

THE PERSONAL Rule of the King was not set up covertly or by degrees. Charles openly proclaimed his intention. "We shall," he said, "account it presumption for any to prescribe any time unto us for Parliaments, the calling, continuing, and dissolving of which is always in our own power."

The least sentimental condition of the Personal Rule was dominant—money. How to get the money? First, an extreme frugality must be practised by the executive—no wars, no adventures of any kind, no disturbances. No large question could be stirred. The King, with his elegant, dignified Court, whose figures are portrayed by the pencil of Van Dyck, whose manners and whose morals were an example to all, reigned on the smallest scale. He was a despot, but an unarmed despot. It is a travesty to represent this period of Personal Rule as a time of tyranny in any effective sense. In later years, under the yoke of Cromwell's Major-Generals, all England looked back to these placid thirties as an age of ease and tranquillity. But man has never sought tranquillity alone. His nature drives him forward to fortunes which, for better or for worse, are different from those which it is in his power to pause and enjoy.

Under a modest frugal regime King Charles managed to do without a Parliament. Many who would have been vehement if the chance had come their way were content to live their life from day to day. The land was good; springtime, summertime, autumn, had their joys; in the winter there were the Yule log and new amusements. Agriculture and fox hunting cast their compulsive or soothing balms upon restless spirits. Harvests were now abundant and the rise in prices had almost ceased. There was no longer a working-class problem. The Poor Law was administered with exceptional humanity. Ordinary gentlefolk might have no share in national government, but they were still lords on their own estates. In Quarter Sessions they ruled the shires, and as long as they kept clear of the law and paid their taxes with a grunt they were left in peace. It required an intense effort by the Parliamentary party to rouse in them under such conditions a national feeling and concern for the State. The malcontents looked about for points which would inflame the inert forces of the nation.

* * *

Presently Charles's lawyers and sleuth-hounds drew attention to an anomaly which had grown with the passage of years. According to the immemorial laws of England—perhaps of Alfred the Great—the whole land should pay for the upkeep of the Fleet. However, for a long time only the maritime counties had paid for the Navy. Yet was not this Navy the shield of all the peace and freedom which thrived in Britain? Why should not all pay where all benefited? There never was a juster demand made of its subjects by an island state than that all counties should share alike in the upkeep of the Fleet. Put properly to a loyal Parliament, it would have passed, with general consent, on its merits apart from ancient tradition. But the abuse of letting the inland counties go untaxed had grown into a custom not broken by Queen Elizabeth even in the days of the Armada. The project commended itself to the King. In August, 1635, he levied "Ship Money" upon the whole country.

Forthwith a Buckinghamshire gentleman, a former Member of Parliament, solidly active against the Crown, stood forth among many others and refused to pay. His assessment was no more than twenty shillings; but upon the principle that even the best of taxes could be levied only with the consent of Parliament he faced the distraint and imprisonment which were the penalties of contumacy. John Hampden's refusal was selected by both sides as a test case. The Parliamentarians, who had no other means of expression, saw in it a trial upon which all eyes would be directed, and welcomed a martyr whose sacrifice would disturb the public tameness. They wished to hear the people groan at tyranny. The Crown, on the other hand, was encouraged by the logic of its argument. The case of Hampden therefore became famous at once and for ever. An obelisk at Princes Risborough records to this day his valiant assertion that the inland counties have no concern for the Royal Navy, except in so far as Parliament shall require them to pay. The Crown prevailed. The judges were justified in their decision. It does not even appear that the law was strained. But the grievance ran far and wide. Ninety per cent of ship money was eventually collected for the year 1637, but only 20 per cent for 1639. Everywhere persons of property looked up from their pleasant life and began to use again the language of the Petition of Right.

*　　*　　*

The Parliamentary party knew that to foster religious agitation was the surest means of waking England from its apathy. Here emerges the figure of the man who of all others was Charles's evil genius—William Laud, Archbishop of Canterbury. He was a convinced Anglican, wholehearted in his opposition both to Rome and to Geneva, and a leader in the movement away from Calvinism. But he had an itch for politics. Laud now found a new source of revenue for the Crown. Under the statutes of Elizabeth everyone was obliged to go to church; they might think as they liked, but they must conform in public worship. This practice had fallen into widespread disuse. Some did not trouble to go; to others it was abhorrent. Now all over England men and women found themselves haled before the justices for not attending church, and fined one shilling a time. Here indeed was something that ordinary men and women could understand. This was no question for lawyers and judges in the court of the Exchequer; it was something new and something teasing. The Puritans, already chafed,

1 7 5

regarded it as persecution.

Prosecutions of Prynne and other Puritan writers, and the pillorying, branding, and cropping of ears which they suffered in punishment, were isolated blots upon a regime mild and good-natured compared with that of other countries in the recent past or the approaching future. Indeed, it is by no means certain that, left to herself, England would have broken into revolt. It was in Scotland, the home of the Stuarts and Charles's birthplace, that the torch was lighted which began the vast conflagration. Laud was dissatisfied with the spiritual conditions prevailing in the Northern kingdom, and he moved the King to make some effort to improve them. The Scots must adopt the English Prayer Book, and enter broadly into communion with their English brethren. When in July, 1637, the dignitaries of Scottish Church and State were gathered in St. Giles's Church in Edinburgh for the first solemn reading of the new Prayer Book, an outburst of fury and insult overwhelmed the Dean when he sought to read the new dispensation. The ceremony became a riot. A surge of passion swept the ancient capital before which the episcopal and royal authorities trembled. Edinburgh had defied the Crown, and no force was found to resist it. A tempest was blowing which bore men forward. It embodied the unalterable resolve of a whole people to perish rather than submit to Popery. Nothing of this sort had ever been intended or dreamed of by the King; but this was the storm he had aroused. He was expostulating with a whirlwind. It was agreed that a General Assembly should be convoked.

*   *   *

The King was confronted with a hostile and organised Assembly, gathered to adjust religious differences, but whose aims were definitely political and whose demand was the actual and virtual abolition of the Episcopacy. He ordered the dissolution of the Assembly. That body declared itself resolved to continue in permanent session. They took this step with full knowledge of what it meant. The refusal of the General Assembly of Scotland in November, 1638, to dissolve upon the demand of the King's commissioner has been compared to that of the French National Assembly in 1789, when for the first time the members resisted the royal will. The facts and circumstances no doubt were different; but both events led by unbroken chains of causation to the same end, namely, the solemn beheading of a king.

In a few months, and long before any effective preparations could be made in England, Scotland had the strongest armed force in the Island. It had military knowledge and good officers. It had more: it was inspired with earnest, slowly roused, and now fanatical religious passion. The preachers, sword at side, carbine in hand, aided the drill-sergeants with their exhortations.

By the end of 1639 Charles saw himself confronted with an independent State and Government in the North, which, though it paid formal homage to him as King, was resolved to pursue its own policy both at home and abroad. It thus challenged not only the King's Prerogative, but the integrity of his dominions. He felt bound to fight. But how?

* * *

At this decisive moment England's monarchy might well have conformed to the absolutism which was becoming general throughout Europe. Events, however, took a different turn. The King concluded that Parliament must be summoned. In his over-confidence he thought that the Commons would prove manageable. He was wrong. But a momentous step was taken. After nearly eleven years of Personal Rule elections were held throughout England. This opened the world-famous struggle of Parliament against the King. From the moment when the new, afterwards called the Short, Parliament met, Pym was the central figure. Charles and Laud found no comfort from the new assembly. On the contrary, they were met by such a temper that by an act of extreme imprudence it was dissolved after a few days. Its calling had served only to excite and engage the whole of England in the controversy.

Presently the Scots crossed the Tweed and met with no opposition until they reached the Tyne. Then the two hosts faced one another. The Scottish leaders were encouraged in their invasion by the Parliamentary and Puritan movements throughout England, and in the centre of this combination stood Pym. For some days little happened, but one morning a Scottish horseman, watering his horse in the river, came too near the English outposts. Some one pulled a trigger; the shot went home; the imprudent rider was wounded; all the Scots cannon fired and all the English army fled. A contemporary wrote that "Never so many ran from so few with less ado."

The King could not defend the country himself. Only Parliament could save the land from what had now become an act of Scottish aggression. At this moment King Charles's moral position was at its worst. He had plumbed the depths of personal failure.

CHAPTER THIRTY-SEVEN

The Revolt of Parliament

INEXORABLE FORCES compelled the King to do what he most feared. There arose from all quarters a cry that Parliament should be summoned. The King had himself arrived at the same conclusion. In these days his outlook underwent a decided change. He recognised that his theory of monarchy must be modified. In summoning the new Parliament he accepted a different relationship between the people and the Crown.

Thus on November 3, 1640, was installed the second longest and most memorable Parliament that ever sat in England. It derived its force from a blending of political and religious ideas. It was upborne by the need of a growing society to base itself upon a wider foundation than Tudor Paternal rule.

The main feature of the Puritan Revolution for our generation is its measured restraint. The issues were fought out with remorseless antagonism, not only in Parliament by men who glared upon one another and were prepared to send each other to the scaffold, but also in the streets of London, where rival mobs or bands came face to face or even mingled. Respect for law and for human life nevertheless prevailed. In this mortal struggle physical violence was long held in check, and even when it broke into civil war all those conventions were observed which protect even the sternest exercise of the human will from the animal barbarism of earlier and of later times.

* * *

The accession of James I had involved the union of the Crowns of England and Scotland; but now in a manner very different from what James or his son had conceived there was a union of the dominant political parties in both countries, and they strove together for a common cause. Here then was an explosive charge, pent in strong cannon and directed upon King Charles and those who were his trusted Ministers. Of these the first and most obnoxious was Strafford who had gone over to the King and become a member of the Privy Council. Pym and Hampden, the leading figures in the new House of Commons, were immediately in command of a large and indignant majority. Strafford possessed convincing proofs of the correspondence carried on by Pym and others with the invading Scots. This was plain treason if the King's writ ran. It was believed that Strafford meant to open this formidable case; but Pym struck first. All the rage of the Parliamentary party, all the rancour of old comradeship forsworn, all that self-preservation dictated, concentrated upon "the wicked Earl" a blast of fury such as was never recorded in England before or since.

On the morning of November 11 the doors of St. Stephen's Chapel were locked; the key placed upon the table; no strangers might enter, no Member might leave. Late in the afternoon Pym and Hampden, attended by three hundred Members, carried the articles of Strafford's impeachment up to the House of Lords. At the King's request Strafford had come to London. In the morning he had been greeted with respect by the peers. Hearing what was afoot, he returned to the Chamber. But now all was changed. He was received with a hollow murmur. Shouts were raised that he should withdraw while the issue was being debated. He was forced to do so. In less than an hour the powerful Minister saw himself transformed into an accused prisoner. He found himself to his own and the general surprise kneeling at the Bar to receive the directions of his peers. He was deprived of his sword and taken into custody by Black Rod. As he went through the crowd on his journey to Black Rod's house the hostility of the populace was terrible.

The trial of Strafford had begun. Proceeding as they did upon admittedly rival interpretations of law and justice, the Commons at once found difficulty in establishing a case against the hated Minister. That he was the arch enemy of all that the majority championed, and indeed of the rights and liberties of the nation, was apparent. But to prove him guilty of the capital offence of treason was not possible. Strafford defended himself with magnificent ability. Each morning he knelt to the Lord Steward and bowed to the lords and to the assembly. Each day by logic and appeal he broke up the heads of accusation.

Now Pym and his colleagues made a deadly stroke. Sir Henry Vane, Secretary of the Privy Council, had a son who purloined a note which his father had preserved of the discussion in the King's Council on May 5, 1640. The cryptic sentiments ascribed to Strafford were: "You have an army in Ireland you may employ here to reduce this kingdom. Confident as anything under Heaven, Scotland shall not hold out five months . . ."

The Commons declared that this convicted Strafford of advising the use of an Irish army to subdue England. A Bill of Attainder passed the House of Commons by two hundred and four votes to fifty-nine. Only half the Lords dared to vote upon the Bill of Attainder, and these sent Strafford to his doom. The cry for "Justice" rang through London streets. A mob of several thousand, many of them armed, appeared before the palace roaring for Strafford's head.

This was the agony of Charles's life, to which none of his other sufferings compared. The question was not now whether he could save Strafford, but whether the royal authority would perish with him. At last Charles made the surrender which haunted him to the last moment of his life. He gave his assent to the Bill of Attainder. But conscience stirred in him still. Abandoning his kingly authority, on the next day he sent the young Prince of Wales to beg the House of Lords to reduce the sentence from death to perpetual imprisonment. Those peers who still attended refused, and even an appeal for a few days of grace in which the victim might settle his worldly affairs was denied.

Strafford died with fortitude and dignity. He was beyond doubt a man conscious of commanding gifts, impelled by high ambition and a desire to rule. He had sought power by the path of Parliament. He had found it in the favour of the Crown. The circumstances of his trial and of the Attainder threw odium upon his pursuers. They slaughtered a man they could not convict. But that man, if given his full career, would have closed perhaps for generations the windows of civic freedom upon the English people.

*   *   *

179

But everything was now fluid, and in that strong-willed, rugged, obstinate England men, without regard to their former actions, looked about them for sure foothold. From the day when Strafford's head fell beneath the axe there began a conservative reaction, partial but nationwide. Charles, who at the meeting of the Parliament had been almost alone with his cluster of hated Ministers, found himself increasingly sustained by strong and deep currents of public feeling. If he had only allowed these to have their flow he might have reached a very good establishment. The excesses and fanaticism of the Puritan party, their war upon the Church, their confederacy with the Scottish invaders, roused antagonisms of which the hitherto helpless Court was but a spectator, but from which the Crown might by patience and wisdom emerge, curtailed certainly but secure. Henceforward the quarrel was no longer between King and people, but between the two main themes and moods which have until the confusion of the modern age disputed for mastery in England. The twentieth century was to dawn before men and women became unable to recognise their political ancestors in this ancient conflict.

Charles now felt that his hope lay in a reconciliation with Scotland. The interplay of the Scots army in the North with the Puritan faction at Westminster was irresistible. He resolved to go to Scotland himself and open a Parliament in Edinburgh. Pym and his adherents could hardly object to this. Charles accepted everything he had most abhorred. He strove to win the hearts of the Covenanters. He listened devoutly to their sermons and sang the psalms in the manner of the Kirk. He assented to the establishment of total Presbyterianism in Scotland. But all was in vain, and the King returned to England crestfallen.

Upon this melancholy scene a hideous apparition now appeared. The execution of Strafford liberated all the elemental forces in Ireland which his system had so successfully held in restraint. The passions of the original inhabitants and of the hungry, down-trodden masses, bursting from all control, were directed upon the gentry, the landowners, and the Protestants, both within and without the Pale. A veritable Jacquerie, recalling the dark times in France, broke upon the land in the autumn of 1641. The propertied classes, their families and dependents, fled to the few garrisoned towns. Cruelties unspeakable were reported on all sides, and the Government, under the Lords Justices, struck back without mercy. A general slaughter of males and a policy of devastation were proclaimed throughout large parts of the countryside. As the tale of these atrocities crept home to England it gave a shock to men's minds which even amid their own preoccupations lasted long. It was deeply harmful to the King's interests. The Puritan party saw, or declared that they saw, in the Irish outrage the fate to which they would be consigned if the Popish tendencies of the bishops were armed with the sword of an absolute sovereign. They regarded the native Irish as wild beasts to be slain at sight, and the cruelties which they in their turn were to wreak in their hour of triumph took their impulse from this moment.

* * *

During September and October conservative reaction had become a tide. Who could accuse the Court of army plots when the English and Irish armies had both been disbanded? Englishmen, irrespective of religious and constitutional convictions, were ill disposed to be taxed for the upkeep of invading Scottish troops. Presbyterianism made little appeal to the bulk of the English people, who, so far as they were not satisfied with the Elizabethan Church tradition, sought spiritual comfort or excitement in the more vehement sects which had sprung up in the general turmoil of the Reformation, or in the Puritan body itself, such as Anabaptism and Brownism, both of which were as much opposed to Presbytery as to Bishops. The House of Commons at the end of 1641 had travelled far. Pym and his supporters were still dominant and more extreme. But there was an opposition equally resolute. The Lords were now at variance with the Commons, and a large majority, when they attended, sided with the King. From being the servants of the national cause, the Puritans had become an aggressive faction. But the argument, even in that persevering age, was becoming too long and harassing for mere words. Men felt their right hands itching to grasp the swords by which alone it seemed their case could be urged.

It was in this stormy weather that Pym and Hampden sought to rally their forces by bringing forward what was called the "Grand Remonstrance." This long document was intended to advertise all that had so far been accomplished by Parliament in remedying old grievances, and to proclaim the future policy of the Parliamentary leaders. Pym would appeal to the people and win complete control for Parliament over the King's Ministers. Here was a sweeping challenge to royal authority. But the King now had at his side very different counsellors from those of a year before, among them Edward Hyde, later famous as the Historian Clarendon, who opened the debate by insisting that the aim must now be peace; if the Remonstrance were carried, and especially if it were published, the disputes would be embittered and prolonged.

The debate was long and earnest, vehement with restrained passion. At last, at midnight, the Remonstrance, somewhat amended, was put to the vote and carried only by eleven votes.

A hitherto little-noticed Member for Cambridge, Oliver Cromwell, rather rough in his manners, but an offshoot of Thomas Cromwell's line, said to Falkland as they left the House, "If the Remonstrance had been rejected

I would have sold all that I had next morning, and never have seen England any more; and I know there are many honest men of the same resolution." He, and Pym also, looked across the ocean to new lands where the cause for which they were prepared to die, or kill, could breathe, albeit in a wilderness. Their sentiments awoke echoes in America that were not to be stilled until more than a century later, and after much bloodshed.

*　　*　　*

The King was now drawn into various contradictory blunders. Charles resolved to prosecute five of his principal opponents in the Commons for high treason. Upon this wild course he was impelled by Queen Henrietta Maria. She taunted him with cowardice, and exhorted him, if he would ever see her again, to lay strong hands upon those who spent their nights and days seeking his overthrow and her life. He certainly convinced himself that Pym meant to impeach the Queen.

Thus goaded, Charles, accompanied by three or four hundred swords-men—"Cavaliers" we may now call them—went down to the House of Commons. It was January 4, 1642. Never before had a king set foot in the Chamber. When his officers knocked at the door and it was known that he had come in person members of all parties looked upon each other in amazement. His followers beset the doors. All rose at his entry. The Speaker quitted his chair and knelt before him. But a treacherous message from a lady of the Queen's Bedchamber had given Pym a timely warning. The accused Members had already embarked at Westminster steps. The King, conscious of his mistake, cast his eyes around the quivering assembly. "I see that the birds are flown," he said lamely, and after some civil reassurances he departed.

Upon this episode the wrath of London became uncontrollable. The infuriated mobs who thronged the streets and bellowed outside the palace caused Charles and his Court to escape from the capital to Hampton Court. He never saw London again except to suffer trial and death. By stages he withdrew to Newmarket, to Nottingham, and to York. There were now two centres of government. Pym, the Puritans, and what was left of the Parliament ruled with dictatorial power in London in the King's name. The King, round whom there gathered many of the finest elements in Old England, became once again a prince with sovereign rights. About these two centres there slowly assembled the troops and resources for the waging of civil war.

The Great Rebellion

THE NEGOTIATIONS between King and Parliament which occupied the early months of 1642 served only to emphasise their differences while both were gathering their forces. On June 1, 1642, Parliament presented nineteen Propositions to the King. This ultimatum, in brief, invited the King to surrender his whole effective sovereignty over Church and State. But underlying the apparently clear-cut constitutional issue was a religious and class conflict.

When the alignment of the parties on the outbreak of the Civil War is surveyed no simple divisions are to be found. Brother fought against brother, father against son. On both sides men went into the fight doubtfully, but guided by their belief in high-souled ideals. On both sides were others—dissolute courtiers, ambitious politicians spoiling for a fight, out-of-work mercenaries, ready to profit from the national dissensions; but, broadly, the contest now became a tragic conflict of loyalties and ideals.

The arrogant tone and ever-growing demands of the Parliamentary party shaped the lines of the struggle and recruited the forces of the King. The greater part of the nobility gradually rallied to the Royalist cause; the tradesmen and merchants generally inclined to the Parliament; but a substantial section of the aristocracy were behind Pym, and many boroughs were devotedly Royalist. The gentry and yeomen in the counties were deeply divided. Those nearer London generally inclined to Parliament, while the North and West remained largely Royalist. Both sides fought in the name of the King, and both upheld the Parliamentary institution. The Roundheads always spoke of "King and Parliament." The orders given to their first Commander-in-Chief, the Earl of Essex, directed him to "rescue" the King and princes, if necessary by force, from the evil counsellors into whose power they had fallen. Charles vowed himself to live as a constitutional monarch and to respect the laws of the realm. Behind all class and political issues the religious quarrel was the driving power. In Cromwell's words, "Religion was not the thing at first contested for, but God brought it to that issue at last; and gave it unto us by way of redundancy; and at last it proved that which was most dear to us."

For more than seventy years absolute peace had reigned in England. Except for a few officers who had seen service on the Continent, no one knew anything about military matters. At first the Cavaliers, trained in fencing, inured to the chase, with their gamekeepers and dependents, had a military advantage over the Roundheads.

Throughout angry England, divided in every shire, in every town, in every village, and often in the very bosom of families, all eyes had been fixed upon the clash and manœuvre of the two main armies. The hopes of both sides were that these would give a decision, and thereafter peace. When it was seen that nothing of the kind would happen, and that a long, balanced struggle lay ahead, all suspended antagonisms started into action. Fighting and pillage spread throughout the country. The constitutional issue, the religious quarrel, and countless local feuds were combined in a new surge of party hatred. The lines of strife correspond geographically in a broad degree to those upon which the Conservative and Liberal Parties voted and vociferated in the nineteenth century. The cleavages of the great Civil War dominated English life for two centuries, and many strange examples of their persistency survive under universal suffrage in English constituencies today.

From the beginning of 1643 the war became general. Classes and interests as well as parties and creeds did their best against one another. The ports and towns, the manufacturing centres, mostly adhered to the Parliament; what might be called Old England rallied to Charles. In the two great areas of the North and the West the King's cause prospered.

Charles set up his standard on August 22 and called his loyal subjects to his aid. The quality of the Parliamentary forces was inferior, but they made up in zeal what they lacked in discipline and military skill. The King struck south for the Thames valley and London. At Edgehill, on October 23, the battle was marked by abundant ignorance and zeal on both sides. After confused and bloody fighting even Charles's own guards were broken. Both sides retired to their morning positions and gazed at each other in doubt and confusion.

At first the decisive action was not in the North, but in the West. In the confused fighting of 1643 the Royalists inflicted a sharp but not a decisive defeat on the Parliamentary army at Lansdown, outside Bath, and moved on to capture Bristol, then the second city of the Kingdom. The warships in the port declared for the King, and hope dawned of a royal squadron which could command the Bristol Channel. King Charles was master of the West. His cause also prevailed in Yorkshire, and in the Midlands as well.

Charles, who possessed a certain strategic comprehension, then planned a general advance on London from the West, the North, and Oxford. First, he felt, he had to reduce Gloucester, the sole stronghold remaining to the Parliament between Bristol and York. On August 5 the city was invested.

Meanwhile in London Pym, the master of Parliament, the heart and soul of the Roundhead war, was in grievous straits. So far all had gone ill, and every hope had been broken. As head of the Government he was obliged to raise money for an increasingly unpopular war by methods as little conformable to the principles he championed as those which Charles had

ENGLAND
DURING THE
CIVIL WAR

COUNTRY HELD BY THE
ROYALISTS AT THE END OF 1643

✕ BATTLES

SCOTLAND

Dunbar ✕
Edinburgh •
Berwick

Newcastle •

Scarborough ·

Bridlington ·

Marston
Moor ✕ •York·
Preston ✕ Hull
Adwalton Moor ✕ Selby
Lathom House ✻ ✕ Winceby

✕ Newark ·
Winnington
Bridge
Nottingham ·

Shrewsbury ·
✕ Naseby Newmarket ·

Edge
Worcester Hill Northampton ·
✕ ✕ Cropredy Bridge
Gloucester Oxford
Chalgrove Field ✕
Brentford · LONDON
✕ Turnham Green

Bristol
Newbury ✕ ·
Landsdowne ✕ Roundway Down

Carisbrooke
Castle

Lostwithiel ✕
✕ Plymouth ·

used against the Scots in 1640. Forced loans and direct taxation of almost everyone were among his devices. Strong currents of Royalism now flowed in the capital. These joined themselves to the peace movement. Even the Commons, by a narrow majority in a thin House, agreed to a Peace resolution.

Pym's life was ebbing to its close. He had cancer. His greatest colleague, Hampden, had died of wounds early in the year after a clash with Rupert's cavalry. The ruin of his cause and the approach of death in an array of disaster seemed to be the only reward of Pym's struggle. Undaunted, he bore up against all; and the last impulse of his life may well have turned the scale. All the Puritan forces in London were roused to repudiate peace. The preachers exhorted their congregations, and warlike crowds beset Westminster. The House of Commons rescinded their conciliatory resolution, and now the relief of Gloucester was the cry.

At Gloucester Governor Massey had failed the King. The King's resources, indeed the art of war in England at this time, afforded no satisfactory method of making a siege. The King had made no progress against the city when, in the early days of September, Essex and the London army drew near in superior numbers. There was no choice but to raise the siege and retire upon Oxford.

*   *   *

The King's large plan for 1643 failed. Nevertheless the campaign had been very favourable to him. He had gained control of a great part of England. His troops were still, on the whole, better fighting-men than the Roundheads. Much ground lost at the beginning of the war had been recovered. Then on December 8 Pym died, uncheered by success, but unwearied by misfortune. He had neglected his private affairs in the public cause, and his estate would have been bankrupt had not Parliament, as some expression of their grief and gratitude, paid his debts. He remains the most famous of the old Parliamentarians, and the man who more than any other saved England from absolute monarchy and set her upon the path she has since pursued.

*   *   *

There was a lull during the winter. Charles, declaring that the Parliament at Westminster was no longer a free Parliament, summoned all who had been expelled or who had fled from it to a Counter-Assembly. The response was remarkable. Eighty-three peers and a hundred and seventy-five Members met in Oxford on January 22, 1644.

But these advantages were overwhelmed by the arrival in England of a Scottish army who crossed the Tweed in January. For this succour the London Parliament paid £31,000 a month and the cost of equipment. Glittering prospects were opened to Scottish ambition. They had the best of both worlds; they were invited to invade a wealthy country at its own expense in the cause of Almighty God and their own particular style of public worship. Punctual cash payments and assured salvation awaited them across the Border. For the honour of Scotland it must be said that the Edinburgh Assembly, which lent itself to such a policy, contained a strong minority. It was effectively suppressed.

CHAPTER THIRTY-NINE

Marston Moor and Naseby

THE KING at the beginning of 1644 had the larger part of the country behind him, and a considerable Parliament of his own which met in Oxford. Military victory in England seemed within his grasp. The Scots reversed the balance. Their ascendancy became decisive.

It was now that Oliver Cromwell came into prominence. The Member for Cambridge was deemed the best officer on the Parliamentary side, though he had not yet held a supreme command. He had triumphed at Gainsborough in a dark hour. His regiment had a discipline and quality surpassing, as it seemed, any other formation on either side. He could not be ignored. He could not be suppressed. The rise of Cromwell to the first rank of power during 1644 sprang both from his triumphs on the battlefield and his resistance to the Presbyterians and the Scots at Westminster. Except for Papists and Episcopalians, he declared for liberty of conscience. All the obscurer Protestant sects saw in him their champion. Thus, not for the first or last time, theology waited upon arms; and in the long run it was the alliance of the Anglican and Presbyterian against their common enemy, the Independent, that restored both the monarchy and the Established Church.

In the North the Marquis of Newcastle had to contend with the Scottish army on one side and the two Fairfaxes on the other. Presently he found himself besieged in York. The loss of York would ruin the King's cause in the North. Charles therefore sent Prince Rupert, with a strong cavalry force which gathered strength as it marched, to relieve the city. Rupert fought his way into Lancashire, striking heavy blows on all sides. Lathom House was freed. Stockport was plundered; Bolton stormed. On June 1 Lord Goring with five thousand horse joined the Prince. Together they took Liverpool. Then Rupert saved York at its last gasp. The Scots and Roundheads withdrew together westwards, covering Leeds and joining forces from East Anglia under Lord Manchester and Cromwell. The three Puritan armies numbering twenty thousand foot and seven thousand horse lay upon a ridge at Marston Moor. Rupert met the Marquis of Newcastle and their united forces reached eleven thousand foot and seven thousand horse. The Royalist army followed the enemy to Marston Moor and on July 2 found themselves near their encampments. The whole day passed in alternating rain and sunshine, with both armies in close contact. Rupert imagined that it rested with him to begin the battle, but he was himself attacked by the whole force of the Roundheads, who outnumbered his infantry by nearly two to one. A heavy column of steel-clad cavalry was seen approaching at a fast trot. It was Cromwell and his Ironsides. The royal army, who, though drawn up, were preparing to eat their evening meal, had neither the advantage of a defensive position nor the impulsion of attack. None the less they made a glorious fight. Goring's cavalry of the left wing beat the Roundhead right, and, falling upon the Scots in the centre, threw them into disorder and retreat. The veteran Alexander Leslie, now Lord Leven, quitted the field, declaring all was lost, and was arrested by a constable ten miles away. But Cromwell, with the help of the remaining Scots under David Leslie, restored the day. Now for the first time the heroic, dreaded Cavaliers met their match, and their master. "We drove the entire cavalry of the Prince off the field," wrote Cromwell. "God made them as stubble to our swords."

Marston Moor was the largest and also the bloodiest battle of the war. Little quarter was given and there were four thousand slain. A disaster of the first magnitude had smitten the King's cause. His Northern army was shattered and the whole of the North was lost.

* * *

Winter approached, but the war did not slacken. The Cavaliers, undiscouraged by their dwindling territory and the superior numbers and resources of the Roundheads, defended themselves in every county where they had a stronghold. Charles re-entered Oxford in triumph. In the teeth of adversity he had maintained himself against odds of two or three to one.

Cromwell rode in from the Army to his duties as a Member of Parliament. He now made a vehement and organised attack on the conduct of the war. He himself was avid for the power and command which he was sure he could wield; but he proceeded astutely.

During the winter months the Army was reconstituted in accordance with Cromwell's ideas. The Roundhead faction now had a symmetrical military organisation led by men who had risen in the field and had no other standing but their military record and religious zeal. In June, 1645, Cromwell was appointed General of the Horse, and was thus the only man who combined high military command with an outstanding Parliamentary position. From this moment he became the dominant figure in both spheres.

Amid these stresses Archbishop Laud, who languished ailing in the Tower, was brought to the scaffold. Roundheads, Scots, and Puritans alike could all combine upon this act of hatred. The House of Commons upon a division rejected his appeal to be decapitated rather than hanged, drawn, and quartered. Overnight, however, this barbarous decision was mitigated, and after he had uttered an unyielding discourse the old man's head was chopped off in a dignified manner.

The desire of all Englishmen for an end to the unnatural strife forced itself upon the most inflamed partisans. Large numbers assembled in many parts of the country, protesting against the exactions and pillage of the contending forces. A parley for a peace settlement was set on foot at Uxbridge, but neither King Charles nor the Roundhead executive had the slightest intention of giving way upon the two main points—Episcopacy and the control of the armed forces. Uxbridge only proved the ferocious constancy of both parties in their struggle for supreme power.

At the same time the Marquis of Montrose sprang upon the scene. He had been a Covenanter, but having quarrelled with Argyll went over to the King. Now he made himself known to history as a noble character and brilliant general. He pledged his faith to Charles, and distracted all Scotland by a series of victories gained against much larger forces, although sometimes his men had only stones to throw before falling on with the claymore. Dundee, Aberdeen, Glasgow, Perth, and Edinburgh were at one time or another in his power. He wrote to Charles assuring him that he would bring all Scotland to his rescue if he could hold out. But a decisive battle impended in the South.

On June 14, 1645, the last trial of strength was made. Charles met Fairfax and Cromwell in the fine hunting country about Naseby. The Cavaliers did not hesitate to attack uphill the Roundhead army of twice their numbers. The action followed what had almost become the usual course. Cromwell drove all before him. Quarter was given, and the butchery was less than at Marston Moor. A hundred Irish women who were found in the Royalist camp were put to the sword by the Ironsides on grounds of moral principle as well as of national prejudice. Naseby was the expiring effort of the Cavaliers in the open field. There still remained many sieges, with reliefs and manœuvrings, but the final military decision of the Civil War had been given.

CHAPTER FORTY

The Axe Falls

BY THE spring of 1646 all armed resistance to the Parliamentary Army was beaten down. The Puritans had triumphed. In the main the middle class, being more solid for Parliament, had beaten the aristocracy and gentry, who were divided. The new money-power of the City had beaten the old loyalties. The townsfolk had mastered the countryside. What would some day be the "Chapel" had beaten the Church. There were many contrary examples, but upon the whole this was how it lay. The Constitution, however, was still unsettled. All that Charles had stood for in the days of his Personal Rule was swept away; but much wider issues, for which the nation and the times were unripe and unready, had been opened. All these focused in the office and the person of the King. Charles was now ready to yield upon the control of the armed forces, but for the sake of the Episcopal establishment of the Church of England he was prepared to continue the struggle singlehanded. The King thought to come to London alone and argue what had been lost in war with his subjects. He apparently had no fear for the security of his person. He had persuaded himself he was a guest; but he soon found he was a prisoner. Kept in hard circumstances, he entered upon nearly a year's tenacious bargainings on the national issues at stake.

The King naturally hoped to profit by the differences between Parliament and the Army and between the English and Scottish Governments. When the Scots had taken their payment Charles was led with the greatest deference southwards. His popularity became at once manifest. The journey was a progress of cheering crowds and clashing bells. To greet the King, to be freed from the cruel wars, to have the Old England back again, no doubt with some important changes, was the national wish. Charles was still incomparably the most important figure in England. Every one was for the King, provided he would do what they wished.

But a third and new partner had appeared upon the English scene. The Ironside Army, twenty-two thousand strong, was not yet the master, but was no longer the servant, of those who had created it. At its head stood its renowned and trusted generals: Thomas Fairfax, Commander-in-Chief; Oliver Cromwell, its sun of glory.

Now that the war was won most Members of Parliament and their leaders had no more need of the Army. But here a matter very awkward on such occasions obtruded itself. The pay of the Army was in arrears. A serious dispute between Parliament and the Army thus began, both sides flushed with the sense of having a victory in their hands for which they deserved a reward.

Even after Marston Moor and Naseby the victorious Ironsides sought a guarantee which would be national and permanent, and for all the tight-knit majority organisation at Westminster this guarantee the kingly office alone could supply. Here is the salient fact which distinguishes the English Revolution from all others: that those who wielded irresistible physical force were throughout convinced that it could give them no security. Nothing is more characteristic of the English people than their instinctive reverence even in rebellion for law and tradition. Deep in the nature of the men who had broken the King's power was the conviction that law in his name was the sole foundation on which they could build.

Cromwell felt that if they could get hold of the King physically, and before Parliament did so, it would be much. If they could gain him morally it would be all. Now in early June, on Cromwell's orders, Cornet Joyce, with near four hundred Ironside troopers, rode to Holmby House, where the King was agreeably residing. In the morning Cornet Joyce intimated with due respect that he had come to remove the King. Charles made no protest. He walked out on to the terrace and eyed the solid buff and steel array with an almost proprietary air. "I have promised," said Joyce to his troopers, "three things in your name. You will do no harm to His Majesty's person; you will force him to nothing against his conscience; you will allow his servants to accompany him. Do you all promise?" "All," was the cry. "And now, Mr. Joyce," said the King, "tell me, where is your commission? Have you anything in writing from Sir Thomas Fairfax?" Cornet Joyce was embarrassed. He looked this way and that, but finally he said, pointing to the regiment, "Here!" "Indeed," said the King, with the compulsive smile and confidence of sovereignty and Divine Right. "It is one I can read without spelling: as handsome and proper a company of gentlemen as I have seen this many a day. . . . Where next, Mr. Joyce?" Off they all rode together, a jingling and not unhappy company, feeling they had English history in their hands.

Behind all this was a great political and personal deal. At this moment there was at finger tips a settlement in the power of the English people and near to their hearts' desire. But, of course, it was too good to be true. Not so easily can mankind escape from the rigours of its pilgrimage.

The only chance for the arrangement between Charles and Cromwell was that it should be carried swiftly into effect. Instead there was delay. The mood of the soldiers became increasingly morose; and the generals saw themselves in danger of losing control over them. The Army marched on London, occupied Westminster, entered the City, and everything except their problems fell prostrate before them.

* * *

191

In the autumn of 1647 the Army held keen debate. At Putney they wrestled with one another and with their ideas long and earnestly for weeks. All sorts of new figures sprang up; these spoke with fervour and power, and every time they hit the bull's eye. Cromwell listened to sentences like these: "The poorest he that is in England hath a life to live as the greatest he," and "a man is not bound to a system of government which he hath not had any hand in setting over him." It was a brew of hot Gospel and cold steel. Cromwell heard all this and brooded over it. His outlook was Elizabethan. He thought such claims would lead to anarchy. His thoughts wandered back to his landed estate. Clearly this was dangerous nonsense. Apart from all political talk, Cromwell had to think of discipline. He still held power. He used it without delay. Under these stresses the combination between the defeated King and the victorious generals finally splintered.

In November the King, convinced that he would be murdered by the soldiery, whom their officers could no longer restrain, rode off in the night, and by easy stages made his way to Carisbrooke Castle, in the Isle of Wight. Here, where a donkey treads an endless water wheel, he dwelt for almost a year, defenceless, sacrosanct, a spiritual King, a coveted tool, an intriguing parcel, an ultimate sacrifice. There still resided in him a principle which must be either exploited or destroyed; but in England he no longer had the power to make a bargain. There remained the Scots. With them he signed a secret Engagement by which Royalism and Presbyterianism were to be allied. From this conjunction there shortly sprang the Second Civil War.

* * *

The story of the Second Civil War is short and simple. King, Lords and Commons, landlords and merchants, the City and the countryside, bishops and presbyters, the Scottish army, the Welsh people, and the English Fleet, all now turned against the New Model Army. The Army beat the lot. And at their head was Cromwell. Their plight at first might well have seemed desperate; but this very fact wiped out all divisions among them. Fairfax, Cromwell, Ireton, were now once again united to their fierce warriors. The Army marched and fought. They marched to Wales; they marched to Scotland, and none could withstand them. A mere detachment sufficed to quell a general rising in Cornwall and the West. They broke the Royalist forces at Colchester. Cromwell, having subdued the Welsh rising, moved swiftly to the North, picked up his forces, and fell on the Scottish army as it was marching through Lancashire. Although David Leslie led it this was not the old Army of Scotland. The trained Scottish forces, under Lord Leven, stood aside. The invaders were cut off, caught, and destroyed at Preston. The Fleet, which had been so potent a few years back against a struggling King, could do little against this all-mastering, furious Army which stalked

Oliver Cromwell

the land in rags, almost barefoot, but with bright armour, sharp swords, and sublime conviction of its wrongheaded mission.

* * *

By the end of 1648 all was over. Cromwell was Dictator. The Royalists were crushed; Parliament was a tool; the Constitution was a figment; the Scots were rebuffed, the Welsh back in their mountains; the Fleet was reorganised, London overawed. King Charles, at Carisbrooke Castle, was left to pay the bill. It was mortal.

* * *

We must not be led by Victorian writers into regarding this triumph of the Ironsides and of Cromwell as a kind of victory for democracy and the Parliamentary system over Divine Right and Old World dreams. It was the triumph of some twenty thousand resolute, ruthless, disciplined, military fanatics over all that England has ever willed or ever wished. Long years and unceasing irritations were required to reverse it. Thus the struggle, in which we have in these days so much sympathy and part, begun to bring about a constitutional and limited monarchy, had led only to the autocracy of the sword. The harsh, terrific, lightning-charged being, whose erratic, opportunist, self-centred course is laid bare upon the annals, was now master, and the next twelve years are the record of his well-meant, puzzled plungings and surgings.

Plainly the fruit of the victory that could most easily be gathered was the head of the King. One stormy evening, with the rain beating down, in the Isle of Wight it was noticed that many boat-loads of Ironside soldiery were being rowed across the Solent and landed at Newport and Cowes. The King's household made inquiries and kept vigilant watch. His trusty friends urged flight. Charles had enough confidence in the strength of his position to reject the opportunity. It was his last. A few days later he was brought to the mainland and confined.

Hitherto his personal dignity and comfort had always been consulted. Now, with scarcely a personal attendant, he found himself shut in the candleless gloom of a small tower prison. And in this darkness the King rose to his greatest height. His troublous, ill-starred reign had shown him in many wrong attitudes; but at the end he was to be granted by Fate the truly magnificent and indisputable role of the champion of English—nay, British, for all the Island was involved—rights and liberty.

The Army meant to have his blood in the manner which would most effectively vindicate their power and their faith. Cromwell, who had nothing else to give his burning legions, could at least present them with an awful and all-dominating scene of expiation. Charles was reassured against murder. All was respect and ceremony. A strange interlude! But now forward to London; much is afoot there. "Will Your Majesty graciously be pleased to set forth?"

The great trial of "the Man of Blood" was to be presented to the nation and to the world. English law and precedent were scoured from the most remote times, but no sanction or even cover for such a proceeding could be found. The slaying of princes had many examples. Edward II at Berkeley Castle, Richard II at Pontefract, had met terrible fates; but these were deeds wrapped in secrecy, disavowed by authority, covered at the time by mystery or the plea of natural causes. Here the victorious Army meant to teach the English people that henceforward they must obey; and Cromwell now saw in Charles's slaughter his only chance of supremacy and survival. An ordinance passed by the docile remnant of the Commons created a court to try the King. The carpenters fitted Westminster Hall for its most memorable scene. This was not only the killing of a king, but the killing of a king who at that time represented the will and the traditions of almost the whole British nation.

*   *   *

The more detail in which the famous trial has been described the greater is the sense of drama. The King, basing himself upon the law and Constitution he had strained and exploited in his years of prosperity, confronted his enemies with an unbreakable defence. He eyed his judges, as Morley says, "with unaffected scorn." He refused to acknowledge the tribunal. To him it was a monstrous illegality. John Bradshaw, the president of the court, could make no logical dint upon this. Cromwell and the Army could, however, cut off the King's head, and this at all costs they meant to do. The overwhelming sympathy of the great concourse gathered in Westminster Hall was with the King. When, on the afternoon of the final sitting, after being refused leave to speak, he was conducted from the Hall it was amid a low, intense murmur of "God save the King." But the soldiers, primed by their corporals, and themselves in high resolve, shouted, "Justice! Justice! Execution! Execution!"

On the morning of January 30, 1649, Charles was conducted from St. James's. Snow fell, and he had put on his warm underclothes. Most of those who had signed the death warrant were aghast at the deed of which they were to bear the weight and the ultimate vengeance.

At one o'clock in the afternoon Charles was informed that his hour had come. He walked through a window of the Banqueting House onto the scaffold. Masses of soldiers, many ranks deep, held an immense multitude afar. The King looked with a disdainful smile upon the cords and pulleys which had been prepared to fasten him down, upon the fantastic assumption that he would carry his repudiation of the tribunal which had condemned him even to physical lengths. He was allowed to speak as he chose. He said that "he died a good Christian, he had forgiven all the world, yea, chiefly those who had caused his death" (naming none). He resigned himself to death, and assisted the executioner in arranging his hair under a small white satin cap. He laid himself upon the block, and upon his own signal his head was struck off at a single stroke. His severed head was shown to the people, and someone cried, "This is the head of a traitor!"

A strange destiny had engulfed this King of England. None had resisted with more untimely stubbornness the movement of his age. He had been in his heyday the convinced opponent of all we now call our Parliamentary liberties. Yet as misfortunes crowded upon him he increasingly became the physical embodiment of the liberties and traditions of England. His mistakes and wrong deeds had risen not so much from personal cravings for arbitrary power as from the conception of kingship to which he was born and which had long been the settled custom of the land. In the end he stood against an army which had destroyed all Parliamentary government, and was about to plunge England into a tyranny at once more irresistible and more petty than any seen before or since. He did not flinch in any respect from the causes in which he believed. Although, no doubt, in bargainings and manœuvres with his enemies he had practised deceit and ill faith, these arose from the malignancy and ever-shifting character of the quarrel, and were amply matched upon the other side. But he never departed from his central theme, either in religion or State. He adhered unswervingly to the Prayer Book of the Reformed Church and to the Episcopacy, with which he conceived Christianity was interwoven. By his constancy, which underlay all the shifts and turns of tumultuous and swiftly changing years, he preserved the causes by which his life was guided. He was not a martyr in the sense of one who dies for a spiritual ideal. His own kingly interests were mingled at every stage with the larger issues. Some have sought to represent him as the champion of the small or humble man against the rising money-power. This is fanciful. He cannot be claimed as the defender of English liberties, nor wholly of the English Church, but none the less he died for them, and by his death preserved them not only to his son and heir, but to our own day.

BOOK SIX

The Restoration

CHAPTER FORTY-ONE

The English Republic

THE ENGLISH Republic had come into existence even before the execution of the King. On January 4, 1649, the handful of Members of the House of Commons who served the purposes of Cromwell and the Army resolved that "the people are, under God, the original of all just power . . . the supreme power in this nation."

It was essential to divide and disperse the Army, and Cromwell was willing to lead the larger part of it to a war of retribution in the name of the Lord Jehovah against the idolatrous and bloodstained Papists of Ireland. He discharged from the Army all men who would not volunteer for the Irish war. He invested his mission not only with martial but with a priestly aspect. He joined the Puritan divines in preaching a holy war upon the Irish.

Cromwell's campaign of 1649 in Ireland was equally cold-blooded and equally imbued with those Old Testament sentiments which dominated the minds of the Puritans. He resolved upon a deed of "frightfulness" deeply embarrassing to his nineteenth-century admirers and apologists. Having unsuccessfully summoned the garrison of the besieged town of Drogheda to surrender, he breached the ramparts with his cannon, and at the third assault, which he led himself, stormed the town. There followed a massacre so all-effacing as to startle even the opinion of those fierce times. All were put to the sword. None escaped; every priest and friar was butchered. The corpses were carefully ransacked for valuables. The Governor, Sir Arthur Ashton, had an artificial leg, which the Ironsides believed to be made of gold; however, it was only in his belt that they found his private fortune. The ferreting out and slaughter of those in hiding lasted till the third day.

In the safe and comfortable days of Queen Victoria, when Liberals and Conservatives, Gladstone and Disraeli, contended about the past, and when Irish Nationalists and Radical Nonconformists championed their old causes, a school grew up to gape in awe and some in furtive admiration at his savage crimes. Men thought such scenes were gone for ever, and that while moving into a broad age of peace, money-making, and debatings they could afford to pay their tributes to the rugged warriors who had laid the foundations of a liberal society. The twentieth century has sharply recalled its intellectuals from such vain indulgence. We have seen the technique of "frightfulness" applied in our own time with Cromwellian brutality and upon a far larger scale. We know too much of despots and their moods and power to practise the philosophic detachment of our grandfathers. It is necessary to recur to the simpler principle that the wholesale slaughter of unarmed or disarmed men marks with a mordant and eternal brand the memory of conquerors, however they may have prospered.

In Oliver's smoky soul there were evident misgivings. He writes of the "remorse and regret" which are inseparable from such crimes. By a terrifying example he believed that he had saved far greater bloodshed. But this did not prove true. Cromwell in Ireland, disposing of overwhelming strength and using it with merciless wickedness, debased the standards of human conduct and sensibly darkened the journey of mankind. Cromwell's Irish massacres find numberless compeers in the history of all countries during and since the Stone Age. It is therefore only necessary to strip men capable of such deeds of all title to honour, whether it be the light which plays around a great captain of war or the long repute which covers the severities of a successful prince or statesman.

We have seen the many ties which at one time or another have joined the inhabitants of the Western island and even in Ireland itself offered a tolerable way of life to Protestants and Catholics alike. Upon all these Cromwell's record was a lasting bane. By an uncompleted process of terror, by an iniquitous land settlement, by the virtual proscription of the Catholic religion, by bloody deeds he cut new gulfs between the nations and the creeds. The consequences of Cromwell's rule in Ireland have distressed and at times distracted English politics down even to the present day. To heal them baffled the skill and loyalties of successive generations. They became for a time a potent obstacle to the harmony of the English-speaking peoples throughout the world. Upon all of us there still lies "the curse of Cromwell."

*   *   *

At the moment when the axe severed the head of Charles the First from his body his eldest son became, in the opinion of most of his subjects and of Europe, King Charles the Second. Hard courses were laid before the young King. If, said the Scottish Government, you will embrace the Covenant and become the champion of the Presbyterian cause not only will we bring all Scotland under your sovereignty, but we will march with you into England. On the Dutch ship before the King landed in Scotland the most precise guarantees were extracted. When the King looked out from the windows of the house in which he was lodged, he found himself virtually a prisoner in the hands of those who had besought him to be their sovereign. He listened to endless sermons, admonitions, and objurgations. We may admire as polished flint the convictions and purposes of the Scots Government and its divines, but one must be thankful never to have been brought into contact with any of them.

There was again an army to fight for the Crown, and both Cardinal Mazarin in France and Prince William of Orange in Holland lent their aid to Scotland. The unhappy young King was forced, by the need to fight and the desire to win, to issue a declaration in which he desired to be "deeply humbled before God because of his father's opposition to the Solemn League and Covenant; and because his mother had been guilty of idolatry," Charles wondered whether he would dare to look his mother in the face again, and in fact she told him she would never again be his political adviser. On this strange foundation a large Scottish army gathered on the Border.

The menace in the North brought Cromwell back from Ireland. The Council of State at last appointed him Commander-in-Chief in form as he had long been in fact. In his Ironside troops, fresh from their Irish slaughters, he grasped a heavy, sharp, and reeking sword.

The pious Scottish army descended and closed down upon Cromwell and his saints. Both sides confidently appealed to Jehovah; and the Most High, finding little to choose between them in faith and zeal, must have allowed purely military factors to prevail. At the first grey light Cromwell, feinting with his right wing, attacked heavily on the left. "Now," he exclaimed, as the sun rose over the sea behind him, "let God arise and let his enemies be scattered." Once the battle was joined the end was speedy. The Scots fled, leaving three thousand dead on the field. Nine thousand were prisoners in Oliver's hungry camp, and the Army of the Presbyters was broken.

*　　*　　*

The disaster carried Scots policy out of the trammels of dogma. National safety became the cry. The plan of marching south, leaving Cromwell behind in Edinburgh, which he had occupied, and rousing the Royalist forces in England, captivated the majority of the Scots Council.

A Scottish army now invaded England in 1651 upon a Royalist rather than a Presbyterian enterprise. It is proof of Cromwell's political and military sagacity that he allowed them to pass. Charles II trod his native soil as King. He marched in a chilling silence at the head of his troops. But Cromwell could now follow easily upon his track, and his concentration of all the forces of the Commonwealth against the Northern invaders was masterly. Charles acquitted himself with distinction. He rode along the regiments in the thick of the fighting, encouraging them in their duty. The struggle was one of the stiffest contests of the civil wars, but it was forlorn, and the Scots and their Royalist comrades were destroyed as a military force. To Charles II it afforded the most romantic adventure of his life. He escaped with difficulty from the stricken field; a thousand pounds was set upon his head. The land was scoured for him. He hid for a whole day in the famous oak tree at Boscobel. Thus after six weeks of desperate peril did the King find himself again in exile. This was the end of the Civil War or Great Rebellion. England was mastered; Ireland was terrorised; Scotland was conquered. The three kingdoms were united under a Government in London which wielded autocratic power. The most memorable chapter in English history was closed by irresistible forces, which ruled absolutely for a while, but settled nothing. In harsh or melancholy epochs free men may always take comfort from the grand lesson of history, that tyrannies cannot last except among servile races. The years which seem endless to those who endure them are but a flick of mischance in the journey. New and natural hopes leap from the human heart as every spring revives the cultivated soil and rewards the faithful, patient husbandmen.

CHAPTER FORTY-TWO

The Lord Protector

THE MONARCHY had gone; the Lords had gone; the Church of England was prostrate; of the Commons there remained nothing but the few survivors contemptuously named the Rump. This Rump prospered only so long as their Lord General was at the wars. When he returned victorious he was struck by their unpopularity. He was also shocked at their unrepresentative character. Above all, he observed that the Army, hitherto occupied about God's business in other directions, looked sourly on their civilian masters and paymasters.

Cromwell accordingly went to the House on April 20, 1653, accompanied by thirty musketeers. He took his seat and for a time listened to the debate. Then, rising in his place, he made a speech which grew in anger as it proceeded. "Come, come," he concluded, "I will put an end to your prating. You are no Parliament." He called in his musketeers to clear the House and lock the doors. Here sank for the moment all the constitutional safeguards and processes built and treasured across the centuries, from Simon de Montfort to the Petition of Right. One man's will now ruled. One puzzled, self-questioning, but explosive spirit became for a spell the guardian of the slowly gathered work of ages, and of the continuity of the English message.

Cromwell, although crafty and ruthless as occasion claimed, was at all times a reluctant and apologetic dictator. He recognised and deplored the arbitrary character of his own rule, but he had no difficulty in persuading himself that his authority sprang both from Above and below. Was he not the new Moses, the chosen Protector of the people of God, commanded to

199

lead them into the Promised Land, if that could indeed be found? Was he not also the only available constable to safeguard "the several forms of godliness in this nation," and especially in the civil sphere the property of God's servants who had been on the right side, against Royalist conspirators or crazy, ravening Levellers? Was he not the Lord General set up by Parliament, now defunct, captain of all the armed forces, the surviving holder of the whole authority of the State, and, as he said, "a person having power over the three nations without bound or limit set"?

Cromwell only desired personal power in order to have things settled in accord with his vision, not of himself or his fame but of the England of his youthful dreams. He was a giant laggard from the Elizabethan age, a "rustic Tudor gentleman, born out of due time," who wished to see Scotland and Ireland brought to their due allegiance, and England "the awe of the Western world, adorned and defended with stout yeomen, honourable magistrates, learned ministers, flourishing universities, invincible fleets." [1] In foreign policy he was still fighting the Spanish Armada, ever ardent to lead his Ironside redcoats against the stakes and faggots of some Grand Inquisitor, or the idolatrous superstitions of an Italian Pope. Were these not now ripe for the sickle; aye, for the same sickle which had shorn down the malignant Cavaliers at Marston Moor and Naseby and had exterminated the Papists of Wexford and Drogheda? He sharpened his heavy sword for Don Quixote and the successors of Torquemada.

In September, 1654, he sent a naval expedition to the West Indies and Jamaica was occupied. This act of aggression led slowly but inevitably to war between England and Spain, and a consequent alliance between England and France. In June, 1658, six thousand veteran English soldiers in Flanders under Marshal Turenne defeated the Spaniards at the Battle of the Dunes and helped to capture the port of Dunkirk. The blockade of the Spanish coasts disclosed the strength of Britain's sea-power, and one of Blake's captains destroyed a Treasure Fleet off Teneriffe. Cromwell's imperial eye rested long upon Gibraltar. He examined schemes for capturing the marvellous rock. This was reserved for the days of Marlborough, but England retained Dunkirk and Jamaica as a result of Cromwell's war with Spain.

Cromwell found no difficulty in reconciling the predatory aims of the Spanish war with his exertions for a European Protestant League. He was ever ready to strike against the religious persecution of Protestants abroad. In the main, however, Cromwell's foreign policy was more successful in helping British trade and shipping than in checking or reversing the Counter-Reformation. The Mediterranean and Channel were cleared of pirates, foreign trade expanded, and the whole world learnt to respect British sea-power. The poet Waller could write:

[1] G. M. Young, *Charles I and Cromwell.*

The sea's our own; and now all nations greet
With bending sails, each vessel of our fleet;
Your power extends as far as winds can blow
Or swelling sails upon the globe may go.

* * *

But how to find a worthy, docile Parliament, with the fear of God and the root of the matter in their hearts, to aid and comfort the Lord Protector in his task? He sought a Parliament whose authority would relieve him from the reproach of a despotism similar to that which he had punished in "the Man of Blood," which would sustain, and within respectful limits correct, his initiative, without of course diverging from his ideals or hampering his sword or signet. But such Parliaments do not exist. Parliaments are awkward things. They have a knack of developing collective opinions of their own, which they derive from those who elect them. Cromwell sought the right kind of Parliament to limit his own dictatorship without crossing his will, and he boxed the compass in his search. He tried in succession a Puritan oligarchy, an upper middle-class Assembly sprinkled with men who had risen through military service, then in despair a naked military dictatorship, and finally a return to constitutional monarchy in all but name. He had expelled the Rump in the cause of an overdue popular election. He replaced it not by an elected but by a handpicked body of Puritan notables, who became known to history as "Barebone's Parliament," after one of their members, Praise-God Barebones. Here he was back at the old and ever-recurring problem. "I am as much for government by consent as any man," he told a critical Republican. "But"—pertinent inquiry—"where shall we find consent?" Military dictatorship supervened, naked if not wholly unashamed. To the mass of the nation the rule of Cromwell manifested itself in the form of numberless and miserable petty tyrannies, and thus became hated as no Government has ever been hated in England before or since. The feast days of the Church, regarded as superstitious indulgences, were replaced by a monthly fast day. Christmas excited the most fervent hostility of these fanatics. Parliament was deeply concerned at the liberty which it gave to carnal and sensual delights. Soldiers were sent round London on Christmas Day before dinnertime to enter private houses without warrants and seize meat cooking in all kitchens and ovens. Everywhere was prying and spying.

All over the country the Maypoles were hewn down, lest old village dances around them should lead to immorality or at least to levity. Walking abroad on the Sabbath, except to go to church, was punished, and a man was fined for going to a neighbouring parish to hear a sermon. It was even proposed to forbid people sitting at their doors or leaning against them on the Sabbath. Bearbaiting and cockfighting were effectually ended by shooting the bears and wringing the necks of the cocks. All forms of athletic sports, horse racing,

201

and wrestling were banned, and sumptuary laws sought to remove all orna-
ments from male and female attire.

What wonder that under the oak leaves, broad and far throughout the
countryside, men dreamed fondly of what they called the good old times
and yearned for the day when "the King shall enjoy his own again"?

The repulsive features fade from the picture and are replaced by colour
and even charm as the summit of power is reached. We see the Lord Protector in his glory, the champion of Protestantism, the arbiter of Europe,
the patron of learning and the arts. We feel the dignity of his bearing to all
men, and his tenderness towards young people. We feel his passion for
England, as fervent as Chatham's, and in some ways more intimate and
emotional. No one can remain unconscious of his desire to find a moral basis
for his power, or of his sense of a responsibility to his country and his God
ranging far beyond the horizon of his life. Although Cromwell easily convinced himself that he had been chosen the Supreme Ruler of the State, he
was ever ready to share his power with others, provided of course that they
agreed with him. He was willing, indeed anxious, to govern through a Parliament, if that Parliament would carry the laws and taxes he required. But
neither his fondlings nor his purgings induced his Parliaments to do his
will. Again and again he was forced to use or threaten the power of the
sword, and the rule which he sought to make a constitutional alternative to
absolutism or anarchy became in practice a military autocracy.

*   *   *

Nevertheless the dictatorship of Cromwell differed in many ways from
modern patterns. Although the Press was gagged and the Royalists ill used,
although judges were intimidated and local privileges curtailed, there was
always an effective vocal opposition, led by convinced Republicans. There
was no attempt to make a party around the personality of the Dictator,
still less to make a party state. Respect was shown for private property,
and the process of fining the Cavaliers and allowing them to compound by
surrendering part of their estates was conducted with technical formality.
Few people were put to death for political crimes, and no one was cast into
indefinite bondage without trial. Believing the Jews to be a useful element
in the civil community, Cromwell opened again to them the gates of England,
which Edward I had closed nearly four hundred years before. There was in
practice comparatively little persecution on purely religious grounds, and
even Roman Catholics were not seriously molested.

Although a very passionate man when fully roused, Cromwell was frequently harassed by inner doubts and conflicts. This uncertainty about himself excused opportunism, and reflected itself in his famous utterance, "No
man goes so high as he who knows not where he is going." His doubts about
political objectives became increasingly marked in his last years.

On September 3, 1658, the anniversary of the Battles of Dunbar and

Worcester and of the massacre of Drogheda, in the crash and howling of a mighty storm, death came to the Lord Protector. He had always been a good and faithful family man, and his heart had been broken by the death of his favourite and least Puritan daughter. He nominated his eldest son, Richard, a harmless country gentleman, as his successor, and for the moment none disputed his will. If in a tremendous crisis Cromwell's sword had saved the cause of Parliament, he must stand before history as a representative of dictatorship and military rule who, with all his qualities as a soldier and a statesman, is in lasting discord with the genius of the English race.

Yet with all his faults and failures he was indeed the Lord Protector of the enduring rights of the Old England he loved against the terrible weapon which he and Parliament had forged to assert them. Amid the ruins of every institution, social and political, which had hitherto guided the Island life he towered up, gigantic, glowing, indispensable, the sole agency by which time could be gained for healing and regrowth.

CHAPTER FORTY-THREE

The Restoration

CROMWELL'S ELDEST son, Richard, "Tumbledown Dick," as his enemies nicknamed him, was a respectable person with good intentions, but without the force and capacity required by the severity of the times. He was at first accepted by the Army and duly installed in his father's seat; but when he attempted to exercise authority he found he had but the form. His brother, Henry, who was both able and energetic, strove to strengthen the civil power. Upon Henry Cromwell's advice Parliament was summoned.

The Commons thought it unbearable that the Army should establish itself as a separate Estate of the Realm. In their conflict they became willing to entrust the chief command to the Protector. This brought the dispute to a head. Within four months of succeeding to his august office Richard Cromwell found himself deserted even by his personal guard. The Army was master. The spirit of the troops had become hostile to the Protectorate. They were resolved upon a pure republic.

But even in this hour of bloodless and absolute triumph the soldiery felt the need of some civil sanction for their acts. But where could they find it? At length the Rump of the Long Parliament was exhumed and exhibited to a bewildered land. Provision was made for Oliver Cromwell's sons, whose acquiescence in the abolition of the Protectorate was desired. Their debts were paid; they were provided with residences and incomes. Richard accepted these proposals at once, and Henry after some hesitation. Both lived unharmed to the end of their days. The Great Seal of the Protectorate was broken in two. A Republican Constitution based on the representative principle was set up, and all the authorities in the land submitted themselves to it.

While these stresses racked the Republican administration in London a widespread Royalist movement broke out in the country. Revolt was so swiftly crushed that Charles II, fortunately for himself, had no chance of putting himself at its head. The clatter of arms reminded the generals of their power, and they were soon again in sharp dispute with the truncated Parliament they had resuscitated.

But obviously this could not last. Someone must set in train the movement which would produce in England a Government which stood for something old or new. It was from another quarter that deliverance was to come.

* * *

The Cromwellian commander in Scotland was a man of mark. Once again England was to be saved by a man who was not in a hurry. George Monk, a Devonshire gentleman, was a soldier of fortune, caring more for plying his trade than for the causes at stake. He had steered his way through all the hazardous channels and storms, supporting in turn and at the right moment Parliament, the Commonwealth, and the Protectorate.

During the autumn of 1659 General Monk was the object of passionate solicitations from every quarter. They told him he had the future of England in his hands, and all appealed for his goodwill. The General received the emissaries of every interest and party in his camp. He listened patiently, as every great Englishman should, to all they had to urge, and with that simple honesty of character on which we flatter ourselves as a race he kept them all guessing for a long time what he would do.

At length when all patience was exhausted Monk acted. At York he received what he had long hoped for, the invitation of the House of Commons, the desperate Rump, to come to London. Unlike Cromwell, Monk decided to tame the Rump by diluting, not by dissolving it. In February he recalled the Members who had been excluded by an earlier purge. These were mainly Presbyterians, most of whom had become at heart Royalists. The restoration of the monarchy came into sight. Monk was satisfied that a free Parliament should be summoned, and that such a Parliament would certainly recall Charles II. He was genuinely convinced after his march from Scotland that the mass of the English people were tired of constitutional experiments and longed for the return of the monarchy. It was most plainly the wish of the people that the King should "enjoy his own again."

Here the latent wisdom of the Island played its part. In the hour of victory there had been excesses, and the principles of the Great Rebellion had been unduly extended. It was necessary to recur to the original position in theory, but not in practice. Monk sent word to Charles II, advising him to offer a free and general pardon, subject only to certain exceptions to be fixed by Parliament. Here was an England where a substantial part of the land, the main source of wealth and distinction, had passed into other hands. These changes had been made good in the field. They could not be entirely undone. The King might enjoy his own again, but not all the Cavaliers. There must be no reprisals. Everyone must start fair on the new basis.

But sacred blood had flowed. The deed of 1649 was contrary to law, against the presumptive will of Parliament, and abhorrent to the nation. Let those who had done it pay the price. This somewhat unheroic solution was found to be in harmony with that spirit of compromise which has played so invaluable a part in British affairs.

The Lords and Commons were restored. It remained only to complete the three Estates of the Realm by the recall of the King. Parliament hastened to send the exiled Charles a large sum of money for his convenience, and soon concerned itself with the crimson velvet furniture of his coaches of State. The Fleet, once so hostile, was sent to conduct him to his native shores. Immense crowds awaited him at Dover. There, on May 25, 1660, General Monk received him with profound reverence as he landed. The journey to London was triumphal. All classes crowded to welcome the King home to his own. They cheered and wept in uncontrollable emotion. They felt themselves delivered from a nightmare. They now dreamed they had entered a Golden Age. Charles gazed about in astonishment. Could this be the same island from which he had escaped so narrowly only a few years back? Still more must Charles have wondered whether he slept or waked when on Blackheath he saw the dark, glistening columns of the Ironside Army drawn up in stately array and dutiful obedience. It was but eight years since he had hidden from its patrols in the branches of the Boscobel oak. The entry to the City was a blaze of thanksgiving. All around, the masses, rich and poor, Cavalier and Roundhead, Episcopalian, Presbyterian, and Independent, framed a scene of reconciliation and rejoicing without compare in history. It was England's supreme day of joy.

*   *   *

The wheel had not, however, swung a full circle, as many might have thought. This was not only the restoration of the monarchy; it was the restoration of Parliament. Indeed, it was the greatest hour in Parliamentary history. The House of Commons had broken the Crown in the field; it had at length mastered the terrible Army it had created for that purpose. It had purged itself of its own excesses, and now stood forth beyond all challenge, or even need of argument, as the dominant institution of the realm. Above all, everyone now took it for granted that the Crown was the instrument of Parliament and the King the servant of his people. Though the doctrine of

Divine Right was again proclaimed, that of Absolute Power had been abandoned. The Restoration achieved what Pym and Hampden had originally sought, and rejected the excesses into which they had been drawn by the stress of conflict and the crimes and follies of war and dictatorship. The victory of the Commons and the Common Law was permanent.

A new conception of sovereignty had now been born. The Common Lawyers had borne the brunt. They had struggled to ensure that the King should be under the law. This meant the law for which Magna Carta was felt to stand—traditional law, the kind of law which made Englishmen free from arbitrary arrest and arbitrary punishment; the law that had for centuries been declared in the courts of Common Law. Parliament had not striven to make itself omnipotent, nor to destroy the traditional powers of the Crown, but to control their exercise so that the liberties of Parliament and of the individual were safeguarded and protected. During the years without a King, and without the Royal Prerogative, the idea had emerged that an Act of Parliament was the final authority. Coke's claim that the fundamental law could not be overborne, even by Crown and Parliament together, and his dream of judges in a Supreme Court of Common Law had been extinguished in England for ever. It survived in New England across the ocean, one day to emerge in an American revolution directed against both Parliament and Crown.

*　　*　　*

"No standing Army" was to be the common watchword of all parties. Everyone, except the soldiers, was agreed about getting rid of the Army; and that this could be done, and done without bloodshed, seemed a miracle. But they yielded themselves to the tide of opinion. They were paid their dues. They returned to their homes and their former callings, and within a few months this omnipotent, invincible machine vanished in the civil population, leaving scarcely a trace behind.

The King fought for clemency for his father's murderers, and Parliament, many of whose Members had abetted their action, clamoured for retribution. The numbers of those executed fell so far short of the public demand that an addition was made to the bloody scene which at any rate cost no more life. The corpses of Cromwell, Ireton, leader and champion of the Army, and Bradshaw, president of the court which had tried Charles I, were pulled out of their coffins in Westminster Abbey, where they had been buried a few years earlier in solemn state, drawn through the streets on hurdles to Tyburn, hanged upon the three-cornered gibbet for twenty-four hours, their heads spiked up in prominent places, and the remains cast upon the dunghill. Pym and twenty other Parliamentarians were also disinterred and buried in a pit. Such ghoulish warring with the dead was enforced by the ferocity of public opinion, to which the King was glad to throw carcasses instead of living men.

The restored King had had a long fight to minimise these gruesome deeds. "I am weary of hanging," he said. In all, through Charles's exertions, and at some expense to his popularity, less than a dozen persons were put to death in this intense Counter-Revolution.

CHAPTER FORTY-FOUR

The Merry Monarch

THE PARLIAMENT which recalled the King was a balanced assembly and represented both sides of the nation. It surmounted the grave political difficulties of the Restoration with success. It had, however, no constitutional validity, since it had not been summoned by royal writ. This was considered to be a fatal defect. At the end of 1660 it was thought necessary to dissolve it.

This concession to a newly recovered respect for law prevented all chance of a religious settlement which would embrace the whole nation. The longest Parliament in English history now began. It lasted eighteen years. From the moment when it first met it showed itself more Royalist in theory than in practice. It rendered all honour to the King. It had no intention of being governed by him.

Since Clarendon as Lord Chancellor was the chief Minister, and preponderant in the Government, his name is identified with the group of Acts which re-established the Anglican Church and drove the Protestant sects into enduring opposition. For good or for ill, the "Clarendon Code" was a parting of the ways. It destroyed all chance of a United National Church.

Charles did not will this great separation. He walked by the easy path of indifference to the uplands of toleration. He was certainly not spiritually minded. If a gentleman was going to be religious perhaps Rome would give him the greatest satisfaction. But then what trouble that would make, and was not the Anglican Church the mainstay of the Throne? He wished to see all the religious fervour cooled and abated. Why distract this world for the sake of the next? "Of this you may be sure," he said to a deputation of Quakers during the Convention Parliament, "that you shall none of you suffer for your opinions or religious beliefs, so long as you live peaceably, and you have the word of a King for it."

Another cleavage was opening. The lines were being drawn in political life between the Conservative and Radical traditions which have persisted down to our own day. We enter the era of conflict between broad party groups, soon to bear the names of Tory and Whig, which shaped the destinies of the British Empire till all was melted in the fires of the Great War of 1914.

For these far-reaching fissures Charles II had no responsibility. Partisans of Parliament should realise that in this crucial period the King's was the only modern and merciful voice that spoke.

But Charles II had need of an Act of Indulgence for himself. Court life was one unceasing flagrant and brazen scandal. His two principal mistresses, Barbara Villiers, created Countess of Castlemaine, and Louise de Kérouaille—"Madame Carwell," as the English called her—beguiled his leisure and amused themselves with foreign affairs. His marriage with Catherine of Braganza, who brought a rich dowry of eight hundred thousand pounds and the naval bases of Tangier and Bombay, in no way interrupted these dissipations. His treatment of his wife was cruel in an extreme degree; he forced her to accept Barbara as her Lady-in-Waiting. The refined, devout Portuguese princess on one occasion was so outraged that the blood gushed from her nostrils and she was borne swooning from the Court. It was with relief that the public learned that the King had taken a mistress from the people, the transcendently beautiful and good-natured Nell Gwyn, who was lustily cheered in the streets as "the Protestant whore." But these were only the more notorious features of a life of lust and self-indulgence which disgraced a Christian throne, and in an Asiatic Court would have been veiled in the mysteries of the seraglio.

The King's example spread its demoralisation far and wide, and the sense of relief from the tyranny of the Puritans spurred forward every amorous adventure. Nature, affronted, reclaimed her rights with usury. The Commonwealth Parliament had punished adultery by death; Charles scourged chastity and faithfulness with ridicule. There can, however, be no doubt that the mass of the nation in all classes preferred the lax rule of the sinners to the rigorous discipline of the saints. The people of England did not wish to be the people of God in the sense of the Puritan God. They descended with thankfulness from the superhuman levels to which they had been painfully hoisted.

It is inevitable that after a period of intense effort there should follow one of exhaustion and disarray. But this was a fleeting view. The race endured, and in Charles's Court, at his side, there was already a young man, an ensign in his Guards, a partner in his games at tennis, an intruder, as he learned with some displeasure, in the affections of Lady Castlemaine, who would one day grasp a longer and brighter sword than Cromwell's and wield it in wider fields only against the enemies of British greatness and freedom. A Dorsetshire squire, Winston Churchill, along with his father, had fought in the Royalist ranks and had been wounded, mulcted, and expropriated by the Roundheads. The King could do little for his faithful adherent, but he found a place at Court for his son as one of his own pages, and for his daughter Arabella in the household of the Duchess of York. Both improved their advantage. John Churchill obtained a commission in the Guards; Arabella became the mistress of the Duke of York, and bore him a son, James Fitz James, afterwards famous as the warrior Duke of Berwick.

For the first seven years of the reign Clarendon continued First Minister. This wise, venerable statesman wrestled stoutly with the licentiousness of the King and Court, with the intrigues of the royal mistresses, with the inadequacy of the revenue, and with the intolerance of the House of Commons.

The rivalry of England and Holland upon the seas, in fishery and in trade, had become intense, and the strength of the Dutch had revived since Cromwell's war. The acquisition of Tangier as part of the dowry of Catherine of Braganza turned the eyes of the Government to Mediterranean and Oriental trade. Since the Portuguese Governor of Bombay was recalcitrant in yielding that part of Catherine's dowry, the English as yet had no sure base in India. Meanwhile, great Dutch fleets, heavily laden, doubled the Cape of Good Hope several times a year. On the West African coast also the Dutch prospered, and their colonies and trading stations grew continually. They had a settlement on the Hudson, thrust among the colonies of New England. It was too much. Parliament was moved by the merchants; the King was roused to patriotic ardour, the Duke of York thirsted for naval glory. War at sea began off the African coast in 1664 and spread to home waters the following year.

In June the English fleet met the Dutch in equal strength off Lowestoft, and a long, fierce battle was fought. The English artillery was markedly superior in weight and skill, and the Dutch withdrew worsted though undismayed.

The return of Admiral De Ruyter from the West Indies restored the fortunes of the Republic. An even greater battle than Lowestoft was fought in June, 1666. Louis XIV had promised to aid Holland if she were attacked. Although Charles protested that the Dutch were the aggressors, France declared war on England. For four days the English and Dutch fleets battled off the North Foreland. But the fourth day was adverse, and Monk and Rupert, with heavy losses, retired into the Thames. De Ruyter had triumphed.

England was now isolated, and even her power at sea was uncertain. But other calamities drained the strength of the Island. From the spring of 1665 the Great Plague had raged in London. Never since the Black Death in 1348 had pestilence spread such ravages. In London at the climax about seven thousand people died in a single week. The Court retired to Salisbury, leaving the capital in the charge of Monk, whose nerves were equal to every kind of strain. Daniel Defoe's *Journal of the Plague Year* reconstructs for us in vivid, searing style the panic and horror. The worst of the plague was over when in September, 1666, the Great Fire engulfed the tormented capital. It broke out near London Bridge, in a narrow street of wooden houses, and, driven by a strong east wind, the flames spread with resistless fury for four whole days. Wild suspicions that the fire was the work of Anabaptists, Catholics, or foreigners maddened the mob. The King, who had returned to London, acquitted himself with courage and humanity. When the fire was at length stopped outside the City walls by blowing up whole streets more than thirteen thousand dwelling-houses, eighty-nine churches, and St. Paul's Cathedral had been devoured. Yet the fire extinguished the plague, and to later times it seems that the real calamity was not so much the destruction of the insanitary medieval city as the failure to carry through Wren's plan for rebuilding it as a unity of quays and avenues centred on St. Paul's and the Royal Exchange. The task of reconstruction was none the less faced with courage, and from the ashes of the old cathedral rose the splendid dome of St. Paul's as it stands today.

Although the war dragged on till 1667 Charles now sought peace both with France and Holland. While negotiations lingered the Dutch, to spur them, sailed up the Medway under Admiral De Witt, brother of the famous John, broke the boom which guarded Chatham harbour, burnt four ships of the line, and towed away the battleship *Royal Charles,* which had destroyed Admiral Opdam in the Battle of Lowestoft. The sound of enemy cannon, this time loud and near, rolled up the Thames. Among the Puritans the plague, the fire, and the disaster at sea were regarded as direct visitations by which the Almighty chastised the immorality of the age, and especially of the Court. Peace, of which both sides had equal need, was made on indifferent terms. England's chief gain in the war was New Amsterdam, now renamed New York.

* * *

CHAPTER FORTY-FIVE

The Popish Plot

THE MEETING of Parliament in February of 1673 had apprised Charles of his subjects' loathing for the war against the Dutch Protestant Republic. The growing antagonism of the Commons to France, the fear of the returning tides of Popery, the conversion of the Duke of York to Rome, all stirred a deep and dangerous agitation throughout the whole country.

All eyes were now fixed upon James, Duke of York. His marriage, after the death of his first wife, to the Catholic princess Mary of Modena had rendered him suspect. Would he dissemble or would he give up his offices? Very soon it was known that the heir to the throne had laid down his post of Lord High Admiral rather than declare his disbelief in the doctrine of Transubstantiation. This event staggered the nation. The Queen was unlikely to give King Charles an heir. The crown would therefore pass to a Papist King, who showed that for conscience' sake he would not hesitate to sacrifice every material advantage.

A marriage was now contrived between Mary, the Duke of York's daughter by his first wife, and now famous Protestant hero, William of Orange. This match was of the highest consequence. Dread of a Papist King had already turned all eyes to the formidable, gleaming figure of the Stadtholder of Holland, Charles I's grandson by his daughter. William's inflexible Protestantism, grave demeanour, high gifts, and noble ancestry had raised him already to a position of eminence in Europe. Married now to the daughter of the Duke of York, the English heir presumptive, he seemed to offer an alternative succession to the Crown. This was by no means the outlook of King Charles II, still less of his brother, James. They did not regard the danger as serious. Thus the marriage was made, and the two maritime nations, which had recently contended in fierce, memorable battles in the Narrow Seas, became united by this remarkable tie. Since then the Dutch and English peoples have seldom been severed in the broad course of European events.

* * *

Rumours about a secret treaty with the French King and the bugbear of the Duke of York's seemingly inevitable succession were now inflamed and fanned by what was called the "Popish Plot." The Duchess of York's private secretary was accused of a conspiracy to murder the King, bring about a French invasion, and cause a general massacre of Protestants. This sensation drove English society into madness. Anglicans and Puritans alike armed themselves with swords or life preservers, and in London everyone talked about expecting a Papist dagger.

* * *

The shadow of his father's fate fell even upon the King's footsteps. And by now the idea of saving the Kingship and of saving himself at all costs was dominant. The brunt fell upon James, Duke of York. The King now advised him to leave the country and the Duke retired to the Low Countries. Charles, thus relieved at home, faced the fury of the anti-Popish hurricane. A reign of terror was instituted against the English Catholic notables. The King made every effort in his power to protect them. When this was in vain he resigned himself to letting the bloody work go on. His cynical but profound knowledge of men and the vicissitudes of his years of exile served him well. Not for mean motives he endured the horrible ordeal which his subjects imposed upon him, of signing the death warrants of men he knew were guiltless. But there was a great change in his conduct. He abandoned his easy, indolent detachment from politics. He saw that his life and dynasty were at stake; he set himself with all his resources and with all the statecraft which modern research increasingly exalts to recover the ground that had been lost. The last five years of his reign are those most honourable to his memory.

The immediate struggle centred upon the Exclusion Bill. To keep the Papist heir from the throne was the main object of the majority of the nation. Anything rather than that. But who then should succeed? Nothing would induce the King to betray the succession. Sensualist, libertine, agnostic, dilettante, he had one loyalty—royal blood, the legitimate succession. However painful it might be for himself and his realm, he conceived it his sacred duty to pass the crown to a brother whose virtues and whose vices alike rendered him of all others the man, as he knew well, least fitted to wear it.

Charles laboured to present a compromise. He could not admit that Parliament should alter the lineal succession to the Crown. But in the prevailing temper no one would believe that any restrictions could be imposed upon a Popish King. The Exclusion Bill passed its second reading by an overwhelming vote, and the King descended upon the Parliament with another dissolution.

Nevertheless, this short-lived legislature left behind it a monument. It passed a Habeas Corpus Act which confirmed and strengthened the freedom of the individual against arbitrary arrest by the executive Government. No Englishman, however great or however humble, could be imprisoned for more than a few days without grounds being shown against him in open court, according to the settled law of the land. Wherever the English language is spoken in any part of the world, wherever the authority of the British Imperial Crown or of the Government of the United States prevails, all law-abiding men breathe freely. The descent into despotism which has engulfed so many leading nations in the present age has made the virtue of this enactment, sprung from English political genius, apparent even to the most thoughtless, the most ignorant, the most base.

The Protestant tide again swept the country, and in all parts men voted against the Duke of York becoming King. The dominant motives of both sides deserve a high respect, and led inexorably to vast and long distresses. In these days, when the Catholic Church raises her immemorial authority against secular tyranny, it is hard to realise how different was the aspect which she wore to the England of 1679, with lively recollection of the fires of Smithfield, the Massacre of St. Bartholomew, the Spanish Armada, and the Gunpowder Plot.

Whig and Tory

AS SOON as the King saw that the election gave him no relief he prorogued the meeting of the resulting Parliament for almost another year. And it is in this interval that we first discern the use of those names Whig and Tory which were to divide the British Island for nearly two hundred years. Although the root of the quarrel was still religious, the reign of Charles II saw the detachment of liberal ideas from their sectarian basis. The collective mind of England was moving forward from the ravines of religious entanglement to broader if less picturesque uplands. The impulse of religious controversy, which had hitherto been vital to political progress, henceforth took the second place. To the sombre warfare of creeds and sects there succeeded the squalid but far less irrational or uncontrollable strife of parties.

If petitions for the exclusion of the Duke of York were signed by many thousands in the cities and towns, so also abhorrence of these demands upon the Crown was widespread in the country. But no parties could live under such labels as Petitioners and Abhorrers. Instead of naming themselves they named each other. The term "Whig" had described a sour, bigoted, canting, money-grubbing Scots Presbyterian. Irish Papist bandits ravaging estates and manor-houses had been called "Tories." Neither side was lacking in power of abuse.

One can see from these expressions of scorn and hatred how narrowly England escaped another cruel purging of the sword. Yet the names Whig and Tory not only stuck, but became cherished and vaunted by those upon whom they were fastened. They were adorned by memorable achievements for the welfare of England, and both had their share in the expansion and greatness which were to come. Orators and famous writers, sure of their appeal, were to point to them in terms of pride.

When Parliament met in October, 1680, Shaftesbury, the leader of the Opposition, again championed the Exclusion Bill, and at this moment he reached his zenith. He seemed to combine in himself the power of a Minister of the Crown and the popularity of a leader of incipient revolt. The Exclusion Bill was carried through the Commons, and the struggle was fought out in the Lords.

That it ended bloodlessly was largely due to the statesman who rendered the word Trimmer illustrious, George Saville, Marquis of Halifax, the opponent alike of Popery and of France. He was one of those rare beings in whom cool moderation and width of judgment are combined with resolute action.

Halifax broke the Exclusion Bill in the House of Lords. The Whigs propagated the fiction that the bastard Monmouth was legitimate after all. Anyhow, the King dearly loved his handsome, dashing son. Might he not, as pressures and perils gathered about him, take the safe and easy course of declaring him legitimate? But this complaisant solution, which Charles would never tolerate, did not appeal to an assembly every man of which owned lands, wealth, and power through the strictest interpretations of hereditary right. The Anglican Church refused to resist Popery by crowning bastardy. By sixty-three votes to thirty the Peers rejected the Exclusion Bill.

*   *   *

The fury against the Popish Plot was gradually slaked, but a trial of strength impended, and none could tell that it would not take a bloody form. The large majority of the Commons was still resolved upon the Exclusion Bill.

It would seem that the King kept two courses of action open, both of which he had prepared. Could he by strict economies "live of his own"? With economy the deficit would not be large. In negotiating with Louis XIV, eventually a hundred thousand pounds a year was obtained upon the understanding that England would not act contrary to French ambitions on the Continent. With this aid it was thought the King could manage independently of the ferocious Parliament. England had now reached a point in its history as low as when King John, in not dissimilar stresses, had made it over as a fief to the Pope. Modern opinion, which judges Charles's actions from the constitutional standpoint, is revolted by the spectacle of a prince selling the foreign policy of his country for a hundred thousand pounds a year. But if present-day standards are to be applied the religious intolerance of Parliament must also be condemned.

Moreover, the King did not intend to adopt this ignominious policy which he had in his pocket, or almost in his pocket, unless he found no hope in Parliament. He made a show of going to extreme lengths to meet the national fear of a Popish King. The sacred principle of hereditary succession must not be destroyed, but short of this every security should be given. James, when he succeeded, should be King only in name. The kingdom would be governed by a Protector and the Privy Council.

Just as James would sacrifice all for his religious faith, so Charles would dare all for the hereditary principle. There was no risk he would not run to prevent his beloved son, Monmouth, from ousting a brother who was the main source of all his troubles.

*   *   *

The absorbing question now was whether there would be civil war. All the Cromwellian forces were astir; indeed, there was a terror in men's hearts that if James came to the throne they would have to choose between turning Papist and being burnt at the stake. Their fears increased when James returned from exile in May, 1682. An ex-officer of the Roundheads, "Hannibal" Rumbold, dwelt in the Rye House by the Newmarket Road, where it ran through a cutting. Fifty zealous Ironsides could easily overpower the small travelling escort of the King and the Duke of York on their return from their pastime of horse racing. Above this dark design, and unwitting of it, was a general conspiracy for armed action. Many, but by no means all, of the forces which were to hurl James from the throne a few years later were morally prepared to fight. The lucky accident of a fire in Newmarket led Charles and James to return some days before the expected date. They passed the Rye House in safety, and a few weeks later the secret of the plot was betrayed.

When the news spread through the land it caught the Royalist reaction upon its strong upturn. It transformed everything. Hitherto the Whigs had exploited the Popish Plot and made common folk believe that the King was about to be butchered by the Roman Catholics. Here was the antidote. Here was a Whig or Puritan plot from the other side to kill the King. All the veneration which Englishmen had for the monarchy, and the high personal popularity of Charles, with his graceful manners and dangerously attractive vices, were reinforced by the dread that his death would make his Papist brother King. From this moment Charles's triumph was complete.

Thus the Whigs now saw their power crippled. It is remarkable that they should have survived as a political force and that the course of events should so soon have restored them to predominance.

Against his own wishes the triumphant King followed meekly the foreign policy which his French paymaster prescribed. He lived with increasing frugality; his mistresses became concerned for their future, and scrambled for pensions solidly secured upon the revenues of the Post Office. Only the Fleet was nursed. Louis continued his aggressions and waged war upon freedom and the Protestant faith. He ruled splendid and supreme in Europe. England, which under Elizabeth and Cromwell had played a great European part, for a while shrank, apart from domestic politics, to a quiescent and contented community, busy with commerce and colonies, absorbed in its own affairs and thankful they were easier.

Across the seas widespread thrusts were taking place, often on the initiative of the men on the spot rather than by planned direction from London. English commerce was expanding in India and on the West Coast of Africa. The Hudson's Bay Company, launched in 1669, had set up its first trading posts and was building up its influence in the northern territories of Canada. On the coasts of Newfoundland English fishermen had revivified the earliest colony of the Crown. On the American mainland the British occupation of the entire eastern seaboard was almost complete. The capture of New York and the settlement of New Jersey had joined in contiguity the two existing groups of colonies that lay to the north and south. Inland, the State of Pennsylvania was beginning to take shape as an asylum for the persecuted of all countries under the guidance of its Quaker proprietor, William Penn. To the south the two Carolinas had been founded and named in honour of the

King. At the end of Charles's reign the American colonies contained about a quarter of a million settlers, not counting the increasing number of Negro slaves, tran-shipped from Africa. The local assemblies of the colonists were sturdily asserting traditional English rights against the interventions of the King's Ministers from London. Perhaps not many Englishmen at the time, absorbed in the pleasures and feuds of Restoration London, foresaw the broad prospects that stretched out before these comparatively small and distant American communities. But all this lay in the future.

*　　*　　*

The King was only fifty-six, and in appearance lively and robust, but his exorbitant pleasures had undermined his constitution. To represent him as a mere voluptuary is to underrate both his character and his intellect. His whole life had been an unceasing struggle. The tragedy he had witnessed and endured in his youth, the adventures and privations of his manhood, the twenty-five years of baffling politics through which he maintained himself upon the throne, the hateful subjugations forced on him by the Popish Plot, now in his last few years gave place to a serene experience. All the fires of England burned low, but there was a genial glow from the embers at which the weary King warmed his hands.

Suddenly in February, 1685, an apoplectic stroke laid him low. The doctors of the day inflicted their tormenting remedies upon him in vain. With that air of superiority to death for which all mortals should be grateful he apologised for being "so unconscionable a time in dying." James was at hand to save his soul. Old Father Huddleston, the priest who had helped him in the days of the Boscobel oak, was brought up the backstairs to rally him to Rome and give the last sacrament. Apart from hereditary monarchy, there was not much in which Charles believed in this world or another. He wanted to be King, as was his right, and have a pleasant life. He was cynical rather than cruel, and indifferent rather than tolerant. His care for the Royal Navy is his chief claim upon the gratitude of his countrymen.

CHAPTER FORTY-SEVEN

The Catholic King

THE STRUGGLE between Crown and Parliament which had dominated English life since the reign of James I had now come back to its starting point. Eighty years of fearful events and the sharpest ups and downs of fortune had brought the monarchy, in appearance and for the practical purposes of the moment, to almost Tudor absolutism. In spite of Marston

Moor and Naseby, after the execution of a King, after Oliver Cromwell, after the military anarchy, after the enthusiasm of the Restoration, after the savage incipient revolution which raged around the Popish Plot, Charles II had been able to reign for three years without the aid of Parliament and to transmit the crown of a Protestant country to a Catholic successor. So vital did the institution of monarchy appear to those who had lived in this strenuous age that even the barrier of a hostile religion could not prevent the lawful heir from ascending the throne amid the respectful homage of his British subjects.

For the last two years of his brother's reign James had played a leading part in the realm. He had exploited the victory which Charles, by compliance, by using time, by an ignominious foreign policy, had gained for the house of Stuart. His accession to the throne seemed to him to be the vindication of the downright conceptions for which he had always stood. All he thought he needed to make him a real King, on the model now established in Europe by Louis XIV, was a loyal Fleet and a standing Army, well trained and equipped. Warlike command appealed strongly to his nature. Here was the key by which all doors might be opened. Prating Parliaments, a proud, politically minded nobility, the restored, triumphant Episcopacy, the blatant Whigs, the sullen, brooding Puritans, all would have to take their place once the King of England possessed a heavy, tempered, sharpened sword. Everyone was awestruck or spellbound by the splendour of France under absolute monarchy. Why should not the British islands rise to equal grandeur by adopting similar methods?

But behind this there swelled in the King's breast the hope that he might reconcile all his people to the old faith and heal the schism which had rent Christendom for so many generations. He was resolved that there should at least be toleration among all English Christians. It is one of the disputes of history whether toleration was all he sought. James was a convert to Rome. He was a bigot, and there was no sacrifice he would not make for his faith. He lost his throne in consequence, and his son carried on after him the conscientious warfare, to his own exclusion. Toleration was the natural first step to the revival of Catholicism. The King was determined that the Catholics should not be persecuted. It is possible that he fortified himself inwardly by asserting that all he wanted was toleration, and by the enlightened use of the dispensing power to be the true father of all his people.

These large plans filled James's resolute and obstinate mind. Protestant opinion has never doubted that if he had gained despotic power he would have used it for his religion in the same ruthless manner as Louis XIV. The English Protestant nation would have been very foolish to trust themselves to the merciful tolerances of James II, once he had obtained the absolute power he sought.

They did not do so. They were quite sure, from his character, from his avowed unshakeable convictions, from the whole character of the Catholic

Church at this time, that once he wielded the sword their choice would be the Mass or the stake.

Events rolled forward on their unresting course. The sudden death of Charles II came as a shattering blow to his well-loved bastard, Monmouth. He was in Holland, a gay prince, dancing and skating, happy with his beautiful mistress. Thus he beguiled the time till Protestant feeling in England and his father's love should win him what he believed was his birthright. Suddenly he found that he must deal henceforward not with a father who would forgive anything, but with an uncle who forgave nothing, and had a long score in his ledger. William of Orange had entertained him agreeably at The Hague, but on the day when Charles's death was known reasons of State supervened and he ordered him to leave the country.

James ascended the throne with all the ease of Richard Cromwell. He took every measure which forethought could enjoin to grasp the royal power, and his earliest declarations carried comfort to an anxious land. Nevertheless, from the moment he felt himself effectively King, on the second Sunday after his accession, he went publicly to Mass in his chapel. The Duke of Norfolk, who carried the sword of state before him, stopped at the door. "My lord," said the King, "your father would have gone farther." "Your Majesty's father would not have gone so far," rejoined the Duke.

On June 11, 1685, Monmouth landed. He had been nineteen days at sea, using up his luck in escaping the English warships. He was at once welcomed by the populace. He issued a proclamation asserting the validity of his mother's marriage and denouncing James as a usurper who had murdered Charles II. Parliament swore to live and die with the King. Monmouth was attainted and a price was placed upon his head. Despite the enthusiasm for his cause among the common people, the unhappy Duke was doomed. All the ruling forces rallied round the Crown. Monmouth and his rebels, who amounted to six or seven thousand ardent men, made a long march towards Bristol, which closed its gates against him. One chance remained—a sudden night attack upon the royal army which had hurried West to meet him. It miscarried. His followers were slaughtered where they stood, and a merciless pursuit, with wholesale executions, ended their forlorn endeavour. Monmouth escaped the field only to be hunted down a few days later. He could claim no mercy, and none did he receive.

Chief Justice Jeffreys was sent into the West to deal with the large number of prisoners. This cruel, able, unscrupulous judge made his name for ever odious by the "Bloody Assizes." Between two and three hundred persons were hanged, and about eight hundred transported to Barbados, where their descendants still survive.

The conduct of William of Orange showed his statecraft. He was under treaty to send three regiments of infantry to James's aid. He fulfilled his obligation with alacrity. He even offered to come in person to command them. On the other hand, he had not tried too hard to stop Monmouth's expedition from sailing. If the Duke won there would be a Protestant King of England, who would certainly join a coalition against Louis XIV. If he failed, the last barrier which stood between William and his wife Mary and the succession to the English throne would be for ever removed. Of the two alternatives that which he most desired came to pass.

James was now at the height of his power. The defeat of the rebels and the prevention of another civil war had procured a nation-wide rally to the Crown. Of this he took immediate advantage. As soon as the Jeffreys' "campaign," as James called it, was ended, he proposed to his Council the repeal of the Test Act and the Habeas Corpus Act. Chief Justice Jeffreys, red-handed from the "Bloody Assizes," was made Lord Chancellor.

Parliament met for its second session on November 9, and the King laid his immediate purpose before it. In his blunt way he declared, with admitted reason, that the militia was useless. They had twice run away before Monmouth's half-armed peasantry. A strong standing Army was indispensable to the peace and order of the realm. He also made it plain that he would not dismiss his Catholic officers on the morrow of their faithful services. These two demands shook the friendly Parliament to its foundations. It was deeply and predominantly imbued with the Cavalier spirit. Its most hideous nightmare was a standing Army, its dearest treasure the Established Church. Fear and perplexity disturbed all Members, assaulted both in their secular and religious feelings; and beneath their agitation anger grew.

James saw plainly that the House of Lords would constitute a massive obstacle to that very dispensing power for the relief and preferment of the Catholics upon which his heart was set. He therefore repeated the stroke by which Charles II had dispersed the Parliament at Oxford in 1681. On November 20 he suddenly appeared in the House of Lords, summoned the Commons to the Bar, and prorogued Parliament. It never met again while he was King.

These actions disturbed the whole realm. The methods of absolutism were being used to restore the Catholic religion, more dreaded than absolutism itself. Lawyers discerned that a direct conflict between statutory law and Royal Prerogative had arisen. Moreover, they now asserted that the King should not only be under the law, but under the law made in Parliament, the law of statute. The Common Lawyers all ranged themselves behind this new claim.

By the end of the year James had driven away many of his most faithful friends and disquieted everybody. The loyal Parliament which had rallied to James against Monmouth could be brought together no more without the certainty of a quarrel. Its lords and squires sat sullen and anxious amidst their tenantry. The Church, the bulwark of legitimacy, the champion of nonresistance, seethed with suppressed alarms. It was plain that the King, with all the downright resolution of his nature, was actively and of set purpose subverting the faith and the Constitution of the land.

James now embarked upon a political manœuvre at once audacious, crafty, and miscalculated. Hitherto he had striven only to relieve his Catholic subjects. He would now bid for the aid of the Dissenters who were equally oppressed. If Whigs and Tories were combined, he would match them by a coalition of Papists and Nonconformists under the armed power of the Crown. In William Penn, the Quaker courtier and founder of the state of Pennsylvania across the seas, influential in both this and the former reign, he found a powerful and skilled agent. Thus did the King break down the national barriers of his throne and try to shore it up with novel, ill-assorted, and inadequate props.

Meanwhile James was raising and preparing his Army. Charles II's forces of about seven thousand men had cost £280,000 a year. Already James was spending £600,000 upon the upkeep of more than twenty thousand men. Every summer a great camp was formed at Hounslow to impress the Londoners. In August, 1686, this contained about ten thousand men. A year later Feversham could assemble fifteen thousand men and twenty-eight guns. The King went often to the camp, seeking to make himself popular with the officers and all ranks. He allowed Mass to be celebrated in a wooden chapel borne on wheels and placed in the centre of the camp between the horse and foot. He watched the drill of the troops, and dined with Feversham, Churchill, and other generals. He continued his infusion of Catholic officers and Irish recruits. He had a parson, Johnson, pilloried and whipped from Newgate to Tyburn for a seditious pamphlet addressed to Protestant soldiers. He comforted himself with the aspect of this formidable Army, the like of which had not been seen since Cromwell, and against which nothing could be matched in England. He increasingly promoted Catholics to key posts. The Duke of Berwick, now eighteen years old, was made Governor of Portsmouth, and Catholics commanded at both Hull and Dover. Eventually a Catholic admiral ruled the Channel Fleet.

CHAPTER FORTY-EIGHT

The Revolution of 1688

WILLIAM OF ORANGE watched the King's proceedings with close attention. His envoy arrived in London partly to exhibit William as pleading with James to moderate his measures, and partly to sound the Opposition leaders. He made it clear that they could count upon William and Mary for help.

The provocations of the royal policy continued. The King had, in modern parlance, set up his political platform. Defenders of James's conduct are concerned to exaggerate the number of English Catholics. It is even claimed that one-eighth of the population still adhered, in spite of generations of persecution, to the Old Faith. The old Catholic families in England, however, apart from favoured individuals, were deeply apprehensive of the headlong adventure upon which the King was launching them. The Pope himself deprecated James's excessive zeal, and his Legate in England urged caution and prudence. But the King hardened his heart and strengthened his Army.

All classes and parties knew the close sympathy and co-operation of the French and the English Courts. They saw all they cared for in this world and the next threatened. They therefore entered, not without many scruples and hesitations, but with inexorable resolve, upon the paths of conspiracy and rebellion.

* * *

In England during the autumn of 1688 everything pointed, as in 1642, to the outbreak of civil war. But now the grouping of the forces was far different from the days when Charles I unfurled his standard at Nottingham. The King had a large, well-equipped regular Army, with a powerful artillery. He believed himself master of the best, if not at the moment the largest, Navy afloat. He could call for powerful armed aid from Ireland and from France. He held the principal seaports and arsenals under trusty Catholic governors. He enjoyed substantial revenues. He assumed that the Church of England was paralysed by its doctrine of nonresistance, and he had been careful not to allow any Parliament to assemble for collective action. Ranged against him on the other hand were not only the Whigs, but almost all the old friends of the Crown. The men who had made the Restoration, the sons of the men who had fought and died for his father at Marston Moor and Naseby, the Church whose bishops and ministers had so long faced persecution for the principle of Divine Right, the universities which had melted their plate for King Charles I's coffers and sent their young scholars to his armies, the nobility and landed gentry whose interests had seemed so bound up with the monarchy—all, with bent heads and burning hearts, must now prepare themselves to outface their King in arms. Never did the aristocracy or the Established Church face a sterner test or serve the nation better than in 1688. They never flinched; they never doubted.

In this wide and secret confederacy there were two main divisions of policy. The moderates, led by Halifax and Nottingham, urged caution and delay. On the other hand stood the party of action, headed by Danby. He was the first man of great position who definitely set himself to bring William and a foreign army into England. With Danby were the Whig leaders—Shrewsbury, Devonshire, and some others. As early as the spring of 1688 they invited William to come over; and William replied that if he received at the right moment a formal request from leading English statesmen he would come, and that he would be ready by September. A nation-wide conspiracy was on foot by the end of May. Detailed plans were made, and the land was full of whisperings and of mysterious comings and goings.

Much now turned upon the Army. If the troops obeyed orders and fought for the King, England would be torn by civil war, the end of which no man could foresee. But if the Army refused to fight, or was prevented from fighting by any means, then the great issues at stake would be settled bloodlessly. It seems certain, though there is no actual proof, that the general revolutionary conspiracy had a definite military core; and that this formed itself in the Army, or at least among the high officers of the Army, step by step with the designs of the statesmen. The supreme object of all the conspirators, civil or military, was to coerce the King without using physical force.

*　　*　　*

At the end of April James issued a second Declaration of Indulgence. He ordered that the Declaration should be read in all the churches. On May 18 seven bishops, headed by the Primate, the venerable William Sancroft, protested against this use of the dispensing power. The clergy obeyed their ecclesiastical superiors and the Declaration was left unread. James, furious at disobedience, and apparently scandalised at this departure, by the Church he was seeking to undermine, from its doctrine of nonresistance, demanded that the bishops should be put on trial for seditious libel. His Minister, Sunderland, now thoroughly alarmed, endeavoured to dissuade him from so extreme a step. Even Lord Chancellor Jeffreys told Clarendon that the King was going too far. But James persisted, the trial was ordered, and the bishops, all of whom refused the proffered bail, were committed to the Tower.

Up to this moment there always lived the hope that the stresses which racked the nation would die with the King. The accession of either Mary, the heir-presumptive, or Anne, the next in order, promised an end to the struggle between a Catholic monarch and a Protestant people. Peaceable folk could therefore be patient until the tyranny was past. The doctrine of nonresistance did not seem a principle of despair. But on June 10, while the trial of the bishops was still pending, the Queen gave birth to a son. Thus there lay before the English people the prospect of a Papist line, stretching out indefinitely upon the life of the future.

The bishops, formerly detested, never popular, now became the idols of the nation. As they stepped on board the barge for the Tower they were hailed by immense crowds with greetings in which reverence and political sympathy were combined. Now for the first time the Episcopacy found itself in alliance with the population of London. The same scenes were repeated when they were brought back to Westminster Hall on June 15, and at their trial on

June 29. The sitting lasted until late in the evening, and the jurors remained together throughout the night. When on the following day the bishops were declared "Not Guilty" the verdict was acclaimed with universal joy. As they left the court masses of people, including lifelong foes of the Episcopacy, knelt down and asked their blessing. But the attitude of the Army was more important. The King had visited them at Hounslow, and as he departed heard loud cheering. "What is that clamour?" he asked. "Sire, it is nothing; the soldiers are glad that the bishops are acquitted." "Do you call that nothing?" said James.

On the same night, while cannon and tumults proclaimed the public joy, the seven leaders of the party of action met at Shrewsbury's town house, and there and then signed and dispatched their famous letter to William. It was cool and businesslike in tone. "If the circumstances stand so with your Highness," it said, "that you believe you can get here time enough, in a condition to give assistance this year, . . . we, who subscribe this, will not fail to attend your Highness upon landing." William began to prepare his expedition. Protestant Europe and England alike looked to him as their champion.

All turned upon the action of France. If the French armies marched against Holland, William and the whole Dutch strength would be needed to face them, and England must be left to her fate. Louis decided that the best he could hope for would be an England impotent through civil war. At the end of September he turned his armies towards the middle Rhine, and from that moment William was free to set forth. The States-General granted him authority for his English descent and James's hour was come.

*   *   *

As the autumn weeks slipped by excitement and tension grew throughout the Island, and the vast conspiracy which now comprised the main strength of the nation heaved beneath the strain of affairs. The King's attempt to bring in some of the Irish Roman Catholic regiments which Tyrconnel had raised for him produced symptoms so menacing that the project was abandoned. The hatred and fears of all classes found expression in one of Lord Wharton's couplets:

> O, why does he stay so long behind?
> Ho! by my shoul, 'tis a Protestant wind.

The Protestant wind was blowing in the hearts of men, rising in fierce gusts to gale fury. Soon it would blow across the North Sea!

The scale and reality of William's preparations and the alarming state of feeling throughout England had terrified Sunderland and Jeffreys. These two Ministers induced the King to reverse his whole policy. Parliament must be called without delay. All further aggressive Catholic measures must be stopped and a reconciliation made with the Episcopal Church. On October 3 James agreed to abolish the Ecclesiastical Commission, to close the Roman Catholic schools, to restore the Protestant Fellows of Magdalen College, to put the Act of Uniformity into force against Catholics and Dissenters. The dismissed Lord-Lieutenants were invited to resume their functions in the counties. Their charters were restored to the recalcitrant municipalities. The bishops were begged to let bygones be bygones. The Tory squires were urged to take their old places in the magistracy. In the last few months of his reign James was compelled to desert the standard he had himself set up and try in vain by the sacrifice of all his objectives to placate the furies he had aroused. But it was too late.

On October 19 William set out upon the seas. His small army was a microcosm of Protestant Europe—Dutch, Swedes, Danes, Prussians, English, and Scotch, together with a forlorn, devoted band of French Huguenots, to the number of fourteen thousand, embarked upon about five hundred vessels, escorted by sixty warships. William had planned to land in the North, where Danby and other nobles were in readiness to join him. But after he had been once driven back by a gale the wind carried him through the Straits of Dover, which he passed in full view of the crowded coasts of England and France. On November 5 he landed at Torbay, on the coast of Devon. Reminded that it was the anniversary of the Gunpowder Plot, he remarked to Bishop Burnet, "What do you think of Predestination now?"

James was not at first greatly alarmed at the news. He hoped to pen William in the West and to hamper his communications by sea. The troops which had been sent to Yorkshire were recalled to the South, and Salisbury was fixed as the point of assembly for the royal Army. At this crisis the King could marshal as large an army as Oliver Cromwell at his height. Nearly forty thousand regular soldiers were in the royal pay. The Scottish troops, about four thousand strong, had only reached Carlisle, the bulk of the three thousand Irish were still beyond Chester, and at least seven thousand men must be left to hold down London. Still, twenty-five thousand men, or nearly double the number of William's expedition, were around Salisbury when the King arrived on November 19. This was the largest concentration of trained full-time troops that England had ever seen.

But now successive desertions smote the unhappy prince. Lord Cornbury, eldest son of the Earl of Clarendon, an officer of the Royal Dragoons, endeavoured to carry three regiments of horse to William's camp. James, warned from many quarters, meditated Churchill's arrest. On the night of November 23, having failed to carry any large part of the Army with them, Churchill and the Duke of Grafton, with about four hundred officers and troopers, quitted the royal camp. At the same time the Princess Anne, attended by Sarah Churchill, and guided by Bishop Compton, fled from Whitehall and hastened northwards. And now revolt broke out all over the

Multituds flying from London by water in boats & barges.

Flying by land.

Burying the dead with a bell before them.   Searchers.

Carts full of dead to bury.

"From the spring of 1665 the Great Plague had raged in London. Never since the Black Death in 1348 had pestilence spread such ravages. In London at the climax about seven thousand people died in a single week. Daniel Defoe's *JOURNAL OF THE PLAGUE YEAR* reconstructs for us in vivid searing style the panic and horror."

The Great Fire of London, seen from the east, upwind of the blaze. From a painting by an unknown Dutch artist who, from the detail shown, is believed to have been an eyewitness of the event. Old St. Paul's can be clearly seen.

country. Danby was in arms in Yorkshire, Devonshire in Derbyshire, Dela-mere in Cheshire. Lord Bath delivered Plymouth to William. Byng, later an admiral, representing the captains of the Fleet, arrived at his headquarters to inform him that the Navy and Portsmouth were at his disposal. City after city rose in rebellion. By one spontaneous, tremendous convulsion the English nation repudiated James.

The King, finding resistance impossible, assembled such peers and Privy Counsellors as were still in London, and on their advice entered into negotiations with the Prince of Orange. Meanwhile the invading army moved steadily forward towards London. James sent his wife and son out of the kingdom, and the night of December 11 stole from the palace at Whitehall, crossed the river, and rode to the coast. He endeavoured to plunge his realm into anarchy. He threw the Great Seal into the Thames, and sent orders to Feversham to disband the Army, and to Dartmouth to sail to Ireland with what ships he could. The wildest rumours of Irish massacres spread through the land. The London mob sacked the foreign embassies, and a panic and terror, known as "Irish Night," swept the capital. Undoubtedly a complete collapse of order would have occurred but for the resolute action of the Council, which was still sitting in London. With some difficulty they suppressed the storm, and, acknowledging William's authority, besought him to hasten his marches to London.

James in his flight had actually got on board a ship, but, missing the tide, was caught and dragged ashore by the fishermen and townsfolk. He was brought back to London, and after some days of painful suspense was allowed to escape again. This time he succeeded and left English soil for ever. But though the downfall and flight of this impolitic monarch were at the time ignominious, his dignity has been restored to him by history. His sacrifice for religion gained for him the lasting respect of the Catholic Church, and he carried with him into lifelong exile an air of royalty and honour.

BOOK SEVEN

England's Advance to World Power

CHAPTER FORTY-NINE

William of Orange

FROM HIS earliest years the extraordinary Prince who in the general interest robbed his father-in-law of the British throne had dwelt under harsh and stern conditions. William of Orange was fatherless and childless. His life was loveless. His marriage was dictated by reasons of State. He was brought up by a termagant grandmother, and in his youth was regulated by one Dutch committee after another. His childhood was unhappy and his health bad. He had a tubercular lung. He was asthmatic and partly crippled. But within this emaciated and defective frame there burned a remorseless fire, fanned by the storms of Europe.

William was cold, but not personally cruel. He wasted no time on minor revenges. His sole quarrel was with Louis XIV. For all his experience from a youth spent at the head of armies, and for all his dauntless heart, he was never a great commander. He had not a trace of that second-sight of the battlefield which is the mark of military genius. He was no more than a resolute man of good common sense whom the accident of birth had carried to the conduct of war. His inspiration lay in the sphere of diplomacy. He has rarely been surpassed in the sagacity, patience, and discretion of his statecraft. The combinations he made, the difficulties he surmounted, the adroitness with which he used the time factor or played upon the weakness of others, his unerring sense of proportion and power of assigning to objectives their true priorities, all mark him for the highest repute.

He never was fond of England, nor interested in her domestic affairs. As a race he regarded the English as inferior in fibre and fidelity to his Dutchmen. Once securely seated on the English throne he scarcely troubled to disguise these sentiments. It was not surprising that such manners, and still more the mood from which they evidently arose, gave deep offence. For the English, although submissive to the new authority of which they had felt the need, were as proud as any race in Europe. No one relishes being an object of aversion and contempt, especially when these affronts are unstudied, spontaneous, and sincere. William's unsociable disposition, his greediness at table, his silence and surliness in company, his indifference to women, his dislike of London, all prejudiced him with polite society. The ladies voted him "a low Dutch bear."

*   *   *

As soon as he learned on the afternoon of December 23, 1688, that by King James's flight he had become undisputed master of England, the Prince of Orange took the step for which he had come across the water. The French Ambassador was given twenty-four hours to quit the Island and England was committed to the general coalition against France. This opened a war which, with an uneasy interlude, gripped Europe for twenty-five years, and was destined to bring low to the ground the power of Louis XIV.

The Whigs, for their part, looked on the Revolution as the vindication of their own political belief in the idea of a contract between Crown and people. By the private advice of John and Sarah Churchill, Princess Anne, Mary's younger sister, surrendered in favour of William her right to succeed to the throne should Mary predecease him. Thus William gained without dispute the Crown for life. He accepted this Parliamentary decision with good grace. Many honours and promotions at the time of the coronation rewarded the Revolutionary leaders. Churchill, though never in William's immediate circle, was confirmed in his rank of Lieutenant-General, and employed virtually as Commander-in-Chief to reconstitute the English Army. He was created Earl of Marlborough. But William knew that he could never have gained the crown of England without the help of the Cavaliers and High Churchmen, who formed the staple of the Tory Party. Moreover, at this time, as a King he liked the Tory mood. Here was a Church devoted to hereditary monarchy. William felt that Whig principles would ultimately lead to a republic.

*   *   *

The British Islands now entered upon a most dangerous war crisis. The exiled James was received by Louis with every mark of consideration which the pride of the Great King could devise. Ireland presented itself as the obvious immediate center of action and, sustained by a disciplined French contingent, James landed in Ireland in March; the whole islands, except for the Protestant settlements in the North, speedily passed under his control. Thus, in 1690 William found himself compelled to go in person with his main force to Ireland, and by the summer took the field at the head of thirty-six thousand men. At the same time the French Fleet gained a victory over the combined fleets of England and Holland off Beachy Head. It was said in London that "the Dutch had the honour, the French had the advantage, and the English the shame." The command of the Channel temporarily passed to the French, and it seemed that they could land an invading army in England.

Queen Mary's Council, of which Marlborough was a member, had to face an alarming prospect. They were sustained by the loyalty and spirit of the nation. Marlborough stood ready to meet the invasion. But the French King had his eyes on Germany. The anxious weeks of July and August passed by without more serious injury than the burning of Teignmouth by French raiders. By the winter the French Fleet was dismantled, and the English and Dutch Fleets were refitted and again at sea. Thus the danger passed. The end of 1690 therefore saw the command of the sea regained. William was thus free to proceed in person to the Continent with strong forces and to assume command of the main armies of the Alliance. He took Marlborough with him at the head of the English troops. But no independent scope was given to Marlborough's genius, and the campaign, although on the greatest scale, was indecisive. Thereafter a divergence grew between the King and Marlborough. Marlborough was the leading British general, and many officers of various ranks resorted to him and loudly expressed their resentment at the favour shown to the Dutch.

At this time almost all the leading men in England resumed relations with James, now installed near Paris. King William was aware of this. He accepted double-dealing as a necessary element in a situation of unexampled perplexity. There was talk of the substitution of Anne for William and Mary, and at the same time the influence of the Churchills with Princess Anne continued to be dominating. The ill-feeling between the royal personages developed rapidly. William treated Anne's husband with the greatest contempt. Anne, who dearly loved her husband, was infuriated by these affronts.

As often happens in disputes among high personages, the brunt fell on a subordinate. The Queen demanded the dismissal of Sarah Churchill from Anne's household. Anne refused with all the obstinate strength of her nature. The next morning at nine o'clock Marlborough, discharging his functions as Gentleman of the Bedchamber, handed the King his shirt, and William preserved his usual impassivity. Two hours later the Secretary of State delivered to Marlborough a written order to sell at once all the offices he held, civil and military, and consider himself as from that date dismissed from the Army and all public employment and forbidden the Court. No reasons were given officially for this important stroke. The Queen now forbade Sarah to come to Court, and Anne retorted by quitting it herself. No pressure would induce Anne to part with her cherished friend, and in these fires of adversity and almost persecution links were forged upon which the destinies of England were presently to hang.

CHAPTER FIFTY

Continental War

NO SOONER had King William set out upon the Continental war than the imminent menace of invasion fell upon the Island he had left denuded of troops. Louis XIV now planned to descend upon England. King James was to be given his chance of regaining the throne.

Fevered but vigorous preparations were made for defence by land and sea. On May 19–20, 1692, the English and Dutch Fleets met Tourville with the main French naval power in the English Channel off Cape La Hogue. Both sides fought hard, and Tourville was decisively beaten. The whole apparatus of invasion was destroyed under the very eyes of the former King whom it was to have borne to his native shore.

The Battle of Cape La Hogue, with its consequential actions, effaced the memories of Beachy Head. It broke decisively for the whole of the wars of William and Anne all French pretensions to naval supremacy. It was the Trafalgar of the seventeenth century.

On land the campaign of 1692 unrolled in the Spanish Netherlands, which we now know as Belgium. It opened with a brilliant French success: Namur fell to the French armies. Worse was to follow. In August William marched by night with his whole army to attack Marshal Luxembourg. The French were surprised near Steinkirk in the early morning. But Luxembourg was equal to the emergency. From all sides the French advanced. The British lost two of their best generals and half their numbers killed and wounded. William, who was unable to control the battle, shed bitter tears as he watched the slaughter, and exclaimed, "Oh, my poor English!" By noon the whole of the Allied army was in retreat, and the French proclaimed their victory throughout Europe.

In July, 1693, was fought the great Battle of Landen, unmatched in Europe for its slaughter except by Malplaquet and Borodino for over two hundred years. After an heroic resistance the Allies were driven from their position by the French but William rallied the remnants of his army, and was able to maintain himself in the field. The war dragged on for two more years. At last Louis, who had long felt the weight of a struggle upon so many fronts, was now disposed to peace. William was unable to resist the peace movement of both his friends and foes. He saw that the quarrel was still unassuaged; his only wish was to prolong it. But he could not fight alone.

*   *   *

At the end of 1694 Queen Mary had been stricken with smallpox, and on December 28 she died, unreconciled to her sister Anne, mourned by her subjects, and lastingly missed by King William. Hitherto the natural expectation had been that Mary would long survive her husband, upon whose frail, fiery life so many assaults of disease, war, and conspiracy had converged. An English Protestant Queen would then reign in her own right. Instead of this, the crown now lay with William alone for life, and thereafter it must come to Anne. This altered the whole position of the Princess, and with it that of the redoubtable Churchills, who were her devoted intimates and champions. From the moment that the Queen had breathed her last Marlborough's interest no longer diverged from William's. He shared William's resolve to break the power of France; he agreed with the whole character and purpose of his foreign policy. A formal reconciliation was effected between William and Anne. Marlborough remained excluded for four more years but with his profound gift of patience and foresight upon the drift of events he now gave a steady support to William.

*   *   *

The Treaty of Ryswick in 1697 marked the end of the first period in this world war. In fact it was but a truce. Many comforted themselves with the hope that it had brought the struggle against the exorbitant power of France to an equipoise. This prospect was ruined by the Tories. The Tories were now in one of their moods of violent reaction from Continental intervention. The Commons plunged into a campaign of economy and disarmament. The moment the pressure of war was relaxed they had no idea but to cast away their arms. England, having made every sacrifice and performed prodigies of strength and valour, now fell to the ground in weakness and improvidence when a very little more perseverance would have made her, if not supreme, at least secure.

The apparent confusion of politics throughout William's reign was largely due to the King's great reluctance to put himself at the disposal of either of the two main party groups. The Whigs were sensitive to the danger of French aggression in Europe. They understood the deep nature of the struggle, and were prepared to form an effective War Government. The Tories, on the other hand, resented the country's being involved in Continental commitments and voiced the traditional isolationism of the people. The political story of the reign is thus a continuous see-saw and the fruits of warfare are incontinently thrown away. In the name of peace, economy, and isolation the Tories prepared the ground for a far more terrible renewal of the war. Their action has been largely imitated in our own times. No closer parallel exists in history than that presented by the Tory conduct in the years 1696 to 1699 with their similar conduct in the years 1932 to 1937. In each case short-sighted opinions, agreeable to the party spirit, pernicious to national interests, banished all purpose from the State and prepared a deadly resumption of the main struggle. These recurring fits of squalor in the Tory record are a sad counterpoise to the many great services they have rendered the nation in their nobler and more serviceable moods.

*   *   *

William was so smitten by the wave of abject isolationism which swept the governing classes of the Island that he contemplated an abdication and return to Holland. He would abandon the odious and intractable people whose religion and institutions he had preserved and whose fame he had lifted to the head of Europe. He would retort to their hatred of foreigners with a gesture of inexpressible scorn. It was a hard victory to master these emotions. Yet if we reflect on his many faults in tact, in conduct, and in fairness during the earlier days of his reign, the unwarrantable favours he had lavished on his Dutchmen, the injustices done to English commanders, his uncomprehending distaste for the people of his new realm, we cannot feel that all the blame was on one side. His present anguish paid his debts of former years. As for the English, they were only too soon to redeem their follies in blood and toil.

William's distresses led him to look again to Marlborough, with whom the future already seemed in a great measure to rest. The King's life and strength were ebbing. Anne would certainly succeed, and with the accession of Anne the virtual reign of Marlborough must begin. Marlborough patiently awaited this unfolding of events. William slowly divested himself of an animosity so keen that he had once said that had he been a private person Marlborough and he could only have settled their differences by personal combat.

Marlborough was restored to his rank in the Army and to the Privy Council. The ice of a long frost once broken, the King felt the comfort in his many troubles of Marlborough's serene, practical, adaptive personality. He used in peace the soldier he had neglected in war; and Marlborough, though stamped from his youth with the profession of arms, became in the closing years of the reign a leading and powerful politician.

In 1700 came the untimely death of the little Duke of Gloucester, Anne's sole surviving son, who succumbed to the fatal, prevalent scourge of small-pox. There was now no direct Protestant heir to the English and Scottish thrones. By an Act of Settlement the house of Hanover was declared next in succession after William and Anne. The Act laid down that every sovereign in future must be a member of the Church of England. It also declared that no foreign-born monarch might wage Continental wars without the approval of Parliament; he must not go abroad without consent, and no foreigners should sit in Parliament or on the Privy Council. Thus were recorded in statute the English grievances against William III. Parliament had seen to it that the house of Hanover was to be more strictly circumscribed than he had been. But it had also gone far to secure the Protestant Succession.

CHAPTER FIFTY-ONE

The Spanish Succession

NO GREAT war was ever entered upon with more reluctance on both sides than the War of the Spanish Succession. Europe was exhausted and disillusioned. But over all hung the long-delayed, long-dreaded, ever-approaching demise of the Spanish Crown and the partitioning of the Spanish Empire, which included the southern Netherlands, much of Italy, and a large part of the New World. There were three claimants. Much was at stake.

The feeble life-candle of the childless Spanish King burned low in the socket. To the ravages of deformity and disease were added the most grievous afflictions of the mind. All the nations waited in suspense upon his failing pulses and deepening mania. Charles had now reached the end of his torments. But within his diseased frame, his clouded mind, his superstitious soul, trembling on the verge of eternity, there glowed one imperial thought—the unity of the Spanish Empire. He was determined to proclaim with his last gasp that his vast dominions should pass intact and entire to one prince and to one alone. In the end he was persuaded to sign a will leaving his throne to the Duke of Anjou. The will was completed on October 7, and couriers galloped with the news from the Escorial to Versailles. On November 1, 1700, Charles II expired.

Louis XIV had now reached one of the great turning points in the history of France. On November 16 a famous scene was enacted at Versailles; Louis, at his levee, presented the Spanish Ambassador to the Duke of Anjou, saying, "You may salute him as your King." The Ambassador gave vent to his celebrated indiscretion, "There are no more Pyrenees."

The House of Commons was still in a mood far removed from European realities. They had just completed the disarmament of England. They eagerly accepted Louis XIV's assurance that, "content with his power, he would not seek to increase it at the expense of his grandson." A Bourbon prince would become King of Spain, but would remain wholly independent of France.

*   *   *

But now a series of ugly incidents broke from outside upon the fevered complacency of English politics. A plan was disclosed for the immediate French invasion of England in the Jacobite cause. William hastened to present this to Parliament as a proof of perfidy. At about the same time Parliament began to realise that the language and attitude of the French King about the separation of the Crowns of France and Spain was at the very least ambiguous. But the supreme event which roused all England to an understanding of what had actually happened in the virtual union of the

232

Crowns of France and Spain was a tremendous military operation effected under the guise of brazen legality.

Philip V had been acclaimed in Madrid. The Spanish Netherlands rejoiced in his accession. A line of fortresses in Belgium, the main barrier of the Netherlands against a French invasion, all passed in a few weeks, without a shot fired, by the lifting of a few cocked hats, into the hands of Louis XIV. All that the Grand Alliance of 1689 had defended in the Low Countries in seven years of war melted like snow at Easter.

The revulsion was rapid. Europe was roused, and at last England was staggered. Once more the fighting men came into their own. William felt the tide had set in his favour. By the middle of the year the parties in opposition to him in his two realms, the Tory majority in the House of Commons and the powerful burgesses of Amsterdam, were both begging him to do everything that he "thought needful for the preservation of the peace of Europe"—that is to say, for war.

This process united William and Marlborough. Though the opportunities of the reign had been marred or missed by their quarrels and misunderstandings, the two warrior-statesmen were at last united. The formation of the Grand Alliance had begun.

*   *   *

It was now, in this deadly atmosphere, that the flash came which produced the British explosion. On September 16, 1701, James II died. Louis announced that he recognised James's son as King of England and would ever sustain his rights. All England was roused by the insult to her independence. Outraged by the arrogance and by the perfidy of the French despot, the whole nation became resolute for war.

The second Grand Alliance now formed must have seemed a desperate venture to those whose minds were seared by the ill-fortune of William's seven-years war. France had gained without a shot fired all the fortresses and territory so stubbornly disputed. The widest Empire of the world was withdrawn from the Alliance and added to the resources of its antagonists. Spain had changed sides, and with Spain not only the Indies, South America, and a great part of Italy, but the cockpit of Europe—Belgium and Luxembourg. Savoy, a deserter, still rested with France, though her greatest prince was an Austrian general. The Archbishopric of Cologne was also now a French ally. Bavaria, constant to the end in the last war, was to be with France in the new struggle. The Maritime Powers had scarcely a friendly port beyond their coasts. The New World, except in the North, was barred against them. The Mediterranean had become in effect a French lake. South of Plymouth no fortified harbour lay open to British and Dutch ships. They had their superior fleets, but no bases which would carry them to the inland sea.

In every element of strategy by sea or by land, as well as in the extent of territory and population, Louis was twice as strong at the beginning of the War of the Spanish Succession as he had been at the Peace of Ryswick. Such was the prospect, as it seemed, of overwhelming adversity which had opened upon the English people largely as the result of their faction and their fickle moods. At this moment death overtook King William. "The little gentleman in black velvet," the hero for a spell of so many enthusiastic Jacobite toasts, now intervened. On February 20, 1702, William was riding in the park round Hampton Court on Sorrel, a favourite horse. Sorrel stumbled in the new workings of a mole, and the King was thrown. The broken collarbone might well have mended, but in his failing health the accident opened the door to a troop of lurking foes. Complications set in, and after a fortnight it was evident to him and to all who saw him that death was at hand. He transacted business to the end. His interest in the world drama on which the curtain was about to rise lighted his mind as the shadows closed upon him.

In his last years he had woven Marlborough into the whole texture of his combinations and policy. In his last hours he commended him to his successor as the fittest man in the realm to guide her councils and lead her armies. William died at fifty-two, worn out by his labours. Marlborough at the same age strode forward against tremendous odds upon the ten years of unbroken victory which raised the British nation to a height in the world it had never before attained.

CHAPTER FIFTY-TWO

Marlborough: Blenheim and Ramillies

THE AGE of Anne is rightly regarded as the greatest manifestation of the power of England which had till then been known. The genius of Marlborough in the field and his sagacity in counsel enabled the growing strength of the nation to make its full effect on Europe. Sarah managed the Queen, Marlborough managed the war, and Godolphin managed the Parliament. The Queen, for five glorious years, threw herself with happiness and confidence into these capable hands, and the whole force of England was applied to the leadership of the then known world.

There was at that time an extraordinary wealth of capacity in the English governing class. All the offices of the State, military or political, could have been filled two or three times over by able, vigorous, daring, ambitious personalities. It was also the Augustan Age of English letters. Addison, Defoe, Pope, Steele, Swift, are names which shine today. There was a vehement outpouring of books, poems, and pamphlets. Art and science flourished. The work of the Royal Society, founded in Charles II's reign, now bore a largesse of fruit. Sir Isaac Newton in mathematics, physics, and astronomy completed the revolution of ideas which had begun with the Renaissance. Architecture was led to noble achievements by Wren, and to massive monuments by Vanbrugh.

The religious passions of former years now flowed into the channels of political faction. Men and parties, conscious of their message and of the magnitude of the opportunity, strove furiously against one another for the control of the State or for a share in its governance. They carried their rivalry to all lengths; but in the earlier years of the reign there was a common purpose of beating France. This was no small undertaking, for at that time England had but five million inhabitants, while the towering French monarchy was master of near twenty millions, united under the Great King. Louis XIV stood triumphant, and, as it seemed, upon the threshold of unmeasured domination. He was now to be broken and humbled, and the later years of the reign of Anne were to be consumed mainly in disputes about the terms to be imposed upon him.

But all this wore a very different aspect when in March, 1702, Anne ascended the throne. She accepted Marlborough's impulse upon the whole policy of the State. In the first momentous days of her reign he was not only her chief but her sole guide. Both main parties admired him for his gifts, and for a time he stood above their warfare. The new reign opened in a blaze of loyalty. It was the "sunshine day" for which the Princess Anne had long waited with placid attention. Marlborough was made Captain-General of her armies at home and abroad. He acted immediately.

This was the great period of the Dutch Republic. But the death of William III shook the entire structure. There were forces in Holland which thought of a native commander for its troops. But all fell into Marlborough's hands. Marlborough and the able Lord Treasurer, Godolphin, who fulfilled many of the duties of a Prime Minister, worked closely and harmoniously together. But unquestioned authority was never granted to them; they always had to walk warily.

*　　*　　*

For the year 1702 Louis had decided to set his strongest army against Holland. He knew the division and uncertainty into which the Republic had been thrown by the death of King William. He believed that the links which joined it to England had been at the least gravely weakened. He counted upon a period of hesitation and loss of contact which, if turned to good account by military action, might break the Dutch and scare off the English. The French High Command therefore did not hesitate to place their main army, as soon as the campaigning season began, within twenty miles of Nimwegen, at the point where the valleys of the Meuse and the Rhine divide. In May Marlborough made for Nimwegen. Although he was baulked of the opportunity to fight what might have been a decisive battle at great advantage, the French were at once thrown on to the defensive. In a brilliant campaign the new Captain-General conquered all the fortresses of the Meuse. The valiant but fruitless efforts of King William were replaced by the spectacle of substantial advances, and the hitherto aggressive French were seen baffled, hesitating, and in retreat. In his very first year the tide of the war was set flowing in the opposite direction, and the whole Alliance, which had seemed about to collapse, was knit together by new bonds of constancy and hope.

*   *   *

The beginning of Queen Anne's reign seemed to open a period of Tory prosperity. The traditional Tory view was that England should not aspire to play a leading part in the Continental struggle. Her true policy was to intervene only by sea-power, and amid the conflicts of Europe to gain many territories overseas in the outer world. The Tories regarded with aversion the sending of large armies to the Continent. They looked with disparaging eyes upon victories in Europe. They groaned or affected to groan under the burden of Army expenses. The Whigs, on the other hand, though banished from office, were ardent advocates of the greatest military efforts. They supported Marlborough in all his courses. The issue was radical, and much to his regret Marlborough found it necessary to use his paramount influence with the Queen against the leaders of the Tory Party.

*   *   *

For the campaign of 1703 Marlborough was able to concentrate the "Grand Army," south of Nimwegen, the starting-point of the previous year. He had set his heart on the capture of Ostend and of Antwerp. This, the "great design," as he called it, did not succeed because the Dutch were not willing to consent to the very severe offensive battle which Marlborough wished to fight. The Tories threw the blame upon the Whig policy of the Continental war, and the Whigs themselves wilted under the double strain of being out of office and yet held responsible. Both at home and abroad the fortunes of the Grand Allies sank to a low ebb in the winter of 1703. Queen Anne here rose to her greatest height. "I will never forsake," she wrote to Sarah, "your dear self, Marlborough, nor Godolphin, and we four must never part till death mows us down with his impartial hand." With this support Marlborough during the winter months planned the supreme stroke of strategy which turned the whole fortune of the war: an invasion into the heart of Germany, where he would join with Prince Eugene, conquer Bavaria, and rescue Vienna.

Prince Eugene, though he had no actual command, represented the supreme military control of the Empire. Now for the first time began that

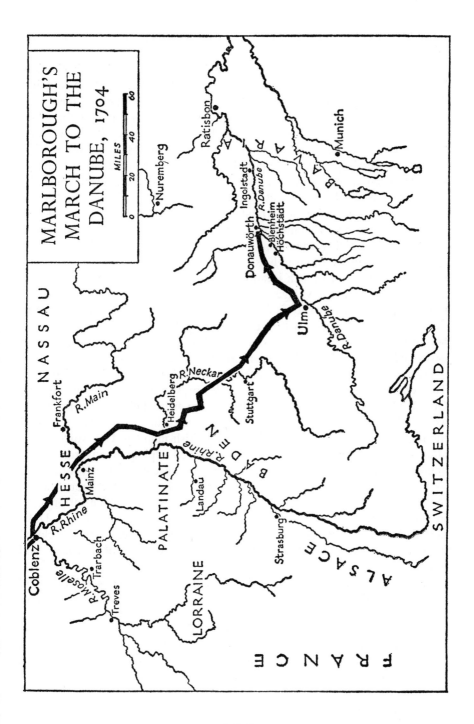

MARLBOROUGH'S MARCH TO THE DANUBE, 1704

MILES
0   20   40   60

NASSAU

Ratisbon

Nuremberg

Munich

Ingolstadt

R. Danube

Donauwörth

Blenheim
Höchstädt

Ulm

R. Danube

HESSE

Frankfort

R. Main

R. Neckar

Heidelberg

Stuttgart

BADEN

Mainz

R. Rhine

PALATINATE

Landau

Coblenz

R. Rhine

R. Moselle

Trarbach

Treves

Strasburg

LORRAINE

ALSACE

SWITZERLAND

FRANCE

237

splendid comradeship of the Duke and Eugene which for seven years continued without jealousy or defeat.

The annals of the British Army contain no more heroic episode than Marlborough's march from the North Sea to the Danube. The twin captains, Prince Eugene and Marlborough—"one soul in two bodies" as they were described—fell upon the French and Bavarian army on the Danube, early in the morning of August 13, 1704. The battle was fought with the greatest fury on both sides. Eugene commanded the right and Marlborough the left and centre. The English attack upon the village of Blindheim—or Blenheim, as it has been called in history—was repulsed, and for several hours the issue hung in the balance; but Marlborough about half-past five in the afternoon, after a series of intricate manœuvres, crossed the Nebel and concentrated an overwhelming force of cavalry against the French centre. At the head of eighty squadrons he broke the centre, routed the French cavalry, drove many thousands to death in the Danube, cut to pieces the remaining squares of French infantry, surrounded the great mass of French troops crowded into the village of Blenheim, and, as dusk fell on this memorable day, was able to write his famous letter to his wife: "I have not time to say more, but to beg you will give my duty to the Queen, and let her know her army has had a glorious victory." The victory of Blenheim almost destroyed the French and Bavarian armies on the Danube.

Over forty thousand men were killed, wounded, captured, or dispersed. The remnant retreated through the Black Forest towards the Upper Rhine. One-third of both armies lay stricken on the field. Thirteen thousand unwounded prisoners, including the most famous regiments of France, passed the night of the 13th in the hands of the British infantry. Ulm surrendered after a brief siege, and Marlborough marched rapidly westwards to the angle of the Rhine, where he was soon able to concentrate nearly a hundred thousand men. With Eugene and the Margrave he drove the French along the left bank towards Strasbourg and set siege to Landau, which surrendered in November. Finally, unwearied by these superb exertions, the Duke marched during October from the Rhine to the Moselle, where he closed a campaign ever a classic model of war by the capture of Trarbach and Treves.

All Europe was hushed before these prodigious events. Louis XIV could not understand how his finest army was not merely defeated, but destroyed. From this moment he thought no more of domination, but only of an honourable exit from the war he had provoked. The whole force of the Grand Alliance was revived and consolidated. The terror of the French arms, which had weighed on Europe for a generation, was broken. Marlborough stood forth, even above his comrade, the great Eugene, as the foremost soldier of the age. England rose with Marlborough to the summit, and the Islanders, who had never known such a triumph since Crécy and

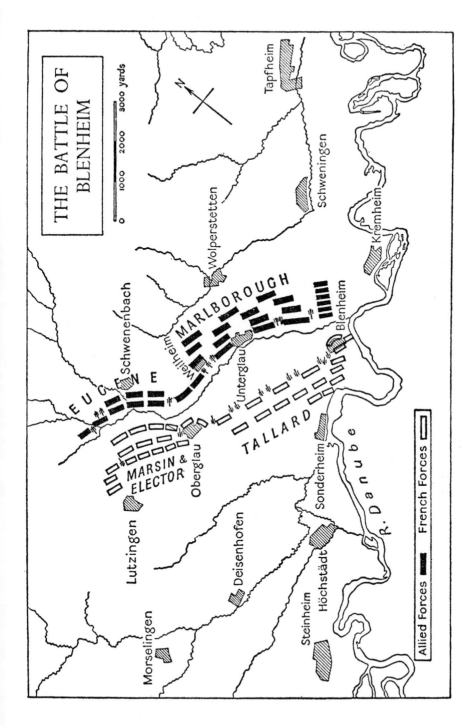

THE BATTLE OF BLENHEIM

3000 yards 2000 1000 0

N

Tapfheim

Schweningen

Wolperstetten

Kremheim

Schwenenbach

MARLBOROUGH

Blenheim

Weilheim

EUGENE

Unterglau

Oberglau

MARSIN &
ELECTOR

TALLARD

Sonderheim

Lutzingen

R. Danube

Deisenhofen

Steinheim

Höchstädt

Morselingen

Allied Forces ▬▬ French Forces ▭

239

Agincourt, four centuries earlier, yielded themselves to transports of joy. Queen Anne, delivered from her perils, enchanted by her glory, loaded him with wealth and honours. On New Year's Day the scores of standards and trophies of victory were borne in stately cavalcade through the streets of London to Westminster Hall.

*   *   *

The same year had seen remarkable successes at sea. The Rock of Gibraltar was then little more than a roadstead, but the possibilities of its commanding position at the gateway of the Mediterranean were already recognised. After bombardment the Rock was taken on August 4, 1704, in the same month as Blenheim, and proved a sure key to maritime power.

*   *   *

In this war a curious rhythm now recurs. When the fortunes of the Allies fell all obeyed Marlborough and looked to him to find the path to safety; but when he produced, infallibly, as it seemed, a new victorious scene the bonds of fear and necessity were relaxed and he was again hampered and controlled. Just as the brilliant campaign of 1702 was succeeded by the disappointments of 1703, so the grand recovery of 1704 gave place to disunity in 1705. The campaign ended again in disappointment and recriminations between the Allies. The Duke returned home to a difficult situation. The triumph of Blenheim seemed overclouded. Once again the fortunes of the Grand Alliance declined, and the central power of the French monarchy regathered its giant strength.

Wearied with the difficulties of co-operating with the Dutch and with the Princes of the Rhine, Marlborough planned through the winter an even more daring repetition of his march to the Danube in 1704. He now schemed to march across Europe with about twenty-five thousand British and British-paid troops by Coblenz, Stuttgart, and Ulm, through the passes of the Alps, to join Eugene in Northern Italy. There amid the vineyards and the olive trees the two great captains would gain another Blenheim and strike into France from the south. It was with melancholy thoughts that he began his most brilliant campaign. "I cross the sea," he wrote to the Imperial Envoy, "with sufficiently sad reflections." "The little concern of the King of Denmark and almost all the other princes give me so dismal thoughts that I almost despair of success," he wrote to Godolphin. But now Fortune, whom Marlborough had so ruefully but sternly dismissed, returned importunate, bearing her most dazzling gift.

Louis XIV had convinced himself that a defensive war could not be maintained against such an opponent. In robust mood he authorised a battle at the beginning of the campaign, with the best-equipped army of France, all clothed in new uniforms and in perfect order. At dawn on May 23, 1706, the two armies were in presence near the village of Ramillies, between Louvain and Liége. After furious fighting, in which forty thousand

240

horsemen were engaged, Marlborough broke the French line, drove their right from the field, and compromised their centre. Forgetting his duty as Commander-in-Chief, he charged into the cavalry battle, sword in hand. He was unhorsed and ridden over by the enemy. His equerry, Colonel Bingfield, while helping him to mount a second charger, had his head carried off by a cannon-ball which passed close to Marlborough's leg as he threw it over the saddle. But he soon resumed his full control of the tremendous event. All the Allied troops now advanced, and the French Army fled from the field in utter ruin. In this masterpiece of war, fought between armies almost exactly equal in strength and quality, the military genius of the English General destroyed and defeated his opponents with great slaughter and thousands of captives. Night shielded the fugitives, but less than a quarter escaped, and all their cannon were abandoned on the field.

*   *   *

The consequences of Ramillies were even more spectacular than those which had followed Blenheim. If, as was said, Blenheim had saved Vienna, Ramillies conquered Belgium. Fortresses, the capture of any one of which would have rewarded the efforts of a long campaign, fell by the dozen. Antwerp and Brussels surrendered, and the astonished Dutch saw themselves again possessors of almost the whole barrier which had been lost in the last year of King William's reign. These immense successes were enhanced by the victories of Prince Eugene in Northern Italy. Marching across the broad base of the Peninsula, he relieved Turin in a wonderful action against heavy odds, and thereafter drove the French completely out of Northern Italy. The "Year of Victory," as it was called in London, may close on this.

CHAPTER FIFTY-THREE

Oudenarde and Malplaquet

IF MARLBOROUGH had merely won the Battle of Ramillies, and perhaps entered Brussels, the campaign of 1706 might have carried the Allied cause to victory in 1707. But he now began to experience a whole series of new resistances and withholdings by the Dutch, as well as their grabbings and graspings, all of which were destined to bring the fortunes of the Allies once again to the lowest ebb. And these Dutch reactions had their counterpart at home. While in the field Marlborough and Eugene carried all before them, a series of English party and personal rivalries prepared a general

241

reversal of fortune. About this time Sarah Churchill's relations with the Queen entered on a perilous phase. She had to bear the brunt of her mistress's repugnance to a Whig infusion in the Cabinet. Anne loathed the Whigs from the bottom of her heart, but her Ministers could not see how it was possible to carry on the war without the Whigs and with only half the Tory Party at their back. Sarah wore out her friendship with the Queen in her duty of urging upon her an administration in harmony with Parliament. Anne's feminine friendships were exacting. Gradually Sarah sought to lighten the burden of this perpetual intercourse. In a poor relation, Abigail Hill, she found an understudy. She brought her into the Queen's life as a "dresser" or lady's maid. The Queen, after a while, took kindly to her new attendant. Sarah experienced relief, went more to the country and lived her family life. Abigail, by the beginning of 1707, had acquired an influence of her own with the Queen destined to deflect the course of European history.

Everything went wrong in 1707. Marlborough's design was that Eugene should debouch from Italy into France and capture Toulon. He used all his power, then at its height, to further this far-reaching plan. Meanwhile great misfortunes happened in Spain. The year had closed with King Philip once more propped up in Madrid, but with the Allies firmly in possession of the eastern quarter of Spain. Now in 1707 the Allied generals fatally divided their forces. A bloody defeat was sustained and the whole Spanish scene, so nearly triumphant in 1706, was now completely reversed.

The great enterprise against Toulon, to which Marlborough had subordinated all other interests, also ended in failure. Eugene was a land animal. He never liked a plan which depended so much upon the sea. After several costly assaults the siege failed. The Imperial army retreated upon Italy. One final disaster remained. Sir Cloudesley Shovel, making the winter passage home, was wrecked in thick and violent weather upon the sharp rocks of the Scillies. Britain's finest admiral, Marlborough's trusted naval leader, perished on the shore.

*   *   *

Marlborough returned from these tribulations to a furious party storm in England. Harley's designs were now apparent, and his strength nourished itself upon the military misfortunes. Marlborough and Godolphin together resolved to drive him from the Cabinet. An intense political crisis supervened. Marlborough demanded Harley's dismissal from his Secretaryship of State. Anne, now completely estranged from Sarah and with Abigail at her elbow, fought a stubborn fight for her favourite Minister. Marlborough tendered his resignation. The news spread far and wide that Marlborough and Godolphin had been dismissed. Both Houses of Parliament decided to conduct no business until they were better informed. The City was in consternation.

This struggle gave Marlborough a final lease of power. He had to a large extent lost the Queen. He had lost the moderate Tories. He must now increasingly throw himself into the hands of the Whigs, and at every stage of this process make wider the breach with the Queen. It was on these perilous foundations that he embarked upon the campaign of 1708. The plan was in principle a renewal of the double invasion of the previous year. This time, however, the effort was to be in the North. Marlborough had hoped to bring Eugene's Rhine army into the Low Countries and by superior numbers to crush the French in the field and pierce the fortress barrier; but a succession of unexpected misfortunes occurred. Conditions on the Rhine compelled Eugene to leave his army behind him. The Dutch rule of the conquered Belgian cities had estranged their inhabitants. By treachery Ghent and Bruges, which together controlled the chief waterways of the Scheldt and the Lys, were delivered to the French. Marshal Vendôme, with whom were the Princes of the Blood, the Dukes of Burgundy and Berri, and the Pretender, the young Prince of Wales, commanded a field army which, after providing for all the garrisons, numbered about eighty thousand men.

For the only time in the Duke's career he bent and bowed under the convergent strains at home and in the field. Eugene, arriving with only a cavalry escort, found him near Brussels in the deepest depression. He was prostrated by fever and so ill that he had to be bled. Here Eugene sustained his comrade. Marlborough rose from his sick-bed, mounted his horse, and the Army was set in motion. By a tremendous march they reached Lessines, on the Dyle. At dawn on July 11 they set out towards the fortress and bridgehead of Oudenarde, on the Scheldt.

The Battle of Oudenarde was in every aspect modern. It more nearly resembled Tannenberg in 1914 than any great action of the eighteenth century. The pace of the battle and its changes prevented all set arrangement. The French fought desperately but without any concerted plan, and a large part of their army was never engaged. The shadows of evening had fallen upon a battlefield of hedges, enclosures, villages, woods, and watercourses, in which the troops were locked in close, fierce fighting, when the Dutch, under the veteran Overkirk, at length traversed the Oudenarde bridges and swung round upon the heights to the north. At the same time Eugene, with magnificent courage, broke through on the right. The opposite wings of the Allies almost met. The French Army was now utterly confused and divided into two parts. In furious anger and consternation, the French Marshal Vendôme ordered a retreat on Ghent. A quarter of his army was destroyed or dispersed. Seven thousand prisoners, many high officers, and a wealth of standards and trophies were in Marlborough's hands when on the morning of July 12 he and his great companion rode their horses into the fine old square of Oudenarde.

This great victory altered the posture of the war. The Allies had recovered the initiative. It was resolved to attack Lille, the strongest fortress of France. The siege of Lille was not only the largest but the most complicated operation of its kind known to the eighteenth century. Eugene conducted the siege, and Marlborough with the covering army held off the largely superior forces which sought to relieve the city.

A brilliant action pierced the gloom of the autumn months and sealed the fate of the city of Lille, which capitulated in October. Bruges was re-captured at the end of December, and Ghent in the first days of January. Thus ended a campaign of struggle and hazard of which Prince Eugene said, "He who has not seen this has seen nothing."

At the same time the capture of Minorca, with its fine harbour at Mahon, gave to the English Navy at last a secure, permanent base in the Mediterranean. Thus the year which had opened in such dismal fashion ended in complete victory for the Allies. The power of France was broken. The Great King was humbled. A terrible frost laid its grip upon tortured Europe. The seed froze in the ground; the cattle died in the fields, and the rabbits in their burrows. The misery of the French people reached the limit of endurance. All sought peace, and all failed to find it.

*　　*　　*

Meanwhile in England the Whigs had at last achieved their long purpose. They had compelled Marlborough and Godolphin to rest wholly upon them. They overbore the Queen. Marlborough, estranged from the Queen, must now conform to the decision of a Whig Cabinet. His reign was ended. Henceforward he had but to serve. There still remained three difficult campaigns, upon a scale larger than any yet seen; but he no longer had control of the policy which alone could render fruitful the sombre struggles of the Army.

When we look upon the long years of terror and spoliation by Louis XIV, great allowances must be made for suspicions in the hour of victory. Nevertheless, the offers now made by France were so ample as to satisfy all reasonable demands of the Allies. In Spain alone did French fortunes prosper. But the Spanish quarrel had developed an independent life of its own. The one thing Louis would not do was to use French troops to drive his grandson out of the kingdom he had made his own. And this was the fatal rock upon which the peace conference was wrecked.

Marlborough had laboured faithfully for peace. He had misgivings, but upon the whole he expected the French to yield. "Are there no counter-proposals?" he asked in surprise when the courier brought the rejection of the Allied ultimatum. With Eugene he made some last efforts; but nothing availed. The disappointment of the Allies found vent in a vain and furious clamour that they had once again been tricked and fooled by Louis XIV. The drums beat in the Allied camps, and the greatest armies those war-

244

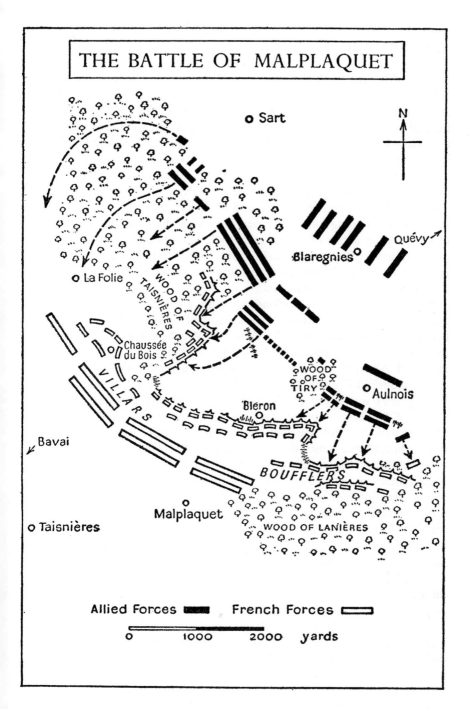

THE BATTLE OF MALPLAQUET

o Sart

N

o La Folie

WOOD OF TAISNIÈRES

Blaregnies o

Quévy

Chaussée du Bois

VILLARS

WOOD OF TIRY

o Aulnois

Bléron

Bavai

BOUFFLERS

o Malplaquet

o Taisnières

WOOD OF LANIÈRES

Allied Forces ▬▬ French Forces ▭

0   1000   2000   yards

worn times had seen rolled forward to the campaign of 1709 and the carnage of Malplaquet.

*   *   *

From this time forth the character of the war was profoundly affected. What had begun as a disjointed, tardy resistance of peoples, Parliaments, and Protestantism to intolerant and aggressive military power had transformed itself gradually and now flagrantly into invasion and subjugation by a victorious coalition. From this moment there was a strange invigoration in the patriotic spirit both of the French and Spanish peoples.

The Allied army had, meanwhile, been raised to its highest strength, and Marlborough and Eugene, concentrating south of Ghent, began the siege of Tournai which surrendered at the end of August. All this time the negotiations had been going forward behind the scenes, but suddenly an explosion of war fury, an access of mental rage, took possession of both Governments and both armies down to the private soldiers. A terrible ardour inspired all ranks. They thirsted to be at each other's throats and slay their foes, and thus bring the long war to an end.

By swift movements Marlborough and Eugene invested Mons, and, advancing south of it, found themselves confronted by Villars in the gap between the woods in which the village of Malplaquet stands, almost along the line of the present French frontier. On September 11 a hundred and ten thousand Allied troops assaulted the entrenchments, defended by about ninety thousand French. The battle was fought with extreme severity, and little quarter was asked or given. Marlborough in the main repeated the tactics of Blenheim. He first attacked both French wings. The Dutch were repelled with frightful slaughter on the left. The right wing, under Eugene, broke through the dense wood, and eventually reached the open country beyond. Under these pressures Villars and his second in command, the valiant Boufflers, were forced to thin their centre. The moment came for which Marlborough was waiting. He launched the English corps under Orkney upon the denuded redoubts, and, having seized them, brought forward his immense cavalry masses, over thirty thousand strong, which had been waiting all day close at hand. With the "Grey" Dragoons and the Scots Greys in the van, the Allied cavalry passed the entrenchments and deployed in the plain beyond. Villars had been grievously wounded, but the French cavalry came forward in magnificent spirit, and a long series of cavalry charges ensued. At length the French cavalry were mastered. Their infantry were already in retreat. "I am so tired," wrote Marlborough to Sarah a few hours later, "that I have but strength enough to tell you that we have had this day a very bloody battle; the first part of the day we beat their foot, and afterwards their horse. God Almighty be praised, it is now in our powers to have what peace we please."

Europe was appalled at the slaughter of Malplaquet. The victors camped upon the field, but the event presented itself to all men as a terrible judgment upon the failure of the peace negotiations. In England the Whigs proclaimed a decisive victory. But the Tories accused them, and also Marlborough, of having thrown away the chance of a good peace to produce a fruitless carnage, the like of which Europe could not remember. Indeed, Malplaquet, the largest and bloodiest battle of the eighteenth century, was surpassed only by Napoleon's barren victory at Borodino a hundred years later.

CHAPTER FIFTY-FOUR

The Treaty of Utrecht

ALL EYES were now turned upon the English Court. It was known throughout Europe that Marlborough's power with the Queen had vanished. The great armies faced one another for the campaign of 1710. Their actual numbers were larger than ever before, but Marlborough and Eugene could not or did not bring Villars to battle. Indeed, it may be thought that Marlborough was so sickened by the slaughter of Malplaquet and so disheartened by the animosities crowding upon him at home that he would henceforward only wage war as if it were a game of chess.

He returned from his ninth campaign to find England in the control of his political and personal foes. But the downfall of Marlborough was also the revival of Louis XIV. From every quarter, therefore, even the most unfriendly, Marlborough was urged, implored, or conjured to serve. Although he was afterwards mocked for love of office and of war, it was his duty to comply. Terms were made between the Tory Ministers and the Captain-General for the tenth year in succession took the field.

* * *

Marlborough in the campaign of 1711 concentrated no fewer than ninety thousand men facing Villars, whose army was still a hundred and twenty thousand strong.

During the winter Villars had constructed an enormous system of entrenchments. He called these lines "Ne Plus Ultra," and at the head of his mobile army courted attack. The great armies formed against each other and the lines of battle were drawn. Everyone expected an onslaught. On August 4 the Duke in person conducted a reconnaissance along the whole front. He allowed large numbers of officers to accompany him and pointed to the positions he would assault. Only his immense prestige prevented out-spoken protests, and may observers condemned the openness with which he spoke of his plans for battle. Marlborough's soldiers had blind faith in a leader who had never led them wrong. But the high command was full of aches and fears. They did not notice that General Cadogan had silently slipped away from the great reconnaissance. They were not informed of the movements behind Marlborough's front.

At length tattoo beat and darkness fell. Orders came to strike tents and stand to arms. Soon staff officers arrived to guide the four columns, and in less than half an hour the whole army was on the march. It was not after all to be a bloody battle. The "Old Corporal" was up to something of his own. All now depended upon marching qualities. "My Lord Duke wishes the infantry to step out."

As the light broadened and the day advanced the troops could see upon their right, across the marshes and streams of the Sensée, that the French were moving parallel to them within half cannon-shot. But they also saw that the head of the French horse was only abreast of the Allied foot. During August 5 the bulk of the Allied army had crossed the Sensée and was drawing up inside the enemy's lines. Thousands of exhausted soldiers had fallen by the way, and large numbers died in the passion of their effort.

In the result Marlborough formed a front beyond the lines, but instead of forcing a battle he moved rapidly and cast his siege-grip on the fortress of Bouchain. The forcing of the "Ne Plus Ultra" line and the siege and capture of Bouchain were judged by Europe to be outstanding manifestations of the military art. It was a siege within a siege. There is no finer example of Marlborough's skill. Bouchain capitulated at the beginning of September. The armies went into winter quarters and Marlborough returned home. For ten years he had led the armies of the Grand Alliance, and during all that period he never fought a battle he did not win or besieged a town he did not take. Nothing like this exists in the annals of war.

*   *   *

It was now impossible to conceal any longer the secret peace negotiations which had all this while been in progress. The Tory leaders were sure they could carry the peace if Marlborough would support it. But the Duke, who was in close association with George of Hanover, the heir to the throne, would not agree to a separate peace in any circumstances.

Parliament opened in the winter of 1711 in intense crisis. The two great parties faced one another upon all the issues of the long war. Marlborough was dismissed from all his offices and exposed to the censure of the House of Commons. The salaries and emoluments he had enjoyed as Captain-General of England, as Deputy Captain-General of Holland, and from many other posts and perquisites had enabled him, with his thrift and acquisitiveness, to build up a large fortune. He was now charged chiefly with converting to his own use during his ten years' command the $2\frac{1}{2}$ per cent levied upon the pay of all foreign contingents in the Allied army. His defence was convincing. But this did not prevent the Tories in the House of Commons from impugning his conduct.

England was now riven in twain upon the issue of peace. A separate peace it must be now, for the Allies one and all repudiated the right of the British Government to abandon the Alliance and provide for themselves. Upon a dark day the British Army, hitherto the most forward in the Allied cause and admired by all, marched away from the camp of the Allies in bitter humiliation and amid the curses of their old comrades. Many of Marlborough's veterans flung themselves on the ground in shame and fury. The outraged Dutch closed the gates of their cities in the face of the deserting Ally. Villars, advancing rapidly, fell upon Eugene's magazines at Denain and inflicted upon him a cruel defeat in which many of his troops were driven into the Scheldt and drowned. Upon this collapse Villars captured all the advanced bases of the Allies and took Douai, Quesnoy, and Bouchain. Thus he obliterated the successes of the past three years, and at the end of the terrible war emerged victorious.

* * *

What is called the Treaty of Utrecht was in fact a series of separate agreements between individual Allied states with France and with Spain. The British Government gained their special terms; the French Court recognised the Protestant succession in Britain, and agreed to expel the Pretender from France, to demolish fortifications and to cede various territories in North America and the West Indies. With Spain the terms were that England should hold Minorca and Gibraltar, thus securing to her, while she remained the chief sea-power, the entry and control of the Mediterranean.

Such were the settlements reached at Utrecht in the spring of 1713, and Chatham, who inherited the consequences, was one day to declare them "an indelible blot upon the age." On this basis Europe subsided into an uneasy peace, and although these terms were not comparable with what the Allies could have gained in 1706, in 1709, or 1710 they none the less ended for a while the long torment to which Christendom had been subjected.

* * *

Marlborough was so much pursued by the Tory Party and harassed by the State prosecutions against him that at the end of 1712 he left the country and lived in self-imposed exile in Holland and Germany till the end of the reign.

The final phase of the Tory triumph was squalid. Anne was now broken with gout and other ailments. For many months her life hung upon a thread. She who had seen so much glory now drew towards an ignominious end. Having enjoyed in the fullest measure the love of her people for many years of splendour, she now found herself the tool of what had become a disreputable faction. Beneath this weight of hostility and reproach the poor

Queen sank in sorrow to the grave. Yet her spirit burned unquenched to the end. The Elector of Hanover, supported by the Dutch and aided by Marlborough, gathered the forces to repeat the descent of William of Orange.

"Good God," exclaimed the Duke of Buckinghamshire (after he had been put out of office), "how has this poor nation been governed in my time! During the reign of King Charles the Second we were governed by a parcel of French whores, in King James the Second's time by a parcel of Popish priests, in King William's time by a parcel of Dutch footmen, and now we are governed by a dirty chambermaid, a Welsh attorney, and a profligate wretch that has neither honour nor honesty."

On July 30, while the Queen was evidently at the point of death, the Privy Council met in the palace. Vigorous measures were taken to ensure the Hanoverian succession. All preparations were made with heralds and Household troops to proclaim King George. When Queen Anne breathed her last at half-past seven on August 1, 1714, it was certain that there would be no Popery, no disputed succession, no French bayonets, no civil war.

Thus ended one of the greatest reigns in English history. It had been rendered glorious by Marlborough's victories and guidance. The Union and the greatness of the Island had been established. The power of France to dominate Europe was broken, and only Napoleon could revive it. The last of the Stuart sovereigns had presided over a wonderful expansion of British national strength, and in spite of the moral and physical failures of her closing years she deserved to bear in history the title of "the Good Queen Anne."

BOOK EIGHT

The First British Empire

CHAPTER FIFTY-FIVE

The House of Hanover

DURING THE late summer of 1714 all England awaited the coming of King George I. On September 18 he landed at Greenwich. This fortunate German prince, who could not speak English, viewed his new realms without enthusiasm. In accepting the throne of the United Kingdom he was conferring, as it seemed to him, a favour upon his new subjects. He was meeting the convenience of English politicians. In return he expected that British power and wealth would be made serviceable to his domains in Hanover and to his larger interests on the European scene. His royal duties would entail exile from home in an island he had only once previously visited and which he did not like. Now on the banks of the Thames he looked about upon the nobles and Ministers who had come to greet him with suspicion and wariness, not unmingled with contempt. Here on English soil stood an unprepossessing figure, an obstinate and humdrum German martinet with dull brains and coarse tastes. As a commander in the late wars he had been sluggish and incompetent, and as a ruler of men he had shown no quickening ability or generosity or spirit. Yet the rigidity of his mind was relieved by a slow shrewdness and a brooding common sense. The British throne was no easy inheritance, especially for a foreign prince. King George took it up grudgingly, and it was ungraciously that he played his allotted part. He owed his crown to the luck of circumstance, but he never let it slip from his grasp.

*   *   *

The political passions of the seventeenth century had spent themselves in the closing years of Queen Anne. The struggle of Whig against Tory had brought the country to the verge of civil war. The issue was who should succeed to the crown, the Catholic son of James II or the Protestant Elector? Now all was settled. There were no more great constitutional issues. George I had come peacefully to the throne. The Tory Party was shattered, and England settled down, grumbling but safe, under the long rule of Whiggism.

The monarchy, too, had lost its lustre. There was no pretence that the Hanoverian kings ruled by Divine Right. They held their position by the express sanction of Parliament. Even the symbolism of royalty was curtailed. The Court was no longer the centre of beauty, rank, and fashion. A certain dowdiness creeps into the ceremonial and the persons of the courtiers. Life in the royal palaces is dominated by the panoply and surroundings of a minor German princeling. The dreary names of the German women are ever present in the memoirs of the time, all soon to deck themselves out with English titles and wealth.

The men who led the Whig Party in the days of Queen Anne were fast retiring from the scene. The greatest figure of them all, John Duke of Marlborough, lived on in splendid isolation in his houses at Blenheim and St. Albans, stricken with a lingering paralysis, until he was released by death in 1722. His wife, Sarah, was doomed to live out her life for twenty years more, a croaking reminder of the high days of the Augustan Age. But she was alone. A new generation of statesmen—Walpole, Stanhope, Carteret, and Townshend—were to ensure the peaceful transition from the age of Anne to the age of the Georges. The first two Georges were preoccupied with European affairs and showed little interest in the home politics of their adopted country. With political power and influence barred except to the favoured few, men turned to other pursuits and new adventures. Financial speculation was encouraged. In 1710 a Tory Ministry had granted a charter to a company trading with the South Seas, and had arranged for it to take over part of the National Debt. This connection had rapidly expanded the wealth of the South Sea Company, and in 1720 a group of Directors approached the Government with a plan to absorb the whole National Debt, then standing at about £30,000,000. The scheme soon came to stink of dishonesty, but the politicians were too greedy to reject it. There was a chance of wiping out the whole debt in twenty-five years. £1,250,000 is said to have been spent in bribes to Ministers, Members of Parliament, and courtiers.

The mania for speculation broke loose. Stock soared in three months from 128 to 300, and within a few months more to 500. Amid the resounding cries of jobbers and speculators a multitude of companies, some genuine and some bogus, was hatched. By June, 1721, the South Sea stock stood at 1,050. Robert Walpole himself had the luck to make a handsome profit on his quiet investments. At every coffee-house in London men and women were investing their savings in any enterprise that would take their money. There was no limit to the credulity of the public. One promoter floated a company to manufacture an invention known as Puckle's Machine Gun, "which was to discharge round and square cannon-balls and bullets and make a total revolution in the art of war," the round missiles being intended for use against Christians and the square against the Turk. Other promoters invited subscriptions for making salt water fresh, for constructing a wheel of perpetual motion, for importing large jackasses from Spain to improve the breed of English mules, and the boldest of all was the advertisement for "a company for carrying on an undertaking of Great Advantage, but no one to know what it is." This amiable swindler set up a shop in Cornhill to receive subscriptions. His office was besieged by eager investors, and after collecting £2,000 in cash he prudently absconded.

The Government took alarm, and the process of suppressing these minor companies began. The South Sea Company was only too anxious to exterminate its rivals, but the pricking of the minor bubbles quickened and precipitated a slump. An orgy of selling began, and by October the South Sea stock stood at 150. Thousands were ruined. The porters and ladies' maids who had bought carriages and fineries found themselves reduced to their former station. Clergy, bishops, poets, and gentry found their life savings vanish overnight. There were suicides daily. Groups of frantic bankrupts thronged the Parliamentary lobbies. There was a general outcry against the cupidity of the German ladies. "We are ruined by Trulls—nay, what is more, by old, ugly Trulls, such as could not find entertainment in the most hospitable hundreds of Old Drury." The brief hour of dreamed-of riches closed in wide-eyed misery. Bringing order to the chaos that remained was the first task of Britain's first Prime Minister.

CHAPTER FIFTY-SIX

Sir Robert Walpole

THE SCANDAL of the South Sea Bubble roused the hopes of the Tories. One man only amid the crash and panic of 1721 could preserve the Whig monopoly. He was Robert Walpole, now established as the greatest master of figures of his generation. Soon he was to become a Knight of the Garter, one of the few Commoners to hold the honour, a leading figure of the Whig Party in the House of Commons.

Walpole, on becoming head of the Government, immediately turned to financial reconstruction. Within a few months the situation improved and England settled down again under another edition of Whig rule. With a business man at the head of affairs the atmosphere of national politics became increasingly materialistic. Walpole's object was to stabilise the Hanoverian regime and the power of the Whig Party within a generation. He was the careful nurse of England's recovery after the national effort under Queen Anne. But men remembered the great age that had passed and scorned the drab days of George I. A policy of security, prosperity, and peace made small appeal to their hearts, and many were ready to attack the degeneration of politics at home and the futility of England abroad. This lure of European politics was too much for several of the men around

Walpole. He meant to do as little as possible: to keep the peace, to stay in office, to juggle with men, to see the years roll by. But others responded to more lively themes. Walpole was forced to quarrel. By his enemies he was now mockingly called the "Prime Minister"—for this honourable title originated as a term of abuse. In 1737 Walpole's staunch ally, Queen Caroline, died. There was steadily growing a reaction, both in the country and in the House of Commons, to the interminable monopoly of political power by this tough, unsentimental squire, with his head for figures and his horror of talent, keeping the country quiet, and, though it was only an incident, feathering his own nest. All that was needed to destroy the mechanism of Walpole's rule was an issue that would stir the country, and which would in its turn stampede the quiescent, half-squared Members of Parliament into a hostile vote against the Minister. The crack came from a series of incidents in Spanish America.

*   *   *

In 1713 the Treaty of Utrecht had granted the English the right to send one shipful of Negro slaves a year to the Spanish plantations in the New World. Such was the inefficiency of Spanish administration that it was easy to run contraband cargoes and the illicit trade grew steadily in the years of peace. But when the Spanish Government began to reorganise, English ships trading unlawfully in the Spanish seas were stopped and searched by the Spanish coastguards. Profits were high, and merchants in London forced Walpole to challenge the right of search. A series of negotiations followed with Madrid.

Spain, nearly bankrupt, was anxious to avoid war. She offered many concessions, and Walpole drastically reduced the claims of English merchants. But the Opposition in Parliament opened a broad attack on the Government's negotiations with Spain. Much was heard of the honour of England and the great traditions of Elizabeth and Cromwell, and there was vehement appeal to national prejudices and sentiments. A captain trading with the Spanish possessions, one Jenkins, was brought before the House of Commons to produce his ear in a bottle, and to maintain that it had been cut off by Spanish coastguards when his ship was searched. "What did you do?" he was asked. "I commended my soul to God and my cause to my country," was the answer put in his mouth by the Opposition. Jenkins's ear caught the popular imagination and became the symbol of agitation.

The Spaniards might have ignored the bellicose Opposition in the British Parliament. Walpole was not strong enough to do so. If the country demanded war with Spain, the Ministers were prepared to ride with them rather than resign. Now opened a mighty struggle, at first with Spain only, but later by the family compact between the Bourbon monarchs involving France. Thus began that final duel between Britain and her nearest neighbour which in less than a century was to see the glories of Chatham, the follies of Lord North, the terrors of the French Revolution, and the rise and fall of Napoleon.

By sure degrees, in the confusion and mismanagement which followed, Walpole's power, as he had foreseen, slipped from him. The operations of the ill-manned Fleet failed. There were riots in London. The Prince of Wales appeared everywhere, to be cheered by opponents of the Government. A new tune was on their lips, with Thomson's resounding words, "Rule, Britannia."

It was February, 1742. Sir Robert had governed England for twenty-one years. During the last days before his fall he sat for hours on end, alone and silent, brooding over the past in Downing Street. He was the first Chief Minister to reside at Number Ten. He had accomplished the work of his life, the peaceful establishment of the Protestant succession in England. He had soothed and coaxed a grumbling, irritated country into acquiescence in the new régime. He had built up a powerful organisation, fed and fattened on Government patronage. He had supervised the day-to-day administration of the country, unhampered by royal interference. The sovereign had ceased after 1714 to preside in person over the Cabinet, save on exceptional occasions—a most significant event, though it was only the result of an accident. One of the charges against Walpole after his fall was that he had sought to become "sole and Prime Minister." He had kept England at peace for nearly twenty years. He was the first great House of Commons man in British history, and if he had resigned before the war with Spain he might have been called the most successful.

CHAPTER FIFTY-SEVEN

The American Colonies

WE MUST now survey the scene presented by the American colonies, which had been quietly and steadily growing for the past hundred and fifty years. Throughout the first half of the seventeenth century Englishmen had poured into the American continent. Legally the colonies in which they settled were chartered bodies subordinate to the Crown, but there was little interference from home, and they soon learned to govern themselves. While distracted by the Civil War the Mother Country left them alone, and although Cromwell's Commonwealth asserted that Parliament was supreme over the whole of the English world its decree was never put into practice, and was swept away by the Restoration. But after 1660 the home Government had new and definite ideas. For the next fifty years successive English administrations tried to enforce the supremacy of the Crown in the American colonies and to strengthen royal power and patronage in the overseas possessions. Thus they hoped to gain credit and advantage. Committees were formed to deal with America. New colonies were founded in Carolina and Pennsylvania, and New Netherland was conquered from the Dutch. Precautions were taken to assure the Crown's authority in these acquisitions. There were efforts to rescind or modify the charters of the older colonies. All this led to unceasing conflict with the colonial assemblies, who resented the threat to royalise and unify colonial administration. Most of these assemblies were representative bodies of freeholders who claimed and exercised the same rights, procedure, and privileges as the Parliament at Westminster. The men who sat in them were many of them bred in a tradition hostile to the Crown. Their fathers had preferred exile to tyranny.

For a long time the English Parliament played no part in the conflict. The struggle lay between the colonies and the King's Ministers in the Privy Council. These officials were determined to call a halt to self-government in America. England's motives were not entirely selfish. Slowly the menace of French imperialism loomed upon the frontiers of her possessions and English statesmen and merchants confronted a deadly competition upon the seas and in the markets of the world. The answer devised was an eminently practical one. British colonial trade must be planned and co-ordinated in London. One of its main objects must be to foster the British Merchant Navy, and to provide a reserve of ships and seamen in the event of war. Colonial trade must travel only in British bottoms, with British crews and to British ports. The colonies were forbidden any outside trade of their own that might hinder the growth of British shipping. The prevailing view of trade was based on the desire for self-sufficiency and on economic nationalism. Colonies were vital. They must produce essential raw materials and afford a market for the home country. The Empire must be a closed economic unit. Such, in brief, was the economic conception enshrined in the legislation of the seventeenth century. There was no room in this scheme for the independent development of the colonies. The system was more irksome on paper than in practice. No seventeenth-century Government could enforce such a code over thousands of miles. American assemblies grumbled but went their own way, ingeniously evading the Westminster restrictions.

The English Revolution of 1688 changed the whole position. Hitherto the colonies had regarded the Parliament in England as their ally against the Crown. But the time was to come when Parliament, victorious over the Crown in the constitutional struggles at home, would attempt to enforce its own sovereignty over America.

The spirit of amity which it was thus hoped to secure fell far short of

The Duke of Marlborough, Victor at Blenheim, Ramillies, Oudenarde and Malplaquet. "The annals of the British Army contain no more heroic episode than Marlborough's march from the North Sea to the Danube."

Blenheim Palace

The seat of John Churchill, Duke of Marlborough, erected It was designed by Sir John Vanbrugh, distinguished soldier, near Oxford at the public expense in the reign of Queen playwright and architect. Here Sir Winston Churchill was

expectation. There were ample reasons for this. Both in outlook and tradition the colonies had been steadily growing apart from the Mother Country. A colonial-born generation now inhabited the American plantations, trained in the harsh struggle with nature, expanding rapidly in the limitless lands stretching westwards from the seaboard, and determined to protect their individuality and their privileges. The doctrines of the English Revolution and the ideas of the seventeenth-century Whigs struck an even deeper echo in the New World than at home. The youthful energies of the Americans found paper obstacles at every turn to the development of their resources. All these causes indisposed them to any great effort on behalf of England. On the other hand, though quick to realise their potential strength and wealth, the colonists were slow to organise; and being still instinctively loyal to their race and conscious of the French menace beyond their own frontiers they were as anxious as Britain to avoid a serious quarrel. They even took an active but ill-organised part in the attempts to conquer French Canada which culminated in the futile expedition of 1711. But, jealous as they were not only of the home Government but of each other, they soon lapsed into quarrelsome isolation.

* * *

These conditions persisted throughout the administration of Walpole, who perceived the necessity for avoiding friction at all costs. But in the course of time the colonists grew more and more resolved to press their advantage, and the middle years of the eighteenth century witnessed a vehement assault by the colonial Assemblies upon the authority of the Imperial Government. They were bent on making themselves into sovereign Parliaments, supreme in the internal government of the several colonies, and free of all restrictions or interference from London. Innumerable struggles took place between the Governors and the legislatures of the colonies. There were many complaints on both sides. The Crown looked upon posts overseas as valuable patronage for its servants, the Government for their supporters. Thus the whole colonial administration was tainted with the prevailing corruption of English public life. Governors, counsellors, judges, and many other officials were all appointed by the Crown, and they were seldom chosen with due regard to the interests of the colonists. "America," said one of her historians, "is the hospital of Great Britain for its decayed M.P.s and abandoned courtiers."

Behind the squabbling of day-to-day administration lay vital developments. Though the colonial Assemblies persistently tried to copy the English pattern, they were hampered at every turn. America was still regarded as existing for the economic benefit of England. The pressure from England grew stronger with the years. The balance of trade turned steadily against the colonies. The colonial merchants could only scrape together enough cash by illegal methods. This drift of money from America was to help keep England solvent in the coming first world war.

The early eighteenth century saw the foundation of the last of the Thirteen Colonies. The philanthropist James Oglethorpe had been painfully moved by the horrible condition of the small debtors in English prisons. After much thought he conceived the idea of allowing these people to emigrate to a new colony. In 1733 the first settlement was founded at Savannah. Small estates were created, and religious toleration was proclaimed for all except Catholics. The first settlers were English debtors, but the foundation promised a new life for the oppressed in many parts of Europe. Bands of Jews quickly arrived, followed by Protestants from Salzburg, Moravians from Germany, and Highlanders from Skye. The polyglot community, named Georgia, soon attracted ardent missionaries, and it was here that John Wesley began his ministering work.

This colony was the last foundation of the Mother Country in the territories that were later to become the United States. Emigration from England had now dwindled to a trickle, but new settlers arrived from other parts. Towards the end of the seventeenth century there had been an influx of Scottish-Irish refugees, whose industrial and commercial endeavours at home had been stifled by the legislation of the English Parliament. They formed a strong English-hating element in their new homes. Pennsylvania received a steady flow of immigrants from Germany, soon to number over two hundred thousand souls. Hard-working and prosperous Huguenots arrived from France in flight from religious persecution. People were also moving from colony to colony. The oases of provincial life were linked up. The population was rapidly doubling itself. Limitless land to the West offered homes for the sons of the first generation. The abundance of territory to be occupied encouraged large families. Contact with primeval conditions created a new and daring outlook. A sturdy independent society was producing its own life and culture, influenced and coloured by surrounding conditions. The Westward march had begun, headed by the Germans and the Ulster Irish in Pennsylvania. The slow trail over the mountains in search of new lands was opening. There was a teeming diversity of human types. On the Western farms which bordered the Indian country were rugged pioneers and sturdy yeomen farmers, and in the New England colonies assertive merchants, lawyers, and squires, and the sons of traders. This varied society was supported in the North by the forced labour of indentured servants and men smuggled away from the press-gangs in English towns, in the South by a mass of slaves multiplied by yearly shiploads from Africa. Events in Europe, of which most Americans were probably scarcely conscious, now came to bear upon the destiny of the Thirteen Colonies.

CHAPTER FIFTY-EIGHT

The First World War

WHEN PITT first joined the Ministry as Secretary of State in November, 1756, Frederick the Great declared, "England has long been in labour, but at last she has brought forth a man."

The winter of 1755–1756 witnessed a great diplomatic revolution towards which the four main powers of Europe had for some time been groping. A convention was signed between Britain and Prussia, shortly followed by a treaty between the French and the Austrians. Thus there was a complete reversal of alliances. A third war with France began with a new and vigorous ally on England's side, the Prussia of Frederick the Great, but with a fumbling Government at Westminster. The mismanagement of the early years of the struggle gave William Pitt his chance. The loss of the island of Minorca raised a national outcry. Pitt's hour had come.

Nothing like it had been seen since Marlborough. From his office in Cleveland Row Pitt designed and won a war which extended from India in the East to America in the West. The whole struggle depended upon the energies of this one man. He gathered all power, financial, administrative, and military, into his own hands. He could work with no one as an equal. His position depended entirely on success in the field. He made no attempt either to consult or to conciliate, but in the execution of his military plans Pitt had a sure eye for choosing the right man. He broke incompetent generals and admirals and replaced them with younger men upon whom he could rely: Wolfe, Amherst, Conway, Howe, Keppel, and Rodney. Thus he achieved victory.

Pitt did not confine himself to a single field of operations. By taking the initiative in every quarter of the globe, Britain prevented the French from concentrating their forces, confused their plan of campaign, and forced them to dissipate their strength. Unless France were beaten in Europe as well as in the New World and in the East she would rise again. Both in North America and in Europe she was in the ascendant. At sea she was a formidable enemy. In India it seemed that if ever a European Power established itself on the ruins of the Mogul Empire its banner would be the lilies and not the cross of St. George. War with France would be a world war—the first in history; and the prize would be something more than a rearrangement of frontiers and a redistribution of fortresses and sugar islands.

In the teeth of disfavour and obstruction Pitt had made his way to the foremost place in Parliament, and now at last fortune, courage, and the confidence of his countrymen had given him a stage on which his gifts could be displayed and his foibles indulged. To call into life and action the depressed and languid spirit of England; to weld all her resources of wealth and manhood into a single instrument of war which should be felt from the Danube to the Mississippi; to humble the house of Bourbon, to make the Union Jack supreme in every ocean; to conquer, to command, and never to count the cost, whether in blood or gold—this was the spirit of Pitt, and this spirit he infused into every rank of his countrymen—admirals and powder-monkeys, great merchants and little shopkeepers; into the youngest officer of the line, who felt that with Pitt in command failure might be forgiven but hesitation never. Life began to tingle in the torpid frame of English administration. So the great years opened, years for Pitt and his country of almost intoxicating glory.

The French were swept out of Hanover; the Dutch, fishing in the murky waters of Oriental intrigue, were stopped by Clive and made to surrender their ships at Chinsura; and Cape Breton was again taken, and the name of the "Great Commoner" stamped on the map at Pittsburgh, Pennsylvania. France's two main fleets, in the Mediterranean and in the Channel, were separately defeated. Admiral Boscawen, fresh from the capture of Louisburg, was detailed to watch the Toulon squadron. He caught it slipping through the Straits of Gibraltar, destroyed five ships, and drove the rest into Cadiz Bay, blockaded and out of action. Three months later, in the short light of a November day, in a high gale and among uncharted rocks and shoals, Admiral Hawke annihilated the Brest fleet. Between these victories Wolfe had fallen at Quebec, leaving Amherst to complete the conquest of Canada, while Clive and Eyre Coote were uprooting the remnants of French power in India.

It is necessary to examine these triumphs and disasters at closer hand. In America Pitt faced a difficult and complex task. The French were moving along the waterways beyond the mountain barrier of the Alleghenies and extending their alliances with the Red Indians in an attempt to link their colony of Louisiana in the South with Canada in the North. Thus the English settlements would be confined to the seaboard and their Westward expansion would stop. Warfare had broken out in 1754. General Braddock was sent from England to re-establish British authority west of the Alleghenies, but his forces were cut to pieces by the French and Indians in Pennsylvania. In this campaign a young Virginian officer named George Washington learnt his first military lessons. Although there were now over a million British Americans, vastly outnumbering the French, their quarrels and disunion extinguished this advantage. Only the tactful handling of Pitt secured their co-operation, for Pitt now bent his mind to the American war. Throughout the winter he studied the maps and wrote dispatches to the officers and governors. A threefold strategic plan was framed for 1758. Loudon was recalled. His successor, Amherst, with Brigadier Wolfe, and naval support from Halifax, was to sail up the St. Lawrence and strike at Quebec. Another army, under Abercromby, was to seize Lake George at the head of the Hudson valley and try to join Amherst and Wolfe before Quebec. A third force, under Brigadier Forbes, would advance up the Ohio valley from Pennsylvania and capture Fort Duquesne, one of a line of French posts along the Ohio and the Mississippi. The Fleet was so disposed as to stop reinforcements leaving France.

A mind capable of conceiving and directing these efforts was now in power at Whitehall, but supervision at a distance of three thousand miles was almost impossible in the days of sail. Amherst and Wolfe hammered at the northern borders of Canada. In July Louisburg was captured. But Abercromby, advancing from Ticonderoga, became entangled in the dense woods; his army was badly beaten and his advance was halted. The Pennsylvanian venture was more successful. Fort Duquesne was taken and destroyed and the place renamed Pittsburgh; but lack of numbers and organisation compelled the British force to retire at the end of the campaign.

Pitt was undaunted. He realised the need for a combined offensive along the whole frontier from Nova Scotia to the Ohio.

According to the new plan, in the coming year the Navy would attack the French West Indies, and the invasion of Canada up the St. Lawrence would be pushed harder than ever, in spite of the bitter experience of the past.

*   *   *

The year 1759 brought fame to British arms throughout the world. In May the Navy captured Guadeloupe, the richest sugar island of the West Indies. In July Amherst took Ticonderoga and Fort Niagara, thus gaining for the American colonies a frontier upon the Great Lakes. In September the expedition up the St. Lawrence attacked Quebec. Wolfe conducted a personal reconnaissance of the river at night, and beguiled the officers by reciting Gray's "Elegy": "The paths of glory lead but to the grave." By brilliant co-operation between Army and Navy Wolfe landed his men, and led them by the unsuspected path, under cover of darkness, up the steep cliffs of the Heights of Abraham. In the battle that followed Montcalm was defeated and killed and the key fortress of Canada was secured. Wolfe, mortally wounded, lived until victory was certain, and died murmuring, "Now God be praised, I will die in peace."

But it needed another year's fighting to gain Canada for the English-speaking world. In May, 1706, the British garrison in Quebec was relieved after a winter siege. With cautious and dogged organisation Amherst converged on Montreal. In September the city fell and the huge province of French Canada changed hands. These were, indeed, the years of victory.

North America was thus made safe for the English-speaking peoples. Pitt had not only won Canada, with its rich fisheries and Indian trade, but had banished for ever the dream and danger of a French colonial empire stretching from Montreal to New Orleans. Little could he know that the extinction of the French menace would lead to the final secession of the English colonies from the British Empire.

*   *   *

Pitt's very success contributed to his fall. Just as Marlborough had been faced by a growing war-weariness after Malplaquet, so now Pitt, an isolated figure, confronted an increasing dislike of the war after the great victories. Among his colleagues there were some who honestly and patriotically doubted the wisdom of continuing the war, from which Britain had gained more than perhaps she could keep; a war which had raised her once more to the height at which she had stood after Ramillies. It was in vain that Pitt attempted to show that no lasting or satisfactory peace could be secured till France was defeated in Europe. Making terms before France was exhausted would only snatch a breathing-space for the next conflict.

In October, 1760, George II died. The temper of the new ruler was adverse. George III had very clear ideas of what he wanted and where he was going. He meant to be King, such a King as all his countrymen would follow and revere. In such a monarchy what was the place of a man like Pitt, who owed nothing to corruption, nothing to the Crown, and everything to the people and to his personal domination of the House of Commons? So long as he was in power he would divide the kingdom with Cæsar. He could not help it. His profound reverence for the person and office of George III could not conceal from either of them the fact that Pitt was a very great man and the King a very limited man. In October, 1761, he was forced to resign, and as the Earl of Chatham retired to private life.

William Pitt ranks with Marlborough as the greatest Englishman in the century between 1689 and 1789. "It is a considerable fact in the history of the world," wrote Carlyle, "that he was for four years King of England." He is the first great figure of British Imperialism.

*   *   *

Within three months of Pitt's resignation the Government were compelled to declare war on Spain. This led to further successes in the West Indies and elsewhere. The British Fleet seized the port of Havana, which commanded the trade routes of the Spanish Main and the movement of the Treasure Fleets. In the Pacific Ocean an expedition from Madras descended upon the Philippines and captured Manila. At sea and on land England was mistress of the outer world. These achievements were largely cast away.

Fifty years after the Treaty of Utrecht Britain signed a new peace with France. Britain's acquisitions under the terms of the Peace of Paris in 1763 were considerable. In America she secured Canada, Nova Scotia, Cape Breton, and the adjoining islands, and the right to navigate the Mississippi, important for Red Indian trade. In the West Indies Grenada, St. Vincent, Dominica, and Tobago were acquired. From Spain she received Florida. In Africa she kept Senegal. In India, the East India Company preserved its extensive conquests.

Historians have taken a flattering view of a treaty which established Britain as an Imperial Power, but its strategic weakness has been smoothly overlooked. Appeasement and conciliation actually won the day. And the sombre verdict of the man who endured the deliberate maiming of his work contained the historic truth. He saw in its terms the seeds of a future war. "The peace was insecure, because it restored the enemy to her former greatness. The peace was inadequate, because the places gained were no equivalent for the places surrendered."

CHAPTER FIFTY-NINE

The Quarrel with America

THE ACCESSION of George III caused a profound change in English politics. In theory and in law the monarchy still retained a decisive influence and power. The personal action of the King had for many centuries been far-reaching, and generally accepted, and only since the installation of the Hanoverian dynasty had the royal influence been largely exercised by the Whig Ministers in Parliament. Walpole and Newcastle had been much more than Ministers; they were almost Regents. Both George I and George II were aliens, their Court was predominantly German. Now all was changed. George III was, or thought he was, an Englishman born and bred. At any rate he tried to be. "George, be King," his mother had said, according to tradition, and George did his best to obey. That he failed in the central problems of his reign may, in the long run of events, have been fortunate for the ultimate liberty of England. Out of the disasters that ensued rose the Parliamentary system of government as we now know it, but the disasters were nevertheless both formidable and far-reaching. By the time that George died America had separated herself from the United Kingdom, the first British Empire had collapsed, and the King himself had gone mad.

*   *   *

The contest with America began to dominate the British political scene. Vast territories had fallen to the Crown on the conclusion of the Seven Years' War. From the Canadian border to the Gulf of Mexico the entire hinterland of the American colonies became British soil, and the parcelling out of these new lands led to further trouble with the colonists. Many of them, like George Washington, had formed companies to buy these frontier tracts from the Indians, but a royal proclamation restrained any purchasing and prohibited their settlement. Washington, among others, ignored the ban.

George III was also determined that the colonies should pay their share in the expenses of the Empire and in garrisoning the New World. For this there were strong arguments. England had supplied most of the men and the money in the struggle with France for their protection, and indeed their survival; but the methods used by the British Government were ineffective and imprudent.

It was resolved to impose a tax on the colonies' imports, and in 1764 Parliament strengthened the Molasses Act of 1733. This Act, imposing a heavy duty on foreign imports, had long been evaded by the colonists. The new regulations were therefore a serious blow. As one merchant put it, "the restrictions which we are laid under by the Parliament put us at a stand how to employ our vessels to any advantage, as we have no prospect of markets at our own islands, and cannot send elsewhere to have anything that will answer in return."

The results were unsatisfactory on both sides of the Atlantic. The British Government found that the taxes brought in very little money; and the English merchants, already concerned at the plight of their American debtors, had no desire to make colonial finance any more unstable. Indirect taxation being so unfruitful, Grenville and his lieutenant Charles Townshend proposed that all colonial legal documents should be stamped, for a fee. There were few protests, although the colonists had always objected to direct taxation, and in 1765 Parliament passed the Stamp Act.

This Act imposed no heavy burden, but it included a tax on newspapers, many of whose journalists were vehement partisans of the extremist party in America. The dispute exposed and fortified the more violent elements in America, and gave them a chance to experiment with organised resistance. The future revolutionary leaders appeared from obscurity—Patrick Henry in Virginia, Samuel Adams in Massachusetts, and Christopher Gadsen in South Carolina. A small, well-organized radical element began to emerge. But although there was an outcry, and protesting delegates convened a Stamp Act Congress in New York, there was no unity of opinion in America. The stamp distributors were attacked and their offices and houses wrecked. But the most effective opposition came from English merchants who denounced the Act as contrary to the true commercial interests of the Empire and a danger to colonial resources.

*   *   *

The personality of George III was now exercising a preponderant influence upon events. He was one of the most conscientious sovereigns who ever sat upon the English throne. Simple in his tastes and unpretentious in manner, he had the superficial appearance of a typical yeoman. But his mind was Hanoverian, with an infinite capacity for mastering detail, and limited success in dealing with large issues and main principles. He possessed great moral courage and an inveterate obstinacy, and his stubbornness lent weight to the stiffening attitude of his Government. His responsibility for the final breach is a high one.

The King sought a political reconciliation. In July, 1765, the Marquis of Rockingham undertook to form a Government, and brought with him as private secretary a young Irishman named Edmund Burke, already known in literary circles as a clever writer and a brilliant talker. He was much more. He was a great political thinker. Viewing English politics and the English character with something of the detachment of an alien, he was able to diagnose the situation with an imaginative insight beyond the range of those immersed in the business of the day and bound by traditional habits of mind. Burke's aim was to correct an effective political party.

He had to overcome the notion, widely prevalent, that party was in itself a rather disreputable thing, a notion which had been strengthened by Pitt's haughty disdain for party business and organisation. On Ireland, on America, on India, Burke's attitude was definite. He stood, and he brought his party to stand, for conciliation of the colonies, relaxation of the restraints on Irish trade, and the government of India on the same moral basis as the government of England. For years Burke was a voice crying in the wilderness, and too often rising to tones of frenzy. An orator to be named with the ancients, an incomparable political reasoner, he lacked both judgment and self-control. He was perhaps the greatest man that Ireland has produced. The same gifts, with a dash of English indolence and irony, might have made him Britain's greatest statesman.

In 1767, Charles Townshend introduced a Bill imposing duties on American imports of paper, glass, lead, and tea. There was rage in America. The Massachusetts Assembly proposed a joint petition with the other colonial bodies against the new duties. Colonial resistance was now being organised on a continental scale and the barriers of provincialism and jealousy were being lowered. Non-importation agreements were concluded and there was a systematic and most successful boycott of English goods. Even so, revolt was still far from their minds; at this stage there were few people who desired secession.

But tempers began to rise. In May, 1768, the sloop *Liberty*, belonging to John Hancock, the most prominent Boston merchant, was stopped and searched near the coast by Royal Customs officers. The colonists rescued it by force. The Cabinet was not seriously apprehensive, but perturbed. It agreed to drop the duties, except on tea. Parliament proclaimed its sovereignty over the colonies by retaining a tax on tea of threepence a pound.

Suddenly by some mysterious operation of Nature the clouds which had gathered round Chatham's intellect cleared. The scene on which he re-opened his eyes was lurid enough to dismay any man. In England a senseless craving for revenge had driven the King to an attack on the rights of electors throughout the country. In America blood had not yet flowed, but all the signs of a dissolution of the Empire were there for those who could read them. But George III, after twelve years' intrigue, had at last got a docile, biddable Prime Minister. Lord North, a charming man, of good abilities and faultless temper, presided over the loss of the American colonies.

In September, 1774, the colonial assemblies held a congress at Philadel-phia. The extremists were not yet out of hand, and the delegates still concen-trated on commercial boycotts. An association was formed to stop all trade with England unless the Coercion Acts were repealed, and the Committees of Correspondence were charged with carrying out the plan. A Declaration of Rights demanded the rescinding of some thirteen commercial Acts passed by the British Parliament since 1763. The tone of this document, which was dispatched to London, was one of respectful moderation. But in London all moderation was cast aside. The "sugar interest" in the House of Com-mons, jealous of colonial competition in the West Indies; Army officers who despised the colonial troops; the Government, pressed for money and blinded by the doctrine that colonies only existed for the benefit of the Mother Country: all combined to extinguish the last hope of peace. The petition was rejected with contempt.

At first all seemed quiet. The American merchants were delighted at the repeal of the import duties, and by the middle of 1770 reconciliation seemed complete, except in Boston. Here Samuel Adams, fertile organiser of resistance and advocate of separation, saw that the struggle was now reaching a crucial stage. Hitherto the quarrel had been at bottom a commer-cial dispute, and neither the American merchants nor the English Ministers had any sympathy for his ideas. Adams feared that the resistance of the colonies would crumble and the British would reassert their authority unless more trouble was stirred up. This he and other Radical leaders pro-ceeded to do.

News that the duties were withdrawn had hardly reached America when the first blood was shed. Most of the British garrison was stationed in Boston. The troops were unpopular with the townsfolk, and Adams spread evil rumours of their conduct. The "lobsters" in their scarlet coats were insulted and jeered at wherever they appeared.

In March, 1770, the persistent snowballing by Boston urchins of an English sentry caused a riot. In the confusion and shouting some of the troops opened fire and there were casualties. This "massacre" was just the sort of incident that Adams had hoped for.

"Committees of Correspondence" were set up throughout Massachusetts, and by the end of the year had spread to seventy-five towns. The Virginian agitators, led by the young Patrick Henry, created a standing committee of their Assembly to keep in touch with the other colonies, and a chain of such bodies was quickly formed. Thus the machinery of revolt was quietly and efficiently created.

In spite of the Boston "massacre," the violence on the high seas, and the commercial squabbles, the agitations of Adams and his friends were beginning to peter out, when Lord North committed a fatal blunder. The East India Company was nearly bankrupt. An Act was passed through Parliament authorising the company to ship tea direct to the colonies, without paying import duties. Thus, in effect, the company was granted a monopoly. The outcry across the Atlantic was instantaneous. The Act succeeded where Adams had failed: it united colonial opinion against the British.

The Radicals, who began to call themselves "Patriots," seized their opportunity to force a crisis. In December, 1773, the first cargoes were lying in Boston. Rioters disguised as Red Indians boarded the ships and destroyed the cases. When the news reached London the cry went up for coercion. In vain Burke and Chatham pleaded for conciliation. Parliament passed a series of "Coercion Acts" which suspended the Massachusetts Assembly, declared the colony to be under Crown control, closed the port of Boston, and decreed that all judges in the colony were henceforth to be appointed by the Crown. These measures were confined to Massachusetts. Thus it was hoped to isolate the resistance. It had the opposite effect.

Events now moved swiftly. The Patriots began accumulating warlike stores at Concord, a village twenty miles from Boston. The Massachusetts Military Governor, General Thomas Gage, decided to seize their ammunition and arrest Samuel Adams and his colleague John Hancock. But the colonists were on the alert. Every night they patrolled the streets of Boston watching for any move by the English troops. On April 18, 1775, eight hundred British troops set off in darkness along the Concord road. But the secret was out. From the steeple of the North Church, messengers were warned with lantern signals. One of the patrols, Paul Revere, mounted his horse and rode hard to Lexington, rousing Adams and Hancock from their beds and urging them to flight.

At five o'clock in the morning the local militia of Lexington, seventy strong, formed up on the village green. As the sun rose the head of the British column, with three officers riding in front, came into view. The leading officer, brandishing his sword, shouted, "Disperse, you rebels, immediately!" The militia commander ordered his men to disperse. The colonial committees were very anxious not to fire the first shot, and there were strict orders not to provoke open conflict with the British regulars. But in the confusion someone fired. A volley was returned. The ranks of the militia were thinned and there was a general *mêlée*. Brushing aside the survivors, the British column marched on to Concord. Now the country-side was up in arms and the bulk of the stores had been moved to safety. It was with difficulty that the British straggled back to Boston, with the enemy close at their heels. The town was cut off from the mainland. The news of Lexington and Concord spread to the other colonies, and Governors and British officials were expelled. With strategic insight the forts at the head of the Hudson valley were seized by Patriot troops under Ethan Allen, leader of the "Green Mountain Boys" from the region that became Vermont, and of Benedict Arnold, a merchant from Connecticut. The British were thus denied any help from Canada, and the War of Independence had begun.

CHAPTER SIXTY

The War of Independence

IN MAY, 1775, a congress of delegates from the American colonies met in the Carpenters' Hall of the quiet Pennsylvanian town of Philadelphia. They were respectable lawyers, doctors, merchants, and landowners, nervous at the onrush of events, and seemingly unfitted to form a revolutionary committee. The first shots had been fired and blood had been shed, but all hope of compromise had not yet vanished, and they were fearful of raising a military Power which might, like Cromwell's Ironsides, overwhelm its creators. They had no common national tradition except that against which they were revolting, no organisation, no industries, no treasury, no supplies, no army. Many of them still hoped for peace with England. Yet British troops under General Sir William Howe were on their way across the Atlantic, and armed, violent, fratricidal conflict stared them in the face.

The centre of resistance and the scene of action was Boston. On May 25 Howe sailed into the harbour with reinforcements which brought the total English troops to about six thousand men. Here Breed's Hill and Bunker Hill dominated the town. If the colonists could occupy and hold these eminences they could cannonade the English out of Boston. On the evening of June 16 Gage determined to forestall them, but next morning a line of entrenchments had appeared upon the heights across the water. Patriot troops, warned by messages from Boston, had dug themselves in during the night. Gage was resolved on a display of force. He had under his command some of the best regiments in the British Army, and he and his fellow-countrymen had acquired a hard contempt for the colonials in earlier wars. He decided to make a frontal attack on the hill, so that all Boston, crowded in its windows and upon its roofs, should witness the spectacle of British soldiers marching steadily in line to storm the rebel entrenchments.

On the hot afternoon of the 17th, in three lines the redcoats moved slowly towards the summit of Breed's Hill. There was silence. The whole of Boston was looking on. At a hundred yards from the trenches there was still not a sound in front. But at fifty yards a hail of buck-shot and bullets from ancient hunting guns smote the attackers. Howe, his white silk breeches splashed with blood, rallied his men, but they were scattered by another volley and driven to their boats. Howe's reputation was at stake. At the third rush, this time in column, the regulars drove the farmers from their line.

This sharp and bloody action sent a stir throughout the colonies, and has been compared in its effects with Bull Run, eighty-six years later. The rebels had become heroes. They had stood up to trained troops, destroyed a third of their opponents, and wiped out in blood the legend of Yankee cowardice. The British had captured the hill, but the Americans had won the glory. Gage made no further attack and in October he was recalled to England in disgrace. Howe succeeded to the command. On both sides of the Atlantic men perceived that a mortal struggle impended.

It was now imperative for the Patriots to raise an army. Massachusetts had already appealed to Congress at Philadelphia for the appointment of a Commander-in-Chief. There had been much talk of whom they were to choose. There was jealousy and dislike of the New Englanders, who were bearing the brunt of the fighting, and largely for political reasons it was decided to appoint a Southerner. Adams's eye centred upon a figure in uniform, among the dark brown clothes of the delegates. He was Colonel George Washington, of Mount Vernon, Virginia. This prosperous planter had fought in the campaigns of the 1750's and had helped extricate the remnants of Braddock's force from their disastrous advance. He was the only man of any military experience at the Congress, and this was limited to a few minor campaigns on the frontier. He was now given command of all the forces that America could raise. Great calls were to be made on the spirit of resolution that was his by nature.

The colonies contained about two hundred and eighty thousand men capable of bearing arms, but at no time during the war did Washington succeed in gathering together more than twenty-five thousand. Jealousy between the colonies and lack of equipment and organisation hampered his efforts. His immediate task was to provide the ragged band at Boston with discipline and munitions, and to this he devoted the autumn and winter months of 1775. Congress nevertheless resolved on an offensive. An expedition was dispatched to Canada under Benedict Arnold, who was to be for ever infamous in American history, and Richard Montgomery, who had once served under Wolfe. They marched along the same routes which the British troops had taken in the campaign of 1759, and they had only eleven hundred men between them. Montgomery captured and occupied Montreal, which was undefended. He then joined Arnold, who after desperate hardships had arrived with the ghost of an army before the fortifications of Quebec. In the depth of winter, in driving snow, they flung themselves at the Heights of Abraham, defended by Sir Guy Carleton with a few hundred men. Montgomery was killed and Arnold's leg was shattered. The survivors, even after this repulse, hung on in their wind-swept camp across the river. But in the spring, when the ice melted in the St. Lawrence, the first reinforcements arrived from England. Having lost more than half their men, the Patriots thereupon trudged back to Maine and Fort Ticonderoga. Canada thus escaped the revolutionary upsurge. French Canadians were on the whole content with life under the British Crown. Soon Canada was to harbour many refugees from the United States who were unable to forswear their loyalty to George III.

Meanwhile Howe was still confined to Boston. He shrank from taking reprisals, and for at least the first two years of the war he hoped for conciliation. Both he and his generals were Whig Members of Parliament, and they shared the party view that a successful war against the colonists was impossible. He was a gallant and capable commander in the field, but always slow to take the initiative. He now set himself the task of overawing the Americans. This, however, needed extensive help from England, and as none arrived, and Boston itself was of no strategic importance, he evacuated the town in the spring of 1776 and moved to the only British base on the Atlantic seaboard, Halifax, in Nova Scotia. At the same time a small expedition under General Clinton was sent southwards to the Loyalists in Charleston in the hope of rallying the Middle and Southern colonies. But the Patriot resistance was stiffening, and although the moderate elements in Congress had hitherto opposed any formal Declaration of Independence the evacuation of Boston roused them to a sterner effort. Until they acquired what would nowadays be called belligerent status they could get no military supplies from abroad, except by smuggling, and supplies were essential. The Conservative politicians were gradually yielding to the Radicals. The publication of a pamphlet called *Common Sense,* by Tom Paine, an English extremist lately arrived in America, put the case for revolution with enormous success and with far greater effect than the writings of intellectuals like Adams.

But it was the British Government which took the next step towards dissolving the tie of allegiance between England and America. Early in 1776 it put in force a Prohibitory Act forbidding all intercourse with the rebellious colonies and declaring a blockade of the American coast. At the same time, it being impossible to raise enough British troops, Hessians were hired from Germany and dispatched across the Atlantic. The resulting outcry in America strengthened the hands of the extremists. At Philadelphia on June 7

Richard Henry Lee, of Virginia, moved the following resolution: "That these united colonies are and of right ought to be free and independent states; that they are absolved from all allegiance to the British Crown, and that all political connection between them and the state of Great Britain is and ought to be totally dissolved." But six of the thirteen colonies still opposed an immediate Declaration. A large-scale British invasion was feared. No foreign alliances had yet been concluded. Many felt that a formal defiance would wreck their cause and alienate their supporters. But at last a committee was appointed, a paper was drafted by Thomas Jefferson, and on July 4, 1776, the Declaration of Independence was unanimously accepted by the Congress of the American colonies.

This historic document proclaimed the causes of the revolt, and enumerated twenty-eight "repeated injuries and usurpations" by the King of Great Britain. The opening is familiar and immortal: "When, in the course of human events, it becomes necessary for one people to dissolve the political bands which have connected them with another, and to assume among the powers of the earth the separate and equal station to which the Laws of Nature and of Nature's God entitle them, a decent respect to the opinions of mankind requires that they should declare the causes which impel them to the separation.

"We hold these truths to be self-evident: that all men are created equal, that they are endowed by their Creator with certain unalienable rights, that among these are life, liberty, and the pursuit of happiness. That to secure these rights Governments are instituted among men, deriving their just powers from the consent of the governed. That whenever any form of government becomes destructive of these ends it is the right of the people to alter or to abolish it, and to institute new government, laying its foundation on such principles and organising its powers in such form as to them shall seem most likely to effect their safety and happiness."

The Declaration was in the main a restatement of the principles which had animated the Whig struggle against the later Stuarts and the English Revolution of 1688, and it now became the symbol and rallying centre of the Patriot cause. Its immediate result was to increase the number of Loyalists, frightened by this splendid defiance. But the purpose of the colonies was proclaimed. The waverers were forced to a decision. There was now no turning back.

*   *   *

All this time the British had remained at Halifax awaiting reinforcements from England and meditating their strategy. Military success hinged on control of the Hudson valley. If they could seize and hold the waterway, and the forts which guarded it, New England would be sundered from the Middle and Southern colonies, which contained two-thirds of the population and most of the food and wealth. The first step was to capture New York, at the river-mouth. Howe could then move northwards, subdue the forts, and join hands with a force from Canada. Thereafter the South, where the settlements lay largely upon the rivers, could be crushed with the help of the Fleet. The plan seemed promising, for the colonists possessed no Navy and Great Britain should have been able to blockade the Atlantic seaboard. But the Fleet was no longer in the high efficiency to which it had been raised by Chatham's admirals. It was able to bring reinforcements across the Atlantic, but in the event New England privateers did much damage to military operations on the coast and harassed transport vessels and supplies. In June, 1776, Howe moved to New York, and began to invest the city, and in July his brother, Admiral Howe, arrived from England with a fleet of over five hundred sail and reinforcements. Howe was now in command of some twenty-five thousand men. This was the largest armed force that had yet been seen in the New World. But Washington was ready. He concentrated his army, now reduced by desertions and smallpox to about twenty thousand men, around the city. From the British camp on Staten Island the American lines could be seen across the bay on the spurs of Long Island, and on the heights of Brooklyn above the East River. In August Howe attacked. The slaughter of Bunker Hill, for thus the action at Breed's Hill is known, had taught him caution and this time he abstained from a frontal assault. He made a feint against the Long Island entrenchments, and then flung his main force to the left of the Americans and descended upon their rear. The stroke succeeded and Washington was compelled to retreat into New York City. Adverse winds impeded the British Fleet and he and his army escaped safely across the East River.

In this disaster Washington appealed to Congress. It seemed impossible to make a stand in New York, yet to abandon it would dismay the Patriots. But Congress agreed that he should evacuate the city without fighting, and after skirmishing on the Harlem heights he withdrew slowly northwards. At this juncture victory lay at Howe's finger-tips. He was master of New York and of the Hudson River for forty miles above it. If he had pursued Washington with the same skill and vigour as Grant was to pursue Lee eighty-eight years later he might have captured the whole colonial army. But for nearly a month Washington was unmolested. At the end of October he was again defeated in a sharp fight at White Plains; but once more the English made no attempt to pursue, and Washington waited desperately to see whether Howe would attack up the Hudson or strike through New Jersey at Philadelphia. Howe resolved to move on Philadelphia. He turned south, capturing as he went the forts in the neighbourhood of New York, and the delegates at Philadelphia fled. Thousands of Americans flocked to the British camp to declare their loyalty. The only hope for the Patriots seemed a mass trek across the Alleghenies into new lands, a migration away from British rule like that of the Boers in the nineteenth century. Even Washington

IN CONGRESS, July 4, 1776

The unanimous Declaration of the thirteen united States of America,

COPY OF THE ORIGINAL SIGNED DECLARATION OF INDEPENDENCE

YOU CAN READ THIS WITH A MAGNIFYING GLASS

The presentation of the Declaration of Independence to the Congress of the American Colonies at the Pennsylvania State House by (standing, centre, left to right) John Adams, Roger Sherman, Robert Livingston, Thomas Jefferson, and Benjamin Franklin. Painting by John Trumbull.

considered such a course. "We must then [*i.e.,* if defeated] retire to Augusta County, in Virginia. Numbers will repair to us for safety and we will try a predatory war. If overpowered we must cross the Allegheny Mountains." [1] Meanwhile he traversed the Hudson and fell back southwards to cover Philadelphia.

The British were hard on his heels and began a rapid occupation of New Jersey. The Patriot cause seemed lost. But Washington remained alert and undaunted and fortune rewarded him. With an imprudence which is difficult to understand, and was soon to be punished, outposts from the British Army were flung about in careless fashion through the New Jersey towns. Washington determined to strike at these isolated bodies before Howe could cross the Delaware River. He selected the village of Trenton, held by a force of Hessians. On Christmas Night the Patriot troops fought their way into the lightly guarded village. At the cost of two officers and two privates they killed or wounded a hundred and six Hessians. The survivors were captured and sent to parade the streets of Philadelphia. The effect of the stroke was out of all proportion to its military importance. It was the most critical moment in the war. At Princeton Lord Cornwallis, a subordinate of Howe's of whom more was to be heard later, tried to avenge the defeat, but was foiled. Washington marched behind him and threatened his line of communications. The year thus ended with the British in winter quarters in New Jersey, but confined by these two actions to the east of the Delaware. Their officers spent a cheerful season in the society of New York. Meanwhile Benjamin Franklin and Silas Deane, first of American diplomats, crossed the Atlantic to seek help from France.

* * *

Posterity should not be misled into thinking that war on the American colonies received the unanimous support of the British people. Burke for one had no illusions. Powerful English politicians denounced not only the military and naval mismanagement, but the use of force against the colonists at all. But in the King's mind all these were traitors. George III grew stubborn and even more intent. He tirelessly struggled to superintend the details of the war organisation, but he was incapable of co-ordinating the activities of his Ministers. These were of poor quality. Rarely has British strategy fallen into such a multitude of errors. Every maxim and principle of war was either violated or disregarded. Instead of concentrating their strength, the British forces were now dispersed over five hundred miles of country, and divided between Burgoyne in Canada, Howe on the Chesapeake, and Clinton in New York.

* * *

Washington, from his winter quarters at Morristown, on the borders of New Jersey, moved hastily south-westwards to screen Philadelphia. Having

[1] J. Fisher, *The Writings of John Fisher* (1902), vol. i.

abandoned New York without a serious fight, he could hardly do the same at the capital of the Congress, but with his ill-disciplined force, fluctuating in numbers, he could only hope to delay the British advance. At the beginning of September Howe advanced with about fourteen thousand men. Washington, with a similar force, drew up his lines on the north bank of the river Brandywine, barring the road to the capital. Howe perceived and exploited the faulty equipment of the army in front of him, its lack of an efficient staff, and its inability to get quick information. He made the same feinting movements which had served so well at Long Island. On the morning of the 11th he divided his army, and, leaving a powerful body to make a frontal attack, marched up-river with Cornwallis, crossed it, and descended on Washington's right flank. His tactics went like clockwork. The attack was successful, disorder spread, and the British troops on the far bank crossed the river and drove the whole American force before them. By sunset Washington was in full retreat. As the Marquis de Lafayette, a young French volunteer in the American army, described it, "Fugitives, cannon, and baggage crowded without order into the road." But here, as at Long Island, Howe refused to pursue and capture the enemy. He was content. On September 26 his advance-guards entered Philadelphia. There was a confused fight to the north of the city at Germantown, but the British pressed on, and soon afterwards the capital fell.

By now, however, the London plans for the northern theatre were beginning to miscarry. Burgoyne, with a few hundred Indians and seven thousand regulars, of whom half were German, was moving through the Canadian forests expecting to join with the British forces from New York. As Burgoyne advanced, the New England militia gathered against him. He was a popular and dashing commander, but the country was difficult. As the autumn rains descended he was cornered at Saratoga, and the New Englanders, their strength daily increasing, closed in. He was only thirty miles from Albany, where he should have met the column from New York, but he could make no headway. Days of hard fighting in the woodlands followed. His supplies ran low, and he was heavily outnumbered. The Americans were operating in their own country by their own methods. Each man fighting mostly on his own initiative, hiding behind bushes and in the tops of trees, they inflicted severe casualties upon some of the best regiments that Europe could muster. The precise drill and formations of Burgoyne's men had no effect. An American deserter brought news that Clinton was moving northwards. It was too late. The Germans refused to fight any longer, and on October 17, 1777, Burgoyne surrendered to the American commander, Horatio Gates. The surrender terms were violated by Congress and the main body of his army were kept prisoners until the signing of the peace. Burgoyne returned to England to attack and be attacked by the Ministry.

* * *

At this point in the struggle the Old World stepped in to aid and comfort the New. Although militarily indecisive in America, Saratoga had an immediate effect in France. At Versailles Benjamin Franklin had been urging an open alliance, but for a year both sides had wavered. The French Ministers hesitated to support the cause of liberty overseas while suppressing it at home. Now all doubts were swept away. The colonists could not survive without French supplies, and the mass of Frenchmen were vehement to avenge the defeats of the Seven Years' War. The French Navy had been strengthened; the British Fleet was disintegrating; and when the news arrived of Saratoga Louis XVI resolved on an official alliance. There was consternation in London, where the Whig opposition had long warned the Government against harsh dealings with the colonists, and the British Ministry formulated a generous compromise. It was too late. On February 6, 1778, before the Congress could be appraised of the new offer, Benjamin Franklin signed an alliance with France.

Thus began another world war, and Britain was now without a single ally. She had lost one army as prisoners in America. There were no more troops to be hired in Germany. Old fears of invasion spread panic through the country. In the agony all minds except the King's turned to Chatham. On April 7 Chatham dragged himself upon crutches to make his last speech against an Opposition address for recalling the Army in America. He had always stood for conciliation and not for surrender. The corpse-like figure, swathed in flannel bandages, tottered to its feet. The House was hushed with the anticipation of death. In whispering sentences, shot through with a sudden gleam of fierce anger, he made his attack "against the dismemberment of this ancient and most noble monarchy." He warned the nation of the dangers of French intervention and the use of German mercenaries. He scourged his countrymen for their inhumanity. "My lords, if I were an American as I am an Englishman, while a foreign troop was landed in my country I never would lay down my arms—never, never, never."

He struggled to speak again, but collapsed senseless in an apoplectic fit. On May 11 he died as his son William was reading to him from Homer the solemn scene of Hector's funeral and the deep despair of Troy. George III displayed his smallness of mind by opposing the plan to erect a monument, which would be, he said, "an offensive measure to me personally"; but the City of London defied him, and Burke's inscription was a fitting memorial: "The means by which Providence raises a nation to greatness are the virtues infused into great men." Such men were very few in the England of Lord North.

CHAPTER SIXTY-ONE

The United States

WASHINGTON IN 1777 took up his winter quarters at Valley Forge, to the north of Philadelphia. At the end of every campaign there were many desertions, and he was now reduced to about nine thousand men, of whom another third were to melt away by the spring. Short of clothing and shelter, they shivered and grumbled through the winter months, while in Philadelphia, a score of miles away, nearly twenty thousand well-equipped English troops were quartered in comfort. The social season was at its height, and the numerous Loyalists in the capital made the stay of Howe and his officers pleasing and cheerful. The British made no move to attack the Patriot army. While Washington could not count on provisions for his men even a day in advance, Howe danced and gambled in Philadelphia. As at Long Island, as at White Plains, as at the Brandywine River, he refused to follow up his victory in the field and annihilate his enemy. Unnerved perhaps by the carnage at Bunker Hill, and still hoping for conciliation, he did nothing. Some inkling of his reluctance may have reached the ears of the Government; at any rate, when news of the French alliance with the rebels reached England at the beginning of the New Year his resignation was accepted.

Howe's successor was Sir Henry Clinton, the former commander of New York, who held very different views on the conduct of hostilities. He perceived that European tactics of march and counter-march and the siege and capture of towns and cities would never prevail against an armed and scattered population. The solution, he thought, was to occupy and settle the whole country. He also made a momentous change of strategy. He resolved to abandon the offensive in the North and begin the process of reduction by subduing the South. Here was the bulk of the population and the wealth, and the main repository of such supplies as the Continent could furnish. Here also were many Loyalists. They must be heartened and organised. A new base would be needed, for New York was too far away, and Clinton's eye rested on Charleston and Savannah. Much could be said for all this, and much might have been achieved if he had been allowed to try it out, but there now appeared a new force which abruptly checked and in time proved deadly to the realisation of these large plans. Savannah was eight hundred miles and fifty days' march from New York. Hitherto Britain had held command of the sea and could shift her troops by salt water far more speedily than the Patriots could move by land, but all was now changed by the intervention of France and the French Fleet. Sea-power was henceforth to dominate and decide the American struggle for independence, and Clinton soon received a sharp reminder that this was now in dispute.

In April, 1778, twelve French ships of the line, mounting, with their attendant frigates, over eight hundred guns, set sail from Toulon. Four thousand soldiers were on board. News of their approach reached Clinton and it became his immediate and vital task to stop them seizing his main base at New York. If they captured the port, or even blockaded the mouth of the Hudson, his whole position on the Continent would be imperilled. On June 18 he accordingly abandoned Philadelphia and marched rapidly across New Jersey with ten thousand troops. Washington, his army swollen by spring recruiting to about equal strength, set off in parallel line of pursuit. At Monmouth Court House there was a confused fight. Clinton beat off the Americans, not without heavy loss, and did not reach New York till the beginning of July. He was only just in time. Shortly after his arrival a French fleet under d'Estaing appeared off the city. They were confronted by a British squadron under Admiral Howe, brother of the superseded military commander, and for ten days the two forces manœuvred outside the harbour. The French attempted to seize Rhode Island, but were frustrated, and Howe in a series of operations which has drawn high praise from American naval historians defeated all efforts by his opponent to intervene. In the autumn d'Estaing abandoned the struggle and sailed for the West Indies. Here also Clinton managed to forestall the French by sending troops forthwith to St. Lucia. D'Estaing arrived too late to intercept them, and this strategic island became a British base.

Nevertheless these successes could not disguise the root facts that Clinton's campaign against the South had been delayed for a year and that Britain was no longer in undisputed command of the sea. The French Fleet dominated the Channel and hindered the transport to New York of men and supplies from Britain, while New England privateers waged a lively and profitable warfare against English commerce. Military operations in America came slowly to a standstill, and although three thousand of Clinton's troops occupied Savannah in Georgia on December 29 his plans for subduing the rebels from a Loyalist base in the South were hampered and curtailed. A furious civil war between Loyalists and Patriots had erupted in these regions, but he could do little to help. Stalemate continued throughout 1779, and for a time the main seat of war shifted from the New World. Both armies in America were crippled, the American from the financial chaos and weak credit of the Congress Government, and the British for want of reinforcements. Fear of invasion gripped the British Government and troops intended for Clinton were kept in the British Isles. The French, for their part, realised that they could get all they wanted in America by fighting Britain on the high seas, and this was anyway much more to the taste of the autocratic Government at Versailles than helping republican rebels. Except for a few volunteers, they did not at this stage send any military or naval help to their allies across the Atlantic; but stores of munitions and clothing preserved the

Patriot cause from collapse. In June the world conflict spread and deepened and another European Power entered the struggle. French diplomacy brought Spain into the war. Britain was still further weakened, her naval communications in the Mediterranean were imperilled, and within a few months Gibraltar was besieged. In the New World she was forced to keep watch against a Spanish incursion into Florida, and American privateers based on the port of New Orleans harassed English commerce in the Caribbean.

In European waters one of these privateers provided a colourful episode. An American captain of Scottish birth named John Paul Jones was supplied by the French with an ancient East India merchantman, which he converted in French dockyards into a man-of-war. It was named the *Bonhomme Richard,* and in September Captain Jones, with a polyglot crew and in company with three smaller vessels, sailed his memorable craft into the North Sea. Off Flamborough Head he intercepted a convoy of merchantmen from the Baltic, and straightway attacked the English escorts, the men-of-war *Serapis* and *Scarborough.* The merchant ships escaped, and on the evening of the 23rd battle commenced between the *Serapis* and the *Bonhomme Richard.* The English vessel was superior in construction, equipment, and guns, but Jones manœuvred his vessel alongside and lashed himself to his adversary. Throughout the night the two vessels rocked together, the muzzles of their guns almost touching, mauling each other with broadsides, musketry volleys, and hand-grenades. At times both ships were on fire. Jones's three smaller vessels circled the inferno, firing broadsides into both ships. The English and American captains fought grimly on. At last, towards dawn, there was a violent explosion in the powder magazine of the *Serapis.* Her guns were wrecked and all abaft the mainmast were killed. The English were forced to surrender; but the *Bonhomme Richard* was so shattered that she sank two days later. The encounter made a lively stir in French and American society and Jones became a hero.

*   *   *

All this time Washington's army had remained incapable of action. They could do little except keep watch on Clinton. Simply to have kept his army in existence during these years was probably Washington's greatest contribution to the Patriot cause. No other American leader could have done as much. In December Clinton decided to try his hand once more at subduing the South. He resolved to capture Charleston, and on the 26th sailed for South Carolina with eight thousand men. For a time he prospered, heartened by news that the French Fleet in the West Indies had been beaten by Admiral Rodney. Bad weather delayed him and the main siege did not begin till the end of March, but in May, 1780, the town fell and five thousand Patriot troops surrendered in the biggest disaster yet sustained by American arms. Then fortune began to turn against Clinton. He had gained a valuable base, but he was confronted with civil war. He found himself faced, not with a regular army in the field, but with innumerable guerrilla bands which harassed his communications and murdered Loyalists. It became evident that a huge army would be needed to occupy and subdue the country. But again sea-power intervened. Rumours that French troops were once more crossing the Atlantic made Clinton hasten back to New York, leaving Cornwallis, his second-in-command, to do the best he could in the South. This was little enough. Washington sent a small force against him under Gates, the victor of Saratoga. Cornwallis defeated Gates at the Battle of Camden and marched into North Carolina, routing the guerrillas as he went, but the countryside rose in arms behind him. There was no crucial point he could strike at, and the only effect of his exertions was the destruction of a quantity of crops which the rebels might have traded to Europe for munitions.

In the North Clinton for the second time found himself in great peril. Another fleet had indeed arrived from France, and this time he was too late to forestall a landing. Over five thousand French troops under the Comte de Rochambeau had disembarked in July at Newport, in Rhode Island. Washington, vigilant and alert, was encamped at White Plains in the Hudson valley; Benedict Arnold, who had led the expedition to Canada in 1776 and fought with distinction at Saratoga, commanded the fort at West Point; at any moment the French might advance inland from the coast and join him. New York, Clinton's base and harbour, seemed lost. But events, in the form of treachery, ran for a time with the British. Arnold had long been dissatisfied with the conduct of the Patriots, and he had recently married a Loyalist lady. He was in debt and he had recently been reprimanded by court-martial for misappropriating Government property. His discontent and his doubts were deepened by the news of Gates's defeat at Camden, and he now offered to surrender West Point to Clinton for the sum of twenty thousand pounds. Its loss would not only destroy Washington's grip on the Hudson valley, but might ruin the whole Patriot power. Clinton seized on the conspiracy as the one chance of retrieving his position in the North, and sent a young major named André in disguise to arrange the details of the capitulation.

On September 21, 1780, André sailed up the Hudson in a sloop, and met Arnold late at night on the west shore not far from Stony Point. Here Arnold gave him written descriptions of the forts, their armaments and stores, the strength of the garrisons, copies of their orders in case of attack, and copies of the proceedings of a council of war recently held at West Point. On his way back across the No Man's Land between the two armies André fell into the hands of some irregular scouts, and was delivered to the nearest American commander. The documents were found in his boots. The commander could not believe in Arnold's treachery, and a request for an explanation was sent to West Point. Arnold escaped, followed by his wife, and was rewarded with a general's commission in King George's service and the command of a British force. He died in disgrace and poverty twenty years after. André was executed as a spy. He wrote a graceful and dignified letter to Washington asking to be shot instead of hanged—in vain. He was a young man of great personal beauty, and in his scarlet uniform, standing upon the gallows, and himself arranging the noose round his neck, he made an appealing sight. His courage reduced to tears the rough crowd that had gathered to see him die. In all the anger of the struggle, with the exasperation of Arnold's desertion hardening every Patriot heart, no one could be found to perform the task of executioner, and in the end a nameless figure, with his face blackened as a disguise, did the work. Forty years later André was re-buried in Westminster Abbey.

Arnold's act of betrayal, though discovered in time, had a marked, if temporary, effect on the sentiment and cohesion of the Patriots. They had been very near disaster. Many Americans were strongly opposed to the war, and Loyalists throughout the country either openly or secretly supported the British. The South was already smitten with hideous civil strife in which American slew American and each man suspected his neighbour. Was the same frightful process to engulf the North, hitherto steadfast in the Patriot cause? If the commander of West Point was a traitor, then who could be trusted? These anxieties and fears were deepened by a reversal of the Patriot fortunes at sea. Admiral Rodney arrived before New York with a substantial fleet and blockaded the French in Newport till the end of the campaigning season. Then he struck again, this time in the West Indies, where the Dutch had been making large fortunes by shipping arms and powder to the Patriots. The centre of their trade was St. Eustatius, in the Leeward Islands. In the autumn news came that Holland had joined the coalition against Great Britain, and Rodney was ordered to seize the island. This he did early in 1781, and a large store of munitions and merchandise consigned to General Washington fell into the hands of the British Fleet.

*   *   *

Strategic divergences between Clinton and Cornwallis now brought disaster to the British and Loyalist cause. Cornwallis had long chafed under Clinton's instructions, which tethered him to his base at Charleston. Clinton judged that the holding of South Carolina was the main object of the war in the South, and that any inland excursion depended on naval control of the coast. Cornwallis on the other hand was eager to press forward. He maintained that the American guerrillas in North Carolina prevented any effective occupation of the South, and until and unless they were subdued the British would have to retire within the walls of Charleston. He held that Virginia was the heart and centre of the Patriot cause and that all efforts should be concentrated on its conquest and occupation. The first

280

step therefore was to overrun North Carolina. There is no doubt he was wrong. Charleston, not Virginia, was the military key to the South. It was the only Southern port of any consequence, and the only place from which he could receive supplies for himself and deny them to the rebels. From here he could not only dominate the state of Georgia to the South, but by establishing small posts in North Carolina, and at Chesapeake Bay, "keep up the appearance," as Washington wrote at the time, "of possessing four hundred miles upon the coast, and of consequence have a pretext for setting up claims which may be very detrimental to the interest of America in European councils." [1] But Cornwallis's military reputation had been in the ascendant since the Battle of Camden, and he was encouraged by the British Government to proceed with his plans, which largely depended for their success on the Southern Loyalists. In spite of their unpromising behaviour in the previous campaign, and in spite of the nomination of Washington's ablest general, Nathanael Greene, to command the Patriot forces in the South, Cornwallis resolved to advance. Thus he marched to destruction.

In January, 1781, he moved towards the borders of North Carolina. His forward detachments clashed with the Americans at Cowpens on the morning of the 17th. The British tactics were simple and costly. Cornwallis had experienced the marksmanship of the American frontiersmen, and knew the inefficiency in musketry of his own troops. He therefore relied on sabre and bayonet charges. The American commander had placed his ill-organised and ill-disciplined militia with the Broad River behind them to stop their dispersing. Washington always doubted the value of these troops, and had declared that no militia would "ever acquire the habits necessary to resist a regular force." But this time, stiffened by Continental troops, they mauled the British.

Cornwallis nevertheless pressed on. He was now far from his base, and Greene's army was still in the field. His only hope was to bring Greene to battle and destroy him. They met at Guilford Court House on March 15. The American militia proved useless, but the trained nucleus of Greene's troops drawn up behind a rail fence wrought havoc among the British regulars. Again and again, headed by their officers, the regiments assaulted the American line. In the end this devoted and disciplined bravery drove the Americans from the field, but the slaughter was indecisive. The Patriot force was still active while the British were far from home and had lost nearly a third of their men. Cornwallis had no choice but to make for the coast and seek reinforcements from the Navy. Greene let him go. His army had done enough. In just under eight months they had marched and fought over nine hundred miles of swampy and desolate country. Outnumbered by three to one, he had reconquered the whole of Georgia except Savannah,

[1] *The Writings of George Washington*, ed. W. C. Ford (1891), vol. ix.

and all but a small portion of South Carolina. He lost the battles, but he won the campaign. Abandoning the wide spaces of North Carolina, he now moved swiftly southwards to raise the country against the British.

Here the fierce civil war in progress between Patriots and Loyalists—or Whigs and Tories as they were locally called—was darkened by midnight raids, seizure of cattle, murders, ambushes, and atrocities such as we have known in our own day in Ireland. While Greene began to subdue the isolated British posts in South Carolina, Cornwallis continued his advance to Virginia. He devastated the country-side in his march, but was fiercely and skilfully harried by Lafayette and a meagre Patriot band.

Throughout these months Clinton lay in New York, and as Cornwallis drew nearer it seemed possible that Clinton might evacuate the Northern base and concentrate the whole British effort on preserving the hold on the Southern colonies. This, if it had succeeded, might have wrecked the Patriot cause, for the Congress was bankrupt and Washington could scarcely keep his army together. But once again the French Fleet turned the scales, this time for ever.

The desperate situation of the Americans was revealed to the French naval commander in the West Indies, De Grasse. In July he sent word to Washington, who had now been joined at White Plains by Rochambeau from Newport, that he would attack the Virginian coast. He called for a supreme effort to concentrate the whole Patriot force in this region. Washington seized the opportunity. Taking elaborate precautions to deceive Clinton, he withdrew his troops from the Hudson and, united with Rochambeau, marched quickly southwards.

Cornwallis in the meantime, starved of supplies, and with ever-lengthening lines of communication, marched to the coast, where he hoped to make direct contact with Clinton by sea. In August he arrived at Yorktown, on Chesapeake Bay, and began to dig himself in. His conduct in the following months has been much criticised. He had no natural defence on the land side of the town, and he made little effort to strike at the enemies gathering round him. The Franco-American strategy was a feat of timing, and the convergence of force was carried out over vast distances. Nearly nine thousand Americans and eight thousand French assembled before Yorktown, while De Grasse blockaded the coast with thirty ships of the line. For nearly two months Cornwallis sat and waited. At the end of September the investment of Yorktown began, and the bombardment of the French siege artillery shattered his earth redoubts. Cornwallis planned a desperate sortie as the defences crumbled. At the end one British cannon remained in action. On October 19, 1781, the whole army, about seven thousand strong, surrendered. On the very same day Clinton and the British squadron sailed from New York, but on hearing of the disaster they turned back.

Thus ended the main struggle. Sea-power had once more decided the issue, and but for the French blockade the British war of attrition might well have succeeded.

In November, his task accomplished, De Grasse returned to the West Indies and Washington was left unaided to face Clinton in New York and the menace of invasion from Canada. Two years were to pass before peace came to America, but no further military operations of any consequence took place.

*   *   *

The surrender at Yorktown had immediate and decisive effects in England. When the news was brought to Lord North his amiable composure slid from him. He paced his room, exclaiming in agonised tones, "Oh, God, it is all over!"

The Opposition gathered strongly in the Commons. There were riotous meetings in London. The Government majority collapsed on a motion censuring the administration of the Navy. An address to stop the American war was rejected by a single vote. In March North informed the Commons that he would resign. "At last the fatal day has come," wrote the King. North maintained his dignity to the last. After twelve years of service he left the House of Commons a beaten man. As the Members stood waiting in the rain for their carriages on that March evening in 1782 they saw North come down the steps and get into his own vehicle, which had been forewarned and was waiting at the head of the line. With a courtly bow to the drenched and hostile Members crowding round him he said, "That, gentlemen, is the advantage of being in the secret," and drove quickly away.

King George, in the agony of personal defeat, showed greater passion. He talked of abdication and retiring to Hanover. The violent feeling in the country denied him all hope of holding a successful election. He was forced to come to terms with the Opposition. Through the long years of the American war Rockingham and Burke had waited in patience for the collapse of North's administration. Now their chance had come. Rockingham made his terms with the King: independence for the colonies and some lessening of the Crown's influence in politics. George III was forced to accept, and Rockingham took office. It fell to him and his colleague, Lord Shelburne, to save what they could from the wreckage of the First British Empire.

CHAPTER SIXTY-TWO

The Indian Empire

THE EIGHTEENTH century saw a revolutionary change in the British position in India. The English East India Company, founded simply as a trading venture, grew with increasing speed into a vast territorial Empire. The great Empire of the Moguls was disintegrating. For two centuries these Moslem descendants of Tamburlaine had gripped and pacified a portion of the world half as large as the present United States. Early in the eighteenth century this formidable dynasty was shaken by a disputed succession. Invaders from the north soon poured across the frontiers. In Central India the fierce fighting tribes of the Mahrattas, bound in a loose confederacy, saw and seized their chance to loot and to raid. The country was swept by anarchy and bloodshed.

Hitherto European traders in India—English, French, Portuguese, and Dutch—had plied their wares in rivalry, but so long as "the Great Mogul" ruled in Delhi they had competed in comparative peace and safety. The English East India Company had grown into a solid affair, with a capital of over a million and a quarter pounds and an annual dividend of 9 per cent. The English Directors had long been reluctant to own any land or assume any responsibilities beyond the confines of their trading stations. About 1740 events forced them to change their tune. The Mahrattas slaughtered the Nawab, or Imperial Governor, of the Carnatic, the five-hundred-mile-long province on the south-eastern coast. They threatened Madras and Bombay, and raided the depths of Bengal. It was becoming impossible for the European traders to stand aside. They must either fight on their own or in alliance with Indian rulers or quit. Most of the Dutch had already withdrawn to the rich archipelago of the East Indies; the Portuguese had long since fallen behind in the race; the French and English resolved to stay. Thus these two European powers were left alone in the field.

As has so often happened in the great crises of her history, France produced a man. Joseph Dupleix, Governor of Pondicherry since 1741, had long foreseen the coming struggle with Britain. He perceived that India awaited a new ruler. The Mogul Empire was at an end, and a Mahratta Empire seemed unlikely to replace it. Why then should not France seize this glittering, fertile prize? Dupleix proceeded to attack Madras and after a five-day bombardment the town surrendered on September 10, 1746. Some of its British defenders escaped to the near-by Fort St. David. Among them was a young clerk of twenty-one, named Robert Clive.

*   *   *

Clive had watched these events with anger and alarm, but hitherto there had been few signs in his career to mark him as the man who would reverse his country's fortunes and found the rule of the British in India. He was the son of a small squire, and his boyhood had been variegated and unpromising. Clive had attended no fewer than four schools, and been unsuccessful at all. In his Shropshire market town he had organised and led a gang of adolescent ruffians who extorted pennies and apples from tradesmen in return for not breaking their windows. At the age of eighteen he was sent abroad as a junior clerk in the East India Company at a salary of five pounds a year and forty pounds expenses. He was a difficult and unpromising subordinate. He detested the routine and the atmosphere of the counting-house. Twice, it is said, he attempted suicide, and twice the pistol misfired. Not until he had obtained a military commission and served some years in the armed forces of the Company did he reveal a military genius unequalled in the British history of India. The siege of Madras and the defence of Fort St. David had given him a taste for fighting. In 1748 a new upheaval gave him the chance of leadership.

At a stroke France had become master of Southern India. The next blow would obviously be against the English. Here was the end of any hope of peaceful trading, or of what would nowadays be called non-intervention in Indian affairs; and it became evident that the East India Company must either fight or die. Clive obtained a commission. He made his way to Trichinopoly, and saw for himself that Mahomet Ali was in desperate peril. If he could be rescued and placed on the throne all might be well. But how to do it? Trichinopoly was beset by a combined French and Indian army of vast numbers. The English had very few soldiers, and were so ill-prepared and so short of officers that Clive, still only twenty-five, was given the chief military command. The struggle lasted for fifty days. Twenty times outnumbered and close to starvation, Clive's puny force broke the onslaught and the siege was lifted. This was the end of Dupleix, and of much else besides.

In 1755 a new struggle was about to open in the North-East. Surajah Dowlah, young, vicious, violent, and greedy, feared, with some justice, that what came to be called the Seven Years' War between Britain and France, lately broken out, would engulf his dominions and reduce him to a puppet like his fellow-princes in the Deccan. He called on both the European communities to dismantle their fortifications. The English, aware that war with France was imminent, had extended their fortifications on the riverbank where the French attack was expected, and ignored his demands. Other frictions increased his anger. In May Surajah Dowlah struck.

Gathering a large army, including guns and Europeans trained to use them, he marched on Calcutta. There was mismanagement and confusion. The small garrison and most of the English civilians fought bravely, but in three days it was all over. A terrible fate now overtook them. A hundred and forty-six Europeans surrendered after the enemy had penetrated the defences under a flag of truce. They were thrust for the night into a prison cell twenty feet square. By the morning all except twenty-three were dead. The victors departed, having looted the Company's possessions. The tragedy of the Black Hole dispelled the last wishful illusion of the British that it might still be possible for them to remain in India as traders and no more. There was an outrage to avenge, and at last they were more than ready to fight.

In January, 1757, with nine hundred European and fifteen hundred Indian soldiers, Clive recaptured Calcutta and repulsed Surajah Dowlah's army of forty thousand men. The war with France now compelled him to retreat. Then fortune came to Clive's aid. Surajah Dowlah's cruelty was too much, even for his own people. A group of courtiers resolved to depose him and place a new ruler, Mir Jafar, on the throne. Clive agreed to help. On June 23 he met Surajah Dowlah at Plassey. He was outnumbered seventeen to one. Clive disposed his force along the edge of a mango grove and awaited the onslaught. Battle there was none. Nevertheless, it was a trial of strength, on which the fortunes of India turned. For four hours there was a cannonade. The enemy dispersed in panic, and a few days later Surajah Dowlah was murdered by Mir Jafar's son. For the loss of thirty-six men Clive had become the master of Bengal and the victor of Plassey. When Clive sailed to England in February, 1760, Britain was the only European Power left in India. Clive had now accumulated a fortune of a quarter of a million pounds. He bought his way into Parliament, as was the custom of the time, and was created an Irish peer.

*   *   *

Modern generations should not mistake the character of the British expansion in India. The Government was never involved as a principal in the Indian conflict. The East India Company was a trading organisation. Its directors were men of business. They wanted dividends, not wars, and grudged every penny spent on troops and annexations. But the turmoil in the great sub-continent compelled them against their will and their judgment to take control of more and more territory, till in the end, and almost by accident, they established an empire no less solid and certainly more peaceful than that of their Mogul predecessors. To call this process "Imperialist expansion" is nonsense, if by that is meant the deliberate acquisition of political power. Of India it has been well said that the British Empire was acquired in a fit of absence of mind.

Clive's triumph created as many problems as it solved, and the years which followed his departure contain some of the most squalid pages in

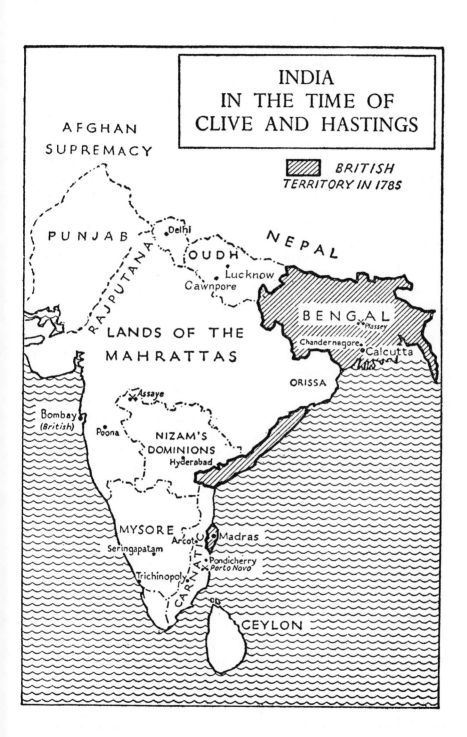

INDIA
IN THE TIME OF
CLIVE AND HASTINGS

BRITISH
TERRITORY IN 1785

AFGHAN
SUPREMACY

PUNJAB

Delhi

NEPAL

OUDH

RAJPUTANA

Lucknow
Cawnpore

BENGAL

×Plassey

Chandernagore
Calcutta

LANDS OF THE
MAHRATTAS

ORISSA

×Assaye

Bombay
(British)

Poona

NIZAM'S
DOMINIONS

Hyderabad

MYSORE

Arcot
Madras

CARNATIC

Seringapatam

Pondicherry
×Porto Novo

Trichinopoly

CEYLON

the history of the British in India. The object of the East India Company was to make profits. How the country was ruled they neither knew nor cared so long as peace was maintained and trade prospered. The ill-paid servants of the Company were both forced and encouraged to take bribes, presents, and every kind of shameful perquisite from the inhabitants. Tales of corruption and the gaining of vast and illicit private fortunes crept back to England. The Directors of the Company suddenly found that they had lost both their dividends and their good name. They appealed to Clive, made him Governor-General of all their Indian territories, and in June, 1764, he sailed to India for the last time. His reforms were drastic, high-handed, and in effect more far-reaching than the victory at Plassey. In January, 1767, he returned to England. The British public were critical and ill-informed. Clive was assailed in the House of Commons.

He defended himself in an eloquent speech. He pointed out that by his exertions the Directors of the East India Company "had acquired an Empire more extensive than any kingdom in Europe. They had acquired a revenue of four millions sterling and trade in proportion." About the gains which he himself had made he exclaimed in a celebrated passage, "Am I not rather deserving of praise for the moderation which marked my proceedings? Consider the situation in which the victory at Plassey had placed me. A great prince was dependent on my pleasure; an opulent city lay at my mercy; its richest bankers bid against each other for my smiles; I walked through vaults which were thrown open to me alone, piled on either hand with gold and jewels. Mr. Chairman, at this moment I stand astonished at my own moderation." The House of Commons unanimously passed a resolution that "Robert Lord Clive rendered great and meritorious services to this country." The vehement, tormented spirit who was the subject of this motion was not appeased. A few years later he died by his own hand.

*   *   *

Clive was soon followed in India by as great a man as himself, but with a somewhat different background. Warren Hastings was poor, but his ancestors had once owned large estates in Worcestershire. The wars of Oliver Cromwell had compelled his great-grandfather to sell the family home at Daylesford, and from early boyhood Hastings dreamed of winning it back. His mother died when he was very young, and an uncle brought him up and sent him to school at Westminster. There he became the senior classical scholar, and the masters wanted him to go to a university. His uncle refused, and sent him to India instead. He was then sixteen years of age.

Warren Hastings held fast to an austere way of life. He desired fame and power, and enough money to buy back Daylesford. The gathering of private fortunes he left to others. Rapacity was not in his nature. In 1772 he be-

The Death of Wolfe
Painting by Benjamin West

"In September [1759] the expedition up the St. Lawrence attacked Quebec. Wolfe conducted a personal reconnaissance of the river at night and beguiled the officers by reciting Gray's *Elegy:* 'The paths of glory lead but to the grave.' By brilliant cooperation between Army and Navy Wolfe landed his men and led them by the unsuspected path, under cover of darkness, up the steep cliffs of the Heights of Abraham. In the battle that followed Montcalm was defeated and killed and the key fortress of Canada was secured. Wolfe, mortally wounded, lived until victory was certain, and died murmuring, 'Now God be praised, I will die in peace.' "

The Canadian Transcontinental Railway

The Dominion was bound together by lines such as this in Alberta near Mount Fitz William.

came Governor of Bengal. By now, however, rich adventurers from the East were making and marring the repute of the new Empire in India. Too wealthy and too arrogant, the "Nabobs," as they were called, were disliked or envied by all classes in Great Britain. Jealousy, ignorance, and sentimentality combined in a cry for reform.

The year after Hastings became Governor of Bengal, Parliament passed a Regulating Act. The administration of British-held territory in India was unified, and Warren Hastings was made the first Governor-General.

By 1783 the only active enemies who remained were the French, and their hopes of progress were stopped by the conclusion of the Treaty of Versailles. England had lost one Empire in America and gained another in India.

Hastings left India in 1785, not without the gratitude of the inhabitants. Unlike many Englishmen in India at this time, he spoke the logical languages well. He enjoyed the society of Indians, and had once been rebuked on this account by the formidable Clive. Though proud of his birth and ancestry, consciousness of race, colour, or religion never influenced or distracted him.

In the beginning Hastings was welcomed and honoured in England. But soon after his return a Parliamentary inquiry into his conduct was set on foot. No personal charge of corruption could be proved against him, but he was arrogant and tactless in his dealings with the politicians of all parties. Parliament resolved to have his blood. The trial opened in Westminster Hall on February 13, 1788. It lasted over seven years. Every aspect and detail of Hastings's administration was scrutinised, denounced, upheld, misunderstood, or applauded. At the end he was acquitted.

Hastings was nearly bankrupt by the cost of defending himself. The Company, however, had given him enough money to buy back Daylesford, and many years later, when he was testifying in the Commons on Indian affairs, the House uncovered in his honour. He never held office again. But at any rate he was more fortunate than his old opponents from France, several of whom had long before been beheaded or made penniless. Posterity has redeemed his name.

* * *

The impeachment of Warren Hastings was a turning-point in the history of the British in India. The chief power was no longer to be grasped by obscure, brilliant servants of the Company who could seize and merit it, and the post of Governor-General was henceforward occupied by personages distinguished on their own account and drawn from the leading families in England. In effect, though not in name, these men were Viceroys, untempted by the hope of financial gain, impatient of restraint by ill-informed Governments in London, and sufficiently intimate with the ruling circles in Britain to do what they thought right and without fear of the consequences.

BOOK NINE

Napoleon

CHAPTER SIXTY-THREE

The American Constitution

THE WAR of Independence was over and the Thirteen Colonies were free to make their own lives. The struggle had told heavily upon their primitive political organisation. The Articles of Confederation to which they had subscribed in 1777 set up a weak central Government enjoying only such authority as the Americans might have allowed to the British Crown. Their Congress had neither the power nor the opportunity in so vast a land of creating an ordered society out of the wreckage of revolution and war.

Agitation and unrest marched with a deepening economic crisis. Demand for revision of the Articles of Confederation grew and in May, 1787, a convention of delegates from twelve of the states met at Philadelphia to consider the matter. The partisans of a strong national Government were in a large majority. Patrick Henry of Virginia refused to attend, and the greatest figure of them all, Thomas Jefferson, was absent as envoy to Paris. One of the leading personalities of the assembly was Alexander Hamilton, who represented the powerful commercial interests of New York City. This handsome, brilliant man had risen rapidly on Washington's staff during the war. He had entered New York society and married well. He was determined that the ruling class, into which he had made his way by his own abilities, should continue to rule, and he now became the recognised leader of those who demanded a capable central Government and limitation of states' powers. A sense of the overhanging crisis in Europe and of the perils of democracy guided these men in their labours, and the debates in the Convention were on a high level. Most of the delegates were in favour of a Federal Government, but methods and details were bitterly contested.

All the delegates came from long-established centres on the Atlantic seaboard, but they realised with uneasiness that their power and influence would soon be threatened by the growing populace of the West. Here, beyond the Ohio and the Alleghenies, lay vast territories which Congress had ordained should be admitted to the Union on an equal footing with the original states as soon as any of them contained sixty thousand free inhabitants. Their population was already expanding, and it was only a question of time before they claimed their rights. Then what would happen to the famous Thirteen States? It was they who had expelled the British, and they felt with some justification that they knew more about politics and the true interests of the Union than the denizens of these remote, half-settled regions. As Gouverneur Morris of Pennsylvania put it: "The busy haunts of men, not the remote wilderness, is the proper school of political talents. If the Western people get the power in their hands they will ruin the Atlantic interests." Both principles were right. The Atlantic communities had the wealth and the experience, but the new lands were fully entitled to join the Union, and to the lasting credit of the Philadelphia delegates no step was taken to prevent them doing so. But one day the clash would come. The power and the future lay with the West, and it was with misgiving and anxiety that the Convention addressed itself to framing the Constitution of the United States.

This was a concise document defining the powers of the new central Government. It established a single executive: a President, appointed indirectly by electors chosen as the state legislatures might decide, and serving for four years, with the right of veto over the acts of Congress, but subject to impeachment; head of the Army and administration, responsible only to the people, completely independent of the legislative power. The Lower House, or the House of Representatives as it was now called, was to be elected for two years, upon a population basis. But this concession to the democratic principle was tempered by the erection of a Senate, elected for six years by the state legislatures. The Senate was to restrain any demagogy of the Lower House, to defend the interests of property against the weight of a Lower House chosen upon the numerical principle, and by its share in the appointing and treaty-making powers of the President to control this powerful functionary. At the summit of the constitutional edifice stood a Supreme Court, composed of judges nominated for life by the President, subject to the ratification of the Senate. It assumed the task of judicial review—namely, a coercive supervision of the Acts not only of Congress, but also of the state legislatures, to ensure their conformity with the Constitution.

A national authority was created, supreme within its sphere. The new nation that had with difficulty struggled into being was henceforth fortified with something unheard of in the existing world—a written Constitution. At first sight this authoritative document presents a sharp contrast with the store of traditions and precedents that make up the unwritten Constitution of Britain. Yet behind it lay no revolutionary theory. It was based not upon the challenging writings of the French philosophers which were soon to set Europe ablaze, but on an Old English doctrine, freshly formulated to meet an urgent American need. The Constitution was a reaffirmation of faith in the principles painfully evolved over the centuries by the English-speaking peoples. It enshrined long-standing English ideas of justice and liberty, henceforth to be regarded on the other side of the Atlantic as basically American.

Of course, a written constitution carries with it the danger of a cramping rigidity. What body of men, however farsighted, can lay down precepts in advance for settling the problems of future generations? The delegates at Philadelphia were well aware of this. They made provision for amendment, and the document drawn up by them was adaptable enough in practice to permit changes in the Constitution. But it had to be proved in argument and debate and generally accepted throughout the land that any changes proposed would follow the guiding ideas of the Founding Fathers. A prime object of the Constitution was to be conservative; it was to guard the principles and machinery of State from capricious and ill-considered alteration. In its fundamental doctrine the American people acquired an institution which was to command the same respect and loyalty as in England are given to Parliament and Crown.

*   *   *

To the leaders of agrarian democracy, the backwoodsmen, the small farmers, the project seemed a betrayal of the Revolution. They had thrown off the English executive. They had gained their local freedom. They were now asked to create another instrument no less powerful and coercive. They had been told they were fighting for the Rights of Man and the equality of the individual. They saw in the Constitution an engine for the defence of property against equality. Jefferson in his diplomatic exile in Paris brooded with misgiving on the new regime. But the party of Hamilton and Morris, with its brilliant propaganda, in a series of public letters called *The Federalist*, carried the day. *The Federalist* letters are among the classics of American literature. Their practical wisdom stands pre-eminent amid the stream of controversial writing at the time. Their authors were concerned, not with abstract arguments about political theory, but with the real dangers threatening America, the evident weakness of the existing Confederation, and the debatable advantages of the various provisions in the new Constitution. Hamilton, Jay, and Madison were the principal contributors. They all agreed upon one point, the importance of creating a collective faith in the Constitution as the embodiment of the American ideal. How well they succeeded and how enduring has been their success is testified by the century and three-quarters that have elapsed since they wrote.

In March, 1789, the new Federal bodies were convened. The first step was to elect a President, and General Washington, the Commander of the Revolution, was the obvious choice. Disinterested and courageous, farsighted and patient, aloof yet direct in manner, inflexible once his mind was made up, Washington possessed the gifts of character for which the situation called. He was reluctant to accept office. Nothing would have

292

pleased him more than to remain in equable but active retirement at Mount Vernon, improving the husbandry of his estate. But, as always, he answered the summons of duty.

There was much confusion and discussion, but the prestige of Washington lent dignity to the new, untried office. On April 30, 1789, in the recently opened Federal Hall in New York, he was solemnly inaugurated as the first President of the United States. A week later the French States-General met at Versailles. Another great revolution was about to burst upon a bewildered world. The flimsy, untested fabric of American unity and order had been erected only just in time.

*   *   *

Many details had yet to be worked out. The first step was the passing of a Bill of Rights. The lack of such fundamental assertions in the Constitution had been a chief complaint of its critics. They were incorporated in ten Amendments. Next the Judiciary Act made the Supreme Court the most formidable part of the Federal machinery.

Administrative departments were quickly set up: Treasury, State, and War. The success of the new Federal Government depended largely upon the men chosen to fill these key offices: Alexander Hamilton, the great Federalist from New York; Thomas Jefferson, the Virginian democrat, now returned from Paris; and, to a lesser extent, General Knox of Massachusetts.

From 1789 to his resignation six years later Hamilton used his brilliant abilities to nourish the Constitution and bind the economic interests of the great merchants of America to the new system. At his inspiration a series of great measures followed. The moneyed interest was overjoyed by this programme, but there was bitter opposition. The clash between capitalist and agrarian glared forth. The planters distrusted the whole idea of public finance.

This cleavage is of durable importance in American history. The beginnings of the great political parties can be discerned, and they soon found their first leaders. Hamilton was quickly recognised as head of the financial and mercantile interest centring in the North, and his opponent was none other than Jefferson, Secretary of State. But the conflict between Jefferson and Hamilton was not confined to economics. A profoundly antagonistic view of politics separated them. They held radically opposed views of human nature. Hamilton, the superbly successful financier, believed that men were guided by their passions and their interests, and that their motives, unless rigidly controlled, were evil. Majority rule and government by the counting of heads were abhorrent to him. There must be a strong central Government and a powerful governing circle, and he saw in Federal institutions, backed by a ruling business class, the hope and future of America. The developing society of England was the ideal for the New World, and such he hoped to create across the Atlantic by his efforts at the Treasury Department. He represents and symbolises one aspect of American development, the successful, self-reliant business world.

Thomas Jefferson was the product of wholly different conditions and the prophet of a rival political idea. Jefferson had been the principal author of the Declaration of Independence and leader of the agrarian democrats in the American Revolution. He was well read; he nourished many scientific interests, and he was a gifted amateur architect. His graceful classical house, Monticello, was built according to his own designs. Like the French school of economists he believed in a yeoman-farmer society. He feared an industrial proletariat as much as he disliked the principle of aristocracy. Industrial and capitalist development appalled him. He believed in his heart that democratic government was only possible among free yeomen. It was not given to him to foresee that the United States would eventually become the greatest industrial democracy in the world.

Jefferson held to the Virginian conception of society, simple and unassailed by the complexity, the perils, and the challenge of industrialism. In France he saw, or thought he saw, the realisation of his political ideas—the destruction of a worn-out aristocracy and a revolutionary assertion of the rights of soil-tilling man. Hamilton, on the other hand, looked to the England of the Younger Pitt as the embodiment of his hopes for America. The outbreak of war between England and France was to bring to a head the fundamental rivalry and conflict between Hamilton and Jefferson and to signalise the birth of the great American parties, Federalist and Republican. Both were to split and founder and change their names, but from them the Republican and Democratic parties of today can trace their lineage.

CHAPTER SIXTY-FOUR

The Younger Pitt

THE SURRENDER of Cornwallis at Yorktown in Virginia had a decisive effect on British opinion. Dark was the scene which spread around the ambitious Island and its stubborn King. Britain was without a single ally; she stood alone amid a world war in which all had gone amiss. Such was the plight to which the obstinacy of George III had reduced the Empire.

The French Government were now close to bankruptcy. They had only aided the American Patriots in the hope of dismembering the British Empire, and, apart from a few romantic enthusiasts like Lafayette, had no wish to help to create a republic in the New World. Although Congress had promised to let France take the lead in peace negotiations, the American Commissioners in Europe realised their danger, and without French knowledge and in direct violation of the Congressional undertaking they signed secret peace preliminaries with England. The most important issue was the future of the Western lands lying between the Allegheny Mountains and the Mississippi. After months of negotiation a frontier was agreed upon which ran from the borders of Maine to the St. Lawrence, up the river, and through the Great Lakes to their head. Everything south of this line, east of the Mississippi, and north of the borders of Florida, became American territory. This was by far the most important result of the treaty.

France now made her terms with England. They gained little that was material. Their main object, however, was achieved. The Thirteen Colonies had been wrested from the United Kingdom, and England's position in the world seemed to have been gravely weakened. Spain was forced to join in the general settlement with the English retaining Gibraltar, the main Spanish objective.

Thus ended what some then called the World War. A new state had come into being across the Atlantic, a great future force in the councils of the nations. The first British Empire had fallen. England had been heavily battered, but remained undaunted.

* * *

The King now seized his chance of regaining popularity. In William Pitt, the son of the great Chatham, the King found the man. His reputation was honourable and clear. By what was certainly the most outstanding domestic action of his long reign, in December, 1783, the King asked Pitt to form a Government. The old Parliamentary machine had failed, and as it broke down a new combination took its place whose efforts were vindicated by the events of the next twenty years.

The revolt of the American colonies had shattered the complacency of eighteenth-century England. Men began to study the root causes of the disaster and the word "reform" was in the air. There was even talk of universal suffrage and other novel theories of democratic representation. But they would all have agreed that Parliament did not and need not precisely represent the English people. To them Parliament represented, not individuals, but "interests"—the landed interest, the mercantile interest, even the labouring interest, but with a strong leaning to the land as the solid and indispensable basis of the national life. No general reform of the franchise was attempted. The individualism of eighteenth-century England assumed no doctrinaire form. The enunciation of first principles has always been obnoxious to the English mind. In England the revolutionary current ran underground and was caught up in provincial eddies.

Nevertheless, England was silently undergoing a revolution in industry and agriculture, which was to have more far-reaching effects than the political tumults of the times. Steam-engines provided a new source of power in factories and foundries, which rapidly multiplied. A network of canals was constructed which carried coal cheaply to new centres of industry. A great upheaval was taking place in society, and the monopoly which the landowners had gained in 1688 could not remain.

There was also a profound change in the emotional and intellectual life of the people. The American Revolution had thrown the English back upon themselves, and a mental stock-taking exposed complacencies and anomalies which could ill stand the public gaze. The religious revival of John Wesley had broken the stony surface of the Age of Reason. Such, in brief, were the turmoils and problems which confronted William Pitt when he became Prime Minister of Britain at the age of twenty-four.

* * *

With all the renown of his father's name behind him, this grave, precocious young man, eloquent, incorruptible, and hard-working, stood upon the uplands of power. Even at this age he had few close acquaintances. But two men were to play a decisive part in his life, Henry Dundas and William Wilberforce. They formed a compact body in the House of Commons, and their prime political aim was the abolition of the slave trade.

Pitt was to need great patience in the coming years. His supporters were stubborn, jealous, and at times rebellious. They frustrated his attempts to reform the Irish Government. From the outset he was overcome by the dead hand of eighteenth-century politics. He failed to abolish the slave trade. He failed to make a settlement in Ireland. He failed to make Parliament more representative of the nation. He saw quite clearly the need and justification for reform, but preferred always to compromise with the forces of resistance.

* * *

It was in the most practical and most urgent problem, the ordering and reconstruction of the finances of the nation, that Pitt achieved his best work, and created that Treasury tradition of wise, incorruptible management which still prevails. His Ministry coincided with a revolution in economic and commercial thought. In 1776 Adam Smith had published *The Wealth of Nations,* which quickly became famous throughout educated circles. Pitt was deeply influenced by his book. The first British Empire was discredited and had almost vanished from the map. Another was gradually growing in Canada, in India, and in the Antipodes, where Cook had just charted the scarce-known Southern Continent. But the conception of a close economic Imperial unit, with the colonies eternally subject in matters of trade to the Mother Country and fettered by comprehensive restrictions upon their commercial intercourse with other nations, had proved disastrous. The times were ripe for an exposition of the principles of Free Trade. In steady, caustic prose Adam Smith destroyed the case for Mercantilism. Pitt was convinced. He was the first English statesman to believe in Free Trade.

Further reform consolidated the revenue. It is to Pitt that we owe the modern machinery of the "Budget." Pitt resolved to acquire a surplus in the revenue and apply it to the reduction of the National Debt. In 1786 he brought in a Bill for this purpose. Here was the famous oft-criticised Sinking Fund. The soundness of the national finances was judged by the amount in the Sinking Fund, which gave an impression of stability to the moneyed classes of the City. Trade revived, prosperity increased, and what then seemed the handsome sum of ten million pounds was paid off in ten years. But perhaps the most striking achievement of Pitt's management was the negotiation of a new commercial treaty with France—the first Free Trade treaty according to the new economic principles.

The hope of further reconstruction and improvement was shattered by war and revolution upon the European scene. For Pitt it was a personal tragedy. His genius lay essentially in business management; his greatest memorials are his financial statements. He was most at home in the world of figures. His mind had set and developed at an unduly early age, without, as Coleridge said, "the ungainliness or the promise of a growing intellect." He found human contacts difficult, and his accession to power cut him off from other men. From 1784 until 1800 he moved exclusively between the narrow world of political London and his house at Putney. He knew nothing of the lives of his countrymen outside the limited area of the Metropolis. Even amid the fellowship of the House of Commons and the political clubs he stood aloof.

It is remarkable to witness the peaceful triteness of English politics, operating almost as if in a vacuum, during the years 1789 to 1793, when the terrible and world-shaking upheavals in Paris and in the provinces of France convulsed men's minds. Pitt was determined to stand clear of the impending European conflict. He was convinced that if the French revolutionaries were left alone to put their house in order as they chose, England could avoid being dragged into war. He maintained an even course of neutrality, and with characteristic obstinacy held to it for over three tumultuous years.

CHAPTER SIXTY-FIVE

Britain Confronts the French Revolution

THE CONVULSION which shook France in 1789 was totally different from the revolutions that the world had seen before. England in the seventeenth century had witnessed a violent shift in power between the Crown and the people; but the basic institutions of State had been left untouched, or at any rate had soon been restored. Nor as yet had there been in England any broadening of popular sovereignty in the direction of universal suffrage. America in her Revolution had proclaimed the wider rights of mankind. In Europe the impulse towards liberty, equality, and popular sovereignty had to come from elsewhere. It came from France. The English Revolution had been entirely a domestic affair. So in the main had the American. But the French Revolution was to spread out from Paris across the whole Continent. It gave rise to a generation of warfare, and its echoes reverberated long into the nineteenth century and afterwards. Every great popular and national movement, until the Bolsheviks gave a fresh turn to events in 1917, was to invoke the principles set forth at Versailles in 1789.

* * *

To the world outside in the summer of 1789, and to foreigners in France, the Revolution seemed to have fulfilled its aims. All was over, it was thought: privilege had been overthrown; the people's rights had been asserted. Burke, meditating in England, was more far-sighted. The convulsion in France, as he eloquently pointed out, was not a dignified, orderly change, carried out with due regard for tradition, like the English Revolution of 1688. A complete break with the past had been made. In the name of reason irrational forces had been let loose. These were not easily to be assuaged. France was fated to undergo every form of revolutionary experience. The pattern has been repeated in other countries, at later times, but with not very different results. France was the crucible in which all the modern elements of Revolution were first put to the test.

In England the Whigs, and especially the reformers and Radicals, had at first welcomed the French Revolution. They were soon repelled by its excesses. Now France gave a frightful demonstration of what happens when the social forces unleashed by reformers break free from all control. Most Englishmen recoiled in horror.

In his Budget speech of 1792 Pitt had announced that he believed in fifteen years of peace for Europe. Non-intervention was his policy. Something more vital to Britain than a massacre of aristocrats or a speech in the Convention, something more concrete than a threat of world revolution, had to happen before he would face the issue of war. The spark, as so often in England's history, came from the Netherlands. On November 28 Antwerp fell into French hands. The whole delicate balance of eighteenth-century international politics was deranged.

Britain was to be at war for over twenty years, and was now confronted with the task of making a major war effort, with her armed forces more crippled, perhaps, than at any time before by lack of equipment, leaders, and men. The conditions of service and the administration of the Army and Navy were so appalling that it is wonderful that anything was achieved at all. For several years British resources were dissipated in ill-manned and ill-planned expeditions to the West Indies. It was with the greatest difficulty that any men could be raised for these mistaken enterprises.

Great hopes had been founded in London upon the French Royalists. In 1793 they seized Toulon, and but for the fact that Dundas, Pitt's close associate, had already assigned all available troops to the West Indies a vital base for future invasion might have been secured.

Something else happened at Toulon. A young lieutenant of the French Army, sprung from a leading Corsican family, well versed in artillery and other military matters, happening to be on leave from his regiment, looked in on the camp of General Dugommier, who commanded the Jacobin besieging army. He walked along the line of batteries, and pointed out that their shot would not reach half-way. This error was adjusted, and the expert lieutenant began to have a say at that incompetent headquarters. Presently orders arrived from Paris prescribing the method of siege according to customary forms. None dared dispute the instructions of the terrible Committee of Public Safety which was now at the head of French affairs. Nevertheless, at the council of war, held in daylight, on bare ground, the expert lieutenant raised his voice. The orders, he said—or so he claimed later—were foolish, and all knew it. There was, however, a way of taking Toulon. He placed his finger on the map where Fort l'Aiguillette on its promontory commanded the entrance to the harbour. "There is Toulon," he said, and all, taking their lives in their hands, obeyed him. He organised and led the assault upon Fort l'Aiguillette. After a hot fight it fell.

On the morning after, the British Fleet was seen to be leaving the harbour. The lieutenant had understood not only the military significance of the captured fort, but the whole set of moral and political forces upon which the Royalist defence of Toulon hung. When these matters were reported to Robespierre and his brother and the Committee in Paris they thought they would like to know more about this competent and apparently well-disposed lieutenant. His name was Napoleon Bonaparte; and, after all, he had taken Toulon.

Meanwhile the Terror rose to its height, and in the political frenzy of Paris no one knew when his hour would come. In a furious convulsion, Robespierre was dragged down and sent where he would have sent the rest. Our lieutenant of Toulon fame was cast back by this event. He was associated with the Robespierres. He was their "maker of plans." By a spin of the coin he might have followed them into the shades. But the extremity of the Terror had died with Robespierre, and the Directorate which succeeded soon had need of him. Placed in command of the military forces, Bonaparte led the French Army against the Austrians in Northern Italy. He animated his ragged and famishing troops by the hopes of glory and booty. He routed the Austrian commanders and conquered the broad base of the Italian peninsula. By these victories he outstripped all rivals in the military field and became the sword of the Revolution, which he was determined to exploit and to destroy.

*   *   *

On the Continent the French were everywhere triumphant. Bonaparte, having reduced Northern Italy, was preparing to strike at Austria through the Alpine passes. Belgium was annexed to France; the Republic of Venice, with a glorious history reaching into the Dark Ages, became an Austrian province. Milan, Piedmont, and the little principalities of Northern Italy were welded into a new Cisalpine Republic. France, dominant in Western Europe, firmly planted in the Mediterranean, safeguarded against attack from Germany by a secret understanding with Austria, had only to consider what she would conquer next. A sober judgement might have said England, by way of Ireland. Bonaparte thought he saw his destiny in a larger field. In the spring of 1798 he sailed for Egypt. Lord Nelson sailed after him.

During the afternoon of August 1 a scouting vessel from Nelson's fleet signalled that a number of French battleships were anchored in Aboukir Bay, to the east of Alexandria. As evening drew near, five British ships passed in succession on the land side of the enemy. The French sailors were many of them on shore and the decks of their vessels were encumbered with gear. They had not thought it necessary to clear the gun ports on their landward side. In the rapidly falling darkness confusion seized their fleet. Relentlessly the English ships, distinguished by four lanterns hoisted in a horizontal pattern, battered the enemy van, passing from one disabled foe to the next down the line. At ten o'clock Brueys's flagship, the *Orient,* blew up. The five ships ahead of her had already surrendered; the rest, their cables cut by shot, or frantically attempting to avoid the inferno of the burning *Orient,* drifted helplessly. In the morning hours three ran ashore and surrendered, and a fourth was burned by her officers. Of the great fleet that had convoyed Napoleon's army to the adventure in Egypt only two ships of the line and two frigates escaped.

Nelson's victory of the Nile cut Napoleon's communications with France

3 0 0

and ended his hopes of vast Eastern conquests. The British Fleet was once again supreme in the Mediterranean Sea. This was a turning-point. But still the British Government could conceive no co-ordinated military plan upon the scale demanded by European strategy. Meanwhile Napoleon, who had escaped back to France, again took charge of the French armies in Italy. In June, 1800, he beat the Austrians at Marengo, and France was once more mistress of Europe. The main contribution of the Island to the war at this time was the vigilance of her fleets and the payment of subsidies to allies. Napoleon's taunt of "a nation of shopkeepers" had some foundation.

*   *   *

Pitt was worn and weary, and perplexed by the uncongenial task of organising England for war. He chose to incur gigantic debts, and to struggle haphazardly through each year until the dismal close of the campaigning season, living from day to day and hoping for the best. But if Pitt was an indifferent War Minister his successors were no improvement.

Indeed, with all his defects William Pitt stood high above his contemporaries. Certainly he held more popular confidence than any other man. Yet Pitt was succeeded by a pinchbeck coalition of King's Friends and rebels from his own party. Masquerading as a Government of National Union, they blundered on for over three years. Their leader was Henry Addington, an amiable former Speaker of the House of Commons whom no one regarded as a statesman.

In March, 1802, Addington's Government made terms with Napoleon by the Treaty of Amiens, and for a time there was a pause in the fighting. English tourists flocked to France eager to gaze upon the scenes of Revolution and to see at first hand the formidable First Consul, as he now was. But the tourist season was short. In May of the following year Napoleon was assembling his forces at Boulogne, intent upon the invasion of England. Pitt was in retirement at Walmer, in Kent. The strain of the past years had broken his health. He was prematurely aged. He had lived a lonely, artificial life, cheered by few friendships. The only time that he ever came in contact with the people was during this brief interval from office, when as Warden of the Cinque Ports he organised the local militia against the threat of invasion. Few things in England's history are more remarkable than this picture of an ex-Prime Minister, riding his horse at the head of a motley company of yokels, drilling on the fields of the South Coast, while a bare twenty miles away across the Channel the Grand Army of Napoleon waited only for a fair wind and a clear passage.

CHAPTER SIXTY-SIX

Trafalgar

IN 1804 Pitt was recalled to power. Feverishly he flung himself into the work of reorganising England's war effort. Since the renewal of war Britain had found herself alone against Napoleon, and for two years she maintained the struggle single-handed during one of the most critical periods in her history. The French had for the moment cowed the Continent into a passive acceptance of their mastery. The opportunity was now at hand to concentrate the whole weight of the armed forces of France against the stubborn Islanders. An enormous army was organised and concentrated at the Channel ports for the invasion of England. At the crest of his hopes Napoleon had himself crowned by the Pope as Emperor of the French. One thing alone was lacking to his designs—command of the sea. As before and since in her history, the Royal Navy alone seemed to stand between the Island and national destruction.

In May, 1803, Nelson had returned to the Mediterranean to resume command of his fleet. Here the fate of his country might be decided. Nelson was well aware of the grim significance of the moment and all his brilliance as a commander was employed on creating a first-class machine. He was not even superior in numbers to the main French Fleet in Toulon harbour. Nelson's burning desire was to lure them out and fight them. Annihilation was his policy. Twice in the course of two years the French attempted a sortie, but retired. Throughout this time Nelson never set foot on shore. He had to cover all escape routes.

In the centre of the web sat Napoleon, and the elaborate scheme for the final blow against England was slowly woven. But the vital instrument in his hand was brittle. In May, 1804, the Emperor had confided the Toulon fleet to Admiral Villeneuve, an excellent seaman. Napoleon would brook no obstacles, and a complicated series of feints was worked out to deceive the British. In the early months of 1805 Napoleon made his final arrangements. The French fleets in the Atlantic and Mediterranean harbours must be concentrated to gain command of the Channel. The Emperor fixed upon the West Indies. Here, after breaking the Mediterranean and Atlantic blockades, and drawing off the British Fleet, as he thought, into the waters of the Western Atlantic, his ships were ordered to gather. The combined French and Spanish fleets would then unite with Ganteaume, the admiral of the Brest squadron, double back to Europe, sail up the Channel, and assure the crossing from Boulogne. The scheme was brilliant on paper, but it took no account of the state of the French ships, and it ignored the vital strategy of concentration always pursued by British admirals when the

302

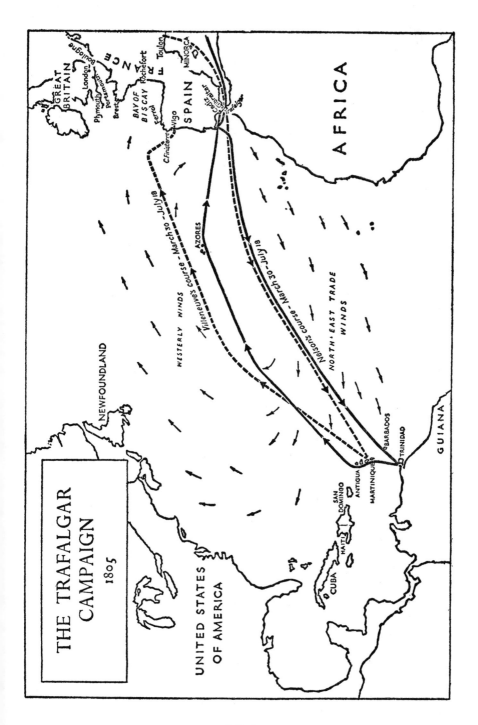

THE TRAFALGAR
CAMPAIGN
1805

GREAT BRITAIN

London
Plymouth
Portsmouth
Brest

FRANCE

Boulogne

Rochefort

Toulon

MINORCA

BAY OF BISCAY

Ferrol

Vigo

C. Finisterre

SPAIN

Cadiz
Gibraltar
Trafalgar

AFRICA

NEWFOUNDLAND

AZORES

WESTERLY WINDS

Villeneuve's course – March 30 – July 18

Nelson's course – March 30 – July 18

NORTH-EAST TRADE WINDS

UNITED STATES
OF AMERICA

CUBA

SAN DOMINGO

HAITI

ANTIGUA

MARTINIQUE

BARBADOS

TRINIDAD

GUIANA

303

enemy was at large.

Villeneuve slipped out of Toulon on the dark night of March 30. The fox was out and the chase began. Fortune seemed against Nelson. All his qualities were now displayed to the full. Out of perplexing, obscure, and conflicting reports he fathomed the French plan. Therefore on May 11 Nelson made the momentous decision to sail westwards himself. The English pursued their quarry, and a game of hide-and-seek followed among the West Indian islands. On the 12th Nelson lay off Antigua, where Villeneuve had lain only four days earlier. He again had to made a crucial decision. Was he right in believing that the French were making for Europe?

Nelson replenished his fleet and sailed for home waters. The crisis was at hand and the outlying squadrons of the Royal Navy instinctively gathered at the mouth of the Channel for the defence of the Island. Nelson went on alone with his flagship, the *Victory,* to Portsmouth. In the following days the campaign reached its climax. Villeneuve sailed again on August 13 in an attempt to enter the English Channel, for Napoleon still believed that the British fleets were dispersed and that the moment had come for invasion. Meanwhile Villeneuve changed his mind. Well aware of the shortcomings of his ill-trained fleet, desperately short of supplies, and with many sick on board, he had abandoned the great venture on August 15 and was already speeding south to Cadiz. The threat of invasion was over.

Amid scenes of enthusiasm Nelson rejoined the *Victory* at Portsmouth and sailed for Cadiz on September 15. All England realised that her fate now lay in the hands of this frail man. His energy and inspiration roused the spirit of his captains to the highest pitch. To them he outlined a new and daring plan of battle. To gain a decisive victory, he was resolved to abandon the old formal line of battle. He would break Villeneuve's line, when it came out of Cadiz harbour, by sailing at right angles boldly into it with two main divisions. After his conference with his captains Nelson wrote, "All approved. It was new, it was singular, it was simple. It must succeed." In a mood of intense exhilaration the fleet prepared for the ordeal ahead. At daybreak on the 21st Nelson saw from the quarterdeck of the *Victory* the battle line of the enemy consisting of twelve Spanish ships and twenty-one French ships of the line. It was seven months since the escape from Toulon, and the first time that Nelson had seen his foes since war had begun in 1803.

The British Fleet lay about ten miles west of the enemy. The clumsy seamanship of his men convinced Villeneuve that flight was impossible, and he hove to in a long sagging line to await Nelson's attack. The English admiral turned to one of his officers. "They have put a good face on it, but I will give them such a dressing as they have never had before." The fleets were drawing nearer and nearer. Another signal was run up upon the *Victory,* "England expects every man will do his duty." When Collingwood saw the flutter he remarked testily, "I wish Nelson would stop signalling, as we all know well enough what we have to do," but when the message was reported to him cheers broke out from the ships in his line. A deathly silence fell upon the fleet as the ships drew nearer. Each captain marked down his adversary, and within a few minutes the two English columns thundered into action. Nelson was pacing as if on parade on his quarterdeck when at 1.15 P.M. he was shot from the mast-head of the *Redoubtable* by a bullet in the shoulder. His backbone was broken, and he was carried below amid the thunder of the *Victory's* guns. The battle was still raging. By the afternoon of October 21, 1805, eighteen of the enemy ships had surrendered and the remainder were in full retreat. Eleven entered Cadiz, but four more were captured off the coast of Spain. In the log of the *Victory* occurs the passage, "Partial firing continued until 4.30, when a victory having been reported to the right Hon. Lord Viscount Nelson, K.B. and Commander-in-Chief, he then died of his wound."

The victory was complete and final. The British Fleet, under her most superb commander, like him had done its duty.

* * *

Napoleon was attracted to other fields. In August, 1805, the camp at Boulogne broke up, and the French troops set out on their long march to the Danube. The campaign that followed wrecked Pitt's hopes and schemes. Austria and Russia were broken at the Battle of Austerlitz. Napoleon's star had once more triumphed, and for England all was to do again.

A personal sorrow now darkened Pitt's life. The House of Commons resolved to impeach his close colleague and lifelong companion, Henry Dundas, for maladministration in the Admiralty. The decisive speech against Dundas was made by none other than Wilberforce. The scene in the House of Commons was poignant. Pitt's eyes filled with tears as he listened to Wilberforce attacking his other greatest friend. Encircled by his supporters, he was led from the House. It was this disgrace, rather than the news of Austerlitz, which finally broke the spirit and energy of the Prime Minister. In January, 1806, he died.

"In an age," runs the inscription on his monument in Guildhall, "when the contagion of ideals threatened to dissolve the forms of civil society he rallied the loyal, the soberminded, and the good around the venerable structure of the English monarchy." This is a fitting epitaph.

CHAPTER SIXTY-SEVEN

The Emperor of the French

WILLIAM PITT'S successors were staunch in the prosecution of war, but even less adept at it than he. The three years between the death of Pitt in January, 1806, and the rise of Wellington in 1809 were uncheered by fortune. The Government's tenure of office was redeemed by Fox's abolition of the slave trade, a measure which ranks among the greatest of British achievements, and from which Pitt had always shrunk. It was Fox's last effort. For forty years his warm-hearted eloquence had inspired the Whigs. Almost his whole Parliamentary life was spent in Opposition. He died as Secretary of State, nine months after his great rival, Pitt, had gone to the grave.

* * *

Napoleon was reaching the height of his career. At Austerlitz he had struck down Russia and Austria. He was already master of the Netherlands, Italy, and the states of the Rhine. At Jena, a year later, he had broken Prussia. The Franco-Russian Alliance, signed at Tilsit on July 7, 1807, was the culmination of his power. He dominated all Europe. The Emperor of Austria was a cowed and obsequious satellite. The King of Prussia and his handsome queen were beggars and almost captives in his train. Napoleon's brothers reigned as Kings at the Hague, at Naples, and in Westphalia. His step-son ruled Northern Italy in his name. Spain lent itself to his system, trusting that worse might not befall. Denmark and Scandinavia made haste to obey. Russia, the great counterpoise, had swung over to his side. Only Britannia remained, unreconciled, unconquered, implacable. There she lay in her Island, mistress of the seas and oceans, ruled by her proud, stubborn aristocracy, facing this immense combination alone, sullen, fierce, and almost unperturbed.

* * *

All through the spring of 1812 the Emperor had been gathering forces on a scale hitherto unknown in Europe, and as the summer came he drew them eastward from all his dominions. For two years past the Emperor's relations with Russia had been growing more and more embittered. The Czar had gradually become convinced that no general European settlement could be made so long as the French Emperor dominated the scene. Napoleon determined to get his blow in first, and to make it a shattering one. Although his generals and Ministers were reluctant and apprehensive, a kind of delirium swept the martial classes of the Empire. Many voices had warned Napoleon of the hardships and difficulties of campaigning in Russia. Nor did he disregard their advice. He had assembled what seemed for those days abundant transport and supply. It proved unequal to the event. His plan was to snatch at the old Russian capital. He confidently expected that the Czar would then treat for peace. All the other sovereigns of Europe in similar circumstances had hastened to bow the knee. But Russia proved a different proposition. Defence, retreat, and winter—on these resources the Russian high command relied. Napoleon had studied the amazing Russian campaigns of the great Swede, King Charles XII. He thought he had profited by his reading. In the twentieth century another more ruthless dictator was to study Napoleon's errors. He, too, thought he had marked the lesson. Russia undeceived them both.

Before Napoleon the Russian armies fell back, avoiding the traps he set for them and devastating the countryside through which the French had to pass. At Borodino, some sixty miles west of the capital, the Russians turned at bay. There in the bloodiest battle of the nineteenth century General Kutusov inflicted a terrible mauling on Napoleon. Both the armies engaged, each of about a hundred and twenty thousand men, lost a third of their strength. Kutusov withdrew once more, and Moscow fell to the French. But the Russians declined to sue for peace. As winter drew near it was forced on Napoleon's mind that Moscow, burnt to a shell by accident or by design, was untenable by his starving troops. There was nothing for it but retreat through the gathering snows—the most celebrated and disastrous retreat in history. Winter now took its dreadful toll. Rearguard actions, however gallant, sapped the remaining French strength. Out of the huge Grand Army launched upon Russia only twenty thousand straggled back to Warsaw. Marshal Ney was said to have been the last Frenchman to quit Russian soil.

On December 5 Napoleon abandoned the remnant of his armies on the Russian frontier and set out by sleigh for Paris. Whatever salvaging could be done he left to his Marshals. For himself he was insensible of disaster. He still put trust in his Star. If he had failed to extend his Empire to the East, he could yet preserve it in the West. By tremendous efforts he would raise new forces and fight again. In the spring of 1813 he once more took the field. Half his men were raw recruits, and France was no longer behind him. Reluctant support was all he could get, and even his Marshals began to waver. Germany rose in the hour of his downfall. The spirit of nationalism, diffused by French armies, sprang up to baffle and betray the master of Europe. Coalitions were formed, backed by the finances of Britain. Napoleon was offered the chance of an honourable peace. Thinking that fate could be reversed by genius in battle, he rejected it. One by one his hesitant allies dropped away. Sweden, ruled by the French Marshal Bernadotte; Prussia, Austria, and even Saxony and Bavaria, his own client states, abandoned him. The Czar was resolved upon a march for the Rhine. Central Europe, so long subservient to France, joined the Russian thrust. A series of gigantic engagements were fought in Saxony and Silesia. At last in the three-day battle of Leipzig in October all Napoleon's foes closed in upon him. Nearly half a million men were involved on each side. In this Battle of the Nations Napoleon was overwhelmed and driven westwards to the frontiers of France. The Allies gathered on the borders of their enemy for the first time since 1793. The great Revolutionary and Imperial adventure was drawing to a close.

* * *

Meantime, by a prodigious effort of arms, and of courage, Lord Wellington had inflicted a series of crushing defeats on French armies in the Iberian Peninsula. In 1811 the French abandoned Madrid and the British occupied the capital. By 1813 he had cleared the whole north of Spain and herded the retreating French into the old mountain kingdom of Navarre. At the battle of Vitoria on June 21 he routed Marshal Jourdan and drove his forces over the Pyrenees. News of this victory heartened the Czar and the Allied armies of Europe. Tenaciously Wellington pursued his purpose of reducing, as he put it, "the power and influence of the grand disturber of Europe." By the spring of 1814 he was on French soil and had occupied Bordeaux.

For Napoleon the end had already come. In the south the front had crumpled; to the east Prussians, Russians, and Austrians were reaching into the heart of France. The combined strength of Europe was too much for him. The forces of opposition to his rule in France openly rose against him. Fouché and Talleyrand, long conspiring in doubt, now put it to themselves that France could only be saved by deserting her Emperor. At the end of March Marshal Marmont, defending Paris, gave up and surrendered the capital. On April 3 Napoleon abdicated and retired to the island of Elba. The long, remorseless tides of war rolled back, and at the Congress of Vienna the Powers prepared for the diplomatic struggle of the peace.

* * *

Britain was represented at Vienna by Castlereagh who was now to take an influential part in the reconstruction of Europe. His voice was foremost in proposing a just and honourable peace. Castlereagh's principal colleagues at Vienna were Metternich, the Austrian Chancellor, and Talleyrand, the spokesman of France. The most urgent problem was the government of France. Napoleon had gone, but who was to replace him? It was Talleyrand who persuaded the Powers to restore the Bourbons in the person of Louis XVIII, brother of the executed King. Louis represented at least a tradition, a fragment of the political faith of France; above all, he represented peace. He was himself a man of mildness and accommodation. The British were principally concerned with the colonial settlement and most with those possessions which had a strategic value as ports of call. For that reason they held on to Malta, and the key of the route to India, the Cape of Good Hope. The gains were scattered and piecemeal, but, taken together, they represented a powerful consolidation of the Imperial structure.

On the Continent the main preoccupation of the Powers was to draw a *cordon sanitaire* around France to protect Central Europe from the infections and dangers of revolution. While Congress danced at Vienna and the statesmen of Europe replotted the map, Napoleon was brooding and scheming in his new retreat at Elba. Long before the wrangling of the Powers had ended he again burst upon the scene.

CHAPTER SIXTY-EIGHT

Washington, Adams, and Jefferson

THE CONFUSED and tumultuous issues of European politics reached America in black and white. Debate on the French Revolution raged throughout the country. Corresponding societies on the Revolutionary model sprang up wherever Jeffersonian principles were upheld, while the Federalist Press thundered against the Jacobins of the New World, and, like Burke in England, denounced them as destroyers of society.

Controversy became less theoretical and much more vehement as soon as American commercial interests were affected. Tempers rose as American ships and merchandise endured the commerce-raiding and privateering of France and Britain. Both parties demanded war—the Federalists against France and the Jeffersonians against England. President Washington was determined to keep the infant republic at peace. His task was smoothed by the antics of the French Revolutionary envoy to the United States, Citizen Genêt, who, finding the Government reluctant to honour the Franco-American alliance of 1778, meddled in American politics, attempted to raise troops, and greatly embarrassed his political allies. In August, 1793, Washington demanded his recall. But, knowing the sharp activity of the guillotine in France, Genêt wisely married an American heiress and subsided peaceably in the New World.

Washington prevailed, and it was he who enumerated the first principle of traditional American foreign policy. In April, 1793, his famous proclamation of neutrality declared that it was "the disposition of the United States to pursue a conduct friendly and impartial towards the belligerent Powers." Infringements would render American citizens liable to prosecution in the Federal courts. But relations with Britain were clouded by unsettled issues. Hamilton's Federalist Party was deeply committed to maintaining a friendly commerce with Britain. The overseas trade of New England was largely financed by London bankers. The carrying trade between the two countries brought great profit to the shipowners of the Eastern states, and they strongly opposed any suggestion of war on the side of Revolutionary France. The farmers and pioneers of the frontier felt differently. To them Britain was the enemy who refused to honour the treaty of 1783 by evacuating the frontier posts on the Canadian border, and was pushing her fur trade from Canada southwards, inciting the Indians against American settlers, and threatening the flank of their own advance to the West. The British in their turn resented the failure of the American Government to settle the large debts still unpaid since before the Revolution. Meanwhile British interference with American shipping, on the plea that it was helping to sustain France, stung public opinion throughout the United States.

Washington decided that the whole field of Anglo-American relations must be revised and settled, and in 1794 he appointed John Jay, Chief Justice of the Supreme Court, as Envoy Extraordinary to London. The British Government felt little tenderness for their late rebels. They knew their military weakness, and Washington's need of the support of Hamilton's party. Moreover, they were considerably aided by Jay's ineptitude in negotiation. A treaty was drawn up which made few concessions to America. The frontier posts were evacuated, and the way to the West thus lay open and unmolested to American pioneers, but no guarantees were given about future British relations with the Indians. Britain paid some compensation for damage done to American ships on the high seas, but refused to modify her blockade or renounce the right to seize ships and cargoes destined for France and her allies. No satisfaction was obtained about the impressment of American seamen for service in the Royal Navy. Worst of all, Jay was forced to yield on the issue of the debts owing to British creditors, and the United States were bound to compensate British claimants for outstanding losses.

The effect on the Federalist Party was most damaging. The Western states were angered by the incomplete arrangements on the Canadian frontier. The Southerners were threatened with serious injury by the debts clause. The treaty revealed and exposed the superiority of British diplomacy and the weakness of the new American Government. The atmosphere was charged afresh with distrust, and the seeds were sown for another war between Britain and the United States.

Washington's second term of office expired in the spring of 1797, and he prepared longingly for his retirement to Mount Vernon. His last days in power were vexed by the gathering assaults of the anti-Federalists and the din of preparations for the new Presidential election. Washington and many of his associates were alarmed by the growth of party spirit. They clung to the view that the diverse interests of the nation were best reflected in a balanced and all-embracing Government. The notion that two great parties should perpetually struggle for power was foreign and repellent to them. Only Jefferson, who had already resigned from the administration, had a clear vision of the rôle that parties should play. He saw the advantages of directing the strife of factions into broad streams and keeping an organised Opposition before the country as a possible alternative Government. But in Washington's mind the dangers of faction were uppermost when in September he issued his Farewell Address to the nation. This document is one of the most celebrated in American history. It is an eloquent plea for union, a warning against "the baneful effects of the Spirit of Party." It is also an exposition of the doctrine of isolation as the true future American policy.

George Washington holds one of the proudest titles that history can bestow. He was the Father of his Nation. Almost alone his staunchness in the War of Independence held the American colonies to their united purpose. His services after victory had been won were no less great. His firmness and example while first President restrained the violence of faction and postponed a national schism for sixty years. His character and influence steadied the dangerous leanings of Americans to take sides against Britain or France. He filled his office with dignity and inspired his administration with much of his own wisdom. To his terms as President are due the smooth organisation of the Federal Government, the establishment of national credit, and the foundation of a foreign policy. By refusing to stand for a third term he set a tradition in American politics which has only been departed from by President Franklin Roosevelt in the Second World War.

For two years Washington lived quietly at his country seat on the Potomac, riding round his plantations, as he had long wished to do. Amid the snows of the last days of the eighteenth century he took to his bed. On the evening of December 14, 1799, he turned to the physician at his side, murmuring, "Doctor, I die hard, but I am not afraid to go." Soon afterwards he passed away.

* * *

John Adams succeeded Washington as head of the American State. He had been nominated by the Federalist Party. Fear of chaos and disorder, a basic distrust of democracy, had cooled his revolutionary ardour and made him a supporter of Hamilton. Of independent mind, he was a thinker rather than a party politician, an intellectual rather than a leader. Though agreeing with Hamilton on the need for strong government and the preservation of property, Adams opposed using the Federal machine for the benefit of particular economic interests and was by no means a wholehearted Federalist. In his judgements he was frequently right, but he lacked the arts of persuasion. He was bad at handling men, and his reputation has suffered accordingly. He was nevertheless one of the ablest political thinkers among American statesmen.

In foreign affairs a new crisis was at hand. The rise of Napoleon Bonaparte dimmed the high regard of Americans for their first ally, France. Fears began to grow that the French might acquire from Spain the provinces of Louisiana and Florida. A vigorous and ambitious European Power would then replace a weak one as a barrier between the expanding United States and the Gulf of Mexico. News also came of extensive French propaganda among the French-speaking inhabitants of Canada. There was a strong reaction, and for the last time the Federalists managed to outdistance their opponents. War hysteria swept the country, and they seized the opportunity to push through legislation which gave the executive extraordinary powers over aliens. The Naturalisation Act of 1798 extended the qualifying period of residence from five to fourteen years, and the Aliens Act gave the President the right to expel foreigners from the country by decree. More pointed was the Sedition Act, which in effect imposed a rigid censorship on the Press and was aimed specifically at the Opposition newspapers. The result was an intense constitutional conflict. It was in vain that Hamilton exhorted his colleagues, "Let us not establish tyranny. Energy is a very different thing from violence." Jefferson was determined to take up the challenge. He drafted resolutions, which were passed both in Kentucky and Virginia, maintaining that a state could review acts of Congress and nullify any measure deemed unconstitutional. This fateful doctrine has been heard since in American history, and these resolves of 1798 became a platform of State Rights in later years.

The Federalists' attack on the liberty of the individual marked the beginning of their fall. Hamilton, who had resigned from the Treasury some years earlier, thought he could now regain power by forcing a war with France. He conceived a vast plan for dividing, in concert with Great Britain, the Spanish colonies in the New World. But the person who extinguished these hopes was the President. Although he was no lover of the masses Adams hated both plutocracy and militarism. Until 1799 he had shown no signs of opposition to the Federalists, but he now realised that war was very near. His complete powers as President over foreign affairs made it easy for him to act swiftly. He suddenly announced the appointment of an envoy to France, and on October 1, 1800, an American mission in Paris concluded a commercial treaty with the French. On the very same day France in secret purchased Louisiana from Spain.

Adams's term of office was now expiring and the Presidential elections were due. They present a complicated spectacle, for there were dramatic splits on both sides. The Federalists had not forgiven Adams for stopping them from going to war with France. Nevertheless he was the only Federalist candidate with any hope of success, and so he won the nomination. Real power in the party, however, still lay with Hamilton, and he in his resentment hampered Adams in every way he could.

Ranged on the Republican side stood Jefferson, flanked for the office of Vice-President by Aaron Burr, a corrupt New York politician. By a curiosity of the American Constitution in those days, which was soon to be remedied, the man who won the largest number of votes became President, while the runner-up was declared Vice-President. Thus it was quite possible to have a President and a Vice-President belonging to opposite parties. Adams was beaten by both Jefferson and Burr, but Jefferson and Burr each gained an equal number of votes. There was little love lost between them. Burr tried to overthrow his chief when the deadlock was referred for decision to the House of Representatives which after many ballots chose Jefferson.

*   *   *

The United States in which Jefferson was inaugurated as President on March 4, 1801, had grown fast during their short existence and were still growing. In the twenty-five years since the Declaration of Independence the population had nearly doubled and was now about five and a half millions. Three new inland states had been set up and admitted to the Union: Vermont in the North, Kentucky and Tennessee in the Central South. Red Indian confederacies that blocked the westward migration had been decisively defeated, and their lands divided into territories which were in their turn to form states. The nation was everywhere thrusting outward from its original Atlantic seaboard. Its commerce upon the high seas now flowed from China, round Cape Horn, to the countries of Europe by way of the fast-rising ports of Boston, Baltimore, and above all New York. Philadelphia remained the greatest of American cities, but it was gradually losing its position as the centre of the life of the Union. It now ceased to be the political capital. Jefferson was the first President to be inaugurated in the new city of Washington, for which spacious plans had been drawn up. As yet only one wing of the Capitol, which housed Congress, had been built and the White House was incomplete; there was a single convenient tavern, a few boarding-houses for Senators and Congressmen, and little else except quagmire and waste land. Jefferson was undaunted by the hardships of his backwoods capital. Thought of the fine city that would one day arise kindled his idealism, and its pioneering life suited his frugal, homely manner.

It was impossible for the President to ignore the world struggle. The farmers whom Jefferson represented depended for their markets upon the Old World, and the Western states and territories needed unhindered transport for their produce down the Mississippi to the Gulf of Mexico. At the

3 1 3

mouth of the great river lay the port of New Orleans, and New Orleans was still in Spanish hands. Rumours of the secret French purchase of Louisiana were now circulating, and were soon given substance. Bonaparte dispatched an expedition to suppress a Negro rising under Toussaint L'Ouverture in the French island colony of Haiti. This accomplished, it was to take possession of Louisiana in the name of the French Government. Thus while the Treaty of Amiens imposed an uneasy peace on Europe trained French troops had arrived once more off the North American continent, and would shortly, it seemed, proceed to the mainland. This, like the French menace from Canada in the eighteenth century, drew the English-speaking nations together. "The day that France takes possession of New Orleans . . ." wrote Jefferson to the American envoy in Paris, "we must marry ourselves to the British Fleet and nation." This was a surprising development in the views of Jefferson, hitherto an admirer of France and opponent of Great Britain. But theoretical opinions must often give way before the facts of international politics. At any rate, it is wise if they do, and Jefferson had his share of practical wisdom.

In the summer of 1802 France compelled the Spaniards to close New Orleans to American produce. The whole West Country was ablaze with anger and alarm. As Jefferson wrote to his envoy in Paris, "There is on the globe one single spot the possessor of which is our natural and habitual enemy. It is New Orleans, through which three-eighths of our produce must pass to market." James Monroe was now sent on a special mission to Paris to try to purchase Louisiana, or at least New Orleans, from the French. While he was on his way American plans were suddenly forwarded by events elsewhere. The French expedition to Haiti ended in disaster, with the loss of thirty thousand men. The renewal of war between France and Britain after the Peace of Amiens was also imminent. With dramatic swiftness Napoleon abandoned all hopes of American empire, and to the astonishment of the American envoy offered to sell all the Louisiana territories which Spain had ceded to France. Monroe arrived in Paris in time to complete the purchase, and for fifteen million dollars Louisiana was transferred to the United States.

At a stroke of the pen the United States had thus doubled its area and acquired vast lands out of which a dozen states later arose. It was to prove the finest bargain in American history. In December, 1803, the American flag was raised upon the Government buildings of New Orleans and the United States entered upon the possession of nine hundred thousand square miles of new territory.

The acquisition of Louisiana brought a new restlessness into American politics and a desire for further advance. West Florida, which stretched along the Gulf of Mexico, still belonged to Spain, and beyond the newly acquired lands the plains of Texas beckoned. Troubles were stirred up between the Western states and territories and the Federal capital. The evil genius of these years is Aaron Burr.

Burr, as we have seen, had missed a chance of becoming President in 1800 largely owing to Hamilton's intervention. Now in 1804 Hamilton's opposition stopped him being selected for the Governorship of New York. He challenged Hamilton to a duel. Hamilton accepted, intending to satisfy honour by firing wide. But Aaron Burr shot to kill, and thus put an end to the life of one of the outstanding figures in the founding years of the American Republic. Discredited in the eyes of all, Burr cast about for means of creating a new American realm of his own. He even sought a large bribe from the British Government. Whether he hoped to detach the Western states from the Union or to carve off a slice of the Spanish dominions is still obscure and disputed, but his career ended abruptly with his arrest and trial for treason. For lack of evidence he was acquitted, and went into voluntary exile.

Jefferson had been triumphantly re-elected President in 1804, but his second term of office was less happy than his first. Under the stress of Westward expansion his party in the East was splitting into local factions. The renewal of European war had also revived the old sinister issues of embargo, blockade, and impressment. Jefferson was faced with the provocations of the British Fleet, which continually arrested ships and took off sailors on the verge of American territorial waters, and sometimes even within them. The British were entitled by the customs of the time to impress British subjects who happened to be serving in American ships; but they also made a practice of impressing American citizens and many sailors whose nationality was doubtful. To this grievance was added another. In retaliation for Napoleon's Berlin Decrees, establishing a Continental blockade of Britain, Orders in Council were issued in London in 1806 imposing severe restrictions on all neutral trade with France and her allies. United States commerce was hard hit by both these belligerent measures. But, as the Battle of Trafalgar had proved, the Royal Navy was much more powerful than the French, and it was at the hands of the British that American shipping suffered most.

Amidst these troubles Jefferson remained serenely determined to preserve the peace. But public opinion was mounting against him. On his recommendation in 1807 Congress passed an Embargo Act which forbade American ships to sail for foreign waters. It prohibited all exports from America by sea or land, and all imports of certain British manufactures. Jefferson hoped that the loss of American trade would oblige the belligerents to come to terms, but in fact his measure proved far more damaging to American commerce than to either the British or French. The economy of New England and all the seaports of the Atlantic coast depended on trade with Britain. From everywhere in the Eastern states protests went up, New

England being particularly vociferous. The Federalists were quick to rally their forces and join in the outcry. Jefferson's own party, the Republicans, revolted and divided against him. After it had been in operation for fourteen months he was forced to withdraw the embargo. Three days later his term of office expired and he retired to his Virginian estate of Monticello.

The failure of his policies in the last two years of his Presidency should not obscure the commanding position of Thomas Jefferson in the history of the United States. He was the first political idealist among American statesmen and the real founder of the American democratic tradition. Contact with the perils of high policy during the crisis of world war modified the original simplicity of his views, but his belief in the common man never wavered. Although his dislike of industrialism weakened in later years, he retained to the end his faith in a close connection between yeoman farming and democracy. His strength lay in the frontier states of the West, which he so truly represented and served in over thirty years of political life.

CHAPTER SIXTY-NINE

The War of 1812

THE NEW President of the United States in March, 1809, was James Madison. As Jefferson's Secretary of State he had had much experience of public office, and he was a political theorist of note. There was a stubborn side to his nature, and his practical skill and judgement were not always equal to that of his predecessor. Madison inherited an inflamed public opinion and a delicate state of relations with Great Britain. At first there were high hopes of a settlement. Madison reached a provisional agreement with the British Minister in Washington which was very favourable to British interests. But for three years Anglo-American relations grew steadily worse. Madison was deceived by Napoleon's revocation of the Berlin Decrees which had closed all European ports controlled by France. He now tried to get England to reciprocate by annulling her Orders in Council against trade with ports in French hands. In vain wiser politicians warned him that Napoleon's action was merely a diplomatic move "to catch us into a war with England."

The unofficial trade war with the United States was telling heavily upon England. The loss of the American market and the hard winter of 1811–1812 had brought widespread unemployment and a business crisis. Petitions were sent to Parliament begging the Government to revoke the Orders in

Council. After much hesitation Castlereagh, now at the Foreign Office, announced in the House of Commons that the Government had done so. But it was too late. The Atlantic crossing took too long for the news to reach America in time. A new generation was entering American politics, headed by Henry Clay from Kentucky and John C. Calhoun from South Carolina. These young men formed a powerful group in the House of Representatives, which came to be known as the "War Hawks." They had no conception of affairs in Europe; they cared nothing about Napoleon's designs, still less about the fate of Russia. Their prime aim and object was to seize Canada and establish American sovereignty throughout the whole Northern continent. Through the influence of Clay the President was won over to a policy of war, and on June 18, 1812, two days after Castlereagh's announcement, Congress declared war on Great Britain. The causes of the conflict were stated in traditional terms: impressment, violations of the three-mile limit, blockades, and Orders in Council. Opinion in America was sharply divided and New England voted overwhelmingly against the declaration of war, but the "War Hawks" with their vociferous propaganda had their way. The frontier spirit in American politics was coming in with a vengeance, and it was sure of itself. Moreover, the frontier farmers felt they had a genuine grievance. There was some good ground for the slogan of "Free Trade and Sailors' Rights" which they adopted. British restrictions on American shipping were holding up the export of their produce. A short expedition of pioneers would set things right, it was thought, and dictate peace in Quebec in a few weeks. Congress adjourned without even voting extra money for the American Army or Navy.

*　　*　　*

On paper the forces were very unequal. The population of the United States was now seven and a half millions, including slaves. In Canada there were only five hundred thousand people, most of them French. But there were nearly five thousand trained British troops, about four thousand Canadian regulars, and about the same number of militia. The Indians could supply between three and four thousand auxiliaries.

The American Regular Army numbered less than seven thousand men, and although with great difficulty over four hundred thousand state militia were called out few were used in Canada. On the American side never more than seven thousand men took part in any engagement, and the untrained volunteers proved hopeless soldiers. Nor was this all. The Seven Years' War had shown that Canada could only be conquered by striking up the St. Lawrence, but the Americans had no sufficient Navy for such a project. They were therefore forced to fight an offensive war on a wide frontier, impassable at places, and were exposed to Indian onslaughts on their columns. Their leaders had worked out no broad strategy. If they had concentrated their troops on Lake Ontario they might have succeeded, but

317

instead they made half-hearted and unco-ordinated thrusts across the borders.

The first American expedition ended in disaster. The ablest British commander, General Isaac Brock, supported by the Indian Confederacy, drove it back. By August the British were in Detroit, and within a few days Fort Dearborn, where Chicago now stands, had fallen. The American frontier rested once more on a line from the Ohio to Lake Erie. The remainder of the year was spent on fruitless moves upon the Niagara front, and operations came to an inconclusive end. The British in Canada were forced to remain on the defensive while great events were taking place in Europe.

The war at sea was more colourful, and for the Americans more cheering. They had sixteen vessels, of which three surpassed anything afloat. These were forty-four-gun frigates, the *Constitution*, the *United States*, and the *President*. They fired a heavier broadside than British frigates, they were heavily timbered, but their clean lines under water enabled them to outsail any ship upon the seas. Their crews were volunteers and their officers highly trained. A London journalist called them "a few fir-built frigates, manned by a handful of bastards and outlaws." This phrase was adopted with glee by the Americans, who gloried in disproving the insult. The British Fleet on the trans-Atlantic station consisted of ninety-seven sail, including eleven ships of the line and thirty-four frigates. Their naval tradition was long and glorious, and, with their memories of Trafalgar and the Nile, the English captains were confident they could sink any American. But when one English ship after another found its guns out-ranged and was battered to pieces the reputation of the "fir-built frigates" was startlingly made. The American public, smarting at the disasters in Canada, gained new heart from these victories. Their frigates within a year had won more successes over the British than the French and Spaniards in two decades of warfare.

These naval episodes had no effect on the general course of the war, and if the British Government had abandoned impressment a new campaign might have been avoided in 1813. But they did not do so, and the Americans set about revising their strategy. The war was continuing officially upon the single issue of impressment, for the conquest of Canada was never announced as a war aim by the United States. Nevertheless Canada was their main objective. By land the Americans made a number of raids into the province of Upper Canada, now named Ontario. Towns and villages were sacked and burnt, including the little capital which has since become the great city of Toronto. The war was becoming fiercer. During the winter of 1812–1813 the Americans had also established a base at Fort Presqu'île, on Lake Erie, and stores were laboriously hauled over the mountains to furnish the American commander, Captain Oliver H. Perry, with a flotilla for fresh-water fighting. In the autumn Perry's little armada sailed to victory. A strange amphibious battle was fought in September, 1813. Negroes, frontier scouts, and militiamen, aboard craft hastily built of new green wood, fought to the end upon the still waters of the lake. The American ships were heavier, and the British were defeated with heavy loss. "We have met the enemy," Perry reported laconically, "and they are ours." But the invasion of Upper Canada on land had been a failure, and the year ended with the Canadians in possession of Fort Niagara.

By the spring of 1814 a decision had been reached in Europe. Napoleon abdicated in April and the British could at last send adequate reinforcements. They purposed to strike from Niagara, from Montreal by way of Lake Champlain, and in the South at New Orleans, with simultaneous naval raids on the American coast. The campaign opened before Wellington's veterans could arrive from the Peninsula. The advance from Niagara was checked by a savage drawn battle at Lundy's Lane, near the Falls. But by the end of August eleven thousand troops from Europe had been concentrated near Montreal to advance by Burgoyne's old route down the Hudson valley. In September, under Sir George Prevost, they moved on Plattsburg, and prepared to dispute the command of Lake Champlain. They were faced by a mere fifteen hundred American regulars, supported by a few thousand militia. All depended on the engagement of the British and American flotillas. As at Lake Erie, the Americans built better ships for fresh-water fighting, and they gained the victory. This crippled the British advance and was the most decisive engagement of the war. Prevost and his forces retired into Canada.

At sea, in spite of their reverses of the previous years, the British were supreme. More ships arrived from European waters. The American coast was defenceless. In August the British General Ross landed in Chesapeake Bay at the head of four thousand men. The American militia, seven thousand strong, but raw and untrained, retreated rapidly, and on the 24th British troops entered the Federal capital of Washington. President Madison took refuge in Virginia. So hasty was the American withdrawal that English officers sat down to a meal cooked for him and his family in the White House. The White House and the Capitol were then burnt in reprisal for the conduct of American militiamen in Canada.

Peace negotiations had been tried throughout the war, but it was not until January, 1814, that the British had agreed to treat. The American Commissioners, among them Henry Clay, reached Ghent in June. At first the British refused to discuss either neutral rights or impressment, and they still hoped for an Indian buffer state in the North-West. It was Wellington's common sense which changed the atmosphere. The previous November he had been asked to take command in America, but he had studied reports of the Battle of Plattsburg and realised that victory depended on naval superiority upon the lakes. He saw no way of gaining it. He held, moreover, that it was not in Britain's interest to demand territory from America on the Canadian border. Both sides therefore agreed upon the *status quo* for the long boundary in the North. Other points were left undetermined. Naval forces on the Great Lakes were regulated by a Commission in 1817, and the disputed boundary of Maine was similarly settled later. By the time the British Navy went to war again impressment had been abandoned.

Thus ended a futile and unnecessary conflict. Anti-American feeling in Great Britain ran high for several years but the United States were never again refused proper treatment as an independent Power. The British Army and Navy had learned to respect their former colonials. When news of peace reached the British Army in the New World one of the soldiers wrote, "We are all happy enough, for we Peninsular soldiers saw that neither fame nor any other military distinction could be acquired by this type of milito-nautico-guerrilla-plundering warfare."

In December the last and most irresponsible British onslaught, the expedition to New Orleans, reached its base. But here in the frontier lands of the South-West a military leader of high quality had appeared in the person of Andrew Jackson. As an early settler in Tennessee he had won a reputation in warfare against the Indians. When the British now tried to subsidise and organise them Jackson pursued them into Spanish West Florida, and occupied its capital, Pensacola.

Meanwhile eight thousand British troops had landed at New Orleans under Sir Edward Pakenham, who had commanded a division at Salamanca. The swamps and inlets in the mouth of the Mississippi made an amphibious operation extremely dangerous. All men and stores had to be transported seventy miles in row-boats from the Fleet. Jackson had hastened back from Florida and entrenched himself on the left bank of the river. His forces were much inferior in numbers, but composed of highly skilled marksmen. On the morning of January 8, 1815, Pakenham led a frontal assault against the American earthworks—one of the most unintelligent manoeuvres in the history of British warfare. Here he was slain and two thousand of his troops were killed or wounded. The only surviving general officer withdrew the army to its transports. The Americans lost seventy men, thirteen of them killed. The battle had lasted precisely half an hour.

The Battle of New Orleans is an important event in American history. It made the career of a future President, Jackson, it led to the belief that the Americans had decisively won the war, and it created an evil legend that the struggle had been a second War of Independence against British tyranny.

The results of the peace were solid and enduring. The war was a turning-point in the history of Canada. Canadians took pride in the part they had played in defending their country, and their growing national sentiment was

"Battle at Bunker's Hill, June 17, 1775" by Henry A. Thomas

The repeal or the Funeral Procession of Miss Americ-Stamp. This contemporary cartoon shows Grenville carrying the coffin of the infant Miss Americ-Stamp to her grave, attended by a few mourners, while in the background commerce flourishes once more.

strengthened. Many disagreements were still to shake Anglo-American relations. Thirty years later, in the dispute over the possession of Oregon, vast territories were involved and there was a threat of war. But henceforward the world was to see a three-thousand-mile international frontier between Canada and the United States undefended by men or guns. On the oceans the British Navy ruled supreme for a century to come, and behind this shield the United States were free to fufil their continental destiny.

CHAPTER SEVENTY

Elba and Waterloo

IN THE New Year of 1815 peace reigned in Europe and in America. In Paris Louis XVIII, a stout, elderly, easy-going Bourbon, sat on the throne of France, oblivious of the mistakes made by his relations, advisers, and followers. The French people, still dreaming of Imperial glories, were ripe for another adventure. After the exertions of twenty years of warfare the Powers of Europe felt they had earned leisure enough to indulge in haggling, bargains, and festivity. A sharp and sudden shock was needed to recall them to their unity of purpose. It came from a familiar quarter.

Napoleon had for nine months been sovereign of Elba. At his capital, he furnished a palace in the grand manner. He still possessed an army: four hundred members of his Old Guard. He also had a navy for which he devised a special Elban ensign; his fleet consisted of a single brig and some cutters. He played cards with his mother and cheated according to his recognised custom. He entertained his favourite sister and his faithful Polish mistress. Only his wife, the Empress Marie Louise, and their son were missing. The Austrian Government took care to keep them both in Vienna. Family Habsburg loyalty meant more to her than her husband.

As the months went by close observers became sure that Napoleon was biding his time. In February, 1815, he saw, or thought he saw, that the Allies were at odds, and that France, discontented, beckoned to him. On Sunday night, the 26th of February, he slipped out of harbour in his brig and at the head of a thousand men, set sail for France and landed near Antibes. The drama of the Hundred Days had begun. Within eighteen days of his landing Napoleon was installed in the capital, had proclaimed his peaceful intention, and at once started shaping his army. He showed all his usual energy. He abounded in self-confidence. But the flashing military judgement of earlier years was dimmed. The gastric ulcer from which he had long suffered caused him intermittent pain.

Yet the Emperor remained a formidable figure and a challenge to Europe. The Powers at Vienna acted with unaccustomed speed and unanimity. They declared Napoleon an outlaw. The British Government, which had led the country and the world against the Corsican, realised that they would have to bear the brunt of a whirlwind campaign. Prussia was the only main ally then in readiness. Wellington recommended the immediate transport of an army to the Netherlands. The King of Great Britain was still King of Hanover. Hanoverian troops, on their way home through the Netherlands, were halted and joined the new army. But the Dutch and Belgian troops put under Wellington's command by the King of the Netherlands looked unreliable. As the summer drew near Wellington assembled a mixed force of eighty-three thousand men, of whom about a third were British. He bluntly cursed, as was his habit, the quality of his untried troops, while bending all his endeavours to train and transform them. The main support for his new adventure must be Marshal Blücher. The Prussians had a force of a hundred and thirteen thousand men, but nearly half of them were untrained militia. Wellington meant to take the offensive. He did not propose tamely to await a Napoleonic onslaught. In his calm, considering way, he worked it all out. As it happened, the Emperor seized his usual initiative.

* * *

Napoleon could not afford to waste a day. Nor did he do so. He must strike immediately at his gathering foes. The moral value of victory would be overwhelming, and the prestige of the British Government would be shaken. Such were his hopes while he applied his intense power of will to rousing the French nation. Assembling a sufficient army threw a heavy strain upon exhausted France. Five corps of about a hundred and twenty-five thousand men were organised on the frontier fortress line.

During the early days of June tension was heightening. It was plain, or at least predictable, that Napoleon would attempt to rout Wellington's and Blücher's armies separately and piecemeal. But where would he land his first blow? Wellington and his great opponent were to cross swords for the first time. They were both in their forty-sixth year. Quietly on June 15 Napoleon struck at the hinge of the Allied armies. The capture of Brussels would be a great forward stride. Possession of a capital city was always a lure for him and a source of strength.

Hours passed before the news reached Wellington. Military intelligence, as so often at the neap of events, was confusing and contradictory. On the night of the 15th, while the French armies massed to destroy the Prussians, the Duchess of Richmond gave a ball in Brussels in honour of the Allied officers. Wellington graced the occasion with his presence. He knew the value of preserving a bold, unruffled face.

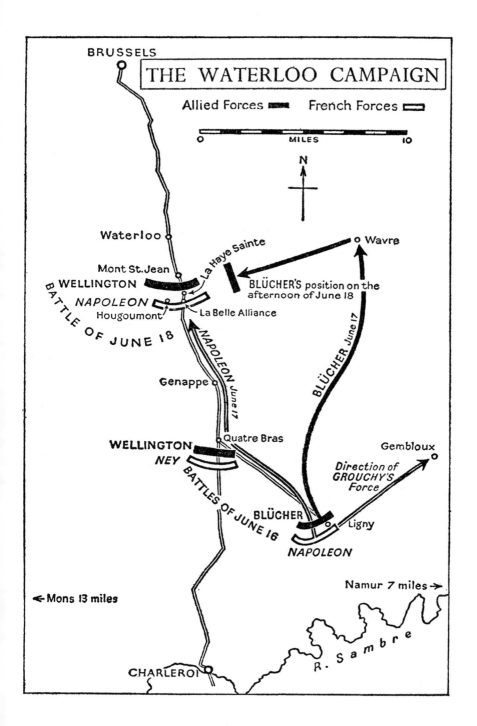

THE WATERLOO CAMPAIGN

Allied Forces ▬▬ French Forces ▭▭

MILES

BRUSSELS

N

Waterloo

La Haye Sainte

Wavre

Mont St. Jean

WELLINGTON

NAPOLEON

BLÜCHER'S position on the
afternoon of June 18

Hougoumont

La Belle Alliance

BATTLE OF JUNE 18

NAPOLEON June 17

BLÜCHER June 17

Genappe

WELLINGTON

NEY

Quatre Bras

Gembloux

Direction of
GROUCHY'S
Force

BATTLES OF JUNE 16

BLÜCHER

Ligny

NAPOLEON

Namur 7 miles →

← Mons 13 miles

R. Sambre

CHARLEROI

For the French everything depended upon beating the Prussians before forcing Wellington to the coast. Napoleon had in mind the vision of a shattered British Army grimly awaiting transports for home in the Flemish ports. He ordered Ney to attack and then meet him that evening in Brussels. But the tardiness and sureness of Wellington's movements deceived him. At two o'clock in the afternoon of the 16th the French went into action. There was little tactical manœuvre in the fierce struggle which swayed backwards and forwards on that June afternoon at the cross-roads on the way to Brussels. It was a head-on collision in which generalship played no part, though leadership did. Wellington was always at his coolest in the hottest of moments. By nightfall Ney had not gained his objective. Brussels was not in his grasp.

Napoleon had gained the advantage at the opening of the campaign. Marshal Blücher was out-generalled, his army split in two, battered by the magnificent French artillery, and driven back. Napoleon decided in the small hours of the 17th to send Marshal Grouchy with thirty-three thousand men to pursue the Prussians while he flung his main weight against Wellington. The crisis of the campaign was at hand.

There seems no doubt that in the opening days Wellington had been surprised. As he confessed at the time, Napoleon's movements had "humbugged" him. But immediately after the battle his methodical mind was in full command of the situation. Wellington himself had inspected this Belgian countryside in the autumn of 1814. He had noted the advantages of the ridge at Waterloo. So had the great Duke of Marlborough a century earlier. Throughout the night of the 16th and 17th a carefully screened retreat began, and by morning the Waterloo position, a line of defence such as Wellington had already tested in the Peninsula, was occupied. Upon the French must be forced the onus of a frontal attack. Wellington knew that time was playing against his adversary. Swift results must be achieved by Napoleon if he was to establish himself again in France. Napoleon, furious to hear of Wellington's skilful withdrawal, pounded in his carriage down the Brussels road with his advance-guard in a desperate attempt to entrap the British rear. The mercy of a violent storm slowed up progress. An angry scene took place upon the meeting of Napoleon and Ney, who was greeted with the words from the Emperor, "You have ruined France!"

* * *

Late in the morning of the 18th of June the French attacked. Napoleon promised his staff they would sleep that night in Brussels. And to Soult, who raised some demur, he said, "You think Wellington a great general because he beat you. I tell you this will be a picnic." Fierce cannonades were launched upon the Allied posts. The battle swayed backwards and forwards upon the grass slopes. In the early afternoon one of the most terrific artillery barrages of the time was launched upon Wellington's infantry. Napoleon, looking through his glasses at the awful *mêlée*, exclaimed,

"Will the English never show their backs?" "I fear," replied Soult, "they will be cut to pieces first." Wellington, too, had much to disturb him. Although the Prussians had been distantly sighted upon the roads in the early afternoon, they were slow in making their presence felt. But by six o'clock in the evening Ney's onslaughts had failed. The French made a final effort, and desperate fighting with no quarter raged again round the farms. The Imperial Guard itself, with Ney at its head, rolled up the hill, but again the fury of British infantry fire held them. The long-awaited moment to counter-attack had come. Wellington had been in the forefront of danger all day. On his chestnut, Copenhagen, he had galloped every-where, issuing brusque orders, gruffly encouraging his men. Now he rode along his much-battered line and ordered the advance. "Go on, go on!" he shouted. "They will not stand!" His cavalry swept from the ridge and sabred the French Army into a disorganized mass of stragglers. Ney, beside himself with rage, a broken sword in his hand, staggered shouting in vain from one band to another. It was too late. Wellington handed over the pursuit to the Prussians. In agony of soul Napoleon followed the road back to Paris.

*　　*　　*

Late that night Blücher and Wellington met and embraced. *"Mein lieber Kamerad,"* said the old German Field-Marshal, who knew not a word of English, *"quelle affaire!"* which was about all the French he could com-mand. This brief greeting was greatly to Wellington's laconic taste. It was a story he delighted to repeat in later years. The Duke rode back to Brussels. The day had been almost too much even for a man of iron. The whole weight of responsibility had fallen on him. Only the power and example of his own personality had kept his motley force together. The strain had been barely tolerable. "By God!" as he justly said, "I don't think it would have been done if I had not been there." As he took tea and toast and had the casualty lists read to him he broke down and wept.

Napoleon had reached his capital three days after the battle. On June 22 he abdicated and retired to Malmaison. On July 6 Blücher and Wellington entered the capital. One of the Duke's first tasks was to restrain the Prus-sians from resentful vengeance.

Two days after the Allies' arrival Louis XVIII appeared. His second restoration was largely of Wellington's making. Wellington had no high regard for the Bourbons, but he was convinced that France under their shaky rule would no longer have the power to disturb the peace of Europe. Louis XVIII was no Grand Monarque and could never aspire to become one. Wellington, like many great soldiers when victory is complete, looked forward to an age of tranquillity. Laurels and bays had been won; it was time to cultivate the olive.

Napoleon left Malmaison at the end of June. He had thoughts of sailing for America, and he ordered a set of travel books about the trans-Atlantic

325

continent. Perhaps a new empire might be forged in Mexico, Peru, or Brazil. The alternative was to throw himself upon the mercy of his most inveterate foe. This is what happened. Captain Maitland in the *Bellerophon* was cruising off Rochefort with orders to prevent any French ships from putting to sea. With him Napoleon entered into negotiation. He hoped he might be kept in pleasant captivity in some English country house or Scottish castle.

The ex-Emperor wrote a flattering letter to the Prince Regent, whom he addressed as "the strongest, the stubbornest, the most generous of my foes." When the Prince read this missive it must have helped to convince him that he and not his generals or his Ministers had really won the war. On this matter he did not need much convincing. The Government, acting for the Allies, decided on exile in St. Helena, an island very mountainous and far away. Escape from it was impossible. On July 26 the Emperor sailed to his sunset in the South Atlantic. He never permitted himself to understand what had happened at Waterloo. The event was everybody's fault but his own. Six years of life in exile lay before him. He spent them with his small faithful retinue creating the Napoleonic legend of invincibility which was to have so powerful an effect on the France of the future.

*   *   *

The Congress of Vienna had completed its work in June. It remained for the emissaries of the Powers to assemble in Paris and compose a new peace with France. The task took three months. The Prussians pressed for harsh terms. Castlereagh, representing Britain, saw that mildness would create the least grievance and guard best against a renewal of war. In this he had the hearty support of Wellington, who now exerted a unique authority throughout Europe.

The second Treaty of Paris, concluded in November, was somewhat stiffer than that of 1814. Yet no intolerable humiliations were involved. In the moderation of the settlement with France the treaty had its greatest success. Wellington took command of the occupying army. For the next three years he was practically a Great European Power in himself. Peace reigned for forty years between the Great Powers, and the main framework of the settlements at Vienna and Paris endured until the twentieth century.

So the scene closes on a protracted peace-making after the longest of the world wars. The impetus of the French Revolution had been spread by the genius of Napoleon to the four quarters of Europe. Ideals of liberty and nationalism, born in Paris, had been imparted to all the European peoples. In the nineteenth century ahead they were to clash resoundingly with the ordered world for which the Congress of Vienna had striven. If France was defeated and her Emperor fallen, the principles which had inspired her lived on. They were to play a notable part in changing the shape of government in every European country, Britain not excepted.

BOOK TEN

Recovery and Reform

CHAPTER SEVENTY-ONE

The Victory Peace

AFTER A generation of warfare peace had come to Europe in the summer of 1815. It was to be a long peace, disturbed by civil commotions and local campaigns, but flaring into no major blaze until the era of German expansion succeeded the age of French predominance. In the Revolutionary and Napoleonic struggles Britain had played an heroic part. The task that had united and preoccupied her people was now at last accomplished. Henceforth they could bend their energies to developing the great resources of industrial and commercial skill which had accumulated in the Island during the past half-century and been tested and sharpened by twenty-two years of war. But the busy world of trade and manufacture and the needs and aspirations of the mass of men, women, and children who toiled in its service were beyond the grasp of the country's leading statesmen on the morrow of Waterloo. The English political scene succumbed to stagnation. Under the shock of the French Terror the English governing classes had closed their minds and their ranks to change. Prolonged exertions had worn out the nation. Convalescence lasted until 1830.

The sea-power, the financial strength, and the tenacity of Britain had defeated Napoleon. In the summer of 1815 Britain under Lord Castlereagh stood at the head of Europe, and upon the terms of the European settlement concluded at the Congress of Vienna the peace of generations depended.

The Congress of Vienna of 1815 stands as a monument to the success of classical diplomacy. The intricacies of its negotiations were immense. Castlereagh was pre-eminent as the genius of the conference. He represented, with its faults and virtues, the equable detached and balanced approach to Continental affairs that was to characterise the best of British foreign policy for nearly a century.

*　　*　　*

Earlier than her neighbours Britain enjoyed the fruits and endured the rigours of the Industrial Revolution. She gained a new domain of power and prosperity. At the same time the growing masses in her ill-built towns were often plunged into squalor and misery, the source of numerous and well-grounded discontents. The skilled man, self-employed, who had hitherto worked in his home, was steadily displaced. Machinery, the rise of population, and extensive changes in employment all presented a formidable social problem. In a society which was rapidly becoming industrial most of them represented the abiding landed interest. They were incapable of carrying out even moderate reforms because of their obsessive fears of bloody revolution.

In the Radical view it was the Government alone, and not chance or Act of God, that was to blame for the misfortunes of the people. The Tory Cabinet, in the face of unprecedented conditions that confronted them, had no idea how to secure the public prosperity. And even if they had hit upon a plan they possessed no experienced body of civil servants to put it into effect. As a result the only remedy for misery was private charity or the Poor Law. Not only was there grinding poverty among the working population, but also a deep-rooted conflict between the manufacturing and agricultural classes.

The economy of the country was dangerously out of balance. The war debt had reached alarming proportions. Agriculture as well as industry quaked at the end of the war. Much capital had been sunk in land for the sake of high profits. Peace brought a slump in the prices fetched by crops, and landowners clamoured for protection against the importation of cheap foreign corn. This had been granted by the Corn Law of 1815, which excluded foreign wheat unless the domestic price per quarter rose above eighty shillings. The cost of bread went up, and the manufacturing classes had to raise wages to save their workers from hunger. The manufacturers in their turn got the income tax abolished, which helped them but imperilled the Budget.

In 1819 an incident took place which increased the unpopularity and quickened the fears of the Government. A meeting of protest was held at St. Peter's Fields, outside Manchester, attended by over fifty thousand people, including women and children. The local magistrates lost their heads, and, after reading the Riot Act, ordered the yeomanry to charge. Eleven people were killed, two of them women, and four hundred were injured. This "massacre of Peterloo," as it was called in ironic reference to the Battle of Waterloo, aroused widespread indignation, which was swelled still further when the Government took drastic steps to prevent the recurrence of disorder. Six Acts were passed regulating public meetings, empowering the magistrates to seize seditious literature, forbidding unauthorised drilling in military formations, imposing a heavy tax upon the Press to restrict the circulation of Radical newspapers, regulating the issue of warrants and the bringing of cases to trial.

Social unrest was gripping all Europe. Compared with most Continental countries, Britain came lightly out of these years of disturbance. By the end of 1819 trade and harvest had improved. Though the landed interests suffered some hardship, not without raising their voices in complaint, it seemed that a corner had been turned.

*   *   *

Once again in English history the personal affairs of the royal family now exploded into public view. King George III had long been intermittently mad, and English politicians had had to reckon with the virtual demise of the Crown for considerable intervals. In 1810 the old King finally sank into incurable imbecility. He lived for another ten years, roaming the corridors of Windsor Castle with long white beard and purple dressing-gown. The Prince became Regent, with unrestricted royal prerogatives. He kept his Tory advisers and prosecuted the war with vigour. Whatever the faults of George IV, his determination as Regent to support Wellington and Castlereagh and to stand up to Napoleon should earn him an honourable place in his country's history.

The atmosphere of the Court was like that of a minor German principality. All was stiff, narrow, fusty. The spirited lad who was to be George IV soon rebelled against his decorous mother and parsimonious father. A gift for facile friendship, often with dubious personages, alienated him still further from the home circle. He soon acquired the attributes of the eighteenth-century English gentleman—the arts of acquiring debts, of wearing fine clothes, and making good conversation. His natural intelligence and good taste went undisciplined and his talent for self-expression was frequently squandered in melodramatic emotion. Self-indulgence warped his judgement and frivolity marred his bearing. When pleasure clashed with royal duty it was usually pleasure that won. The loneliness of his position, both as Regent and King, cast a harsh emphasis upon his not unamiable weaknesses.

At the bidding of his parents in 1795 he was wedded to Caroline of Brunswick, a noisy, flighty, and unattractive German princess. George was so appalled at the sight of his bride that he was drunk for the first twenty-four hours of his married life. A high-spirited, warm-hearted girl was born of their brief union, Princess Charlotte, who found her mother quite as unsatisfactory as her father.

The Government were perturbed about the problem of the succession. Princess Charlotte married Prince Leopold of Saxe-Coburg, but in 1817 she died in childbirth. Her infant was stillborn. George's brothers lacked not only charm, but lawful issue. But they had a cash value to the Government on the royal marriage market. For a sum, the Duke of Kent made a German marriage, and retired to Gibraltar to exercise his martial talents upon the Rock. The offspring of this alliance was the future Queen Victoria.

In January, 1820, the mad old King died. Popular feeling against the conditions of England was now diverted into a national inquiry into the condition of the monarchy. The characters of the royal personages concerned came under merciless scrutiny. In July, 1821, George IV was crowned in pomp at Westminster Abbey. Caroline attempted to force her way into the Abbey, but was turned away because she had no ticket. A month later she died.

The agitation over the Queen had been essentially the expression of discontent. It marked the highest point of the Radical movement in these post-war years. Towards the end of 1820, however, industry and trade revived and popular disturbances subsided. The mass of the country was instinctively Royalist and the personal defects of the sovereign had little effect upon this deep-rooted tradition. The Tory administration, however, which consisted largely of ageing reactionaries, had been gravely weakened. The people began henceforth to renew their interest in Parlimentary Reform, which soon became the question of the hour.

CHAPTER SEVENTY-TWO

Canning and the Duke

MODERN SCHOLARS, delving deeply into family connections and commercial interests, have sought to show that there was no such thing as a two-party system in eighteenth-century Britain. If caution must be the hallmark of history, all that may be said is that the men in power were vigorously opposed by the men who were out, while in between stood large numbers of neutral-minded gentlemen placidly prepared to support whichever group held office. It is not much of a conclusion to come to about a great age of Parliamentary debate. The ins and outs might as well have names, and why not employ the names of Whig and Tory which their supporters cast at one another? At any rate, in the 1820's a Government of Tory complexion had been in power almost without interruption for thirty years.

This Government had successfully piloted the country through the longest and most dangerous war in which Britain had yet been engaged. It had also survived, though with tarnishing reputation, five years of peace-time unrest. But the nineteenth century called for a fresh interpretation of the duties of Government. New principles and doctrines were arising which were to break up the old political parties and in the Victorian age reshape and recreate them. Meanwhile Robert Peel became Canning's rival for the future leadership of the Tories. Canning had played a leading part in the conception and launching of the Peninsular War. Brilliant, witty, effervescent, he had a gift for sarcasm which made him many enemies. A legend of unreliability grew up, his seniors thought him an intriguer, and when he resigned in 1820 a Tory lord declared with relish, "Now we have got rid of those confounded men of genius." In August, 1822, Canning was offered the post of Governor-General of India. He reconciled himself to this honourable exile; his political life seemed at an end. But then Fate took a hand. As the ship came up the Thames to take him to the East, Castlereagh, his mind unhinged by overwork, cut his throat in the dressing-room of his home. Canning's presence in the Government was now essential: he was appointed Foreign Secretary, and in this office he dominated English politics until his death five years later.

The following years saw a more enlightened period of Tory rule. Canning, Peel, and Huskisson pursued bold policies which in many respects were in advance of those propounded by the Whigs. The penal code was reformed by Peel, and the London police force is his creation. Huskisson overhauled the tariff system, and continued Pitt's work in abolishing uneconomic taxes and revising the customs duties. Canning urged a scaling down of the duty on corn as the price rose at home. This was bound to bring conflict in the Tory ranks. He realised the distress and the political danger it would cause in the country, and declared on one occasion, "We are on the brink of a great struggle between property and population. . . . Such a struggle is only to be averted by the mildest and most liberal legislation." This soothing task he set before himself, but it was Peel who had to face the crisis when it came.

A crisis in Spain confronted Canning with his first task as Foreign Secretary. He had backed the Spanish national rising in 1808, and was naturally sympathetic, but Metternich and the Holy Alliance saw the revolt, which soon spread to the Bourbon Kingdom of Naples, as a threat to the principle of monarchy and to the entire European system. A Congress at Verona in the autumn of 1822 discussed intervention in Spain on behalf of the Bourbons. Wellington had gone out as British representative with instructions from Castlereagh that Britain was to play no part in such a move. Canning vehemently agreed with this view and gave it wide publicity in England, and indeed the whole tradition of British foreign politics was against intervention in the domestic affairs of other states.

A much larger issue now loomed beyond the European scene. Britain had little direct interest in the constitution of Spain, but for two centuries she had competed for the trade of Spain's colonies in South America. Their liberties were important to her. During the wars with Napoleon these colonies had enjoyed the taste of autonomy. They had no relish, when the Bourbons were restored in Madrid, for the revival of royal Spanish rule. Up and down the whole length of the Andes campaigns were fought for

South American liberation. By Canning's time at the Foreign Office most of the republics that now figure on the map had come into separate if unstable existence. In the meanwhile British commerce with these regions had trebled in value since 1814. If France or the Holy Alliance intervened in the New World, if European troops were sent across the Atlantic to subdue the rebels, all this was lost, and much besides. These dangers gave Canning great anxiety. The business elements in England, whose support he was keen to command, were acutely sensitive to the peril. He acted with decision. He urged the United States to join Britain in opposing European interference in the countries across the Atlantic. While the Americans meditated on this proposal Canning also made an approach to the French. France had no desire to start an overseas quarrel with Britain. She disclaimed the use of force in South America and forswore colonial ambitions there. Thus was the Holy Alliance checked. As Canning later declared in a triumphant phrase, he had "called the New World into existence to redress the balance of the Old."

The New World meanwhile had something of its own to say. The United States had no wish to see European quarrels transferred across the ocean. They had already recognised the independence of the principal Latin-American republics. They did not want aspiring princes of the royal houses of Europe to be ferried over and set up as monarchs on the democratic continent. Still less would they contemplate European reconquest and colonisation. Canning's suggestion for a joint Anglo-American declaration began to grow attractive. Two honoured ex-Presidents, Jefferson and Madison, agreed with President Monroe that it would be a welcome and momentous step. They all had in mind Russian designs in the Pacific Ocean, as well as menaces from Europe; for the Russians occupied Alaska, and the territorial claims of the Czar stretched down the Western coast of America to California, where his agents were active. Monroe, however, had in John Quincy Adams a Secretary of State who was cautious and stubborn by temperament and suspicious of Britain. Adams distrusted Canning, whom he earnestly thought to possess "a little too much wit for a Minister of State." He believed that the United States should act on their own initiative. If at some future time Cuba, or even Canada, desired to enlist in the Great Republic, might not a joint statement with Britain about the inviolability of the Continent prejudice such possibilities? It was wiser for America to keep her hands free. As Adams noted in his diary, "It would be more candid, as well as more dignified, to avow our principles explicitly to Russia and France, than to come as a cock-boat in the wake of the British man-of-war." Hence there was propounded on December 2, 1823, in the President's annual message to Congress, a purely American doctrine, the Monroe Doctrine, which has often since been voiced in trans-Atlantic affairs. "The American continents," Monroe said, "by the free and independent condition they have assumed and maintain, are henceforth not to be considered as subjects for future colonisation by any European Powers. . . . We should consider any attempt on their part to extend their [political] system to any portion of this hemisphere as dangerous to our peace and safety." These were resounding claims. Their acceptance by the rest of the world depended on the friendly vigilance of the "British man-of-war," but this was a fact seldom openly acknowledged. For the best part of a century the Royal Navy remained the stoutest guarantee of freedom in the Americas. Thus shielded by the British bulwark, the American continent was able to work out its own unhindered destiny.

Monroe's famous message conveyed a warning to Britain as well as to the authoritarian Powers. Canning understood the risks of competition and dispute with the United States upon the Continent in which the Americans now claimed predominance. He was determined to avert all conflicts which might embarrass Britain and harm her own proper interests. There was no purpose, however, in arguing about dangers which still lay largely in the future. His private comment was short and to the point. "The avowed pretension of the United States," he wrote, "to put themselves at the head of the confederacy of all the Americas and to sway that confederacy against Europe (Great Britain included) is not a pretension identified with our interests, or one that we can countenance or tolerate. It is, however, a pretension which there is no use in contesting in the abstract, but we must not say anything that seems to admit the principle."

Soon afterwards Britain officially recognised the independence of the South American states. King George IV, who bore no love for republics, and many of Canning's colleagues in the Government, had strenuously opposed this step. Even now the King refused to read the Royal Speech containing the announcement. It was read for him by a reluctant Lord Chancellor. So Canning's view prevailed. His stroke over South America may probably be judged his greatest triumph in foreign policy.

Another crisis erupted in the Eastern Mediterranean. After four centuries of subjection to the Turks the spirit of liberty was stirring among the Greeks. They broke into revolt, and in 1822 declared their independence. In England there was widespread enthusiasm for their cause. It appealed to the educated classes who had been brought up on the glories of Thermopylae and Salamis. Enlightened circles in London were eager for intervention. Subscriptions were raised, and Byron and other British volunteers went to the aid of the Greeks. Before he met his death at Missolonghi Byron was deeply disillusioned. After complicated negotiations Britain, France, and Russia agreed in 1827 on terms to be put to the Turks. British and French squadrons were sent to Greek waters to enforce them. This was the last achievement of Canning's diplomacy. Had Canning been granted a longer spell of life the group he led might have founded a new political allegiance. But on August 8, after a short illness, Canning died. He was killed, like Castlereagh, by overwork. Canning had played a decisive part in the shaping of the new century. In war and in peace he had proved himself a man of large views and active determination. His quick mind and hasty temper made him an uneasy party colleague. As his friend Sir Walter Scott said of him, he wanted prudence. Through Canning, however, the better side of the Pitt tradition was handed on to the future. In many ways he was in sympathy with the new movements stirring in English life. He was also in close touch with the Press and knew how to use publicity in the conduct of government. As with Chatham, his political power was largely based on public opinion and on a popular foreign policy. Disraeli bore witness to this striking man. "I never saw Canning but once. I remember as if it were but yesterday the tumult of that ethereal brow. Still lingers in my ear the melody of that voice."

*   *   *

Canning's death at a critical moment at home and abroad dislocated the political scene. The Government, rent by Whig intrigues, abruptly disappeared. There was no question of a purely Whig Government. That party was weak and indifferently led. Wellington and Peel were instructed to form an administration. This they did. Wellington became Prime Minister. The old Tories were to fight one more action. It was a stubborn rearguard. In June, 1830, King George IV died. "The first gentleman of Europe" was not long mourned by his people. This once handsome man had grown so gross and corpulent that he was ashamed to show himself in public. His extravagance had become a mania, and his natural abilities were clouded by years of self-indulgence. No tyrant by nature, he yet enjoyed fancying himself as an autocrat. His memory was bespattered by the Victorians. He was not in his conduct much worse or better than most contemporary men of fashion.

*   *   *

George IV was succeeded on the throne by his brother, the Duke of Clarence, the most eccentric and least obnoxious of the sons of George III. He had been brought up in the Navy, and had passed a life of total obscurity, except for a brief and ludicrous interval when Canning had made him Lord High Admiral in 1827. Good-nature and simplicity of mind were William IV's in equal measure. The gravest embarrassments he caused his Ministers sprang from his garrulity. The Queen was not a beauty, but her quiet homeliness was a welcome change after the domestic life of George IV. "Sailor William" needed every ounce of fairness. There were heavy seas ahead. Revolution had again broken out in France, and the Bourbon monarchy was at an end. As the news swept across the Channel there were mutterings of a coming storm in England.

334

CHAPTER SEVENTY-THREE

Reform and Free Trade

IN 1830 the Liberal forces in Europe stirred again. The July Revolution in France set up a constitutional monarchy under the house of Orleans. The new King, Louis Philippe, was a wiser and more honourable man than his father. He was to keep his uneasy throne for eighteen years, and he also kept his head. Encouraged by events in Paris, the Belgians rebelled against the Kingdom of the Netherlands in which they had been incorporated by the peace treaties of 1815. Britain had played a big part in this arrangement. It had long been British policy, and still is, to support the independence of the Low Countries and prevent any of their provinces from passing under the control of a menacing Power. The twentieth century needs no reminding of the great wars that have been fought with this as a leading cause. Much diplomatic activity ensued before a peaceful solution was eventually found.

These agitations on the European continent, largely orderly in character and democratic in purpose, were much acclaimed in England; and their progress was closely and excitedly studied. The Whigs suspected the Duke of Wellington of intending to restore the Kingdom of the Netherlands by force. This was not true, but the rumour was enough to inflame the hot tempers of the times. Poverty in the villages and on the farms had already led to rioting in South-East England. In the growing towns and cities industrial discontent was driving men of business and their workers into political action. Turmoil, upheaval, even revolution, seemed imminent. Instead, there was a General Election.

At the polls the Whigs made gains, but the result was indecisive. The Whig leader was Earl Grey. It is given to few men to carry out late in life a great measure of reform which they have advocated without success for forty years. Such was to be Grey's achievement. He and his colleagues perceived that the agitation which had shaken England since Waterloo issued from two quite separate sources—the middle classes, unrepresented, prosperous, respectable, influenced by the democratic ideas of the French Revolution, but deeply law-abiding in their hunger for political power; and on the other side a bitter and more revolutionary section of working men, smitten by the economic dislocation of war and its aftermath, prepared to talk of violence and perhaps even to use it. An alliance with the middle classes and a moderate extension of the franchise would suffice, at any rate for a time, and for this Grey prepared his plans.

Wellington hoped that the Whigs were too disorganised to form a Government, but his own party was even more disunited. Those who had followed Canning would have nothing more to do with the Tory "Old

Guard," and now made common cause with the Whigs. The Tories were defeated and King William IV asked Grey to form a Government. With one brief interval the Whigs had been out of office for nearly fifty years. Now at a bound they were at the summit of power and influence.

They were confronted with an ugly scene. French threats to intervene in Belgium made it imperative but unpopular to increase the military estimates. The Chancellor of the Exchequer failed to provide an effective Budget. Law and order were breaking down in the south-eastern counties, and Lord Melbourne, the new Home Secretary, acted decidedly. Over four hundred farm workers were sentenced to transportation. The Radicals were indignant and disillusioned. Only Parliamentary Reform could save the Government, and to this they now addressed themselves.

In March, 1831, Lord John Russell rose in the House of Commons to move the first Reform Bill. It was proposed to abolish over a hundred "rotten" and "pocket" boroughs and replace them with new constituencies for the unrepresented areas of the Metropolis, the industrial North, and the Midlands. To the Tories this was a violation of all they stood for, an affront to their deepest political convictions, a gross attack on the rights of property. A seat was a thing to be bought or sold like a house or an estate, and a more uniform franchise savoured of an arithmetical conception of politics dangerously akin to French democracy. Many Whigs, too, who had expected a milder measure were at first dumbfounded by the breadth of Russell's proposals. They soon rallied to the Government when they saw the enthusiasm of the country, for the Whigs believed that Reform would forestall revolution. The Tories, on the other hand, feared that it was the first step on the road to cataclysm. To them, and indeed to many Whigs, English government meant the rule, and the duty to rule, of the landed classes in the interests of the community. A wider franchise would mean the beginning of the end of the old system of administration by influence and patronage. Agitation spread throughout the country. In the House of Commons the Tories fought every inch of the way. The Government was by no means sure of its majority, and although a small block of Irish votes controlled by O'Connell, leader of the emancipated Catholics, was cast for Grey the Bill was defeated. A roar of hatred and disappointment swept the country. Grey asked the King for a dissolution, and William IV had the sense to realise that a refusal might mean revolution. The news caused uproar in the Lords, where a motion was introduced asking the King to reconsider his decision, but as the shouting rose from the benches and peers shook their fists across the floor of the House the thunder of cannon was heard as the King left St. James's to come in person to pronounce the dissolution.

Excited elections were held on the single issue of Reform. It was the first time a mandate of this kind had been asked of the British people. They re-

George Washington and the Marquis de Lafayette with Martha Washington,
her daughter-in-law and grandchildren at Mount Vernon

Surrender of Lord Cornwallis at Yorktown, Virginia, October 19, 1781. Washington is mounted, near the center front. Washington is afoot in the center front. French officers are to the left, American officers the American flag. From a painting by Colonel Trumbull

turned an unmistakable answer. The Tories were annihilated in the county constituencies and the Whigs and their allies gained a majority of one hundred and thirty-six in the House of Commons. When Parliament reassembled the battle was shifted to the House of Lords. Wellington rose again and again to put the case against Reform. "A democracy," he declared, "has never been established in any part of the world that it has not immediately declared war against property, against the payment of the public debt, and against all the principles of conservation, which are secured by, and are in fact the principal objects of, the British Constitution as it now exists. Property and its possessors will become the common enemy."

On the night of October 7, 1831, the critical division took place. The peers were sharply divided, and it was the twenty-one bishops in the Upper House who decided the issue; they were against Reform. Thus the Tories triumphed. The Bill was defeated and a new constitutional issue was raised—the Peers against the People.

Next morning the newspapers, bordered in black, proclaimed the news. Rioting broke out in the Midlands; houses and property were burned; there was wild disorder in Bristol. The associations of Reformers in the country, called Political Unions, strove to harness enthusiasm for the Bill and to steady the public temper. Meanwhile the Government persevered. In December Russell introduced the Bill for the third time, and the Commons carried it by a majority of two to one. In the following May it came again before the Lords. It was rejected by forty-four votes. There was now no question of another dissolution and Grey realised that only extreme remedies would serve. He accordingly drove to Windsor and asked the King to create enough new Peers to carry the Bill. The King refused and the Cabinet resigned. William IV asked Wellington and Peel to form an administration to carry Reform. Feeling in the country became menacing. Plans were made for strikes and a general refusal of taxes. Banners and placards appeared in the London streets with the caption "To Stop the Duke Go for Gold," and there was a run on the Bank of England. Radical leaders declared they would paralyse any Tory Government which came to power, and after a week the Duke admitted defeat. On the afternoon of May 18 Grey and Brougham called at St. James's Palace. The king authorised them to draw up a list of persons who would be made Peers and could be counted on to vote for the Whigs. At the same time he sent his private secretary to tell the leading Tories of his decision and suggest that they could avoid such extremities by abstaining. When the Bill was again introduced the Opposition benches were practically empty. It was carried by an overwhelming majority, and became law on June 7, 1832.

*   *   *

The new electors and the Radicals were not content and during the next five years the younger politicians forced through an equally extensive reform of public administration. Grey, feeling he had done enough, retired in 1834. The new leaders were Lord Melbourne and Lord John Russell. Russell was a Whig of the old school. He saw the need for further reforms in the sphere of government, but the broadening paths of democracy did not beckon him. Melbourne accepted the office of Prime Minister with reluctance, genuinely wondering whether the honour was worth while. Once in power his bland qualities helped to keep his divided team together. But his administration wore an eighteenth-century air in the midst of nineteenth-century stress.

One of Melbourne's ablest colleagues was Lord Palmerston, who held the Foreign Office for nearly eleven years. Under the wise guidance of Lord Grey, Palmerston had secured a settlement of the Belgian problem which still endures. The neutrality of the country was guaranteed by international treaty. Thus was a pledge given which was to be redeemed with blood in 1914. There was a jaunty forthright self-assurance about everything Palmerston did which often gave offence in the staider chancelleries of Europe, but his imperturbable spirit gradually won the admiration of the mass of his fellow-countrymen. He was in these years building up the popularity which later made him appear the embodiment of mid-Victorian confidence.

Some quarter of a million voters had been added by the Reform Bill to the electorate, which now numbered nearly seven hundred thousand persons. This meant that about one adult male in six had the vote. However, they by no means gave their undivided support to the Whigs. The strange habit of English electors of voting against Governments which give them the franchise now made itself felt. Nevertheless the legislation and the commissions of these years were by no means unfruitful. The slaves in the West Indies were finally emancipated in 1833. For the first time in English history the Government made educational grants to religious societies. The first effective Factory Act was passed, though the long hours of work it permitted would horrify the twentieth century and did not satisfy the humanitarians of the time. The Poor Law was reformed on lines that were considered highly advanced in administrative and intellectual circles, though they did not prove popular among those they were supposed to benefit.

The whole system of local government was reconstructed and the old local oligarchies abolished. Politics meanwhile centred on the position of the Established Church and the maintenance of order in Ireland, and it was their failure to deal with these issues and to balance their Budgets that in due course ruined the Whigs. Moreover, great forces were at work outside the House of Commons. A large mass of the country still remained unenfranchised. The relations of capital and labour had scarcely been touched by the hand of Parliament, and the activities of the early trade unions frightened the Government into oppressive measures. The most celebrated case was that of the Tolpuddle "Martyrs" of 1834, when six labourers from that Dorsetshire village of curious name were sentenced to transportation for the technical offence of "administering unlawful oaths" to members of their union. Public agitation eventually secured their pardon, but not until they had served two years in New South Wales. While unrest for many reasons spread, the position of the monarchy itself showed signs of weakness. The Whigs were not the men to bridge the gulf which seemed to yawn between official political circles and the nation.

*   *   *

In 1837 King William IV died. Humorous, tactless, pleasant, and unrespected, he had played his part in lowering esteem for the monarchy, and indeed the vices and eccentricities of the sons of George III had by this time almost destroyed its hold upon the hearts of the people. The new sovereign was a maiden of eighteen. The country knew nothing of either her character or her virtues. "Few people," wrote Palmerston, "have had opportunities of forming a correct judgement of the Princess; but I incline to think that she will turn out to be a remarkable person, and gifted with a great deal of strength of character." He was right. On the eve of her accession the new Queen Victoria wrote in her diary: "Since it has pleased Providence to place me in this station, I shall do my utmost to fulfil my duty towards my country; I am very young, and perhaps in many, though not in all things, inexperienced, but I am sure that very few have more real good will and more real desire to do what is fit and right than I have." It was a promise she was spaciously to fulfil.

Meanwhile Lord Melbourne, who had little faith in law-making, with grace and pleasantness was doing nothing. On top of this there appeared towards the end of the year the first signs of a great economic depression. Chartism, as it was called, in which some historians discern the beginnings of socialism, was the last despairing cry of poverty against the Machine Age. The Chartists, believing, like the agitators for Reform before 1832, that an extension of the franchise would cure all their miseries, demanded annual Parliaments, universal male suffrage, equal electoral districts, the removal of the property qualification for Membership of Parliament, the secret ballot, and the payment of Members. Their only hope of success was to secure, as the Radicals had done, the backing of a Parliamentary party and of the progressive middle classes. But they deliberately refused to bid for middle-class support. Their leaders quarrelled among themselves and affronted respectable people by threatening and irresponsible speeches. They had no funds, and no organisation such as the Catholic Association had found in the parishes of the Irish clergy, or the Labour Party was to find later in the trade unions. For a time England was flooded with petitions and pamphlets.

The ferment varied in warmth from one part of the country to another.

339

Whenever conditions improved the popular temper cooled. Agitation revived from time to time, but in the end the whole muddled, well-intentioned business came to nothing.

In 1839 Melbourne offered to resign, but for another two years Victoria kept him in office. His charm had captured her affections. He imparted to her much of his wisdom on men and affairs, without burdening her with his scepticism, and she refused to be separated from her beloved Prime Minister. In February of the following year a new figure entered upon the British scene. The Queen married her cousin, Prince Albert of Saxe-Coburg. The Prince was an upright, conscientious man with far-ranging interests and high ideals. He and the Queen enjoyed for twenty-one years, until his early death, a happy family life, which held up an example much in accord with the desires of her subjects. After the excesses of George IV and his brothers, the dignity and repute of the monarchy stood in need of restoration, and this was Victoria and Albert's achievement. The patronage which he earnestly extended to science, industry, and the arts, and to good causes of many kinds, gradually won him a wide measure of public respect. Together the Queen and the Prince set a new standard for the conduct of monarchy which has ever since been honourably observed.

Peel, unlike Melbourne, had given the Queen an impression of awkwardness and coldness of manner; but at last in 1841 a General Election brought him to power. Once again the sky seemed clear at Westminster. But a storm was gathering in Ireland.

The immediate issue was the price of bread. To promote foreign commerce Peel had reduced import duties on everything except corn. Dear bread, however, meant either high wages or misery for the masses, and Peel gradually realised that cheap imported food could alone sustain the continued prosperity of the nation. Free Trade in corn seemed imperative, but the political obstacles were formidable. The Tory Party leaned heavily on the votes of the landowners who had invested much capital in their properties during the Napoleonic wars. Peace had brought cheaper corn from abroad, and the cry for protection had led in 1815 to a prohibition of the import of foreign grain except when the price in the home market was abnormally high. The repeal or modification of this and later Corn Laws now overclouded all other issues. The landowners were accused of using their power in Parliament to safeguard their interests at the expense of the rest of the community. The enmity of the manufacturers and industrialists sharpened the conflict, for the Corn Laws not only caused great distress to the working classes, but angered many employers. Protection in their view prevented them from building up new markets overseas and from competing on fair terms in old ones.

Hostility to the Corn Laws had grown during the depression of 1838–1842. An Anti-Corn Law League was formed at Manchester to press for their abolition. It soon exerted a powerful influence on public opinion, and produced two remarkable leaders and organisers who became the Free Trade prophets of nineteenth-century England, Richard Cobden, a calico printer, and John Bright, a Quaker mill-owner. Meetings were held throughout the land. The propaganda was effective and novel: a few simple ideas hammered into the minds of audiences by picked lecturers and speakers. Never had there been such a shrewdly conducted agitation. Monster petitions were sent to Parliament. Cobden persuaded prosperous townspeople to buy forty-shilling freeholds in the county constituencies and thus secure a double vote. This so increased the number of Anti-Corn Law electors that instead of only petitioning Parliament from outside, the League started influencing it from within.

In August, 1845, the potato crop failed in Ireland. Famine was imminent and Peel could wait no longer, but when he put his proposals to the Cabinet several of his colleagues revolted and in December he had to resign. The Whig leader Russell refused to form an administration, and Peel returned to office to face and conquer the onslaught of the Tory Protectionists. Their spokesman, the hitherto little-known Benjamin Disraeli, denounced him not so much for seeking to abolish the Corn Laws as for betraying his position as head of a great party. But Peel maintained that his duty to the nation was higher than his duty to his party, and he believed it was his mission to carry the abolition of the Corn Laws. On June 25, 1846, with the help of Whig and Irish votes, the Corn Laws were repealed. Disraeli immediately had his revenge. Turmoil in Ireland destroyed Peel's Government, and by a vote on the same night the great Ministry, one of the strongest of the century, came to an end. Peel had been the dominating force and personality in English politics since the passing of the great Reform Bill. Whether in Opposition or in office, he had towered above the scene. He was not a man of broad and ranging modes of thought, but he understood better than any of his contemporaries the needs of the country, and he had the outstanding courage to change his views in order to meet them. It is true that he split his party, but there are greater crimes than that. The age over which he presided was one of formidable industrial advance. It was the Railway Age. By 1848 some five thousand miles of railroads had been built in the United Kingdom. Speed of transport and increasing output were the words of the day. Coal and iron production had doubled. Engineering was making great, though as yet hesitating, strides. All the steps were being taken, not by Government, but by enterprisers throughout the country, which were to make Britain the greatest industrial Power of the nineteenth-century world. Peel had a practical sense of these vast developments. Free trade, he knew, was no cure-all for the pangs and anguish of a changing society. But the days of the land-owning predominance were doomed. Free trade seemed essential to manufacture, and in manufacture Britain was entering upon her supremacy. All this Peel grasped. His Government set an example of initiative which both the Conservative and Liberal Parties honoured by imitation in the future. Of his own methods of government he once said, "The fact is, people like a certain degree of obstinacy and presumption in a Minister. They abuse him for dictation and arrogance, but they like being governed." High words perhaps, but they fitted the time.

Early in 1850, after he had watched with restraint and composure the totterings of his Whig successors, Peel fell from his horse while riding in the Green Park and was fatally injured. So died one of the great shapers of British politics in the Victorian Age.

CHAPTER SEVENTY-FOUR

England and the Crimean War

IN 1848 Thomas Babington Macaulay, who had been a Minister of the Crown and served the Government of India in high office, published the first volumes of his *History of England*. This great work, with all its prejudiced opinions and errors of fact, provided the historical background for the sense of progress which was now inspiring Victorian Britain. Macaulay set out to show that the story of England since the Whig Revolution of 1688 was one of perpetual and limitless advance. In his opening chapter he wrote: "The history of our own country in the last hundred and sixty years is eminently the history of physical, moral, and intellectual improvement." This was a heartening note, much appreciated by contemporary readers. Optimism reigned throughout the land. An even more shining future, Macaulay implied, lay before the United Kingdom. So indeed it did. His views were widely shared, and were soon given form in the Great Exhibition of British achievement which justly gratified the nation.

Prince Albert sponsored the idea. There had already been small exhibitions of manufactures, in which he had taken an interest. In 1849, after opening the new Albert Dock in Liverpool, the Prince had been so much impressed by the surging vigour of British industry, and its maritime cause and consequence, that he adopted with enthusiasm a plan for an exhibition on a far larger scale than had ever been seen before. It would display to the country and the world the progress achieved in every field. It would also be international, proclaiming the benefits of free trade between nations and looking forward to the universal peace which it was then supposed must inevitably result from the unhampered traffic in goods.

Few people foresaw the war with Russia that was soon to break out.

For two years, against considerable opposition, the Prince headed a committee to further his project. In 1851 the Great Exhibition was opened in Hyde Park. Nineteen acres were devoted to the principal building, the Crystal Palace, designed by an expert glasshouse gardener, Joseph Paxton. Housing most of the exhibits, and enclosing whole trees within its glass and iron structure, it was to be the marvel of the decade. In spite of prophecies of failure, the Exhibition was a triumphant success. Over a million people a month visited it during the six months of its opening. Nearly fourteen thousand exhibits of industrial skill and craft were shown, of which half were British. The Prince was vindicated, and the large profit made by the organisers was invested and put to learned and educational purposes. Queen Victoria described the opening day as "one of the greatest and most glorious in our lives." Her feelings were prompted by her delight that Prince Albert should have confounded his critics, ever ready to accuse him of meddling in national affairs, but there was more to it than that. The Queen paid many visits to the Crystal Palace, where her presence aroused in the scores of thousands of subjects with whom she mingled a deep loyalty and a sense of national pride. Never had the Throne been so firmly grounded in the affections of the people. Prosperity, however unevenly its blessings fell, gave Britain a self-assurance that seemed worth more than social legislation and further reform. From mills and mines and factories flowed the wealth that was making life easier for the country. And this the country recognised.

The mid-century marks the summit of Britain's preponderance in industry. In another twenty years other nations, among whom industrial progress had started later, had begun to cut down her lead. Until 1870 Britain had mined more than half the world's coal, and in that year her output of pig-iron was still greater than the rest of the world's put together. Foreign trade stood at a figure of nearly seven hundred millions sterling, as compared with three hundred for the United States, three hundred and forty for France, and three hundred for Germany. But the proportions were rapidly changing. Railways greatly assisted the growth of industry in Germany and America, where coal and iron resources were separated from each other by considerable distances. A challenge was also presented to British agriculture, now that prairie-grown American wheat could be carried to American ports by railroad and shipped across the ocean to European markets. Nevertheless there was no slowing down of industry in Britain. Textiles, the backbone of British exports, filled an insatiable demand in Asia, and the future of the mighty steel and engineering industries seemed assured for a long time to come. In England the rapidly expanding Midlands and North were blackened by the smoke and dust of the pits and forges.

Critics were not wanting of the age of mass production that was now taking shape. Charles Dickens in his novels revealed the plight of the poor, holding up to pity the conditions in which many of them dwelt and ridiculing the State institutions that crudely encompassed them. John Ruskin was another. In the midst of his long life he turned from the study of painting and architecture to modern social problems. His heart lay in the Middle Ages, which he imagined to be peopled by a fraternity of craftsmen harmoniously creating works of art. Peering out upon the Victorian scene, this prophetic figure looked in vain for similar accomplishment. Bad taste in manufacture, bad relations between employers and men, aroused his eloquent wrath. His was a voice that cried the way both to new movements in the arts and to socialism in politics.

*   *   *

Foreign affairs and the threat of war now began to darken the scene. Turkey had troubled the statesmen of Europe for many years. The military empire, which for three centuries had dominated the Eastern world from the Persian Gulf to Budapest, and from the Caspian to Algiers, seemed now on the edge of disruption and collapse. What then would become of its vast territories? To whom would fall the wide, fertile Turkish provinces in Europe and Asia? The urgency and imminence of such questions were sharpened by the evident determination of Russia to seize the Danubian lands, Constantinople, and the Black Sea. England could not ignore the threat. The shadow of Russia, already a formidable Asiatic Power, appeared to be creeping over India.

The ruling politicians of England now attempted to check Russian expansion by propping up the decaying system of Turkish rule in South-East Europe. The conflict which came to a head was precipitated by the claim of the Russian Czar for a general protectorate over the Christians in the Turkish Empire. This, if granted, would have given Russia authority over the many millions of Rumanians, Serbs, Bulgarians, Greeks, and Armenians within the Ottoman domains. The balance of power, which British governments always sought in the Near East, as elsewhere, would have been destroyed.

The Turks rejected the Russian demands, and on June 2, 1853, the Russian attitude had become so menacing that the Cabinet ordered the British fleet to Besika Bay, outside the Dardanelles. Napoleon III, eager for British approval and support, agreed to provide a French squadron.

Thus England drifted into war. In February, 1854, Nicholas I recalled his ambassadors from London and Paris, and at the end of March the Crimean War began, with France and Britain as allies of Turkey.

The operations were ill-planned and ill-conducted on both sides. The conditions of service in the British Army were intolerable; the administration was bad, the equipment scanty, the commanders of no outstanding ability. The French and British between them had only fifty-six thousand

3 4 4

troops in the Crimea in the terrible winter of 1854–1855. Nearly fourteen thousand of them went to hospital, and many died for want of medical supplies. Most of these casualties were British. The French were much better provided for, while the Russians, who accepted official mismanagement as a matter of course, perished in uncounted numbers on the long route marches through the snow southwards to the Crimea. At Balaclava in October, 1854, the British cavalry distinguished themselves by two astonishing charges against overwhelming odds. The second of these was the celebrated charge of the Light Brigade, in which six hundred and seventy-three horsemen, led by Lord Cardigan, rode up the valley under heavy fire, imperturbably, as if taking part in a review, to attack the Russian batteries. They captured the guns, but only a third of the brigade answered the first muster after the charge. Lord Cardigan calmly returned to the yacht on which he lived, had a bath, dined, drank a bottle of champagne, and went to bed. His brigade had performed an inspiring feat of gallantry. But it was due, like much else in this war, to the blunders of commanders. The Light Brigade had charged the wrong guns.

In September, 1855, the great Crimean port of Sebastopol at last fell to the Allies. The futility of the plan of campaign was now revealed. It was impossible to invade Russia from the Crimea. What should the next move be? France by now had four times as many troops in the field as England, and Napoleon III was threatening to withdraw them. A peace party in Paris was making its views felt. The French Emperor was inclined to negotiate, meanwhile reducing operations against Russia to a mere blockade. If the war was to continue, he felt, other Powers would have to be drawn in, and an appeal made to the national sentiments of Poles, Swedes, and other hereditary enemies of the Czar. This was too grandiose even for Lord Palmerston, and he realised the war must stop. Threatened by an Austrian ultimatum, Russia agreed to terms, and in February, 1856, a peace conference opened in Paris.

With one exception few of the leading figures emerged from the Crimean War with enhanced reputations. Miss Florence Nightingale had been sent out in an official capacity by the War Minister. She arrived at Scutari and there organised the first base hospital of modern times. With few nurses and scanty equipment she reduced the death-rate at Scutari from forty-two per hundred to twenty-two per thousand men. Her influence and example were far-reaching.

The treaty of Paris, signed at the end of March, removed the immediate causes of the conflict, but provided no permanent settlement of the Eastern Question. Within twenty years Europe was nearly at war again over Russian ambitions in the Near East. The fundamental situation was unaltered: so long as Turkey was weak, so long would her empire remain a temptation to Russian Imperialists and an embarrassment to Western Europe.

CHAPTER SEVENTY-FIVE

Palmerston

WITH ONE short interval of Tory government, Lord Palmerston presided over the English scene throughout the decade that began in 1855. Not long after the signing of peace which ended the misguided and inconclusive Crimean War he was confronted with another emergency which also arose in the East, but this time in Asia. The Indian Mutiny made, in some respects, a more lasting impact on England than that war. It paved the way for Empire.

After it was over Britain gradually and consciously became a world-wide Imperial Power. The causes of the Mutiny lay deep in the past. About the beginning of the nineteenth century a new generation of British administrators and soldiers appeared in India, austere, upright, Bible-reading men, who dreamed of Christianising and Europeanising the sub-continent, and for a while gained a brief promise of success. Hitherto the English, like the Romans in the provinces of their empire, had a neutral policy on religion. In England missionary zeal was stirring, and respect for alien creeds gradually succumbed to the desire for proselytisation. *Suttee,* the burning of widows; *Thugee,* the strangling of travellers by fanatics who deemed it a religious duty; and female infanticide were suppressed. Measures were taken to make English learning available to the higher-ranking and more wealthy Indians. All this was unsettling, and played its part in the terrible events which now occurred.

A more immediate cause of the rising was a series of defeats and reverses suffered by the British. The Russian threat to India had begun to overhang the minds of Englishmen. It was in fact a gross exaggeration to suppose that Russian armies could have crossed the ranges of the Hindu-Kush in force and arrived in the Indus valley. But the menace seemed real at the time. When it was learnt that a small body of Russians had penetrated into the fringes of Afghanistan a British expedition was dispatched in 1839 to Kabul and a British candidate placed on the Afghan throne. The result was disaster. The country rose up in arms. In December, 1841, under a promise of safe-conduct, the British garrison of some four thousand troops, accompanied by nearly three times as many women, children, and Afghan camp-followers, began to withdraw through the snow and the mountain passes. The safe-conduct was violated, and nearly all were murdered or taken prisoners. A single survivor reached India on January 13.

Another defeat soon followed in the Punjab, the most northerly of the Indian provinces at that time. Here the warrior Sikhs, a reformed Hindu sect, forbidden to touch tobacco or cut their hair above the waist, had long held sway. Encouraged by the news from Afghanistan, and restless after the death of their great leader, Ranjit Singh, who had hitherto held them in check, they resolved to try their hand at invading the Company's territory. In 1845 they crossed the boundary river of the Sutlej, and were met and repulsed two hundred miles north of Delhi. The British installed a regency. Three years later the Sikhs tried to overthrow it. There was a desperate drawn battle deep within the province at Chilianwala, in which three British regiments lost their colours. Shortly afterwards the British forces redeemed their name and the Sikh army was destroyed. The Punjab was pacified by John and Henry Lawrence.

This was a period of confident expansion in India, generally undertaken by men on the spot and not always approved by opinion in Britain. Two other major annexations completed the extension of British rule.

The East India Company's army of Bengal had long been of ill-repute. The Company's British officers were often of poor quality, for the abler and more thrusting among them sought secondment to the more spacious fields of civil administration. There were grievances about pay and pensions. Other developments, unconnected with this military unrest, added their weight. By the 1850's railways, roads, posts, telegraphs, and schools were beginning to push and agitate their way across the countryside, and were thought by many Indians to threaten an ancient society whose inmost structure and spirit sprang from a rigid and unalterable caste system. If everyone used the same trains and the same schools, or even the same roads, it was argued, how could caste survive? Unfounded stories spread that the Government intended to convert India forcibly to Christianity. The disasters in Afghanistan and the slaughter of the Sikh wars cast doubt on the invincibility of British arms. Thus a legacy of troubles confronted Dalhousie's successor, Lord Canning. He had been in India little more than a year when the introduction of a new type of ammunition provided a spark and focus for the mass of discontent.

Rumours began to flow that the cartridges for the new Enfield rifle were greased with the fat of pigs and cows, animals which Moslem and Hindu respectively were forbidden to eat. The cartridges had to be bitten before they could be inserted in the muzzle. In the spring of 1857 some cavalry troopers were court-martialled and imprisoned for refusing to touch the cartridges. Three regiments mutinied, captured the prison, killed their British officers, and marched on Delhi. For three weeks there was a pause, and then the mutiny spread. British officers would not believe in the disloyalty of their troops and many were murdered. The rebels turned on Lucknow. Here also there was a desperate struggle. Seventeen hundred troops, nearly half of them loyal sepoys, held the Residency against sixty thousand rebels.

Food was short and there was much disease. On September 25 Havelock and Outram fought their way in, but were beset in their turn, Havelock dying of exhaustion a few days later. In November the siege was raised by Sir Colin Campbell, the new Commander-in-Chief appointed by Lord Palmerston. The British troops took horrible vengeance. Muntineers were blown from the mouths of cannon, sometimes alive, or their bodies sewn up in the skins of cows and swine. At Cawnpore there was a horrible massacre. For twenty-one days nine hundred British and loyal Indians, nearly half of them women and children, were besieged and attacked by three thousand sepoys with the Nana Sahib at their head. At length, on June 26, they were granted safe-conduct. As they were leaving by boat they were fired upon, and all the men were killed. Such women and children as survived were cast into prison. On the night of July 15 a relieving force under Sir Henry Havelock, a veteran of Indian warfare, was barely twenty miles away. The Nana Sahib ordered his sepoys to kill the prisoners. They refused. Five assassins then cut the captives to death with knives and threw the bodies into a well.

Elsewhere the rising was more speedily crushed. The recapture of Delhi destroyed all semblance and pretence that the mutiny was a national revolt. On November 1 the Governor-General proclaimed with truth that Queen Victoria was now sovereign of all India. The rule of the East India Company, which had long ceased to be a trading business in India, was abolished. Thus, after almost exactly a century, the advice which Clive had given to Pitt was accepted by the British Government. Henceforward there were to be no more annexations, no subsidiary treaties, no more civil wars. Religious toleration and equality before the law were promised to all. Indians for a generation and more were to look back on the Queen's Proclamation of 1858 as a Magna Carta.

The scale of the Indian Mutiny should not be exaggerated. Three-quarters of the troops remained loyal; barely a third of British territory was affected; there had been risings and revolts among the soldiery before; the brunt of the outbreak was suppressed in the space of a few weeks. It was in no sense a national movement, or, as some later Indian writers have suggested, a patriotic struggle for freedom or a war of independence. The idea and ideal of the inhabitants of the sub-continent forming a single people and state was not to emerge for many years. But terrible atrocities had been committed by both sides. From now on there was an increasing gulf between the rulers and the ruled. The easy-going ways of the eighteenth century were gone for ever, and so were the missionary fervour and reforming zeal of the early Victorians and their predecessors. British administration became detached, impartial, efficient. Great progress was made and many material benefits were secured. The frontiers were guarded and the peace was kept. Starvation was subdued. The population vastly increased. The Indian army, revived and reorganised, was to play a glorious part on Britain's side in two world wars. Nevertheless, the atrocities and reprisals of the blood-stained months of the Mutiny left an enduring and bitter mark in the memory of both countries.

* * *

While these events unrolled in India the political scene in England remained confused and for twenty years Governments of mixed complexion followed one another. Prosperity was spreading through the land, and with it went a lull in the fiercer forms of political agitation. Dignity and deference were the values of the age. If the gentleman was still the admired ideal, the self-made man was also deeply respected, and educating the manual labourer began to seem more important than rousing him to revolution. With this view large numbers of working men happily concurred. All this made for a feeling of stability, with which a sense of steady progress was allied.

Religion in its numerous varieties cast a soothing and uplifting influence on men's minds. The virtues of toleration had been learnt, though toleration did not mean lukewarmness. But thinking men were also disturbed by a new theory, long foreshadowed in the work of scientists, the theory of evolution. It was given classic expression in *The Origin of Species,* published by Charles Darwin in 1859. This theory and its emphasis on the survival of the fittest in the history of life upon the globe was a powerful adjunct to mid-Victorian optimism. It lent fresh force to the belief in the forward march of mankind.

Palmerston seemed to his fellow-countrymen the embodiment of their own healthy hopes and his patriotic sentiments appealed to the self-confidence of the nation. But it was Palmerston's desire, for all his strong language and sometimes hasty action, to keep the general peace in Europe.

* * *

In home politics, meanwhile, a sublime complacency enveloped the Government. Palmerston, like Melbourne before him, did not believe in too much legislation. Good-humour and common sense distinguished him. Disraeli, chafing on the Opposition benches, vented his scorn and irritation on this last of the eighteenth-century politicians. Disraeli had become the leader of his party in the House of Commons. His struggle for power was hard and uphill. A Jew at the head of a phalanx of country gentlemen was an unusual sight in English politics.

Standing apart both from the Whigs and Tories was William Gladstone. Having started his Parliamentary career in 1832 as a strict Tory, he was to make a long pilgrimage into the Liberal camp. The son of a rich Liverpool merchant with slave-owning interests in the West Indies, Gladstone came from the same class as his old leader, Peel, and believed, like him, in the new arguments for Free Trade. But, like Disraeli, his progress was slow. It was fortunate for him that supreme power did not come too soon.

Long years of waiting made Gladstone sure of himself. In 1859, at the age of fifty, Gladstone joined the Whigs and the pilgrimage was over. As Chancellor of the Exchequer under Palmerston his golden period began— great Budget speeches in the House of Commons, a superb handling of administrative detail. His finance was a remarkable success and it was soon apparent who would succeed to the leadership of the party. In 1865, in his eighty-first year, Palmerston died. The eighteenth century died with him. The later Victorian age demanded a new leader, and at long last he had arrived. When Gladstone next appeared before his electors he opened his speech by saying, "At last, my friends, I am come among you, and am come among you unmuzzled." But the Whigs still hesitated. Gladstone, like Disraeli, wanted to extend the franchise to large sections of the working classes; he was anxious to capture the votes of the new electorate. He prevailed upon the Government, now headed by Russell, to put forward a Reform Bill, but the Cabinet were so divided that they resigned. A minority administration under Derby and Disraeli followed, which lasted for two and a half years.

Disraeli now seized his chance. He introduced a fresh Reform Bill in 1867, which he skilfully adapted to meet the wishes of the House, and nearly a million new voters were added to an existing electorate of about the same number. Derby called it "a leap in the dark." Even the Radicals were anxious about how the uneducated masses would behave. In February, 1868, Derby resigned and Disraeli was at last Prime Minister—as he put it, "at the top of the greasy pole." He had to hold a General Election. The new voters gave their overwhelming support to his opponents, and Gladstone formed the strongest administration that England had seen since the days of Peel.

CHAPTER SEVENTY-SIX

The Migration of the Peoples

1: CANADA AND SOUTH AFRICA

OCCUPATION OF the empty lands of the globe was violently accelerated by the fall of Napoleon. The long struggle against France had stifled or arrested the expansion of the English-speaking peoples. Their energies and their hopes had been concentrated on survival and on victory. There had been no time for dreams of emigration, and no men to spare if it had been possible. Suddenly all this was changed by the decision at Waterloo. Once again the oceans were free. Once more the New World offered an escape from the hardships and frustrations of the Old. The war was over. Fares were cheap and transport was plentiful. The result was the most spectacular migration of human beings of which history has yet had record and a vast enrichment of the trade and industry of Great Britain.

News began to spread among the masses that fertile unoccupied and habitable lands still existed, in which white men could dwell in peace and liberty, and perhaps could even better themselves. The increasing population of Britain added to the pressure. The numbers grew, and the flow began: by the middle of the century no fewer than eight million people had left the British Isles.

The motives, methods, and character of the movement were very different from those which had sustained the Pilgrim Fathers and the Stuart plantations of the seventeenth century. Famine drove at least a million Irishmen to the United States and elsewhere. Gold lured hardy fortune-hunters to Australia, and to the bleak recesses of Canada. Hunger for land and for the profits of the wool trade beckoned the more sober and well-to-do. All this was largely accomplished in the face of official indifference and sometimes of hostility. Thus, as in India, the Second British Empire was founded almost by accident, and with small encouragement from any of the main political parties.

*   *   *

Of the new territories Canada was the most familiar and the nearest in point of distance to the United Kingdom. In Lower Canada the French were deeply rooted, a compact, alien community, uninterested and untouched by the democratic ideas of liberal or revolutionary Europe. Beyond them, to the north-west, lay Upper Canada, settled by Englishmen who had left the United States towards the end of the eighteenth century rather than live under the American republic. These proud folk had out of devotion to the British Throne abandoned most of their possessions, and been rewarded with the unremunerative but honourable title of United Empire Loyalists. The Mohawk tribe, inspired by the same sentiments, had journeyed with them. They had hacked a living space out of the forests, and dwelt lonely and remote, cut off from Lower Canada by the rapids of the St. Lawrence, and watchful against incursions from the United States. Then there was a vast emptiness till one reached a few posts on the Pacific which traded their wares to China.

These communities, so different in tradition, character, and race, had been rallied into temporary unity by invasion from the United States in the three-year struggle between 1812 and 1814. Then trouble began. The two Provinces started to quarrel with each other. Differences over religion added to the irritations. French politicians made vehement speeches. In Upper Canada the new settlers struggled for political equality with the Loyalists.

In the following year both Provinces rebelled, Lower Canada for a month and Upper Canada for a week. There were mobs, firing by troops, shifty compromises, and very few executions. Everything was on a small scale and in a minor key and no great harm was done, but it made the British Government realise that Canadian affairs required attention. In 1838 Lord Durham was sent to investigate. His instructions were vague and simple, "To put things right." He produced, or at least lent his name to, the famous report in which he diagnosed and proclaimed the root causes of the trouble and advocated representative government, carried on by Ministers chosen from the popular Assembly, a united Canada, and planned settlement of the unoccupied lands. These recommendations were largely put into effect by the Canada Act of 1840, which was the work of Lord John Russell.

Thereafter Canada's progress was swift and peaceful. Her population had risen from about half a million in 1815 to a million and a quarter in 1838. A regular steamship service with the British Isles and cheap trans-Atlantic postage were established in the same year. There were hesitations and doubts in England at the novel idea of making colonies almost completely free, but the appointment of Durham's son-in-law, Lord Elgin, as Governor-General in 1847 was decisive. When he laid down his office seven years later the principle had been firmly accepted by Canadians of all persuasions that popular power must march with popular responsibility, that Ministers must govern and be obeyed so long as they enjoyed the confidence of the majority and should resign when they had lost it.

There was hardly any talk now of leaving the Empire or dividing Canada into separate and sovereign units or joining the American Republic. On the contrary, the Oregon Treaty with the United States in 1846 extended the 49th parallel right across the continent as a boundary between the two countries and gave the whole of Vancouver Island to Great Britain.

In the mid-century a movement for the federation of all the Canadian Provinces began to grow and gather support. The Civil War in the United States helped to convince Canadians that all was not perfect in their neighbour's constitution, and the victory of the North also aroused their fears that the exultant Union might be tempted to extend its borders farther still. Canada had already turned her gaze westwards. Between the Province of Ontario and the Rocky Mountains lay a thousand miles of territory, uninhabited save by a few settlers in Manitoba, a roaming-place for Indians, trappers, and wild animals. It was a temptation, so it was argued, to the land-hunger of the United States. Discharged Irish soldiers from the Civil War had already made armed raids across the border which Congress had declared itself powerless to arrest. Might not the Americans press forward, occupy these vacant lands by stealth, and even establish a kind of squatter's right to the prairies? The soil was believed to be fertile and was said to offer a living for white men. In 1867 America purchased the remote and forbidding expanse of Alaska from the Russians for the sum of seven million two hundred thousand dollars, but here, on the door-step of the Republic, lay a prize which seemed much more desirable and was very easy of access. No one ruled over it except the Hudson's Bay Company, founded in the reign of Charles II, and the Company, believing that agriculture would imperil its fur-trade, was both hostile to settlers and jealous of its own authority. Eleven years before, however, the discovery of gold on the Fraser River had precipitated a rush of fortune-hunters to the Pacific coast. The Company's officals had proved powerless to control the turmoil, and the Government in London had been compelled to extend the royal sovereignty to this distant shore. Thus was born the Crown colony of British Columbia, which soon united with the Island of Vancouver and demanded and obtained self-rule. But between it and Ontario lay a no-man's-land, and something must be done if it was not to fall into the hands of the United States. How indeed could Canada remain separate from America and yet stay alive?

These considerations prompted the British North America Act of 1867, which created the first of the self-governing British Dominions beyond the seas. Thus the way was made easy for the absorption of new territories and Provinces, and on the eve of her Railway Age and westward expansion the political stability of Canada was assured. The obvious, immediate step was to buy out the Hudson's Bay Company. This was done two years later for the sum of £300,000. The Company kept its trading rights, and, indeed, retains them to this day, but it surrendered its territorial sovereignty to the Crown.

Manitoba became a Province of the Dominion in 1870, and in the next year British Columbia was also admitted. By themselves, however, these constitutional steps would not have sufficed to bind the broad stretches of Canada together.

The challenging task that faced the Dominion was to settle and develop her empty Western lands before the immigrant tide from America could flood across the 49th parallel. The answer was to build a transcontinental railway. Helped by government funds, a Scotsman, Donald Smith, better known as Lord Strathcona, carried out the plan and the Canadian Pacific Railway was opened in 1885. Other lines sprang up, and corn, soon counted in millions of bushels a year, began to flow in from the prairies. Canada had become a nation, and shining prospects lay before her.

*   *   *

South Africa, unlike America, had scanty attractions for the early colonists and explorers. As the half-way house to the Indies many broke their voyage there, but few cared to stay. The Gulf of St. Lawrence made it easy to reach the interior of Canada, but the coastline of South Africa, short of natural harbours and navigable rivers, mostly consisted of cliffs and sand-hills washed by strong currents and stormy seas. Inland a succession of mountain ranges, running parallel to the coast, barred the way. From the west the ascent was comparatively gradual, but the country was barren and waterless. From the south and east range after range, in many places sheer and precipitous, had to be climbed. Few lands have been more difficult for Europeans to enter than South Africa, and for them it long remained the "Tavern of the Seas," a port of call on the route to the East.

In the seventeenth century the fleets of the Dutch East India Company, sailing for the Indies or returning home to Amsterdam and Rotterdam, were the most frequent visitors to the Cape, and Table Bay was their halting-place. The establishment of a permanent settlement was discussed, but nothing was done till 1652, when, at the height of their power and in the Golden Age of their civilisation, the Dutch sent three ships to take possession of Table Bay. Colonisation was no part of the plan: they merely wanted to found a port of call for the Company's ships, and almost all the inhabitants were servants of the Company, forbidden to strike out into the new land. After twenty years there were no more than sixty-four free burghers at Table Bay.

The change came at the turn of the seventeenth century, when settlers were encouraged to come out from Holland and take up grants of land. Not all were Dutch; many were Huguenots, Germans, or Swedes, driven into exile by religious persecution; but the Dutch gradually assimilated them. The little community was served and sustained by a local population of Negro slaves.

Throughout the eighteenth century the colony prospered and grew. In 1760 the first European crossed the Orange River, and by 1778 the Fish River had been made its eastern boundary. By the end of the century the population numbered about fifteen thousand, and there were three areas of settlement. Cape Town, or "Little Paris" as the settlers called it, was a town and port of five thousand inhabitants, and the Company's headquarters.

But Holland had now been slowly overtaken by Britain, and as the century drew to its close it became clear that the Imperial future lay, not with the Dutch, but either with the British or the French. In 1782 the Dutch East India Company had paid its last dividend, and twelve years later declared its bankruptcy, with a deficit of £10,000,000. When the Dutch were defeated by the French, the British seized Cape Colony as enemy territory. It was finally ceded to them under the peace settlement of 1814 in return for an indemnity of £6,000,000.

It was now the turn of the British. Emigration coincided with a change of policy. Convinced that South Africa was destined to become a permanent part of the British Empire, the Government resolved to make it as English as they could. In 1820 and 1821 nearly five thousand settlers were brought out from Great Britain. English began to replace Dutch as the official language. In 1828 the judicial system was remodelled on the English pattern, Dutch currency was replaced by English, and the English began to dominate the churches and the schools. Thus was born a division which Canada had surmounted.

With the same religion, a similar language, a common stock, and kindred political and social traditions, the British and the Dutch Boers nevertheless plunged into racial strife. British methods of government created among the Boers a more bitter antagonism than in any other Imperial country except Ireland. Anglicisation was not only ill-conceived, it was unsuccessful. The English were to discover, as the Spaniards had learnt in the sixteenth century, that no race has ever clung more tenaciously to its own culture and institutions than the Dutch.

At this time there was much enthusiasm in England for good works. The missionaries believed and preached that black men were the equals of white men; the settlers regarded the natives primarily as farmhands and wanted to control them as strictly as possible. When the missionaries got slavery abolished in 1833, the settlers were indignant.

The first crisis came in 1834, when hordes of Bantu swept over the frontier, laying waste the country and destroying the farms. The Governor, Sir Benjamin D'Urban, drove them back, and to prevent another attack he annexed the territory between the rivers Keiskamma and Kei, expelled the native raiders, and compensated the settlers by offering them land in this new province, which was named after Queen Adelaide. This roused the missionaries, and they persuaded the Colonial Secretary, Lord Glenelg, to repudiate D'Urban and abandon the new province. The settlers lost all compensation, and insult was added to injury when it became known that Glenelg considered that the Kaffirs had an ample justification for the war into which they had rushed. Thus was provoked the Great Trek.

In small parties, accompanied by their women and children and driving their cattle before them, about five thousand Boers set out into the unknown, like the Children of Israel seeking the Promised Land. They were soon followed by many others. Some journeyed over a thousand miles to the banks of the Limpopo, many were attacked by the Matabele and the Zulu, all endured thirst and famine, yet in the unyielding spirit of their Calvinist religion they marched on. The Great Trek was one of the remarkable feats of the nineteenth century, and its purpose was to shake off British rule for ever.

In a great battle at Blood River, in 1838, they crushed the fierce Zulu warriors, and after their victory they established the Republic of Natal around the little town of Pietermaritzburg, with Andries Pretorius as its first President.

Their freedom was brief. The British refused to recognise the republic, and after a short struggle in 1845 made it a province of Cape Colony. But the Government in London did not care to extend its responsibilities, and in 1852 it recognised the independence of the Transvaal settlers. Two years later the British withdrew from beyond the Orange River and the Orange Free State was formed. By 1857 there were five separate republics and three colonies within the territory of the present Union of South Africa.

The old colony of the Cape meanwhile prospered, as the production of wool increased by leaps and bounds, and in 1853 an Order in Council established representative institutions in the colony, with a Parliament in Cape Town, though without the grant of full responsible government. Here we may leave South African history for a spell of uneasy peace.

CHAPTER SEVENTY-SEVEN

The Migration of the Peoples

2: AUSTRALIA AND NEW ZEALAND

AUSTRALIA HAS a long history in the realms of human imagination. From the days of Herodotus mankind has had its legends of distant lands, seen for a moment on the horizon, inhabited by strange monsters and rich with the fabulous wealth of Solomon's Ophir and Tarshish. How the ships of the King of Israel in the tenth century before Christ could have reached the South Pacific Ocean is beyond conjecture. But the geographers and navigators of the Renaissance conceived themselves to be inspired by Biblical example. Yet the sixteenth century had ended before landfall was made in Australia by Europeans, and the men who found it were hard-headed, unromantic Dutch traders.

The extent of the continent was not accurately known until the middle of the eighteenth century, when Captain James Cook made three voyages between 1768 and 1779. Cook was a surveyor trained in the Royal Navy. His reports were official, accurate, and detailed. His news reached Britain at a timely moment. English convicts had long been transported to America, but since the War of Independence the Government had nowhere to send them and many were now dying of disease in the hulks and gaols of London. Why not send the prisoners to the new continent?

The younger Pitt's administration shrank from colonial ventures after the disasters in North America, but delay was deemed impossible, and in January, 1788, seven hundred and seventeen convicts were anchored in Botany Bay. A hundred and ninety-seven were women. The Bay had been so named by Sir Joseph Banks, a distinguished amateur of science, who accompanied Cook on one of his voyages. There was not much botany about it now. The convicts were soon moved a few miles north to Port Jackson, within the magnificent expanse of Sydney Harbour. Famine crouched above the settlement, and for long the colony could not supply all its own food. Without training, capital, or the desire to work, the forgers and thieves, poachers and Irish rebels, criminals and political exiles, had neither the will nor the ability to fit themselves to the new land. "The convict barracks of New South Wales," wrote an Australian Governor, "remind me of the monasteries of Spain. They contain a population of consumers who produce nothing." The region had been named by Captain Cook after South Wales. He thought he had detected a resemblance in coastline. But hard-working Wales and its antipodean namesake had very little else in common at the time. The population changed from about fifteen thousand convicts and twenty-one thousand free settlers in 1828 to twenty-seven thousand convicts and over a hundred thousand free settlers in 1841. Free men soon demanded, and got, free government. Transportation to New South Wales was finally abolished in 1840, and two years later a Legislative Council was set up, most of whose members were elected by popular vote.

Wool founded the prosperity of the country. The turning-point had been the discovery of the Bathurst Plains, beyond the Blue Mountains. Here and to the south of Sydney, and on the Darling Downs to the north, were great sheep-runs, mile after mile of lonely grazing land, open, grassy downs, inhabited only by a few shepherds and thousands upon thousands of silent, soft-footed sheep moving ever farther into the interior. The flocks multiplied swiftly: by 1850 there were more than sixteen million sheep in Australia. This was over sixteen times more sheep than there were men and women.

The British Government claimed that all land under British rule was Crown property. "Squatters," who needed thousands of acres for their sheep-runs and neither could nor would pay a pound, or even five shillings, for their grazing, struck out into the emptiness and took what they wanted. The Colonial Office surrendered to the pressure of events. The squatters were there to stay, and soon became the most important section of the community.

*   *   *

Long before 1850 the settlement of other parts of Australia had begun. Tasmania developed in much the same way as New South Wales, and had become a separate colony in 1825. Prosperity came from wool and whaling, and brought a solid upsurge in population, which reached sixty-eight thousand by 1840, mostly free. In 1851 the new colony of Victoria, complete with representative institutions, was established, with its capital at Melbourne. The young Queen gave her name to this new offshoot of the English-speaking peoples. Its capital commemorates the Whig Prime Minister whom she had found to be the most agreeable of her advisers, and who was now no more.

The third offspring of New South Wales was Queensland. It grew up around the town of Brisbane, but developed more slowly and did not become a separate colony until 1859. By then two other settlements had arisen on the Australian coasts, both independently of New South Wales and the other colonies. In 1834 a body known as "the Colonisation Commissioners for South Australia" had been set up in London, and two years later the first settlers landed near Adelaide. The city was named after William IV's Queen. South Australia was never a convict settlement. It was organised by a group of men under the influence of Gibbon Wakefield, whose elaborate theories were now put into practice. On the whole they succeeded, though a system of dual control by which responsibility was divided between the Government and the Colonisation, or Land, Commissioners gave so much trouble that the Commissioners were abolished in 1842. Within seven years the colony numbered fifty-two thousand inhabitants, and had been substantially enriched by the discovery of copper deposits. Along with the eastern colonies, it was presently granted representative institutions.

The other colony, Western Australia, had a very different history. Founded in 1829, it nearly died at birth. With much less fertile soil than the eastern colonies and separated from them by vast and uninhabitable desert, it suffered greatly from lack of labour. Convicts, which the other colonies deemed an obstacle to progress, seemed the only solution, and the British Government, once again encumbered with prisoners, eagerly accepted an invitation to send some out to Perth. In 1849 a penal settlement was established, with much money to finance it. Thus resuscitated, the population trebled within the next ten years, but Western Australia did not obtain representative institutions until 1870, after the convict settlement had been abolished, nor full self-government till 1890.

* * *

Early in 1851 a certain Edward Hargraves noticed that the gold-bearing rocks of California resembled those near Bathurst, in New South Wales. News of the discovery leaked out, and within a few weeks the Australian Gold Rush had begun. The gold fever swept the eastern colonies. The whole of Australia seemed to be on the move, marching out to Bathurst, Ballarat, or Bendigo, with picks and shovels on their shoulders, pots and basins around their waists, an excited, feverish crowd, pouring into mining towns that had sprung up overnight, fully equipped with gambling saloons, bars, and brothels. Not all were "diggers," as the miners came to be called, and the hotel-keepers, store-keepers, prostitutes, and other toilers usually fared best. Horses were shod with golden shoes, men lit their pipes with banknotes, so the stories ran, and a bridal party attended a wedding in bright pink velvet. When fortunes could be made and lost overnight there seemed no point in steady employment. Squatters lost their shepherds, business houses their clerks, ships their crews. Early in 1852 there were only two policemen left in Melbourne; more than fifty had gone off to the goldfields. Wages doubled and trebled; prices rose fantastically, and the values of land changed with bewildering rapidity. The other colonies, including New Zealand, lost great numbers of men to the goldfields. In a single year ninety-five thousand immigrants entered Victoria; in five months four thousand men out of a total population, including women and children, of fifty thousand left Tasmania for Victoria.

Keeping the peace, settling disputed claims, providing transport, housing, and enough food to stop famine was a grievous burden for the new administration at Melbourne, most of whose staff had also deserted to the goldfields. But in the next few years independent diggers were replaced by mining companies, which alone had the resources to carry on underground work. Between 1851 and 1861 £124,000,000 worth of gold was raised. A more permanent enrichment was the increase in Australian population, which now rose to over a million.

Wool and agriculture at first were deeply smitten by the rush for gold, and squatters who lost their shepherds cursed its discovery. But Australia gained in the end. Food was needed, and over a million acres were soon under cultivation. The economy of the country, hitherto far too dependent on wool, thus achieved a balance.

The political repercussions were far-reaching. The increase of population, trade, and revenue made it imperative to reform the makeshift constitutions of 1850, and after long discussion in the colonies a number of schemes were laid before the Colonial Office and approved by the home Government. Between 1855 and 1859 two-chamber Parliaments, elected by popular vote and with Ministers responsible to the Lower House, were introduced in all the antipodean states except Western Australia, where, as already related, self-government came later.

Great changes were still to unroll, and Australia as we now know it was born in 1901 by the association of the colonies in a Commonwealth, with a new capital at Canberra. Federation came late and slowly to the southern continent, for the lively, various, widely separated settlements cherished their own self-rule. Even today most of the Australian population dwells in the settlements founded in the nineteenth century. The heart of the country, over a million square miles in extent, has attracted delvers after metals and ranchers of cattle, but it remains largely uninhabited. The silence of the bush and the loneliness of the desert are only disturbed by the passing of some transcontinental express, the whirr of a boomerang, or the drone of a pilotless missile.

* * *

Twelve hundred miles to the east of Australia lie the islands of New Zealand. Here, long before they were discovered by Europeans, a Polynesian warrior race, the Maoris, had sailed across the Pacific from the northeast and established a civilisation notable for the brilliance of its art and the strength of its military system. When Captain Cook visited them towards the end of the eighteenth century he judged that they numbered about a hundred thousand. This was a formidable obstacle to European colonisation, a cultured people long in possession of the land, independent in spirit and skilled in warfare. Soon after Cook's discovery a small English community gained a footing but they were mostly whalers and sealers, shipwrecked mariners, and a few escaped convicts from Australia, enduring a lonely, precarious, and somewhat disreputable existence. Resistance to English colonisation was fortified by the arrival of Christian missionaries.

The missionaries struggled to defeat the power of the traders opposing, in the interest of the Maoris, the admission of English immigrants. For a time they succeeded, and the Australian colonies had been established for half a century before the first official English settlement was founded. News that France was contemplating the annexation of New Zealand compelled the British Government to act. In February, 1840, the Maoris ceded to Great Britain all the rights and powers of sovereignty in return for confirmation in "the full and exclusive possession of their lands and estates."

Two powers were thus established, the Governor at the top of the North Island, and a private joint-stock company at Wellington. The company wanted land, as much and as soon as possible. The treaty and the Colonial Office said it belonged to the Maoris. The two authorities struggled and bickered throughout the forties. "By woman and land are men lost" ran the Maori proverb, and the older chiefs realised that if they lost their land their tribal life would be extinguished. The ingenuity of their laws exasperated settlers who had innocently purchased land for hard cash and found themselves denied possession because the tribe's inalienable rights over the soil were unaffected by private bargains. Nevertheless by 1859 the settlers had occupied seven million acres in the North Island and over thirty-two million acres in the South, where the Maoris were fewer.

The result was Maori wars, a series of intermittent local conflicts lasting from 1843 to 1869. The Maoris fought magnificently, and the admiration of the Regular officers for their opponents sharpened their dislike of the settlers. But by 1869 the Maoris realised that the British had come to stay.

Despite these years of strife, the colony continued to expand. Gibbon Wakefield, an advocate of systematic colonisation, was anxious to overcome the opposition of the missionaries, and persuaded both the Free Church of Scotland and the Church of England to co-operate in establishing two new settlements. These, at Otago and Canterbury, were remarkable applications of his theories. Both were in the South Island, and from 1860 to 1906 it was the South Island, prosperous and comparatively immune from the Maori wars, which contained most of the population. By 1868 the British numbered only about a quarter of a million; twelve years later they were nearly twice as many.

Peace brought prosperity. Great flocks of sheep were reared on the famous Canterbury Plains of the South Island, and a native Corriedale cross-breed was evolved. In the eighteen-sixties gold was found in Otago and Canterbury and there was a temporary boom. The Australian gold discoveries and the swift rise in prices in Melbourne and Sydney gave the island agriculture a flying start. Despite a depression in the eighties, the prosperity of New Zealand has continued to grow ever since. The invention of the refrigerator enabled the colony to compete with European and English producers thirteen thousand miles away. The co-operative movement, especially in dairy-farming, helped small farmers with little capital to build up an industry of remarkable magnitude, and the Dominion of New Zealand soon possessed the highest external trade in proportion to its numbers of any nation in the world.

* * *

New Zealand's political development was no less rapid. Founded in the days of the Durham Report and the first experiments with colonial self-government in Canada, she obtained by the Constitution Act of 1852 a broad measure of independence. Her problems did not, as in the older colonies, centre on the demand for responsible government, but on relations between the central and provincial administrations. Inland travel was so difficult that until late in the nineteenth century the colony remained a number of small, scattered settlements, all differing in the circumstances of their foundation and the character of their interests. This was recognised in the Constitution Act, which set up a number of provincial councils on a democratic basis, each to a considerable extent independent of the General Assembly.

Conflict between the provincial assemblies and the central administration troubled New Zealand politics for twenty years. Some provinces were wealthy, others less so. Otago and Canterbury, stimulated by the discovery of gold, became rich and prosperous, while the settlers in the North Island, harassed by the Maori wars, grew more and more impoverished. At one time Otago and Canterbury wanted to secede. Reform came in 1875, when

the constitution was modified, the provinces were abolished, local administration was placed in the hands of county councils, and the powers of the
central Government were greatly increased. Thus, on a smaller scale, New
Zealand faced and mastered all the problems of federal government thirty
years before Australia. Indeed her political vitality is no less astonishing
than her economic vigour. The tradition and prejudices of the past weighed
less heavily than in the older countries. Many of the reforms introduced
into Great Britain by the Liberal Government of 1906, and then regarded
as extreme innovations, had already been accepted by New Zealand. Industrial arbitration, old-age pensions, factory legislation, State insurance and
medical service, housing Acts, all achieved between 1890 and the outbreak
of the First World War, and State support for co-operative production,
testified to the survival and fertility, even in the remote and unfamiliar
islands of the Pacific, of the British political genius.

BOOK ELEVEN

The Great Republic

CHAPTER SEVENTY-EIGHT

American Epic

THE YEAR 1815 had marked the end of a period of American development. Up to this time the life of the continent had been moulded largely by forces from Europe, but with the conclusion of the War of 1812 against England America turned in upon herself and with her back to the Atlantic looked towards the West. The years following the Peace of Ghent are full of the din of the Westward advance. In politics the vehement struggles of Federalist and Republican were replaced by what a contemporary journalist called "the era of good feelings." But underneath the calm surface of the first decade lay the bitter rivalry of sectional interests which were soon to assume permanent and organised party forms.

The ties with Europe were slowly and inexorably broken. Outstanding disputes between England and America were settled by a series of commissions. The boundaries of Canada were fixed, and both countries agreed to a mutual pact of disarmament upon that storm centre, the Great Lakes. In 1819, after straggling warfare in Spanish Florida, led by the hero of New Orleans, Andrew Jackson, the Spanish Government finally yielded the territory to the United States for five million dollars. Spain had withdrawn from the Northern continent for ever.

But the turmoils of European politics were to threaten America once again for the last time for many years to come. The sovereigns of the Old World were bound together to maintain the principle of monarchy and to cooperate in intervening in any country which showed signs of rebellion against existing institutions. Rumours spread to Washington that the reactionary Powers of Europe, having supported the restoration of the Bourbons in Spain, might promote similar activities in the New World to restore Bourbon sovereignty there. In South America lay the Spanish colonies, which had in their turn thrown off the yoke of their mother country.

The British Government under Canning offered to co-operate with the United States in stopping the extension of this threatening principle of intervention to the New World. Britain announced that she recognised the sovereignty of the Latin republics in South America. Meanwhile President Monroe acted independently and issued his message to Congress proclaiming the principles later known as the Monroe Doctrine. With this valedictory message America concentrated upon her own affairs. A new generation of politicians was rising. The old veterans of the days of the Constitution had most of them vanished from the scene, though Jefferson and Madison lingered on in graceful retirement in their Virginian homes.

*   *   *

Westward lay the march of American Empire. Within thirty years of the establishment of the Union nine new states had been formed in the Mississippi valley, and two in the borders of New England. As early as 1769 men like Daniel Boone had pushed their way into the Kentucky country, skirmishing with the Indians. By 1790 there were thirty-five thousand settlers in the Tennessee country, and double that number in Kentucky. By 1800 there were a million Americans west of the mountain ranges of the Alleghenies. From these new lands a strong, self-reliant Western breed took its place in American life. Modern American democracy was born and cradled in the valley of the Mississippi. The foresight of the first independent Congress of the United States had proclaimed for all time the principle that when new territories gained a certain population they should be admitted to statehood upon an equality with the existing partners of the Union. It is a proof of the quality and power of the Westerners that eleven [1] of the eighteen Presidents of the United States between 1828 and 1901 were either born or passed the greater part of their lives in the valley of the Mississippi.

America was swelling rapidly in numbers as well as in area. Between 1790 and 1820 the population increased from four to nine and a half millions. Thereafter it almost doubled every twenty years. Nothing like such a rate of growth had before been noted in the world. The settlement of great bodies of men in the West was eased by the removal of the Indian tribes from the regions east of the Mississippi. They had been defeated when they fought as allies of Britain in the War of 1812. Now it became Federal policy to eject them. The lands thus thrown open were made available in smaller units and at lower prices than in earlier years to the incoming colonists—for we might as well use this honourable word about them, unpopular though it may now be. Colonisation, in the true sense, was the task that engaged the Western pioneers. Farmers from stony New England were tilling the fertile empty territories to the south of the Great Lakes, while in the South the Black Belt of Alabama and Mississippi proved fruitful soil for the recent art of large-scale cotton cultivation.

But this ceaseless expansion to the West also changed the national centre of gravity, and intense stresses arose of interest as well as of feeling. The Eastern states, North and South alike, presently found their political power challenged by these settler communities, and the lure of pioneering

[1] Jackson, Harrison, Polk, Taylor, Lincoln, Johnson, Grant, Hayes, Garfield, Harrison, McKinley.

created the fear of a labour shortage in the Eastern factories. In fact the gap was filled by new immigrants from Europe. As the frontier line rolled westward the new communities rising rapidly to statehood forced their own problems and desires upon the exhilarated but also embarrassed Federal Government. The East feared the approaching political dominance of the democratic West. The West resented the financial and economic bias of the Eastern moneyed classes. The forces of divergence grew strong, and only the elasticity of the Federal system prevented the usual conflict between a mother country and its sturdy children.

The political history of these years between 1815 and 1830 is confused but by 1830 the situation cleared and the great parties of the future stood opposed. With the growth of Federal legislation and the creation of a national economic framework of tariffs, banks, and land policies the Union felt the stress of state jealousies and rival interests. The expansion to the West tilted the political balance in favour of the new Western states, and strenuously the older forces in the North and South resisted the rising power of democracy within the Federal State. They had to confront not only the desires of the West, but also those of the small planters in the South and of the working men in the industrial North. Many of these people now for the first time began to receive the vote as universal manhood suffrage was more widely adopted. The electorate was expanding and eager to make its voice heard. At the same time the convention system was introduced into American politics. Candidates for the Presidency and for lesser public office in the states gradually ceased to be nominated by restricted party caucuses. Instead they were selected at meetings of delegates representing a variety of local and specialised opinion. This obliged the would-be President and other public office-holders to be more responsive to the divergences of popular will. Politicians of conservative mind like Henry Clay and John C. Calhoun feared the menacing signs of particularism and the consequent threat to the Union. These men formulated what they called the "American System." But their policy was merely a re-expression of the ideas of Hamilton. They sought to harmonise economic interests within a Federal framework.

Public works were set on foot; steamboats appeared upon the Mississippi, and the concentration of trade in the Gulf of Mexico roused alarm in the Atlantic states, who saw themselves being deprived of profitable markets. But they hastened themselves to compete with this increasing activity. In 1817 the state of New York began the construction of the Erie Canal, which was to make New York City the most prosperous of the Eastern seaports. The great Cumberland high-road across the Ohio to Illinois was built with Federal money, and a network of roads was to bind the eager West to the Eastern states. But the history of the American nineteenth century is dominated by the continually threatened cleavage of East and

West, and, upon the Atlantic seaboard, of the Northern and Southern states. In the early years of the century the keynote of politics was the rival bidding of Northern and Southern politicians for the votes and support of the Western states.

*   *   *

The issue of slavery was soon to trouble the relations of the North and South. In 1819 a Bill was tabled in Congress to admit Missouri as a state to the Union. This territory lay inside the bounds of the Louisiana Purchase, where the future of slavery had not so far been decided by Federal law. As the people of Missouri proposed to allow slavery in their draft constitution the Northerners looked upon this Bill as an aggressive move to increase the voting power of the South. A wild campaign of mutual recrimination followed. But with the increasing problem of the West facing them both, North and South could not afford to quarrel, and the angry sectional strife stirred up by this Bill ended in a compromise which was to hold until the middle of the century. Missouri was admitted as a slave-holding state, and slavery was prohibited north of latitude 36° 30′ within the existing territories of the Union which did not yet enjoy statehood. As part of the compromise Maine, which had just severed itself from Massachusetts, was admitted as a free state, making the division between slave and free equal, being twelve each. Far-seeing men realised the impending tragedy of this division. John Quincy Adams noted in his diary, "I considered it at once as the knell of the Union. I take it for granted that the present question is a mere preamble—a title-page to a great, tragic volume."

It was this cultured New Englander, son of the second President of the United States, who succeeded Monroe in 1825. The so-called era of good feelings was coming to a close, and the four years of his Presidency were to reveal the growth of lively party politics. All the political and economic interests of the Eastern states were forced on to the defensive by the rapid expansion of the West.

The West grouped itself around the figure of the frontier General Andrew Jackson, who claimed to represent the true Jeffersonian principles of democracy against the corrupt moneyed interests of the East. Adams received the support of those classes who viewed with alarm the growing power of the farmers and settlers of the frontier. The issue between the two factions was joined in 1828, when Jackson stood as rival candidate against Adams's re-election. In the welter of this election two new parties were born, the Democrats and the National Republicans, later called the Whigs. It was the fiercest campaign since Jefferson had driven the elder Adams from office in 1800. As the results came in it was seen that Adams had won practically nothing outside New England, and that in the person of Andrew Jackson the West had reached controlling power. Here at last was an American President who had no spiritual contacts whatever with the Old World, who represented at the White House the spirit of the American frontier. To many it seemed that democracy had triumphed indeed.

To the men of the West Jackson was their General, marching against the political monopoly of the moneyed classes. The complications of high politics caused difficulties for the backwoodsman. His simple mind, suspicious of his opponents, made him open to influence by more partisan and self-seeking politicians. In part he was guided by Martin Van Buren, his Secretary of State. But he relied even more heavily for advice on political cronies of his own choosing, who were known as the "Kitchen Cabinet," because they were not office-holders. Jackson was led to believe that his first duty was to cleanse the stables of the previous régime. His dismissal of a large number of civil servants brought the spoils system, long prevalent in many states, firmly into the Federal machine.

Two great recurring problems in American politics, closely related, demanded the attention of President Andrew Jackson—the supremacy of the Union and the organisation of a national economy. Protection favoured the interests of the North at the expense of the South, and in 1832 the state of South Carolina determined to challenge the right of the Federal Government to impose a tariff system, and, echoing the Virginia and Kentucky resolutions of 1798, expounded in its most extreme form the doctrine of state rights. In the party struggles which followed the votes of the Western states held the balance. Their burning question was the regulation of the sale of public land by the Federal Government.

The debates on these themes in the American Senate contained the finest examples of American oratory. In this battle of giants the most imposing of them all was Daniel Webster, of Massachusetts. He it was who stated the case for the Union and refuted the case of South Carolina in one of the most famous of American speeches. His words enshrined the new feeling of nation-wide patriotism that was gathering strength, at least in the North. A broader sense of loyalty to the Union was developing. "It is to that Union," Webster declared in the Senate, "we owe our safety at home, and our consideration and dignity abroad. It is to that Union that we are chiefly indebted for whatever makes us most proud of our country. That Union we reached only by the discipline of our virtues in the severe school of adversity . . .

"While the Union lasts we have high, exciting, gratifying prospects spread out before us, for us and our children. Beyond that I seek not to penetrate the veil. God grant that in my day at least that curtain may not rise! God grant that on my vision never may be opened what lies behind! When my eyes shall be turned to behold for the last time the sun in heaven, may I not see him shining on the broken and dishonoured fragments of a once glorious Union; on states dissevered, discordant, belligerent; on a land rent with civil feuds, or drenched, it may be, in fraternal blood! Let their last feeble and lingering glance rather behold the gorgeous ensign of the Republic, now known and honoured throughout the earth, still full high advanced, its arms and trophies streaming in their original lustre, not a stripe erased or polluted, not a single star obscured, bearing for its motto no such miserable interrogatory as 'What is all this worth?' nor those other words of delusion and folly, 'Liberty first and Union afterwards,' but everywhere, spread all over in characters of living light, blazing on all its ample folds, as they float over the sea and over the land, and in every wind under the whole heavens, that other sentiment, dear to every true American heart— Liberty *and* Union, now and for ever, one and inseparable!"

On the Indiana frontier a young man was moved by this speech. His name was Abraham Lincoln.

President Jackson himself was impressed, and in his war-like approach to politics was prepared to coerce South Carolina by force. But a tactful compromise was reached. The tariff was lowered but rendered permanent, and the Force Act, authorising the President to use the Army if necessary to collect the customs duties, was declared null and void by South Carolina. Here then for a space the matter was left. But the South Carolina theory of "nullification" showed the danger of the Republic, and with the prophetic instinct of the simple frontiersman Jackson pointed to the future: "The next pretext will be the Negro or slavery question."

* * *

The westward tide rolled on, bearing with it new problems of adjustment. The generation of the 1840's saw their culmination. During these years there took place the annexation of Texas, a war with Mexico, the conquest of California, and the settlement of the Oregon boundary with Great Britain. Adventurous Americans in search of land and riches had been since 1820 crossing the Mexican boundary into the Texas country, which belonged to the Republic of Mexico, freed from Spain in 1821. While this community was growing, American sailors on the Pacific coast, captains interested in the China trade, established themselves in the ports of the Mexican Province of California. Pioneers pushed their way overland in search of skins and furs, and by 1826 reached the mission stations of the Province. The Mexicans, alarmed at the appearance of these settlers, vainly sought to stem the flood; for Mexican Governments were highly unstable, and in distant Provinces their writ hardly ran. But there appeared on the scene a new military dictator, Santa Anna, determined to strengthen Mexican authority, and at once a revolt broke out. In November, 1835, the Americans in Texas erected an autonomous state and raised the Lone Star flag. The Mexicans, under Santa Anna, marched northwards. At the Mission House of the Alamo in March, 1836, a small body of Texans, fighting to the last man, was exterminated in one of the epic fights of American history by a superior Mexican force. The whole Province was aroused. Under the leadership of General Sam Houston from Tennessee a force was raised, and in savage fighting the Mexican army of Santa Anna was in its

Horatio, Viscount Nelson
by Lemmel Abbott

On the morning of October 21, 1805, before the Battle of Trafalgar, Nelson gave a signal to bear down on the enemy in two lines. Having seen that all was as it should be, Nelson retired to his cabin and wrote the following prayer:

Monday, October 21st

At daylight saw the Enemy's Combined Fleet from East to E.S.E. bore away; made the signal for Order of Sailing, and to Prepare for Battle; the Enemy with their heads to the Southward; at seven the Enemy wearing in succession. May the Great God, Whom I worship, grant to my Country, and for the benefit of Europe in general, a great and glorious Victory; and may no misconduct in anyone tarnish it; and may humanity after Victory be the predominant feature in the British Fleet. For myself, individually, I commit my life to Him who made me, and may His blessing light upon my endeavors for serving my Country faithfully. To Him I resign myself and the just cause which is entrusted me to defend. Amen. Amen. Amen.

turn destroyed and its commander captured at San Jacinto River. The Texans had stormed the positions with the cry "Remember the Alamo!" The independence of Texas was recognised by Santa Anna. His act was repudiated later by the Mexican Government, but their war effort was exhausted, and the Texans organised themselves into a republic, electing Sam Houston as President.

For the next ten years the question of the admission of Texas as a state of the Union was a burning issue in American politics. As each new state demanded entry into the Union so the feeling for and against slavery ran higher. The great Abolitionist journalist, William Lloyd Garrison, called for a secession of the Northern states if the slave state of Texas was admitted to the Union. The Southerners, realising that Texan votes would give them a majority in the Senate if this vast territory was admitted as a number of separate states, clamoured for annexation. The capitalists of the East were committed, through the formation of land companies, to exploit Texas, and besides the issue of dubious stocks by these bodies vast quantities of paper notes and bonds of the new Texan Republic were floated in the United States. The speculation in these helped to split the political opposition of the Northern states to the annexation. Even more important was the conversion of many Northerners to belief in the "Manifest Destiny" of the United States. This meant that their destiny was to spread across the whole of the North American continent. The Democratic Party in the election of 1844 called for the occupation of Oregon as well as the annexation of Texas, thus holding out to the North the promise of Oregon as a counterweight to Southern Texas. The victory of the Democratic candidate, James K. Polk, was interpreted as a mandate for admitting Texas, and this was done by joint resolution of Congress in February, 1845.

It remained to persuade Mexico to recognise this state of affairs, and also to fix the boundaries of Texas. President Polk was determined to push them as far south as possible, and war was inevitable. It broke out in May, 1846. Meanwhile a similar train of events was unfolding on the other side of the continent. All this time American penetration of the West had continued, often with grim experiences of starvation and winter snows. Nothing could stop the migration towards the Pacific. The lure of the rich China trade and the dream of controlling the Western Ocean brought the acquisition of California to the fore, and gave her even more importance in American eyes than Texas. In June, 1846, the American settlers in California, instigated from Washington, raised the Bear Flag as their standard of revolt and declared their independence on the Texan model. Soon afterwards American forces arrived and the Stars and Stripes replaced the Bear.

The American advance was rapidly gathering momentum. The Mexican army of the North was twice beaten by General Zachary Taylor, a future

President. A force under General Winfield Scott was landed at Vera Cruz and marched on Mexico City. The capital fell to the Americans after a month of street fighting in September, 1847. On this expedition a number of young officers distinguished themselves. They included Captain Robert E. Lee, Captain George B. McClellan, Lieutenant Ulysses S. Grant, and Colonel Jefferson Davis.

Mexico sued for peace, and by the treaty which followed she was obliged not only to recognise the annexation of Texas, but also to cede California, Arizona, and New Mexico. Lieutenant Grant confided his impressions to his memoirs: "I do not think there was ever a more wicked war than that waged by the United States on Mexico. I thought so at the time, when I was a youngster, only I had not moral courage enough to resign." But the expansive force of the American peoples was explosive. "Manifest Destiny" was on the march, and it was unfortunate that Mexico stood in the path. The legend of Imperialism and the belief in the right of the United States to exploit both continents, North and South, which sprang from the Mexican War henceforward cast their shadow on co-operation between the South American republics and the United States.

*   *   *

The immediate gains were enormous. While the commissioners were actually debating the treaty with Mexico an American labourer in California discovered the first nugget of gold in that region. The whole economy of a sleepy Mexican province, with its age-old Spanish culture, was suddenly overwhelmed by a mad rush for gold. In 1850 the population of California was about eighty-two thousand souls. In two years the figure had risen to two hundred and seven thousand. A lawless mining society arose upon the Pacific coast. From the cities of the East and from the adjoining states men of all professions and classes of society flocked to California, many being murdered, killed in quarrels, by cold and famine, or drowned in the sea voyage round Cape Horn. The gold of California lured numbers to their death, and a few to riches beyond belief.

> Oh! California,
> That's the land for me;
> I'm off to Sacramento
> With my washbowl on my knee.

The anarchy of the gold rush brought an urgent demand for settled government in California, and the old perplexing, rasping quarrel over the admission of a new state was heard again at Washington. For the moment nothing was done, and the Californians called their own state convention and drew up a temporary constitution.

During all this time, farther to the north, another territory had been coming into being. The "Oregon Trail" had brought many men from the more crowded states of the North-East to find their homes and establish their farms along the undefined Canadian frontier to the Pacific. With the prospect of war in the South for the acquisition of Texas and California, the American Government was not anxious to embark upon a quarrel with Great Britain upon its Northern frontier. There was strong opposition by the Southerners to the acquisition of Oregon, where the Northern pioneers were opposed to slavery. Oregon would be another "free soil state." Negotiations were opened with Britain, and in spite of electioneering slogans of "Fifty-four forty or fight" the boundary was settled in June, 1846, by peaceful diplomacy along the forty-ninth parallel. This solution owed much to the accommodating nature of the Foreign Secretary in Peel's Government, Lord Aberdeen. The controversy now died down, and in 1859 the territory of Oregon reached statehood.

Among the many settlements which lay dotted over the whole of the American continent was the Mormon colony at Salt Lake City. In the spring of 1847 members of this revivalist and polygamist sect started from the state of Illinois under their prophet leader, Brigham Young, to find homes free from molestation in the West. By the summer they reached the country round Salt Lake, and two hours after their arrival they had begun establishing their homes and ploughing up the soil. Within three years a flourishing community of eleven thousand souls, combining religious fervour, philoprogenitiveness, and shrewd economic sense, had been established by careful planning in the Salt Lake country, and in 1850 the territory received recognition by the Federal Government under the name of Utah.

With the establishment of this colony the settlement of the continent was comprehensive. The task before the Federal Government was now to organise the Far Western territory won in the Mexican War and in the compromise with Britain. From this there rose in its final and dread form the issue of bond and free.

CHAPTER SEVENTY-NINE

Slavery and Secession

IN THE years following 1850 the prospects of the United States filled America with hope and Europe with envious admiration. The continent had been conquered and nourished. Exports, imports, and, most of all, internal trade, had been more than doubled in a decade. The American mercantile marine outnumbered the ships under the British flag. More than thirty thousand miles of railway overcame the vast distances, and added economic cohesion to political unity. Here democracy seemed at last to have achieved both prosperity and power. The abounding industrialism of the Eastern states was balanced and fed by an immense agriculture of yeomen farmers. In all material affairs the American people surpassed anything that history had known before.

Yet thoughtful men and travellers had for some years observed the approach of a convulsion which would grip not only the body but the soul of the United States. Of the three races who dwelt in North America, the Whites towered overwhelming and supreme. The Red men, the original inhabitants, age-long product of the soil and climate, shrank back, pushed, exploited, but always disdainful, from the arms, and still more from the civilisation, of the transplanted European society by which they were ousted and eclipsed. The Black men presented a problem, moral, social, economic, and political, the like of which had never before been known. The proud Redskin was set upon his road to ruin by an excessive liberty. Almost all the four million Negroes were slaves.

In regions so wide and varied as those of the Union extreme divergences of interest, outlook, and culture had developed. South of the fortieth parallel and the projecting angle formed by the Mississippi and the Ohio the institution of Negro slavery had long reigned almost unquestioned. Upon this basis the whole life of the Southern states had been erected. It was a strange, fierce, old-fashioned life. An aristocracy of planters, living in rural magnificence and almost feudal state, and a multitude of smallholders, grew cotton for the world by slave-labour. Of the six million white inhabitants of the so-called "slave states" less than three hundred and fifty thousand owned slaves, and only forty thousand controlled plantations requiring a working unit of more than twenty field hands. But the three or four thousand principal slave-owners generally ruled the politics of the South as effectively as the medieval baronage had ruled England. Beneath them, but not dissociated from them, were, first, several hundred thousand small slave-owners, to whom "the peculiar institution," as it had already come to be called, was a domestic convenience; second, a strong class of yeomen farmers similar to that existing in the North; and, thirdly, a rabble of "mean whites" capable of being formed into an army.

It is almost impossible for us nowadays to understand how profoundly and inextricably Negro slavery was interwoven into the whole life, economy, and culture of the Southern states. The tentacles of slavery spread widely through the Northern "free" states, along every channel of business dealing and many paths of political influence. One assertion alone reveals the powerlessness of the community to shake itself free from the frightful disease which had become part of its being. It was said that over six hundred and sixty thousand slaves were held by ministers of the Gospel and members of the different Protestant Churches. Thus the institution of slavery was not only defended by every argument of self-interest, but many a Southern pulpit championed it as a system ordained by the Creator and sanctified by the Gospel of Christ.

Meanwhile the North, once largely indifferent to the fate of slaves, had been converted by the 1850's to the cause of anti-slavery. For twenty years William Lloyd Garrison's newspaper, *The Liberator,* had been carrying on from Boston a campaign of the utmost virulence against the institution of slavery. This public print was not very widely read, but its language enraged the South. At the same time the American Anti-Slavery Society in New York and other humanitarian bodies were issuing vigorous tracts and periodicals. They employed scores of agents to preach Abolition up and down the land. The result was a hardening of sentiment on both sides of the question. It was hardened still further in 1852, when Harriet Beecher Stowe published *Uncle Tom's Cabin.* Her work was frankly propagandist; she used every weapon. In its pages the theoretical and religious arguments are bandied to and fro, but there was one method in which she excelled all other assailants of the evil. She presented to her readers a succession of simple, poignant incidents inseparable from a system of slavery: the breaking up of the Negro's home and family, the parting of husband and wife, the sale of the baby from the breast of its mother; the indiscriminate auction of the slaves on the death of a good employer; the impotence of the virtuous slave-owner, the cruelties of the bad; the callous traffic of the slave-dealers, and the horrors of the remote plantations, the whipping establishments to which fine ladies sent their maids for chastisement for minor faults; the aggravated problem of the quadroon and the mulatto; the almost-white slave girl sold and resold for lust; the bringing into the world of slave children indistinguishable in their colour from the dominant race—all these features of the life of a civilised, educated, modern Christian community, occupying enormous fertile regions of the earth, were introduced with every trapping of art and appeal into her pages.

Such advocacy was devastating. By the end of the year hundreds of thousands of copies of *Uncle Tom's Cabin* had been sold in the United States. In September, it is said, ten thousand copies of it were being supplied every day to a single firm of English booksellers. By the end of 1852 more than a million copies had been sold in England, probably ten times as many as had ever been sold of any other work except the Bible and the Prayer Book. *Uncle Tom's Cabin* rolled round the world in every language and was read with passion and emotion in every country. It was the herald of the storm.

*   *   *

The moral surge of the age had first suppressed, by naval power, the slave trade on the seas, and thereafter abolished the status of slavery throughout the British Empire. The same temper stirred alike the New England states of the Atlantic shore and the powerful, swiftly growing population of the Middle West of the American Union. A gulf of sentiment and interest opened and widened between the Northern and Southern states. Across this gulf there flashed for some years the interchanges of thought, of argument and parley. In the North many of the leaders, religious and secular, felt intensely that the whole future of the noble continent they had won lay under a curse. If it could not at once be lifted, at least it must be prevented from spreading. Nor was this passion in any degree excited, in its earliest phase, by commercial rivalry. There was no doubt that slave labour could not hold its own with free labour in tilling the soil where the climatic conditions were similar. The contrast between the activity and progress of a free state on the Ohio and the stagnation of a slave state on the opposite bank was glaringly apparent to all beholders. It was the contrast between the nineteenth century and the seventeenth. The Northern states were not undersold by the competition of the South. They also needed the cotton crop in which alone slave labour was an economic advantage. The issue was not economic, but moral. It was also social. The slave-owning aristocracy in much of the South felt a class-superiority to the business, manufacturing, and financial society of the North. The Puritan stock of the North regarded the elegant gentry of the South with something of the wrath and censure of Cromwell's Ironsides for Rupert's Cavaliers. Indeed, at many points the grim struggle which impended resembled and reproduced in its passions the antagonisms of the English Civil War.

But the actual occasion of quarrel was political and constitutional. The North held tenaciously to the Federal conceptions of Alexander Hamilton. In the South sovereign state rights was paramount. Many of the Southern Generals, like Joseph E. Johnston, Ambrose P. Hill, and FitzHugh Lee, had never owned a slave. A Virginian colonel of the United States Army serving in Texas, Robert E. Lee, wrote that slavery was "a moral and political evil in any country," as few in an enlightened age could but acknowledge. But upon the constitutional issue all these men of the highest morale and virtue deemed themselves bound to the death to the fortunes and sovereign independence of their states. The North, it was said, was enriching itself at the expense of the South. The Yankees were jealous of a style and distinction to which vulgar commercialism could never attain. They had no right to use the Federal Constitution which the great Virginians Washington and Madison had largely founded, in order to bind the most famous states of the Union to their dictates. They did not understand the totally different conditions of Southern life. They maligned and insulted a civilisation more elevated in manners, if not in worldly wealth, than their own. They sought to impose the tyranny of their ideas upon states which had freely joined the Union for common purposes, and might as freely

374

depart when those purposes had been fulfilled.

The old Missouri compromise of 1820 no longer satisfied the passions now aroused. By the Mexican War extensive new territories had been acquired; what principle should be applied to them? The Southerners, still dominated by John C. Calhoun, held that the territories belonged to the states united, not to the United States, that slaves were Common Law property, and that Congress had no right to prohibit slavery in the Territories. The demand of California for admission to the Union precipitated the crisis. Many moderates had wanted to prolong the line of the Missouri compromise across the continent to the Pacific. But in California it did not meet the case. It would have run right through the middle of the state. Besides, the constitution of California prohibited slavery, and its introduction would set a precedent in those states which were to be created out of the conquests from Mexico. In January, 1850, the gathering storm-clouds of slavery and secession evoked in the Senate the last of the great oratorical debates in which Calhoun, Clay, and Webster vied with one another. Henry Clay produced his last compromise in resolutions to postpone collision. California should be admitted to the Union immediately as a "free" state; the territorial Governments in New Mexico and Utah should be organised without mentioning slavery; a stringent Fugitive Slave Law would appease the South, and the assumption of the Texas National Debt by the Federal Government the bond-holders of the North. By these mutual concessions Clay hoped to preserve the political unity of the continent. On this last occasion he rose and spoke for nearly two days in the Senate. Calhoun was dying, and sat grimly silent in the Senate. One of his colleagues spoke his plea for him. "I have, Senators, believed from the first that the agitation of the subject of slavery would, if not prevented by some timely and effective measure, end in disunion. . . . The cords that bind the states together are snapping."

Daniel Webster rose three days later: "I speak today for the preservation of the Union. Hear me for my cause." The voices of Webster and Clay prevailed and the compromise was adopted. Passions were for the moment stilled by what was called the "principle of popular sovereignty." This meant that when the new Territories became states the settlers should decide for themselves for or against slavery. Calhoun was already dead, and within two years Clay and Webster passed from the scene. They left behind them an uneasy calm. Meanwhile the continent developed at dizzy speed. By 1850 nine thousand miles of railway had been built; by 1861 over thirty thousand. German and Irish immigrants from Europe streamed into the new lands of the West. Agricultural machinery changed the settler type. The prairie farmer replaced the backwoodsman, and the cultivation of the Great Plains began in earnest.

*   *   *

375

The anti-slavery forces in the North were determined to resist the introduction of slavery into the new territories. In May the Kansas-Nebraska Act was passed by the Senate. The new territories of the Great Plains were to be divided into Kansas and Nebraska, and the principle of "popular sovereignty" was affirmed. This Act was a signal for outbursts of agitation and violence in the Northern states. Under the Fugitive Slave Law Federal agents had already been instructed to arrest and send back to their masters slaves who had escaped into the free states. There had been innumerable minor incidents, but now, on the morrow of the Kansas-Nebraska Act, the patience of the North was at an end. The day after it came into force a Boston mob attempted to rescue a fugitive slave, Anthony Burns, who was detained for deportation to the South. It took a battalion of artillery, four platoons of marines, the sheriff's posse, and twenty-two companies of the militia to line the streets and bring the slave to the ship at Boston wharf. "It cost the United States about a hundred thousand dollars to return the slave to his master. The real bill came later, and it was paid in blood." [1]

In the new territory of Kansas there was murderous fighting between the free-soil and pro-slavery partisans. Slavery-men sacked the free-soil town of Lawrence, and three days later John Brown, a Puritanical mystic and militant Abolitionist from Ohio, with his four sons, dragged five slavery-men from their beds and slaughtered them as a reprisal. Over two hundred lives were lost in this local reign of terror, but John Brown escaped. At every point, in every walk of life, the opposing causes came into conflict. Charles Sumner, Senator from Massachusetts, was beaten over the head with a cane in the Senate by a South Carolina Representative till he was unconscious. All the anti-slavery elements in the North and West had coalesced after the passing of the Kansas-Nebraska Act in a new Republican Party upon the platform of anti-slavery. Feeling ran high in the Presidential elections of 1856. But Democratic influences nominated "a Northern man with Southern principles," James Buchanan of Pennsylvania, and for the last time Southern influences had their voice at Washington.

The savage struggle between free-soil and slavery in the Great Plains brought from the backwoods into national politics a new figure. Abraham Lincoln, a small-town lawyer from Springfield, Illinois, was stirred to the depths of his being by the passing of the Kansas-Nebraska Act. He had already served a term in Congress; now he stood for the Senate. He espoused the duty of opposing by the moral force of his personality the principle of slavery. " 'A house divided against itself cannot stand.' I believe this Government cannot endure permanently half slave and half free. I do not expect the Union to be dissolved—I do not expect the house to fall—but I do expect it will cease to be divided. It will become all one thing or all the other. Either the opponents of slavery will arrest the further

[1] Morison and Commager, *Growth of the American Republic,* vol. i, p. 622.

spread of it, and place it where the public mind shall rest in the belief that it is in the course of ultimate extinction; or its advocates will push it forward till it shall become alike lawful in all the states, old as well as new, North as well as South." In a series of public debates and speeches Lincoln fought Senator Stephen A. Douglas throughout the prairie towns of Illinois in the summer and autumn of 1858, and although he was beaten for the Senatorship he had already become a national figure. He had made slavery a moral and not a legal issue, and he had propounded the disruptive idea of overriding a Supreme Court decision in the case of Dred Scott and of outlawing slavery in the new territories. He felt instinctively the weakness and impermanence of this new concession to the susceptibilities of the South. He realised that as the agitation for abolition grew, so the Southerners would demand further guarantees to protect their own peculiar slave society. President Buchanan and the Democratic circle around the White House talked of conquering Cuba and Nicaragua in the hope of adding new slave-owning territories to the Union. Southern business men urged reopening the slave trade owing to the high price of slaves, while all the time the North, in a series of disturbing incidents, defied the Fugitive Slave Act of 1850.

It needed but a spark to cause an explosion. In October, 1859, the fanatic John Brown, with his sons and a dozen followers, seized the Federal arsenal at Harpers Ferry, on the slavery frontier, declared war upon the United States, and liberated a number of bewildered slaves. He was attacked by the Federal marines under Colonel Robert E. Lee, and after some loss of life was captured, severely wounded. He was tried and hanged with four of his adherents. The South, declaring the outrage the work of the Republican Party, was convulsed with excitement. In the North millions regarded John Brown as a martyr. His body lay mouldering in the grave, but his soul went marching on.

CHAPTER EIGHTY

The Union in Danger

NOW CAME the fateful Presidential election of 1860. In February the Southern Senator Jefferson Davis demanded that the Northern states should repeal their Personal Liberty Laws and cease to interfere with the Fugitive Slave Law of 1850. Chief Justice Taney's decision of the Supreme Court in the Dred Scott case that slavery could not be prohibited by the

Federal Government in the Territories of the United States must be obeyed. The Federal Government, Davis demanded, should protect slavery in those areas. Against this, Abraham Lincoln, in New York and elsewhere, unfolded in magnificent orations, calm, massive, and magnanimous, the anti-slavery cause. In this crisis the Democratic Party split. When Douglas, their Presidential candidate, carried a set of compromise proposals in the party meeting at Charleston the Alabama delegation marched out of the hall, followed by those of seven other cotton states. Lincoln would probably in any case have been elected, but the division among the Democrats made his victory certain. The cotton states put forward as their candidate John C. Breckinridge, of Kentucky, who was at that moment Vice-President. He stood as a Southern Rights Democrat. The scene was further complicated by the appearance of a fourth aspirant, Senator John Bell, of Kentucky, who called himself a Constitutional Unionist and was an old-fashioned Whig. Secession was not the issue, though everyone felt that the South would in fact secede if Lincoln won. Slavery was the dominating and all-absorbing topic. Lincoln and the Republicans wanted to reverse the Dred Scott decision, prohibit slavery in the Territories and confine it within its existing limits. Douglas and the official Democrats were for non-intervention in the Territories and "popular sovereignty" by the settlers. Breckinridge and his supporters demanded that slavery in the Territories should be protected by law. Bell tried to ignore the issue altogether in the blissful hope that the nation could be made to forget everything that had happened since the Mexican War. On November 6, 1860, Lincoln was elected. Douglas, just as ardently for the Union, was the runner-up on the popular vote. Breckinridge, who was reputed to be the Secessionist candidate in spite of his assurances of loyalty to the Union, came third. Even in the slave states he failed to win a majority of the votes.

In spite of this great majority against breaking the Union, the state of South Carolina, where the doctrines of Calhoun were cherished, passed by a unanimous vote at Charleston on December 20 its famous Ordinance of Secession, declaring that the Union of 1788 between South Carolina and all other states, Northern and Southern alike, was dissolved. This precipitate and mortal act was hailed with delirious enthusiasm. The cannons fired; the bells rang; flags flew on every house. The streets were crowded with cheering multitudes. The example of South Carolina was followed by the states of Mississippi, Florida, Alabama, Georgia, Louisiana, and Texas. Delegates from these sovereign states, as they regarded themselves, met in Alabama in February and organised a new Confederacy, of which Jefferson Davis was chosen President. A new constitution, similar in almost all respects to that of the United States, but founded explicitly upon slavery, was proclaimed. A Confederate flag—the Stars and Bars—was adopted. Jefferson Davis was chosen Provisional President and was authorised to raise an army of a hundred thousand men, large sums were voted, and a delegation of three was sent abroad to seek recognition and friendship in Europe. All the leading figures concerned in this decision harboured grave illusions. They thought the North would not try to coerce them back into the Union. If it made the attempt they believed the Yankees would be no match for Southern arms. And if the North imposed a blockade the Confederates expected that the Powers of Europe would intervene on their behalf. They cherished the notion that "King Cotton" was so vital to Britain and France that neither country could peaceably allow its supplies to be cut off.

Buchanan was still President of the United States, and Lincoln, President-Elect, could not take office till March. For four months the dying administration gaped upon a distracted land. Buchanan, longing for release, tried desperately to discharge his duties and follow a middle course. All counter-preparations in the North were paralysed. On the other hand, he refused to recognise the validity of secession. Practically all the Federal posts, with their small garrisons, in the Southern states had passed without fighting into the possession of the Confederacy. But the forts of Charleston harbour, under the command of Major Anderson, a determined officer, continued to fly the Stars and Stripes. When called upon to surrender he withdrew to Fort Sumter, which stood on an island. His food ran low, and when a ship bearing supplies from the North arrived to succour him Confederate batteries from the mainland drove it back by cannon-fire. Meanwhile strenuous efforts at compromise were being made. Many Northerners were prepared for the sake of peace to give way to the South on the slavery issue. But Lincoln was inflexible. He would not repudiate the platform on which he had been elected. He could not countenance the extension of slavery to the Territories. This was the nub on which all turned. In this tense and tremendous situation Abraham Lincoln was sworn President on March 4, 1861. Around him the structure of Federal Government was falling to pieces. Officials and officers were every day leaving for their home states in the South. Hands were clasped between old comrades for the last time in friendship.

The North, for all its detestation of slavery, had by no means contemplated civil war. Between the extremists on both sides there was an immense borderland where all interests and relationships were interlaced by every tie of kinship and custom and every shade of opinion found its expression. So far only the cotton states, or Lower South, had severed themselves from the Union. Missouri, Arkansas, Kentucky, Tennessee, North Carolina, Maryland, Delaware, and above all the noble and ancient Virginia, the Old Dominion, the birthplace of Washington, the fountain of American tradition and inspiration, still hung in the balance. Lincoln appealed for patience and conciliation. He declared himself resolved to hold the forts and property of the United States. He disclaimed all intention of invading the South. He announced that he would not interfere with slavery in the Southern states. He revived the common memories of the North and South, which, like "mystic cords, stretch from every battlefield and patriot grave to every living heart . . . over this broad land." "In your hands," he exclaimed, "my dissatisfied fellow-countrymen, and not in mine, is this momentous issue of civil war. The Government will not assail you. You can have no conflict without yourselves being the aggressors. You have no oath registered in Heaven to destroy the Government, while I shall have the most solemn one to preserve and defend it."

On April 8 Lincoln informed the Governor of South Carolina of his intention to re-victual Major Anderson and his eighty-three men in Fort Sumter. Thereupon President Davis ordered General Beauregard, who commanded seven thousand men at Charleston, to demand the immediate surrender of the fort. Anderson, admitting that famine would reduce him in a few days, nevertheless continued constant. Vain parleys were held; but before dawn on April 12 the Confederate batteries opened a general bombardment, and for thirty-four hours fifty heavy cannon rained their shells upon Fort Sumter. Anderson and his handful of men, sheltering in their bomb-proof caverns, feeling that all had been done that honour and law required, marched out begrimed and half suffocated on the 14th, and were allowed to depart to the North. No blood had been shed, but the awful act of rebellion had occurred.

The cannonade at Fort Sumter resounded through the world. It roused and united the people of the North. All the free states stood together. Party divisions were effaced. Douglas, Lincoln's rival at the election, with a million and a half Democratic votes at his back, hastened to the White House to grasp Lincoln's hand. Ex-President Buchanan declared, "The North will sustain the administration almost to a man." Upon this surge and his own vehement resolve, Lincoln issued a proclamation calling for "the militia of the Union to the number of seventy-five thousand" to suppress "combinations" in seven states "too powerful to be suppressed by the ordinary course of judicial proceedings." Here, then, was the outbreak of the American Civil War.

*　　　*　　　*

Upon Lincoln's call to arms to coerce the seceding states Virginia made without hesitation the choice which she was so heroically to sustain. She would not fight on the issue of slavery, but stood firm on the constitutional ground that every state in the Union enjoyed sovereign rights. On this principle Virginians denied the claim of the Federal Government to exercise coercion. On the 17th of April the Virginia Convention at Richmond, by a vote of one hundred and three to forty-six, took that state out of the Union, and placed her entire military forces at the disposal of the Confed-

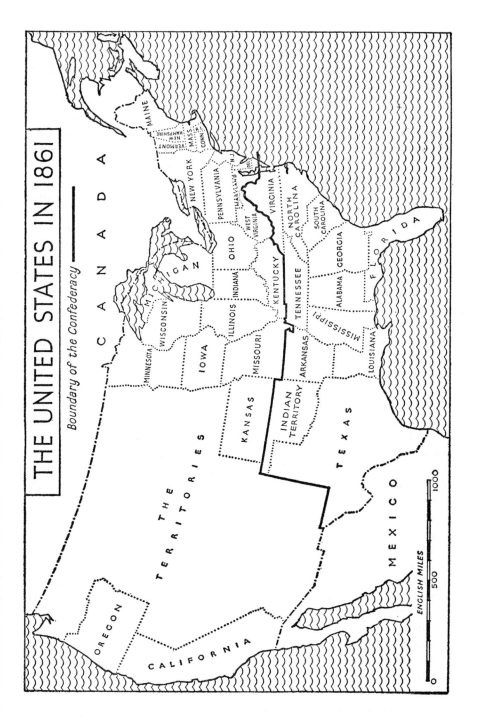

THE UNITED STATES IN 1861

Boundary of the Confederacy ———

CANADA

MAINE

VERMONT
NEW HAMPSHIRE
MASS.
CONN.

NEW YORK

PENNSYLVANIA

N.J.

MARYLAND

WEST VIRGINIA

VIRGINIA

NORTH CAROLINA

SOUTH CAROLINA

GEORGIA

FLORIDA

ALABAMA

MISSISSIPPI

TENNESSEE

KENTUCKY

OHIO

INDIANA

ILLINOIS

MICHIGAN

WISCONSIN

MINNESOTA

IOWA

MISSOURI

ARKANSAS

LOUISIANA

KANSAS

INDIAN TERRITORY

TEXAS

THE TERRITORIES

OREGON

CALIFORNIA

MEXICO

ENGLISH MILES

1000

500

0

eracy. This decided the conduct of one of the noblest Americans who ever lived, and one of the greatest captains known to the annals of war.

Robert E. Lee stood high in American life. A graduate of West Point and Staff-Officer in the Mexican War, he had served for more than twenty-five years in the United States Army with distinction. His noble presence and gentle, kindly manner were sustained by religious faith and an exalted character. As the American scene darkened he weighed carefully, while commanding a regiment of cavalry on the Texan border, the course which duty and honour would require from him. He was opposed to slavery and thought that "secession would do no good," but he had been taught from childhood that his first allegiance was to the state of Virginia. Summoned to Washington during March, 1861, he had thus expressed himself to an intimate Northern friend: "If Virginia stands by the old Union, so will I. But if she secedes (though I do not believe in secession as a constitutional right, nor that there is sufficient cause for revolution), then I will still follow my native state with my sword, and if need be with my life."

He reached the capital in the fevered days of March, and General Scott, his old chief, wrestled earnestly with him in a three hours' interview. By Lincoln's authority he was offered the chief command of the great Union army now being raised. He declined at once, and when Virginia seceded he resigned his commission, bade farewell for ever to his home at Arlington, and in the deepest sorrow boarded the train for Richmond. Here he was immediately offered the chief command of all the military and naval forces of Virginia, and he accepted his new task. Some of those who saw him in these tragic weeks, when sometimes his eyes filled with tears, emotion which he never showed after the gain or loss of great battles, have written about his inward struggle. But there was no struggle; he never hesitated. The choice was for the state of Virginia. He deplored that choice; he foresaw its consequences with bitter grief; but for himself he had no doubts at the time, nor ever after regret or remorse.

Those who hold that the fortunes of mankind are largely the result of the impact upon events of superior beings will find it fitting that Lee's famous comrade in arms, "Stonewall Jackson," should be mentioned at this point. Lee was fifty-four in the crisis, Jackson but thirty-seven. Like Lee, he was a trained professional soldier who had served gallantly in the Mexican War. He had devoted himself to the theoretical study of the military art. He was at this time a professor at the Virginia Military Institute. Jackson came of Ulster stock, settled in Virginia. His character was stern, his manner reserved and usually forbidding, his temper Calvinistic, his mode of life strict, frugal, austere. He might have stepped into American history from the command of one of Cromwell's regiments. Black-bearded, pale-faced, with thin, compressed lips, aquiline nose, and dark, piercing eyes, he slouched in his weather-stained uniform a professor-warrior; yet greatly beloved by the few who knew him best, and gifted with that strange power of commanding measureless devotion from the thousands whom he ruled with an iron hand.

Against Lee and his great lieutenant, united for a year of intense action in a comradeship which recalls that of Marlborough and Eugene, were now to be marshalled the overwhelming forces of the Union.

*   *   *

Both sides set to work to form armies. Trained officers and men were few, weapons and munitions scanty. The American people had enjoyed a long peace, and their warfare had been to reclaim the wilderness and draw wealth from the soil. On neither side was there any realisation of the ordeal that lay before them. The warlike spirit ran high in the South, and their gentry and frontier farmers, like the Cavaliers, were more accustomed to riding and shooting than their compeers in the commercial North. Proud and ardent, their manhood rallied to the newly forming regiments, confident that they would conquer, sure at least that they were unconquerable.

At first sight, to foreign observers, the disparity between the combatants was evident. Twenty-three states, with a population of twenty-two millions, were arrayed against eleven states, whose population of nine millions included nearly four million slaves. But as the Southern states only claimed the right to go their own way their policy would be defensive; the North, which denied this right and was determined to keep them in the Union by force, had to take the offensive. A formidable task confronted the aggressors.

Nothing short of the subjugation of the entire South would suffice. The issue was not to be settled by two or three battles; the whole country would have to be conquered piecemeal. The Confederacy embraced an area which extended eight hundred miles from north to south and seventeen hundred from east to west. The railways were few and badly conditioned; the roads no better. The region was sparsely inhabited, and the invader would have for the most part to bring his own supplies. He would have enormously long lines of communication to guard in his march through a hostile country. Most of the slaves, who might have been expected to prove an embarrassment to the South, on the contrary proved a solid help, tending the plantations in the absence of their masters, raising the crops which fed the armies, working on the roads and building fortifications, thus releasing a large number of whites for service in the field.

The seven states of the Lower South had seceded after Lincoln's election. Lincoln's call for troops after Sumter was followed by the secession of four states of the Upper South. There remained the attitude of the border slave states, Kentucky, Missouri, Maryland, and Delaware. Of these Kentucky was the most important on account of its geographical position, and because Missouri was likely to follow its example. Indeed, the issue of the war seemed perhaps to turn upon Kentucky. Lincoln, like Jefferson Davis, a Kentuckian by birth, is reported to have said, "I should like to have God on my side, but I must have Kentucky." But Kentucky, loyal to the memory of Henry Clay, "the Great Compromiser," tried to remain neutral. Neither combatant could tolerate this attitude for long; yet both feared lest any violent act of aggression might throw the state into the other's arms. Lincoln proved the more astute diplomatist, and by keeping the control of policy in his own hands secured Kentucky for the Union in September. This was the first real victory for the North.

In Missouri, as in the sister state, there was a majority in favour of neutrality; but the extremists on both sides took control and civil war resulted. The Governor was a rabid Secessionist, and, supported by the legislature, endeavoured to take the state out of the Union. The Union leader was one of the powerful Blair family, and his brother a member of the Cabinet. He invoked the aid of General Lyon, commander of the Federal troops in St. Louis, and with his help the Governor's separatist designs were defeated.

In Maryland the issue was more quickly settled. The Secessionists were strong in Baltimore, and gained temporary control of the city. They destroyed the railway bridges on the two northern lines, and for a few days Washington found itself dangerously isolated. Reinforcements from Massachusetts were assaulted in their march through the streets, and a bloody collision occurred. But without help from Virginia the Maryland Secessionists were not capable of making head against the national capital, and the Loyalist Governor gained time, until on May 13 General Butler, with a small Federal force, made a sudden dash, and, taking the Secessionists by surprise, occupied Baltimore. This ended the secession in Maryland. A fourth slave state, Delaware, also stayed in the Union. Its Legislature had Southern leanings, but geography ruled otherwise.

Lincoln not only secured four slavery states as allies, but also detached an important section from the seceding state of Virginia. West Virginia, separated by the Alleghenies from the rest of the state, and geographically and economically a part of the Ohio valley, had long chafed under the oppression of the state Government at Richmond, which ignored its interests and exploited it for the benefit of the "Tidewater" section. It now seized the opportunity to secede from Secession. When in May the popular vote of Virginia ratified the Ordinance of Secession it broke away, and with the help of its powerful neighbour, Ohio, established its independence under the title of the state of Kanawha, which two years later was formally admitted to the Union as the state of West Virginia.

* * *

In the task of preparing for war the Southern President had advantages over his rival. A West-Pointer, he had served in the Regular Army for several years and had fought in the Mexican War; he had afterwards been Secretary of War in President Pierce's administration, and then chairman of the Senate Military Affairs Committee. He had an inside knowledge of the officer corps, and could make the best use of the material at his disposal. Not only did he select with a few exceptions the right men, but he supported them in adversity. The principal Confederate Generals who were in command at the beginning of the war, if not killed, were still in command at its end.

Lincoln, on the other hand, was without military experience; his profession of the law had not brought him in contact with Army officers. His appointments were too often made on political grounds. He was too ready, especially at first, to yield to the popular clamour which demanded the recall of an unsuccessful general. Few, having failed once, were given a second chance. After each defeat a change was made in the command of the Army of the Potomac. None of the Generals in command of Federal armies at the end of the war had held high commands at the beginning. The survivors were very good, but the Federal cause was the poorer for the loss of those who had fallen by the way. But the Federal Government, gaining power steadily at the expense of the states, rapidly won unquestioned control over all the forces of the Union. The Southern "Sovereign States," on the other hand, were unable even under the stress of war to abandon the principle of decentralisation for which they had been contending. Some State Governors, though loyal to the Confederate cause, were slow to respond to central direction, and when conscription was decided upon by the Confederate Congress in 1862 there was much opposition and evasion by the state authorities.

* * *

By what paths should the North invade the South to reconquer it for the Union? The Allegheny Mountains divided the Mississippi valley from the broad slopes which stretched eastward to the Atlantic. The Mississippi and its great tributary, the Ohio, with the Cumberland and the Tennessee Rivers, offered sure means of carrying the war into the heart of the Confederacy and rending it asunder. The mechanical and material resources of the North ensured the control of these waterways. The South could not organise any river forces capable of coping with the Federal flotillas. The one lateral line of communication within Confederate territory, the Charleston–Memphis railroad, which passed through the key position of Chattanooga on the Tennessee, at the junction of four railway lines, would be speedily threatened. Waterways could not be cut by cavalry raids; the current of the rivers was with the North, and there was no limit except shipping to the troops and the supplies which could be carried. Old Winfield Scott, the Federal General-in-Chief, saw in this Western theatre the true line of strategic advance. But the initial neutrality of Kentucky confused the Northern view, and when at the end of September Kentucky was gained the main Union forces were differently engaged.

Upon Virginia joining the Confederacy Jefferson Davis made Richmond the Southern capital. It was within a hundred miles of Washington. It controlled, or might control, the estuaries of the James and York Rivers, with their tributaries. It covered the powerful naval base at Norfolk. Between Richmond and the enemy flowed in successive barriers the broad outlets of the Potomac and the Rappahannock, with its tributary the Rapidan. Here, then, upon this advanced battleground, rather than in the interior, must the Confederacy maintain itself or fall. Thus the two capitals stood like queens at chess upon adjoining squares, and, sustained by their combinations of covering pieces, they endured four years of grim play within a single move of capture.

The Confederates hoped at first to defend the line of the Potomac, which marked the northern frontier of Virginia. They had seized the Federal arsenal and army depot at Harpers Ferry, where the Shenandoah joins the Potomac, and for several months, while the Union forces were gathering, Colonel Jackson, and later General Joseph E. Johnston, with a few thousand men, maintained themselves there. In front of the railway junction of Manassas, by the Bull Run stream, only thirty miles from Washington, stood General Beauregard, of Sumter repute, with the main Confederate army. Thus the summer of 1861 came. "How long," cried the politicians in Washington, and the turbulent public opinion behind them in the North, "should the United States tolerate this insolent challenge?" The three-months volunteers whom Lincoln had summoned at the end of April must be made to strike a blow before their time expired. General Scott wished to wait till trained armies were formed. But do not all regulars despise militia and volunteers? Pressed beyond resistance, Scott yielded to the entreaties of Lincoln and his Cabinet. Harpers Ferry had already been recovered, and Joseph E. Johnston, with eleven thousand men, had withdrawn up the Shenandoah. Scott therefore sent fifteen thousand men to hold off Johnston in the valley, while Irvin McDowell, a competent soldier, with thirty-five thousand, moved to attack Beauregard, who mustered twenty-two thousand. The essence of this plan was that Johnston's army, held by superior force, should not join Beauregard before McDowell attacked him.

The Federal advance had originally been fixed for July 9, but it was not till a week later that it actually began. The two Confederate Generals were both expecting to be attacked by the superior forces on their respective fronts, and each was asking for reinforcements from the other. But the Union General in the valley, Patterson, allowed Johnston to slip away unobserved, and he joined Beauregard with two brigades on the day before the battle. But McDowell virtually achieved a surprise, and his much superior force threatened to overwhelm the weak Confederate left before reinforcements could arrive. In this crisis Jackson's brigade, standing "like a stone wall" on the Henry Hill, stopped the Federal advance, until the arrival by rail of another of Johnston's brigades turned the tide of battle.

The combat, though fierce, was confused, and on both sides disjointed. The day was hot, the troops raw, the staffs inexperienced. The Northerners retreated; the Confederates were too disorganised to pursue; but the retreat became a rout. Members of the Cabinet, Senators, Congressmen, even ladies, had come out from Washington to see the sport. They were involved in a panic when thousands of men, casting away their arms and even their coats, fled and never stopped till they reached the entrenchments which surrounded Washington. Not more than five thousand men were killed or wounded on both sides in the action, but the name Bull Run rang far and wide. Europe was astonished; the South was overjoyed; and a wave of fury swept the Union, before which the passions which had followed the attack on Fort Sumter seemed but a ripple.

It is still argued that the Confederates should have struck hot-foot at Washington. But Johnston at the time thought the Confederate army more disorganised by victory than the Federals by defeat. He had not seen the rout. Jackson and other Confederate Generals were eager to advance on Washington. Who shall say?

* * *

The day after this ignominious affair a new commander replaced Mc-Dowell. One of Lee's comrades on Scott's staff in Mexico, General George B. McClellan, a Regular officer with many remarkable qualities, was summoned from West Virginia, where he had been active and forward, to take command. And when at the end of October General Scott retired, McClellan became General-in-Chief of all the armies of the Republic, and bent himself with zeal and capacity to forming brigades, divisions, army corps, with artillery, engineers, and supply trains, according to the best European models.

The year 1861 ended with the Confederacy intact and almost unmolested. Along the immense front, with its deep borderlands and debatable regions, more than a hundred and fifty skirmishes and petty actions had been fought without serious bloodshed. Although the Confederate commanders realised that the time would soon come when McClellan would take the field against them with an army vastly superior in numbers, well disciplined and well equipped, they did not dare, with only forty thousand men, however elated, to invade Maryland and march on Baltimore. They did not even attempt to recover West Virginia.

So far the war had appeared to Europe as a desultory brawl of mobs and partisans which might at any time be closed by politics and parley. Napoleon III sympathised with the Confederates, and would have aided them if the British Government had been agreeable. Queen Victoria desired a strict neutrality, and opinion in England was curiously divided. The upper classes, Conservative and Liberal alike, generally looked with favour upon the South, and in this view Gladstone concurred. Disraeli, the Conservative leader, was neutral. The Radicals and the unenfranchised mass of the working classes were solid against slavery, and Cobden and Bright spoke their mind. But the Northern blockade struck hard at the commercial classes, and Lancashire, though always constant against slavery, began to feel the cotton famine. The arrest on a British ship, the *Trent,* of the Confederate agents, Mason and Slidell, by a United States cruiser roused a storm. The Foreign Secretary, Lord John Russell, penned a hard dispatch which the Prince Consort persuaded the Prime Minister, Lord Palmerston, to modify. A clause was inserted which enabled the Federal Government without loss of honour to declare their cruiser's action unauthorised. President Lincoln took some persuading, but in the end he sagely remarked "One war at a time," liberated the captives, and all remained in sullen suspense. Blockade-running, both in cotton outwards and arms inwards, developed upon a large scale; but not a single European Government received the envoys of the Confederate states. No one in Europe imagined the drama of the terrific war which the year 1862 would unfold. None appraised truly the implacable rage of the antagonists. None understood the strength of Abraham Lincoln or the resources of the United States. Few outside the Confederacy had ever heard of Lee or Jackson.

CHAPTER EIGHTY-ONE

The Campaign Against Richmond

THE NEW Year opened grievously for the South, and a bitter tide of disillusion chilled its people. In the Cabinet and headquarters at Richmond, where facts and figures told their sombre tale, the plight of the Confederacy already seemed grave. The Union blockade froze the coasts. Hostile armies, double or triple the numbers the South could muster, were assuming shape and quality, both in the Atlantic and Mississippi theatres. The awful weight of the North, with its wealth and munition-making power, lay now upon the minds of President Davis, his colleagues and Generals. The Southern states had no arsenals, little iron and steel, few and small factories from which boots, clothing, equipment could be supplied. The magazines were almost empty. Even flintlock muskets were scarce. The smooth-bore cannon of the Confederate artillery was far out-ranged by the new rifled guns of the Union. Nor was there any effectual means by which these needs could be met. It is upon this background that the military prodigies of the year stand forth.

Disaster opened in the Mississippi valley. Masses of blue-clad soldiers began to appear upon the three-hundred-mile front from the great river to the mountain ranges, and all kinds of queer craft cased in steel and carrying cannon and mortars glided slowly down the riverways from the north. The fighting line retreated southwards to the Cumberland and Tennessee Rivers, and to a Confederate fortress called Island No. 10 on the Mississippi.

The Federal General, Henry W. Halleck, who commanded the Western Department was a model of caution. Fortunately among his Generals there was a retired Regular officer, Ulysses S. Grant, who since the Mexican War had lived in obscurity, working for a time in his father's leather store in Illinois. The Confederates sought to block the Mississippi at Island No. 10, the Tennessee at Fort Henry, and the Cumberland at Fort Donelson, and their advanced forces garrisoned these armed posts. Fort Henry was weak, and Fort Donelson was an entrenched camp which required a considerable army for its defence. Grant proposed a winter advance up the Tennessee River and an attack upon Fort Henry. Halleck approved. Grant made the advance, and the advance made Grant. Albert Sidney Johnston, Commander of the Confederate forces in the West, foresaw with perfect clarity a Federal winter offensive while the rivers were well filled. He clamoured for reinforcements, both to President Davis and the Governors of the Western states. The former could not and the latter did not supply them. In February, 1862, Grant seized Fort Henry. It was but ten miles across the tongue of land between the rivers to Fort Donelson, on the Cumberland. Without authority, and in severe frost, Grant struck at Fort Donelson, which was defended by seventeen thousand Confederates under Floyd, the former United States Secretary for War. After four days' fighting and confrontation Fort Donelson surrendered, with fourteen thousand prisoners and sixty guns. Floyd, apprehending a charge of treason, escaped the night before. He was probably wise.

Johnston, now at last furnished with the beginnings of an army, gathered the remnants of his former front at Corinth, behind the Tennessee, and Polk fell back down the Mississippi to Memphis.

* * *

At Washington McClellan, General-in-Chief, laboured to prepare his army, and resisted by every means the intense political pressures which demanded an advance "on to Richmond." He exaggerated the strength of the enemy and strove to gain time to drill his men by repeated promises to advance. As month succeeded month and the swarming Army of the Potomac made no movement the enthusiasm which had greeted McClellan in

July, 1861, waned. He had long been devising a plan for an amphibious movement down Chesapeake Bay to some point on the coast of Virginia close to the rebel capital. He imparted these ideas to Lincoln in general terms early in December. Availing himself of sea-power, he proposed to transport an army of a hundred and fifty thousand men down Chesapeake Bay and disembark it at Urbana, on the Lower Rappahannock, where it would be only a few days' march from Richmond. He expected to cut off General J. B. Magruder and the Confederate troops defending the Yorktown peninsula, and he hoped to reach Richmond before Johnston could retreat thither.

No one can asperse the principle of this conception. It utilised all the forces of the Union Government; it turned the flank of all the Confederate positions between Washington and Richmond; it struck at the forehead of the Confederacy. President Lincoln had one overpowering objection to the whole idea of a maritime expedition. It would uncover Washington; and Joseph E. Johnston, for the strength of whose army he probably accepted McClellan's own figures, to say nothing of "Stonewall" Jackson, would at once swoop down on the defenceless capital. Hard bargaining ensued upon the number of troops to be left to guard the capital and the mouth of the Shenandoah valley, where at Harpers Ferry the river flows into the Potomac. This was agreed at forty thousand. Eventually on February 27 Lincoln gave a reluctant assent, and everything was set in train for the tremendous enterprise. At the same time Lincoln resolved to keep supreme control, relieved McClellan of the general direction of the United States armies, and restricted him to the command of the Army of the Potomac. For this there were also sound military reasons.

It was, however, a mistake not to appoint a new General-in-Chief. All the Generals in command of armies were ordered to take their instructions from the Secretary of War. For the last two months this office had been held by Edwin M. Stanton. Stanton, like McClellan, was a Democrat, and during the last days of the Buchanan administration had held the post of Attorney-General. At the outset Stanton had professed unbounded devotion to McClellan, but the General soon began to doubt the sincerity of his professions and thought that he detected a deliberate design to debar him from free access to the President.

*　　*　　*

The Confederates lost their best chance of victory when they failed to use the autumn and winter of 1861. Their success at Bull Run proved as injurious as a reverse. Believing with their President that foreign intervention was near at hand, and arrogantly confident that they could beat the North in the field if need arose, they relaxed their efforts. The volunteers who came forward after the first battle could not be armed. Recruiting fell off; the soldiers in the field began to go home. Efforts to fill the ranks by grants of bounties and furloughs were ineffectual. By the beginning of 1862 the position was desperate. Nearly two-thirds of the Confederate Army consisted of one-year volunteers. In May the terms of enlistment of the hundred and forty-eight regiments which they formed would expire. These regiments were the backbone of the Army. Invasion was imminent. Conscription was contrary to the theory of state independence and sovereignty. But the Confederate Congress rose manfully to the occasion, and on April 16 by a vote of more than two to one passed an Act declaring every ablebodied white man between the ages of eighteen and thirty-five subject to military service. The armies were nevertheless filled by volunteers seeking to escape the stigma of serving under compulsion rather than by the Act itself. Indeed, the Act proved unpopular in the States and was difficult to enforce. Full use was made of its exemption clauses by the disaffected in order to escape service.

Throughout this period President Jefferson Davis rigorously adhered to the passive-defensive. Determined to keep the control of military operations in his own hands, he devoted his attention to the East, and largely ignored the West, where chaos reigned until Albert Sidney Johnston's appointment to the supreme command in September. Lee was sent to organise the coast defences. When a large expedition under the Union General Ambrose E. Burnside entered the inland waters of North Carolina the Confederates were ill-prepared, and lost Roanoke Island and New Bern. President Davis was more than ever determined to maintain at their full strength the garrisons in the threatened states. He recalled General Lee from his coastal defence work in the Carolinas, and employed him in a somewhat ill-defined capacity as his chief military adviser at headquarters.

In the middle of March Halleck, who had been appointed to the sole command in the Western theatre, directed Don Carlos Buell to combine with Grant, who had William T. Sherman with him, on the western bank of the Tennessee, thirty miles from Corinth near Shiloh, and attack Albert Sidney Johnston. But before Buell's men were across the river Johnston struck. In the early morning of April 6 he surprised the advanced Federal troops in their tents near Shiloh, and the largest and most bloody battle yet seen in the war was fought. Johnston at first carried all before him; and Grant, who was late in reaching the field, was by nightfall in grave danger. But Johnston, exposing himself with reckless gallantry at the head of an infantry charge, was wounded and bled to death from a main artery in a few minutes. Whatever results his great personality and wonderful energy could have gained on the morrow were lost; Beauregard, who succeeded him, drew off the Confederate troops. Each side lost in this furious action ten thousand men; but the proportion of loss was far heavier in the thinner Confederate ranks. A combined naval and military expedition could easily at this time have lunged far to the south and secured the fortress of Vicksburg in Mississippi. But Halleck accommodated himself readily to the President's wish for action in East Tennessee. He moved slowly against Corinth, and spent a month in trying to surround Beauregard, who escaped by a swift and long retreat. By the summer the Union line in the West had moved southwards by two hundred miles on a three-hundred-mile front.

* * *

The stage was now set for the military drama of the Richmond-Yorktown peninsula. At the beginning of April McClellan's army began to land in large numbers at the Federal Fortress Monroe, which served as a bridgehead. As soon as this movement became evident Joseph E. Johnston, to the surprise and relief of the Federal Government, abandoned Manassas Junction, crossed the Upper Rappahannock, and stood in the rugged wilderness country behind its tributary the Rapidan. Now behind the Rapidan he was in close touch with Richmond, so that McClellan's strategy, vindicated in principle, was baulked in practice. In the middle of April Johnston, leaving his main army eighty miles to the westward, arrived at Yorktown, and assumed the additional command of the troops in the peninsula. He thus enjoyed interior lines and could concentrate all his forces for the defence of Richmond. The Union Navy, after a heavy combat, found itself unable to face the plunging fire of the batteries on the bluffs of the York River on McClellan's right flank. The Confederate entrenchments stretched before him across the peninsula. He conceived himself outnumbered by the enemy, and if Davis had consented to give Johnston the garrisons of the Atlantic towns he would have been.

In these depressing circumstances McClellan acted with more than his habitual deliberation. He spent a month in a formal siege of Yorktown. Lincoln, on the other hand, urged him to vigorous action. "I always insisted," he wrote drily, on April 9, "that going down the bay in search of a field instead of fighting at or near Manassas was only shifting and not surmounting a difficulty; that we would find the same enemy, and the same or equal entrenchments, at either place." Eventually, after the surrender of Yorktown, which opened the York River to his ships, McClellan advanced upon the Confederate lines. And by the middle of May McClellan had progressed sixty miles up the York, and arrived at White House, on the Richmond–West Point railway, twenty-five miles from the rebel capital.

However, President Davis had in April been persuaded by Lee to reinforce "Stonewall" Jackson for an offensive diversion in the Shenandoah valley. With only sixteen thousand men against four Federal Generals, Banks, Shields, Frémont, and Milroy, who disposed of over forty thousand, Jackson fought the brief, brilliant campaign which reinforced his first renown. Striking right and left at the superior forces on either side of him, running daily risks of capture, making enormous marches, sometimes dividing his small force, he gained a series of sharp actions, which greatly

The Eastern
THEATRE OF WAR
1861-65

0   25   50   75   100
Miles

perturbed President Lincoln and his advisers. Lincoln had at last promised McClellan McDowell's corps; but six days later, when the Union Army was half across the swampy river Chickahominy, a telegram brought the General the news that McDowell's movement was "suspended." McClellan paused in his advance; violent rains flooded the Chickahominy, and the Union Army found itself divided, with two corps only on the southern side. This was clearly Johnston's opportunity. With his whole force he attacked the two isolated Union corps. President Davis, with Lee at his side, rode out to watch the resulting battle of Seven Pines, or Fair Oaks as it is sometimes called. The Confederate attack miscarried. The battle was severe but indecisive, costing each side about six thousand men. McClellan was checked, and heavy rains made him all the more ready to remain inactive. He stood fast with his outposts five miles from Richmond. Lincoln, having learned that Jackson was now in retreat up the valley, again promised McDowell's corps. But when Jackson turned on his pursuers and defeated them on two successive days, June 8 and 9, at Cross Keys and Port Republic, he changed his mind again and would not let McDowell go.

Far more important than the fighting was the fact that General Joseph E. Johnston was severely wounded on the first day at Seven Pines, and President Davis on June 1 appointed Lee to command what was henceforward to bear the deathless title of the Army of Northern Virginia.

*　　*　　*

Lee now made the first of his offensive combinations, and immediately his hand was felt in the whole conduct of the war. He procured from Davis the gathering of the Atlantic garrisons which Johnston had been denied. He played upon the fears of Washington by sending seven thousand men to strengthen Jackson in the valley. This ensured the further paralysis of McDowell. Jackson rode in from his army to concert the plans. He was ordered to leave his "enfeebled troops" in the valley, and come secretly with his main force to Ashland, fifteen miles north of Richmond and on the Richmond-Fredericksburg railway. He could thence by advancing turn the flank and the rear of the Union armies and cut their communications with West Point. He was to be ready to act by dawn on June 26. But McClellan made no change in his array, which still lay in sight of Richmond astride the Chickahominy. Lee's army, counting Jackson, was now over seventy-five thousand strong. McClellan mustered eighty-seven thousand; but of these only the corps of General Fitz-John Porter, twenty-five thousand strong, was now north of the Chickahominy. Lee resolved to move the bulk of his force across that river, and, joined by Jackson, to concentrate fifty-six thousand men against Porter's corps, turn its right flank, destroy it, sever McClellan's communications with West Point, and thereafter cross the Chickahominy in his rear and bring him to ruin. There would be left in the entrenchments defending Richmond only sixteen thou-

394

sand men. It would be open to McClellan, when he saw what was afoot, to march with sixty thousand men straight upon the Richmond lines and assault them with a superiority of nearly four to one. Lee, who knew McClellan well, and judged him rightly, was sure he would not do this.

During the night of June 25 two Confederate corps crossed the Chickahominy, formed to their right, and fell upon Porter at Mechanicsville. Porter, surprised, made a stubborn resistance. His batteries of rifled cannon wrought havoc in the Confederate ranks. Jackson did not appear upon the scene. The difficulties of the route had delayed him by a day. Porter, having inflicted a loss of over two thousand men upon his assailants, was able to fall back upon his reserves at Gaines's Mill, four miles farther downstream, where the onslaught was renewed with the greatest fury on June 27. Gaines's Mill was the first battle in which Lee commanded personally. It was bitterly contested. Again the power of the Union artillery was manifest. The Confederates were several times repulsed at all points, and the country on Porter's right was so obstructed with forest and swamp that when Jackson came into action in the late afternoon he could not turn the flank. Lee, however, did not despair. He appealed to his troops. He launched J. B. Hood's gallant Texans at the centre, and as the shadows lengthened ordered the whole army to attack. The Texans broke the centre of Porter's hard-tried corps. The Union troops were driven from the field. Twenty guns and several thousand prisoners were already taken when night fell. Where would Porter go? McClellan had remained immobile opposite Magruder during the two days' fighting. What would he do? His communications were cut. His right wing was crushed. Lee's long, swinging left arm, of which Jackson was at last the fist, must curve completely round the right and rear of the Federal Army. Surely the stroke was mortal?

But McClellan was a skilful soldier. When his generals met him at headquarters on the night of Gaines's Mill he informed them that he had let go his communications with West Point and the York River; that, using seapower, he was shifting his base from the York to the James; that the whole army would march southwards to Harrison's Landing on that river, where all supplies would await them. He had, we now know, made some preparations for such a change beforehand. But he ran a grave risk in leaving the decision till the last moment. What was called, from its shape, a "grapevine bridge" had been built across the swamps and stream of the Chickahominy, and by this tortuous, rickety structure Porter made good his escape, while the whole Federal Army prepared to make a difficult and dangerous flank march across the White Oak Swamp to the southern side of the peninsula. It was now Magruder's turn to advance and strike at this vulnerable army. He broke in upon them on the 28th at Savage Station, capturing their field hospitals and large supplies. But Lee could not yet be sure that McClellan was really making for the James. He might as well be retreating by the Williamsburg road on Fortress Monroe. Lee therefore delayed one day before crossing the Chickahominy in pursuit. It was not till the 30th that he brought McClellan to battle at Glendale, or Frayser's Farm. This was the main crisis.

It is almost incredible that McClellan spent the day conferring with the Navy and arranging the new base on the James. He left the battle to fight itself. On the Confederate side many things went wrong. The maps were faulty; the timing failed; the attacks were delivered piecemeal; Jackson, from whom so much had been hoped, appeared in physical eclipse. Out of seventy-five thousand men with whom Lee had proposed to deal the final blow barely twenty thousand were really launched. These, after frightful losses, broke the Union centre; but night enabled the army to continue its retreat. At Malvern Hill, in a position of great strength, with the James River behind them to forbid further retreat, and the fire of the Navy and its gunboats to cover their flanks, McClellan stood at bay. Once again at the end of this week of furious fighting Lee ordered the attack, and his soldiers charged with their marvellous impetuosity. Loud roared the Union cannonade; high rose the rebel yell, that deadly sound *"Aah-ih!"* so often to be heard in these bloody years. But all was in vain. McClellan was saved. Frustrated, beaten, driven into retreat, his whole campaign wrecked, with a loss of enormous masses of stores and munitions, sixty cannon and thirty-six thousand rifles, with Richmond invincible, McClellan and his brave army nevertheless finished the Battle of the Seven Days by hurling back their pursuers with the loss of five thousand men.

Victory in the Seven Days' Battle rested with Lee. The world saw the total failure of the immense Federal plan. This also was the impression at Washington. McClellan, who was undaunted, proposed to move across the James to Petersburg and attack Richmond "by the back door," as Grant was to do in 1864–1865. His proposals were not accepted. But to Lee the adventure was hardly less disappointing. He had failed by a succession of narrow chances, arising largely from the newness of his staffs, to annihilate his foe. He had lost over twenty thousand of the flower of his army, against seventeen thousand on the Union side with its overflowing man-power.

Lincoln and his advisers now sought to return to their original plan of massing overwhelming forces on the overland route between Washington and Richmond and breaking through by weight of numbers. But their armies were divided, and Lee at Richmond stood directly between them. The President ordered McClellan to withdraw from the peninsula and bring his troops up the Potomac to the neighbourhood of Washington. Halleck was appointed General-in-Chief; he brought General Pope, who had done well in the Mississippi valley, to command what was to be called "the Army of Virginia." Pope was a harsh, vainglorious man, puffed up with good fortune in the Western theatre, and speaking in derogatory terms of the armies of the East and their achievements. He would show them how war should be waged. McClellan was ordered to hand over his troops, who parted from him in outspoken grief, and was relegated to the defence of the Washington lines.

The strategic situation offered advantages to Lee and his lieutenant. Before McClellan's army could be brought round from the Yorktown peninsula they would deal with Pope. How they treated him must be recounted.

*   *   *

An historic naval episode had meanwhile occurred. When in the spring of 1861 the Federal Government had lightly abandoned the Navy yard at Norfolk to the seceding state of Virginia some stores and several vessels of the United States Navy had been burned. One of these, the frigate *Merrimac* was repaired and refashioned in a curious way. It was given steam-engines to propel it, and above its deck a low penthouse of teak was erected. This was covered with two layers of railway iron hammered into two-inch plates. These layers were riveted transversely upon each other, making an ironclad shelter four inches thick. A heavy metal ram was fastened to the prow, and a battery of ten seven-inch rifled guns, firing through portholes, was mounted in the penthouse. Many had thought of this sort of thing before; now it came upon the scene.

This strange vessel was only finished on March 7, 1862. She had never fired a gun, nor had her engines been revolved, when on March 8 she went into action against the all-powerful Navy of the United States, which from Fortress Monroe was blocking the estuaries of the York and James Rivers. The engines, described as the worst possible, were found to make only five knots an hour, and the vessel swam and steered like a waterlogged ship. Out she came, and with no hesitation engaged the two nearest ships of the blockading fleet, the *Cumberland* and the *Congress*. These delivered broadsides which would have sunk an ordinary frigate. Besides this, all other United States ships in range and the shore batteries at Sewell's Point concentrated their fire upon her. Without paying the slightest attention to this bombardment, the *Merrimac*, rechristened the *Virginia*, steered straight for the *Cumberland*, and struck her almost at right angles. On board the *Merrimac* the collision was hardly perceptible. The ram broke off; the *Cumberland* heeled over, and, firing her cannon to the last, soon foundered, with most of her crew. The *Merrimac* then turned upon the *Congress*, and at two hundred yards' range smashed her to pieces and set her on fire. After an hour the *Congress* hoisted the white flag, and every effort was made by various small Confederate ships to rescue her crew. The *Minnesota*, which was aground, would have shared her fate if the ebb tide had not prevented the *Merrimac*, which drew twenty-two feet of water, from approaching her. Although the *Merrimac* was for a long time under the fire of at least a hundred heavy guns her armour was hardly damaged. Nothing outside the armour escaped. The funnel and two of the muzzles of the guns were shot off. Inside only twenty-one men were killed or wounded by splinters through the portholes. Her triumphant crew lay down by the side of their guns, expecting to destroy the rest of the United States fleet the next morning.

But when daylight came and steam was raised a strange-looking vessel was seen to be protecting the *Minnesota*. "She appeared," wrote one of the *Merrimac's* crew, "but a pigmy compared with the lofty frigate which she guarded." This was Ericsson's *Monitor,* of which there had been much talk, now at last ready. The *Merrimac* had made the naval revolution, but the *Monitor,* one day later, was a whole lap ahead of her. She carried only two guns; but they were eleven-inch, and mounted in a revolving iron turret nine inches thick. She had a turtle deck, heavily protected, almost flush with the water-line. As she drew only twelve feet of water she had an advantage in manœuvre.

Both these ironclad monsters approached each other, while the stately ships of the United States fleet watched spellbound. They came to the closest quarters, and the *Merrimac,* now ramless, struck the *Monitor.* None of the *Merrimac's* shells pierced the *Monitor's* armour; but when the two eleven-inch guns hit the *Merrimac* amidships the whole side was driven in several inches, and all the guns' crews bled at the nose from concussion. For six hours these two ironclads battered each other with hardly any injury or loss on either side, and both withdrew at close of day, never to meet again. As the *Merrimac* had no armour below the water-line her crew considered her lucky. She returned to the dock-yard to have this defect and many others repaired. The *Monitor,* which was so unseaworthy that she had nearly foundered on the way to the fight, also required attention. As soon as the news reached Europe it was realised that all the war-fleets of the world were obsolete. The British Admiralty, by an intense effort, in the course of a few years reconstructed the Royal Navy so as to meet the altered conditions. But even now there are fools who build large ships to fight at sea with hardly any armour.[1] The combat of the *Merrimac* and the *Monitor* made the greatest change in sea-fighting since cannon fired by gunpowder had been mounted on ships about four hundred years before.

When Norfolk was evacuated by the Confederates efforts were made to take the *Merrimac* up the James River for the defence of Richmond; but although she was so lightened as to become defenceless her draught prevented her escape. By the orders of her captain she was therefore burned and sunk. The joy which her exploit evoked throughout the Confederacy now turned to grief and anger. But the Confederate court-martial upon

[1] Written in 1939.

the captain declared that "The only alternative, in the opinion of the court, was to abandon and burn the ship then and there; which in the judgement of the court was deliberately and wisely done by order of the accused."

CHAPTER EIGHTY-TWO

Lee and McClellan

GENERAL POPE reached the front on August 1, 1862. The new commander's task was plainly to gain as much ground as he could without being seriously engaged until McClellan's army could return from the James River and join him. Pope had already forty thousand men; in six weeks he would have a hundred and fifty thousand. He was full of energy, and very sanguine. He hoped to capture both Gordonsville and Charlottesville even before his main force arrived, and then finish off Richmond.

As soon as Lee saw that McClellan had no further bite he sent Jackson, in the middle of July, with two divisions (eleven thousand men) to Gordonsville, and raised him by the end of the month to twenty-four thousand. This was a lot for Jackson, who had barely two to one to face. He found Pope's army moving hopefully towards him by the three roads which joined at Culpeper. On August 9 he fell upon General Banks, commanding Pope's leading corps, seven miles south of Culpeper, at Cedar Mountain. He used twenty thousand men against Banks's nine thousand, drove them from the field with the loss of a quarter of their number, and left the rest in no condition to do more than guard the baggage. But before Culpeper he found himself confronted with the other two corps of Pope's army, and in harmony with Lee's conceptions he fell back to Gordonsville.

On August 13 Lee learnt that McClellan's army was being re-embarked at Fortress Monroe. This was the signal for which he was waiting. Before this splendid army could make its weight tell with Pope in Northern Virginia, a period of a month at the outside, he must win a great battle there. He at once ordered General James Longstreet with twelve brigades, the bulk of the Richmond forces, to join Jackson at Gordonsville, and by the 17th he had fifty-five thousand men concentrated in the woods behind Clark's Mountain, within striking distance of Culpeper, where Pope was now established. Pope was unaware of his peril, and might well have been destroyed. But Lee waited a day to bring up his cavalry, and in the meantime a Confederate officer was captured with papers which opened Pope's eyes. Favoured by the morning mist, he retreated forthwith behind the

Rappahannock. Lee's first right-handed clutch had failed. He now scooped with the left hand. Jackson crossed the Upper Rappahannock by Sulphur Springs. But the river rose after his first brigade was over, and a second time Pope was saved.

Lee now knew that his brief period of superiority had passed, and that he must expect, in a week or ten days, overwhelming forces to be massed against him. He knew that the leading divisions of McClellan's former army were already ashore at Aquia Creek. How could the Army of Northern Virginia cope with a hundred and fifty thousand men, once they were concentrated? He therefore resolved with Jackson upon a daring and, since it was successful, brilliant manœuvre. In the face of a superior and rapidly growing enemy he divided his army. Before dawn on August 25 Jackson began another of his famous marches. With twenty thousand men, after covering twenty-six miles, he reached Salem, far behind Pope's right flank, and the next day by another twenty-five-mile march through Thoroughfare Gap in the hills he cut the Alexandria Orange railway, upon which Pope depended for his supplies, a few miles south of Manassas Junction. On the 27th he seized the Junction. Here the whole supply of Pope's army was heaped. Food, equipment, stores of every kind, dazzling to the pinched Confederates, fell into his hands. He set guards upon the liquor and let his men take what they could carry. Most of them reclothed themselves. But this booty might be bought at a fatal price. On every side superior Federal forces lay or were approaching. The cutting of Pope's communications was an incident and not the aim of Jackson and his chief. Nothing short of a great battle won was of any use to them. He therefore delivered the Junction and its depot to the flames. Looking northwards, Pope perceived the night sky reddened by the immense conflagration. It was Jackson's part to keep him puzzled and occupied till Lee could come round with Longstreet and the main army and join him.

There was now no danger of Pope marching on towards Richmond. He was hamstrung. He must retreat. But with the great forces arriving by every road to join him he would still have a large preponderance. He might even close Thoroughfare Gap to Lee and the rest of the Confederate Army. It was a dire hazard of war. Jackson withdrew from Manassas Junction northward into the woods by Sudley Springs. Pope, believing that he had him in his grip at the Junction, marched upon it from every quarter. The Junction was found in ashes and empty. During the 28th neither side knew all that was happening; but Jackson was aware that Longstreet was thrusting through Thoroughfare Gap with Lee and the main Confederate Army. Pope's orders to his disjointed army were to annihilate Jackson, now located south of Sudley Springs, and for this purpose he set seventy thousand men in motion. He thought only of Jackson. He seemed to have forgotten Longstreet and Lee, who were already massing into line on Jackson's right.

General Robert E. Lee

A photograph by Matthew B. Brady
made on the porch of Lee's home.

Taking the Rampart, by Gilbert Gaul

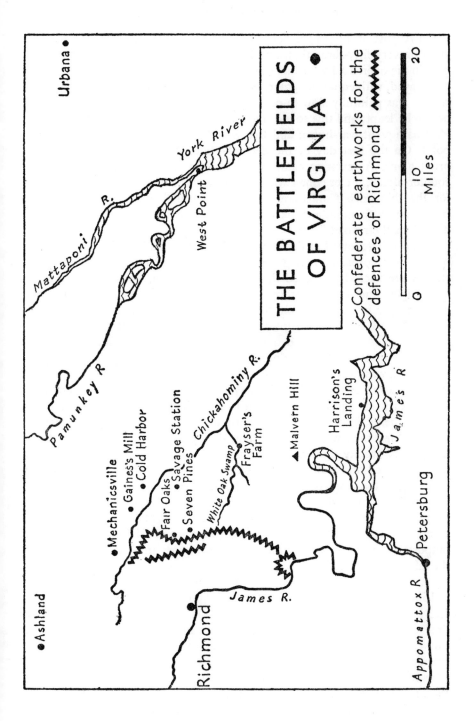

THE BATTLEFIELDS
OF VIRGINIA

● Confederate earthworks for the
defences of Richmond ⌇⌇⌇⌇

0 ――――― 10 ――――― 20
Miles

401

On August 30 began the Second Battle of Bull Run, or Manassas. With great bravery fifty-three thousand Federals in five successive assaults grappled in the open field with Jackson's twenty thousand. To and fro the struggle swayed, with equal slaughter. Longstreet, already in line, but still unperceived, was painfully slow in coming into action. He always wished to look before he leapt; and this sound maxim was far below the level of the event. He was a great war-horse, and Lee would not press him beyond a certain point. On the first day of the Second Manassas Jackson bore the whole brunt alone. As evening came, when his last reserves had delivered their counter-attack, a clergyman with whom he was friendly expressed his fears for the thin-worn Confederate left. "Stonewall," measuring the struggle from minute to minute, took one long look at the field and said, "They have done their worst."

Battle was renewed at dawn on the 31st. Pope had received the support of two new corps, marching up from Aquia. Still unconscious of Longstreet's presence, he ordered the ill-starred General, Porter, to turn Jackson's right, and Porter's troops responded loyally. But now Longstreet, massive once he was in action, threw in the main weight of the Confederate Army. Pope's array was ruptured. On a four-mile front the new, unexpected Confederate Army debouched magnificently from the woods. The two corps of Pope's left, outnumbered and outflanked, retreated. Porter, enveloped, was overwhelmed, and subsequently victimised by court-martial. Although even at the end of the day Pope commanded seventy thousand faithful men, he had no thought but to seek shelter behind the Washington entrenchments, into which he also carried with him a final reinforcement of ten thousand men which reached him during the night. Lee had captured thirty guns, twenty thousand precious rifles, and seven thousand prisoners, and had killed and wounded thirteen thousand five hundred Federals, at a total cost to the Confederacy of ten thousand men. He had utterly defeated seventy-five thousand Union troops with less than fifty-five thousand in his own hand. It was exactly four months since President Davis had given him command. Then McClellan was within five miles of Richmond. Now Lee's outposts were within twenty miles of Washington. In this decisive manner the tables were turned.

*　　*　　*

Lincoln wanted an aggressive General who would energetically seek out Lee and beat him. McClellan for all his qualities of leadership lacked the final ounces of fighting spirit. Lincoln with his shrewd judgement of men knew this. But he also knew that McClellan was probably the ablest commander available to him. When, on September 2, Pope and his beaten army seemed about to collapse upon Washington, and panic lapped around him, the President offered McClellan the command of all the forces. The flouted commander at once undertook to save the city. History has never allowed

McClellan to rise above the level of competent and courageous mediocrity; but it must not be forgotten that when he rode out to meet the retreating army they received him with frantic enthusiasm. The long, jaded, humiliated columns of brave men who had been so shamefully mishandled broke their ranks and almost dragged their restored commander from the saddle. Thus fortified, McClellan restored order to the army and turned its face again to the foe.

Lee, after the second Confederate victory at Manassas, did what ought to have been done after the first. He invaded Maryland to give that state a chance to come over, if it still would or could. Always seeking the decisive and final battle which he knew could alone save the Confederacy, he marched north, crossed the Potomac, and arrived in the neighbourhood of Frederick, abreast of Baltimore. He knew he had never the slightest chance of taking Washington; but there were prizes to be won in the open field. At Harpers Ferry in the Shenandoah valley there was a great Union depot of supply. Lee's design was to capture Harpers Ferry, into which the two smaller garrisons withdrew. Accordingly he marched west from Frederick through the range of hills called the South Mountains, sent Jackson looping out by Martinsburg, and on September 13 closed down on Harpers Ferry from all sides.

McClellan, hoping to save Harpers Ferry, now started after Lee with nearly ninety thousand men, including two fine corps that had not yet suffered at all. By a stroke of luck a Northern private soldier picked up three cigars wrapped in a piece of paper which was in fact a copy of Lee's most secret orders. McClellan learned on the 13th that Lee had divided his army and that the bulk of it was closing on Harpers Ferry. He therefore advanced with very good assurance to attack him. Everything now became a matter of hours. Could Jackson capture Harpers Ferry before Lee was beaten in the passes of the South Mountains?

McClellan wasted many of these precious hours. But considering that members of the Government behind him could only gape and gibber and that his political foes were avid of a chance to bring him to ruin it is not surprising that he acted with a double dose of his habitual caution. By overwhelming forces Lee was beaten back from the two gaps in the South Mountain range on the 14th. He now had to make a great decision. At first he thought to gather his spoils and laurels and re-cross the Potomac into Virginia. But later, feeling that nothing but victory would suffice, he resolved to give battle behind the Antietam stream, with his back to the Potomac, believing that Jackson would capture Harpers Ferry in the meanwhile and rejoin him in time.

Harpers Ferry surrendered early on the 15th. Seventy-three guns, thirteen thousand rifles, and twelve thousand five hundred prisoners were gathered by Jackson's officers. He was himself already marching all through the afternoon and night to join Lee, who stood with but twenty thousand men against the vast approaching mass of McClellan. This worthy general was unable to free himself from the Washington obsession. Had he been as great a soldier or as great a man as Lee he would have staked all on the battle. But to make sure of not running undue risks, he lost a day, and failed to win the battle.

It was not till September 17 that he attacked. By this time Jackson had arrived and was posted on Lee's left, and the rest of the Confederate divisions, having cleaned up Harpers Ferry, were striding along to the new encounter. Lee fought with his back to the Potomac, and could scarcely, if defeated, have escaped across its single bridge by Sharpsburg. This horrible battle was the acme of Federal mismanagement. McClellan, after riding down the line, fought it from his headquarters on what was called "the Commander-in-Chief idea." This meant that he made his dispositions and left the battle to fight itself. But Jackson stood in the line, and Lee rode his horse about the field controlling the storm, as Marlborough, Frederick the Great, and Napoleon were wont to do. The Confederate left, under Jackson, was practically destroyed, but only after ruining double their numbers, two whole corps of the Federal Army. All here came to a standstill, till Jackson was reinforced by Lee from his hard-pressed right and centre. The Union centre then attacked piecemeal, and their leading division was torn to pieces, half falling smitten. Burnside, who with the Union left was to cross the Antietam and cut Lee's line of retreat, would have succeeded but for the arrival of Lee's last division, under A. P. Hill, from Harpers Ferry. Striking the right flank of the assailants from an unexpected direction, he ended this menace; and night fell upon a drawn battle, in which the Federals had lost thirteen thousand men, a fourth of the troops they engaged, and one-sixth of those they had on the field, and the Confederacy nine thousand, which was about a quarter.

When darkness fell Lee faced his great lieutenants. Without exception they advised immediate retreat across the Potomac. Even Jackson, unconquerable in action, thought this would be wise. But Lee, who still hoped to gain his indisputable, decisive battle, after hearing all opinions, declared his resolve to stand his ground. Therefore the shattered Confederates faced the morning light and the huge array of valiant soldiers who seemed about to overwhelm them. But McClellan had had enough. He lay still. There was no fighting on the 18th. Lee put it hard across Jackson to take the offensive; but when Jackson, after personal reconnaissance with the artillery commander, declared it impossible Lee accepted this sagacious judgement, and his first invasion of Maryland came to an end.

War had never reached such an intensity of moral and physical forces focused upon decisive points as in this campaign of 1862. The number of battles that were fought and their desperate, bloody character far surpassed any events in which Napoleon ever moved. From June 1, when Lee was given the command, the Army of Northern Virginia fought seven ferocious battles—the Seven Days, Cedar Run, the Second Manassas, South Mountain, Harpers Ferry, the Antietam, and later Fredericksburg—in as many months. Lee very rarely had three-quarters, and several times only half, the strength of his opponents. These brave Northerners were certainly hampered by a woeful political direction, but, on the other side, the Confederates were short of weapons, ammunition, food, equipment, clothes, and boots. It was even said that their line of march could be traced by the bloodstained footprints of unshod men. But the Army of Northern Virginia "carried the Confederacy on its bayonets" and made a struggle unsurpassed in history.

* * *

Lincoln had hoped for a signal victory. McClellan at the Antietam presented him with a partial though important success. But the President's faith in the Union cause was never dimmed by disappointments. He was much beset by anxieties, which led him to cross-examine his commanders as if he were still a prosecuting attorney. The Generals did not relish it. But Lincoln's popularity with the troops stood high. They put their trust in him. They had a sense, however, of his natural resolution and generosity of character. He had to draw deeply on these qualities in his work at the White House. Through his office flowed a stream of politicians, newspaper editors, and other men of influence. Most of them clamoured for quick victory, with no conception of the hazards of war. Many of them cherished their own amateur plans of operation which they confidently urged upon their leader. Many of them, too, had favourite Generals for whom they canvassed. Lincoln treated all his visitors with patience and firmness. His homely humour stood him in good stead. A sense of irony helped to lighten his burdens. In tense moments a dry joke relieved his feelings. At the same time his spirit was sustained by a deepening belief in Providence. When the toll of war rose steeply and plans went wrong he appealed for strength in his inmost thoughts to a power higher than man's. Strength was certainly given him. It is sometimes necessary at the summit of authority to bear with the intrigues of disloyal colleagues, to remain calm when others panic, and to withstand misguided popular outcries. All this Lincoln did.

The Antietam and the withdrawal of Lee into Virginia gave the President an opportunity to take a momentous step. He proclaimed the emancipation of all the slaves in the insurgent states. The impression produced in France and Britain by Lee's spirited and resolute operations, with their successive great battles, either victorious or drawn, made the Washington Cabinet fearful of mediation, to be followed, if rejected, by recognition of the Confederacy. The North was discouraged by disastrous and futile losses and by the sense of being out-generalled. Recruitment fell off and desertion was rife. Many urged peace, and others asked whether the Union was worthy of this slaughter, if slavery was to be maintained. By casting down this final challenge and raising the war to the level of a moral crusade Lincoln hoped to rally British public opinion to the Union cause and raise a new enthusiasm among his own fellow-countrymen.

It was a move he had long considered. Ever since the beginning of the war the Radicals had been pressing for the total abolition of slavery. Lincoln had misgivings about the effects on the slave-owning states of the border which had remained loyal. He insisted that the sole object of the war was to preserve the Union. Meanwhile he was meditating on the constitutional difficulties that stood in the way. He believed he had no power to interfere with slavery in the border states. He felt his Proclamation could be legally justified only as a military measure, issued in virtue of his office as Commander-in-Chief of the Army and Navy. Its intention was to deprive the Confederacy of a source of its strength. When the Proclamation was published, with effect from January 1, 1863, it therefore applied only to the rebel states. Slavery in the rest of the Union was not finally abolished until the passing of the Thirteenth Amendment in December, 1865. In the South the Proclamation only came into force as the Federal armies advanced. Nor were the broader results all that Lincoln had hoped. In Britain it was not understood why he had not declared Abolition outright. A political manœuvre on his part was suspected. In America itself the war assumed an implacable character, offering to the South no alternative but subjugation. The Democratic Party in the North was opposed to the Emancipation Edict, and General McClellan, who might be expected to become the Democratic candidate for the Presidency, had two months earlier sent Lincoln a solemn warning against such an action. At the Congressional elections in the autumn of 1862 the Republicans lost ground. Many Northerners thought that the President had gone too far, others that he had not gone far enough. Great, judicious, and well-considered steps are thus sometimes at first received with public incomprehension.

Lee withdrew by easy marches up the Shenandoah valley. He did not hesitate to divide his army in the face of McClellan's great hosts. He left Jackson in the valley to keep Washington on tenterhooks, and rested himself with Longstreet, near Culpeper Court House. If pressed he could fall back to Gordonsville, where he judged Jackson could join him in time. McClellan, however, had now at length prepared his blow. He planned to strike Lee with overwhelming strength before Jackson could return. At this moment he was himself taken in rear by President Lincoln. On the night of November 7, 1862, he was ordered to hand over his command to General Burnside, and at the same time Porter, his most competent subordinate, was placed under arrest.

There was almost a mutiny in the Union Army when McClellan's dismissal was known. He himself acted with perfect propriety, and used all his influence to place his successor in the saddle. He was never employed again. There remained for him a vivid political struggle where numbers, which alone count in such affairs, were found upon the other side. General Porter, although he had rendered good service in the intervening Maryland campaign, was tried by court-martial for his conduct at the Second Manassas, condemned, and dismissed from the United States Army. This injustice was repaired after the lapse of years.

We have seen several times in this obstinate war President Lincoln pressing for battle and for frontal attack. "On to Richmond" was his mood; and now at last in Burnside he had found a General who would butt straight at the barrier. Burnside followed a simple plan. He chose the shortest road which led on the map to Richmond, and concentrated his army along it upon the crossing of the Rappahannock at Fredericksburg.

He took a fortnight in order to do this as well as possible. Meanwhile Lee brought in Jackson and other reinforcements. Hitherto Lee had always fought in the open field; even against the heavy odds of the Antietam he had not used the spade. He now applied the fortnight accorded him to fortify his position above Fredericksburg with every then-known device. Breastworks revetted with logs and stone walls covered by solid earth were prepared. Nearly a hundred and fifty cannon were comfortably sited. Rifle-pits abounded, and good lateral roads were cut through the scrubby forest behind the line. On December 11 Burnside occupied Fredericksburg, crossed the river with a large part of his army, and deployed for battle. He had a hundred and eighteen thousand men, against Lee's eighty thousand. On the 13th he delivered his assault. He attacked both the Confederate left wing and its right piecemeal. Then he attacked in the centre. The Northern soldiers showed an intense devotion. Brigade after brigade, division after division, they charged up the slopes under a murderous fire. As evening fell the Union Army recoiled with a loss of nearly thirteen thousand men. The Confederate casualties, mostly in Jackson's command, were under six thousand. Burnside, who now thought chiefly of dying at the head of his troops, wished to renew the battle next day. He was restrained by universal opinion at the front and at the capital; and soon after was superseded in chief command by one of his lieutenants, General Joseph Hooker.

Lee had not wished to fight at Fredericksburg at all. The Federal Army was so near its salt-water base at Aquia Creek that no counter-stroke was possible. He had advised President Davis to let him meet Burnside thirty miles back on the North Anna River, where there was room for him to use Jackson and Stuart in terrible revenge upon the communications of a repulsed army. But although Davis's relations with the Confederate Generals were on a high plane he had hampered his champion most sadly, cramping him down to a strict defensive, and thus the shattering blow of Fredericksburg had no lasting consequences. If these two Presidents had let McClellan and Lee fight the quarrel out between them as they thought best the end would have been the same, but the war would have been less muddled, much shorter, and less bloody.

* * *

In the West nothing decisive had happened up till the end of 1862. By November General Joseph E. Johnston, having recovered from the wounds he got at Seven Pines, was appointed to the chief Confederate command in this theatre, but with only a partial authority over its various armies. When it was evident that Grant was preparing for the invasion of Mississippi and an attack upon Vicksburg Johnston urged that the Arkansas army of some fifty thousand should cross the Mississippi and join Pemberton. This would have secured a Confederate superiority. Jefferson Davis vetoed this desirable, and indeed imperative, measure. The President insisted instead that General Braxton Bragg should send ten thousand men from Chattanooga to strengthen Pemberton in defending Vicksburg. This was accordingly done.

Early in December Grant made a renewed attempt against Vicksburg, sending General Sherman from Memphis, with about thirty thousand men, and Admiral Porter's Naval Squadron, to enter the Yazoo River and occupy the heights to the north of the city. Sherman assaulted the Confederate defences at Chickasaw Bluff on December 29, and in less than an hour was repulsed with the loss of nearly two thousand men, the Confederates losing only a hundred and fifty. Meanwhile the weakening of Bragg's army in Tennessee brought about, on the last day of the year, a severe battle at Murfreesboro, in which the greatest bravery was displayed by both sides. The Federals, under Rosecrans, lost over nine thousand killed and wounded, as well as nearly four thousand prisoners and twenty-eight guns. But for this Bragg paid over ten thousand men. The Federal hold on Tennessee and its capital Nashville was unshaken. Bragg withdrew his disappointed troops into winter quarters covering Chattanooga.

The armies in the different states still confronted each other on fairly equal terms, and although the Union Navy declared its ability to run the gauntlet of the Confederate batteries when required the great riverway remained barred to Federal transports and traffic. But now there was to be a profound change in the balance.

408

CHAPTER EIGHTY-THREE

Chancellorsville and Gettysburg

THE SPRING of 1863 found the Army of the Potomac and the Army of Northern Virginia still facing each other across the Rappahannock. At the end of January, when he was appointed, Hooker found the Federal Army in a sorry plight. More than three thousand officers and eighty thousand men were either deserters or absent with or without leave. Blows like Fredericksburg are hard to sustain. It was not till April that reorganisation was complete; reinforcements had poured in, and the absentees had returned from their Christmas at home. He was now at the head of over a hundred and thirty thousand men, rested and revived, splendidly equipped, and organised in six army corps. He formed besides a cavalry corps ten thousand strong, and he felt himself able to declare that he led "the finest army on the planet."

In meeting the offensive, which he knew must come, Lee was gravely hampered by President Davis's policy of the strict defensive and the dispersal of the Confederate troops to cover a number of places. Thus, for one reason or another, in the spring of 1863, Lee's nine divisions were reduced by three, and two of his four cavalry brigades were south of the James to gather forage. His infantry was less than half and his cavalry a quarter of the forces he had to encounter. He therefore abandoned the idea of an offensive into Pennsylvania by way of the Shenandoah valley, which he had had in mind, and awaited events.

Hooker's preponderance enabled him to act with two armies. His plan was, first, a fortnight in advance of the main move, to send his cavalry round Lee's left by the upper fords of the Rappahannock; then to turn Lee's left with three corps, while the two others, under General John Sedgwick, crossed the river below Lee's right at Fredericksburg. Even then he had another corps in reserve. He expected that Lee would be forced to abandon his lines and retreat, in which case he meant to follow him up by the direct road to Richmond. In the middle of April these movements began.

At first all went well with Hooker. His three army corps, about seventy thousand strong, crossed the Rappahannock, and by the night of the 30th of April a Federal army of ninety thousand men was concentrated at or near Chancellorsville. The Federal cavalry, in enormous, though not as it proved overwhelming, strength, were already moving towards the Virginia Central Railway, forty-five miles in rear of Lee's army, and one of his main lines of supply, which it was their mission not only to cut but to destroy. At the same time General Sedgwick, commanding the two corps opposite

Fredericksburg, crossed the river and deployed to attack Jackson's three divisions under General Jubal A. Early, which held the old trenches of the former battle.

Lee was thus taken in pincers by two armies, each capable of fighting a major battle with him, while at the same time his rear was ravaged and his communications assailed. The advance of either Federal Army would render his position untenable, and their junction or simultaneous action in a single battle must destroy him. Nothing more hopeless on the map than his position on the night of the 30th can be imagined, and it is this which raises the event which followed from a military to an historic level.

The great commander and his trusty lieutenant remained crouched but confident amid this tremendous encirclement. Beset upon both flanks by hostile armies which were for the moment disconnected, and unable to retreat without yielding vital positions, Lee naturally sought to hold off one assailant while striking at the other. Which to choose? Jackson was for falling upon Sedgwick and driving him into the river; but Lee knew that nothing less than the defeat of the main Union Army would save him. Hooker had taken command in person of this mighty array, and Lee, as soon as he learned where he was, left only a division to delay Sedgwick and marched at once to attack him. Meanwhile "Jeb" Stuart manœuvred against the Federal General Stoneman's cavalry to such good purpose that Stoneman played no part in the battle.

*　　*　　*

Chancellorsville stands on the edge of a wild region of forest and tangled scrub which still deserves the name of Wilderness. Roads or paths cut through this alone rendered movement possible. On May 1 Hooker, having brought up all his troops, ordered a general advance eastwards along the Turnpike and the Plank road. As he advanced into the Wilderness he met large enemy forces, who began at once to attack him. These were Stonewall Jackson's corps handled with its general's usual vigour. Now "Fighting Joe," so famous as a subordinate, bent under the strain of supreme command. He had expected that his well-executed strategy would compel Lee to retreat. He now conceived himself about to be attacked by the whole Confederate Army. He turned at once and fell back upon the entrenched line he had already prudently prepared before Chancellorsville. It was late in the afternoon of the 1st when the advancing Confederates, emerging from the woodland, came within sight of this formidable position with its masses of troops. Thus the night set in.

Lee and Jackson sat together, and knew that they had one day before them. Unless they could beat Hooker at odds of two to one during May 2 they would be attacked front and rear by overwhelming forces. Frontal attack was impossible. Their only chance was to divide their small army and swing round Hooker's right. This meant that Jackson with twenty-six

4 1 0

thousand men would march round Hooker's right to attack him, while Lee faced nearly eighty thousand Federals with seventeen thousand. At 4 A.M. Jackson was on the march. It seemed vital that his movement should be unperceived, but an unexpected gap in the forest revealed about eight o'clock to the Federal troops at Hazel Grove a long column moving towards the right of their wide front. Hooker, convinced that he was safe within his fortifications and that his strategy was successful, made no move, while the hours slipped away. It was six o'clock in the evening before Jackson reached the end of his march. He had not only turned Hooker's flank, but was actually in rear of his right-hand corps. He deployed into line, facing Lee about four miles away on the other side of the Federal Army. The surprise was complete. The soldiers of the Eleventh Federal Corps were eating their supper and playing cards behind their defences when suddenly there burst from the forest at their backs the Confederate line of battle. In one hour the Eleventh Corps, attacked by superior forces in this battle, although as a whole their army was two to one, was dashed into rout and ruin.

Night was falling, but Jackson saw supreme opportunity before him. He was within half a mile of the road leading to United States Ford, the sole line of retreat for Hooker's whole army, and between him and this deadly thrust no organised force intervened. He selected the point which he must gain by night and hold to the death at dawn. The prize was nothing less than the destruction of the main Federal Army. They must either overwhelm him the next day or starve between the Wilderness and his cannon. All this he saw. He rode forward with a handful of officers along the Plank road to the skirmish line to see what he could of the ground. He had often risked his life in this way, and now the forfeit was claimed. As he returned, his own men, Carolinians proud to die at his command, mistaking in the darkness the small party for hostile cavalry, fired a volley. Three bullets pierced the General's left arm and shoulder. He fell from his horse, and when, after an agonising passage, he reached the field hospital he was too much weakened by loss of blood to concentrate his mind. His staff officer, who was to lead A. P. Hill's division to the vital point, had been killed by the same volley. Hill, on whom the command devolved, hastening forward after vainly questioning his swooning chief, was almost immediately himself wounded. It was some hours before Stuart, from the cavalry, could be brought to the scene. No one knew Jackson's plan, and he was now unconscious. Thus on small agate points do the balances of the world turn.

Stuart fought a fine battle during the night, and on May 3, with wild shouts of "Remember Jackson!" the infuriated Confederates assaulted the Federal line. They drove it back. They captured Hazel Grove. They joined hands again with Lee. But the chance of the night was gone for ever. Hooker now had masses of men covering his line of retreat to the ford. He now thought of nothing but retreat. He did not even keep Lee occupied upon his front. He was morally beaten on the 2nd, and during the battle of the 3rd a solid shot hitting the pillar of a house by which he stood stunned him, which was perhaps a merciful stroke.

Lee now turned on Sedgwick, whose position south of the river was one of great peril. He had fought hard during the whole of the 3rd, and found himself on the 4th with the river at his back and only twenty thousand effective men, attacked by Lee, with at least twenty-five thousand. But the Confederate soldiers were exhausted by their superhuman exertions. Sedgwick, though beaten and mauled, managed to escape by his pontoons at Fredericksburg. Here he was soon joined by the Commander-in-Chief and the rest of the magnificent army which nine days before had seemed to have certain success in their path, but now stood baffled and humbled at their starting-point. They were still twice as numerous as their opponents. They had lost seventeen thousand men out of one hundred thirty thousand and the Confederates twelve thousand five hundred out of sixty thousand.

Chancellorsville was the finest battle which Lee and Jackson fought together. Their combination had become perfect. "Such an executive officer," said Lee, "the sun never shone on. Straight as the needle to the pole, he advances to the execution of my purpose." "I would follow General Lee blindfold" is a remark attributed to Jackson. Now all was over. "Could I have directed events," wrote Lee, ascribing the glory to his stricken comrade, "I should have chosen for the good of the country to be disabled in your stead." Jackson lingered for a week. His arm was amputated. Pneumonia supervened. On the 10th he was told to prepare for death, to which he consented with surprise and fortitude. "Very good, very good; it is all right." Finally, after some hours, quietly and clearly: "Let us cross over the river and rest under the shade of the trees." His loss was a mortal blow to Lee and to the cause of the South.

*   *   *

The initiative in the field now passed to Lee, who resolved to carry out his long-planned invasion of Pennsylvania. But Vicksburg, on the Mississippi, was in dire straits, and unless Joseph E. Johnston could be largely reinforced its fall was imminent. A proposal was made to stand on the defensive in Virginia, to send Lee himself with Longstreet's two divisions to the Mississippi, and other troops to Middle Tennessee, perhaps forcing Grant to abandon his campaign against Vicksburg. Lee refused point-blank to go. Squarely he put the issue before the Council of War: the risk had to be taken of losing Mississippi or Virginia. His view prevailed, and on May 26, three weeks after Chancellorsville, the invasion of Pennsylvania was sanctioned. Lee's object in 1863, as in the previous year, was to force the Army of the Potomac to fight under conditions in which defeat

412

would spell annihilation. In this he saw the sole hope of winning Southern independence.

At first the campaign went well for Lee. Ewell on the 10th of June left Culpeper for the valley, and, marching with a speed worthy of "Stonewall" Jackson, cleared the Federal garrisons out of Winchester and Martinsburg, capturing four thousand prisoners and twenty-eight guns, and on the 15th was crossing the Potomac. On the 22nd he was ordered to advance farther into Pennsylvania and capture Harrisburg, a hundred miles north of Washington, if it "came within his means."

On the 27th Ewell reached Carlisle, and his outposts next day were within four miles of Harrisburg. The other two Confederate corps were at Chambersburg. As far as Chambersburg Lee had been following the Cumberland valley, with his right flank shielded by the South Mountain range, and as yet he knew nothing of Hooker's movements. Stuart was riding gaily round the Federal rear and only rejoined Lee with his men and horses utterly exhausted on the afternoon of July 2. Thus for a whole week Lee had been deprived of the "eyes" of his army; and much had happened meanwhile.

As soon as Lee began his movement to the north Hooker proposed to march on Richmond. But Lincoln forbade him, and rightly pointed out that not Richmond but Lee's army was his proper objective. In thus deciding the President did what Lee had expected. Halleck and Stanton had agreed after Chancellorsville that Hooker must not be in command of the army in the next battle. When therefore the General tendered his resignation it was promptly accepted. Early in the morning of June 28 General George G. Meade, commander of the Fifth Corps, who was now appointed to the chief command, decided to move his whole army by forced marches northwards to the Susquehanna to prevent Lee from crossing that river, and at the same time to cover Baltimore and Washington. Meade was a safe, dogged commander, with no political affiliations. He could be relied upon to avoid acts of folly, and also anything brilliant.

Lee now ordered a concentration at Cashtown, close to the eastern foot of South Mountain. He did not hurry, and "the march was conducted with a view to the comfort of the troops." At the outset of the campaign he had been in agreement with Longstreet that the strategy should be offensive and the tactics defensive, and he had no intention of fighting a battle except under favourable conditions. But chance ruled otherwise.

On June 30 a brigade of Hill's corps advanced eight miles from Cashtown to Gettysburg, partly to look for shoes, partly to reconnoitre a place through which Ewell's corps might be moving next day. Gettysburg was found in the hands of some Federal cavalry, which had just entered. The Confederate brigade thereupon turned back without ascertaining the strength of the hostile force. Buford, the Federal cavalry commander, who bore the Christian names of Napoleon B., seems to have been the first man in either army to appreciate the strategical importance of Gettysburg, the meeting-place of some dozen roads from all points of the compass. He moved his division to the west of the town, where he found a strong position behind a stream and called upon the First and the Eleventh Corps to come to his aid with all speed.

On July 1 severe fighting began with the leading Confederate troops, and presently Ewell, coming down from the north-east, struck in upon the Federal flank, driving the Eleventh Corps through Gettysburg to seek shelter on higher ground three miles southwards, well named Cemetery Ridge. On this first day of battle fifty thousand men had been engaged, and four Confederate divisions had defeated and seriously injured two Federal corps. It now became a race between Lee and Meade, who could concentrate his forces first. Neither Lee nor Meade wished to fight decisively at this moment or on this ground; but they were both drawn into the greatest and bloodiest battle of the Civil War. Lee could not extricate himself and his supply trains without fighting Meade's army to a standstill, and Meade was equally committed to a field he thought ill-chosen.

Lee wished to open the second day of the battle with an attack by Ewell and Hill on Cemetery Ridge, which he rightly regarded as the key to the Federal position. He was deterred by their objections. Longstreet, when he arrived, argued at length for a manœuvre round Meade's left to place Lee's army between Meade and Washington. Such a movement in the absence of Stuart's cavalry would certainly have been reckless, and it is not easy to see how Lee could have provisioned his army in such a position. Finally Lee formally ordered Longstreet to attack the Federal left at dawn. Longstreet, who entirely disapproved of the rôle assigned to him, did not come into action till four in the afternoon. While he waited for an additional brigade two corps joined the Union Army. Lee, who imagined that the Federal left rested upon the Emmetsburg road, expected that Longstreet's advance up this road would roll up the Federal line from left to right. But at this point the Federal corps commander, Sickles, had taken up an advanced position on his own authority, and his flank was not the end of the Federal line. When this was discovered Longstreet obstinately refused to depart from the strict letter of his orders, though he knew that Lee was not aware of the true position. All that he achieved after several hours' fierce fighting was to force Sickles back to Meade's main line. On this day the greater part of Hill's corps took no part in the battle. Ewell, who was to have attacked the north end of the ridge as soon as he heard Longstreet's guns, did not get into action till 6 P.M. There were no signs of any co-ordination of attacks on the Confederate side on July 2. Although Lee had failed to make his will prevail, and the Confederate attacks had been unconnected, the losses

THE
GETTYSBURG
CAMPAIGN

Miles

0   10   20   30   40   50

415

of the Federal Army were terrible, and Meade at the Council of War that night was narrowly dissuaded from ordering a general retreat.

The third day began. Lee still bid high for victory. He resolved to launch fifteen thousand men, sustained by the fire of a hundred and twenty-five guns, against Meade's left centre, at the point where one of Hill's brigades had pierced the day before. Ewell's corps would at the same time attack from the north, and if the assault under General George E. Pickett broke the Federal line the whole Confederate Army would fall on. Again the attack was ordered for the earliest possible hour. It was the Federals, however, who opened the third day by recapturing in the grey of the dawn some of the trenches vacated the previous evening, and after hard fighting drove the Confederates before noon entirely off Culp's Hill. Exhausted by this, Ewell made no further movement. Longstreet was still arguing vehemently in favour of a wide turning movement round Meade's left. The heavy losses which his corps had suffered on the 2nd made this more difficult than ever.

The morning passed in utter silence. It was not till one in the afternoon that the Confederates began the heaviest bombardment yet known. Longstreet, unable to rally himself to a plan he deemed disastrous, left it to the artillery commander, Alexander, to give the signal to Pickett. At half-past two the Confederate ammunition, dragged all the way from Richmond in tented wagons, was running short. "Come quick," Alexander said to Pickett, "or my ammunition will not support you properly." "General," said Pickett to Longstreet, who stood sombre and mute, "shall I advance?" By an intense effort Longstreet bowed his head in assent. Pickett saluted and set forty-two regiments against the Union centre. We see today, upon this battlefield so piously preserved by North and South, and where many of the guns still stand in their firing stations, the bare, slight slopes up which this grand infantry charge was made. In splendid array, all their battle flags flying, the forlorn assault marched on. But, like the Old Guard on the evening of Waterloo, they faced odds and metal beyond the virtue of mortals. The Federal rifled artillery paused till they were within seven hundred yards; then they opened again with a roar and cut lanes in the steadfastly advancing ranks. On they went, without flinching or disorder; then the deadly sound, like tearing paper, as Lee once described it, rose under and presently above the cannonade. But Pickett's division still drove forward, and at trench, stone wall, or rail fence closed with far larger numbers of men, who, if not so lively as themselves, were at least ready to die for their cause. All three brigadiers in Pickett's division fell killed or mortally wounded. General L. A. Armistead with a few hundred men actually entered the Union centre, and the spot where he died with his hand on a captured cannon is today revered by the manhood of the United States.

But where were the reserves to carry through this superb effort? Where were the simultaneous attacks to grip and rock the entire front? Lee at Gettysburg no more than Napoleon at Waterloo could win dominance. The victorious stormers were killed or captured; the rest walked home across the corpses which encumbered the plain amid a remorseless artillery fire. Less than a third came back. Lee met them on his horse Traveller with the only explanation, which they would not accept, "It is all my fault." Longstreet, in memoirs written long afterwards, has left on record a sentence which is his best defence: "As I rode back to the line of batteries, expecting an immediate counter-stroke, the shot and shell ploughed the ground around my horse, and an involuntary appeal went up that one of them would remove me from scenes of such awful responsibility."

But there was no counter-stroke. The Battle of Gettysburg was at an end. Twenty-three thousand Federals and over twenty thousand Confederates had been smitten by lead or steel. As after the Antietam, Lee confronted his foe on the morrow and offered to fight again. But no one knew better that it was decisive. With every personal resource he gathered up his army. An immense wagon train of wounded were jolted, springless, over sixteen miles of crumpled road. On the night of the 4th Lee began his retreat. Meade let him go. The energy for pursuit had been expended in the battle. The Potomac was found in flood; Lee's pontoon bridge had been partially destroyed by a raid from the city of Frederick. For a week the Confederates stood at bay behind entrenchments with their backs to an unfordable river. Longstreet would have stayed to court attack; but Lee measured the event. Meade did not appear till the 12th, and his attack was planned for the 14th. When that morning came, Lee, after a cruel night march, was safe on the other side of the river. He carried with him his wounded and his prisoners. He had lost only two guns, and the war.

The Washington Government were extremely discontented with Meade's inactivity; and not without reason. Napoleon might have made Lee's final attack, but he certainly would not have made Meade's impotent pursuit. Lincoln promoted Meade only to the rank of Major-General for his good service at Gettysburg. Lee wended his way back by the Shenandoah valley to his old stations behind the Rappahannock and the Rapidan. The South had shot its bolt.

Up to a certain point the Gettysburg campaign was admirably conducted by Lee, and some of its objects were achieved; but the defeat with which it ended far more than counterbalanced these. The irreparable loss of twenty-eight thousand men in the whole operation out of an army of seventy-five thousand forbade any further attempts to win Southern independence by a victory on Northern soil. Lee believed that his own army was invincible, and after Chancellorsville he had begun to regard the Army of the Potomac almost with contempt. He failed to distinguish between bad troops and good troops badly led. It was not the army but its commander that had been beaten on the Rappahannock. It may well be that had Hooker been allowed to retain his command Lee might have defeated him a second time. Fortune, which had befriended Lee at Chancellorsville, now turned against him. Stuart's long absence left him blind as to the enemy's movements at the most critical stage of the campaign, and it was during his absence that he made the fatal mistake of moving to the east side of the mountains. Lee's military genius did not shine. He was disconcerted by Stuart's silence, he was "off his balance," and his subordinates became conscious of this mood. Above all he had not Jackson at his side. Longstreet's recalcitrance had ruined all chance of success at Gettysburg. On Longstreet the South laid the heavy blame.

There was no other battle in the East in 1863, and the armies were left for the winter facing each other on the Rapidan.

*   *   *

We must now turn to the West, where great battles were fought, and many fell. From the West, it is true, the eventual thrust came which split and devastated the South. But its importance in 1862 and 1863 lay chiefly in the advance of Grant to the supreme unified command of the Union armies. The objective was the clearance or barrage of the Mississippi. In April, 1862, Admiral Farragut, a Southerner, who adhered to the Union, had become prominent at the head of the Federal Navy. With a fleet of all kinds of vessels, partly armoured or naked, he had run past the forts guarding the approaches to New Orleans, the largest city and the commercial capital of the Confederacy, which fell next day. He had then continued the ascent of the river, and reached Vicksburg on May 18. Finding no Federal troops at hand to support him, he retired to run the batteries again on June 25, and join hands with the Federal flotilla at Memphis. It was therefore known by the end of 1862 that the Confederate batteries could not stop the Union ships. As for the torpedoes, a new word, of which there was then much talk, Farragut was to say, "Damn the torpedoes!" and be justified. Thenceforward the Union flotillas could move up and down the great river, through its entire course, by paying a toll. This was a substantial aid to the Federal Army on either bank. Here in the Mississippi valley was almost a separate war. The Western states of the Confederacy claimed a great measure of autonomy from Jefferson Davis and his Government at Richmond, while clamouring for its help. At Washington the Western theatre was viewed in much the same way as was the Eastern front by the Allied and associated Powers in the First World War. It was secondary, but also indispensable. It was not the path to victory, but unless it was pursued victory would be long delayed.

In December, 1862, Grant reassembled his army on the right bank of the Mississippi. Vicksburg was still his first aim, but the floods of the

4 1 8

Yazoo basin prevented at this season all operations except by water. Having by numerous feints deceived the Confederate General, Pemberton, who with a field army was defending Vicksburg, Grant successfully ferried forty-five thousand men across the Mississippi below the Grand Gulf batteries, thirty-six miles down-stream from Vicksburg. He surprised and drove back Pemberton's troops, and on May 3 established himself at Grand Gulf, in a safe position on the uplands, with his left flank protected by the wide Black River, and in touch with the Federal flotillas. Here he was joined four days later by his third corps, under Sherman. He now began a cautious movement towards Vicksburg and the railway which joined it to the town of Jackson. General Joseph E. Johnston was hurried to the scene. His only thought now was to extricate Pemberton's army; he ordered that General to march at once to join him before Grant could interpose his three corps between them. Pemberton resolved to disobey this order. He not only disobeyed, he miscalculated. Dropping his links with Grand Gulf, Grant pressed Johnston back with his right hand, and then turned on Pemberton in great superiority. After a considerable battle at Champion's Hill, in which over six thousand men fell, Pemberton was driven back into Vicksburg. With the aid of the flotilla the Union General opened a new base north of the city, and after two attempts to storm its defences, one of which cost him four thousand men, commenced a regular siege. Large reinforcements presently raised his army to over seventy thousand men. Johnston, with twenty-four thousand, could do nothing to relieve Pemberton. Vicksburg was starved into surrender, and its Confederate garrison and field army, more than thirty thousand strong, capitulated on July 4, at the very moment of Lee's defeat at Gettysburg. Five days later Port Hudson, in Louisiana, also reduced by famine, surrendered with seven thousand men to General Banks, and the whole course of the Mississippi was at last in Federal hands. "The Father of Waters," said Lincoln, "again goes unvexed to the sea." These were stunning blows to the South.

*   *   *

The main fury of the war was now transferred to the West. Until the fall of Vicksburg was certain the highly competent Rosecrans, with about sixty thousand men, forming the Union Army of the Cumberland, was content from the scene of his success at Murfreesboro to watch Bragg, who stood across the railway line between him and Chattanooga. This city and railway centre, protected by the deep and wide Tennessee River on the north and the high ridges of the Appalachian Mountains, a western chain of the Alleghenies, on the south, was the key not only to the mastery of the Mississippi valley, but to the invasion of prosperous, powerful, and hitherto inviolate Georgia. When Rosecrans, at the end of June, advanced along the railway to Chattanooga, and Burnside, with another army of forty thousand men, a hundred miles to the east, struck at Knoxville, great and far-reaching operations were afoot. Burnside captured Knoxville, cutting one of the sinew railways of the Confederacy. Rosecrans manœuvred Bragg out of all his defensive lines astride the Nashville–Chattanooga railway, and by September 4 gained Chattanooga without a battle.

Rosecrans now made the disastrous mistake of supposing that the resolute, agile army in his front was cowed. Bragg, who was one of the worst generals, hated by his lieutenants, and nearly always making the wrong decision, was none the less a substantial fighter. South of Chattanooga the mountain ridges spread out like the fingers of a hand. Bragg lay quiet at Lafayette with an army now reinforced to sixty thousand men. By September 12 Rosecrans realised the appalling fact that his three corps were spread on a sixty-mile front, and that Bragg lay in their midst three times as strong as any one of them. Bragg, overbearing and ill-served, missed this opportunity, which Lee or Jackson would have made decisive for the whole of the West. Rosecrans recoiled, and concentrated towards Chattanooga; but he was too late, even against Bragg, to escape a battle on ground and under conditions far from his choice.

At Chickamauga, across the border of Georgia, on September 18 Bragg fell upon his enemy. Longstreet, from Virginia, with two divisions and artillery, had reached him, together with other heavy reinforcements, so that he had the rare fortune for a Confederate General of the weight of numbers behind him. Seventy thousand Confederates attacked fifty-five thousand Federals. The two days' battle was fought with desperate valour on both sides. Bragg tried persistently to turn the Federal left and cut Rosecrans from Chattanooga, but when this wing of the Union Army, commanded by General George H. Thomas, had drawn to its aid troops from the centre and right, Longstreet, with twenty thousand Virginian veterans, assaulted the denuded parts of the Union front, and drove two-thirds of Rosecrans' army, with himself and the corps commanders, except Thomas, in ruin from the field. Longstreet begged Bragg to put all his spare weight behind a left-handed punch; but the Commander-in-Chief was set upon his first idea. He continued to butt into Thomas, who had built overnight breastworks of logs and railway iron in the woodland. Night closed upon a scene of carnage surpassed only by Gettysburg. Thomas, "the rock of Chickamauga," extricated himself and his corps and joined the rest of the Federal Army in Chattanooga.

The casualties in this battle were frightful. Sixteen thousand Federals and over twenty thousand Confederates were killed, wounded, or missing. The Confederates, who had captured forty guns and the battlefield, and who for the moment had broken the enemy's power, had gained the victory. It might have been Ramillies or Waterloo. It was Malplaquet.

Bragg now blockaded and almost surrounded Rosecrans and the Army of the Cumberland in Chattanooga. He held the two heights which domi-

ARKANSAS TENNESSEE

Nashville

Memphis

Corinth Shiloh

Arkansas R.

Mississippi R.

Tennessee R.

Yazoo R.

MISSISSIPPI

Yazoo City

ALABAMA

Vicksburg

Grand Gulf

Port Hudson

LOUISIANA

Mobile

FLORIDA

New Orleans

Gulf *of* *Mexico*

Miles

0   50   100   150

THE
MISSISSIPPI
THEATRE

nated Lookout Mountain and Missionary Ridge. For a time he barred all supplies by the Tennessee River. In early October it looked as if the Army of the Cumberland would be starved into surrender.

The Washington Government now began to lean heavily upon General Ulysses Grant. His faults and weaknesses were apparent; but so also was his stature. On the Union side, baffled, bewildered, disappointed, weary of bloodshed and expense, Grant now began to loom vast and solid through a red fog. Victory had followed him from Fort Donelson to Vicksburg. Here were large rebel surrenders—troops, cannon, territory. Who else could show the like? On October 16 Grant was given command of the departments of the Ohio, Cumberland, and Tennessee Rivers, with his lieutenant, Sherman, under him at the head of the Army of Tennessee.

By a series of intricate measures Grant freed the Tennessee River, stormed both Missionary Ridge and Lookout Mountain, and drove Bragg and the Confederate Army in thorough disorder away from Chattanooga. The frontiers of the Confederacy rolled southwards in another long lap. Vicksburg had cut it in two along the line of the Mississippi. Chattanooga cut the eastern half again along the range of the Alleghenies. By December, 1863, the Confederates were driven back into Georgia, and the whole Mississippi valley was recovered for the Union. All these convulsive events might have taken a different grip if President Davis had made Lee Supreme Commander of the Confederate Army after Chancellorsville, or, better still, in 1862, and if he had devoted his authority and fine qualities wholly to the task of rallying behind the chief General the loyal, indomitable, but woefully particularist energies of the South. By the end of 1863 all illusions had vanished. The South knew they had lost the war.

CHAPTER EIGHTY-FOUR

The Victory of the Union

THE CONFEDERACY was defeated, and the last long phase of the war was one of conquest and subjugation. During the winter of the year which had witnessed Chancellorsville and Gettysburg, Vicksburg, Chattanooga, and Chickamauga, there was a pause. The North gathered its overwhelming strength for a sombre task. The war-leadership of President Davis was gravely questioned in the South. He had kept in his own hands not only the enormous business of holding the Confederacy together and managing its political and economic life, but he had exercised an overriding control upon its military operations. He had obdurately pursued a defensive policy and strategy against odds which nothing but decisive victory in the field could shorten. This had led logically and surely to ruin.

On March 9, 1864, President Lincoln appointed Ulysses Grant to the command of all the armies of the United States, raising him to the rank of Lieutenant-General. At last on the Northern side there was unity of command, and a General capable of exercising it. Grant's plan was brutal and simple. It was summed up in the word "Attrition." In intense fighting and exchange of lives weight of numbers would prevail. To Meade, who nominally retained the command of the Army of the Potomac, he gave the order, "Wherever Lee goes you will go also." To Sherman, his friend and brother officer, who had risen with him, he confided the command in the West with similar instructions, but with an addition: "To move against Johnston's army, to break it up, and to get into the interior country as far as you can, inflicting all the damage you can against their war resources." If either Johnston or Lee, profiting by interior lines, showed signs of trying to join the other no exertion was to be spared to follow him.

With the approach of spring Grant, having launched the Union Army, came to grips with Lee on the old battle-grounds of the Rappahannock and the Rapidan, where the traces of Chancellorsville remained and memories of "Stonewall" Jackson brooded. He took the field at the beginning of May with a hundred and twenty thousand men against Lee with sixty thousand. He crossed the Rapidan by the fords which "Fighting Joe" Hooker had used the year before. There in the savage country of the Wilderness was fought a battle worthy of its field. In two days of intricate and ferocious fighting, May 5 and 6, Grant was repulsed with a loss of eighteen thousand men, Lee himself losing about ten thousand, the most part in a vehement counter-stroke. Grant then passaged to his left, and in a series of confused struggles from the 8th to the 19th sought to cut the Confederates from their line of retreat upon Richmond. This was called the Battle of Spotsylvania Court House, in which the Federal armies suffered another loss of over eighteen thousand men, or double that of their opponents. Undeterred by this slaughter, Grant repeated his movement to the left, and prolonged heavy fighting followed in the wild regions of the South Anna stream and afterwards on the Pamunkey River. Grant, for all the courage of his men, could never turn Lee's right flank, and Lee and his devoted soldiers could never overcome odds of two to one. They could only inflict death and wounds in proportion to their numbers. According to Grant's war-thought, this process, though costly, had only to be continued long enough to procure the desired result. "I propose to fight it out on this line," he wrote to Halleck at Washington, "if it takes all summer." But other factors, less arithmetical in their character, imposed themselves.

At Cold Harbour, on the ground of the "Seven Days" in 1862, the

Federal Commander-in-Chief hurled his army through the blasted, undulating woodland against the haggard, half-starved, but elated Confederate lines. It was at this battle that Lee conversed with the Postmaster-General of the Confederacy, who had ridden out to see the fighting, and asked, "If he breaks your line what reserve have you?" "Not a regiment," said Lee, "and that has been my condition since the fighting commenced. If I shorten my lines to provide a reserve he will turn them; if I weaken my lines to provide a reserve he will break me." But the result of the day ended Grant's tactics of unflinching butchery. After seven thousand brave blue-coated soldiers had fallen in an hour or so the troops refused to renew the assault. More is expected of the high command than determination in thrusting men to their doom. The Union dead and wounded lay between the lines; the dead soon began to stink in the broiling sun, the living screamed for water. But Grant failed to secure a truce for burial and mercy. It was not till the third day after the battle that upon a letter from Lee, saying he would gladly accord it if asked, formal request was made, and for a few hours the firing ceased. During the World Wars through which we have lived no such indulgences were allowed, and numbers dwarfing the scale of the American Civil War perished in "no-man's-land," in long, helpless agony where they fell. But in that comparatively civilised and refined epoch in America Cold Harbour was deemed a horror almost beyond words.

The Army of Northern Virginia had inflicted upon Grant in thirty days a loss equal to its own total strength. He now saw himself compelled to resort to manœuvre. He did exactly what McClellan had done on the same ground two years earlier. By a skilful and daring march, which Lee was too weak to interrupt, he moved his whole army across the peninsula, and, again using sea-power, crossed the James River and established a new base on the south bank. He set himself to attack Richmond by the "back door," as McClellan had wished to do. Repulsed at Petersburg, he laid siege with an army now reinforced to a hundred and forty thousand men to the trench lines covering that stronghold and the lines east of Richmond. He failed again to turn Lee's right flank by movements south of the James, and at the end of June resigned himself to trench warfare attack by spade, mine, and cannon. There was no investment, for Lee's western flank remained open. There static conditions lasted till April, 1865. These performances, although they eventually gained their purpose, must be regarded as the negation of generalship. They were none the less a deadly form of war.

* * *

Meanwhile, in the West, Sherman, who enjoyed a superiority of almost two to one, had begun in May to fight his way south along the railway from Chattanooga to Atlanta, deep in Georgia. He was faced by Joseph E. Johnston, with three strong Confederate corps. A remarkable duel ensued

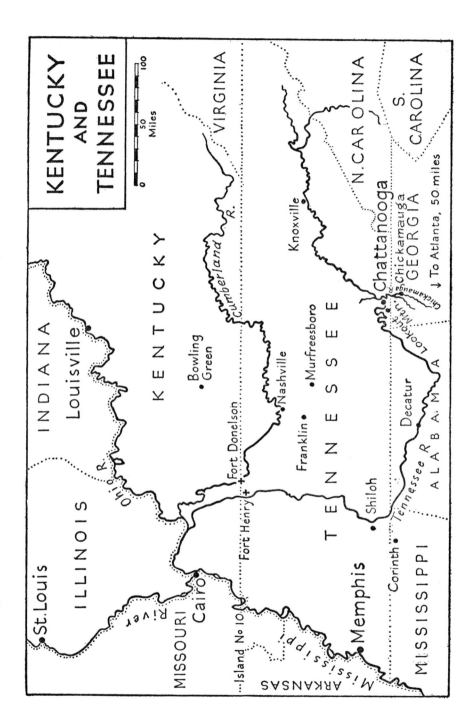

KENTUCKY AND TENNESSEE

INDIANA
Louisville
ILLINOIS
St.Louis
MISSOURI
Cairo
ARKANSAS
Island No.10
Fort Henry
Fort Donelson
Memphis
Mississippi River
Corinth
Shiloh
MISSISSIPPI
KENTUCKY
Bowling Green
Cumberland R.
Nashville
Franklin
Murfreesboro
TENNESSEE
VIRGINIA
Knoxville
N. CAROLINA
S. CAROLINA
Chattanooga
Chickamauga
GEORGIA
↓ To Atlanta, 50 miles
Lookout Mtn.
Tennessee R.
Decatur
ALABAMA
Ohio R.
100
50
Miles
0

425

between skilful adversaries. Sherman avoided frontal attacks, and by flanking movements manœuvred Johnston out of one strong position after another. Fierce fighting was continuous on the outpost lines, and in a minor engagement one of Johnston's corps commanders, General Leonidas Polk, was killed by a cannon-shot. Only at Kenesaw Mountain did Sherman assault. He was repulsed with the loss of two thousand five hundred men. But meanwhile the spectacle of this remorseless advance and his unwillingness to force a battle cost Johnston the confidence of Jefferson Davis. At the moment when he had resolved to stand at Peach Tree Creek he was superseded by John B. Hood. The Confederate Army, impatient of long retreats, acclaimed the change; but military opinion has always regarded the removal of Johnston as one of the worst mistakes of President Davis in his anxious office. At Peach Tree Creek, Decatur, and East Point Hood gave full range to the passion for on offensive which inspired the Government he served and the army he led. The Confederates, defending their native soil, hurled themselves against the invader, and suffered irreparable losses. At Decatur alone they lost ten thousand men, without inflicting a third of that loss upon the enemy. After East Point, where five thousand Confederates fell, both the Army of the West and the Richmond Government were convinced that Johnston had probably been right. Hood was directed to return to the defensive, and after some weeks of siege was driven from Atlanta. In the four months' fighting Sherman had carried the Union flag a hundred and fifty miles into the Confederacy, with a loss of thirty-two thousand men. The Confederate loss exceeded thirty-five thousand. Thus Sherman could claim a solid achievement.

This victory prepared another. Indeed, the most important conflict of 1864 was fought with votes. It was astonishing that in the height of ruthless civil war all the process of election should be rigidly maintained. Lincoln's first term was expiring, and he must now submit himself to the popular vote of such parts of the American Union as were under his control. Nothing shows the strength of the institutions which he defended better than this incongruous episode. General McClellan, whom he had used hardly, was the Democratic candidate. His platform at Chicago in August was "that after four years of failure to restore the Union by the experiment of war . . . immediate efforts be made for the cessation of hostilities . . . and peace be restored on the basis of a Federal Union of the states." This proposal was known as the Peace Plank. Republicans had no difficulty in denouncing it as disloyal. In fact, it represented the views of only a section of the Democrats. The worst that can be said about it is that it was absurd. All knew that the South would never consent to the restoration of the Federal Union while life and strength remained. In Lincoln's own Cabinet Salmon P. Chase, Secretary of the Treasury, a man of proved ability, became his rival for the Republican nomination. This was one of a number of moves made by Republican malcontents to displace their leader by someone whom they imagined would be a more vigorous President. Lincoln's political foes, gazing upon him, did not know vigour when they saw it. These were hard conditions under which to wage a war to the death. The awful slaughters to which Grant had led the Army of the Potomac and the prolonged stalemate outside Richmond made a sinister impression upon the North. But the capture of Atlanta, and a descent by Admiral Farragut upon the harbour of Mobile, the last Confederate open port, both gave that surge of encouragement which party men know how to use. Four million citizens voted in November, 1864, and Lincoln was chosen by a majority of only four hundred thousand. Narrow indeed was the margin of mass support by which his policy of the remorseless coercion of the Southern states to reincorporation was carried. This did not mean that all Democrats wanted peace at any price. McClellan had made it plain when he accepted nomination that the South must offer to return to the Union before an armistice could be negotiated. But the founders of the American Constitution, which was now based upon the widest male suffrage, had so devised the machinery that the choice of the President should be indirect; and in the electoral college Lincoln, who carried every Union state except New Jersey, Delaware, and Kentucky, commanded two hundred and twelve delegates against only twenty-one for McClellan.

In order to placate or confuse the pacifist vote Lincoln had encouraged unofficial peace parleys with the South. Horace Greeley, of the *New York Tribune,* was the President's representative. He met the Southern emissaries in Canada at Niagara Falls. Greeley soon discovered that they had no authority to negotiate a peace. The move would in any case have failed, since Lincoln's conditions now included the abolition of slavery as well as Reunion. The fourth winter of this relentless moral and physical struggle between communities who now respected and armies who had long admired one another came on.

Although Atlanta had fallen, Hood's army of forty-four thousand bitter men was still active in the field and free to strike at Sherman's communications. With him were also ten thousand cavalry under Nathan B. Forrest, a new figure who gleamed in the sunset of the Confederacy. Forrest could hardly read or write, but by general account he possessed military qualities of the highest order. His remark that the art of war consists of being "Firstest with mostest" is classic. All these forces were at large around and behind Sherman. On November 12 that General, having persuaded a naturally anxious Washington Cabinet, cast his communications to the winds and began his grim march through Georgia to the shores of the Atlantic. When the Northern blockade had practically stopped the export of cotton from the Confederacy the women, with the slaves, who obeyed and respected them, had sowed the fields with corn. Georgia was full of food in this dark winter. Sherman set himself to march through it on a wide front, living on the country, devouring and destroying all farms, villages, towns, railroads, and public works which lay within his wide-ranging reach. He left behind him a blackened trail, and hatreds which pursue his memory to this day. "War is hell," he said, and certainly he made it so. But no one must suppose that his depredations and pillage were comparable to the atrocities which were committed during the World Wars of the twentieth century or to the barbarities of the Middle Ages. Searching investigation has discovered hardly a case of murder or rape. None the less a dark shadow lies upon this part of the map of the United States.

Meanwhile Hood, with the Confederate Army of the West, not only tore up Sherman's communications with the United States, so that he was not heard of for a month, but with an army of nearly sixty thousand men struck deep into the Northern conquests. He invaded Tennessee, Thomas, who had been left by Sherman to watch him, retiring. It looked as if the Confederates might once more break through to the Ohio. But, pressing on, they were defeated and routed by Thomas on December 15 in the Battle of Nashville. Hood returned in much disorder to the South. Sherman, after vicissitudes, reached Savannah on the ocean coast in time to send the news of its fall as a "Christmas present" to the re-established President Lincoln.

* * *

The end was now in sight. Sherman planned for 1865 a more severe punishment for South Carolina than had been inflicted upon Georgia. Here was a state which by its arrogance had let loose these years of woe upon the American people. Here were the men who had fired upon the Stars and Stripes at Fort Sumter. In Lincoln's Cabinet Ministers spoke of obliterating Charleston and sowing the foundations with salt. Sherman marched accordingly with extreme vigour. But meanwhile outside Richmond Lee's powers of resistance were exhausted. He had not been deterred by Grant's arrival on the south bank of the James from sending General Early with a strong detachment into the Shenandoah valley. In July, 1864, Early defeated the Federal commanders in the Jackson style, and once again Washington had heard the cannon of an advancing foe. But now the Shenandoah had been cleared and devastated by Sheridan with overwhelming forces. The Petersburg lines before Richmond had long repelled every Federal assault. The explosion of a gigantic mine under the defences had only led to a struggle in the crater, in which four thousand Northerners fell. But the weight which lay upon Lee could no longer be borne.

It was not until the beginning of February, 1865, in this desperate strait, that President Davis appointed him Commander-in-Chief. In the same month another attempt was made at negotiation. The Vice-President of the Confederacy, A. H. Stephens, was empowered to meet the President of the United States on board a steamer in Hampton Roads, at the mouth of the

James River. It offers a strange spectacle, which has not been repeated since, that two opposed belligerent leaders should thus parley in the midst of war. Moreover, the Southern representative had not so many years ago been an acquaintance of Lincoln's. But neither side had the slightest intention of giving way on the main issue. Jefferson Davis in his instructions spoke of a treaty "whereby our two countries may dwell in peace together." Lincoln offered a wide generosity, but only if the United States were again to be one country. It was as he had predicted. The South could not voluntarily re-accept the Union. The North could not voluntarily yield it.

Lee meanwhile had at once restored Joseph E. Johnston to the command of the Western Army. No rule can be laid down upon the High Command of states and armies in war. All depends upon the facts and the men. But should a great general appear the civil Government would be wise to give him full scope at once in the military sphere. After the Second Manassas, or after Chancellorsville at the latest, Lee was plainly discernible as the Captain-General of the South. But that was in the spring of '62; it was now the spring of '65. Every Confederate counter-offensive had been crushed. The forces of the North ravaged the doomed Confederacy, and at last Grant closed upon its stubborn capital.

On Sunday, April 2, after the Battle of Five Forks and the turning of the Petersburg lines, President Davis sat in his pew in the church at Richmond. A messenger came up the aisle. "General Lee requests immediate evacuation." Southwards then must the Confederate Government wander. There were still some hundreds of miles in which they exercised authority. Lee had still a plan. He would march swiftly south from Richmond, unite with Johnston, break Sherman, and then turn again to meet Grant and the immense Army of the Potomac. But all this was for honour, and mercifully that final agony was spared. Lee, disengaging himself from Richmond, was pursued by more than three times his numbers, and Sheridan, with a cavalry corps, lapped around his line of retreat and broke in upon his trains. When there were no more half-rations of green corn and roots to give to the soldiers, and they were beset on three sides, Grant ventured to appeal to Lee to recognise that his position was hopeless. Lee bowed to physical necessity. He rode on Traveller to Appomattox Court House to learn what terms would be offered. Grant wrote them out in a few sentences. The officers and men of the Army of Northern Virginia must surrender their arms and return on parole to their homes, not to be molested while they observed the laws of the United States. Lee's officers were to keep their swords. Food would be provided from the Union wagons. Grant added, "Your men must keep their horses and mules. They will need them for the spring ploughing." This was the greatest day in the career of General Grant, and stands high in the story of the United States. The Army of

Northern Virginia, which so long had "carried the Confederacy on its bayonets," surrendered, twenty-seven thousand strong; and a fortnight later, despite the protests of President Davis, Johnston accepted from Sherman terms similar to those granted to Lee. Davis himself was captured by a cavalry squadron. The armed resistance of the Southern states was thus entirely subdued.

Lincoln had entered Richmond with Grant, and on his return to Washington learned of Lee's surrender. Conqueror and master, he towered above all others, and four years of assured power seemed to lie before him. By his constancy under many varied strains and amid problems to which his training gave him no key he had saved the Union with steel and flame. His thoughts were bent upon healing his country's wounds. For this he possessed all the qualities of spirit and wisdom, and wielded besides incomparable authority. To those who spoke of hanging Jefferson Davis he replied, "Judge not that ye be not judged." On April 11 he proclaimed the need of a broad and generous temper and urged the conciliation of the vanquished. At Cabinet on the 14th he spoke of Lee and other Confederate leaders with kindness, and pointed to the paths of forgiveness and goodwill. But that very night as he sat in his box at Ford's Theatre a fanatical actor, one of a murder gang, stole in from behind and shot him through the head. The miscreant leapt on the stage, exclaiming, *"Sic semper tyrannis,"* and although his ankle was broken through his spur catching in an American flag he managed to escape to Virginia, where he was hunted down and shot to death in a barn. Seward, Secretary of State, was also stabbed at his home, though not fatally, as part of the same plot.

Lincoln died next day, without regaining consciousness, and with him vanished the only protector of the prostrate South. Others might try to emulate his magnanimity; none but he could control the bitter political hatreds which were rife. The assassin's bullet had wrought more evil to the United States than all the Confederate cannonade. The death of Lincoln deprived the Union of the guiding hand which alone could have solved the problems of reconstruction and added to the triumph of armies those lasting victories which are gained over the hearts of men.

> Who overcomes
> By force hath overcome but half his foe.

Thus ended the great American Civil War, which must upon the whole be considered the noblest and least avoidable of all the great mass-conflicts of which till then there was record.

BOOK TWELVE

The Victorian Age

CHAPTER EIGHTY-FIVE

Gladstone and Disraeli

WE NOW enter upon a long, connected, and progressive period in British history—the Prime Ministerships of Gladstone and Disraeli. These two great Parliamentarians in alternation ruled the land from 1868 to 1885. For nearly twenty years no one effectively disputed their leadership, and until Disraeli died in 1881 the political scene was dominated by a personal duel on a grand scale.

When Gladstone became Prime Minister in 1868 he was deemed a careful and parsimonious administrator who had become a sound Liberal reformer. But this was only one side of his genius. What gradually made him the most controversial figure of the century was his gift of rousing moral indignation both in himself and in the electorate. In two great crusades on the Balkans and on Ireland his dominant theme was that conscience and the moral law must govern political decisions. Such a demand, strenuously voiced, was open to the charge of hypocrisy when, as so often happened, Gladstone's policy obviously coincided with the well-being of the Liberal Party. But the charge was false; the spirit of the preacher breathed in Gladstone's speeches. He was willing to break his party rather than deny his conscience. Soon after his conversion to Home Rule for Ireland he said to his lieutenant, Sir William Harcourt, "I am prepared to go forward without anybody." It was a spirit which was to mismanage men and split the Liberals, but it won him a place in the hearts of his followers of which Britain had never seen the like.

To face Gladstone Disraeli needed all the courage and quickness of wit with which he had been so generously endowed. Many Tories disliked and distrusted his reforming views, but he handled his colleagues with a rare skill. He has never been surpassed in the art of party management. In all his attitudes there was a degree of cynicism; in his make-up there was not a trace of moral fervour. Large sections of the working classes were held to Church, Crown, Empire, and aristocracy by practical interests which could be turned to party advantage. Or so he saw it. He never became wholly assimilated to English ways of life, and preserved to his death the detachment which had led him as a young man to make his own analysis of English society. It was this which probably enabled him to diagnose and assess the deeper political currents of his age. Long handicapped by his own party, he led it in the end to an electoral triumph, and achieved for a period the power he had always desired.

* * *

Gladstone always said that his Cabinet of 1868 to 1874 was "one of the best instruments of government that ever was constructed." Driven by his boundless energy, it put into effect a long-delayed avalanche of reforms. This was the Golden Age when Liberalism was still an aggressive, unshackling force, and the doctrine of individualism and the philosophy of *laissez-faire* were seeking out and destroying the last relics of eighteenth-century government. The Civil Service, the Army, the universities, and the law were all attacked and the grip of the old landed interest began to crumble. The power of what James Mill had called the "sinister interests" shrivelled bit by bit as the public service was gradually but remorselessly thrown open to talent and industry. Freedom was the keynote, *laissez-faire* the method; no undue extension of Government authority was needed; and the middle class at last acquired a share in the political sphere equal to their economic power. Gladstone came in on the flood; a decisive electoral victory and a country ready for reform gave him his opportunity. The Liberal Party, for a rare moment in equilibrium, was united behind him. The scale and scope of his policy, directed at a series of obvious abuses, was such that Radicals, moderate Liberals, and even Whigs were brought together in agreement. He began with Ireland. "My mission," he had said when the summons from the Queen reached him at his country home in Hawarden, "is to pacify Ireland," and, in spite of bitter opposition and in defiance of his own early principles, which had been to defend property and the Anglican faith, he carried, in 1869, the disestablishment of the Protestant Church of Ireland. This was followed next year by a Land Act which attempted to protect tenants from unfair eviction. But Ireland was not so easily to be pacified.

In England the Government found no lack of work to do. After the Electoral Reform of 1867 Robert Lowe, now Chancellor of the Exchequer, had said that "We must educate our masters." Voters ought to know at least how to read and write, and have opened to them the paths to higher knowledge. Thus the extension of the franchise and the general Liberal belief in the value of education led to the launching of a national system of primary schools. This was achieved by W. E. Forster's Education Act of 1870, blurred though it was, like all education measures for some decades to come, by sectarian passion and controversy. At the same time patronage was finally destroyed in the home Civil Service. Entrance to the new administrative class was henceforth possible only through a competitive examination which placed great emphasis on intellectual attainment. Ability, not wealth or family connection, was now the means to advance. In the following year all religious tests at Oxford and Cambridge were abolished. The universities were thrown open to Roman Catholics, Jews, Dissenters, and

President Abraham Lincoln with Major General John A. McClernand
and Major Allan Pinkerton of the Secret Service. The photograph was
taken by Mathew B. Brady at Antietam, Maryland, early in October, 1862.

Lieutenant General Ulysses S. Grant
from a photograph by Barr and Young

young men of no belief. The ancient intricacies of the judicial system, so long a nightmare to litigants and a feeding ground for lawyers, were simplified and modernised by the fusion of courts of law and equity. All this was accompanied by a generally sound administration, and, what was perhaps closest to Gladstone's own heart, a policy of economy and low taxation.

The sufferings and disgraces of the Crimea had made it evident that the great Duke of Wellington's practices, in the hands of lesser men, had broken down. The Prussian victories in the war with France administered a shock to military and civilian opinion. Reforms were long overdue at the War Office. Flogging was abolished. An Enlistment Act introduced short service, which would create an efficient reserve. In 1871 the purchase of commissions was prohibited. The infantry were rearmed with the Martini-Henry rifle, and the regimental system was completely reorganised on a county basis. The War Office was overhauled, though a General Staff was not yet established.

All this was achieved in the space of six brilliant, crowded years, and then, as so often happens in English history, the pendulum swung back. Great reforms offend great interests. The Anglicans were hit by several measures; the Nonconformists found little to please them in the Education Act. The working classes were offered little to attract them apart from a Ballot Act which allowed them to exercise the newly won franchise in secret and without intimidation. The settlement for fifteen million dollars of the *Alabama* dispute with the United States, though sensible, was disagreeable to a people long fed on a Palmerstonian diet. They began to suspect that Gladstone was half-hearted in defending British interests. An unsuccessful Licensing Bill, prompted by the Temperance wing of the Liberal Party, estranged the drink interest and founded an alliance between the brewer and the Conservative Party. Gladstone was soon to complain that he had been borne down from power "in a torrent of gin and beer." Parliament was dissolved in 1874.

Gladstone fought the election on a proposal to abolish the income-tax, which then stood at threepence in the pound, and to the end of his life he always regretted his failure to achieve this object. But the country was now against him and he lost. He went into semi-retirement, believing that the great reforming work of Liberalism had been completed. Most of his Whig friends agreed. The Radicals thought otherwise. All of them were wrong. "The Grand Old Man" was soon to return to politics, and return in a setting and amid a storm which would rend and disrupt the loyalties and traditions of English public life in a manner far more drastic than any of them yet conceived.

*   *   *

While his great adversary devoted his leisure to felling trees at Hawarden and writing articles about Homer, Disraeli seized his chance. He had long waited for supreme power. He saw clearly that although many of the new electors were attracted by the ideas of tradition, continuity, and ordered social progress such feelings would never ripen into electoral advantage under the inert conservatism of his own back-benchers. He had not only to win over the electorate, but also to convert his own party.

Disraeli's campaign began long before Gladstone fell. He concentrated on social reform and on a new conception of the Empire, and both prongs of attack struck Gladstone at his weakest points. The Empire had never aroused his interest, and though passionate in defence of the political rights of the working class he cared little for their material claims. Disraeli, on the other hand, proclaimed that "the first consideration of a Minister should be the health of the people." Liberals tried to laugh this off as a "policy of sewage." In his first full session after reaching office Disraeli proceeded to redeem his pledge. A Trade Union Act gave the unions almost complete freedom of action, an Artisan's Dwelling Act was the first measure to tackle the housing problem, a Sale of Food and Drugs Act and a Public Health Act at last established sanitary law on a sound footing. Disraeli succeeded in persuading much of the Conservative Party not only that the real needs of the electorate included healthier conditions of life, better homes, and freedom to organise in the world of industry, but also that the Conservative Party was perfectly well fitted to provide them. Well might Alexander Macdonald, the miners' leader, declare that "The Conservative Party have done more for the working classes in five years than the Liberals have in fifty."

The second part of the new Conservative programme, Imperialism, had also been launched before Disraeli came to power. Gladstone's passion for economy in all things military, his caution in Europe, and his indifference to the Empire jarred on a public which was growing ever more conscious of British Imperial glory. Disraeli's appeal was perfectly tuned to the new mood and at first he was brilliantly successful. The Suez Canal had been open for six years, and had transformed the strategic position of Great Britain. No longer was the Cape of Good Hope the key to the route to India and the Far East. The Foreign Office had been curiously slow to appreciate this obvious fact and had missed more than one opportunity to control the waterway. In 1875 Disraeli, on behalf of the British Government, bought, for four million pounds, the shares of the Egyptian Khedive Ismail in the Canal. This Turkish satrap was bankrupt and glad to sell; his holding amounted to nearly half the total issue. The route to India was safeguarded, a possible threat to British naval supremacy was removed, and—of fateful importance for the future—Britain was inexorably drawn into Egyptian politics. In the following year Queen Victoria, to her great pleasure, was proclaimed Empress of India. Such a stroke would never have occurred to Gladstone, or, indeed, to the next generation of Imperialists. But Disraeli's Oriental, almost mystical, approach to Empire, his emphasis on Imperial symbols, his belief in the importance of outward display, gave his policy an imaginative colour never achieved by his successors. His purpose was to make those colonies which he had once condemned as "millstones round our necks" sparkle like diamonds. New storms in Europe distracted attention from this glittering prospect.

* * *

In 1876 the Eastern Question erupted anew. Most of the Balkans still remained under Turkish rule, and all attempts to improve the Ottoman administration of Christian provinces had foundered on the obstinacy of the Sultan and the magnitude of the task. Slavs, Rumanians, and Greeks were united in their detestation of the Turk. Revolt offered little hope of permanent success, and they had long looked to the Czar of Russia as their potential liberator.

Rebellion broke out in Bosnia and Herzegovina. Germany, Austria, and Russia proposed that Turkey should be coerced into making serious reforms. Disraeli resisted these plans, arguing that they "must end very soon in the disintegration of Turkey," and to emphasise British support of Turkey a fleet was dispatched to the Dardanelles. Europe waited for war to break out between Russia and Turkey. When it came in the summer of 1877 the mood of the country quickly changed. Gladstone, whose onslaught on the Turks had at first carried all before it, was now castigated as a pro-Russian. Feeling rose as, month after month, in spite of heroic Turkish resistance, especially at Plevna in Bulgaria, the mass of Russian troops moved ponderously towards the Dardanelles. At last, in January, 1878, they stood before the walls of Constantinople. Public opinion reached fever-point. The music-hall song of the hour was:

> We don't want to fight, but by jingo if we do
> We've got the ships, we've got the men, we've got the money too!
> We've fought the Bear before, and while we're Britons true
> The Russians shall not have Constantinople.

In February, after considerable prevarication, a fleet of British ironclads steamed into the Golden Horn. They lay in the Sea of Marmora, opposite the Russian Army, for six uneasy months of truce; the whale, as Bismarck said, facing the elephant.

In March Turkey and Russia signed the Treaty of San Stefano. Andrassy, the Austrian Foreign Minister, in anger called it "an orthodox Slavic sermon." It gave Russia effective control of the Balkans, and was obviously unacceptable to the other Great Powers. War again seemed likely. A conference of the Great Powers met at the Congress of Berlin in June and July. Business was dominated by Andrassy, Beaconsfield, Bismarck, and the Russian Minister Gortchakov, a quartet whose combined diplomatic talents would have been difficult to match. The result was that Russia gave up much of what she had momentarily gained at San Stefano. By a separate Anglo-Turkish convention Great Britain received Cyprus and guaranteed the territorial integrity of Turkey-in-Asia in return for yet another pledge by the Sultan to introduce proper reforms. Beaconsfield returned from Berlin claiming that he had brought "peace with honour." He had, indeed, averted war for the moment. Russia, blocked in the Balkans, turned her gaze away from Europe to the Far East.

* * *

While the duel between Disraeli and Gladstone held the centre of the stage far-reaching movements were taking shape below the surface of Parliamentary politics. The Reform Act of 1867, in granting the vote to virtually every adult male resident in a borough, killed the modified eighteenth-century régime which had persisted since 1832. The emergence of a mass electorate called for a new kind of politics. Sheer numbers rendered the old techniques ineffective in the large cities. Two things were required: a party policy which would persuade the electors to vote, and an efficient organisation to make sure that they did so. Of the two leaders Gladstone was slow to see the implications of the new age. The great demagogue was bored by the ordinary everyday business of party. Disraeli, on the other hand, produced both a policy and an organisation. The Conservative Party was completely overhauled. The Central Office was established and a network of local associations was set up, combined in a National Union. The transition was remarkably smooth, and although there were to be storms in the early 1880's the system created by Disraeli still largely remains at the present time.

In the Liberal camp the situation was very different. Gladstone's coolness and Whig hostility prevented the building of a centralised party organisation. The impulse and impetus came not from the centre, but through the provinces. In 1873 Joseph Chamberlain had become Mayor of Birmingham. A National Liberal Federation was born. The aim of its promoters was to make the Federation the Parliament of the Liberal movement, which would work out a Radical programme and eventually replace the Whigs by a new set of leaders drawn from its own ranks. This was a novel phenomenon. Unlike Chartism and the anti-Corn Law League, movements for reform need no longer operate on the fringe of party. Radicalism was now powerful enough to make a bid for control. This change was greatly aided by the clustering of the parties round opposite social poles, a process well under way by 1880, and which Gladstone recognised in the course of his election campaign. "I am sorry," he declared, "to say we cannot reckon upon the aristocracy. We cannot reckon upon what is called the landed interest. We cannot reckon upon the clergy of the Established Church either in England or in Scotland. . . . We cannot reckon upon the wealth of the country nor upon the rank of the country. . . . In the main these powers are against us. . . . We must set them down among our most determined foes."

At the election Chamberlain and his followers put forward a programme of reform which was unacceptable to the Whigs, and indeed to Gladstone. Their success exposed and proclaimed the wide changes which the new franchise had wrought in the structure of the party system.

* * *

Gladstone and Disraeli had done much to bridge the gap between aristocratic rule and democracy. They both believed that Governments should be active, and the Statute Books for the years between 1868 and 1876 bulge with reforming measures. Elections gradually became a judgement on what the Government of the day had accomplished and an assessment of the promises for the future made by the two parties. By 1880 they were being fought with techniques which differ very little from those used today. Gladstone's Midlothian Campaign, the first broad appeal to the people by a potential Prime Minister, underlined the change. It shocked the Queen that he should make a speech about foreign policy from a railway carriage window, but her protest echoed an age that had already passed. This was the way to become "the People's William."

Beaconsfield died a year later. His great task, taken on almost single-handed, had been to lead the Conservative Party out of the despair of the period after 1846, to persuade it to face the inevitability of democracy, and to endow it with the policies which would meet the new conditions. That he was successful is a remarkable indication of his skill in all matters related to party. He made the Conservatives a great force in democratic politics. The large-scale two-party system with its "swing of the pendulum" begins with him. Tory democracy—working men by hundreds of thousands who voted Conservative—became the dominant factor. The extension of the franchise which had hitherto threatened to engulf the past bore it proudly forward. Whereas the Whigs vanished from the scene, the Tories, though they were slow to realise it, sprang into renewed life and power with a fair future before them. Such was the work of Disraeli, for which his name will be duly honoured.

CHAPTER EIGHTY-SIX

American "Reconstruction"

ACROSS THE Atlantic the victory of Northern arms had preserved American unity. But immense problems had now to be faced. The most urgent was that of restoring order and prosperity to the defeated Confederacy. Great areas in the South, along the line of Sherman's march, and in the valley of Virginia, had been devastated. Atlanta, Columbia, Charleston,

Richmond, and other cities had been grievously damaged by bombardment and fire. The life of the South had come to a standstill. Farming, denied a market by the Northern blockade, had fallen into stagnation, despite the heroic efforts of Southern women and the faithful slaves to keep the land in cultivation. The blockade had also caused severe shortages in many common goods, and the breakdown of transport within the Confederacy had brought all within the grip of famine. The entire and inflated Southern banking system had collapsed. Confederate paper money and securities were now worthless. The whole region was reduced to penury. As the ragged, hungry soldiers of the Confederacy made their way homeward after Appomattox they were everywhere confronted by scenes of desolation and ruin.

Reconstruction was the word. But a prime difficulty in reconstructing the South was the future of the Negro. Lincoln's Proclamation of 1863 nominally freed the slaves in the rebellious states, but further action was needed, especially since doubts were expressed in many quarters about the constitutional rightness of Lincoln's Proclamation and of the Act passed by Congress in 1862 abolishing slavery in the Territories. The Thirteenth Constitutional Amendment was therefore proposed, prohibiting slavery in all areas within the jurisdiction of the United States.

But here was a complication. The American Constitution provided that no amendment was valid until it had been ratified by three-quarters of the states. As the Union now consisted of thirty-six states, some at least of the eleven former Confederate states would have to ratify if the Thirteenth Amendment was to become effective. The position of the states which had seceded from the Union had to be defined. If they had in fact left the Union should they return as the equals of their conquerors? If so, on what conditions?

While the war was still in progress Lincoln had dismissed the question of the legal status of the Confederate states as a "pernicious abstraction." He had been concerned only with restoring them to their "proper practical relation with the Union." In December, 1863, he had set out a plan for their readmission. Pardon was offered, with a few exceptions, to all adherents of the Confederacy who would take an oath of loyalty to the Union. When such oaths had been taken by 10 per cent of the electorate of any state it remained only for state Governments to be established which were prepared to abolish slavery. Then they would be readmitted. Lincoln's "10 per cent plan" was never carried out. Reconstructed Governments were set up in 1864 in three of the Confederate states which had fallen under the control of Union armies, but Congress refused to seat the Senators and Representatives whom they sent to Washington.

*   *   *

Congress believed that Reconstruction was its business, and not the President's. The Radical Republicans who dominated Congress did not wish to smooth the path of the South's return to her allegiance. They wanted a harsh and vengeful policy, and they especially desired the immediate enfranchisement of the Negro. Radical vindictiveness sprang from various causes. The most creditable was a humanitarian concern for the welfare of the Negro. These feelings were shared only by a minority. There was another and nearer point. The Radicals saw that if the Negro was given the vote they could break the power of the Southern planter and preserve the ascendancy over the Federal Government that Northern business interests had won since 1861. To allow the Southern states, in alliance with Northern Democrats, to recover their former voice in national affairs would, the Radicals believed, be incongruous and absurd. It would also jeopardise the mass of legislation on tariffs, banking, and public land which Northern capitalists had secured for themselves during the war. To safeguard these laws the Radicals took up the cry of the Negro vote, meaning to use it to keep their own party in power.

Even if Lincoln had lived to complete his second term he would have met with heavy opposition from his own party. The magnanimous policy he had outlined in April, 1865, in the classic address delivered from the White House, was shattered by the bullet that killed him a few days later. The new President, Andrew Johnson of Tennessee, though sharing Lincoln's views on Reconstruction, was markedly lacking in political gifts. Nevertheless, from Lincoln's death until the end of the year, while Congress was in recess, Johnson was able to put into effect a Reconstruction plan closely resembling Lincoln's. Each Southern state, in conventions chosen by loyal electors, could qualify for readmission to the Union by repealing the Ordinances of Secession, repudiating the Confederate war debt, and abolishing slavery. The South, anxious, in the words of General Grant, "to return to self-government within the Union as soon as possible," was quick to comply. Southerners then proceeded to elect state legislatures and officials, chose Senators and Representatives to go to Washington, and ratified the Thirteenth Amendment, which went into force in December, 1865.

When Congress reconvened in that same month it declined to seat the elected Representatives of the South. Ignoring Johnson's work, Congress went on to put its own ideas into practice. Its first step was to set up a Joint Committee on Reconstruction, charged with the task of collecting information about Southern conditions. Early in the new year this body, under Radical control, reported that drastic measures were necessary to protect the emancipated Negro. Congress promptly took action. First came the Freedmen's Bureau Bill, which prolonged the life and greatly extended the powers of an agency set up earlier to assist Negroes to make the transition

439

to freedom. This was followed by a Civil Rights Bill, conferring citizenship on the Negroes and granting them equality of treatment before the law. The Radicals aimed at making doubly sure of their purposes by incorporating its provisions in the Fourteenth Amendment.

The quarrel between Johnson and the Radicals was now open and bitter, and the Congressional elections of 1866 witnessed a fierce struggle between them. The Radical leaders carried more conviction with the Northern electors than did Johnson, whose undignified outbursts during a speaking tour lost him much support. The result was a resounding victory for the Radicals, who obtained a two-thirds majority in both Houses of Congress. The way was now clear for them to carry out their own plan of Reconstruction, for they were strong enough to override the President's vetoes. A series of harsh and vengeful Reconstruction Acts was passed in 1867. The South was divided into five military districts, each under the command of a Federal Major-General. The former Confederacy was to be subjected to Army rule of the kind that Cromwell had once imposed on England. In order to be readmitted to the Union the Southern states were now required to ratify the Fourteenth Amendment and to frame state constitutions which provided for Negro suffrage—and this in spite of the fact that very few of the Northern states had as yet granted the Negro the vote.

Not content with these successes, the Radical leaders then tried to remove the President from office by impeachment. This would have suited them well, for as the law then stood Johnson would have been replaced by the President of the Senate, who was himself a leading Radical. According to the Constitution, the President could be thus dismissed on conviction for treason, bribery, or other high crimes and misdemeanours. Yet Johnson's opposition to Radical policies had never overstepped constitutional limits, and his enemies were put to some difficulty in framing charges against him. After vain endeavours to find any evidence of treason or corruptibility, the Radicals put forward as a pretext for his impeachment Johnson's effort, in August, 1867, to rid himself of his Secretary of War, Edwin M. Stanton. This unscrupulous politician had long merited dismissal. But when Johnson demanded his resignation Stanton refused to comply. For some months he continued to conduct the business of the War Department, in which he finally barricaded himself. Stanton justified his conduct by reference to the Tenure of Office Act, a measure recently adopted over Johnson's veto as part of the Radical effort to diminish the powers of the Presidency. No Cabinet officers, the Act had declared, were to be dismissed without the consent of the Senate. Failure to obtain consent was punishable as a high crime.

Thus in March, 1868, the Radical leaders were able to induce the House to adopt eleven articles impeaching Andrew Johnson at the bar of the Senate. In the event they failed by a single vote to obtain the two-thirds majority in the Senate which they needed to convict the President. Seven Republican Senators, withstanding immense and prolonged pressure, refused to allow the impeachment process to be debased for party ends. They voted for acquittal.

By the narrowest possible margin a cardinal principle of the American Constitution, that of the separation of powers, was thus preserved. Had the impeachment succeeded the whole course of American constitutional development would have been changed. Power would henceforth have become concentrated in the legislative branch of the Government, and no President could have been sure of retaining office in the face of an adverse Congressional majority. Nevertheless the Radicals were strong enough in Congress during the rest of Johnson's term to be able to ignore his wishes. A further Republican victory at the polls in 1868 brought General Ulysses S. Grant to the White House. The triumph of the Radicals was now complete, for the ineptitude in high office of the victorious Union commander made him their tool.

The political reconstruction of the South ground forward in strict accordance with the harsh legislation of 1867. Between 1868 and 1871 "carpet-bag" and "scalawag" Governments, supported by the Negro vote and by Federal bayonets, were installed in all the Southern states. When these states were deemed to have complied with the Radical requirements they were allowed to return to the Union.

To bolster up the "carpet-bag" Governments Congress initiated the Fifteenth Amendment, which laid down that suffrage could not be denied to any citizen on grounds of "race, colour, or previous condition of servitude." A series of laws placed Congressional elections under Federal management, and authorised the use of military force to suppress violence in the Southern states. These measures were prompted by the vigorous efforts of white Southerners, both by legal methods and by threats to Negro voters from secret societies like the Ku Klux Klan, to overthrow the "carpet-bag" Governments and restore white supremacy. For a time repression achieved its purpose, but gradually state after state was recaptured by white voters. This success was partly due to the stubbornness of Southern resistance and partly to a change in Northern sentiment. By the early 1870's the Northern business man wanted an end to unsettled conditions, which were bad for trade. Northerners became weary of upholding corrupt minority Governments by force. They began to withdraw their support from the Radical programme.

By 1875 the Radical Republicans had so far lost control that only South Carolina, Florida, and Louisiana were still in the hands of the "carpet-baggers." In the following year a way was opened for these states to recover control of their own affairs. After the Presidential election of 1876 disputes arose in these three states over the validity of the election returns.

The matter was extremely important, since the nineteen electoral votes at stake were sufficient to decide the Presidential contest. The Democratic candidate, Samuel J. Tilden, had obtained one hundred and eighty-four electoral votes, or one short of a majority. The Republican, Rutherford B. Hayes, therefore needed all the disputed nineteen. As a sop to Democratic opinion generally, and to the South in particular, Hayes's supporters promised that Federal troops would be withdrawn from the South as soon as Hayes took office. Mollified by this concession, the South abandoned its opposition to Hayes. In April, 1877, a month after Hayes assumed the Presidency, and twelve years after Lee's surrender at Appomattox, the last Federal garrisons left the South. The remaining "carpet-bag" Governments promptly collapsed, white supremacy was everywhere restored, and the period of Radical Reconstruction was over.

Reconstruction left in the South a legacy of bitterness and hatred greater by far than that produced by four years of war. Remembering the Republicans as the party of Negro rule, the white South for the next fifty years would vote almost to a man for the Democratic Party. The Negro himself gained little lasting benefit from Reconstruction. His advancement had been the plaything of self-seeking and cynical men, and was set back for an incalculable period.

*　　*　　*

From the end of Reconstruction until the closing decade of the century American politics lacked interest. The issues of the war itself were dead, and unreplaced. No major questions divided the parties, no new policies were initiated, and scarcely a measure deserving the attention of the historian was placed on the Statute Book. Nor were the political personalities of the time any more exciting than the events in which they took part. A succession of worthy, mediocre men filled the Presidency, the chief virtue of their administrations being the absence of the corruption which had disgraced the two terms of the unfortunate General Grant.

Yet if the politics of the period were insignificant its economic developments were of the first importance. Throughout the generation that followed the Civil War the pace of economic change quickened and the main outlines of modern America emerged. Between 1860 and 1900 the population of the Union soared from thirty-one to seventy-six millions. This increase was due in part to the heavy influx of European immigrants, who within forty years totalled fifteen millions. Cities grew fast. Great mineral deposits were discovered and exploited, giving rise to vast new industries. "No other generation in American history," it has been remarked, "witnessed changes as swift or as revolutionary as those which transformed the rural republic of Lincoln and Lee into the urban industrial empire of McKinley and Roosevelt."

Even in the South a revolution was afoot. A great number of Southern whites for the first time became landowners. The old sprawling plantations disappeared, and were replaced by small farms, engaged for the most part in growing the same crops as before the war. Negroes, however, continued as in the days of slavery to provide the bulk of the labour for cotton cultivation. Because they lacked capital few of the coloured freedmen were able to buy farms or to pay rent. A novel form of tenantry known as "share-cropping" therefore came into being. Furnished by the farmer with land and equipment, the Negro—and later the landless white—gave their labour in return for one-third of the crop they produced. By these means Southern agriculture slowly revived.

This period saw also the beginnings of large-scale industry in the South. The Southern textile industry, very small before 1860, managed in time to recover and then to expand. The tobacco industry flourished in North Carolina and Virginia, and the discovery of coal and iron deposits in Tennessee and Alabama led to the rise of a Southern iron industry. Yet the South remained predominantly agricultural, and the growth of Southern industry was insignificant compared with that of the North.

The Civil War had given a great impetus to Northern output. The Federal armies had needed huge quantities of arms and equipment, clothing and footwear. Fortified by Government contracts, Northern manufacturers embarked on large-scale production. Furthermore, in the absence of Southern representatives Congress passed into law the protective measures demanded by Northern industrialists and financiers. But the assistance thus afforded did no more than speed the coming of the American Industrial Revolution.

Each decade saw new levels of output in the iron and steel mills of the Pittsburgh area, the oil refineries of Ohio, Pennsylvania, and elsewhere, the flour mills of Minneapolis and St. Paul, the meat-packing plants of Chicago and Cincinnati, the clothing and boot and shoe factories of New England, and the breweries of Milwaukee and St. Louis, to mention only the biggest of American industrial enterprises. In each of these fields great captains of industry arose, the most powerful of whom were Rockefeller in oil and Carnegie in steel. With untiring energy and skill, and with ruthless disregard for competitors, these men built up economic empires which gave them great wealth and a formidable power over the life of the community. Carnegie and Rockefeller, together with Morgan in finance and Vanderbilt and Harriman in railroads, became the representative figures of the age, in striking contrast to the colourless actors upon the political scene. By 1900, owing to their vigorous efforts, American industry was concentrated in a number of giant corporations, each practically a monopoly in its chosen field. Meanwhile the United States had ceased to depend on European manufactures; they were even invading Europe with their own. Thus America passed through a gilded age of which the millionaire seemed, at least to

European eyes, the typical representative. Yet it was at the same time an age of unrest, racked by severe growing pains. There was much poverty in the big cities, especially among recent immigrants. There were sharp, sudden financial panics, causing loss and ruin, and there were many strikes, which sometimes broke into violence. Labour began to organise itself in Trade Unions and to confront the industrialists with a stiff bargaining power. These developments were to lead to a period of protest and reform in the early twentieth century. The gains conferred by large-scale industry were great and lasting, but the wrongs that had accompanied their making were only gradually righted. All this made for a lively, thrusting, controversial future.

CHAPTER EIGHTY-SEVEN

America as a World Power

WHILE THE United States were growing into the world's leading industrial Power their people were busily completing the settlement of the continent. At the beginning of the Civil War, after two and a half centuries of westward advance from the Atlantic coast, the frontier of settlement had reached roughly the line of the 97th meridian, which runs through Nebraska, Kansas, Oklahoma, and Texas. Between this frontier and the towns and cities of the Pacific seaboard lay a thousand miles of wilderness. Here were the Great Plains, about a million square miles in extent, where roamed many Indian tribes, and little else except the immense herds of buffalo on which they lived. The sparse rainfall of the Great Plains and lack of timber had made them seem unsuitable for farming and unlikely ever to be peopled. Yet in less than a generation large parts of this huge area were settled by white men and the natural frontier disappeared. The population west of the Mississippi rose in thirty years from about five millions in 1860 to almost eighteen millions, while the number of states in the Union increased from thirty-three to forty-four. By 1890 only four more states remained to be carved out of the West. These were Utah, Oklahoma, New Mexico, and Arizona, all admitted to the Union by 1912, when the political shape of the country became complete.

White settlement of the Great Plains was first prompted by the discovery of precious metals. In 1859 gold was found at Pikes Peak, on the eastern slopes of the Rockies, and miners began to flock into Colorado. As fresh deposits of gold, silver, and copper came to light there was a rush to

444

Nevada, Arizona, Idaho, and Montana, and finally to the Black Hills of South Dakota. These sudden migrations in search of wealth did not always create lasting settlements, for many of the booms were short-lived. When precious ores ran low the whole population of the mining camps moved on elsewhere, leaving ghost towns to mark the site of their "diggings." Yet by speeding the political organisation of the West and encouraging the building of railroads the discovery of gold and silver did much to open up the Great Plains.

It was the railway indeed, more than any other factor, which threw wide the Plains to settlers. This was the great age of American railroad construction. At the close of the Civil War the United States had possessed about thirty-five thousand miles of tracks, but in less than ten years that figure had been doubled, and by 1890 doubled again. The most prodigious feat was the building of a number of transcontinental railways. The first to cross the continent was completed in May, 1869, when a link was made in Utah between the lines of the Union Pacific, stretching westward from Iowa, and the Central Pacific, reaching out eastward from California. This project was financed by a grant from Congress to the two companies of millions of acres of public land, a method which was also used elsewhere. Towards the end of the century three more transcontinental routes had been added, and other great lines had opened up the country. Many of the railroad companies took a direct part in peopling the West, for they realised that their lines could hardly pay until the country on either side of the tracks was settled. An extensive campaign to popularise the West was undertaken both in the Eastern states and in Europe. Because transport was cheap and land could be acquired on credit thousands of settlers were induced to seek new homes in the Great Plains.

The settlement of the West could only take place if the Indian barrier were removed. Already by the time of the Civil War the Indian had been obliged to retreat across half the continent in the face of white advance. Now, as the Redman was harried out of his last refuge, a further tragic chapter was added to his story. The threat to their hunting grounds, and indeed to their whole existence, delivered by the onrush of civilisation impelled the nomadic tribes of the Great Plains to resist the invaders with determination and savagery. From the Sioux and the Crows of the North to the Comanche and Apache of the South, these warlike tribesmen were magnificent horsemen and intrepid fighters. Their bows and arrows were much more effective than the muzzle-loading rifles with which the Federal troops were at first equipped. Yet their final defeat was inevitable. The introduction of the Winchester repeating rifle and the Colt revolver gave armed supremacy to the whites, who were already superior in organisation, numbers, and strategy. But the fatal blow was the wholesale slaughter of the buffalo, chiefly by professional hunters employed by Eastern leather manufacturers. By the early 1870's between two and three million buffalo were being killed annually for their hides, and ten years later a museum expedition seeking specimens could find only two hundred in the whole of the West. On the buffalo the Indian of the Plains had relied not only for food, but for a great variety of other things, from clothing to fuel. When the buffalo was virtually exterminated nomadic life became impossible. The Indians had to comply with the Government's plans and be herded into reservations.

Means had still to be found in the semi-arid West for making agriculture pay. The miner was at first succeeded not by the farmer but by the rancher, who for twenty years after the Civil War used the Great Plains as pasture for his cattle on the long drive from Texas to the Middle West. Although the journey involved passing through territory inhabited by hostile Indians, who frequently stampeded the cattle, vast herds were led each year from the ranches of the South-West to the cattle centres of Kansas and Nebraska. Then, after being fattened for market, the cattle were shipped to the stock-yards and canneries of Kansas City or Chicago. But the farmer still hung back from the Great Plains. In this extensive grassland there were very few trees, and no lumber for building houses, barns, and fences. More serious still, the annual rainfall between the 98th meridian and the Rockies was usually below the twenty-inch minimum needed for agriculture.

Science now stepped in. A technique known as dry farming was developed. Deep ploughing loosened the soil sufficiently to allow water to move upwards, and frequent harrowing prevented evaporation. New strains of wheat were introduced from Russia, which were resistant to drought and to the disease of wheat-rust, then common on the Plains. But it was large-scale industry that really made farming possible. A wide range of mechanical farm implements, reapers, harvesters, threshers, and improved types of plough enabled the Western farmer to cultivate large enough tracts of land to offset the low yield per acre. Moreover, the invention of barbed wire, though it ended the great cattle drives, solved the problem of fencing.

During the last quarter of the century large numbers of emigrant farmers were flowing into the Great Plains. By 1890 "the frontier"—which officially meant a region inhabited by more than two but less than six persons per square mile—had disappeared. The formerly unsettled area, the superintendent of the census explained, had now "been so broken into by isolated bodies of settlement that there [could] hardly be said to be a frontier line." The colonisation begun at Jamestown, Virginia, almost three centuries before was now complete. Hitherto the frontier had been America's safety-valve. Through it had passed ardent ambitions and bold, restless spirits. Now the safety-valve was shut, and the problems and pressures of dynamic growth within the United States were greatly intensified.

*   *   *

446

Since the fall of Napoleon the American people had been so engrossed in settling the continent and in exploiting its natural resources that foreign affairs had interested them little. Now, with the process of settlement complete, and the work of economic development well in hand, they sought fresh fields in which to labour. By the 1890's the idea of Empire had taken hold of all the great industrial Powers. Britain, France, and Germany were especially active in acquiring new colonies and new markets. This European example was not lost upon America. For these and other reasons a vigorous spirit of self-assertion developed, which first became manifest in the Venezuelan boundary dispute with Britain in 1895.

Ever since the end of the Civil War Anglo-American relations had been distinctly cool. In spite of the settlement of the *Alabama* claims by Gladstone's Government, Britain's sympathy for the South during the great conflict had left its mark upon the Union. Constant bickering agitated the two countries over such matters as seal-fishing in the Bering Sea, the rights of American fishermen in Canadian waters, and interpretations of the Clayton-Bulwer Treaty of 1850 about the proposed Panama Canal. But all these disputes paled before the question of the Venezuelan boundary. The frontier between this South American republic and British Guiana had long been unsettled, and although the United States had frequently offered mediation her advances had always been declined by Britain. In the summer of 1895 the American State Department sent what President Cleveland described as "a twenty-inch gun note." Britain was accused of violating the Monroe Doctrine, and was required to give a definite answer as to whether she would accept arbitration. Lord Salisbury rejected arbitration and told the American Government that its interpretation of the Monroe Doctrine was at fault. At this Cleveland sent Congress a message announcing that America would fix the boundary line independently and oblige the disputants to accept her decision.

For a few days war with Britain seemed possible, and even imminent. But the first patriotic outburst in America soon gave way to more sober feelings. In Britain opinion had reacted less violently. Too involved in Europe and South Africa to think of quarrelling with America, the British Government agreed to arbitration. Their claims in Guiana were largely conceded by the tribunal. There followed a steady improvement in Anglo-American relations, chiefly because Britain was awakening to the dangers of her isolation. Her growing alarm at German naval expansion led her to make friendly overtures to which the United States were fully ready to respond.

The exuberant pride of Americans could not long be held in check. In the Cuban revolt against Spanish rule it found an outlet. Ever since this revolt began in 1895 American popular sentiment had sympathised with the rebel fight for independence. In 1898 popular clamour for war with

Spain reached its height. In February the American battleship *Maine,* sent to Cuba to protect American lives and property, was blown up by a mine in Havana harbour, with the loss of most of her crew. At this the Spanish Government hastily made concessions to the United States, which President McKinley was at first disposed to accept. But public indignation was too strong for him, and on April 11 war was declared.

The conflict lasted only ten weeks, and was marked by a succession of overwhelming American victories. In Cuba an American expeditionary force, despite complaints about the mismanagement of the War Department and incompetent leadership in the field, won a series of rapid battles which brought about the surrender of all the Spanish forces in the island. At sea Commodore Dewey immobilised the main Spanish fleet in an engagement in Manila Bay in the distant Philippines on May 1. The Caribbean squadron of the Spanish Navy was sunk outside the Cuban port of Santiago. In August Spain sued for peace, and in December a treaty was signed at Paris whereby Cuba became independent. The United States acquired Puerto Rico, Guam, and the Philippines.

All this did much to heal the wounds remaining from the Civil War. The venture also showed that the American people were now fully aware of their own strength as a world Power. Their new colonial rôle was further stressed by the acquisition between 1898 and 1900 not only of the territory wrested from Spain, but of Hawaii, part of Samoa, and the vacant island of Wake in the Pacific. The United States, though not yet abandoning isolation, henceforward became less preoccupied by home affairs. They began to play an important rôle in the international scene. The Spanish War helped to promote a new and warmer friendship with Britain, for Britain, alone of the European nations, sympathised with the United States in the conflict. This the Americans appreciated, and as the nineteenth century drew to its end the foundations were laid for a closer concert between the two peoples in facing the problems of the world.

CHAPTER EIGHTY-EIGHT

Home Rule for Ireland

WHEN GLADSTONE in 1880 became Prime Minister for the second time, his position was not the comfortable one he had held twelve years before. Almost as soon as the House assembled the Speaker remarked that Gladstone had "a difficult team to drive." So it was to prove. Few periods of office have begun with higher hopes; none has been more disappointing in its outcome. Gladstone was to find himself in direct clash and conflict with his own colleagues in the Cabinet on the main political, Imperial, and foreign issues of the day, and above all on Ireland. A Cabinet with such deep cleavages was unlikely to prove an effective instrument of government. Over it ruled the Grand Old Man, as he was already considered at the age of seventy-one, his force and energy undimmed, his passions and enthusiasms growing more intense with every year that passed. He towered above his colleagues. When he was away from Cabinet, wrote one of them, it was as though he had "left us mice without the cat."

These were strange years for party warfare. The upsurge of the new forces, Radicalism and Tory Democracy, was playing havoc with the old Parliamentary system. The confusion was not to be resolved until Gladstone, using Home Rule for Ireland like an axe, divided the political world by forcing men to make a clear and sharp decision about a single great proposal.

* * *

It was a constant complaint among Liberals that whenever they succeeded the Tories in office they fell heirs to a set of Imperial complications which involved them in enterprises hateful to their anti-Imperialist sentiments. So it was in 1880. One of their first troubles sprang from South Africa. There the Boer Republic of the Transvaal had long been in difficulties. To save it from ruin and possible extinction Disraeli's Government had annexed it. Disraeli looked forward to a union of all the white communities of South Africa in a self-governing Confederation on the Canadian model, but the times were not yet ripe. A fierce desire for renewed independence began to stir among the Transvaal Boers, and they looked for an opportunity to throw off British rule. At the end of 1880 the Boers revolted and a small British force was cut to pieces at Majuba Hill. Gladstone declined to bow to the outcry for retaliation and continued with the negotiations that had already been under way. The outcome gave virtual independence to the Transvaal. This application of Liberal principles provided the foundation of Boer power in South Africa.

Meanwhile, at Cape Town, Cecil Rhodes had entered politics, resolved to create a vast, all-embracing South African dominion, and endowed by nature with the energy that often makes dreams come true. From these events sprang consequences which have yet to run their course.

* * *

As Gladstone had foreseen at the time, Disraeli's purchase of shares in the Suez Canal, brilliant stroke though it was, soon brought all the problems of Egypt in its wake. At the end of 1881 Anglo-French control was shattered by a nationalist revolt led by Colonel Arabi Pasha. A sudden twist in the domestic politics of France forced her to stand aside, and the other European Powers remained aloof. The cabinet decided to dispatch an army under Sir Garnet Wolseley to Egypt. The decision was crowned by military success, and Arabi's army was decisively defeated. Gladstone delighted in the victory, but was troubled in his conscience. The Liberal instinct was now to withdraw, but Egypt could not be left a vacuum. To annex her was too repugnant to the Liberal conscience. Gladstone therefore chose the worst of both worlds. The odium of occupation remained on the British.

Intervention in Egypt led to an even more perplexing entanglement in the Sudan. This huge territory, more than a thousand miles deep, stretched along the torrid banks of the Nile from the borders of Egypt down almost to the Equator. In spite of the efforts of British advisers it was woefully misgoverned by Pashas from Cairo. During the same year that the Egyptians revolted the Sudanese rebelled against the Egyptians. They were led by the Mahdi, a Moslem fanatic who quickly destroyed an Egyptian army, was soon in control of most of the Sudan, and whose blood-lust spread terror everywhere in their advance. Either the Sudan must be reconquered or it must be evacuated, and the Government in London chose evacuation.

On January 14, 1884, General Charles Gordon, who had achieved fame in Chinese wars, left London charged by the Cabinet with the task of evacuation. Gordon had himself served in the Sudan, and had played a notable part in attempts to suppress the slave trade. He also had a conscience. It was to cost him his life. He arrived in Khartoum, and once there he judged that it would be wrong to withdraw the garrisons and abandon the country to the mercy of the Mahdi's Dervishes. The Government might have foreseen that a commander cast in heroic mould would not readily lend himself to withdrawal. Retreat was never to Gordon's liking. He was resolved to remain in Khartoum until his self-imposed mission was accomplished. Help for Gordon was to be long in coming, in spite of his urgent appeals. By May Gordon was cut off in Khartoum. Throughout the spring and summer public opinion in England mounted, and large meetings were held demanding that Gordon must be saved. His stern religious faith, his Bible-reading, his assaults on slavery, his charitable work for the children of the poor, as well as his military prowess, had made him a popular figure, as gallant and noble as one of King Arthur's Knights.

Eventually the Government were induced to rescue him and in September General Wolseley hastened to Cairo. Speed was essential, but disaster could not be risked. Wolseley was aware that time was fatally short. He felt the eyes and anxieties of England focused upon Gordon and himself, and on the distance that lay between them.

Not until the 28th of January did they reach Khartoum. It was too late. Gordon's flag no longer flew over the Residency. He was dead; the city had fallen two days before, after a prodigious display of valour by its defender.

He had fallen alone, unsuccoured and unsupported by any of his own countrymen. In the eyes of perhaps half the nation Gladstone was a murderer. Gordon became a national martyr. Thirteen years went by before Gordon was avenged.

* * *

Speculation about the future of English politics was abruptly cut short by the announcement of Gladstone's conversion to the policy of Home Rule. To comprehend the significance and impact of this event we must look back upon the melancholy story of Ireland. In the years since the Great Famine of the 1840's, Ireland had continued in her misery. Her peasants, especially in the West, lived in a state of extreme poverty and degradation. Ireland was, and is, a poor country, and in spite of famine and emigration she was still overpopulated. But these misfortunes were greatly aggravated by the policies of the English Government. The Irish peasant was crushed by a land system which he hated. It was not just a matter of material poverty, of life passed in a one-roomed hut on a diet of potatoes. He felt he had been robbed of his heritage. For most of the nineteenth century the English answer was to ignore the hate and crush the crime which it produced.

It must not be supposed that the Irish picture can be seen from Britain entirely in black and white. The landlords were mostly colonists from England and of long standing; they believed themselves to be, and in many ways were, a civilising influence in a primitive country. They had often had to fight for their lives and their property. The deep hold of the Roman Catholic Church on a superstitious peasantry had tended on political as well as religious grounds to be hostile to England. Ireland more than once since the days of Queen Elizabeth had threatened to become a stepping-stone to the invasion of Great Britain from the Continent. Rick-burning, the assassination of landlords, and other acts of terrorism had contributed to a general acceptance in England of the landlord's case. It was hard to grasp that the vicious circle of unrest, heavy-handed repression, and rebellion could only be broken by remedying fundamental grievances.

From the moment when he first took office as Prime Minister, Gladstone made Irish affairs his special concern, until at last they came to dominate his mind to the exclusion of almost everything else.

In 1873 the Irish founded a Home Rule League to achieve Home Rule by peaceful methods. Effective leadership of the Home Rule movement soon passed into the hands of Charles Stewart Parnell, a newcomer to Parliament. From his mother, the daughter of an American admiral who had won distinction fighting the British, he had acquired a hatred and contempt for English ways and institutions. A patrician in the Irish party, he was a born leader, with a power of discipline and a tactical skill that soon converted Home Rule from a debating topic into the supreme question of the hour.

451

A grave fall in world crop prices in the late seventies and a series of bad harvests accelerated the number of evictions as the impoverished peasants failed to pay their rents. And in the last quarter of 1880 nearly two thousand outrages were committed. A new weapon appeared when Parnell advised his followers to make life unbearable for anyone who violated peasant law and custom "by isolating him from his kind as if he were a leper of old." One of the first victims was a land agent, Captain Boycott, whose name has passed into the English language.

The Government then decided both to strike at terrorism and to reform the land laws. In March, 1881, a sweeping Coercion Act was followed immediately by a Land Act which conceded almost everything that the Irish had demanded, the "three F's"—Fair Rents, Fixity of Tenure, and Free Sale. This was far more generous than anything the Irish had expected, but Parnell, driven by Irish-American extremists and by his belief that even greater concessions could be extracted from Gladstone, set out to obstruct the working of the new land courts. The Government had no alternative but to arrest him. This it did in October. He was asked who would take his place. His reply was "Captain Moonlight." His prophecy was justified. Crime and murder multiplied.

The English nation was shocked, the hand of the coercion party was strengthened, and all hope of any immediate conciliation was quenched. Parnell, for his part, was content to bide his time, and for three years Ireland was relatively quiet and peaceful.

* * *

Thus we return to the year 1885. When the election came in November Parnell, unable to extract a clear promise of support from Gladstone, ordered the Irish in Britain to vote Conservative. Ireland was not an important issue at these hustings. The result could not have been more unfortunate. The position was exactly what Lord Salisbury had described as "low-water mark—*i.e.*, Tories + Parnellites = Liberals." For Parnell the outcome was a disaster. His support had made the Conservatives a present of thirty seats. It proved to be a gift to the enemy.

By Christmas, 1885, the die was cast, and on January 26, 1886, Salisbury's Government announced that it would introduce a Coercion Bill of the most stringent kind. Without hesitation, almost without consultation with his colleagues, Gladstone brought about its defeat on an amendment to the Queen's Speech. There was no doubt that the new Government would be a Home Rule Government.

A Home Rule Bill was introduced into the Commons on April 8, 1886, by Gladstone in a speech which lasted for three and a half hours. He put the case for Home Rule as one of justice for Ireland and freedom for her people. It was an impressive performance, outstanding even in Gladstone's dazzling Parliamentary career. But his appeal to the Liberal principles of liberty and self-government struck against deep emotions. His sudden conversion to the new policy, his dependence upon the Irish vote for continuance in office, and the bitter memories of Irish crimes combined to deepen the fears and prejudices of his opponents. The emotions of race, religion, class, and economic interest all obscured the Liberal arguments which Gladstone used. Fire evoked fire.

The Bill was defeated on the second reading two months after its introduction. Gladstone chose to dissolve Parliament and to fight the new election on the single issue of Home Rule. His zeal, enthusiasm, and energy were not enough to overcome the mighty forces arrayed against him, and Salisbury again took office.

Apart from one short spell the Conservatives were to remain in power for twenty years. The long period of Liberal-Whig predominance which had begun in 1830 was over. It had been brought to an end by Whig distaste for social reform and by Gladstone's precipitate conversion to Home Rule. The turn of the wheel had brought fortune to the Conservatives, whose prospects had seemed so gloomy in 1880. The opponents whom they had feared as the irresistible instruments of democracy had delivered themselves into their hands.

CHAPTER EIGHTY-NINE

Lord Salisbury's Government

IT WAS not immediately perceived in the summer of 1886 that the controversy over Home Rule for Ireland had wrought a deep change in the allegiance of English political parties. It was tacitly accepted, after the failure of a Round Table Conference between the leaders of the two sides, held at the beginning of 1887, that the gulf was too wide to be bridged. This decisive split produced strange bedfellows. At the age of thirty-seven Lord Randolph Churchill became Leader of the House and Chancellor of the Exchequer. His career had reached its pinnacle. In the course of six years his skill in debate and political tactics had carried him beyond all his rivals. Lord Randolph's ideas on Tory Democracy struck no spark in Salisbury's traditional Conservatism. The Prime Minister had no great faith in betterment by legislation. He believed that the primary business of government was to administer the existing order, and that the Conservatives owed their first duty to the classes who relied upon them to defend their interests. The differences between the two men, both in character and policy, were fundamental. The final collision occurred over a comparatively trivial point, Lord Randolph's demand for a reduction in the Army and Navy Estimates. He resigned on the eve of Christmas, 1886, at the wrong time, on the wrong issue, and he made no attempt to rally support. He lived for another nine years, enduring much ill-health, but already his career lay in ruins.

* * *

Salisbury's interest and that of a large section of public opinion lay in the world overseas, where the Imperialist movement was reaching its climax of exploration, conquest, and settlement. Livingstone, Stanley, and other travellers had opened up the interior of darkest Africa. Their feats of exploration paved the way for the acquisition of colonies by the European Powers. The Prime Minister never lost sight of the need to preserve peace while the colonial map of Africa was being drawn. The task of forwarding British interests was largely carried out by men like Cecil Rhodes who, in spite of the indifference of the Government at home, carved out a great new empire.

When Salisbury took office he himself promoted no great schemes of Imperial expansion, but he was prepared to back up the men on the spot. The work of consolidation and political control was entrusted, after the Elizabethan model, to chartered companies. The Royal Niger Company operated in Nigeria, the British East Africa Company controlled what is now Kenya and Uganda, and the British South Africa Company acquired the territory of the Rhodesias. All were launched between 1886 and 1889. Rhodesia is the only self-governing member of the British Commonwealth which bears the name of the man who founded it, and foresaw its future. Its capital, Salisbury, commemorates the Prime Minister. Many border disputes with the other colonising Powers arose, but Salisbury pursued a steady policy of settlement by negotiation. The key to Salisbury's success lay in his skilful handling of the innumerable complications that arose between the Powers in an age of intense national rivalries. He once said that "British policy is to drift lazily downstream, occasionally putting out a boat-hook to avoid a collision." By 1892 he had largely succeeded in his aims. No British Foreign Secretary has wielded his diplomatic boat-hook with greater dexterity.

* * *

The relentless question of a sullen and embittered Ireland overshadowed domestic politics. In his nephew, A. J. Balfour, who became Irish Secretary in 1887, Salisbury found a man capable of putting into practice the notion that all could be solved by "twenty years of resolute government." The situation that Balfour faced was very difficult. Agricultural prices were steadily falling, but the Government had rejected Parnell's argument that the only way to prevent mass evictions was to reassess rents. The Irish

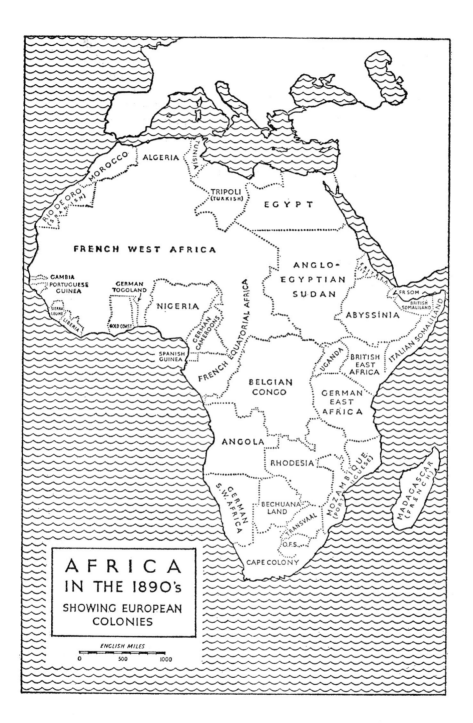

RIO DE ORO
(SPANISH)
MOROCCO
ALGERIA
TUNISIA
TRIPOLI
(TURKISH)
EGYPT

FRENCH WEST AFRICA

ANGLO-
EGYPTIAN
SUDAN

GAMBIA
PORTUGUESE
GUINEA
GERMAN
TOGOLAND
NIGERIA
ERITREA
FR SOM
BRITISH
SOMALILAND
ABYSSINIA

SIERRA
LEONE
LIBERIA
GOLD COAST
GERMAN
CAMEROONS
FRENCH EQUATORIAL AFRICA
ITALIAN SOMALILAND

SPANISH
GUINEA
UGANDA
BRITISH
EAST
AFRICA

BELGIAN
CONGO
GERMAN
EAST
AFRICA

ANGOLA

RHODESIA
MOZAMBIQUE
(PORTUGUESE)
MADAGASCAR
(FRENCH)

GERMAN
S.W. AFRICA
BECHUANA
LAND
TRANSVAL
O.F.S.
CAPE COLONY

AFRICA
IN THE 1890's
SHOWING EUROPEAN
COLONIES

ENGLISH MILES
0   500   1000

peasants had taken matters into their own hands by launching the "Plan of Campaign." The basis of the Plan was that tenants in a body should ask for a reduction of rent. If the landlord refused rents were to be withheld and the money paid into a campaign fund. The Plan was enforced with the terrorist methods which had now become an implacable feature of Irish land disputes. Balfour stretched his authority to the limit and acted with a determination that fully matched the ruthlessness of his Irish opponents. In defending his actions in the House of Commons he displayed such skill and resource that he rose rapidly to the front rank of Parliamentarians.

Liberal prospects, which had been bright in 1889, were now badly clouded. When the election came in the summer of 1892, the result was a Home Rule majority of only forty, dependent on the Irish Members. Gladstone was resolute. Work began immediately on a second Home Rule Bill, and in February, 1893, he introduced it himself. At the age of eighty-four he piloted the Bill through eighty-five sittings against an Opposition led by debaters as formidable as Chamberlain and Balfour. There have been few more remarkable achievements in the whole history of Parliament. It was all in vain. Passing through the Commons by small majorities, the Bill was rejected on the second reading in the Lords by four hundred and nineteen votes to forty-one. Thus perished all hope of a united, self-governing Ireland, loyal to the British Crown. A generation later civil war, partition, and the separation of the South from the main stream of world events were to be Ireland's lot.

The immediate reaction in England was one of indifference. Gladstone fell increasingly out of sympathy with his colleagues. They refused to support his scheme for a dissolution and an attack on the Lords. He resigned on March 3, 1894, fifty-two and a half years after his swearing in as a Privy Counsellor. His parting with his Ministers was affecting. Gladstone, who remained unmoved, afterwards referred to this meeting as "that blubbering Cabinet." He died in 1898. His career had been the most noteworthy of the century, leaving behind innumerable marks on the pages of history. He was the greatest popular leader of his age, and he has hardly been equalled in his power to move the people on great moral issues. He stands, too, in the very front rank of House of Commons figures. Few of his conceptions were unworthy. Gladstone's achievements, like his failures, were on the grand scale.

* * *

In January, 1893, the Independent Labour Party had been founded at a conference at Bradford. The aims of the I.L.P., as it was called, were the popularisation of Socialist doctrine and the promotion of independent working-class candidates at Parliamentary elections. Here was a sign, not much noticed in the great world of politics, of new forces which were coming to the surface in the industrial areas of Britain. An early manifesta-

456

tion in 1881 was the emergence of the Fabian Society, run by a group of young and obscure but highly gifted men, Sidney Webb and George Bernard Shaw among them. They damned all revolutionary theory and set about the propagation of a practical Socialist doctrine. The stream of publications which flowed from the Fabian pens did much to shape the course of Labour politics. The outlook, in the main, was practical and empirical, owing little to dogmatic theory and nothing to Marx.

Most working men knew little of these higher intellectual activities. They were absorbed in efforts to raise their standards of living. The greatest difficulty for Socialist groups was that their fervent beliefs evoked no response either among the mass of working men or among Trade Union leaders. On February 27, 1900, it was decided to set up a Labour Representation Committee, with Ramsay MacDonald as its secretary. The Labour Party had been founded. MacDonald in the twentieth century was to become the first Labour Prime Minister. He was to split his party at a moment of national crisis, and die amid the execrations of the Socialists whose political fortunes he had done so much to build.

*   *   *

Gladstone had been succeeded as Prime Minister by Lord Rosebery. Rosebery had the good luck to win the Derby twice during his sixteen months of office. Not much other fortune befell him. His was a bleak, precarious, wasting inheritance and the years that followed were dark ones for the Liberal Party. At the General Election of 1895 the Conservative-Liberal Unionist alliance won a decisive victory.

Lord Salisbury thereupon formed a powerful administration. He once again combined the offices of Prime Minister and Foreign Secretary, and his position in his own party and in the country was unrivalled. His methods of dispatching business were by now unorthodox. It is said that he sometimes failed to recognise members of his Cabinet when he met them on rare social occasions. He loved to retire to the great Cecil house at Hatfield, whence he discharged his vast responsibilities by a stream of letters written in his own hand. He enjoyed riding a stately tricycle around his park. His authority and prestige derived in part from the air of patrician assurance which marked his public speech and action. In character he presented the aristocratic tradition in politics at its best. He cared little for popular acclaim, and such disinterestedness in a democratic age was accepted and even approved.

But the man who in the public eye dominated the Government was the Liberal Unionist leader, Joseph Chamberlain, now at the height of his powers and anxious for the office which had been denied to him for so long. By his own choice Chamberlain became Colonial Secretary. The excitement of politics lay in the clash of Imperial forces in the continents of Africa and Asia, and it was there that Chamberlain resolved to make his mark. From the moment he took office projects of reform were pushed into the background by the constant eruption of questions inseparable from a policy of expansion.

The situation in Nigeria was difficult. The French, by moving overland to the south of the Sahara Desert, were attempting to confine the British to the coastal areas by using their superior military strength. Chamberlain, who, as Salisbury said, hated to give anything away, retaliated. Skilful diplomacy backed resolute action, and the Anglo-French Convention drew boundary lines in West Africa which were entirely satisfactory to the British.

In 1898 a far more dangerous dispute broke out between Britain and France over the control of the Upper Nile. Since the death of Gordon the Dervishes had held unquestioned sway in the Sudan. Their prophet, the Mahdi, was dead, but his successor, the Khalifa as he was called, kept their loose military empire in his grip. French moves towards the source of the Nile were already taking place, and must be forestalled; the Italian settlements on the Red Sea needed support; the slave-trade, which the Dervishes had revived, called for suppression; and at home Lord Salisbury's Government was not averse to an Imperial advance. In March Sir Herbert Kitchener, Sirdar of the Egyptian Army, launched his campaign for the avenging of Gordon and the reconquest of the Sudan. This vast tract of African territory could no longer be left a prey to barbarous rule, or remain a magnet for European rivalries.

The desert and the harsh tropical climate presented a formidable challenge to Kitchener's expedition, and he left nothing to chance. His great capacity, now to be displayed, was his foresight in organisation. The River War on the banks of the Nile was a painstaking operation, well planned and well directed. It was largely an engineers' war, enlivened by many short, fierce, gallant actions. The Khalifa's forces were at least three times as numerous, devoted to their cause, ferociously brave, and wily in the ways of the desert. After two and a half years the Dervish Army was finally confronted and destroyed outside Khartoum at the Battle of Omdurman on September 2, 1898. The Khalifa and his surviving lieutenants were gradually hunted down, and the Sudan then entered upon a period of constructive rule.

Five days after the Battle of Omdurman news reached Khartoum that there were Europeans at Fashoda, a post high upon the White Nile. For a time the French flag flew alongside the British and the Egyptian at Fashoda fort while matters were referred to London and Paris. In both capitals there was a flurry of talk about war. But the French gave way, and the watershed of the Congo and the Nile was fixed as the boundary separating British and French interests. This was virtually the last of the colonial disputes which for some decades had poisoned relations between Britain and France. Henceforward, under the growing menace of Germany, the two countries found themselves in constantly increasing harmony.

CHAPTER NINETY

The End of the Victorian Era

BRITAIN ENTERED the twentieth century in the grip of war. The conflict in South Africa, which began as a small colonial campaign, soon called for a large-scale national effort. Its course was followed in Britain with intense interest and lively emotion. The years of the Boer War saw a surge of patriotism among the vast majority of the British people, and a widespread enthusiasm for the cause of Empire.

Of course there were vehement critics and dissentients, the pro-Boers, as they were derisively called. They included some influential Liberal leaders, and in their train a rising young Welsh lawyer named Lloyd George, who now first made himself known to the nation by the vigour of his attacks upon the war and the Government. Nevertheless, the general feeling in the country was staunchly Imperialist. There was pride in the broad crimson stretches on the map of the globe which marked the span of the British Empire, and confidence in the Royal Navy's command of the Seven Seas. Europe was envious. Most of the Powers made plain their sympathy for the Boers, and there were hints of an allied combination against the Island kingdom. She might not have been allowed to escape from her colonial war with an easy victory, but her dominion of the seas caused second thoughts. On the outbreak of war a flying squadron of the Royal Navy was mobilised at Portsmouth, and this upon consideration from many angles proved effective in overawing Europe. The lesson was not lost upon the German Kaiser. The spectacle of British sea-power exercising unchallengeable authority made him redouble his efforts to create a mighty ocean-going German battle fleet. Dire consequences were to flow from his spirit of emulation.

*   *   *

The South African War had its roots deep in the past. Two landlocked Boer Republics, owing a vague suzerainty to Britain, were surrounded on all sides by British colonies, protectorates, and territories. Yet conflict was not at first inevitable. The large Dutch population in Cape Colony appeared reconciled to British rule and supported Cecil Rhodes as their Premier. The Orange Free State was friendly, and even in the Transvaal, home of the dourest frontier farmers, a considerable Boer party favoured co-operation with Britain. Hopes of an Anglo-Boer federation in South Africa were by no means dead. But all this abruptly changed during the last five years of the nineteenth century.

The Transvaal had been transformed by the exploitation of the extremely rich gold fields on the Witwatersrand. This was the work of foreign capital and labour, most of it British. Within a few years Johannesburg had developed into a great city. The Uitlanders—or Outlanders, as foreigners were called—equalled the native Boers in number, but the Transvaal Government refused to grant them political rights, even though they contributed all but one-twentieth of the country's taxation. Paul Kruger, the President of the Republic, who had taken part in the Great Trek and was now past his seventieth year, determined to preserve the character and independence of his country. He headed the recalcitrant Dutch, unwilling to make common cause with the British, and opposed to the advance of industry, though ready to feed on its profits. The threat of a cosmopólitan gold field to a close community of Bible-reading farmers was obvious to him. But his fears were intensified by the encircling motions of Rhodes's British South Africa Company which already controlled the territories to the north that were to become the Rhodesians, and was now trying to acquire Bechuanaland to the west. Rhodes, who had large financial interests on the Rand, dreamt of a United South Africa and a Cape-to-Cairo railway running through British territory all the way.

The political and economic grievances of the Uitlanders made an explosion inevitable. Rhodes had worked out a scheme for an uprising of the British in Johannesburg to be reinforced by the invasion of the Transvaal by a Company force. This was to be led by the Administrator of Rhodesia, Dr. Leander Starr Jameson. At the last moment the rising in Johannesburg failed to take place, but Jameson, not having counter-instructions from Rhodes, invaded the Transvaal with five hundred men on December 29. It ended in the failure which it deserved. On January 2 Jameson and his force surrendered to the Boers at Doornkop. The raid was a turning-point; the entire course of South African history was henceforth violently diverted from peaceful channels. The atmosphere of the country was poisoned by national and racial prejudice; the Dutch at the Cape, in natural sympathy with the Transvaal Boers, began to growl at the British. Rhodes was forced to resign his Premiership; but his great popularity in England served only to sharpen Boer suspicion of a deep-laid plot against the life of their republics.

In 1897 Sir Alfred Milner, an outstanding public servant, became High Commissioner in South Africa. Within a few months he had made up his mind; he wrote to Chamberlain, "There is no ultimate way out of the political troubles of South Africa except reform in the Transvaal or war. And at present the chances of reform in the Transvaal are worse than ever." But Chamberlain was anxious to avoid war, except as a last resort, and even then he hoped that the responsibility for its outbreak could be fixed on the Boers. He believed, as did Rhodes, that Kruger, under pressure, would yield. They underestimated the pioneers of the veldt.

A conference at Bloemfontein in June between Kruger and Milner settled nothing. Milner was convinced that the Boers, now armed to the teeth, were aiming at the establishment of a Dutch United States of South Africa. Kruger was equally convinced that the British intended to rob the Boers of their freedom and independence. "It is our country you want," he said, as tears ran down his face. Chamberlain made several attempts to come to an agreement, but by this time both sides were pressing ahead with military preparations. On October 9 the Boers delivered an ultimatum while the British forces in South Africa were still weak. Three days later their troops moved over the border.

*   *   *

At the outbreak of the war the Boers put thirty-five thousand men, or twice the British number, in the field, and a much superior artillery derived from German sources. They crossed the frontiers in several directions. Their army was almost entirely mounted. Within a few weeks they had invested Ladysmith to the east, and Mafeking and Kimberley to the west. At Mafeking a small force commanded by Colonel Baden-Powell was encircled by many times its number under Pete Cronje. At Kimberley Cecil Rhodes himself and a large civilian population were beset. The countryside was friendly to the Boer cause. World opinion was uniformly hostile to the British. Meanwhile a British Army corps of three divisions was on the way as reinforcement.

The British Army corps, as it arrived, was distributed by Buller in order to show a front everywhere. One division was sent to defend Natal, another to the relief of Kimberley, and a third to the north-eastern district of Cape Colony. Within a single December week each of them advanced against the rifle and artillery fire of the Boers, and was decisively defeated with, for those days, severe losses in men and guns. Although the losses of under a thousand men in each case may seem small nowadays, they came as a startling and heavy shock to the public in Britain and throughout the Empire, and indeed to the troops on the spot. But Queen Victoria braced the nation in words which have become justly famous. "Please understand," she replied to Balfour when he tried to discuss "Black Week," as it was called, "that there is no one depressed in *this* house. We are not interested in the possibilities of defeat. They do not exist." Lord Roberts of Kandahar was made the new Commander-in-Chief, Lord Kitchener of Khartoum was appointed his Chief of Staff, and in a few months the two already illustrious generals with an ever-increasing army transformed the scene.

The new British command saw clearly that forces must be used on a large scale and in combination; and the Boer capitals, Bloemfontein and then Pretoria, became their sure objective. On March 13 Roberts reached Bloemfontein, on May 31 Johannesburg, and on June 5 Pretoria fell. Mafeking was liberated after a siege which had lasted two hundred and seventeen days, and its relief provoked unseemly celebrations in London. Kruger fled. The Orange Free State and the Transvaal were annexed, and in the autumn of 1900 Roberts went home to England. After almost exactly a year of lively fighting, and with both the rebel capitals occupied, it seemed to the British people that the Boer War was finished, and won. Yet the war dragged on for another eighteen months. Not until March, 1902, did the Boers finally sue for peace.

The provisions of the peace signed at Vereeniging on May 31, 1902, may be judged magnanimous in the extreme. Thirty-two commandos remained unbeaten in the field. Two delegates from each met the British envoys, and after much discussion they agreed to lay down their arms and ammunition. None should be punished except for certain specified breaches of the usages of war; self-government would be accorded as soon as possible, and Britain would pay three million pounds in compensation. Such, in brief, were the principal terms, of which the last may be reckoned as generous, and was at any rate unprecedented in the history of modern war. Upon the conclusion of peace Lord Salisbury resigned. The last Prime Minister to sit in the House of Lords, he had presided over an unparalleled expansion of the British Empire. He died in the following year, and with him a certain aloofness of spirit, now considered old-fashioned, passed from British politics. All the peace terms were kept, and Milner did much to reconstruct South Africa. Nearly half a million British and Dominion troops had been employed, of whom one in ten became casualties. The total cost in money to the United Kingdom has been reckoned at over two hundred and twenty million pounds.

* * *

On January 22, 1901, Queen Victoria died. She lay at Osborne, the country home in the Isle of Wight which she and Prince Albert had designed and furnished fifty-five years before. Nothing in its household arrangements had been changed during the Queen's long widowhood. She had determined to conduct her life according to the pattern set by the Prince; nor did she waver from her resolution. Nevertheless a great change had gradually overtaken the monarchy. The Sovereign had become the symbol of Empire. At the Queen's Jubilees in 1887 and 1897 India and the colonies had been vividly represented in the State celebrations. The Crown was providing the link between the growing family of nations and races which the former Prime Minister, Lord Rosebery, had with foresight christened the Commonwealth. Disraeli's vision and Chamberlain's enthusiasm

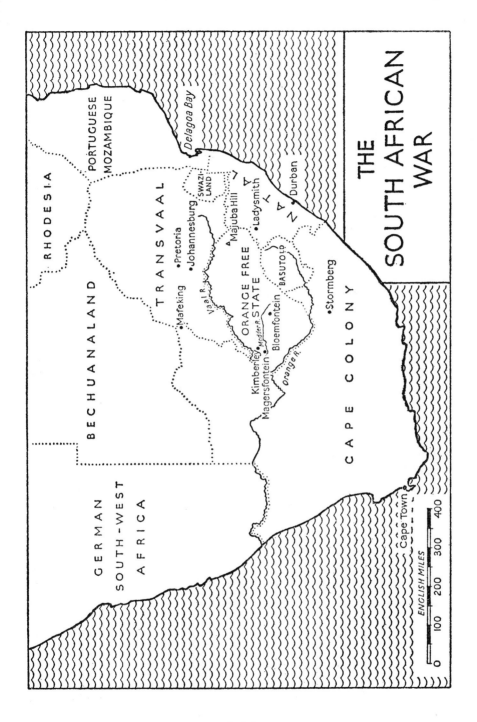

THE
SOUTH AFRICAN
WAR

ENGLISH MILES

0   100   200   300   400

RHODESIA

PORTUGUESE
MOZAMBIQUE

Delagoa Bay

BECHUANALAND

GERMAN
SOUTH-WEST
AFRICA

TRANSVAAL

•Pretoria
•Johannesburg

•Mafeking

SWAZI-
LAND

▲Majuba Hill
•Ladysmith

•Durban

ORANGE FREE
STATE

Vaal R.

Kimberley•
Magersfontein• •Bloemfontein
    Modder R.

Orange R.

BASUTOLD

CAPE COLONY

•Stormberg

Cape Town•

463

had both contributed to this broadening Imperial theme. The Queen herself was seized with the greatness of her rôle. She sent her sons and grandsons on official tours of her ever-increasing dominions, where they were heartily welcomed. Homage from a stream of colonial dignitaries was received by her in England. She appointed Indian servants to her household, and from them learnt Hindustani. Thus she sought by every means within her power to bind her diverse peoples together in loyalty to the British Crown, and her endeavours chimed with the Imperial spirit of the age. One of her last public acts, when she was over eighty years of age, was to visit Ireland. She had never believed in Irish Home Rule, which seemed to her a danger to the unity of the Empire. Prompted by a desire to recognise the gallantry of her Irish soldiers in South Africa, she travelled to Dublin in April, 1900, wearing the shamrock on her bonnet and jacket. Her Irish subjects, even the Nationalists among them, gave her a rousing reception. In Ireland a fund of goodwill still flowed for the Throne, on which English Governments sadly failed to draw.

In England during the Queen's years of withdrawal from the outward shows of public life there had once been restiveness against the Crown, and professed republicans had raised their voices. By the end of the century all this had died away. High devotion to her royal task, domestic virtues, evident sincerity of nature, a piercing and sometimes disconcerting truthfulness—all these qualities of the Queen's had long impressed themselves upon the minds of her subjects. In the mass they could have no knowledge of how shrewd she was in political matters, nor of the wisdom she had accumulated in the course of her dealings with many Ministers and innumerable crises. But they justly caught a sense of a great presiding personage. Even Ministers who in private often found her views impulsive and partisan came to respect the watchful sense of duty that always moved her. She represented staunchness and continuity in British traditions, and as she grew in years veneration clustered round her. When she died she had reigned for nearly sixty-four years. Few of her subjects could remember a time when she had not been their Sovereign. But all reflecting men and women could appreciate the advance of British power and the progress of the British peoples that had taken place during the age to which she gave her name. The Victorian Age closed in 1901, but the sense of purpose and confidence which had inspired it lived on through the ordeals to come.

* * *

We have now reached in this account the end of the nineteenth century, and the modern world might reasonably have looked forward to a long period of peace and prosperity. The prospects seemed bright, and no one dreamed that we had entered a period of strife in which command and ascendancy by a single world Power would be the supreme incentive. Two fearful wars, each of about five years' duration, were to illustrate the magnitude

Queen Victoria in the dress she wore
at her Jubilee in July, 1887

Waiting for the Queen

"In 1851 the Great Exhibition was opened in Hyde Park. Nineteen acres were devoted to the principal building, the Crystal Palace. Housing most of the exhibits and enclosing whole trees within its glass and iron structure, it was to be the marvel of the decade."

which developments had reached during the climax of the Victorian era. The rise of Germany to world Power had long been accompanied by national assertiveness and the continuous building up of armaments. No one could attempt to measure the character and consequences of the impending struggles. To fight on till victory was won became the sole objective, and in this the power of the nations engaged was to prove astounding. It seemed so easy in the course of the closing years of the passing century to take as a matter of course the almost universal system of national armies created by general conscription and fed by the measureless resources of industrial progress. Order and organisation were the salient features of modern life, and when Germany threw all her qualities into the task the steps became obvious, and even inevitable. Nay, it could be argued, and perhaps even proved, that the wise and normal method of modern progress, which all the Continent of Europe adopted in one form or another, was the principle of rearmament on the highest scale. Such was the vitality of the human race that it nevertheless flourished undeterred.

Alone of the Great Powers of Europe, which ordained that every man should be trained as a soldier and serve for two or even three years, Great Britain availed herself of her island position and naval mastery to stand outside the universal habit—for such it had become. And yet this abstention was by no means to allay the growth of the danger. On the contrary, in South Africa Britain took, unconsciously no doubt, a leading part in bringing about the crisis. She exhibited herself to all the nations as supreme. For three long years the process of conquering the Boers continued, leaving the rest of Europe and America the facts of Empire and much else to meditate upon. All the Powers began to think of navies in a different mood. Germany saw that her world preponderance would not be achieved without warships of the greatest strength and quality, and France and other nations followed her example. It was indeed a new outlet for national pride and energy, of which Japan, at the opposite side of the globe, took eager advantage. To the vast military staffs were added naval formations which pointed out the logic and importance of all their doings. The conquest of the air was also on the way. Britain would have been content to rule alone in moderation.

Nearly a hundred years of peace and progress had carried Britain to the leadership of the world. She had striven repeatedly for the maintenance of peace, at any rate for herself, and progress and prosperity had been continuous in all classes. The franchise had been extended almost to the actuarial limit, and yet quiet and order reigned. Conservative forces had shown that they could ride the storm, and indeed that there was no great storm between the domestic parties. The great mass of the country could get on with their daily tasks and leave politics to those who were interested as partisans without fear. The national horse had shown that the reins could be thrown on his neck without leading to a furious gallop in this direction or that. No one felt himself left out of the Constitution. An excess of self-assertion would be injurious. Certainly the dawn of the twentieth century seemed bright and calm for those who lived within the unequalled bounds of the British Empire, or sought shelter within its folds. There was endless work to be done. It did not matter which party ruled: they found fault with one another, as they had a perfect right to do. None of the ancient inhibitions obstructed the adventurous. If mistakes were made they had been made before, and Britons could repair them without serious consequences. Active and vigorous politics should be sustained. To go forward gradually but boldly seemed to be fully justified.

The United States remained, save in naval matters, largely aloof from these manifestations. Her thoughts were turned inwards on her unlimited natural resources, as yet barely explored and still less exploited. Her population still owed much of its amazing increase to immigrants from Europe, and these, out of temper with the continent of their origins and perhaps misfortunes, had no wish to see their new home entangled in the struggles of the old. The vast potentialities of America lay as a portent across the globe, as yet dimly recognised, save by the imaginative. But in the contracting world of better communications to remain detached from the preoccupations of others was rapidly becoming impossible. The status of world Power is inseparable from its responsibilities. The convulsive climax of the first Great War was finally and inseparably to link America with the fortunes of the Old World and of Britain.

*   *   *

Here is set out a long story of the English-speaking peoples. They are now to become Allies in terrible but victorious wars. And that is not the end. Another phase looms before us in which alliance will once more be tested and in which its formidable virtues may be to preserve Peace and Freedom. The future is unknowable, but the past should give us hope. Nor should we now seek to define precisely the exact terms of ultimate union.

Index

474